Heritage Signature® Auct

U.S. Coin

February 4,5 & 7, 2010 | Long Beach, California

Featuring: THE STAN BURGER COLLECTION, PART TWO • THE CHANDLER COLLECTION, PART TWO
THE LONGFELLOW COLLECTION • THE ALFRED V. MELSON COLLECTION, PART TWO • THE SOUTH TEXAS COLLECTION

LOT VIEWING

Long Beach Convention Center • Room 104 A
300 East Ocean Blvd. • Long Beach, CA 90802

Tuesday, February 2, 2010 • 11:00 AM - 7:00 PM PT
Wednesday, February 3, 2010 • 8:00 AM - 7:00 PM PT
Thursday, February 4, 2010 • 8:00 AM - 7:00 PM PT
Friday, February 5, 2010 • 8:00 AM - 7:00 PM PT
Saturday, February 6, 2010 • 8:00 AM - 12:00 PM PT

View Lots and Video Lot Descriptions Online at HA.com/Coins

LIVE FLOOR BIDDING

Bid in person during the floor sessions.

LIVE TELEPHONE BIDDING *(floor sessions only)*

Phone bidding must be arranged on or before Wednesday, February 3, 2010, by 12:00 PM CT. Client Service: 866-835-3243.

HERITAGE Live!™ BIDDING

Bid live from your location, anywhere in the world, during the Auction using our HERITAGE Live!™ program at HA.com/Live

INTERNET BIDDING

Internet absentee bidding ends at 10:00 PM CT the evening before each session. HA.com/Coins

FAX BIDDING

Fax bids must be received on or before Wednesday, February 3, 2010, by 12:00 PM CT. Fax: 214-409-1425

MAIL BIDDING

Mail bids must be received on or before Wednesday, February 3, 2010.

Please see "Choose Your Bidding Method" in the back of this catalog for specific details about each of these bidding methods.

LIVE AUCTION
SIGNATURE® FLOOR SESSIONS 1-3

(Floor, Telephone, HERITAGE Live!,™ Internet, Fax, and Mail)

Long Beach Convention Center • Room 103 B
300 East Ocean Blvd. • Long Beach, CA 90802

SESSION 1

Thursday, February 4, 2010 • 7:00 PM PT • Lots 1–501

SESSION 2

Friday, February 5, 2010 • 1:00 PM PT • Lots 502–952

SESSION 3

Friday, February 5, 2010 • 6:00 PM PT • Lots 953–1877

NON FLOOR/NON PHONE BIDDING SESSION 4

(HERITAGE Live!,™ Internet, Fax, and Mail only)

SESSION 4

Sunday, February 7, 2010 • 2:00 PM CT • Lots 7001–8721

AUCTION RESULTS

Immediately available at HA.com/Coins

LOT SETTLEMENT AND PICK-UP

Friday, February 5, 2010 • 10:00 AM - 1:00 PM PT
Saturday, February 6, 2010 • 9:00 AM - 12:00 PM PT

Extended Payment Terms available. See details in the back of this catalog.

Lots are sold at an approximate rate of 200 lots per hour, but it is not uncommon to sell 150 lots or 250 lots in any given hour.

This auction is subject to a 15% Buyer's Premium.

THIS AUCTION IS PRESENTED AND CATALOGED BY HERITAGE NUMISMATIC AUCTIONS, INC.

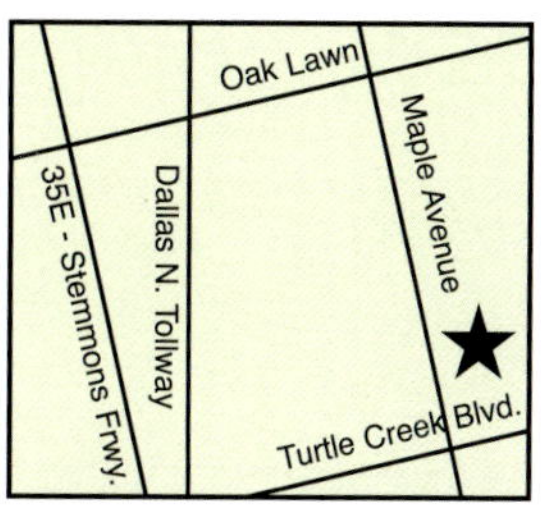

Heritage World Headquarters

HERITAGE HA.com
Auction Galleries

Home Office • 3500 Maple Avenue, 17th Floor • Dallas, TX. 75219
Design District Annex • 1518 Slocum Street • Dallas, TX. 75207
Beverly Hills Office • 9478 W. Olympic Blvd., First Floor • Beverly Hills, CA. 90212
214.528.3500 | 800.872.6467 | 214.409.1425 (fax)
Direct Client Service Line: Toll Free 1.866.835.3243 • Email: Bid@HA.com

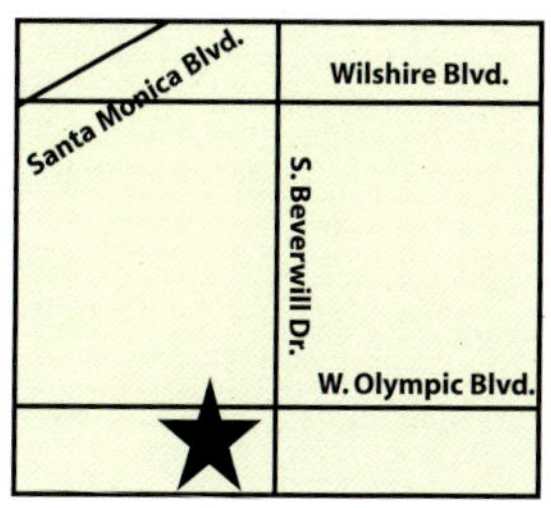

Beverly Hills Office
9478 W. Olympic Blvd., First Floor
Beverly Hills, CA. 90212

18539

U.S. Coin Specialists

Steve Ivy
CEO
Co-Chairman of the Board

Jim Halperin
Co-Chairman of the Board

Greg Rohan
President

Paul Minshull
Chief Operating Officer

Todd Imhof
Executive Vice President

Leo Frese
Vice President

David Mayfield
Vice President,
Numismatics

Jim Stoutjesdyk
Vice President,
Numismatics

3500 Maple Avenue, 17th Floor • Dallas, Texas 75219
Phone 214-528-3500 • 800-872-6467
HA.com/Coins

DIRECTORY FOR DEPARTMENT SPECIALISTS AND SERVICES

COINS & CURRENCY

COINS – UNITED STATES

HA.com/Coins

Leo Frese, Ext. 1294
Leo@HA.com
David Mayfield, Ext. 1277
DavidM@HA.com
Jessica Aylmer, Ext. 1706
JessicaA@HA.com
Diedre Buchmoyer, Ext. 1794
DiedreB@HA.com
Win Callender, Ext. 1415
WinC@HA.com
Bert DeLaGarza, Ext. 1795
BertD@HA.com
Chris Dykstra, Ext. 1380
ChrisD@HA.com
Sam Foose, Ext. 1227
SamF@HA.com
Jason Friedman, Ext. 1582
JasonF@HA.com
Shaunda Fry, Ext. 1159
ShaundaF@HA.com
Jim Jelinski, Ext. 1257
JimJ@HA.com
Katherine Kurachek, Ext. 1389
KK@HA.com
Bob Marino, Ext. 1374
BobMarino@HA.com
Mike Sadler, Ext. 1332
MikeS@HA.com

RARE CURRENCY

HA.com/Currency

Len Glazer, Ext. 1390
Len@HA.com
Allen Mincho, Ext. 1327
Allen@HA.com
Dustin Johnston, Ext. 1302
Dustin@HA.com
Michael Moczalla, Ext. 1481
MichaelM@HA.com
Jason Friedman, Ext. 1582
JasonF@HA.com

U.S. COINS PRIVATE TREATY SALES

HA.com/Coins

Todd Imhof, Ext. 1313
Todd@HA.com

U.S. COINS PURCHASED

HA.com/Coins

Jim Stoutjesdyk, Ext. 1310
JimS@HA.com

WORLD & ANCIENT COINS

HA.com/WorldCoins

Warren Tucker, Ext. 1287
WTucker@HA.com
Cristiano Bierrenbach, Ext. 1661
CrisB@HA.com
Scott Cordry, Ext. 1369
ScottC@HA.com

COMICS & COMIC ART

HA.com/Comics

Ed Jaster, Ext. 1288
EdJ@HA.com
Lon Allen, Ext. 1261
LonA@HA.com
Barry Sandoval, Ext. 1377
BarryS@HA.com
Todd Hignite, Ext. 1790
ToddH@HA.com

FINE ART

AMERICAN & EUROPEAN PAINTINGS & SCULPTURE

HA.com/FineArt

Edmund P. Pillsbury, Ph.D., Ext. 1533
EPP@HA.com
Ed Jaster, Ext. 1288
EdJ@HA.com
Courtney Case, Ext. 1293
CourtneyC@HA.com
Marianne Berardi, Ph.D., Ext. 1506
MarianneB@HA.com
Ariana Hartsock, Ext. 1283
ArianaH@HA.com

ART OF THE AMERICAN WEST

HA.com/WesternArt

Michael Duty, Ext. 1712
MichaelD@HA.com

FURNITURE & DECORATIVE ART

HA.com/Decorative

Tim Rigdon, Ext. 1119
TimR@HA.com
Meredith Meuwly, Ext. 1631
MeredithM@HA.com
Nicholas Dawes, Ext. 1605
NickD@HA.com

ILLUSTRATION ART

HA.com/Illustration

Ed Jaster, Ext. 1288
EdJ@HA.com
Todd Hignite, Ext. 1790
ToddH@HA.com

MODERN & CONTEMPORARY ART

HA.com/Modern

Frank Hettig, Ext. 1157
FrankH@HA.com

SILVER & VERTU

HA.com/Silver

Tim Rigdon, Ext. 1119
TimR@HA.com

TEXAS ART

HA.com/TexasArt

Atlee Phillips, Ext. 1786
AtleeP@HA.com

20TH-CENTURY DESIGN

HA.com/Design

Christina Japp, Ext. 1247
CJapp@HA.com
Nicholas Dawes, Ext. 1605
NickD@HA.com

VINTAGE & CONTEMPORARY PHOTOGRAPHY

HA.com/ArtPhotography

Ed Jaster, Ext. 1288
EdJ@HA.com

HISTORICAL

AMERICAN INDIAN ART

HA.com/AmericanIndian

Delia Sullivan, Ext. 1343
DeliaS@HA.com

AMERICANA & POLITICAL

HA.com/Historical

Tom Slater, Ext. 1441
TomS@HA.com
Marsha Dixey, Ext. 1455
MarshaD@HA.com
John Hickey, Ext. 1264
JohnH@HA.com
Michael Riley, Ext. 1467
MichaelR@HA.com

CIVIL WAR AND ARMS & MILITARIA

HA.com/CivilWar

Dennis Lowe, Ext. 1182
DennisL@HA.com

HISTORICAL MANUSCRIPTS

HA.com/Manuscripts

Sandra Palomino, Ext. 1107
SandraP@HA.com

RARE BOOKS

HA.com/Books

James Gannon, Ext. 1609
JamesG@HA.com
Joe Fay, Ext. 1544
JoeF@HA.com

SPACE EXPLORATION

HA.com/Space

John Hickey, Ext. 1264
JohnH@HA.com
Michael Riley, Ext. 1467
MichaelR@HA.com

TEXANA

HA.com/Historical

Sandra Palomino, Ext. 1107
SandraP@HA.com

JEWELRY & TIMEPIECES

FINE JEWELRY

HA.com/Jewelry

Jill Burgum, Ext. 1697
JillB@HA.com

WATCHES & FINE TIMEPIECES

HA.com/Timepieces

Jim Wolf, Ext. 1659
JWolf@HA.com

MUSIC & ENTERTAINMENT MEMORABILIA

HA.com/Entertainment

Doug Norwine, Ext. 1452
DougN@HA.com
John Hickey, Ext. 1264
JohnH@HA.com
Garry Shrum, Ext. 1585
GarryS@HA.com
Jim Steele, Ext. 1328
JimSt@HA.com
Kristen Painter, Ext. 1149
KristenP@HA.com

NATURAL HISTORY

HA.com/NaturalHistory

David Herskowitz, Ext. 1610
DavidH@HA.com

RARE STAMPS

HA.com/Stamps

Harvey Bennett, Ext. 1185
HarveyB@HA.com
Steven Crippe, Ext. 1777
StevenC@HA.com

SPORTS COLLECTIBLES

HA.com/Sports

Chris Ivy, Ext. 1319
CIvy@HA.com
Peter Calderon, Ext. 1789
PeterC@HA.com
Mike Gutierrez, Ext. 1183
MikeG@HA.com
Lee Iskowitz, Ext. 1601
LeeI@HA.com
Mark Jordan, Ext. 1187
MarkJ@HA.com
Chris Nerat, Ext. 1615
ChrisN@HA.com
Jonathan Scheier, Ext. 1314
JonathanS@HA.com

VINTAGE MOVIE POSTERS

HA.com/MoviePosters

Grey Smith, Ext. 1367
GreySm@HA.com
Bruce Carteron, Ext. 1551
BruceC@HA.com
Isaiah Evans, Ext. 1201
IsaiahE@HA.com

TRUSTS & ESTATES

HA.com/Estates
Mark Prendergast, Ext. 1632
MPrendergast@HA.com

CORPORATE & INSTITUTIONAL COLLECTIONS/VENTURES

Jared Green, Ext. 1279
Jared@HA.com

AUCTION OPERATIONS

Norma Gonzalez, Ext. 1242
V.P. Auction Operations
Norma@HA.com

CREDIT DEPARTMENT

Marti Korver, Ext. 1248
Marti@HA.com
Eric Thomas, Ext. 1241
EricT@HA.com

MARKETING

Debbie Rexing, Ext. 1356
DebbieR@HA.com

MEDIA & PUBLIC RELATIONS

Noah Fleisher, Ext. 1143
NoahF@HA.com

BEVERLY HILLS OFFICE

9478 W. Olympic Blvd., First Floor
Beverly Hills, CA 90212
Leo Frese
310-492-8600
Leo@HA.com

HOUSTON OFFICE

Mark Prendergast
713-899-8364
MPrendergast@HA.com

CORPORATE OFFICERS

R. Steven Ivy, Co-Chairman
James L. Halperin, Co-Chairman
Gregory J. Rohan, President
Paul Minshull, Chief Operating Officer
Todd Imhof, Executive Vice President
Leo Frese, Vice President

FOR THE EXTENSIONS ABOVE, PLEASE CALL 800-872-6467 | FOR TOLL-FREE DIRECT CLIENT SERVICE, CALL 866-835-3243

HERITAGE HA.com
Auction Galleries

Dear Bidder,

Heritage held its first Official Auction at the Long Beach Coin Expo in 1985, and for a quarter century, with the support of our consignors and bidders, we have held an incredible series of successful numismatic auctions. We have set record-after-record, as our auctions at the Long Beach Coin Expo earned their reputation for prices realized leadership and an exciting show location. We hope that you have come in person to one – *or all* – of the thrice annual Long Beach shows, to enjoy the best that numismatics has to offer. Our ties to the Southern California collecting community will now be strengthened with the opening of our new gallery and auction room in Beverly Hills.

A wonderful array of American numismatic rarities awaits you in this catalog, the pride of more than 200 consignors. In the Long Beach floor sessions (and the subsequent Final Session offerings) we will be auctioning about 3,400 lots of numismatic treasures. Of course, with well in excess of 475,000 registered bidder-members, there will be plenty of demand in play for these coins. We are especially mindful of the trust that both bidders and consignors have placed in Heritage. In return, we exert every effort to deliver the highest possible prices in an increasingly global marketplace.

We invite you to read about this Long Beach's anchor consignors.

The Stan Burger Collection, Part Two

Heritage offered early gold and silver highlights from the Stan Burger Collection in our FUN 2010 Signature® Auction. In this Long Beach, Part Two contains additional selections that are particularly strong in Colonials and high-quality type coins. Specialists and generalists alike will find attractive coins of interest herein. Mr. Burger started collecting coins at the age of eight, inspired by the change of the reverse of the Lincoln cent. He searched through the "coin jars" of family friends and relatives. Although inclined to simply collect coins out of circulation (his best early find was a 1950-D nickel!) rather than *buy* coins, he did begin to purchase proof sets from the Mint. Ultimately, with the rise of third-party grading and the ability to invest more significantly, he began to buy more important coins with investment potential. His first choice was coins that were "big, old, and gold, followed by big, old, and silver." Like most numismatists, he also fell in love with the colonial series, with all of their challenges and rewards. We offer at Long Beach more of the results of two-plus decades of dedicated collecting.

He encourages every collector "to buy the best coin possible; it will increase their satisfaction and investment return, as well as prove their wives wrong!"

The Chandler Collection, Part Two

Heritage was proud to offer Part One of The Chandler Collector at FUN 2009, and Part Two at FUN 2010. Now we offer a few additional rarities out of that last consignment. The late – and very private – numismatist who assembled this magnificent collection traced his numismatic inspiration to a very specific source. Following the death of his wife's grandfather, the family discovered three wonderful proof sets (dated around the turn of the twentieth century) among his effects. They had been unaware that their grandfather had any interest in coins, but the spark was soon ignited in them as well as they followed in his collecting footsteps. Collectors continue to enthuse over these fresh-to-market coins.

The Alfred V. Melson Collection, Part Two

In our FUN 2010 auction, we offered an initial selection of exotic error rarities out of Alfred Melson's world-class collection, with many from the 1943/44 transition years. Included in this auction are additional Lincoln errors (led by his 1943-S cent struck on a bronze planchet, certified VF35 by PCGS) and some appealing Indian quarter eagles. More Philadelphia Mint 1943 bronze cents are known than D-mint and S-mint errors put together, putting this among the rarest of the rare errors. This specimen was unknown to David Lange in 1996, when he published his *Complete Guide to Lincoln Cents*, only becoming known to the market in August 1999. This rarity is also unusual in having circulated for so long. The new owner will enjoy the research opportunities provided. Mint workers have made mistakes as long as coins have been produced, and collectors enjoy them as much – if not more – than perfect productions.

The Longfellow Collection

Specialists in the gold dollar series will be enthusiastic bidders when the 65 specimens in the Longfellow Collection come onto the auction block at Long Beach. All numismatists (and not just Charlotte collectors) will be anxious to examine his 1849-C Open Wreath gold dollar, certified XF45 by NGC. This is a major rarity by any measure, with only four confirmed examples (with a fifth rumored). Other exceptional gold dollars are his: 1849-C Closed Wreath Variety 1 (MS64 NGC, tied for finest certified); 1853-D Variety 5-G (MS66 NGC, CAC; the only 66, with none finer); 1855 (MS66 PCGS, CAC); and an 1875 (MS66 PCGS, CAC).

The consignor of this magnificent collection had previously assembled a world-class collection of three dollar gold pieces, and then decided to focus on gold dollars because he "liked the way they looked." Eye-appeal is obviously mixed with a deep sense of their historic context. The better part of a decade was spent collecting, with constant upgrading. The consignor's favorite, and the source of much pride, is his 1853-D; a difficult pursuit that resulted in owning the finest known. Proceeds from this auction will be spent on the consignor's other love – a new airplane to enjoy his weekly travels.

The South Texas Collection

The 20 lots of the South Texas Collection reflect the aspirations of many advanced coin collectors, containing classic rarities. Early gold is especially well represented, with his 1795 half eagle Small Eagle BD-1 (MS60 NGC) among the best. A matched pair of 1907 High Relief double eagles (Wire Rim MS62 PCGS and Flat Rim MS63 NGC, CAC) will also be popular. His 1798 Large Eagle dollar, Pointed 9, B-27, BB-113 (AU58 NGC) will not disappoint early silver specialists. The collector chose to buy rare coins for their history and diversification of his portfolio, motivators understood by most serious collectors, but his methodology is surprising -- in the oil and gas business, our consignor would take his first income check from a new well and buy one coin. As can be discerned, he has been most successful in both his vocation and hobby.

We invite you to use the world's best research tool – our free *Auction Archives* at HA.com – to do your homework on bid prices. It now contains detailed full-color images, lot descriptions, and prices realized for far more than one million numismatic items sold in our prior auctions. This is the world's most incredible numismatic pricing library. It contains information that will truly help you maximize your success when bidding at auction. Heritage has made it easy to add exciting items to your important collection.

We have made it equally easy to participate once your research is concluded. While we continue to have successful mail bidders in every Signature® auction, this is simply not the most practical way to participate. Successful bidding participation – and controlling the size of your invoice – is made much easier when you participate through our unique Interactive Internet™ bidding system at HA.com; by providing a continual flow of information on the success of your bids, you know when to bid higher or focus on your most desired lots. Of course, before the floor sessions begin, you can also bid by Fax or by e-mail. During the floor sessions, increasing numbers of successful bidders are participating through our HERITAGE Live! bidding system at HA.com/Live; you will definitely want to try this at your first opportunity, so that you are familiar with it before a major auction. You can also bid by agent or by phone during the floor sessions. We always recommend that you join us in Long Beach for these exciting auctions – and curiously, many bidders still participate by computer or phone to maximize their social time! However you choose to bid, we wish you good luck!

Please stop by the Heritage tables on the Long Beach bourse to say hello, or visit us in the lot viewing room.

Sincerely,

Greg Rohan
President

Todd Imhof
Executive Vice President

Denomination Index

SESSION ONE

Floor, Telephone, Heritage Live!™, Internet, Fax, and Mail Signature® Auction #1137
Thursday, February 4, 2010, 7:00 PM PT, Lots 1-501
Long Beach, California

A 15% Buyer's Premium ($14 minimum) Will Be Added To All Lots

Visit HA.com to view full-color images and bid.

COLONIALS

Very Rare Noe-29 1662 Oak Tree Twopence, XF

1 **1662 Oak Tree Twopence XF40 PCGS.** Small Date. Crosby 1-A2, Noe-29, W-240, R.6. 10.0 gn. The small and distant 2 identifies this rare Noe variety. A nicely detailed example with apple-green and rose patina. Softness of strike is limited to the right reverse border. The obverse is misaligned toward 4:30, affecting a few peripheral letters. A pair of thin marks are noted at 3 o'clock on the reverse. Listed on page 36 of the 2010 *Guide Book*. (#17)

XF Sharpness 1652 Oak Tree Shilling Crosby 2-D, Noe-5, W-470

2 **1652 Oak Tree Shilling—Environmental Damage—NGC. XF Details.** 'IN' at bottom. Crosby 2-D, Noe-5, W-470, R.2. 67.7 gn. Silver-gray and charcoal hues prevail on this lightly worn coin, which shows evidence of possible burial and later unearthing. The letters in NEW on the obverse and the last T in MASATHVSETS on the reverse are cut off by the irregularly shaped flan. (#20)

Desirable 1652 Noe-33 Pine Tree Sixpence, XF40

3 **1652 Pine Tree Sixpence XF40 PCGS.** Pellets at trunk. Crosby 1-A, Noe-33, W-670, R.3. The weight is not recorded on the PCGS holder. This pleasing gray-brown example has bold design details with hints of steel and maroon patina. The surfaces are minutely rough as often seen. Listed on page 37 of the 2010 *Guide Book*. Population: 5 in 40, 24 finer (1/10). (#22)

Noe-17 1652 Pine Tree Shilling Small Planchet, VF25

4 **1652 Pine Tree Shilling, Small Planchet VF25 PCGS.** Crosby 22-L, Noe-17, W-840, R.3. 69.0 grains. A pleasing example of the Small Planchet variety with attractive medium to dark gray surfaces. The design is imperfectly centered, as commonly seen on these pieces. However, the entire obverse and reverse legends are on the planchet. Listed on page 37 of the 2010 *Guide Book*. (#24)

5 **(1670-75) St. Patrick Farthing Fine 15 PCGS.** Breen-208. Light brown overall with somewhat darker toning near the borders. A circulated but mark-free example of this Old World import. The gold-colored splasher is off center but overlaps the upper left portion of the crown. Listed on page 39 of the 2010 *Guide Book*. (#42)

MS62 American Plantations Token Newman 4-E, W-1155

6 **(c. 1828) American Plantations 1/24 Part Real, Restrike MS62 PCGS.** Newman 4-E, W-1155, R.5. One of the two Restrike marriages per the recent Whitman Early American reference, although often designated as an Original striking by PCGS since it lacks the prominent obverse die break seen on Newman 5-D. The surfaces are smooth and cream-gray aside from a pair of small darkly toned border areas on the reverse. Listed on page 39 of the 2010 *Guide Book*. (#52)

Sharp 1722 Rosa Americana Halfpenny D. G. REX, AU58

7 **1722 Rosa Americana Halfpenny, D. G. REX AU58 PCGS.** Breen-133. UTILE DULCI. Stops after REX and 1722. A sharply struck olive-brown piece with a dash of mauve patina on the obverse center. The obverse is beautifully smooth, while the reverse has only a couple of unimportant marks. A touch of wear on the rose accounts for the grade. Listed on page 40 of the 2010 *Guide Book*.
Ex: FUN Signature (Heritage, 1/2007), lot 48, which realized $2,875. (#101)

8 **1723 Hibernia Farthing, D:G:REX MS62 Brown PCGS.** Martin 1.1-Bc.1, W-12240, High R.4. A strongly detailed cinnamon-brown example with smooth surfaces for the grade. This briefly issued legend subtype is seldom encountered in Mint State. Listed on page 42 of the 2010 *Guide Book*.
From The Stan Burger Collection, Part Two.(#173)

W-13470 1723 Hibernia Halfpenny MS66 Brown

9 **1723 Hibernia Halfpenny MS66 Brown PCGS. CAC.** Martin 4.14-Fb.2, R.4. W-13470. A chocolate-brown Premium Gem with undisturbed surfaces and a precise strike. Hints of mint red remain within the obverse legend. A remarkable example of this Irish import. Listed on page 43 of the 2010 *Guide Book*. Population: 1 in 66 Brown, 2 finer as 66 Red and Brown (1/10). (#180)

10 **1723 Hibernia Halfpenny MS64 Red and Brown PCGS.** No pellet before H, Small 3, 11 harpstrings, Breen-157, W-13120, Martin 4.57-Gc.13, R.3. Medium-brown surfaces show glimpses of blue and faded orange at the margins. Softly defined through the central reverse but pleasing otherwise. Housed in a green label holder. Listed on page 43 of the 2010 *Guide Book*.
From The Stan Burger Collection, Part Two.(#181)

11 **1739-BB French Colonies Sou Marque MS65 NGC.** Breen-608. Vlack-250, R.2. Strasbourg Mint. A remarkable Gem that appears virtually the same today as when it was issued. The undisturbed ivory-gray fields are lustrous and offer traces of tan toning. Evenly struck, and without planchet issues. It would take a Herculean effort to find a superior sou marque of any date or mint. The obverse die is moderately misaligned toward 1:30. Listed on page 51 of the 2010 *Guide Book*.(#158671)

12 **1764-A French Colonies Sou Marque MS65 NGC.** Breen-425, Vlack-48a, second semester. The 1764-A French sou marque pieces are among the common issues of the extensive series. Breen claims in his *Complete Encyclopedia* that examples are plentiful from both semesters, while Vlack states that no first semester pieces have ever been reported. This amazing Gem has lustrous pewter-gray surfaces with hints of steel toning. Listed on page 51 of the 2010 Guide Book.(#158675)

13 **1766 Pitt Halfpenny VF20 PCGS.** Betts-519, Breen-251, W-8350, R.3. A dark steel-gray representative with clear types and generally legible legends, although the right reverse inscriptions are partly off the flan. Moderately granular, but inoffensive as such. Listed on page 48 of the 2010 *Guide Book*.
Ex: Jones Beach Collection (Heritage, 1/2007), lot 90.(#236)

14 **1766 Pitt Halfpenny XF45 PCGS.** Betts-519, Breen-251, W-8350, R.3. A medium brown Choice XF representative that has an unabraded appearance and a hint of charcoal-gray patina in protected areas. Listed on page 48 of the 2010 *Guide Book*. (#236)

15 **1773 Virginia Halfpenny, Period MS64 Brown PCGS.** Newman 22-S, W-1550, R.5. Though labeled as "Brown," this rare Virginia halfpenny has considerable copper-orange at the left obverse rim. Softly struck but with smooth surfaces, particularly at the blue-brown centers. Housed in a green label holder. Listed on page 43 of the 2010 *Guide Book*.
From The Stan Burger Collection, Part Two.(#240)

16 **1773 Virginia Halfpenny, Period MS64 Brown NGC.** Newman 25-M. Designated as Brown, but considerable orange-gold remains, especially on the reverse. Evenly struck and attractive with trivial contact on the right obverse deciding the grade. Listed on page 43 of the 2010 *Guide Book*. Census: 13 in 64 Brown, 3 finer (1/10). (#240)

17 **1773 Virginia Halfpenny, Period MS65 Brown PCGS.** Newman 25-M. Both sides display glimpses of the initial orange-red luster, although most of this lovely Gem is toned chocolate-brown. Evenly struck and impressively preserved. Clashed on the upper obverse and lower reverse, as struck at the Tower Mint in London. Listed on page 43 of the 2010 *Guide Book*. Population: 3 in 65 Brown, 1 finer (1/10).(#240)

18 **1773 Virginia Halfpenny, Period MS64 Red and Brown PCGS.** Newman 25-M, W-1580, R.2. A surprising amount of pale copper-orange remains on this Choice coin. The portrait shows violet-brown influences, however, and the margins on each side display minor carbon. Listed on page 43 of the 2010 *Guide Book*.
From The Stan Burger Collection, Part Two.(#241)

19 **1773 Virginia Halfpenny, No Period MS64 Brown PCGS.** Newman 3-F, W-1455, High R.4. A Seven Harpstrings variety. Sharp with glossy brown surfaces that have a golden aura on the obverse and elements of peach on the reverse. High eye appeal. Listed on page 43 of the 2010 *Guide Book*.
From The Stan Burger Collection, Part Two.(#243)

MS66 Brown 1773 Virginia Halfpenny
No Period, Newman 3-F

20 **1773 Virginia Halfpenny, No Period MS66 Brown PCGS.** Newman 3-F. Seven harpstrings. The 1 in the date is repunched. An exquisitely detailed and beautifully preserved Premium Gem representative with splendidly smooth surfaces. Each side shows rich chocolate-brown toning along with noticeable remnants of the initial fire-red, particularly on the reverse. Listed on page 43 of the 2010 *Guide Book*. (#243)

1787 Massachusetts Half Cent, Ryder 2-A
Scarce MS62 Brown

21 **1787 Massachusetts Half Cent MS62 Brown NGC.** Ryder 2-A, W-5910, R.3. Faded mint red fills the legends and outlines the devices, while the open fields are deep brown. A nice strike with the usual inexactness at the centers. A few faint vertical hairlines can be made out with a glass, and protected areas have a few specks of green-gray debris. Listed on page 57 of the 2010 *Guide Book*. Census: 6 in 62 Brown, 8 finer (1/10).
Ex: Long Beach Signature (Heritage, 9/2005), lot 527, which realized $2,300.
From The Stan Burger Collection, Part Two. (#296)

Impressive MS63 Brown Ryder 1-B
1788 Massachusetts Half Cent

22 **1788 Massachusetts Half Cent MS63 Brown PCGS.** Ryder 1-B, W-6010, R.2. A lovely chocolate-brown piece that has no indication of abrasions. The strike is above average, although the centers show hints of the planchet texture. Certified in a green label holder. Listed on page 57 of the 2010 *Guide Book*. Population: 4 in 63 Brown, 9 finer (12/09).
From The Stan Burger Collection, Part Two. (#308)

AU50 W-2355 African Head
1785 Connecticut Copper

23 **1785 Connecticut Copper, African Head AU50 PCGS.** Miller 4.1-F.4, W-2355, R.1. A mildly worn example of the generally available but distinctive and popular variety. Surfaces are luminous blue-brown with few abrasions. A planchet void present at the right reverse rim adds visual interest. Population: 6 in 50, 3 finer (12/09). Listed on page 59 of the 2010 *Guide Book*. (#319)

24 **1787 Connecticut Copper, Horned Bust AU55 PCGS.** Miller 4-L, W-2810, R.1. The late die stage with a full-fledged "horn" die break attached to the mailed bust. Chocolate-brown overall with gunmetal high points. A thin mark is noted between the AU in AUCTORI. Listed on page 59 of the 2010 *Guide Book*. Population: 7 in 55, 5 finer (1/10).(#364)

Choice VF 1785 Vermont Copper
Ryder-2, Bressett 1-A, W-2005

25 **1785 Vermont Copper, VERMONTS VF35 PCGS.** RR-2, Bressett 1-A, W-2005, R.2. An unabraded medium brown Republic copper that has pleasing detail and several noticeable flan laminations. The tornado-shaped die break above the 8 in the date indicates an intermediate die state. Listed on page 68 of the 2010 *Guide Book*. Population: 6 in 35, 12 finer (1/10). (#539)

26 **1787 Vermont Copper, BRITANNIA XF45 PCGS.** RR-13, Bressett 17-V, R.1. Boldly defined for this *Guide Book* type. Medium-brown with a hint of obverse verdigris. A couple of light handling marks are on the lower left reverse. The reverse legends and device are indistinct, as always for the variety, the reverse die long in use prior to its pairing with the Bressett 17 obverse. Listed on page 68 of the 2010 *Guide Book*.
Ex: FUN Signature (Heritage, 1/2006), lot 450.(#554)

27 **1783 Nova Constellatio Copper, Pointed Rays, Large US AU50 NGC.** Crosby 1-A, W-1860, R.4. Offering smooth medium brown surfaces with excellent eye appeal, this attractive problem-free piece is sure to please most collectors. Listed on page 52 of the 2010 *Guide Book*.(#804)

28 **1787 Fugio Cent, STATES UNITED, 4 Cinquefoils, Pointed Rays VF35 NGC.** Newman 9-T, W-6755, R.4. A midgrade Fugio with unabraded tan-brown surfaces. Obverse retained flan laminations, as made, are noted at 1 and 5 o'clock. A scarcer variety that is seldom seen any finer. Listed on page 83 of the 2010 *Guide Book*.(#883)

Prized 1787 STATES UNITED Fugio Cent Newman 13-X, W-6855, MS62 Brown

29 **1787 Fugio Cent, STATES UNITED, 4 Cinquefoils, Pointed Rays MS62 Brown ANACS.** Newman 13-X, W-6855, R.2. Newman's Obverse 13 with considerable clash marks, paired with the X reverse showing a die crack up from near 6 o'clock at the rim. Glossy, minimally abraded surfaces are chocolate-brown with prominent blueberry overtones. Strong eye appeal for this more available die pair. Listed on page 83 of the 2010 *Guide Book*.
From The Stan Burger Collection, Part Two. (#883)

Popular MS62 Brown 1787 Fugio Copper Pointed Rays, Newman 12-X

30 **1787 Fugio Cent, STATES UNITED, 4 Cinquefoils, Pointed Rays MS62 Brown PCGS.** Newman 12-X, W-6820, R.3. A chocolate-brown Fugio that boasts shimmering luster and a mark-free appearance. The left border is incompletely brought up, minor planchet flaws include a small void on the reverse rim at 11 o'clock, and the 2 o'clock ring has a gray spot. Encased in a green label holder and listed on page 83 of the 2010 *Guide Book*.
From The Stan Burger Collection, Part Two. (#883)

Pointed Rays Newman 8-X 1787 Fugio Cent MS62 Brown, STATES UNITED

31 **1787 Fugio Cent, STATES UNITED, 4 Cinquefoils, Pointed Rays MS62 Brown PCGS.** Newman 8-X, W-6750, R.3. The advanced obverse die break near 6 o'clock readily attributes this Newman variety, which participated in the Bank of New York hoard along with other "X" reverse Fugios such as 11-X and 12-X. This medium brown example has comprehensive satin luster and no visible marks, although the obverse displays a few narrow darkly toned laminations of mint origin. Listed on page 83 of the 2010 *Guide Book*. (#883)

MS62 Brown 1787 Fugio Cent, Newman 8-B UNITED STATES, Cinquefoils

32 **1787 Fugio Cent, UNITED STATES, Cinquefoils MS62 Brown PCGS.** Newman 8-B, W-6740, R.3. An unabraded medium brown Fugio "cent" that has a couple of inconsequential flan flaws on the reverse. Well struck at the centers, while border elements are incompletely brought up. Housed in a green label holder. Listed on page 83 of the 2010 *Guide Book*.
From The Stan Burger Collection, Part Two. (#889)

33 **1787 Fugio Cent, Club Rays, Rounded Ends VF20 NGC.** Newman 3-D. A tan-brown example that has even wear and pleasing surfaces. The few narrow flan striations are of mint origin. Listed on page 84 of the 2010 *Guide Book*.(#904)

Important Uniface Auctori Plebis Token Breen-1152, Choice Very Fine

34 **Uniface Obverse Auctori Plebis Token VF35 NGC.** Breen-1152, "extremely rare." The bust faces right and a period and two cinquefoils follows PLEBIS, but without other ornamentation in the legend. Lovely light chestnut-tan toning. A difficult issue to grade, since the presence of raised die lines in the fields suggests minimal circulation wear, but the profile is featureless (as intended by the maker), which gives an incorrect impression of long use in commerce. (#966)

35 **1789 Mott Token, Thick Planchet, Plain Edge MS62 Brown PCGS.** Breen-1020. The late die state with a huge die break from the clock corner and indistinct detail on the eagle's shield. This token is in much better shape than its dies, since the generally golden-brown surfaces are pleasing. Listed on page 70 of the 2010 *Guide Book*. Population: 10 in 62 Brown, 15 finer (1/10). (#603)

36 **(1792-94) Kentucky Token, Plain Edge MS64 Brown PCGS. CAC.** Breen-1155, W-8800, R.1. The Kentucky token ranks among the common Colonial issues, with Mint State pieces seen frequently, although usually in lower grades than this example. Satiny olive and steel-brown surfaces retain traces of original mint red on both sides. Listed on page 71 of the 2010 *Guide Book*. (#614)

37 **1794 Franklin Press Token MS64 Brown NGC.** Breen-1165, W-8850, R.1. Struck in London, this token emanated from a printing shop where Benjamin Franklin once worked, explaining its popularity with American collectors. This pleasing piece is lustrous with hints of light green peripheral toning over chocolate-brown surfaces. Census: 3 in 64 Brown, 1 finer (1/10). Listed on page 72 of the 2010 *Guide Book*.(#630)

38 **1795 Talbot Allum & Lee Cent MS64 Brown PCGS.** Fuld-1, W-8620, R.1. Smooth chocolate-brown surfaces show flecks of deeper color and divergent accents. Cinnamon-peach elements grace the obverse, while the reverse assumes a violet cast. Listed on page 72 of the 2010 *Guide Book*.
From The Stan Burger Collection, Part Two.(#640)

PR63 Red and Brown Fuld-1
1795 Talbot, Allum & Lee Cent

39 **1795 Talbot, Allum & Lee Cent PR63 Red and Brown NGC.** Fuld-1, Breen-1035. Mellowed mint red and powder-blue grace the obverse. The reverse is ocean-blue and olive with peripheral rose tints. Well struck and flashy with a few faint hairlines on the lower right obverse. Business strikes are listed on page 72 of the 2010 *Guide Book*. (#90641)

40 **1783 Georgivs Triumpho Token AU50 PCGS.** Baker-7, W-10100, R.3. Many Washington varieties were struck in 19th century despite 18th century dates, but the Georgivs Triumpho token is believed struck in 1783. Deep golden-brown with clean surfaces aside from four faint vertical pinscratches on the upper reverse. Listed on page 75 of the 2010 *Guide Book*. Population: 11 in 50, 25 finer (1/10).(#664)

41 **1783 Washington & Independence Cent, Small Military Bust, Plain Edge AU55 PCGS.** Baker-4A, W-10155, R.5. A bold medium brown representative that exhibits an interesting clash mark (as made) above the olive branch. A wispy slide mark is noted in the right obverse field. The Small Military Bust is noticeably scarcer than its Large Military Bust Baker-4 counterpart. Listed on page 75 of the 2010 *Guide Book*. Population: 5 in 55, 5 finer (1/10). (#670)

42 No lot.

43 **1783 Washington & Independence Cent, Draped Bust, No Button, Copper Restrike, Engrailed Edge PR65 Brown PCGS. CAC.** Baker-3, W-10370, R.5. A chocolate-brown Gem proof with suggestions of violet. Sharply struck with excellent surface quality. Listed on page 76 of the 2010 *Guide Book*. Population: 31 in 65 Brown, 14 finer (1/10).(#685)

1783 Washington & Independence Copper
Draped Bust, Engrailed Edge, Baker-3, PR67 Brown

44 **1783 1C Washington & Independence Cent, Draped Bust, No Button, Copper Restrike, Engrailed Edge PR67 Brown PCGS.** Baker-3, W-10370, R.5. Incorrectly certified by PCGS as the Plain Edge restrike (Baker-3C). The large 3 in the date is diagnostic for the W.S. Lincoln restrike. This is a splendid, glossy milk-chocolate Superb Gem proof example. Listed on page 76 of the 2010 *Guide Book*. Population: 5 in 67 Brown, 0 finer (1/10). (#685)

45 **Undated Washington Double Head Cent AU58 PCGS.** Baker-6, W-11200, R.2. An impressive near-Mint medium brown example of this popular Washington variety. Only minimally abraded, and high-point wear is slight. Listed on page 76 of the 2010 *Guide Book*. Population: 14 in 58, 5 finer (1/10).(#692)

46 **1793 Washington Ship Halfpenny, Copper, Lettered Edge AU55 PCGS.** Breen-18, W-10855, R.4. A lovely Choice AU example of this scarce Washington copper. The deep chocolate-brown fields and devices are impressively free from marks or spots. A relatively early die state, the reverse field is swollen (as made) but the dies are not clashed and the die sinking along the lower right reverse border is very limited. Listed on page 79 of the 2010 *Guide Book*. (#734)

Lettered Edge Washington Ship Halfpenny
Baker-18, MS61 Brown

47 **1793 Washington Ship Halfpenny, Copper, Lettered Edge MS61 Brown PCGS.** Baker-18, W-10855, R.4. A satiny and surprisingly mark-free example of this scarce Washington type. The upper reverse has a series of minute to small strike-throughs, as made, and lavender verdigris passes through the N in PRESIDENT. Encapsulated in a green label holder. Listed on page 79 of the 2010 *Guide Book*. Population: 5 in 61 Brown, 2 finer (12/09).
From The Stan Burger Collection, Part Two. (#734)

48 **1795 Washington Grate Halfpenny, Large Buttons, Reeded Edge MS64 Red and Brown PCGS.** Baker-29A, W-10955, R.1. The reeded edge slopes to the right. A lustrous violet-brown and blue-brown piece with considerable faded orange close to the rims. Housed in a green label holder. Listed on page 79 of the 2010 *Guide Book*.
From The Stan Burger Collection, Part Two.(#747)

49 **1795 Washington Grate Halfpenny, Large Buttons, Reeded Edge MS64 Red and Brown PCGS.** Baker-29AA, W-10955. The edge reeding, partially visible through the holder, slopes down to left. This well struck near-Gem has substantial fire-red throughout the legends. The open fields are apple-green aside from a few gray freckles near PEACE. One long thin vertical mark on the central reverse. Listed on page 79 of the 2010 *Guide Book*.(#747)

50 **1795 Washington Grate Halfpenny, Large Buttons, Reeded Edge MS64 Red and Brown PCGS.** Baker-29AA, W-10955. This well struck near-Gem retains the initial fire-red near design recesses, while the fields and highpoints are toned brown. Faint curved lines seen on the central reverse were on the planchet prior to the strike, and are found on many Uncirculated examples of this popular Washington type. Population: 18 in 64 Red and Brown, 1 finer (1/10).(#747)

Bust Left Baker-30 Washington 'Penny' Liberty & Security, MS64 Red and Brown

51 **Undated Washington Liberty & Security Penny MS64 Red and Brown PCGS.** Baker-30, W-11050, R.2. Plain rims, Asylum lettering on edge. Though considerable copper-orange luster remains on this near-Gem, it is tempered with violet-brown through the portrait area on the obverse and on most of the reverse. Well struck with strong eye appeal. Listed on page 80 of the 2010 *Guide Book*. Population: 12 in 64 Red and Brown, 3 finer (12/09). (#768)

52 **Undated Washington Success Medal, Large Size, Reeded Edge AU53 PCGS.** Baker-266, W-10915, R.6. Pleasing medium-brown patina covers the obverse, while the reverse has mostly tan coloration. A number of shallow scratches are noted on the right obverse, but they are nearly imperceptible without a loupe. Listed on page 80 of the 2010 *Guide Book*.(#780)

Baker-265 Washington Success Medal Large Size, Reeded Edge, MS63

53 **Undated Washington Success Medal, Large Size, Reeded Edge MS63 PCGS.** Baker-265, W-10900, R.5. Cracked at upper obverse, as usually seen. Strong brassy yellow-orange color with strong luster and rose accents through the right obverse. Minimally abraded and visually impressive. Listed on page 80 of the 2010 *Guide Book*. Population: 4 in 63, 1 finer (12/09). (#780)

Undated Baker-267 Washington Success Medal Small Size, Reeded Edge, MS63

54 **Undated Washington Success Medal, Small Size, Reeded Edge MS63 NGC.** Baker-267. The present lot is the single finest certified reeded edge small size Washington Success medal. Light golden-brown and dove-gray toning drapes the nicely struck surfaces. Thin marks on the reverse border near SUCCESS TO THE emerge beneath a loupe. Listed on page 80 of the 2010 *Guide Book*. (#783)

HALF CENTS

Prized VF C-2 1793 Half Cent

55 **1793 VF20 PCGS.** C-2, B-2, R.3. The obverse with Liberty's cap distant from the Y in her name, and the reverse with the 1 in the numerator well-centered over a denominator with the digit 2 high. This is a moderately worn representative from the historic first year of Philadelphia Mint coinage, the smaller of just two denominations struck in 1793. Deep walnut-brown surfaces show few overt abrasions, though numerous planchet flaws can be found across the obverse, as well as through the lower and right reverse. Nonetheless, a pleasing coin sure to delight the winning bidder. MRB Fine 12. (#1000)

Popular 1793 Half Cent, C-3, VF30

56 **1793 VF30 PCGS.** C-3, B-3, R.3. The 7 is short and the L in LIBERTY is low, identifying the obverse. The reverse is distinguished by a crowded fraction. Having the sharpness of XF, this piece is net graded because of a few tiny rim bruises on each side. Otherwise, the surfaces are pleasing with intermingled tan and darker olive. Trivial marks on each side are consistent with the grade. In addition, there is a natural planchet crack at 7 o'clock that remains from the time this piece was minted in 1793. The strike is sharp and nicely centered with full obverse and reverse borders, although the planchet was apparently narrow, leaving little margin outside the border beads. MRB Fine 12. (#1000)

57 **1797 Plain Edge Fine 12 PCGS.** C-2, B-2, R.3. An ebony-brown Liberty Cap half cent with bold obverse legends and several faint letters on the reverse, particularly the ICA in AMERICA. Minutely granular and only minimally abraded. MRB VG10. (#1036)

Attractive C-3 1805 Half Cent, Fine 15

58 **1805 Small 5, Stems Fine 15 PCGS.** C-3, B-3, R.4. Manley Die State 2.0 with an obvious bulge on the right obverse field. Cohen-3 is notoriously difficult to procure nice. Manley states "the finest known [is]reported as Extremely Fine." This medium brown example has moderate verdigris on the reverse, while the obverse is only mildly granular. Minimally abraded despite its service in circulation. MRB VG8. Population: 6 in 15, 6 finer (12/09). (#1087)

C-3 1805 Small 5, Stems Half Cent, Fine 15

59 **1805 Small 5, Stems Fine 15 PCGS.** C-3, B-3, R.4. The combination of a Small 5 obverse with a Stems reverse is the scarcest among 1805 half cents, though ironically, the same combination is the only one represented by multiple die pairs. This well-worn example is surprisingly luminous with generous cinnamon-rose accents against the chocolate surfaces. MRB VG10. (#1087)

Red Uncirculated 1806 Half Cent Large 6, Stems, C-4

60 **1806 Large 6, Stems MS61 Red PCGS.** C-4, B-4, R.1. Orange-red luster dominates although the open fields display hints of olive-gray. A good strike despite the expected softness on portions of the wreath. Infrequent minor spots are of little import, as are subtle marks above the H in HALF. MRB MS63. (#1101)

61 **1828 13 Stars MS64 Red and Brown PCGS. CAC.** C-3, B-2, R.1. The most frequently available of the three 1828 half cent varieties. Though violet-brown color dominates the central obverse, the margins show glimpses of original copper-orange, which prevails through most of the reverse. MRB MS63.(#1148)

62 **1849 Large Date MS65 Brown NGC.** C-1, B-1, R.1. Large Date, as with all business strikes. Mild olive-brown coloration defines the eye appeal of this well-defined Gem. Smooth surfaces are carefully preserved. MRB MS60.(#1218)

63 **1854 MS65 Red and Brown PCGS. CAC.** C-1, B-1, R.1. A pleasing Braided Hair half cent, this Gem has full satiny cartwheel luster. Considerable red mint luster is blended with attractive brown patina that is accented by pale blue and violet toning. MRB MS63. Population: 10 in 65 Red and Brown, 1 finer (1/10). (#1231)

LARGE CENTS

1793 S-4 Periods Chain Cent, VF Details

64 **1793 Chain Periods PCGS Genuine** S-4, B-5, R.4. The PCGS number ending in .97 suggests Environmental Damage as the reason, or perhaps one of the reasons, that PCGS deemed this coin not gradable. In our opinion, this coin has the details of a VF specimen that has been corroded.

The rough and wavy dark chocolate surfaces of this piece suggest that it was buried, and then burnished to diminish the rough appearance of ground corrosion. A few minor rim bruises are evident on each side, but they are of little concern. The net result is a sharply detailed piece that still retains a modicum of desirability. MRB VG8. (#91341)

Good S-6 1793 Wreath Cent Vine and Bars Edge

65 **1793 Wreath Cent, Vine and Bars Good 4 PCGS.** S-6, B-7, R.3. A deep chocolate-brown example of this coveted first-year type. All legends are clear, aside from the lower half of the date. A few minor rim dings are expected of the grade, along with occasional tiny peripheral pits. A thin mark appears above the wreath, but otherwise this piece is refreshingly free from pinscratches. In an old green label holder. MRB AG3. (#1347)

XF Details 1793 Wreath Cent Vine and Bars, S-10

66 **1793 Wreath Cent, Vine and Bars—Damaged—NGC. XF Details.** S-10, B-10, R.4. A well struck blue-brown example of this very scarce variety. Though a diagonal bar-shaped gouge crosses half of Liberty's neck and juts into the field, the remainder of the coin is minimally abraded. Beading at the right obverse border also shows a degree of anomalous flatness. MRB Fine 12. (#1347)

67 **1794 Head of 1794 VF20 NGC.** S-29, B-11, R.2. This attractively detailed cent offers light brown and ice-blue toning. The surfaces are minutely granular, and the only thin marks worthy of mention are above the 9 in the date and through the NE in ONE. MRB Fine 12.(#901374)

68 **1794 Head of 1794—Corrosion—NGC. XF Details.** S-25, B-15, R.3. Circulation wear is minimal, but this ebony-brown Liberty Cap cent is lightly burnished and has distributed verdigris. Mint luster is noticeable within the hair curls. MRB VG8.(#901374)

69 **1796 Liberty Cap—Rim Damage—NGC. VF Details.** S-89, B-10, R.3. While the surfaces show minor marks, corrosion, and rim bruises, this is a pleasing example of the S-89 die combination. Both sides are medium to dark brown with full borders and nice centering. MRB VG10.(#1392)

70 **1796 Liberty Cap VF25 PCGS.** S-83, B-4, R.4. This scarce Liberty Cap marriage is distinguished by obverse die cracks between the ERT in LIBERTY and in front of Liberty's mouth. CENT is softly brought up, but the neck curls are well detailed, and the deep brown surfaces are refreshingly problem-free. MRB Fine 12.(#1392)

71 **1797 Reverse of 1797, Stems—Environmental Damage—NCS. VF Details.** S-122, B-9, High R.5. A deep blue-brown example of this rare variety with moderate detail remaining. The extensive pitted texture on each side suggests burial and later unearthing. MRB VG7.(#1422)

Uncirculated Details 1797 Cent
Reverse of 1797, Stems, S-138

72 **1797 Reverse of 1797, Stems—Environmental Damage—NGC. Unc Details.** S-138, B-20, R.1. A sharp cinnamon-brown example of this available die pair with no trace of wear. A pinscratch does pass below Liberty's eye, and the surfaces show porosity that is the result of environmental damage, such as burial and later unearthing. Still, a readily collectible example. MRB VF30. (#1422)

73 **1798 Second Hair Style XF45 NGC.** S-166, B-32, R.1. Rosewood and medium-brown surfaces show suggestions of violet. A minimally abraded coin with smooth visual appeal. For the various Second Hair Style die pairs, Census: 5 in 45, 22 finer (1/10). MRB VF20. (#1434)

Attractive AU53 1800 Cent, S-212

74 **1800 AU53 NGC.** S-212, B-20, R.3. Among the top dozen or so examples of the variety. The S-212 variety is sometimes called the "Chips" variety, named for the die chips at the base of the 00. The appearance is similar to, and sometimes confused with, S-197, which is known as the "Q" variety. This piece has lightly abraded surfaces with deep steel and olive toning. MRB VF35. (#1449)

Choice XF No Stems 1802 Cent, S-231

75 **1802 No Stems XF45 PCGS.** S-231, B-9, R.1. One of two No Stems die marriages, further identified by an arc-shaped die crack in front of the profile. This deep medium brown Choice XF example lacks significant marks, and the only obvious spot is relegated to the reverse border at 4 o'clock. MRB VF30. Population: 5 in 45, 6 finer (12/09). (#1476)

76 **1803 Small Date, Small Fraction XF40 NGC.** S-251, B-8, R.2. Despite light overall wear, this teak-brown survivor shows impressive detail in the recesses of Liberty's hair. Smooth and pleasing. MRB VF30.(#1482)

77 **1805 XF40 NGC.** S-267, B-1, R.1. A blunt 1 in the date and the leaf pair left of the second S in STATES attribute the variety, which is indicated on the insert. Medium brown patination bathes both sides, each of which is appropriately defined and free of significant marks. Quite attractive for an early large cent that saw some circulation. MRB VF30.(#1510)

78 **1810 XF45 NGC.** S-282, B-3, R.2. A charming example of the conditionally challenging Classic Head type. Medium to deep brown with a smooth reverse and a few minor abrasions on the left obverse. MRB XF40.(#1549)

79 **1810—Improperly Cleaned—NGC. AU Details.** S-283, B-4, R.2. Well struck for a Classic cent with only minor wear overall. Blue-brown and mahogany surfaces show scattered abrasions and evidence of a past cleaning. MRB VF30.(#1549)

Near-Mint S-292 1813 Large Cent

80 **1813 AU58 NGC.** S-292, B-2, R.2. On the reverse, the second S in STATES is vertically aligned with the leaftip below. Just a touch of rub affects the high points of this Classic cent, which offers better-than-average detail and caramel overtones against the dominant chocolate hues of the smooth surfaces. MRB XF45. (#1570)

81 **1820 Large Date MS64 Brown NGC.** N-13, R.1. Grellman Die State b, with signature cracks through date and all stars. Though classified as Brown, this generally violet-brown piece does show traces of muted orange near the rims. MRB MS60.(#1615)

82 **1820 Large Date MS65 Red and Brown NGC.** N-13, R.1. A lovely example of the popular and plentiful N-13 variety that is almost certainly from the famous Randall Hoard. This variety is an ideal candidate for a type collection due to its availability. MRB MS63.(#1616)

83 **1823/2 VF25 NGC.** N-1, Low R.2. While not scarce in an absolute sense, this date has considerable fame, overdate or not. The present midrange representative offers plum overtones on rich chocolate-brown surfaces showing light to moderate abrasions. MRB VF20.(#1630)

84 **1837 Plain Cords, Medium Letters MS65 Brown NGC.** N-8, R.1. Bold crisp denticles, a bold dot between EN of CENT, die scratches over ERIC, a spindly die crack on the upper reverse from 11 to 1 o'clock, and a light crack down from the right base of the E in ONE confirm the variety. Lustrous tan-brown surfaces display tints of purple and sharply struck design elements, save for the typical softness in the centers of the left and upper border stars. A highly attractive large cent. MRB MS60+. Census for the issue: 56 in 65 Brown, 23 finer (12/09).(#1735)

85 **1837 Plain Cords, Medium Letters MS63 Red and Brown PCGS.** N-1, R.3. Both sides have peripheral die cracks that provide ready attribution. This suitably struck representative displays faded orange-red near the margins. The lower left obverse quadrant has a couple of unobtrusive marks, and a small spot is on the bottom loop of the 8 in the date. MRB MS60+.(#1736)

86 **1839/6 VG8 NGC.** N-1, High R.3. From early dies without any evidence of the eventual heavy die crack between stars 3 and 4. The sole Newcomb marriage for this scarce blundered date *Guide Book* variety. A lightly abraded deep brown example that has minor granularity on the upper reverse periphery. MRB Good 6.(#1756)

Distinctive Undated Braided Hair Large Cent Struck on Half Cent Planchet, Fine Details

87 **Undated Braided Hair Large Cent—Struck on a Half Cent Planchet, Scratches—NCS. Fine Details.** 4.69 gm. All of STATES on the reverse, as well as parts of UNITED and OF on that side and most of the date on the obverse, are off the flan. Luminous chocolate-brown surfaces show a number of long scratches through the fields, and each side exhibits significant wear. Still, a highly desirable example of an early wrong-planchet error. MRB VG8.

Gem Red and Brown 1841 Cent, Newcomb-3

88 **1841 MS65 Red and Brown NGC. CAC.** N-3, R.2. Grellman Die State d. Crimson-red outlines the stars, legends, and hair, but the open fields, cheek, and neck are toned deep brown. Well struck and unabraded with only minor carbon. NGC has yet to certify an example as full Red. Housed in a former generation holder. MRB MS63. (#1833)

Undated (1847 N-1) Mature Head Large Cent Struck 35% Off-Center, MS64 Brown

89 **Undated Mature Head Cent—Struck 35% Off-Center—MS64 Brown NGC.** No date visible, but die markers, including a short diagonal line on Liberty's jaw, lines at RTY, and a lump on the base of E in CENT, identify this piece as 1847 N-1. Struck off-center just to the left of 6 o'clock; the unstruck arcs have an olive-gold cast, while deeper copper-blue and violet hues are present at the struck areas. A bold and intriguing error. MRB AU50.

Dramatic N-31 1848 Large Cent Error Struck 70% Off-Center, MS63 Brown

90 **1848 Large Cent—Struck 70% Off-Center—MS63 Brown NGC.** N-31, R.2. Though this large cent error was struck about 70% off-center toward 11 o'clock, this leaves two important pieces of information on the flan: first the date, and second the tiny die line between the ES in STATES that identifies the variety. Mushroom-brown surfaces show elements of blue and violet. MRB AU55.

91 **1849 MS64 Red and Brown PCGS.** N-3, R.4. Grellman Die State g. Grellman lists 22 distinct die states in his standard reference, due to crumbling of the reverse die. The borders are orange-red, while the centers are brown. Unabraded and beautifully preserved. MRB MS60+.(#1887)

92 **1851 MS64 Red and Brown PCGS.** N-2, R.1. Much closer to Red than Brown, although the cheek and obverse field are slightly too mellowed to command a Red designation. Lustrous and crisply struck with minor carbon and a solitary graze near the profile. MRB MS60+.(#1893)

Splendid 1853 N-3 Cent, MS66 Red and Brown

93 **1853 MS66 Red and Brown PCGS.** N-3, R.1. This lovely Premium Gem has considerable original red mint luster with considerable blue-brown toning, about 50% of each. The surfaces are smooth and frosty, with flowlines on the obverse and clashmarks on both sides, as struck. MRB MS64. Population: 5 in 66 Red and Brown, 0 finer (1/10). (#1902)

94 **1854 MS65 Red and Brown NGC.** N-14, Low R.2. Grellman die state b. Predominantly orange-gold, but some mellowing has occurred over the past 150+ years, especially on the central reverse. Impressively unabraded, and only one small spot is noted, near star 4. MRB MS64.(#1905)

Exquisite Red Gem 1855 Cent, N-4, Upright 5s

95 **1855 Upright 5s MS65 Red PCGS.** N-4, R.1. Grellman Die State a. This lustrous Gem has consistent brick-red color and is devoid of abrasions. A few minute spots require close attention to locate. Well struck aside from a few upper left star centers. This splendid Braided Hair cent type coin is certified in a green label holder. MRB MS65. (#1909)

96 **1857 Large Date MS65 Brown PCGS. CAC.** N-1, R.1. Sole Large Date die pair for the year. Despite the "Brown" designation, considerable faded red remains at the margins of this Gem. Solid centers but softly struck stars. MRB MS60.(#1928)

97 **1857 Small Date MS64 Brown PCGS.** N-4, R.1. The lines down from the earlobe allow for identification. The obverse has chocolate-brown color with glimpses of peripheral orange, while the reverse is 50% Red. Crisply struck except for the stars. MRB MS60+. Population: 8 in 64 Brown, 0 finer (1/10).(#1931)

98 **1857 Small Date MS65 Red and Brown NGC.** N-4, R.1. This Small Date example from the final year of the large cent offers a lovely blend of fresh copper-orange and rich violet colors. Smooth and attractive. MRB MS63.

FLYING EAGLE CENTS

99 **1857—Reverse Die Clash With Seated Quarter, Improperly Cleaned—NGC. AU Details.** FS-901, formerly FS-005. Snow-8. The reversed outline of the eagle's neck and wings from a Seated Liberty quarter is clearly visible in the area through and above ONE on the Flying Eagle cent reverse. Olive-brown surfaces with dark outlines at the obverse margins show the aftereffects of a past cleaning.

100 **1857 MS64 PCGS.** Lustrous salmon-pink and orange surfaces host well struck devices. A small carbon spot is noted below the second S in STATES, and on the reverse, a tiny mark is visible below the T in CENT.(#2016)

Appealing 1857 Gem Flying Eagle Cent

101 **1857 MS65 NGC.** Light tan-gold patination resides on the lustrous surfaces of this Gem and a well executed strike delivers sharp definition to the design elements, including the breast, wings, and bow knot. A couple of minute flecks on the reverse are undisturbing. Both sides present nice overall eye appeal. (#2016)

102 **1858 Large Letters MS64 NGC.** Low Leaves, Open E in ONE. A crisply struck and shimmering Choice type coin with blended almond-gold and steel-gray toning. Marks are insignificant, and the obverse margin displays interesting slender die cracks. (#2019)

Attractive MS65 1858 Small Letters Cent

103 **1858 Small Letters MS65 NGC.** Low Leaves Reverse, Closed E in ONE. The Small Letters variety with clear separation between all letters in AMERICA. This Gem offers smooth eye appeal with light honey-gold surfaces showing occasional elements of deeper copper-peach. A small dark spot below the eagle's beak is of little concern when compared to the overall eye appeal. (#2020)

PROOF FLYING EAGLE CENTS

Snow-3 1856 Flying Eagle Cent PR10

104 **1856 PR10 PCGS. CAC.** Snow-3. Although designated as a proof by PCGS, this is the business strike variety coined in 1856 for distribution to Washington officials. This tan-brown representative is evenly circulated and minutely granular. No marks are remotely consequential save for tiny rim ticks at 4 o'clock on the obverse and 1:30 on the reverse. (#2037)

Famous 1856 Flying Eagle Cent, PR62

105 **1856 PR62 PCGS. Eagle Eye Photo Seal, Card Included.** Snow-9, a variety associated with proof production of this historic issue that has been avidly sought since its debut more than 150 years ago. An intricately struck and satiny specimen that has a single identifier, a small thin mark on the right border of the T in UNITED. Careful examination also reveals a faint retained lamination near the obverse border at 8 o'clock. The obverse is golden-brown, and the reverse has dusky blended walnut and olive toning. The price of an 1856 Flying Eagle cent climbs relatively slowly with grade on a percentage basis, indicating that unworn, unimpaired examples provide excellent value relative to their circulated counterparts. (#2037)

Select Proof 1856 Flying Eagle Cent

106 **1856 PR63 PCGS.** Snow-9, a familiar variety for the surprisingly high-mintage Flying Eagle cent patterns of 1856. The date is popularly collected as part of the regular series, though the coins' pattern status is unquestioned. The present Select proof is sharply struck with a mixture of dusky gold-orange and light brown color on the surfaces. The obverse shows a handful of minor flyspecks, including one just along the lower line of the eagle's body. On the reverse, the disturbance around the EN in CENT is a planchet flaw which does not influence the technical grade, though the field to the right of ONE does show a shallow contact mark. (#2037)

1858 Large Letters Flying Eagle Cent, PR66
Approximately 20 Times Rarer Than the 1856

107 **1858 Large Letters PR66 NGC.** Snow PR-1. High Leaves, Closed E in ONE. An incredibly rare small cent issue, one of only 80 examples of the Large Letters Flying Eagle cent struck in proof format, a mintage figure that automatically makes this date about *20 times rarer than the 1856 Flying Eagle cent*. On top of that, perhaps only 50 or 60 pieces from that original production figure of 80 coins can be traced today. By way of contrast, the 1858 Small Letters proof coinage amounted to 200 pieces, and for the 1857 nearly 500 specimens were issued. The reflective, sunset-orange surfaces show considerable faded red around the obverse periphery and most of the reverse, which adds accents of aqua and indigo. All design elements are sharp and crisp, and one must search diligently with a loupe to detect even the smallest detrimental marks or flecks. A collection highlight in the making. Census: 2 in 66, 0 finer (1/10). (#2042)

Spectacular Cameo Proof 1858 Large Letters Cent, PR67

108 **1858 Large Letters PR67 Cameo NGC.** Snow-PR1, the obverse with small die chips in the denticles below the date, which slopes up and to the right; these chips are weakened but visible. The reverse is the High Leaves variety, as with all proof 1858 Large Letters cents. Richard Snow lists an estimated mintage of 100 Large Letters proofs in his *Guide Book of Flying Eagle and Indian Head Cents*.

As might be expected a mintage of just 100 pieces, high-grade specimens are rarities; in the NGC *Census Report*, there are only four proof Flying Eagle cents at the 67 grade level, regardless of issue or contrast designation, with none finer (1/10). Of the four pieces, three are of the 1858 Large Letters Variety, two Cameo and one Ultra Cameo, and the possibility of a multiple submission among the three 1858 Large Letters coins cannot be ruled out entirely. In addition, the PCGS *Population Report* shows no 1858 Large Letters pieces in PR67 or higher.

Snow notes for the issue in his *Guide Book*, "The Proofs of this year are usually exceptional with deep mirror fields and outstanding strikes." True to those words, this Superb Gem has remarkably reflective surfaces, rose-accented copper-gold with pale lilac-blue peripheral elements. Lightly frosted, fully struck devices supply considerable contrast that meets more than the minimum needed for a Cameo designation. A small contact mark below the second S in STATES serves as a pedigree marker, and a minor strike-through is visible below the trailing ribbon to the left of the knot on the reverse. (#82042)

INDIAN CENTS

109 **1860 Pointed Bust MS64 PCGS.** FS-401, formerly FS-006.4. A satiny and evenly struck near-Gem with light tan-gold color and virtually no marks aside from a solitary tick on the N in ONE. Population: 75 in 64, 35 finer (12/09).(#2056)

Lovely MS66 1860 Cent

110 **1860 MS66 PCGS.** A lovely Premium Gem example of the more available Rounded Bust version of the 1860 cent, light peach-tan in color with occasional elements of olive. Well struck with all four diamonds on Liberty's ribbon sharp and complete. PCGS has certified a mere eight finer representatives (1/10). (#2058)

Remarkable MS66 ★ 1861 Cent

111 **1861 MS66 ★ NGC.** Unusual and exciting color defines the eye appeal of this Premium Gem. Gold-orange, rose-violet, and blue-green elements mingle on the surfaces, which sparkle with luster. An uncommonly beautiful and delightfully preserved example of this copper-nickel Indian cent issue. NGC has graded a mere three numerically finer pieces (1/10). (#2061)

112 **1862 MS65 PCGS. CAC.** Copper-gold luster envelops both sides of this Gem, each of which is devoid of significant marks. Generally well struck, except for the usual softness in the feather tips. All four diamonds are sharp. Housed in a green label holder. (#2064)

Very Rare Copper-Nickel 1864 With L Cent
Sharpness of AU

113 **1864 L On Ribbon—Struck on a Copper-Nickel Planchet, Corroded—ANACS. AU50 Details.** This well struck medium-brown and rose example has little if any actual wear but is moderately porous and has distributed tiny freckles of ebony verdigris. The progression of 1864 cents is Copper-Nickel, Bronze No L, Bronze L On Ribbon. A few Copper-Nickel L On Ribbon pieces exist. Richard Snow, in the second edition of his 1859-1869 attribution guide, states that three examples are known: two pieces from proof dies and a single business strike. The present piece, discovered after the publication of the aforementioned guide, is also a business strike and matches none of the three L On Ribbon proof obverse dies. The Copper-Nickel L On Ribbon pieces are difficult to classify. They are listed as Judd-358 but could also be considered off-metal errors, similar to the famous 1943 bronze cent. However, since they were struck on regular issue dies in an alloy used for circulation that year, they are technically a regular issue rather than a mint error or pattern. If so, Snow notes, "they would certainly be one of the rarest regular issue coins in all numismatics."

114 **1865 Plain 5 MS65 Red and Brown PCGS.** Snow-6, 865/865. Repunching is visible under the tops of the digits. Richard Snow writes in the second edition of his *1859-1869 Attribution Guide:* "This variety is slightly scarce. The finest seen is MS-65RB." Copper-gold luster shows through whispers of light tan patina on this well struck Red and Brown Gem. Devoid of mentionable marks and spots. Population for the issue: 14 in 65 Red and Brown, 0 finer (12/09).(#92083)

115 **1866 MS65 Red and Brown PCGS.** Light tan patination resides on the golden surfaces of this well impressed Gem. A nicely preserved piece with no significant marks. Population: 61 in 65 Red and Brown, 1 finer (12/09).(#2086)

Attractive 1867 Cent, MS65 Red
Important Condition Rarity

116 **1867 MS65 Red NGC. CAC.** The 1867 is an important rarity in Red Gem condition and virtually unobtainable any finer. Attractive copper-gold luster invigorates both sides, each of which exhibits sharply struck design motifs, including the feather tips and all four diamonds. Devoid of significant marks or spots. Census: 2 in 65 Red, 0 finer (1/10). (#2090)

117 **1868 MS66 Brown PCGS.** Attractive and lustrous bluish-brown surfaces retain traces of original mint red near the borders. This is the single finest "Brown" example of the date.(#2091)

Desirable 1869 Cent, Snow-4, MS64 Red

118 **1869 MS64 Red PCGS. CAC.** Snow-4. The 69 in the date is lightly repunched north. Copper-gold luster enlivens both sides of this near-Gem, each of which exhibits well struck design features. A few minuscule flecks are undisturbing. All in all, a highly attractive coin, appropriately recognized by CAC. Population: 45 in 64 Red, 35 finer (12/09). (#2096)

119 **1870 Doubled Die Obverse MS64 Red and Brown PCGS. CAC.** FS-101, formerly FS-008.6. Snow-1, paired with a reverse that shows minor die doubling on the upright of the E in CENT. The obverse is repunched and exhibits a widely die doubled TY in LIBERTY. Bold N in ONE. Golden-brown overall with glimpses of sea-green on the portrait highpoints. Well struck and unabraded. (#2098)

120 **1873 Open 3 MS65 Red and Brown PCGS. CAC.** Whispers of reddish-tan and sky-blue run over the lustrous surfaces of this well cared-for Gem. Sharply struck, including the feather tips and all four diamonds. Only the upper part of the shield shows some minor softness. Population: 50 in 65 Red and Brown, 3 finer (1/10). (#2107)

121 **1877 VF30 NGC.** The slightly deeper brown fields of this key date representative nicely highlight the lighter design motifs. Great overall definition despite light, even wear. The letters LI and RTY of LIBERTY are sharp, as are the tops of BE. Attractive, clean surfaces add to the coin's appeal.(#2127)

Popular 1877 Cent, XF40

122 **1877 XF40 NGC.** A deeply toned walnut-brown representative of this perennial collector favorite, lightly worn with only a few scattered digs in and around the portrait. As always on circulation-strike pieces, the lower corner of the N in ONE is softly defined. A great coin for a similarly graded or slightly higher-condition date set. (#2127)

1877 Cent, MS63 Red and Brown

123 **1877 MS63 Red and Brown PCGS. Eagle Eye Seal, Card Included.** Shallow N in ONE, characteristic of business strikes of this famous series key. Orange-gold fills the borders and design recesses, while the open fields and face are brown. The strike is good, although the feather tips and the bow knot exhibit incompleteness. Unabraded aside from a pair of nearly imperceptible thin marks through the bonnet ribbon and the M in AMERICA. Carbon is limited to the field beneath STATES. (#2128)

124 **1892 MS66 Red and Brown PCGS.** Lustrous copper-tan surfaces exhibit sharply struck design elements, including crispness on the diamonds and about half of the feather tips. A couple of minute obverse marks do not detract. Population: 1 in 66 Red and Brown, 0 finer (1/10).(#2182)

125 **1895 MS66 Red NGC.** A bold strike and rich orange luster characterize this Premium Gem Indian cent. A splash of olive toning is visible on the obverse. Census: 32 in 66 Red, 8 finer (1/10).(#2192)

126 **1895 MS66 Red NGC.** Even, fiery red mint luster covers both sides of this impressive, high grade type coin. The striking details are strong throughout, and the only mentionable flaw is a tiny speck of carbon at 6 o'clock on the lower reverse. Census: 32 in 66 Red, 8 finer (1/10).(#2192)

Amazing MS67 Red 1902 Indian Cent

127 **1902 MS67 Red PCGS.** Phenomenal quality in an Indian cent and undoubtedly one of the finest type coins available on the market today in this "common" series. Indian cents are only common until one begins to search for a coin of this quality. That is when it becomes apparent how great the demand is and how tightly held such pieces are. This example has totally original surfaces. The obverse is even orange-red, while the reverse is a deeper, almost cherry-red. The abrasions and carbon spots usually seen on Indian cents are absent here, and the strike is sharp. Population: 9 in 67 Red, 0 finer (1/10). (#2213)

PROOF INDIAN CENTS

128 **1863 PR64 PCGS. CAC.** Both sides show a pattern of peripheral copper-orange giving way to a lavender infusion in the center. On the obverse, additional umber elements are present at the upper and right margins.(#2262)

129 **1866 PR64 Red and Brown PCGS.** Reddish-tan freckles with an occasional sky-blue dapple run over each side of this near-Gem proof. Mirrored fields nicely set off the sharply struck devices. Some unobtrusive marks prevent the attainment of Gem classification. Population: 75 in 64 Red and Brown, 50 finer (1/10). (#2286)

130 **1867 PR65 Red and Brown PCGS.** A flashy and fully struck Gem that displays deeply variegated peach-red, forest-green, and honey-gold. One tiny spot is near the M in AMERICA. In an old green label holder.(#2289)

131 **1867 PR64 Red NGC.** Slight mellowing of the brilliant mint red color is evident on this attractive proof Indian cent. Both sides have traces of violet toning close to the borders.(#2290)

132 **1868 PR64 Red PCGS.** This delightful proof has fully brilliant pale orange surfaces with hints of toning on each side. A few minor spots preclude an even finer designation. The reverse is rotated approximately 170 degrees clockwise. Population: 28 in 64 Red, 9 finer (12/09).(#2293)

Red Gem Proof 1870 Cent

133 **1870 PR65 Red PCGS. CAC.** Shallow N in ONE. A lovely example of this elusive date. The pumpkin-gold surfaces are virtually unmellowed, and are clean aside from a fleck beneath the F in OF. The strike appears full, even on the tips of the headdress. A highly attractive Gem proof Indian cent. Population: 23 in 65 Red, 4 finer (12/09). (#2299)

134 **1871 PR65 Red and Brown PCGS. Eagle Eye Photo Seal, Card Included.** Shallow N in ONE. The color is primarily apricot, although the centers exhibit mild lilac or jade-green hues. This well struck Gem has a few distributed pinpoint flecks.(#2301)

135 **1872 PR65 Red and Brown PCGS. CAC.** Bold N in ONE. This precisely struck Gem approaches full Red, since the coin is predominately orange and sun-gold. Satiny and undisturbed aside from a pinpoint spot at 5 o'clock on the reverse.(#2304)

136 **1873 Closed 3 PR64 Red and Brown PCGS. Eagle Eye Seal, Card Included.** This needle-sharp Choice proof cent displays cobalt-blue, apple-green, and violet at the centers, while the borders are sun-gold. A popular, lower mintage date.(#2307)

Stunning 1873 Cent, Closed 3, PR66 Red

137 **1873 Closed 3 PR66 Red NGC.** This stunning Premium Gem displays a degree of field-motif contrast at various angles, especially on the obverse. The copper-gold surfaces are imbued with traces of crimson and sky-blue on the reverse and exhibit razor-sharp definition on the design elements. Devoid of significant contacts or spots. Census: 2 in 66 Red, 0 finer (12/09). (#2308)

138 **1875 PR66 Red and Brown PCGS.** A appealing woodgrain effect dominates the eye appeal, with speckled purple-violet and red-gold patina across both sides. Crisply struck with watery reflectivity in the fields and impressive surface preservation. Several tiny die lines and die lumps (as struck) appear just beneath Liberty's earlobe. Population: 8 in 66 Red and Brown, 0 finer (1/10).(#2313)

Lovely PR65 Red 1875 Cent

139 **1875 PR65 Red PCGS.** Bold copper-orange color shows occasional subtle variations, such as tiny milk-white spots through the upper borders. Strongly mirrored for a copper proof of the era with bold definition and no singularly mentionable flaws. PCGS has graded just two finer Red specimens (12/09). (#2314)

Dynamic PR65 Red 1876 Cent

140 **1876 PR65 Red PCGS. CAC.** A needle-sharp Centennial-year Gem, noteworthy for its field reflectivity and its radiant yellow-gold and ruby-red color. A few minute flecks beneath the shoulder curl fail to distract. Encased in an old green label holder. Population: 20 in 65 Red, 8 finer (12/09). (#2317)

Elegant 1876 Cent, Red Gem Proof

141 **1876 PR65 Red PCGS.** An amazing Red Gem struck during America's Centennial celebrations, an event that coincided and arguably presaged the elevated proof mintages seen in later proof Indian cent issues. Strong lemon-gold color dominates the obverse, while the upper fringes of that side and most of the reverse show a deeper peach hue. The surfaces never approach Red and Brown territory. Population: 20 in 65 Red, 8 finer (1/10). (#2317)

Popular PR63 Red 1877 Cent

142 **1877 PR63 Red PCGS.** This Select proof shows considerable variation in color, from lemon-gold to hazel, honey to cherry, yet no shade falls into strictly "Brown" territory. Aside from a handful of flyspecks and hairlines, an entirely pleasing example of this popular proof issue, made famous by its low-mintage business strike counterpart. (#2320)

143 **1878 PR65 Red PCGS.** Bold copper-orange color has remained steadfast for more than a century. A remarkably appealing Gem specimen with a crisp strike. Population: 36 in 65 Red, 9 finer (12/09).(#2323)

Prized PR66 Red Cameo 1881 Cent

144 **1881 PR66 Red Cameo NGC.** The mirrored fields highlight the devices on this Premium Gem Red Cameo proof, and an exacting strike leaves sharp definition on the design features. Copper-gold surfaces are devoid of mentionable contact marks, though a few tiny light flecks are visible on each side. Great overall eye appeal. (#82332)

145 **1886 Type Two PR65 Red and Brown NGC.** Fantastic magenta, cherry, violet, and olive-brown hues enliven this sharply struck Gem. A carefully preserved specimen with amazing eye appeal. (#92346)

146 **1889 PR65 Red and Brown PCGS.** Vivaciously toned in shades of aqua-blue, lilac-red, and apple-green. Nicely struck and unabraded with no obvious carbon. An affordable high grade 19th century type coin.(#2355)

147 **1891 PR65 Red PCGS.** Certified in a green-label holder with the expected needle-sharp strike, this pleasing Red Gem proof boasts a consistent brick-red appearance with lighter golden color on the high points. Population: 15 in 65 Red, 4 finer (12/09). (#2362)

148 **1893 PR65 Red PCGS.** Rich orange, gold, and olive dominate, but a blush of crimson-lilac iridescence is noted over Liberty's headdress. A few minute obverse flecks correspond with the assigned grade. A conditionally scarce issue. Housed in a green label holder. Population: 26 in 65 Red, 8 finer (12/09).
Ex: Joshua Collection (Heritage, 1/2001), lot 6298.(#2368)

149 **1897 PR66 Red and Brown NGC.** From cherry-red to magenta through violet and blueberry, this Premium Gem proof's eclectic and electric patina should appeal to the toning enthusiast. Carefully preserved with outlandish eye appeal. Census: 14 in 66 Red and Brown, 4 finer (12/09).(#2379)

150 **1898 PR67 Red and Brown NGC.** The fire-red color that fills the obverse center has subtle lime hues at the fringes. The more deeply toned reverse exhibits plum, gold, and olive colors. Exquisitely struck, as expected of a proof striking. Carefully preserved with minimal carbon.(#2382)

151 **1902 PR64 Red and Brown PCGS.** This precisely struck and glossy near-Gem displays cherry-red, canary-gold, and olive-green hues. Encapsulated in an old green label holder.(#2394)

LINCOLN CENTS

152 **1909 VDB Doubled Die Obverse MS65 Red and Brown PCGS.** FS-1101, formerly FS-012. The date and the RTY in LIBERTY are nicely die doubled. A splendid Gem with considerable orange mint color, especially on the obverse.(#82424)

Impressive 1909 VDB Cent, MS66 Red FS-1101, Doubled Die Obverse

153 **1909 VDB Doubled Die Obverse MS66 Red PCGS.** FS-1101, formerly FS-012. Portions of LIBERTY and the date are strongly die doubled on the FS-1101, not to be confused with the other obverse doubled die variety listed in the *Cherrypickers' Guide*, FS-1102, which is less impressive. Putting aside considerations of the variety, this example is a fire-red Premium Gem with an exemplary strike and no individually distracting marks. Thorough perusal beneath a glass eventually encounters a few pinpoint flecks, but the overall eye appeal is amazing for the grade. Population: 7 in 66 Red, 1 finer (1/10). (#82425)

154 **1909-S VDB XF45 NGC.** A minimally marked and attractive teak-brown example of the famous 1909-S VDB cent. A small dot of deeper color is centered on the left side of the M in AMERICA on the reverse.(#2426)

155 **1909-S VDB—Environmental Damage—NGC. AU Details.** This sharply struck key date cent has substantial luster and minimal wear. Streaks of steel-blue and gunmetal-gray fail to overlie all traces of the initial pumpkin-gold color. One hair-thin horizontal mark near the ear, but the surfaces show only unobtrusive granularity. (#2426)

156 **1909-S VDB MS63 Brown NGC.** Gold luster shows through the thin veil of semi-streaked light tan patination. A decisive strike leaves strong definition on the design elements, including the date, mintmark, and designer initials. A few minuscule ticks are unimportant. An appealing piece for the grade and color designation.(#2426)

157 **1909-S VDB MS64 Brown NGC.** Copper-gold luster shows through the whispers of light tan patina and a decisive strike leaves sharp detail on the design elements, including the date, mintmark, and designer's initials. Very pleasing for a near-Gem and the Brown color designation.(#2426)

Pleasing 1909-S VDB Cent, MS64 Red and Brown

158 **1909-S VDB MS64 Red and Brown NGC. CAC.** Soft mint-green, crimson, and gold patination assumes slightly deeper hues on the reverse of this near-Gem. Lustrous surfaces exhibit well struck design features, though the VDB initials are somewhat mushy. A few light marks take nothing from the pleasing overall eye appeal. (#2427)

Attractive 1909-S VDB Cent, MS65 Red and Brown

159 **1909-S VDB MS65 Red and Brown PCGS.** A mix of attractive purple, orange, mint-green, and sky-blue patination adorns both sides of this Gem. A well executed strike delivers strong definition to the design elements, though the VDB initials are a tad soft. Devoid of mentionable marks or spots. (#2427)

Sharp 1909-S VDB Cent, MS66 Red and Brown

160 **1909-S VDB MS66 Red and Brown PCGS.** This Premium Gem key date representative exhibits sharply defined design elements, including the bow tie and wheat stalks and the all-important mintmark and VDB initials. A blend of gold, maroon, and sky-blue patination bathes well cared-for surfaces. Population: 28 in 66 Red and Brown, 0 finer (12/09). (#2427)

Dazzling 1909-S VDB Cent, MS65 Red

161 **1909-S VDB MS65 Red NGC. CAC.** Dazzling luster and beautiful orange-red color confirm the exemplary quality of this key date Gem. The strike is sharp, even on the often blurry initials. Unabraded, and only the rare pinpoint fleck denies perfection. Encased in a prior generation holder. (#2428)

Appealing 1909-S VDB Red Gem Cent

162 **1909-S VDB MS65 Red PCGS.** Uniform copper-gold luster invigorates both sides of this key-date Gem representative. An exacting strike delivers crisp delineation to the design features, readily apparent in the date, mintmark, and VDB initials. No mentionable contact marks or spots take away from the great overall eye appeal. (#2428)

163 **1909-S MS65 Red PCGS. CAC.** Like nearly all surviving examples, this Gem is fully brilliant with golden mint luster and bold design definition. A few darker toning splashes on each side do little to diminish the excellent eye appeal.(#2434)

164 **1912-S MS65 Red and Brown PCGS.** Copper-orange coloration with hints of light green bathes both sides of this Gem and a well executed strike leaves sharp detail on the design elements save for softness in the right wheat stalk. What appears to be a linear planchet flaw is visible on the shoulder. Population: 26 in 65 Red and Brown, 2 finer (1/10).(#2457)

165 **1914-D XF45 PCGS.** Attractive medium-brown color with subtle blue overtones on the obverse. Only a few stray marks are present on this lightly circulated better-date cent. Previously graded XF45 by NGC; insert accompanies lot.(#2471)

Exceptional 1914-D Cent, MS64 Brown

166 **1914-D MS64 Brown NGC.** Light to medium brown surfaces display hints of underlying reddish-orange luster and a well executed strike leaves strong definition on the design elements, including the hair and lettering, areas sometimes showing weakness. No significant spots are visible. This is an exceptional key date representative in the Lincoln cent series. Census: 45 in 64 Brown, 17 finer (1/10). (#2471)

Well Struck 1914-D Cent, MS64 Red and Brown

167 **1914-D MS64 Red and Brown PCGS. CAC.** This near-Gem key-date representative displays a better strike than usually seen, including strong detail in Lincoln's hair, the lettering, and the wheat stalks. A few light freckles of purplish-tan visit the copper-gold lustrous surfaces. Devoid of significant marks or flecks. Red and Brown pieces are difficult to locate any finer. (#2472)

Full Red 1914-S Lincoln Cent, MS65
One of the Great Color Rarities in the Series

168 **1914-S MS65 Red PCGS.** As David Lange explains in his series reference, the problem with the scarcity of full Red 1914-S cents lies in the generally poor planchet stock used. He also points out a conundrum: "It seems that sharply struck coins are invariably dark, while the few bright examples tend to be mushy." This coin is the exception to the rule. It has wonderful, bright red color and is fully struck. The mattelike surfaces show no mentionable abrasions on either side. This is a coin for the advanced collector to seriously consider. Population: 32 in 65 Red, 3 finer (12/09). (#2476)

Magnificent 1919 Cent, MS67 Red

169 **1919 MS67 Red PCGS.** The 1919 is available with little trouble through MS65 Red, and even Premium Gems with that color designation can be located with little difficulty. Superb Gems are much more challenging, and finer-grade specimens are nearly unobtainable. Orange-gold luster imbued with tints of light green endows this MS67 offering. Sharply struck and impeccably preserved. Population: 58 in 67 Red, 15 finer (12/09). (#2515)

Red Gem 1919-D Cent

170 **1919-D MS65 Red NGC.** The obverse of this MS65 1919-D cent offers amazing copper-orange color that shines boldly with occasional suggestions of rose. While the reverse displays a degree of spotting through the upper obverse, the present example displays well. Census: 21 in 65 Red, 0 finer (1/10). (#2518)

171 **1922 No D Strong Reverse VF20 PCGS.** FS-401, formerly FS-013.2. Die Pair 2. This pleasing olive-brown example has all of the hallmarks of Die Pair 2, considered the only true 1922 "Plain" Lincoln cent. The obverse has the usual weak strike while the reverse is bold. The surfaces are smooth with only a few grade-consistent marks.(#3285)

172 **1922 No D Strong Reverse VF25 NGC.** FS-401, formerly FS-013.2. Die Pair 2. This chocolate-brown VF coin shows occasional rose-violet and gold overtones. Bold lines in the reverse wheat ears identify its prized variety.(#3285)

Outstanding MS67 Red 1925 Cent

173 **1925 MS67 Red PCGS.** Strong lemon-gold and copper-orange hues dominate the centers, while the margins fade back to pale peach. All colors on this Superb Gem are thoroughly Red, however, and thoroughly attractive. A boldly struck and carefully preserved cent. Population: 55 in 67 Red, 0 finer (12/09). (#2560)

174 **1926 MS67 Red PCGS.** Pale copper-peach surfaces come alive with splashes of electric tangerine. A dynamic Superb Gem example of this much-favored Lincoln cent issue. Population: 77 in 67 Red, 0 finer (12/09).(#2569)

175 **1926 MS67 Red PCGS.** PCGS has graded no finer Red representatives than this stunning MS67 coin (12/09). Fresh orange and lemon luster adds an element of pale sea-green at the right margins.(#2569)

176 **1926 MS67 Red PCGS.** A bright and shining Superb Gem with bold copper-orange luster and crisp definition. Only a few tiny disturbances in the fields preclude an even finer designation. Tied for the finest Red example certified by NGC or PCGS (12/09). (#2569)

177 **1926-D MS64 Red PCGS.** Attractive copper-gold luster invigorates both sides of this near-Gem cent and a solid strike brings out strong definition on the design elements. A few inoffensive marks preclude Gem status. PCGS has certified fewer than 50 pieces finer (1/10).(#2572)

1943-S Cent Struck in Bronze, VF35
An Amazing Branch Mint Error Rarity

178 **1943-S Cent—Struck on a Bronze Planchet—VF35 PCGS.** Coming on the heels of Heritage's offering of a 1943 bronze cent struck at Philadelphia in our January 2010 FUN Auction, we are now proud to present this 1943-S bronze cent for the February 2010 Long Beach Auction. More Philadelphia Mint 1943 bronze cents are known than D-mint and S-mint errors put together; most recent censuses state that only one 1943-D bronze cent is known, plus seven 1943-S bronze cents. The latter figure, however, may overstate the actual population by one or even two pieces, since most of the known survivors are clustered in a narrow range from AU to low Mint State.

In that respect, this coin is unusual by virtue of its Choice VF grade. It is also a relatively recent entrant to the numismatic marketplace; it was unknown to David Lange in 1996, when he published his *Complete Guide to Lincoln Cents*, having been "kept for decades" privately by the owner, but sold alongside the Dr. Carl A. Minning, Jr. Collection in an August 1999 auction by Bowers and Merena. How the coin came to be VF, unlike its fellows, remains unclear.

As expected for a VF35 coin, this piece shows light to moderate wear over each side, and the surfaces show a number of light digs and abrasions under magnification. That said, the overall eye appeal is far better than the preceding sentence might suggest. The coin's glossy olive-gold and mushroom-brown color, accented in cobalt-blue, is highly redeeming, as is the strike. In short, a memorable opportunity for the Lincoln cent enthusiast, which could be either a second chance at a 1943-dated bronze cent or the second step to assembling a "date set" of these famous 20th century rarities.
Ex: The Dr. Carl A. Minning, Jr. Collection (and Other Properties) (Bowers and Merena, 8/1999), lot 1122; The Collections of Phillip Flannagan et al. (Bowers and Merena, 11-12/2001), lot 6076.
From The Alfred V. Melson Collection, Part Two.

179 **1955 Doubled Die Obverse—Improperly Cleaned—NGC. AU Details.** FS-101, formerly FS-021.8. A lightly worn example of the famous doubled die. Rose-violet and olive-brown surfaces are glossy from a past cleaning, though there are few overt abrasions. (#2825)

1955 Doubled Die Obverse Cent, MS64 Brown

180 **1955 Doubled Die Obverse MS64 Brown PCGS.** FS-101, formerly FS-021.8. Blue influences add eye appeal to the smooth walnut-brown surfaces of this Choice 1955 Doubled Die Obverse cent. The strike is as bold as the spread on the obverse. A tiny spot of deep color appears along the right obverse rim, and the upper reverse shows a faint fingerprint, but these are minor quibbles in context. (#2825)

Lustrous MS64 Brown 1955 Cent Doubled Die Obverse

181 **1955 Doubled Die Obverse MS64 Brown PCGS.** FS-101, formerly FS-021.8. This richly toned Choice Doubled Die cent displays deep powder-blue, lilac, and olive-brown shades. Lustrous, crisply struck, and carefully preserved. The Lincoln cent, Wheat Reverse collection in Brown offers many opportunities as well as challenges in the current market environment. PCGS has certified only six Brown examples finer (1/10). (#2825)

Heralded 1955 Doubled Die Obverse Cent MS64 Red and Brown

182 **1955 Doubled Die Obverse MS64 Red and Brown NGC.** FS-101, formerly FS-025.5. No magnifying glass is required to appreciate the dramatic die doubling on the famous 1955 *Guide Book* variety. Most survivors are circulated or toned brown, but the present near-Gem has substantial orange-red, although the portrait high points are lilac. Lustrous and unabraded. (#2826)

Famous 1955 Doubled Die Obverse Cent MS64 Red

183 **1955 Doubled Die Obverse MS64 Red PCGS.** FS-101, formerly FS-021.8. Remarkable copper-orange luster with minimal obverse carbon, though the reverse shows scattered flyspecks. The doubling on the obverse is bold, as is the strike. Fully Red examples of this famous doubled die variety are highly elusive, and PCGS has graded just 18 finer pieces in the Red category (1/10). (#2827)

184 **1960-D Small Over Large Date MS66 Red PCGS.** FS-101, formerly FS-025.5. The recut D is not noted on the PCGS holder, nevertheless, the second D is distinct and nearly complete, although faint, north of the more prominent mintmark. The doubled date, the result of hub doubling, is plainly visible under magnification. Beautiful orange-gold luster is imbued with hints of crimson. Sharply struck and well cared for. Population: 11 in 66 Red, 0 finer (1/10).(#82869)

185 **1971 Doubled Die Obverse MS64 Red PCGS.** FS-101, formerly FS-031. All obverse legends are die doubled, most prominently on the IBER in LIBERTY. Many times rarer than the better known 1972 Doubled Die Obverse. A lustrous and only lightly abraded orange-gold near-Gem with a few small gray freckles on the left reverse. Population: 27 in 64 Red, 22 finer (1/10).(#82941)

Notable 1971 Doubled Die Cent, MS65 Red

186 **1971 Doubled Die Obverse MS65 Red PCGS.** FS-101, formerly FS-031. Broad doubling through the lower letters and digits, and to a lesser extent on IN GOD WE TRUST. A bright copper-orange Gem example of this popular *Guide Book* variety, minimally marked but with minor spotting noted in the field below the Lincoln Memorial. (#82941)

PROOF LINCOLN CENTS

187 **1909 PR64 Red and Brown PCGS.** Predominantly fire-red, although the high points are lavender-red. An undisturbed and intricately struck Choice matte proof from the eventful first year of the long-lived series. Encapsulated in a green label holder. (#3304)

Richly Toned PR66 Red and Brown 1909 Lincoln Cent

188 **1909 PR66 Red and Brown PCGS.** Electric colors dominate the eye appeal of this post-VDB 1909 Lincoln cent matte proof. Colors range from pale pink accents to the dominant cherry-rose and elements of magenta-violet at the margins. Precisely struck with minimally disturbed surfaces. Population: 23 in 66 Red and Brown, 2 finer (12/09). (#3304)

1909 PR66 Lincoln Cent, Full Red With Attractive Peripheral Toning

189 **1909 PR66 Red PCGS.** The boldly impressed devices are contact-free, and the granular fields range from bright copper-gold to warm sunset-orange, with a few tiny carbon spots at the lower reverse periphery. While the matte finish employed on these pieces was popular for medals, most contemporary numismatists disliked the finish, and the change is an often-cited culprit for the end of proof production in 1916. Population: 39 in 66 Red, 6 finer (12/09). (#3305)

Exceptional PR66 Red 1910 Lincoln Cent

190 **1910 PR66 Red PCGS.** The matte proof cents from 1910 are a challenging issue to locate in both high grade and with full red mint luster still intact. Proof cents were sold as part of minor, silver, and gold proof sets, but apparently they were not distributed individually. The total number of proofs struck according to the National Archives was 4,083 pieces, much higher than previously believed. Nevertheless, only a handful exist today in full Red because the Mint distributed the coins in sulfur-laden tissue paper that quickly toned the surfaces. This bright, sparkling example has a yellowish tinge to the red. Each side shows pronounced granularity, indicative of an earlier striking. The details are intricately brought up on each side, and there are no mentionable or noticeable contact marks. Population: 20 in 66 Red, 3 finer (12/09). (#3308)

191 **1911 PR65 Brown PCGS.** A medley of tan, lime-green, crimson, and sky-blue patina adorns both sides of this Gem, and a well executed strike leaves crisp definition on the design elements. This is truly a super-looking coin. Population: 27 in 65 Brown, 8 finer (1/10).(#3309)

192 **1912 PR65 Brown PCGS.** Despite the generous mintage of 2,172 pieces, 1912 proof cents are scarce. The glossy surfaces of this Brown Gem display crisply struck devices. Multicolored obverse toning cedes to olive-brown on the reverse. Free of mentionable marks or spots. Population: 35 in 65 Brown, 10 finer (1/10).(#3312)

193 **1912 PR64 Red and Brown NGC.** A needle-sharp matte proof cent that has streaky cherry-red, ruby, forest-green, and sun-gold toning. One thin mark noted above LIBERTY. Encased in a prior generation holder.(#3313)

194 **1913 PR65 Red and Brown PCGS.** Lustrous copper-gold obverse surfaces cede to a bluish-gray, crimson, and copper-gold reverse. Crisply struck, and revealing some light flecks over each side. Population: 66 in 65 Red and Brown, 15 finer (1/10). (#3316)

195 **1913 PR65 Red and Brown PCGS.** Lustrous surfaces exhibit decisively struck design elements and are covered with an array of gold, purple, green, and bluish-purple toning. A few flecks are scattered over each side. Population: 66 in 65 Red and Brown, 15 finer (1/10).(#3316)

Beautiful 1936 Satin Finish Cent, PR65 Red

196 **1936 Type One—Satin Finish PR65 Red PCGS.** Rich orange luster with satin surfaces are accompanied by a trace of deeper toning on this delightful satin Gem. Both sides of this beauty are pristine with few obvious spots or surface marks. Population: 54 in 65 Red, 24 finer (1/10). (#3332)

197 **1939 PR67 Red NGC.** An absolutely beautiful cent, this Superb Gem proof has fully brilliant orange color with deeply mirrored fields and exceptional aesthetic appeal. Only a few trivial specks prevent an even higher grade. Census: 27 in 67 Red, 0 finer (1/10). (#3344)

198 **1956 PR67 Red Deep Cameo PCGS.** Radiant devices and legends exhibit considerable contrast with the glass fields. The pumpkin-gold color is unmellowed, and the strike is unimprovable. A couple of nearly microscopic flecks deny numismatic perfection. Population: 35 in 67 Red Deep Cameo, 6 finer (1/10). (#93377)

199 **1958 PR68 Red Cameo PCGS.** A flashy and razor-sharp orange-gold Superb Gem with essentially pristine preservation. Obvious cameo contrast sets the present piece apart from the usual 1950s proof cent. Population: 22 in 68 Red Cameo, 0 finer (1/10). (#83383)

Rare Close AM 1998-S Cent
PR69 Red Deep Cameo

200 **1998-S Close AM PR69 Red Deep Cameo PCGS.** Proof 1998-S cents were supposed to have been struck from a different reverse hub than 1998-dated business strikes. Proofs should have the FG initials close to the Lincoln Memorial, and the AM in AMERICA should be normally spaced. A handful of proofs were struck from a business strike hub with a distant FG and a close AM. These are coveted by Registry Set collectors, especially when the coin is as close to perfect as the present specimen. Population: 39 in 69 Red Deep Cameo, 0 finer (1/10). (#93529)

TWO CENT PIECES

201 **1864 Large Motto MS65 Red PCGS.** Fresh copper-peach luster with no suggestion of turning and only a handful of flyspecks. This Red Gem is ideal for the type enthusiast.(#3578)

202 **1866 MS66 Red and Brown NGC.** Light tan patina resides on the softly lustrous surfaces of this Premium Gem two cent piece and a well executed strike delivers strong definition to the design elements. Devoid of significant marks or spots. Census: 8 in 66 Red and Brown, 0 finer (1/10).(#3589)

PROOF TWO CENT PIECES

203 **1866 PR64 Red and Brown NGC. CAC.** A flashy and razor-sharp near-Gem with lime and fire-red color. One small spot clings to a vertical shield stripe. A meager 725 proofs were struck. In an old prehologram holder.(#3631)

Splendid 1870 Two Cent, PR65 Red

204 **1870 PR65 Red PCGS.** Splendid copper-gold color displays hints of light orange, and an exacting strike delivers crisp delineation to the design elements. A few small spots are visible on the obverse. From a mintage of 1,000 or so pieces. Population: 37 in 65 Red, 9 finer (12/09). (#3644)

205 **1871 PR64 Red PCGS.** A shimmering salmon-pink near-Gem. Unabraded and crisply struck. Distributed minor carbon decides the grade. TRUST is die doubled, diagnostic of this proof issue. Housed in a first-generation holder. Population: 41 in 64 Red, 49 finer (1/10).(#3647)

PR66 Red and Brown 1872 Two Cent

206 **1872 PR66 Red and Brown NGC. CAC.** The year 1872 saw the end of the business strike two cent piece, yet the proof coinage for that year, as in the low-mintage years of 1870 and 1871, was near the series peak. This well-preserved specimen, which boasts considerable copper-orange in addition to blue-brown, is solidly defined and immensely appealing. (#3649)

Attractive 1872 Two Cent, PR66 Red and Brown

207 **1872 PR66 Red and Brown NGC.** Bluish-purple and orange colors compete for territory on the obverse of this Premium Gem while the former palette dominates the reverse. The design elements are exquisitely struck and reveal pleasing variance with the reflective obverse fields. No mentionable contact marks or spots are evident on the well preserved surfaces. Census: 35 in 66 Red and Brown, 4 finer (1/10). (#3649)

208 **1872 PR65 Red NGC.** Pale copper color with occasional suggestions of peach or toning. This riveting Red Gem offers great eye appeal for the issue. Census: 20 in 65 Red, 5 finer (12/09). (#3650)

Bold 1873 Closed 3 Two Cent, PR64 Brown

209 **1873 Closed 3 PR64 Brown PCGS.** From a minuscule proof mintage of 600 pieces, the 1873 two cent piece is a scarce coin in all grades. Golden-tan and purple coloration runs over both sides of this near-Gem and an exacting strike emboldens the design motifs. One tiny fleck in the lower middle shield is concealed within the toning. Population: 34 in 64 Brown, 14 finer (12/09). (#3651)

Closed 3 1873 Two Cent, PR65 Red and Brown

210 **1873 Closed 3 PR65 Red and Brown NGC.** The Closed 3 or "Original" examples of this proof-only issue number just 600 pieces, and examples are prized regardless of grade. This Gem proof exhibits considerable light copper-orange color through each side, though dusky reddish-brown color appears at the right obverse and blue-brown elements are present within the wreath. (#3652)

THREE CENT SILVER

211 **1851-O MS64 PCGS.** A delicate blend of lime-green, rose, brown, and gray patination bathes the lustrous surfaces of this near-Gem. Well struck except for the usual minor softness in the obverse center. The only branch mint three cent silver piece. Population: 88 in 64, 61 finer (1/10).(#3665)

212 **1853 MS65 PCGS. CAC.** Occasional splashes of sky-blue visit the golden-gray lustrous surfaces of this Gem, being a tad deeper in hue on the obverse. Sharply struck except for weakness in the stars along the reverse border. Nicely preserved and highly appealing. (#3667)

213 **1853 MS66 PCGS. CAC.** An immensely lustrous Premium Gem charmer with subtle gold-green peripheral toning and light blue-violet centers. PCGS has certified just five finer pieces (12/09). (#3667)

214 **1862 MS65 PCGS. CAC.** The 1862 is a relatively common issue, although the typical example is circulated or lower Mint State, while Gem survivors are scarce and desirable. This piece has satiny luster with reflective fields beneath lovely rainbow toning. (#3680)

Colorful MS67 1862 Three Cent Silver

215 **1862 MS67 NGC.** The 343,000 business strikes for the 1862 three cent silver make it the last issue of its kind to be readily available across most grades. "Most grades," however, does not include MS67, where this example is one of 33 pieces tied for numerically finest in the combined certified population (1/10). Both sides are strongly lustrous beneath blankets of multicolored toning, with azure, plum, fire-orange, and rose-gold hues prominent. (#3680)

216 **1871 MS65 PCGS.** Semiprooflike fields highlight the well struck motifs of this attractive Gem. Pastel multicolored toning covers both sides, each of which is devoid of mentionable marks. Population: 13 in 65, 26 finer (1/10).(#3692)

PROOF THREE CENT SILVER

217 **1870 PR64 Cameo PCGS. CAC.** A fully brilliant near-Gem, this three cent piece has fully and deeply mirrored fields that frame the lustrous devices. Slight gold toning is evident on otherwise untoned silver surfaces. Population: 9 in 64 Cameo, 8 finer (1/10). (#83721)

218 **1872 PR64 Cameo PCGS.** Light silver-gray and white color overall with dots of green-gold at parts of the margins. A pleasing specimen of this penultimate three cent silver proof issue. Population: 12 in 64 Cameo, 10 finer (12/09).(#83723)

THREE CENT NICKELS

219 **1869 MS66 PCGS.** This piece is highly lustrous with light gold-gray patina over both sides. Boldly struck with a near-absence of marks, and tied for numerically finest known to NGC or PCGS (12/09).(#3735)

220 **1872 MS66 NGC. CAC.** Light gold and peach hues add color to otherwise pale nickel-gray surfaces. A smooth Premium Gem example of this three cent nickel issue. Census: 3 in 66, 0 finer (1/10).(#3738)

221 **1872 MS66 PCGS.** Light gray surfaces imbued with traces of gold-tan display nice luster and sharply struck design elements, including all lines in the III denomination. There are no mentionable marks to report. Population: 13 in 66, 0 finer (1/10).(#3738)

Elusive 1880 Three Cent Piece, MS67

222 **1880 MS67 PCGS.** A lustrous and razor-sharp Superb Gem with pristine surfaces and light almond-gold toning. Just 21,000 pieces were struck, and high grade business strikes are much scarcer than their proof counterparts. Encased in a green label holder. Population: 32 in 67, 0 finer (1/10). (#3748)

223 **1888 MS66 PCGS.** A definite circulation strike with fields that show no trace of reflectivity. Only 36,501 such pieces were struck in 1888. Light golden toning is seen over each side. Fully struck. Population: 50 in 66, 34 finer (1/10).(#3757)

PROOF THREE CENT NICKELS

224 **1870 PR65 Cameo PCGS.** Satiny and untoned with exemplary preservation. The strike is precise save for minor blending at the center of the first denominational column. Population: 24 in 65 Cameo, 7 finer (1/10).(#83766)

225 **1871 PR66 NGC.** Whispers of light gold color visit the well preserved surfaces of this Premium Gem. The design features are exquisitely brought up, including all lines in the III denomination, and yield a degree of contrast with the mirrored fields at various angles. Census: 29 in 66, 8 finer (1/10).(#3767)

226 **1873 Closed 3 PR65 NGC.** Strongly reflective and largely nickel-white with occasional turquoise and green elements. A charming and well-preserved Gem.(#3769)

Sharp 1877 Three Cent Nickel, PR64 Cameo Key to the Series

227 **1877 PR64 Cameo NGC.** The proof-only 1877 is the key to the three cent nickel series. Faint violet and beige-gold color shows up under magnification, mostly in the fields that highlight the mildly frosted devices. A decisive strike sharpens the design elements, including the lines in the III denomination. A handful of minuscule marks denies Gem status. (#83773)

228 **1878 PR67 Cameo NGC.** An impressive, contrasting Superb Gem with brilliant light gray surfaces. This example is a wonderful representative of the second consecutive proof only issue after 1877. Census: 27 in 67 Cameo, 0 finer (1/10).(#83774)

229 **1881 PR67 NGC. CAC.** This boldly defined proof has brilliant light gray surfaces with exceptional mirrored fields. There is no evidence of toning on either side. It is a near-Cameo example. Census: 51 in 67, 8 finer (1/10).(#3777)

230 **1885 PR67 NGC.** Butter-gold and ice-blue toning drapes this satiny and virtually carbon-free Superb Gem. Fully struck save for slight sloping of the dentils toward the field. The 1885 has a mintage of less than 5,000 pieces when proofs and business strike production are combined. Census: 23 in 67, 0 finer (1/10). (#3781)

231 **1886 PR67 Cameo NGC. CAC.** A sensational example of this proof-only three cent nickel piece, tied for the finest certified Cameo proof. Both sides are brilliant light gray with untoned surfaces and bold design definition. Census: 14 in 67 Cameo, 0 finer (1/10).(#83782)

Superb Gem Proof 1887 Three Cent Nickel

232 **1887 PR67 NGC.** As the single finest nonoverdated proof 1887 three cent nickel certified by NGC (1/10), this Superb Gem specimen is of obvious interest to the Registry collector. Any series enthusiast, however, can just as easily appreciate the profound mirrors and mild contrast. The minimally toned reverse shows a handful of planchet flaws scattered around the III within the wreath. (#3783)

Impressive 1888 Three Cent Nickel, PR67 Cameo

233 **1888 PR67 Cameo PCGS.** Struck in the penultimate year of production for the three cent nickel, the 1888 is generally only available in proof format. Proof production spiked in 1888 with 4,582 pieces minted, second highest in the series. The bright, mirrorlike surfaces have just a hint of rose toning on each side; there are no obvious contact marks. Population: 7 in 67 Cameo, 0 finer (12/09). (#83785)

SHIELD NICKELS

Attractive MS65 1871 Shield Nickel

234 **1871 MS65 PCGS. CAC.** Peach and violet shadings grace this lustrous Shield nickel Gem, with the former color dominant on the obverse and the latter prevailing on the reverse. Well-defined overall with only slight shallowness on certain lines through the stars on the reverse. Population: 28 in 65, 8 finer (1/10). (#3798)

235 **1876 MS65 NGC.** Dazzling luster and light straw-gold toning ensure the originality of this boldly struck Gem. A loupe reveals occasional minute carbon. The date exhibits minor repunching. Unabraded, and scarce in such formidable quality. Census: 34 in 65, 6 finer (12/09).(#3805)

PROOF SHIELD NICKELS

236 **1874 PR66 NGC.** Hints of ice-blue and beige-gold patina reside on the luminous, well cared-for surfaces of this Premium Gem nickel. The design elements are sharply impressed. Census: 36 in 66, 4 finer (1/10).(#3828)

237 **1876 PR66 PCGS.** Violet, lilac, and champagne-gold obverse coloration cedes to dominant champagne-gold on the reverse. Sharply struck design elements stand out against the mirrored fields. Devoid of mentionable contacts or spots. Population: 29 in 66, 1 finer (1/10).(#3830)

Dazzling PR66 Ultra Cameo 1876 Shield Nickel

238 **1876 PR66 Ultra Cameo NGC.** Proof Shield nickels from 1876 exist in fair quantities. As David Bowers (2006) indicates, however, some searching is required to locate one with deep mirrors and nice eye appeal, but the present coin is one such. Mirrored fields highlight the crisply struck, frosty motifs, and the untoned surfaces are virtually unimprovable. A highly appealing coin in all respects. Census: 4 in 66 Ultra Cameo, 1 finer (1/10). (#93830)

239 **1879/8 PR66 PCGS. CAC.** The *Guide Book* overdate variety of the proof 1879 Shield nickel commands a distinct premium over its "normal" counterpart. This gleaming Premium Gem has charming lavender-blue peripheral toning surrounding muted golden centers. (#3834)

240 **1879/8 PR67 PCGS. CAC.** Breen-2514, "very scarce." An absolutely exquisite example of this popular overdate variety, listed both in Breen and the *Guide Book*. Fully struck and virtually pristine, with untoned, impeccably preserved surfaces. Population: 24 in 67, 7 finer (12/09).(#3834)

241 **1882 PR66 PCGS.** Light green-gold shadings vary over the surfaces of this later Shield nickel proof. Excellent strike and preservation combine for great eye appeal. PCGS has certified 38 finer specimens (1/10).(#3837)

242 **1883 PR66 PCGS.** Nearly untoned surfaces display a degree of field-motif contrast, especially on the obverse. An exacting strike delivers virtually complete definition to the design features. Well preserved with no significant marks or spots. Nice overall eye appeal.(#3838)

243 **1883 PR66 Cameo PCGS. CAC.** Nearly untoned surfaces exhibit sharply struck devices and strong cameo contrast. A few light flecks are unimportant. Population: 44 in 66 Cameo, 5 finer (12/09). (#83838)

LIBERTY NICKELS

244 **1885—Improperly Cleaned—NGC. AU Details.** The light gray surfaces of this key date representative have been dulled somewhat by the cleaning and some faint obverse hairlines show under magnification. A well defined piece with no significant contact marks.(#3846)

Choice AU 1885 Liberty Nickel

245 **1885 AU55 PCGS. CAC.** A lightly circulated and luminous example of this popular Liberty nickel key, well-defined for the issue but with luster and striking characteristics of a business strike, rather than an impaired proof. Peach and gold overtones grace surfaces that are otherwise light nickel-gray. (#3846)

246 **1886 MS63 PCGS.** The 1886 is one of the keys to the Liberty Head nickel series. This lustrous Select example displays soft golden-gray patina and shows some localized strike weakness, particularly the star centers, hair over the forehead, and elements left of the bow knot. Some minor planchet roughness is noted. (#3847)

Outstanding MS66 1886 Liberty Nickel
Tied for Finest Certified

247 **1886 MS66 PCGS.** Little has been written about the 1886 nickel and its rarity, residing as it does in the shadow of the much better-known 1885. Both are key issues, along with the 1912-S, and the best reason we have for the rarity of the 1886 is taken from what we know about the scarcity of the 1885 and extending the logic one more year. In a 2003 *Coin World* article by Bob Julian, he states:

> "Coinage continued at a heavy pace throughout the rest of 1883 and well into 1885. However, in March 1885 the Treasury suspended nickel coinage because large numbers were flowing into the Subtreasuries and very few pieces leaving. This was the same situation as had prevailed from 1876 through 1881. For this reason, the 1885 nickel is the most difficult date of this series to acquire."

Even though mintage picked up in 1886, it was not impressively so in the context of the series. Only 3.3 million pieces were coined in that year, versus the tiny 1.4 million in 1885. Few were saved, and the 1886 has slowly acquired the status of a key date even though it is chronologically closest to the #1 key in the series.

This piece is brilliant throughout, with amazingly bright, vibrant mint luster on each side. The surfaces show only a few tiny marks, visible with a strong magnifier. The striking details are full in all areas except the left ear of corn. This piece is tied as finest certified at both of the major services. Only five other pieces have been so graded at PCGS, while NGC has certified four at the MS66 level (1/10). (#3847)

248 **1891 MS66 NGC.** Although the left ear of corn in the wreath is weak as usual, all other design aspects of this Premium Gem are bold. The surfaces are attractive light gray with frosty luster. The obverse has pale blue and gold patina while the reverse is brighter gold. Census: 16 in 66, 1 finer (1/10).(#3852)

249 **1912 MS66 PCGS. CAC.** Lovely golden-bronze toning adorns the intensely lustrous, virtually pristine surfaces of this Premium Gem example. The striking definition is extremely bold, and only the left ear of corn shows noticeable weakness. Population: 24 in 66, 0 finer (12/09).(#3873)

250 **1912-S XF40 PCGS.** Dusky nickel-gray surface show arcs and spots of deep olive. A lightly circulated, fundamentally pleasing example of this mintmarked Liberty nickel key.(#3875)

Beautifully Patinated 1912-S Nickel, MS64

251 **1912-S MS64 PCGS.** An attractive blend of violet, ice-blue, lavender, gold, and greenish-tan patina adorns the lustrous surfaces of this near-Gem. Sharply struck design features complement the beautiful coloration, with only the left corn ear showing minor softness. Devoid of mentionable contact marks. One of three keys to the always-popular Liberty nickel series with a mintage of only 238,000 pieces. (#3875)

PROOF LIBERTY NICKELS

252 **1883 No Cents PR66 Cameo PCGS.** A gleaming Cameo Premium Gem proof of this one-year-only design type. Both sides are minimally toned with easily appreciated contrast. Population: 55 in 66 Cameo, 11 finer (12/09).(#83878)

253 **1884 PR66 Cameo NGC.** FS-301, formerly FS-013.8. The 1 in the date is widely repunched. This needle-sharp Premium Gem has flashy fields and a frosty portrait. Each side has light to moderate chestnut toning. Census: 27 in 66 Cameo, 18 finer (12/09). (#83882)

Superb Cameo Proof 1888 Liberty Nickel
With Outstanding Contrast

254 **1888 PR67 Cameo NGC.** Only rarely do we see early Liberty nickels with the contrast present on this piece. Most likely this coin was one of the first struck from a new pair of dies, rather than having been intentionally produced with this white-on-black effect. Each side is bright and sparkling, just a shade from brilliant, with a pale overlay of golden present. Fully struck and problem-free. Census: 1 in 67 Cameo, 0 finer (12/09). (#83886)

255 **1892 PR67 ★ Cameo NGC.** Inspection of NGC/PCGS population figures indicates that 1892 proof nickels are readily available, even in the better levels of preservation. Cameos, on the other hand, are more difficult to locate, and Cameos with NGC's Star are elusive. Indeed, a mere three Cameos are given the Star designation, the present Superb Gem coin tied with one other for the finest. The design elements are exquisitely brought up and stand out against the mirrored fields. Untoned surfaces are impeccably preserved. (#83890)

256 **1902 PR67 NGC.** An impressive proof striking that shows unfathomably deep mirrors in the fields on each side. Also, both sides display bright reddish-golden toning. A magnificent, high grade proof Liberty nickel. Census: 15 in 67, 1 finer (1/10). (#3900)

Brilliant PR67 ★ 1907 Liberty Nickel

257 **1907 PR67 ★ NGC. CAC.** This brilliant Superb Gem has a cameo reverse, and Liberty's hair is also frosted. The glassy fields appear immaculate, and the strike is complete aside from a few grains on the left ear of corn. The lowest mintage regular proof issue. Census: 3 in 67 ★, 0 finer (10/08). (#3905)

258 **1908 PR66 Cameo PCGS.** Fantastically mirrored with distinct contrast despite a lack of thick frost, as is common for later proof Liberty nickel issues. This Premium Gem has amazing visual appeal. Population: 10 in 66 Cameo, 4 finer (1/10).(#83906)

BUFFALO NICKELS

259 **1914 MS66 PCGS.** The highly lustrous surfaces of this Premium Gem display a wonderful blend of ice-blue, lavender, and gold-beige patina. A well executed strike delivers strong delineation to the design elements. A couple of trivial spots are noted in the lower left obverse quadrant.(#3924)

260 **1915-D MS65 PCGS.** Gold toning imbued with hints of lavender bathes the lustrous surfaces of this D-mint Gem. Sharply struck and minimally abraded. PCGS has seen only 30 pieces finer. Housed in a green label holder.(#3928)

Lustrous 1915-S Gem Nickel

261 **1915-S MS65 PCGS.** Soft rainbow toning graces the lustrous surfaces of this Gem S-mint. The design elements are sharply struck, including the braid, horn, and bison's head. Well preserved surfaces reveal no contact marks or spots worthy of note. Housed in a green label holder. (#3929)

262 **1917-D MS65 PCGS.** A medley of yellow-gold, violet, ice-blue, and lime-green bathes the obverse of this Gem D-mint, while the same color palette is dominated by violet on the reverse. Above-average detail with the horn particularly sharp. PCGS has graded 13 finer examples (12/09).(#3935)

263 **1917-D MS65 NGC.** Satiny gray surfaces have light gold accents on this lovely Gem Buffalo nickel. The 1917-D is scarce at the Gem level, and seldom encountered any finer. Census: 46 in 65, 7 finer (1/10).(#3935)

Superb Gem 1918 Nickel

264 **1918 MS67 PCGS. CAC.** An exceptional 1918 nickel in every respect. The issue is infamous for poor striking quality, yet this example offers crisp design definition on the portrait, and only slight softness is evident on the bison's shoulder. The decidedly above-average luster brings the dappled rose-violet and yellow patina over each side to life. The last (and perhaps most obvious) exceptional aspect of this Superb Gem is its impressive preservation. Neither side shows any individually mentionable marks. All things considered, a remarkable example for the high-end Buffalo nickel enthusiast. Population: 7 in 67, 0 finer (12/09). (#3937)

265 **1918-D MS64 PCGS.** The lustrous light gray surfaces exhibit hints of soft violet and gold. Generally well struck and revealing just a few trivial marks. This is a delightful near-Gem. The '18-D can be difficult to locate above MS64.(#3938)

266 **1918/7-D Good 4 PCGS.** FS-101, formerly FS-016.5. Just enough of the date is visible to positively identify the overdate feature on this example. Although well worn, the surfaces are mostly smooth and attractive with natural light gray patina.(#3939)

267 **1918/7-D Good 6 NGC.** FS-101, formerly FS-016.5. Though extensively worn, this nickel shows a clear date, and a clear overdate by extension. The lowest curve of the bison's horn remains visible on this medium-gray piece.(#3939)

268 **1918-S MS63 ICG.** Nickel-pink and pale orange shadings dominate the eye appeal of this softly struck Select S-mint example. Minimally abraded for the grade assigned.(#3940)

269 **1920-D MS64 NGC.** Solidly struck with above-average luster and quality. The key to this near-Gem is the patina, deep peach and magenta with lighter green-gold at the centers.(#3945)

270 **1920-S MS63 NGC.** Attractive shades of orange-gold, fuchsia, and sage grace each side of this lovely Select coin. While the luster is subtle, the strike is better than expected on this semikey coin, and other distractions are virtually nil.(#3946)

Beautifully Toned 1923 Nickel, MS67 ★

271 **1923 MS67 ★ NGC.** Ex: Yankee Collection. While one of the more frequently encountered P-mints from the 1920s, seldom is a 1923 found with such profound mint luster and toning. Each side has ice-blue centers with golden toning around the margins. The color is enlivened by bright, sparkling mint luster, and the strike is full. Census: 2 in 67 ★, 0 finer (1/10). (#3949)

Wonderful, High-End 1924-D Nickel, MS65

272 **1924-D MS65 PCGS. CAC.** This remarkable coin displays thick, silky mint luster and a virtual absence of abrasions. Each side has light rose-colored toning with an accent of lilac over the bison on the reverse. The 1924-D is never found fully struck; the present example shows slight softness just above the knot in the Indian's braid, and the head and tail of the bison are incompletely brought up. Nevertheless, this is a coin for the collector who is realistic enough to know that a fully struck Gem will not be available, making this a wonderful acquisition for an advanced set. (#3952)

Low Mintage 1924-S Nickel, MS64

273 **1924-S MS64 PCGS.** This low-mintage issue (1.437 million pieces) is scarce in all grades. The present near-Gem offering shows typical striking characteristics, in that portions of the Indian's hair and the bison's head are weak. The date, LIBERTY, horn, and mintmark are crisp, however. Champagne-gold lustrous surfaces display violet and lavender accents. A few minute marks preclude Gem status. (#3953)

274 **1925-D MS64 PCGS.** This medium-gold and reddish-violet D-mint example reveals slightly better detail than is average for the issue, especially on the reverse. No significant abrasions or spots interrupt the generally well preserved surfaces.(#3955)

275 **1925-D MS64 NGC.** A challenging coin in the Buffalo nickel series, especially with a decent strike. This piece has varying average to above average definition. The satiny surfaces have even rose colored toning over each side.(#3955)

Elusive 1925-D Gem Nickel

276 **1925-D MS65 PCGS.** The 1925-D is elusive in Mint State, especially at the higher levels. Soft golden-beige patina rests on the lustrous, well preserved surfaces of this Gem example. The design elements are generally well struck save for the usually-seen localized weakness. The horn, however, is sharp. Housed in a green label holder. Population: 68 in 65, 3 finer (12/09). (#3955)

Lustrous 1925-S Five Cent, MS64

277 **1925-S MS64 PCGS.** The lustrous surfaces of this near-Gem yield light gold patina. The design features are typically struck, revealing incompleteness on the letters in LIBERTY and CENTS, the mintmark, and portions of the motif on both sides. Generally well preserved, and difficult to locate any finer. (#3956)

278 **1926-D MS64 PCGS.** As is the case with all Denver Mint issues from its decade, the 1926-D is scarce in all grades, and desirable in Mint State. This undisturbed Choice example has medium autumn-gold toning and a decidedly above average strike.(#3958)

279 **1926-S XF45 PCGS.** Soft violet-gray color with hints of light gold resides on the semigloss surfaces of this Choice XF coin. Well defined for the issue, with most of the bison's horn present, though the tip is a tad short of complete. There are no marks worthy of note on this pleasing better-date representative with a mintage less than 1 million pieces.(#3959)

Choice AU 1926-S Nickel

280 **1926-S AU55 PCGS.** Soft luster enlivens the surfaces, which offer luminous peach and orange-rose hues over a base of sage. Only minor rub is noted on the highest design elements, and the well-defined devices are minimally abraded. Great eye appeal for the grade and the issue of fewer than a million pieces. (#3959)

Attractively Toned MS64 1926-S Buffalo Nickel

281 **1926-S MS64 NGC.** The 1926-S nickel had a mintage of 970,000 pieces. And yet it is not rare or valuable in low grades, indicating that the issue spent considerable time in circulation before being pulled out by collectors. The price increases from one grade to the next are dizzying. Low grade circulated coins are affordable by collectors of any means, but examples in mint condition are only available to those who can shell out multiple thousands of dollars. This is an especially pleasing, problem-free specimen. The devices are strongly struck, and the overall appearance is well-balanced from side to side. Attractive rose and lilac toning is interspersed over each side, and there are no obvious or detracting marks. (#3959)

282 **1927-S MS63 PCGS.** This better date Buffalo nickel displays soft multicolored toning and is somewhat better struck than ordinarily seen, though the hair on the bison's head is weak. The most potent luster resides in the areas around and the interstices of the motifs. Housed in a first generation holder.(#3962)

Near-Gem 1927-S Five Cent

283 **1927-S MS64 PCGS.** Softly struck with quicksilver luster, as this San Francisco issue is usually seen, yet the overall eye appeal is more impressive than those elements might suggest. Key to its attractiveness is a generous portion of liquid-gold color that covers most of the otherwise nickel-gray surfaces. Housed in a first-generation holder. PCGS has graded only 20 coins finer (1/10). (#3962)

284 **1928-S MS64 NGC. CAC.** Splashes of violet, ice-blue, gold, and light green patina visit the lustrous surfaces of this attractive near-Gem. Generally well struck and devoid of significant marks. Nice overall eye appeal.(#3965)

Colorful MS67 1934 Nickel

285 **1934 MS67 NGC.** Rich and dynamic gold and orange patina embraces much of each side of this shining Superb Gem. The central obverse and reverse also show elements of sage toning. Exquisitely preserved for this high-mintage but little-saved Depression-era issue. Census: 13 in 67, 0 finer (1/10). (#3972)

Splendid, Thickly Lustrous 1935-S Nickel, MS67

286 **1935-S MS67 NGC.** This appealing Superb Gem is essentially blemish-free, as expected for the assigned grade. Pretty golden patina on the Indian's hair complements tinges of ice-blue appearing on the face. The piece has a sharp strike, if a trifle short of full, and similar coloration appears on the reverse. Among the finest few dozen certified at either service (1/10). (#3976)

287 **1937-D Three-Legged XF45 PCGS.** FS-901, formerly FS-020.2. The bison's hip and hair display moderate wear, but the caramel-gold and gunmetal surfaces retain glimpses of luster. A lightly abraded example of this famous lapped die mint error.(#3982)

288 **1937-D Three-Legged XF45 ANACS.** FS-901, formerly FS-020.2. A Choice XF piece with orange and olive toning where luster remains. Devoid of relevant marks, and an impressive example of this well known *Guide Book* variety.
Ex: Dallas Signature (Heritage, 11/2006), lot 409, which realized $977.50.(#3982)

289 **1937-D Three-Legged AU55 NGC.** FS-901, formerly FS-020.2. A briefly circulated gold-gray example of this ever-popular later Buffalo nickel variety. Just a touch of rub is present on the highest points of the faintly abraded surfaces.(#3982)

290 **1937-D Three-Legged AU58 NGC.** FS-901, formerly FS-020.2. Dusky peach and pink-gray hues grace this Three-Legged nickel. Just a touch of friction affects the high points, and the coin is minimally abraded overall.(#3982)

Appealing 1937-D Three-Legged Select Nickel

291 **1937-D Three-Legged MS63 NGC.** FS-901, formerly FS-020.2. A melange of gold, lavender, aqua-blue, mint-green, and gray patination resides on the lustrous surfaces of this popular Three-Legged representative. Generally well struck and revealing just a few minor reverse marks. Nice overall eye appeal for the Select grade level. (#3982)

Superlative 1938-D Buffalo, MS68

292 **1938-D MS68 NGC.** Collectors and the general public knew that the Buffalo nickel design would end its run in 1938, and they hoarded many examples of the Denver coins of that year. In fact, despite a comparatively small mintage of just over 7 million pieces, the 1938-D is the definitive type coin for its series. This applies even in the lofty grade of MS68, where NGC and PCGS have certified a combined 23 pieces (6/09). The one offered here has impeccable surfaces that shine beneath deep golden-orange patina. The detail is crisp, and the overall effect is pleasing. An amazing example that would make a statement in any type or date set. Census: 15 in 68, 0 finer (1/10). (#3984)

293 **1938-D/S MS67 NGC.** FS-511, formerly FS-20.5. OMM-1. There are several overmintmarked dies, but this is the most significant among them, since the S mintmark can be seen both above and within the D mintmark, which is crisply repunched at the base. Beautifully toned in rose-gold, powder-blue, and lemon-gold. Census: 86 in 67, 5 finer (12/09).(#3985)

Magnificent MS68 1938-D/S Nickel

294 **1938-D/S MS68 NGC.** FS-511, formerly FS-20.5. OMM-1. While San Francisco struck no 1938-dated Buffalo nickels, Denver did, and several S-mint reverse dies had their mintmarks punched-over for use in Colorado. This is a stunning MS68 representative of the most prominent of the overmintmarks. Light yellow-green outer toning gives way to light blue and violet colors through the centers. Amazingly lustrous and a visual delight. Census: 4 in 68, 0 finer (1/10). (#3985)

PROOF BUFFALO NICKELS

295 **1914 PR66 PCGS.** Soft greenish-gold patina on the obverse cedes to violet and light nickel-gray on the reverse. Impeccably preserved surfaces exhibit sharply struck motifs. Great quality. PCGS has graded just 79 finer specimens (12/09).(#3991)

296 **1936 Type One—Satin Finish PR67 NGC.** Strong nickel-gray satin luster offers occasional suggestions of gold or iridescence. A sharp Superb Gem proof with noteworthy visual appeal. NGC has certified 22 numerically finer Satin proofs (12/09).(#3994)

297 **1936 Type Two—Brilliant Finish PR64 NGC.** Iridescent gold, champagne, and violet patina bathes the luminous surfaces of this near-Gem proof, augmented by speckles of deeper green, orange, and charcoal. Exquisitely struck and revealing no significant marks. (#3995)

298 **1937—Environmental Damage—NGC—Proof.** A layer of champagne-gold patina resides on the obverse of this proof, while the reverse displays a veneer of champagne and violet-blue coloration. Tiny black carbon flecks are interspersed with minuscule toning spots on both sides. Really a decent looking piece despite the NGC disclaimer.(#3996)

299 **1937 PR66 ★ NGC. CAC.** The bright surfaces display hints of field-motif contrast at most angles, and possess a veneer of soft violet and gold color. Exquisitely struck and devoid of mentionable marks or spots. NGC's coveted Star and the CAC green label attest to the outstanding eye appeal.(#3996)

300 **1937 PR66 NGC.** Gorgeous toning with progressions from gold-orange through violet and blue patina. Excellent reflectivity and dynamic eye appeal.(#3996)

301 **1937 PR67 PCGS. CAC.** The quicksilver surfaces of this splendid Superb Gem proof are essentially devoid of color other than the expected silver-gray, but that only serves to emphasize its many charms. The strike is full as expected, and essential contact is absent. The reverse is rotated a few degrees counterclockwise with respect to the obverse. Difficult to improve upon; PCGS has certified only 11 pieces finer (1/10).(#3996)

JEFFERSON NICKELS

302 **1938-D MS67 Full Steps PCGS.** Soft champagne-gold color resides on the lustrous surfaces of this Superb Gem. This is a sharply struck and nicely preserved specimen. Population: 30 in 67 Full Steps, 0 finer (12/09).(#84001)

303 **1939 Reverse of 1940 MS67 Full Steps PCGS.** A magnificent blend of light violet, gold-orange, and mint-green patination drapes the lustrous surfaces of this sharply struck Superb Gem. Impeccable preservation enhances even more the coin's outstanding eye Appeal. Population: 20 in 67 Full Steps, 0 finer (1/10).(#894003)

304 **1939 Reverse of 1940 MS67 Full Steps PCGS.** A virtually brilliant Superb Gem that has a mark-free appearance and a bold strike. An outstanding representative of this transitional date. The PCGS number on the insert is 84003, but this coin is the Straight Steps, Reverse of 1940 subtype. Population: 20 in 67 Full Steps, 0 finer (1/10).(#894003)

305 **1939 Doubled MONTICELLO MS66 PCGS.** FS-801, formerly FS-022. A great Premium Gem example of the much-favored *Guide Book* classic. Surfaces have dusky peach-gold color with occasional glints of nickel-white. Population: 32 in 66, 4 finer (1/10).(#4004)

Sharp MS66 Full Steps 1939 Nickel Doubled Die Reverse, Ex: Compradore

306 **1939 Doubled MONTICELLO MS66 Full Steps PCGS.** Ex: Compradore Collection. FS-801, formerly FS-022. One of the most pronounced Jefferson nickel varieties, with prominent doubling on MONTICELLO and FIVE CENTS. This shining representative shows delicate peach tints in the fields of this otherwise nickel-white example. Razor-sharp striking definition further enhances the remarkable visual appeal. Population: 7 in 66 Full Steps, 0 finer (1/10). (#84004)

307 **1939-D Reverse of 1938 MS66 Full Steps PCGS.** Rich golden toning overall with dots of caramel and deeper shadings through the "sky" above Monticello. Razor-sharp striking definition and amazing eye appeal.(#84005)

308 **1939-D Reverse of 1940 MS66 Full Steps PCGS.** Peach-gold, powder-blue, and lavender patina graces this highly lustrous Premium Gem. Exactingly struck with grand eye appeal. Population: 29 in 66 Full Steps, 2 finer (12/09).(#894005)

309 **1939-D Reverse of 1940 MS66 Full Steps PCGS.** The "Straight Steps" confirm the Reverse of 1940. Blazing luster exudes from surfaces softly toned in violet, gold, and light blue. Sharply struck and showing some minute toning spots on each side. Population: 29 in 66 Full Steps, 2 finer (1/10).(#894005)

310 **1939-S Reverse of 1938 MS66 Full Steps PCGS.** The steps are "wavy" and the top one is thin on this variety. Soft gold-tan color resides on the lustrous surfaces of this Premium Gem. This is a sharply struck and minimally marked piece. Population: 16 in 66 Full Steps, 0 finer (12/09).(#84006)

311 **1939-S Reverse of 1940 MS66 Full Steps PCGS.** A thin veil of tan-gold and powder-blue color adheres to the lustrous surfaces of this lovely Premium Gem. Both sides are sharply struck and minimally marked. Population: 14 in 66 Full Steps, 0 finer (1/10). (#894006)

Superb 1940-S Nickel, MS67 Full Steps

312 **1940-S MS67 Full Steps PCGS.** Ex: Compradore Collection. Minimally toned with vibrant luster and remarkable eye appeal for this challenging earlier issue. The strike is bold, as expected for the Full Steps designation, and the luster is delightful. Carefully preserved and incredibly appealing. Population: 8 in 67 Full Steps, 0 finer (1/10). (#84009)

313 **1941 MS67 Full Steps PCGS.** This Superb Gem specimen is highly lustrous with pale gold, blue, and olive-yellow over brilliant nickel-gray surfaces. Five full steps are visible on this example, which tied for the finest certified by PCGS. Population: 16 in 67 Full Steps, 0 finer (12/09).(#84010)

314 **1941-S Large S MS66 PCGS.** FS-501, formerly FS-024.5. Green-gold overtones grace glossy nickel-gray surfaces. A challenging issue any finer, regardless of mintmark size.

Important MS65 1942-D/D Nickel 'D Over Horizontal D' Variety

315 **1942-D D Over Horizontal D MS65 PCGS.** FS-501, previously FS-027. Frosty on the obverse with delicate pastel-blue and champagne patina. The detail is strong, particularly on the steps (which are a few light marks away from a Full Steps designation), though die lapping is evident at Jefferson's shoulder. The all-important overmintmark is plain under magnification, and the portrait is clean, though a minor graze affects the left-central pillar of Monticello. One of just five Gems certified by PCGS, with none finer (1/10). (#4015)

Notable MS67 Full Steps 1942-S Nickel

316 **1942-S MS67 Full Steps PCGS.** Ex: Compradore Collection. An impressive example with light champagne toning over reflective gray surfaces. Heavy die polish on both sides imparts a prooflike appearance. The reverse has five full steps with about half of the sixth step visible. Extremely rare so sharp. Population: 9 in 67 Full Steps, 0 finer (1/10). (#84017)

317 **1943-P Doubled Die Obverse MS66 PCGS.** FS-106, formerly FS-029. This boldly doubled obverse has made its way into the *Guide Book*. A great Premium Gem example of the variety, silver-white with faint blue accents and a handful of diagonal streaks on the obverse.(#4174)

318 **1943-P Doubled Die MS65 Full Steps PCGS.** FS-106, formerly FS-029. A noteworthy Full Steps Gem example of this *Guide Book* classic. Brightly lustrous surfaces show hints of gold. (#84174)

319 **1943-P Doubled Die Obverse MS66 Full Steps PCGS.** Ex: Compradore Collection. FS-106, formerly FS-029. Jefferson's eye and all obverse legends are clearly die doubled. Brilliant silver-gray surfaces are accented by subtle champagne toning. Better than five full steps are visible; this piece nearly qualifies as a six-step example. Population: 13 in 66 Full Steps, 2 finer (1/10).(#84174)

Prominent 1943/2-P Nickel, MS66 Full Steps

320 **1943/2-P MS66 Full Steps PCGS.** FS-101, formerly FS-028. This is a brilliant Premium Gem example of the popular overdate variety with light gold toning over silvery surfaces. The overdate feature (i.e. the digit 2 beneath the 3) is extremely prominent, even with just a five-power magnifier. Population: 22 in 66 Full Steps, 2 finer (1/10). (#84019)

321 **1944-S MS67 Full Steps PCGS.** Soft champagne coloration adorns the lustrous surfaces of this Superb Gem war nickel. Exquisitely struck and preserved. Population: 27 in 67 Full Steps, 0 finer (1/10).(#84024)

322 **1945-P Tripled Die Reverse MS66 PCGS.** FS-804, formerly FS-030.5. This Tripled Die Reverse variety is also a notable repunched mintmark, according to the *Cherrypickers' Guide*. This Premium Gem offers frosty silver-white color with a touch of peach.

323 **1945-P Minor Doubled Die Reverse MS66 PCGS.** FS-803, formerly FS-030.3. Fantastically lustrous with a touch of gold. This Premium Gem example of the minor FS-803 doubled die has great eye appeal.

324 **1945-S MS66 Full Steps PCGS.** Champagne-gold and ice-blue coloration resides on the highly lustrous surfaces of this sharply struck Premium Gem. There are no serious marks or spots to report. Population: 83 in 66 Full Steps, 4 finer (1/10).(#84027)

325 **1946 MS66 Full Steps PCGS.** A medley of gold-beige, ice-blue, and lavender patination adorns the highly lustrous surfaces of this remarkable Premium Gem. This exquisitely struck piece reveals just a few minor grade-consistent marks. Population: 17 in 66 Full Steps, 0 finer (1/10).(#84028)

Impressive 1946-D/D Nickel, FS-501, MS66

326 **1946-D D Over Horizontal D MS66 PCGS.** FS-501, previously FS-031. This piece represents excellent value in this rare variant. The only difference between this and the Full Steps MS66 coin also in this auction is slight, almost imperceptible softness on the lowest steps of Monticello. The inverted mintmark is plain, and the thickly lustrous surfaces are covered with lilac and rose toning. A splendid, high grade example. Population: 1 in 66, 0 finer (1/10). (#38507)

Rarely Seen 1946-D/D Nickel, FS-501 MS66 Full Steps

327 **1946-D D Over Horizontal D MS66 Full Steps PCGS.** Ex: Compradore Collection. FS-501, previously FS-031. The mintmark is dramatically repunched, with the first punch inverted. This valuable repunched mintmark is considered the second rarest of the original Jefferson "Top 10" in Mint State, second only to the 1942-D Over Horizontal D. This is only the second Full Steps example we have handled, and it is the finest. The mint luster on this piece is thick and frosted, more suggestive of a San Francisco product than a Denver piece, in our opinion. The surfaces are lightly toned with a pale golden overlay of patina on each side. The only mentionable abrasions are a couple of shallow marks on Jefferson's coat. Population: 13 in 66 Full Steps, 0 finer (1/10).

1946-D Over Inverted D Nickel, MS66 Full Steps

328 **1946-D D Over Horizontal D MS66 Full Steps PCGS.** FS-501, formerly FS-031. This mispunched mintmark is actually a D Over Inverted D. It was discovered by Adolf Weiss, founder of the PAK Full Step Nickel Club. It is a surprisingly rare coin, especially in Uncirculated grades. More, of course, could be found as original rolls are broken up in the future. Five step coins, such as this one, have a survival rate of 1:20. This is a pleasing coin with thick mint luster and a light overlay of lilac-golden toning. Population: 13 in 66 Full Steps, 0 finer (1/10). (#894029)

Pleasing MS66 Full Steps 1948 Nickel

329 **1948 MS66 Full Steps PCGS.** Fantastically lustrous with elements of gold and peach toning over otherwise nickel-white surfaces. The patina is more prominent on the smooth reverse, over and above the sharply struck image of Monticello. Challenging so fine with Full Steps: PCGS has certified only 11 such coins at the MS66 level and none finer (1/10). (#84034)

330 **1949 MS65 Full Steps PCGS.** Ex: Compradore Collection. Despite a large mintage, few high quality 1949 nickels exist, as there were few collectors who saved rolls at the time of issue. This piece has incredible light gold toning over satiny luster, with full underlying mint brilliance. Population: 17 in 65 Full Steps, 0 finer (1/10).(#84037)

331 **1949-S MS66 Full Steps PCGS.** Variegated champagne-gold and ice-blue patination rides over the lustrous surfaces of this sharply struck Premium Gem. A few light, grade-consistent marks do not detract from the coin's nice overall eye appeal. Population: 14 in 66 Full Steps, 1 finer (12/09).(#84040)

332 **1951 MS66 Full Steps PCGS.** An impeccable, satiny example accented in golden patina. All design motifs are sharply defined. Population: 13 in 66 Full Steps, 0 finer (1/10).(#84043)

333 **1951-S MS66 Full Steps PCGS.** The design elements are fully brought up and the steps of Monticello are especially crisp. Satiny and well preserved; the surfaces show few marks and variegated pastel coloration on both sides. Population: 19 in 66 Full Steps, 0 finer (1/10).(#84045)

Scarce 1953 Nickel, MS65 Full Steps

334 **1953 MS65 Full Steps PCGS.** According to Bernard Nagengast (2002), "one of the rarest P mints in full strike condition ... ." This example is sharply struck, with bright luster, rich olive-gold toning, and just a few wispy marks on Jefferson's jaw and cheekbone that are difficult to discern without magnification. Population: 7 in 65 Full Steps, 0 finer (1/10). (#84049)

335 **1953-D MS67 PCGS.** An extraordinary Superb Gem with frosty luster beneath rainbow iridescence. The strike is a trifle weak as usual, with only partial step detail remaining.(#4050)

336 **1953-S MS64 Full Steps PCGS.** According to Bernard Nagengast, the appearance frequency of the Five Step variety is only 1 in 5,000; six steps are unverified. We suspect this ratio might be slightly conservative. A fully brilliant specimen; only a few inconsequential contact marks limit the grade. A "must-see" coin for the Jefferson nickel specialist. Population: 15 in 64 Full Steps, 2 finer (1/10). (#84051)

Elusive 1956-D Nickel, MS66 Full Steps

337 **1956-D MS66 Full Steps PCGS.** The 1956-D is a challenging coin to locate in high grade and with Full Steps. Nagengast (2002) estimates that only one coin in 150 is found fully struck. This is a lovely example. The satiny surfaces display variegated rose and lilac toning on each side, and the fields are bright from obvious die polishing, the evidence of which can be seen with magnification. Population: 6 in 66 Full Steps, 0 finer (1/10). (#84060)

Interesting 1957 Nickel, MS66 Full Steps

338 **1957 MS66 Full Steps PCGS.** While the 1957 nickel is available as singles and even in rolls, it is a noteworthy strike rarity. Probably no more than one out of 10 Uncirculated pieces shows Full Steps. This is such a coin, visually impressive with thick mint luster radiating beneath even golden toning that covers each side. The reverse die shows significant signs of deterioration and heavy metal flow on the reverse, yet that side is fully struck. The obverse has die striae in the fields. An interesting coin for the specialist. Population: 9 in 66 Full Steps, 0 finer (1/10). (#84061)

339 **1957-D MS66 Full Steps PCGS.** Variegated sky-blue, lavender, and beige-gold toning resides on the intensely lustrous surfaces of this sharply struck Premium Gem. Great overall eye appeal. Population: 9 in 66 Full Steps, 0 finer (1/10).(#84062)

Magnificent 1958-D Nickel, MS67 Full Steps

340 **1958-D MS67 Full Steps PCGS.** Fully brilliant, without a trace of color to distract from the original, unimpeded magnificence of this stunning Superb Gem specimen. Blazing luster spills from both the immaculate, flashy silk-textured fields and the snow-white glow of the delicately frosted devices. Fully struck with razor-sharp detailed devices and bold legends, and the ever important steps of Monticello are deeply impressed and boldly defined. Population: 7 in 67 Full Steps, 0 finer (1/10). (#84064)

341 **1959 MS66 Full Steps PCGS.** Lustrous pale gray surfaces are accented by soft champagne-gold toning. This is a sharply struck Gem with excellent eye appeal. Population: 14 in 66 Full Steps, 0 finer (12/09).(#84065)

Important 1959-D Jefferson, MS66 Full Steps

342 **1959-D MS66 Full Steps PCGS.** The fields of this boldly defined Jefferson nickel are brilliant and satiny, with a hint of reflectivity adding to its eye appeal. Faint champagne toning enhances its overall appearance. Like most Full Steps Jefferson nickels of the last half century, this is an extremely rare issue in high grade. Collectors new to the field will need to become accustomed to the rarity of such coins, while those who have specialized in the current nickel series find the rarity unsurprising. Population: 6 in 66 Full Steps, 0 finer (1/10). (#84066)

Gem Full Steps 1960 Nickel

343 **1960 MS65 Full Steps PCGS.** Frosty nickel-white luster tending to blue dominates the centers, while the margins show occasional glints of golden color. A sharply impressed piece, not only at the steps but also on many of the subtler features of the Jefferson portrait and Monticello. Population: 7 in 65 Full Steps, 1 finer (1/10). (#84067)

1961 Nickel, MS65 Full Steps
A Rare Find With Full Steps

344 **1961 MS65 Full Steps PCGS.** Ex: Compradore Collection. Deep gold and iridescent toning appears over satiny surfaces. Typical for the issue is a poor strike and rough surfaces, although the present piece is a desirable exception. Bowers estimates that only one coin out of 150 exists with Full Steps. Population: 10 in 65 Full Steps, 0 finer (1/10). (#84069)

Rarely Seen 1963-D Nickel, MS65 Full Steps

345 **1963-D MS65 Full Steps PCGS.** Ex: Compradore Collection. A reflective Gem with exceptional eye appeal and bold design types. Both sides have light gold toning with slightly reflective fields. Here is another Full Steps example that is rarely seen, with a ratio of 1 to 3,000, according to Bowers. Population: 2 in 65 Full Steps, 0 finer (1/10). (#84074)

Elusive 1964 Jefferson, MS66 Full Steps

346 **1964 MS66 Full Steps PCGS.** Ex: Compradore Collection. The Philadelphia Mint struck more than 1 billion nickels in 1964, and about 1 of every 30 examples (or 30 million) had full steps. While such a quantity seems sufficient, the connoisseur will find the search for an example as nice as this piece to be a difficult road. Fully lustrous with satin surfaces and pale gold toning. Population: 5 in 66 Full Steps, 0 finer (1/10). (#84075)

1968-S Nickel With Full Steps, MS66

347 **1968-S MS66 Full Steps PCGS.** Although 1968-S nickels are sometimes available by the roll in Mint State, they invariably feature little or no definition on the all-important steps. The present Premium Gem is a noteworthy exception. Mauve and apricot patina embraces this satiny and nearly undisturbed example. Population: 3 in 66 Full Steps, 0 finer (1/10). (#84081)

348 **1974 MS66 Full Steps PCGS.** Ex: Compradore Collection. Pastel blue, violet, gold, and beige patina covers lustrous surfaces. The design elements are sharply impressed, culminating in Full Steps. A couple of minute marks are noted on Jefferson's cheek and Monticello. Population: 12 in 66 Full Steps, 0 finer (12/09). (#84092)

349 **1976 MS67 Full Steps PCGS.** Pretty ice-blue and apricot-rose toning blankets each side. The nearly mark-free surfaces are sharply defined throughout. This coin is tied with one other PCGS '76 nickel for the finest certified (12/09).(#84096)

350 **1981-P MS66 Full Steps PCGS.** Occasional violet splashes visit the highly lustrous champagne surfaces of this attractive Premium Gem. Nicely struck with no significant marks. Population: 5 in 66 Full Steps, 0 finer (12/09).(#84106)

351 **1992-P MS67 Full Steps PCGS.** Ex: Compradore Collection. Brilliant and lustrous with a full strike except on Jefferson's jaw. Carefully preserved and attractive. Population: 2 in 67 Full Steps, 0 finer (1/10).(#84128)

352 **2000-D MS67 Full Steps PCGS.** Exceptionally bright with reflective surfaces and fully struck devices. Trivial abrasions are noted on Jefferson's portrait. Population: 11 in 67 Full Steps, 0 finer (1/10).(#84147)

SMS JEFFERSON NICKEL

353 **1994-P SMS MS70 Full Steps PCGS.** The special finish matte Jefferson nickel was originally available only in the 1993 Jefferson 250th Anniversary Set (indicated on insert). Pristine surfaces reveal just the barest hint of tan-gold color. Population: 11 in 70 Full Steps (12/09).(#84230)

PROOF JEFFERSON NICKELS

Singular 1939 Reverse of 1940 Nickel FS-901, PR66 Cameo PCGS

354 **1939 Reverse of 1940 PR66 Cameo PCGS.** FS-901, formerly FS-023. The 1940 Reverse is characterized by crisp, straight steps to Monticello, while the 1938 Reverse has the steps wavy. Most 1939 proof Jefferson nickels have the 1938 Reverse, with less than 100 of the 1940 Reverse certified by PCGS. The Premium Gem Cameo proof offered here is the only 1939 Jefferson nickel that PCGS has certified as a Cameo proof. NGC has certified three pieces as Cameo proof, meaning that both services combined can only provide four examples to collectors. The current auction record for an example of this variety is $4,888, and we fully expect that the current offering will exceed that price level. Fully brilliant and pristine proof surfaces exhibit excellent contrast, with no evidence of toning on either side. Population: 1 in 66 Cameo, none finer (1/10). (#94176)

Flashy, Deeply Mirrored 1939 Nickel Rare Reverse of 1940, PR67

355 **1939 Reverse of 1940 PR67 PCGS.** FS-901, formerly FS-023. The reflective fields highlight the mildly frosted devices, particularly on the reverse. The seemingly brilliant surfaces are almost devoid of any hint of toning, the only exception is a tiny speck of golden color between Jefferson's chin and the D in GOD. A rare variety as a proof with the "straight steps" Reverse of 1940. Population: 16 in 67, 0 finer (1/10). (#94176)

Finest Certified 1942 Type One Nickel PR66 Cameo

356 **1942 Type One PR66 Cameo PCGS.** Extremely rare, as are all 1936-1942 proofs with any degree of contrast. This is a boldly struck and nearly untoned Type One Gem with good cameo contrast. There is just the slightest hint of color on each side with good reflectivity in the fields. Jefferson's jaw has a small planchet flaw, as made, and the dies are slightly rotated counterclockwise. The finest of only two pieces certified as Cameo by PCGS. None have been certified as Deep Cameo. Population: 1 in 66 Cameo, 0 finer (1/10). (#84179)

357 **1951 PR68 Cameo PCGS.** A veneer of uniform champagne patina rides over the virtually pristine surfaces of this wonderful five cent piece. The design elements are exquisitely impressed. Population: 4 in 68 Cameo, 0 finer (1/10).(#84183)

Deep Cameo 1952 Nickel, PR67 One of the Keys to the Deep Cameo Series

358 **1952 PR67 Deep Cameo PCGS.** The 1952 is one of the keys to the series with strong cameo contrast. To quote Rick Tomaska (1991), "Well-preserved examples are so scarce with ultra-heavy contrasted devices that few cameo dealers or collectors have ever even seen one." This piece shows extraordinarily deep mirrors on each side with starkly contrasted devices. Each side has a thin layer of golden-rose toning, and the surfaces are essentially perfect. Population: 10 in 67 Deep Cameo, 1 finer (1/10). (#94184)

Starkly Contrasted 1954 Nickel, PR68 Deep Cameo

359 **1954 PR68 Deep Cameo PCGS.** A hint of ice-blue near the rims offsets the practically black-and-white brilliance of this brightly mirrored specimen. The ivory devices have rich, delightful frost and contrast markedly against the illimitable depth of reflectivity in the fields. Population: 5 in 68 Deep Cameo, 0 finer (1/10). (#94186)

360 **1955 PR68 Deep Cameo PCGS.** Magnificent icy-white devices rise above the darkly mirrored fields. A dab of gray appears inside the C in AMERICA, but otherwise this is a perfect example of the proof issue. Population: 22 in 68 Deep Cameo, 0 finer (1/10). (#94187)

361 **1959 PR68 Deep Cameo PCGS.** Light gold color visits this razor-sharp Superb Gem. The devices are radiant and frosty, and the surfaces appear pristine. Traces of retained laminations, as made, are noted near FIVE CENTS. Although more than 1 million proofs were struck, few among these pieces displayed significant white on black contrast. Generally, only the initial pieces struck from freshly installed dies exhibited this quality. Population: 10 in 68 Deep Cameo, 1 finer (1/10).(#94191)

362 **1961 PR69 Deep Cameo PCGS.** A veneer of barely discernible yellow-gold patina runs over both sides of this immaculately preserved piece, each of which yields stunning field-motif contrast and an excellent strike. Superb eye appeal throughout. Population: 12 in 69 Deep Cameo, 0 finer (1/10).(#94193)

PR69 Cameo 1971 No S Nickel

363 **1971 No S PR69 Cameo PCGS.** While the proof Roosevelt dime series has a number of No S varieties, only one such variety is recognized for the larger Jefferson nickel. This high-end No S proof from 1971 has outstanding contrast and virtually flawless surfaces. The mirrors in particular are remarkable. Population: 8 in 69 Cameo, 0 finer (1/10). (#84204)

364 **1979-S Type Two PR70 Deep Cameo PCGS.** Type Two is the clear S mintmark, introduced during the year to replace a worn punch. Both sides of this amazing pristine Deep Cameo display stone-white and black contrast. Population: 25 in 70 Deep Cameo (1/10).(#94213)

365 **1990-S Doubled Die Obverse PR69 Ultra Cameo NGC.** DDO-001. IN GOD WE TRUST is nicely die doubled in a clockwise direction. The variety is currently unlisted in *Cherrypickers'*, but that oversight will eventually be corrected. This flawless specimen is razor-sharp and has delicate honey-gold toning near the borders.

MERCURY DIMES

Key-Date 1916-D Dime, MS65 Full Bands

366 **1916-D MS65 Full Bands NGC.** The key-date 1916-D Mercury dime had a mintage of only 264,000 coins, which was in stark contrast to the large number of ten cent pieces made at the Philadelphia and San Francisco mints in 1916 (22.1 million and 10.4 million pieces, respectively). The entire 1916-D dime issue, according to David Lange (2005), was released in November 1916. He writes that the coinage of dimes was then halted at Denver so that the presses could be redirected to produce a large order for quarters the Treasury Department had placed.

The radiantly lustrous surface of this Gem are lightly toned with splashes of champagne-gold, sky-blue, and gray-violet patina. An impressive strike leaves sharp detail on the design features, culminating in full central bands. A few minuscule reverse marks do not subtract from the coin's great overall appeal. Census: 24 in 65 Full Bands, 7 finer (12/09). (#4907)

Delicately Patinated 1917 Dime, MS67
The Single Finest Certified Example

367 **1917 MS67 NGC.** The 1917 dime mintage exceeded 55 million pieces, making the issue common in all grades through MS65. The present Superb Gem displays dappled gold-tan and greenish-gold patina resting on lustrous surfaces. The design elements are well struck and each side reveals just a few minuscule marks. This piece is the single finest certified by either NGC or PCGS (1/10). (#4910)

Fantastic MS67 Full Bands 1917 Dime

368 **1917 MS67 Full Bands PCGS.** Though over 55 million dimes were struck at Philadelphia in 1917, the issue was little-saved, and today, sharply defined Superb Gems are in short supply. This impressively lustrous example has charming peach-to-gold toning over most of each side, with glints of silver-white at parts of the margins. Population: 14 in 67 Full Bands, 0 finer (1/10). (#4911)

369 **1917-D MS64 Full Bands NGC.** Decisively struck with above-average luster. Pale silver centers yield to green-gold and orange peripheral hues that are strongest at the lower reverse. Census: 68 in 64 Full Bands, 16 finer (12/09).(#4913)

370 **1917-S MS66 Full Bands PCGS.** Ex: Scheppman Collection. A hint of gold toning visits this lustrous and splendidly preserved Premium Gem. The strike is precise, and the eye appeal is unassailable. Population: 63 in 66 Full Bands, 10 finer (12/09). (#4915)

371 **1918-D MS63 Full Bands PCGS.** Soft gold and violet patina rests on the lustrous surfaces of this exquisitely struck D-mint dime. Minor marks, more so on the reverse, preclude a finer grade. (#4919)

Semikey 1919-D Dime, MS64 Full Bands

372 **1919-D MS64 Full Bands PCGS. CAC.** Boldly struck with a pair of peripheral die cracks noted on the obverse, at 11:30 and 3 o'clock. Lovely apricot-gray toning adorns both sides, and a mixture of additional colors decorates the lower reverse. A pleasing, high-end example for the grade. Population: 67 in 64 Full Bands, 17 finer (1/10). (#4925)

373 **1919-S MS62 Full Bands PCGS.** Attractive forest-green and yellow-tan color graces the obverse, while the reverse shows mostly even golden color. Though a number of small ticks account for the grade, no single mark warrants individual mention.(#4927)

374 **1920 MS67 Full Bands NGC.** An array of medium intensity colors adorns the highly lustrous surfaces of this charming Superb Gem. A decisive strike transcends the Full Bands to include crispness on the remaining design elements. A couple of minuscule reverse marks are in concert with the designated grade. Census: 14 in 67 Full Bands, 2 finer (1/10).(#4929)

375 **1921-D AU50 PCGS.** Lightly toned and briefly circulated with attractive surfaces and only a hint of incompleteness of strike at the borders. The 1921-D has one of the lowest mintages of the series, since the Denver Mint was occupied with large-scale silver dollar production. Encased in a green label holder.(#4936)

Colorful 1925 Dime, MS66 Full Bands

376 **1925 MS66 Full Bands PCGS.** This well-preserved 1925 dime has a surprisingly bold strike, which lends the coin added importance. Strongly lustrous surfaces are silver-white beneath areas of canary-gold, mustard, and peach patina. Smooth and attractive. PCGS has graded a mere 25 finer Full Bands representatives (12/09). (#4949)

Lovely MS66 Full Bands 1925 Dime

377 **1925 MS66 Full Bands PCGS.** Light silver and powder-blue colors give way to streaky green-gold at the right sides of both the obverse and reverse. A shining Premium Gem with impressive detail, including full separation on the bands across the fasces. Challenging with Full Bands despite a mintage of over 25 million pieces. (#4949)

1925 Premium Gem Dime With Full Bands

378 **1925 MS66 Full Bands PCGS.** Razor-sharp striking definition across the bands on the reverse. This Premium Gem offers excellent eye appeal. Baby-blue toning shows thin lines of reddish-gold color at parts of the obverse margins, and elements of canary gold are present near the centers. Population: 47 in 66 Full Bands, 25 finer (12/09). (#4949)

Bold 1925 Dime, MS67 Full Bands

379 **1925 MS67 Full Bands PCGS.** An extraordinarily bold strike defines the eye appeal of this shining Superb Gem. Light blue toning graces much of the centers, while the margins show small streaks of gold and tan color. Highly challenging any finer with Full Bands; PCGS has certified just three such coins (12/09). (#4949)

MS67 Full Bands 1925 Dime

380 **1925 MS67 Full Bands PCGS.** A sharp Superb Gem example of this challenging issue, one Lange notes as "an exception" to the norm of 1920s Mercury dimes having strong central detail. This delightful coin, however, shows sharp definition throughout. Lustrous surfaces show a pale blue cast overall with streaks of violet and tan color at the upper obverse and lower reverse. Population: 22 in 67 Full Bands, 3 finer (12/09). (#4949)

Superb Gem Full Bands 1925 Dime

381 **1925 MS67 Full Bands PCGS.** Pale blue glints grace the outer zones of this crisply struck Superb Gem, while the centers show a subtle aura of gold, which is deeper on the reverse. Attractively lustrous with a few streaks of peripheral tan and russet along the bottom of the reverse and the top of the obverse. Population: 22 in 67 Full Bands, 3 finer (12/09). (#4949)

Astounding MS68 Full Bands 1925 Dime

382 **1925 MS68 Full Bands PCGS.** For the collector who missed the opportunity to own the MS68 Full Bands 1925 dime in Heritage's January 2010 FUN Auction, consider the offering of this example a second chance. The 1925 is among the most challenging Philadelphia dates of the decade with Full Bands, due to general striking softness that seems almost anachronistic. This coin, by contrast, is delightfully sharp with satiny surfaces, generally pale silver-gray with subtle blue and gold hues. A few streaks of russet appear at the left reverse margin. Population: 3 in 68 Full Bands, 0 finer (12/09). (#4949)

383 **1925-S MS65 NGC.** A frosty S-mint with light silver-gray surfaces that show occasional suggestions of blue. Well struck overall with excellent quality. Census: 8 in 65, 6 finer (12/09).(#4952)

384 **1927-D MS64 Full Bands PCGS.** Lustrous silver-gray surfaces exhibit sharply struck design elements culminating in Full Bands. A few minuscule marks preclude Gem status. Population: 44 in 64 Full Bands, 56 finer (1/10).(#4963)

Gem Full Bands 1927-D Dime

385 **1927-D MS65 Full Bands PCGS.** Light gold and peach peripheral tints add color to this Full Bands Gem, which shows only a suggestion of silver-blue toning otherwise. Decisively struck and fantastically lustrous, an excellent representative of this Roaring Twenties issue. PCGS has graded a mere nine finer Full Bands coins (1/10). (#4963)

386 **1929-D MS67 Full Bands PCGS.** Vibrant luster exudes from the frosty surfaces of this lovely Superb Gem. Nearly color free save for an occasional wisp of gold-tan that shows up under magnification. A decisive strike leaves bold definition on the design motifs, and both sides reveal impeccable preservation. Population: 30 in 67 Full Bands, 1 finer (12/09).(#4975)

387 **1930-S MS67 NGC.** Beautiful luster envelops this nearly untoned near-Gem. Sharply struck, including good (though not full) separation in the middle bands. Census: 4 in 67, 0 finer (1/10). (#4980)

388 **1930-S MS66 Full Bands PCGS.** Always popular because of its low mintage of 1.8 million pieces. Most were unneeded at the time of issue and distributed to the public only later, in the mid-1930s. This piece has the usual dazzling mint brilliance and is brilliant throughout. Population: 55 in 66 Full Bands, 9 finer (1/10).(#4981)

389 **1935-D MS67 Full Bands NGC.** The radiantly lustrous surfaces of this Superb Gem display dappled orange-brown and lime-green on the obverse and splashes of orange-gold, yellow-gold, and violet on the reverse. Exquisitely struck and lovingly preserved. Census: 5 in 67 Full Bands, 0 finer (1/10).(#4995)

390 **1942/1 AU55 NGC.** FS-101, formerly FS-010.7. Luster shimmers throughout the borders and devices of this lightly circulated key date dime. The overdate is obvious, and no marks are consequential. A few freckles of jade-green patina are noted near the rims.(#5036)

391 **1942/1 AU58 NGC.** FS-101, formerly FS-010.7. The cartwheel luster is unmistakable, although slightly subdued across the open fields. This unmarked Borderline Uncirculated dime has dappled tan-gold and jade-green toning. A dramatic overdate *Guide Book* variety that is very scarce relative to demand.(#5036)

392 **1942-D MS68 Full Bands PCGS.** A few hints of light gold are visible on the lustrous surfaces of this Sharply struck Superb Gem. Impeccably preserved. Population: 17 in 68 Full Bands, 0 finer (1/10).(#5039)

Terrific 1942/1-D Dime, MS67 Full Bands Tied Atop the Condition Census

393 **1942/1-D MS67 Full Bands NGC.** FS-101, formerly FS-010.8. In a numismatically less-sophisticated era, coin collectors believed that the cause of overdates, even those of the 20th century, was the hand-alteration of a working die—the repunching by hand, usually of a single digit, for a later year over that of an earlier one. The belief was certainly not without justification, as in an earlier time from the late 18th century to the first few decades of the 19th century, Philadelphia Mint employees were known to do just that, with the numerous Bust half overdates the most eloquent evidence of the practice. But after 1836, the Mint's new steam presses largely obviated the need for hand-production of working dies, other than the punching in of dates from two-, three-, or four-digit logotypes. Afterward, the production of overdates was confined to those rare situations, usually close to the end of the year, when the Mint was making working dies for two different years. The repeated "squeezes" or impressions required between work-hardenings or annealings occasionally saw working hubs of two different years intervening, creating an overdated die via a dual-hubbing mishap.

Such is the case with the 1942/1 overdate Mercury dimes from the Philadelphia and Denver mints. The resemblance largely ends there, however. The Philadelphia variety was discovered within months of its production, and a photograph of the error was published in the May 1943 issue of *Numismatic Scrapbook*. The Philadelphia variety can be clearly seen with the naked eye—probably the boldest overdate of the 20th century. The Denver variant is more subtle, showing only traces of a 1 beneath the 2 and a small extra bit of metal beneath the 4. The Denver overdate was also publicized much later, in 1962.

The present Superb Gem Full Bands example is unquestionably among the finest available today in the numismatic marketplace. NGC has certified two such Full Bands examples, and the highest-certified Full Bands examples at PCGS are 13 pieces in MS66 (1/10). This piece stretches the limits of the meaning of satin luster, veering nearly to frosty. The piece appears to be an early die state as well, with a clear bottom to the 1 below the 2 and pronounced doubling of the 4. There are absolutely no abrasions worthy of mention. The surfaces are brilliant throughout and silver-white, simply a terrific coin. Census: 2 in 67 Full Bands, 0 finer (1/10). (#5041)

394 **1944-D MS68 Full Bands PCGS.** This immaculate Superb Gem is perfect save for trivial incompleteness of strike on the tops of the LI in LIBERTY. Delicate olive and almond-gold toning. In a green label holder. Population: 76 in 68 Full Bands, 0 finer (1/10). (#5053)

PROOF MERCURY DIMES

395 **1936 PR64 PCGS.** Luminous surfaces display speckled russet, purple, and sky-blue toning and are sharply struck. Devoid of mentionable marks.(#5071)

396 **1936 PR65 NGC.** Yellow-green, reddish-gold, and orange streaks and splashes provide a highly attractive color palette on the well preserved surfaces of this Gem proof. An exacting strike delivers complete detail to the design elements.(#5071)

Seemingly Perfect PR68 1938 Mercury Dime

397 **1938 PR68 NGC.** The 1938 is an overlooked date in the 1936-1942 proof series. The 1936 is the key to the series of course, but the 1938 dime only had a production run of 8,728 proofs. This is a stunning example that is completely brilliant throughout. The fields are deeply mirrored on each side. We see this coin as perfect, and as Michael Sherman once said, "How can there be two grading points higher than this?" (#5073)

398 **1939 PR68 NGC.** Brilliant surfaces displaying whispers of light gold on the reverse reach out to the observer. An exquisitely struck and marvelously preserved example of this Superb Gem proof dime. Census: 67 in 68, 0 finer (12/09).(#5074)

399 **1942 PR68 NGC.** The mirrored fields are slightly subdued by an almost imperceptible iridescent toning seen over each side. The surfaces are essentially perfect in terms of preservation. Considered the "common" date for the type, but the mintage was still only 22,329 proofs, a tiny fraction of the collectors who would like such a coin for a type set.(#5077)

ROOSEVELT DIMES

400 **1947-S MS67 Full Torch Prooflike NGC.** The Trumpet Tail mintmark is clearly repunched. A virtually pristine Superb Gem, sharply struck and only faintly toned almond-gold. This is the finest of only two 1947-S dimes certified by NGC as both Full Torch and Prooflike. The other example is graded MS65.(#85087)

1949-D Roosevelt Dime, MS68 With Richly Variegated Toning

401 **1949-D MS68 PCGS.** Wondrously toned in every color imaginable. The underlying mint luster is thick and enlivens the colors even more. The surfaces appear flawless. This is one of the finest examples known of this early issue and will undoubtedly end up in a premier set of Roosevelt dimes. Population: 5 in 68, 0 finer (1/10). (#5092)

402 **1949-S MS68 ★ NGC.** An absolutely stunning Superb Gem, this 1949-S Roosevelt dime has full rainbow toning with pastel green, yellow, russet, blue, and steel on both sides. This piece is the finest 1949-S Roosevelt dime that we have ever offered, aptly recognized by the NGC Star label.(#5093)

1951-D Dime, MS68 Full Bands Among the Finest Known

403 **1951-D MS68 Full Bands PCGS.** Along with the 1949-D in this sale, these two pieces (from the same source) would form core coins to a high-grade set of Roosevelt dimes. The surfaces of this piece are highly lustrous and greatly enhance the rose, lime-green, and original brilliance seen on each side. As one would imagine from the grade, the coin is essentially perfect. Population: 3 in 68 Full Bands, 0 finer (1/10). (#85098)

PROOF ROOSEVELT DIME

404 **1970 No S PR68 Cameo PCGS.** Moderately contrasted with an excellent cameo effect. Untoned surfaces are blemish-free. Population: 29 in 68 Cameo, 2 finer (1/10).(#85248)

STANDING LIBERTY QUARTERS

Famous 1916 Standing Liberty Quarter

405 **1916 PCGS Genuine.** The PCGS number ending in .92 suggests Cleaning as the reason, or perhaps one of the reasons, that PCGS deemed this coin not gradable. In our opinion, this coin has the details of a VF specimen that has environmental damage and has been cleaned. This midrange coin is oddly luminous, with the silver-blue surfaces showing hairlines from a past cleaning. A streak of dark toning crosses Liberty's body diagonally, across the shield. (#5704)

Desirable VF30 1916 Standing Liberty Quarter

406 **1916 VF30 NGC.** An appealing midrange example of the classic first-year Standing Liberty quarter key date, medium-gray on the obverse with the rose and gold accents on that side growing more overt on the reverse. Significantly worn on the high points, but smooth with ample detail in the recesses.
From The South Texas Collection. (#5704)

Gorgeous 1916 Gem Standing Liberty Quarter

407 **1916 MS65 PCGS.** The 1916 Standing Liberty quarter owes its key date status, at least in part, to design issues that delayed its production until the end of the year. In a September 24, 2007 *Coin World* article titled "1916 Standing Liberty 25c Differs From 1917 Designs," Eric von Klinger writes that Mint officials sought modifications to Hermon MacNeil's obverse design through the latter part of 1916. Finally, Mint Director F.J.H. von Engelken wrote Philadelphia Mint Superintendent Adam Joyce on November 11 that Treasury Secretary William McAdoo decided "to let the quarter go as it is," despite wanting the figure of Liberty to be brought out more clearly. Von Klinger says that this resulted in a short production run of only 52,000 coins on December 16 at the Philadelphia Mint.

Dazzling luster envelops both sides of this magnificent Gem, each of which displays just a few wisps of barely discernible light tan-gold color under magnification. The design elements are strongly impressed, including clarity of the rivets, the inner shield outline, and most of its horizontal stripes. Liberty's head, though not full, still exhibits good detail, as does most of the eagle's plumage. A few minute grade-consistent marks fail to take away from the coin's gorgeous eye appeal. Population: 25 in 65, 7 finer (12/09). (#5704)

408 **1917 Type One MS65 Full Head NGC. CAC.** This lustrous, sharply struck Gem displays light to medium intensity yellow-gold toning accented with deep electric-blue and purple at the margins. Nicely preserved, though we mention a graze on Liberty's chest for complete accuracy.(#5707)

409 **1917 Type One MS65 Full Head PCGS.** Strong definition and luster are the only shared characteristics between the two sides of this Gem. The obverse has only faint tan peripheral toning around a broad silver-white center, while the reverse offers dappled violet and olive-gray patina.(#5707)

410 **1917 Type One MS65 Full Head PCGS.** Marvelous frosty luster endows this Gem, and a well executed strike sharpens the design elements. Not only is the the head fully struck, but the horizontal and vertical lines in the shield are crisp, as are the rivets. A few grade-consistent marks are visible on the untoned surfaces. (#5707)

411 **1917 Type One MS65 Full Head NGC.** Warm peach and rose tints cover much of each side, with the reverse showing more of the underlying silver-white. A well-defined and attractive Type One type coin.(#5707)

412 **1917-D Type One MS66 Full Head PCGS.** A rare degree of eye appeal is seen on this gorgeous Premium Gem. Lovely mattelike surfaces display ample frostiness and pinpoint detailing. An edging of reddish-golden-brown toning frames the obverse, while similar coloration affects all but the high points and the lower border of the reverse.(#5709)

413 **1917-D Type One MS66 Full Head NGC.** This Premium Gem is boldly defined with full head and shield details. Both sides have heavy toning with predominate lilac and russet, accented by blue-green and gold. Census: 75 in 66 Full Head, 20 finer (1/10). (#5709)

Pleasing 1917-S Type One Quarter, MS66 Full Head

414 **1917-S Type One MS66 Full Head PCGS. CAC.** Soft, barely discernible violet patina is joined on the reverse by blue-green and purple dapples around the margins. Both sides yield pleasing frosty luster and are nicely preserved. All design elements are sharply impressed, though the inner shield is somewhat weak. Population: 60 in 66 Full Head, 9 finer (12/09). (#5711)

Magnificent 1917-S Type One Quarter Full Head Premium Gem

415 **1917-S Type One MS66 Full Head PCGS.** Occasional splashes of light gold-tan patina visit the highly lustrous surfaces of this magnificent Premium Gem. In addition to the Full Head, design completeness is apparent on the rivets, Liberty's toes, and the eagle's plumage. Impeccable preservation reaches out to the observer. Population: 60 in 66 Full Head, 9 finer (12/09). (#5711)

416 **1917 Type Two MS66 Full Head PCGS.** Rich reddish-orange patina embraces most of each side, though small slivers of silver-white also appeal. Excellent detail and strong eye appeal for this popular type issue. Population: 63 in 66 Full Head, 7 finer (1/10). (#5715)

417 **1917-S Type Two MS64 Full Head NGC.** Occasional splashes of yellow-green and reddish-gold adhere to the lustrous surfaces of this near-Gem. Nicely struck save for the usual softness in the rivets at Liberty's hip. Devoid of mentionable contact marks.(#5719)

Important MS66 Full Head 1918-D Quarter

418 **1918-D MS66 Full Head PCGS. CAC.** An uncommonly sharp example of this earlier Denver issue, profoundly lustrous with rich and intriguing veils of pink-purple and yellow-green over a pale silver base. Carefully preserved and memorably appealing. Tied for the finest Full Head example of the issue certified by NGC or PCGS (12/09). (#5723)

419 **1918-S MS63 Full Head PCGS.** The 1918-S is a very scarce issue in the series with a Full Head, and an MS63 coin is definitely a worthwhile acquisition. The brilliant surfaces show the usual thick, frosted mint luster. There are a couple of smaller abrasions that account for the grade as well as a larger one to the left of the eagle. (#5725)

Bright 1918-S Quarter, MS64 Full Head

420 **1918-S MS64 Full Head PCGS.** Bright luster endows the color-free surfaces of this near-Gem. The design elements are generally well impressed, though a couple of rivets near Liberty's hip are soft. A few minute marks prevent a Gem grade, but this piece is nevertheless a great-looking Full Head S-mint quarter. (#5725)

Choice Full Head 1918-S Quarter

421 **1918-S MS64 Full Head PCGS. CAC.** Virtually untoned and immensely lustrous with a sharp head and only two soft rivets on the shield. Both sides of this near-Gem show evidence of clash marks and lapping, with the reverse fields exhibiting prominent die polish. PCGS has graded 39 finer Full Head examples (12/09). (#5725)

Near-Gem 1918/7-S Quarter

422 **1918/7-S MS64 PCGS.** FS-101, formerly FS-008.5. The 1918/7-S Standing Liberty quarter went unnoticed—surprisingly so, for such a bold overdate—until 1937, when the first known example was offered in a Barney Bluestone sale (12/1937, lot 741), a Mint State coin that brought a then-remarkable $26.25. At the time the coin was thought to be unique. Even today, Mint State pieces are quite rare, and Full Head coins even more so.

The 1918/7-S quarter has numerous die diagnostics that aid in authentication:

—Most examples show a small, raised die chip above the step, just to the left of the lowest star on the right.

—A clash mark from the E of AMERICA is at Liberty's right knee.

—Clashing and die polishing appear at AME on the reverse.

—A clash from the eagle's wing runs diagonally through the first T of TRUST.

All of these features are present on the near-Gem representative offered here. Brightly lustrous surfaces are minimally toned with few marks, and while the coin shows typical softness at Liberty's head and shield and the eagle's body, the strike does not detract from the eye appeal. PCGS has graded only five finer non-Full Head examples of the overdate (1/10). (#5726)

423 **1919 MS67 NGC.** Whispers of olive-green visit the lustrous surfaces of this lovely Superb Gem. Sharply struck, particularly the chain mail, vertical shield stripes, and rivets. There are no mentionable marks to report. Census: 15 in 67, 2 finer (1/10). (#5728)

424 **1919-D MS63 PCGS.** If one were to assemble a set of Standing Liberty quarters based on value alone, this piece would certainly merit consideration. The 1919-D is one of the keys to the Full Head series, and this piece is well defined even though it does not merit the coveted Full Head designation. Also, the mint luster is bright, even semireflective on the reverse. Just a few tiny abrasions explain the grade.(#5730)

Original Light Gray 1920 Quarter, MS64 Full Head

425 **1920 MS64 Full Head PCGS. CAC.** An original coin, the surfaces are oyster-gray with numerous small specks of russet scattered mostly around the obverse. As usual, the mint luster is outstanding and there are remarkably few abrasions for an MS64 (which undoubtedly explains the CAC designation). The strike is strongly defined in all areas. (#5735)

426 **1920-S MS65 PCGS.** A fully original Gem, this remarkable 1920-S quarter has frosty luster beneath silver-gray patina with splashes of iridescent toning. A scarce Standing Liberty quarter that represents excellent value with mostly complete head definition versus a technical Full Head coin. Population: 40 in 65, 17 finer (1/10). (#5738)

Choice Full Head 1920-S Quarter

427 **1920-S MS64 Full Head PCGS.** Dusky olive hues form an arc on either side of Liberty's well-defined head, while the rest of the coin is pale silver-gray with a suggestion of blue. An elegantly appealing near-Gem representative of this challenging San Francisco issue. Population: 30 in 64 Full Head, 22 finer (1/10). (#5739)

428 **1921 XF45 NGC.** Freckles of grayish-purple patina are somewhat more prevalent on the obverse of this Choice XF quarter. Nicely defined for the issue and grade. One of the scarcer dates in the Standing Liberty series.(#5740)

Shining 1923 Quarter, MS66 Full Head

429 **1923 MS66 Full Head PCGS. CAC.** Fantastic luster with an above-average overall strike, even by Full Head standards; only one rivet is soft. The obverse is minimally toned save for a hint of canary-yellow, but that color and pale blue are more prominent across the reverse. Population: 24 in 66 Full Head, 2 finer (12/09). (#5743)

430 **1924-D MS65 PCGS.** Golden-rose toning covers each side of this well, but not fully struck quarter. Strong mint luster also shines through the toning. This is an early die state, and scarce as such, with no trace of the horizontal die crack that later develops through the date and subsequent weakness at the tops of the digits. (#5748)

431 **1924-S MS65 PCGS.** This piece just misses Full Head status, only lacking the hole in Liberty's ear. Both sides shimmer with frosted mint luster that enhances the medium density golden-rose toning. (#5750)

Full Head MS66 1925 Quarter

432 **1925 MS66 Full Head PCGS.** Light silver-gray centers show elements of blue and gold, and the margins show deeper amber-tan colors. Carefully preserved with a strongly detailed shield with complete rivets, as well as the Full Head noted in the grade. Housed in a green label holder. PCGS has graded just six finer Full Head coins (1/10). (#5753)

Full Head Near-Gem 1926-D Quarter

433 **1926-D MS64 Full Head PCGS. CAC.** A relatively available issue, but not at all so in MS64 Full Head; this piece is one of 27 so certified at PCGS, with 29 finer (12/09). This lustrous silver-white piece shows amazing head definition, with sharp delineation of the hairline all the way down to the ear. A couple of the shield rivets are missing, and interesting parallel marks on Liberty's torso appear Mint-made. (#5757)

434 **1927 MS66 NGC.** Soft multicolored toning endows the lustrous surfaces of this Premium Gem. This is a sharply struck piece with minimal marks. Census: 21 in 66, 3 finer (1/10).(#5760)

435 **1927-D MS66 PCGS. CAC.** Dappled blue, canary-gold, and violet hues grace this D-mint Premium Gem. Only slight softness in the ear area precludes Full Head status. Population: 26 in 66, 0 finer (12/09).(#5762)

436 **1927-D MS63 Full Head PCGS. CAC.** A pale silver-gray example with thin skeins of blue toning running through the fields. Well-defined and minimally abraded for the grade assigned. (#5763)

437 **1927-S XF45 PCGS. CAC.** Hints of luster and good detail show on the silver-gray surfaces. A pleasing Choice XF example of this late semikey date in the Standing Liberty quarter series. (#5764)

438 **1928-S MS66 Full Head PCGS.** The brilliant surfaces of this Premium Gem offer scintillating satiny luster. The strike is razor-sharp on the head, and there is only minor weakness on a couple of shield rivets. PCGS has certified only 12 finer Full Head examples (12/09).(#5771)

Appealing MS67 Full Head 1928-S Quarter

439 **1928-S MS67 Full Head NGC.** A brightly lustrous Superb Gem example of this later S-mint quarter issue, far above-average on head detail, if slightly soft on the shield and the eagle's breast feathers. Each side is practically silver-white, with only occasional suggestions of gold at the central obverse. Census: 35 in 67 Full Head, 2 finer (1/10). (#5771)

440 **1929 MS66 Full Head PCGS. CAC.** Golden color dominates the centers, while russet and violet elements are present at the borders. Crisply struck overall with only slight softness at the lower shield. PCGS has graded just seven finer Full Head coins (12/09). (#5773)

Impressive 1929-D Quarter, MS65 Full Head

441 **1929-D MS65 Full Head PCGS. CAC.** Just a trace of light champagne toning on each side accents the frosty silver brilliance of this bold Gem. As a date, the 1929-D is scarce, but as a sharp Gem example, it is a condition rarity. Here is a remarkable opportunity for the avid Standing Liberty quarter collector to acquire an important addition. Population: 36 in 65 Full Head, 10 finer (12/09). (#5775)

442 **1930 MS66 Full Head PCGS. CAC.** The lustrous obverse has strong golden overtones, while on the reverse the same colors are a mere accent. Decidedly above-average detail for this final-year issue.(#5779)

443 **1930 MS66 Full Head NGC.** The ultimate type coin in the Standing Liberty series. This coin has it all: fully struck; bright, shimmering mint luster; just a trace of light, original toning; and surfaces clean enough to rate MS66.(#5779)

Lustrous 1930 Quarter, MS67 Full Head

444 **1930 MS67 Full Head NGC. CAC.** Attractive luster emanates from silver-gray surfaces accented with violet dapples at the obverse border and splashes of gold-tan on the reverse. In addition to the Full Head, relatively strong definition is visible on the chain mail and vertical stripes on the shield. A nicely preserved piece. Census: 29 in 67 Full Head, 0 finer (12/09). (#5779)

Sharp 1930 Quarter, MS67 Full Head

445 **1930 MS67 Full Head NGC.** Delicate gold patination joined by light green, gray, and lavender on the obverse resides on the highly lustrous surfaces of this Superb Gem. Sharply struck and culminating in Full Head; the usual softness is visible in a couple of rivets adjacent to Liberty's hip. An impeccably preserved piece. Census: 29 in 67 Full Head, 0 finer (1/10). (#5779)

WASHINGTON QUARTERS

446 **1932-D MS63 PCGS. CAC.** Strong silver-white luster is the base of this Select D-mint key, though both sides also exhibit minor gold elements. A well struck and minimally abraded coin.(#5791)

447 **1932-D MS63 PCGS.** Deep golden-brown and iridescent toning masks the frosty luster of this key-date 1932-D quarter. Here is an opportunity to acquire that long missing piece and cross another one off the want list.(#5791)

Near-Gem 1932-D Quarter, Upper-End Coin That Represents Great Value

448 **1932-D MS64 PCGS. CAC.** The price difference between MS64 and MS65 in the 1932-D quarter is huge. And that price differential makes this upper-end, CAC-certified example an especially good buy. The surfaces have original hazy gray patina with occasional dabs of golden on the obverse, while the reverse is almost completely golden-toned. Close examination with a loupe shows two tiny marks on Washington's lower cheek. There is also a dab of deeper golden toning on the high point of the cheek that looks like a surface flaw, but it is nothing more than toning in that area. (#5791)

Gem 1932-D Washington Quarter

449 **1932-D MS65 PCGS.** Silver-gray centers give way to varying levels of tan and umber peripheral toning on each side. The obverse has extensive coverage with an additional small patch on Washington's neck, while the reverse has patina only at the top and bottom, deepest at the mintmark. Population: 64 in 65, 1 finer (12/09). (#5791)

450 **1932-S MS64 PCGS. CAC.** Whispers of apple-green, crimson, and violet patination are somewhat more extensive in territory and deeper on the obverse of this near-Gem Washington key date representative. Lustrous, well struck, minimally marked, and highly appealing.(#5792)

451 **1936-D MS65 NGC.** Shining and slightly frosty, a primarily silver-white coin with touches of peripheral gold and tan. Well-defined and strongly appealing. NGC has graded just 65 numerically finer pieces (1/10).(#5801)

Attractive 1942-D Doubled Die Obverse Washington Quarter, FS-101, MS63

452 **1942-D Doubled Die Obverse MS63 PCGS.** FS-101, formerly FS-015. Doubling is most noticeable as notching on the L and E of LIBERTY and extremely thick letters on all obverse legends. Splashes of golden-tan are more prevalent on the margins. Highly lustrous, sharply struck, and minimally abraded. Population: 4 in 63, 1 finer (1/10). (#95818)

453 **1943-D MS68 NGC.** Vibrant luster invigorates this D-mint Superb Gem and an exacting strike leaves strong definition on the design elements. Crimson, forest-green, and yellow-gold patination is much more extensive and deeper on the obverse. Immaculately preserved throughout. The single finest certified specimen (1/10). (#5821)

454 **1947-S MS67 PCGS.** Golden-brown, navy-blue, and lime-green consume the margins of this lustrous and mark-free Superb Gem. Light dove-gray and apricot toning adorn the fields and devices. PCGS has certified just three pieces finer (1/10).(#5835)

455 **1950-S/D MS65 PCGS.** FS-601, formerly FS-022. This *Guide Book* variety clearly shows both mintmarks. A serif of the D is noted near the upper left of the S, and the curve of the D dominates the right border of the overmintmark. Lustrous and lightly toned with a sharp strike and smooth surfaces. Encased in a green label holder. Population: 47 in 65, 32 finer (1/10).(#5845)

456 **1952-S MS67 PCGS.** The toning on this coin suggests it was originally housed in a Mint set holder. The obverse has deeply speckled blue, golden, and rose toning; while the reverse is ice-blue in the center with golden-russet around the margin. Superior mint luster.(#5851)

Memorable MS68 ★ 1954 Quarter

457 **1954 MS68 ★ NGC. CAC.** Spectacular cherry-red, jade-green, and golden-brown patina is prominent on both sides, although the central reverse is only faintly toned. An immaculate and lustrous Superb Gem, worthy of the finest Registry holding. Census: 2 in 68 ★, none finer (1/10). (#5855)

PROOF WASHINGTON QUARTERS

458 **1936 PR65 NGC.** The bright surfaces of this Gem proof display occasional splashes of green, yellow-orange, purple, and blue. Well defined and nicely preserved.(#5975)

First-Year PR66 1936 Quarter

459 **1936 PR66 NGC.** The first year of the proof Washington quarter series and perennially popular as such, due in part to the low mintage of 3,837 pieces. This Premium Gem proof offers silver centers with accents of copper radiating outward. Generous luster emanates beneath the light patina. NGC has certified only 20 examples finer (1/10). (#5975)

WALKING LIBERTY HALF DOLLARS

460 **1916-D MS64 PCGS.** Variegated violet and champagne coloration adorns the lustrous surfaces of this well struck near-Gem. A few unimportant ticks do not detract.(#6567)

Near-Gem 1916-S Half Dollar

461 **1916-S MS64 NGC.** A near-Gem San Francisco Walker from the first year of issue, satiny yet surprisingly bright. Though the strike is soft, with little definition on the branch hand or the high points of the eagle, there is no trace of wear, and on the obverse, only a shallow abrasion in the right obverse field warrants individual mention. (#6568)

462 **1917 MS65 NGC.** Golden-brown patina displays reddish-purple accents at the margins of this sharply struck, strongly lustrous Gem. The only mark worthy of note is a reverse rim cut at 11 o'clock. (#6569)

463 **1917-D Reverse MS63 PCGS.** Bright luster emanates from the untoned surfaces of this Select D-mint half. A well struck specimen with a few minute marks.(#6571)

Brilliant MS63 1918-D Walking Liberty Half

464 **1918-D MS63 PCGS.** In Gem condition, the 1918-D is the third rarest issue in the Walking Liberty series. This MS63 example represents excellent value and has most of the eye appeal of an MS64. The surfaces are brilliant throughout, and the striking details, while incomplete, are certainly above-average for the issue. The mint luster is softly frosted, rather than the usual satiny variant. An exceptionally attractive coin for the grade. (#6575)

Lustrous 1918-D Near-Gem Half Dollar

465 **1918-D MS64 PCGS.** Both sides of this near-Gem D-mint representative yield full luster and display soft grayish patina. The design elements are well struck, including good detail in Liberty's branch hand. A few light grazes preclude Gem classification. PCGS has seen fewer than 30 pieces grading higher (1/10). (#6575)

466 **1920 MS64 PCGS. CAC.** A charming near-Gem bathed in pleasing luster. The chestnut-gray toning is original and moderate. Sharply struck and impressively devoid of significant marks. (#6580)

Charming MS66 1920-D Half Dollar

467 **1920-D MS66 PCGS.** With over 1.5 million pieces struck, the 1920-D is not one of the low-mintage rarities commonly touted as a key date. Yet above the MS65 level, it is impossible to deny the issue's condition rarity: NGC has graded only one such coin and PCGS has certified just six, for a total of seven at the MS66 level and none finer (12/09). This example's inherent quality is obvious at first glance, with light golden toning blanketing uncommonly lustrous surfaces. The top of the obverse adds an arc of peach. Liberty's head and branch hand offer uncommonly strong (though incomplete) detail, and only a few tiny marks are visible. (#6581)

Delicately Toned 1920-S Half Dollar, MS62

468 **1920-S MS62 PCGS.** Delicate almond-gold luster bathes this scarce San Francisco Walking Liberty half. The branch hand shows expected blending, but the strike is good for the facility. Both sides are refreshingly unmarked save for a vertical thin line west of HALF. An opportunity to acquire a nice Uncirculated example. (#6582)

Near-Gem 1920-S Half Dollar

469 **1920-S MS64 PCGS. CAC.** Bright silver-white luster with undercurrents of blue and occasional tan accents close to the rims. The strike is typically soft on Liberty's head and hands and the eagle's body, yet the pillowy detail somehow ties into the coin's impressive eye appeal. PCGS has certified 48 finer examples (1/10). (#6582)

Shining MS65 1933-S Half Dollar

470 **1933-S MS65 PCGS.** Some collectors consider the 1933-S the last issue of the early series of Walkers while others consider it the first issue of the late series. Regardless, it is scarce in Gem or finer grades. The present example has full brilliance with sharp details and faint traces of pale gold toning. PCGS has only certified 82 finer examples (1/10). This piece is housed in a first generation holder. (#6591)

471 **1934 MS67 NGC.** Fantastic flashy luster with eye appeal that cannot be ignored. This sharply struck and dynamic Superb Gem has minimally toned centers framed by peach and green-gold patina. Housed in a prior generation holder. NGC has graded just eight numerically finer pieces (12/09).(#6592)

472 **1934 MS67 PCGS. CAC.** Splashes of lime-green, orange, and ice-blue adorn the lustrous surfaces of this beautiful, sharply struck Superb Gem. A few minute marks are in line with the designated grade.(#6592)

Stunning MS68 1934 Half Dollar

473 **1934 MS68 NGC.** With a mintage of nearly 7 million pieces, the 1934 is available in all grades through sharply struck Gem. In this lofty grade, however, the 1934 is nearly unobtainable. This specimen exhibits a sharp strike, including excellent definition on Liberty's left thumb and adjacent branches, and on the gown lines. Radiantly lustrous surfaces offer delicate whispers of cobalt-blue, golden-brown, and lavender. Nearly pristine surfaces reveal just a few minor, unobtrusive marks. Census: 8 in 68, 0 finer (1/10). (#6592)

474 **1935-S MS65 NGC.** Slightly frosty with a golden aura over much of the soft silver-white surfaces. An attractive Gem, though the pillowy detail on the devices is typical. NGC has graded 53 numerically finer examples (12/09).(#6597)

Satiny 1935-S Half Dollar, MS66

475 **1935-S MS66 PCGS.** The lustrous satinlike surfaces of this Premium Gem display whispers of champagne-gold around the borders. The design elements exhibit somewhat better definition than usually seen, including above-average detail on Liberty's head and branch hand. Some milling marks are noted on the obverse portrait. Population: 92 in 66, 2 finer (12/09). (#6597)

476 **1937-D MS66 PCGS. CAC.** Bold orange, violet, and umber shadings cover most of the outer areas, while the centers glitter under pale silver-blue patina with dots of deep crimson on the reverse. PCGS has graded just 36 finer pieces (12/09). (#6602)

477 **1939-D MS67 NGC.** Rich rose, peach, and silver-blue toning graces this highly lustrous Superb Gem. The strike is above average, although the branch hand is incomplete, as nearly always seen. Census: 86 in 67, 2 finer (1/10).(#6607)

478 **1941-S MS66 NGC.** A bright, slightly frosty Premium Gem example of this popular short-set issue. Gold-kissed surfaces are minimally marked, though the devices show a degree of the usual softness. NGC has graded 17 numerically finer pieces (12/09). (#6613)

479 **1944-D MS67 NGC.** Bright luster envelops this Superb Gem. The only apparent color shows as light gold-tan on portions of the reverse. Well struck and revealing just a few minute grade-consistent marks.(#6622)

480 **1946 Doubled Die Reverse MS64 PCGS.** FS-801, formerly FS-011.1. Doubling is most prominent on the eagle's feathers and on E PLURIBUS UNUM. Currently the only die variety of the series that receives a separate *Guide Book* listing. Untoned and lustrous with a good strike and a well preserved reverse. Population: 48 in 64, 19 finer (1/10).(#6632)

481 **1947 MS67 PCGS.** Soft golden-brown patination runs over the strongly lustrous surfaces of this Superb Gem and an impressive strike leaves good detail on the design motifs, including Liberty's branch hand. Both sides have been well cared for.(#6630)

PROOF WALKING LIBERTY HALF DOLLARS

Attractive 1936 Half Dollar, PR65

482 **1936 PR65 NGC.** Soft ice-blue and gold-tan patina on the obverse of this key-date representative in the short Walking Liberty proof series cedes to a layer of rose coloration on the reverse dappled with olive-green. Some faint obverse marks may well preclude an even finer numerical grade. (#6636)

Delicately Toned 1936 Half Dollar, PR66

483 **1936 PR66 NGC.** The 1936 is the key to the Walking Liberty half series. Splashes of yellow-gold are joined by whispers of apple-green on the reverse of this Premium Gem example, and a powerful strike imparts bold definition to the design elements. Impeccably preserved throughout. (#6636)

Original 1936 Half Dollar, PR67

484 **1936 PR67 PCGS.** This challenging first-year issue had a mintage limited to a mere 3,901 proofs. A large percentage of this production run was later cleaned by non-numismatists, and as a result high grade, original coins are elusive and always eagerly sought by collectors. This is such a coin. Each side is problem-free and totally original. A small center of original brilliance is seen on the obverse, while the reverse has a much larger center of brightness. The margins display a subtle iridescence that is most appealing. (#6636)

485 **1937 PR65 PCGS. CAC.** Fantastic mirrors with considerable cameo contrast for a coin not certified as such. Peripheral cream-gold tints on the obverse extend into the fields on the reverse. (#6637)

486 **1937 PR66 NGC.** Luminous, well cared-for surfaces display hints of violet and champagne color and occasional deep purple freckles. Sharply struck throughout.(#6637)

487 **1937 PR66 NGC.** The obverse displays barely discernible freckles of gold and gray while the reverse takes on deeper shades of gold-tan, yellow-gold, and purple. A decisive strike leaves strong definition on the design elements.(#6637)

488 **1938 PR67 NGC.** The nearly untoned obverse on this Superb Gem is replaced on the reverse with yellow-gold, violet, sea-green, and reddish-gold. Well struck and impeccably preserved. (#6638)

489 **1939 PR67 NGC. CAC.** The full brilliance of this Superb Gem appears to reach out to the observer. Decisively struck and impeccably preserved.(#6639)

Colorful PR68 1939 Half Dollar

490 **1939 PR68 NGC.** Though the impressive mirrors of this PR68 specimen are never overpowered by the colorful toning over each side, its pastel-yellow, turquoise, and rose-violet hues are always eye-catching and seemingly omnipresent. Marvelous eye appeal in all respects. NGC has graded only one numerically finer example (1/10). (#6639)

491 **1940 PR67 NGC.** The champagne-gold surfaces of this Superb Gem proof display occasional splashes of sky-blue, slightly more so on the obverse. Sharply struck and lovingly preserved. (#6640)

Nearly Perfect PR68 1940 Walker

492 **1940 PR68 NGC.** This is an essentially perfect proof Walker, and even a loupe fails to reveal any mentionable contact marks. These early proof sets were packaged in cellophane envelopes, and with the passing years they became more and more brittle; eventually, many of them split on the side(s). This piece appears to have come from an envelope that split on the right side, as both obverse and reverse are deeply toned in that area, while brilliant elsewhere. An interesting and impressive type coin. Census: 51 in 68, 0 finer (1/10). (#6640)

Brilliant 1941 Half Dollar, PR68

493 **1941 PR68 NGC.** Stunning brilliance appear to reach out to the observer of this superb Gem proof Walker, and a well executed strike imparts crisp definition to the design elements. Immaculately preserved surfaces exhibit no mentionable contact marks or spots. Both sides yield tremendous eye appeal. Census: 67 in 68, 0 finer (1/10). (#6641)

494 **1942 PR67 NGC. CAC.** A veneer of yellow-gold and ice-blue patina runs over both sides of this sharply struck Superb Gem proof, accented with a sliver of purple on the lower right margin of the reverse. An impeccably preserved piece.(#6642)

Stunning 1942 Walker, PR68

495 **1942 PR68 NGC.** A gorgeous Walking Liberty half dollar, this Superb Gem proof has bold devices and light contrast that results from the combination of lustrous devices and mirrored fields. Both sides are graced with lovely golden toning with brilliant blue around a portion of the obverse periphery. NGC has only certified four finer examples (1/10). (#6642)

Lovely 1942 Walker, PR68

496 **1942 PR68 NGC.** This fully brilliant Superb Gem proof Walking Liberty half dollar has exceptionally deep mirrored fields around satiny devices, with slight contrast visible. Both sides have outstanding eye appeal with bright, untoned silver surfaces. NGC has certified four finer pieces (1/10). (#6642)

FRANKLIN HALF DOLLAR

Important 1960 Franklin Half Dollar MS66 Full Bell Lines

497 **1960 MS66 Full Bell Lines PCGS.** Here is a lovely 1960 Franklin half dollar that is destined for a Set Registry collection, as it is tied for the finest Full Bell Lines pieces that PCGS has certified. Both sides have gold, olive, and iridescent toning over frosty luster. Population: 34 in 66 Full Bell Lines, 0 finer (1/10). (#86678)

PROOF FRANKLIN HALF DOLLARS

498 **1950 PR67 PCGS.** A Superb Gem example of this initial Franklin half dollar proof issue, sharply struck but with a degree of cartwheeling to the luster. Silver-white overall with reddish-tan peripheral elements.(#6691)

499 **1953 PR66 Deep Cameo PCGS.** Intensely mirrored fields show remarkable black-on-white contrast against the snow-white devices. A number of milk spots in the fields limit the grade, but there are virtually no marks on either side. PCGS reports just seven Deep Cameo pieces finer than this sharply struck specimen (1/10). (#96694)

500 **1961 Doubled Die Reverse PR64 PCGS.** FS-801, formerly FS-013. A near-Gem proof example of this only Franklin half doubled die listed in the *Guide Book*. Modestly contrasted with minor milk spots and hairlines on otherwise silver-white surfaces. Population: 13 in 64, 38 finer (1/10).(#6689)

PR66 1961 Doubled Die Reverse Half

501 **1961 Doubled Die Reverse PR66 PCGS.** FS-801, formerly FS-013. Dramatic die doubling is evident on UNITED and E PLURIBUS UNUM, as well as on other reverse letters. The gleaming surfaces exhibit slight cameo contrast on the obverse. The strike is razor-sharp, and aside from a degree of peripheral milk-spotting, both sides are virtually pristine. A fantastic example of this underrated variety. (#6689)

End of Session One

SESSION TWO

Floor, Telephone, Heritage Live!™, Internet, Fax, and Mail Signature® Auction #1137
Friday, February 5, 2010, 1:00 PM PT, Lots 502-952
Long Beach, California

A 15% Buyer's Premium ($14 minimum) Will Be Added To All Lots

Visit HA.com to view full-color images and bid.

MORGAN DOLLARS

502 **1878 8TF MS65 PCGS.** VAM-16. A pleasing Gem of this first design of the first year of the new Morgan dollar issue, a brilliantly mirrored silver-white coin with good eye appeal and generous cartwheel luster. Seldom seen finer, as PCGS has certified only 31 pieces in higher grade (1/10).(#7072)

Impressive 1878 Eight Tailfeathers Morgan Dollar, MS66

503 **1878 8TF MS66 PCGS.** VAM-16. An immensely lustrous and dynamically toned Premium Gem example of this one-year-only design type. The left obverse shows rainbow arcs of emerald, indigo, violet, magenta, yellow, and finally turquoise. The rest of the coin has faint gold-gray toning that thickens near the rims. Well struck devices are softly frosted beneath the patina. Population: 29 in 66, 2 finer (12/09). (#7072)

504 **1878 7/8TF Strong MS65 PCGS.** VAM-37. A prominent 7/4 Tailfeathers variety adds interest to this first-year coin. An impressively lustrous Gem, softly struck but richly toned blue-green and gold-orange with additional cobalt and pale silver-gray elements on the reverse.(#7078)

Rare 1878 7/8 Tailfeathers Dollar MS63 Deep Mirror Prooflike

505 **1878 7/8TF Strong MS63 Deep Mirror Prooflike PCGS.** VAM-38. The 7/8 Tailfeathers is always desirable with Prooflike, or in this case Deep Mirror Prooflike fields. The die polishing that gives this piece its DMPL status is abundantly clear on the design elements. Portions have been polished away on Liberty's hair, the eagle's wings, and the eagle's legs. The surfaces are brilliant except for a light accent of golden around the perimeters. The devices are sharply struck and there are no large or objectionable abrasions. Population: 43 in 63 Deep Mirror Prooflike, 31 finer (1/10). *From The Classic Collection*. (#97079)

Seldom Seen 1878 7/8 Tailfeathers Dollar MS63 Deep Mirror Prooflike

506 **1878 7/8TF Weak MS63 Deep Mirror Prooflike PCGS.** VAM-34. The 7/8 Tailfeathers variety has long been a highly respected issue with Prooflike or Deep Mirror Prooflike fields. This is an especially pleasing example for the grade that is brilliant throughout. The striking details are complete in the centers on each side, and there are only the light, scattered abrasions one would expect from an MS63. Population: 46 in 63 Deep Mirror Prooflike, 34 finer (1/10). *From The Classic Collection*. (#97071)

507 **1878 7TF Reverse of 1878 MS65 PCGS.** A swath of rainbow toning occurs on the upper obverse of this highly lustrous Gem. Well struck and nicely preserved.(#7074)

508 **1878-CC MS65 PCGS.** This is a brilliant example of this first-year CC Morgan dollar, and always a popular issue as such. The striking details are complete on both sides and there are no detracting abrasions on this impressive Gem.(#7080)

509 **1878-CC MS65 PCGS.** A brilliant silver-white Gem of this always-popular issue, the first Morgan dollars produced at the fabled Carson City Mint. Generous cartwheel luster and a bold strike complete the obvious eye appeal. A nice choice for a Gem set.(#7080)

510 **1878-S MS66 PCGS.** A frosty Premium Gem with dramatic obverse toning, deep olive, blue, and yellow-green over most of the left obverse with a sharp line and abrupt shift to silver. The reverse shows only light gold-orange peripheral toning around a near-brilliant center.(#7082)

511 **1878-S MS66 PCGS.** Intense luster shows through dappled medium intensity multicolored toning. An exacting strike imparts strong detail to the devices including the hair over Liberty's ear and the eagle's breast feathers. Both sides have been well cared for. (#7082)

512 **1879 MS66 PCGS.** Ex: Jack Lee. The silvery surfaces of this Premium Gem dollar possess full luster and reveal just a few minor grade-consistent marks. A well executed strike leaves strong definition on the design elements, including the breast feathers, features that are often weak. Population: 85 in 66, 1 finer (12/09). (#7084)

513 **1879 MS66 PCGS.** Light gold peripheral toning is joined by electric-blue and lavender on the obverse margins. Adequately struck, save for some weakness in the obverse center. A few minute obverse marks are noted. Population: 86 in 66, 1 finer (1/10). (#7084)

514 **1879-CC PCGS Genuine.** The PCGS number ending in .92 suggests Cleaned as the reason, or perhaps one of the reasons, that PCGS deemed this coin not gradable. In our opinion, this coin has the details of an XF specimen that has been cleaned and exhibits obverse damage. The damage consists of several small but relatively deep marks on the chin and jaw. This lightly toned semikey Carson City dollar has ample bright luster, and the cleaning is relatively inoffensive.(#7086)

515 **1879-CC XF45 NGC.** Hints of light gold visit this Choice XF Morgan. Fairly clean surfaces exhibit well defined devices. (#7086)

Brilliant 1879-CC Dollar, MS62

516 **1879-CC MS62 ANACS.** VAM-2b. This is the Normal Mintmark variety with no die defects around the CC. It is a frosty Mint State piece with brilliant silver surfaces beneath light champagne toning. The 1879-CC is the second rarest Carson City Morgan dollar, and always in demand in all Mint State grades. (#7086)

Choice Mint State 1879-CC Dollar

517 **1879-CC MS64 PCGS.** Soft luster filters through the dusky blue-gray shadings that drape this Carson City near-Gem. An attractive example of a challenging issue with above-average definition on the hair over Liberty's ear. A small patch of roughness is noted above the A in STATES. Elusive any finer, with PCGS certifying only 93 such pieces (1/10). (#7086)

518 **1879-CC Capped Die XF45 PCGS.** VAM-3. A Top 100 Variety. Gold-orange rim toning does not reach into the pale silver-gray centers, which retain considerable luster. Light wear and abrasions are present mostly on the devices. A pleasing example of this repunched mintmark variant in a better circulated grade. (#7088)

519 **1879-CC Capped Die AU53 PCGS.** VAM-3. A Top 100 Variety. Luster outlines all design elements of this better date Carson City dollar. The centers display light wear, but the nearly untoned surfaces lack consequential marks.(#7088)

Lustrous 1879-CC Morgan, MS62
Capped Die Variety

520 **1879-CC Capped Die MS62 ANACS.** VAM-3. A Top 100 Variety. The Capped Die variety, actually a doubled mintmark with an engraver's attempt to remove the smaller mintmark resulting in myriad tiny raised lumps around the mintmark. This frosty Mint State piece has considerable silver brilliance with faint lilac and gold toning. (#7088)

Shining Gem 1879-O Dollar

521 **1879-O MS65 PCGS. CAC.** Though not strictly Prooflike, owing to the prominent cartwheels and uneven reflectivity of the silver-white fields, the overall appearance of this Gem is suggestive. Solidly struck central devices offer delightful silver-white frost. PCGS has certified just 13 finer examples (1/10). (#7090)

522 **1879-S MS67 PCGS. CAC.** Electric-blue, purple, and gold-orange patina gravitates to the margins of this lovely Superb Gem. Lustrous surfaces are impeccably preserved.(#7092)

523 **1880-CC MS66 PCGS.** Well struck, essentially untoned surfaces yield pleasing luster. Light obverse grazes are unimportant. PCGS has seen only 27 finer examples (1/10).(#7100)

524 **1880-CC MS66 PCGS. CAC.** A wisp or two of light grayish-tan occurs on each side of this Premium Gem. Lustrous surfaces exhibit sharply struck design elements and are minimally abraded. (#7100)

525 **1880-CC 8 Over High 7 MS65 NGC.** VAM-5. A Top 100 Variety. Although undesignated as such on the insert, this is one of the three major 1880-CC dollar overdate varieties. Each of the three VAMs receives a separate *Guide Book* listing. A lustrous Gem that has peripheral glimpses of peach toning. The fields are well preserved, while the cheek has a few faint grazes.(#7102)

526 **1880-CC 8 Over High 7 MS65 Prooflike PCGS.** VAM-5. A Top 100 Variety. Among the most obvious silver dollar overdate varieties. Almond-gray toning visits impressively smooth surfaces. The fields are unabraded and flashy, particularly on the reverse. Population: 14 in 65 Prooflike, 0 finer (12/09).(#7103)

Premium Gem 8 Over Low 7 VAM-6
1880-CC Dollar, Top 100

527 **1880-CC 8 Over Low 7 MS66 NGC.** VAM-6. A Top 100 Variety. The variety and overdate are undesignated on the NGC holder. Each side is mostly untoned on this lustrous and nicely struck Carson City dollar. Minor facial grazes are of little import. Several overdate VAMS are known for 1880-dated Morgan dollars, but the 1880-CC VAM-4 through VAM-6 are the most prominent. (#7104)

MS66 1880-CC Silver Dollar
Popular 8 Over Low 7

528 **1880-CC 8 Over Low 7 MS66 PCGS.** VAM-6. A Top 100 Variety. The underdigit 7 is unmistakable within both loops of the 8, and also extends beneath the base of that digit. A nicely struck and lustrous Carson City Premium Gem that has a hint of caramel-gold toning on each side. The fields are exceptionally smooth, and the portrait has only wispy grazes. Population: 30 in 66, 0 finer (1/10). (#7104)

529 **1880/79-CC Reverse of 1878 MS64 NGC.** VAM-4. A Top 100 Variety. The underdigits 79 are bold beneath the 80, and the reverse has the Parallel (top) Arrow Feather style of 1878. Barely discernible gold peripheral color on the reverse cedes to slightly deeper purple, electric-blue, and gold on the obverse. Lustrous surfaces are sharply struck and reveal just a few minor marks precluding Gem status.(#7108)

530 **1880/79-CC Reverse of 1878 MS64 PCGS. CAC.** VAM-4. A Top 100 Variety. Essentially untoned surfaces yield pleasing luster and sharply impressed design elements. Several obverse grazes define the grade.(#7108)

531 **1880/79-CC Reverse of 1878 MS64 PCGS.** VAM-4. A Top 100 Variety. A nearly brilliant Choice Carson City overdated dollar with booming luster. Abrasions are few and inconsequential, although a fingerprint trace is noted near 3 o'clock on the reverse. (#7108)

532 **1880/79-CC Reverse of 1878 MS65 PCGS.** VAM-4. A Top 100 Variety. Well struck with strong luster. Untoned surfaces are minimally abraded.(#7108)

533 **1880/79-CC Reverse of 1878 MS65 PCGS.** VAM-4. A Top 100 Variety. While traces of the underdigits are sometimes not visible or weakly defined, on this piece all that is required is light magnification to make out the outlines of the 7 and 9 underdigits. The coin is brilliant and highly lustrous and the striking details are fully brought up.(#7108)

534 **1880-O MS64 PCGS.** Micro O. Whispers of peripheral gold and purple are joined by golden-tan on the central reverse. Fully lustrous and sharply struck with just a few minute grade-consistent marks. Difficult to locate any finer.(#7114)

535 **1880-O MS64 NGC.** Cobalt-blue, lavender, and gold-tan patina runs over the lustrous surfaces of this well struck near-Gem. Light marks are visible on the cheek and neck.(#7114)

536 **1880-O MS64 NGC.** Micro O. Both sides are covered in patches of violet, dove-gray, olive-green, and amber, which complement the sharply struck details. Some grade-defining marks are noted on Liberty's cheek, on the eagle's breast, and in the upper reverse field. NGC reports just 21 examples finer (12/09). Housed in a prior generation holder.(#7114)

537 **1880-O MS64 PCGS.** Micro O. This well struck near-Gem has a nearly brilliant reverse. The obverse features dusky chestnut toning. Lustrous and attractive with minimal marks. Much scarcer in better Mint State grades than its 1880 Carson City counterpart. (#7114)

538 **1880/79-O MS63 Deep Mirror Prooflike PCGS.** VAM-4. A Top 100 Variety. Micro O reverse. The overdate feature is unlisted on the PCGS insert of the green label holder. The 1880-O is a remarkably scarce coin with Deep Mirror Prooflike fields, and it is certainly a worthy acquisition in MS63. This piece is brilliant throughout and the deeply mirrored fields establish a "black" background for the white, frosted devices. A few obverse abrasions are noted, but this is a premium example of this prooflike rarity. Fully struck.
From The Classic Collection.(#97117)

539 **1880-S MS67 ★ NGC. CAC.** Large S. The 1880-S is plentiful in the better grades of Mint State, but locating a Superb Gem with *both* the NGC Star and the CAC green label, as is the case with the present offering, is extremely difficult. Radiant luster emanates from its impeccably preserved, untoned surfaces, and a decisive strike delivers strong definition to the design elements. This coin possesses super all-around eye appeal.(#7118)

540 **1880-S MS67 Prooflike NGC. CAC.** Medium S. Freckles of purple concentrate at the margins of this Superb Gem and sharply struck design motifs stand out against the prooflike fields. A wonderfully preserved specimen with strong eye appeal.(#7119)

541 **1880-S MS66 Deep Mirror Prooflike PCGS. CAC.** Large S. Flashy and gorgeous with thickly frosted devices and deeply reflective mirrors. The obverse is minimally toned, though the upper left reverse shows an area of amber. PCGS has only certified 28 finer (12/09).(#97119)

Dazzling 1880-S Morgan
MS67 Deep Mirror Prooflike

542 **1880-S MS67 Deep Mirror Prooflike NGC.** Medium S. This stone-white Superb Gem obtains its remarkable eye appeal from a combination of deeply frosted motifs and immaculate glassy fields. Crisply struck and exceptionally attractive. Census: 17 in 67 Deep Mirror Prooflike, 3 finer (1/10). (#97119)

543 **1880/9-S MS67 PCGS. CAC.** VAM-11, A Hot 50 Variety. Remnants of the former 9 are visible within the 0 in the date. Brightly lustrous and untoned. Adequately struck and impeccably preserved. Population: 22 in 67, 1 finer (1/10).(#7122)

544 **1881-CC MS66 NGC.** Pleasing luster radiates from the silver-gray surfaces of this Premium Gem. Excellent design detail is apparent throughout. A few grade-consistent grazes are undistracting. (#7126)

545 **1881-CC MS66 PCGS. CAC.** This sharply struck, highly lustrous Premium Gem generates excellent eye appeal. Both sides are color-free. Housed in a green label holder.(#7126)

546 **1881-CC MS66 NGC. CAC.** Both sides of this Premium Gem are awash with radiant luster and are completely devoid of color. Sharply struck, including the hair at Liberty's ear and the eagle's breast feathers. Well preserved throughout.(#7126)

547 **1881-CC MS66 PCGS. CAC.** Ebullient luster exudes from the untoned surfaces of this attractive Premium Gem. Boldly struck on the devices, and devoid of mentionable marks.(#7126)

548 **1881-CC MS66 PCGS.** A lovely example of this ever-popular Carson City Morgan dollar, well-defined with subtly frosted high points. Ample silver-gray haze drapes the beautifully preserved surfaces.(#7126)

Spectacular MS67 1881-CC Morgan Dollar

549 **1881-CC MS67 PCGS.** The 1881-CC has an impressively low mintage of only 296,000 pieces, but a very high survival rate because most of the production was stored for 80 years in government vaults. Unlike most of the GSA dollars seen this example was not extensively abraded. In fact, the thick mint luster shows only a few inconsequential luster grazes on each side. The strike is full, as one would expect, and the centers are untoned and surrounded by a light accent of golden patina at the margins. (#7126)

550 **1881-CC MS65 Deep Mirror Prooflike NGC.** Deeply mirrored fields accentuate the sharply struck, mildly frosted devices. Untoned surfaces reveal a few light to moderate abrasions over each side. Census: 60 in 65 Deep Mirror Prooflike, 11 finer (1/10). (#97127)

551 **1881-O MS63 Deep Mirror Prooflike PCGS.** This is a splendid, heavily contrasted white-on-black cameo that is completely brilliant. The devices are fully struck on each side.
From The Classic Collection.(#97129)

552 **1881-O MS64 Deep Mirror Prooflike PCGS. CAC.** Essentially color-free surfaces exhibit strong field-device contrast and are sharply struck. While a few minute grazes preclude Gem status, MS64 is the finest grade most collectors will encounter. PCGS has seen only seven examples graded higher (12/09).(#97129)

553 **1881-O MS64 Deep Mirror Prooflike PCGS. CAC.** Deeply mirrored fields highlight frosty, sharply struck motifs. Color-free surfaces reveal a few minor grade-defining grazes. Very difficult to locate any finer.(#97129)

554 **1881-O MS64 Deep Mirror Prooflike PCGS.** A wondrous coin that exhibits unfathomably deep mirrors in the fields. Set against these mirrors are the thick, lustrous devices that establish the Deep Mirror Prooflike designation. The surfaces are brilliant throughout and the devices are notably lacking in the abrasions that usually accompany DMPL dollars. Essentially unobtainable any finer, only 11 pieces have been certified better than this piece (1/10).
From The Classic Collection.(#97129)

555 **1881-S MS67 Prooflike PCGS. CAC.** Prooflike fields yield pleasing contrast with the sharply struck design elements. Untoned surfaces are well cared for. Population: 64 in 67 Prooflike, 1 finer (1/10).(#7131)

556 **1882 MS66 NGC. CAC.** The color-free surfaces of this Premium Gem exhibit remarkable smoothness. Pleasing luster with a reasonable strike.(#7132)

557 **1882 MS66 PCGS. CAC.** A frosty Premium Gem with the look of a Carson City dollar, rather than a Philadelphia Mint product. This piece has brilliant luster and sharp design features with no evidence of toning on either side. PCGS has only certified six finer examples of the date (1/10).(#7132)

558 **1882 MS66 PCGS.** The obverse of this lovely Premium Gem is fully brilliant with faint gold toning at the border, while the reverse is deeply toned in dark gold and iridescent shades. PCGS has only certified six finer pieces (1/10).(#7132)

559 **1882-CC MS66 PCGS. CAC.** Whispers of light peripheral gold are more extensive and deeper on the reverse of this Premium Gem Morgan. Generally well struck and minimally abraded. (#7134)

560 **1882-CC MS66 PCGS. CAC.** Medium intensity multicolored toning covers most of the obverse of this Premium Gem, leaving the reverse color-free. Well cared for surfaces exhibit sharply struck devices, including the hair over Liberty's ear and the eagle's breast feathers.(#7134)

561 **1882-CC MS66 PCGS. CAC.** The untoned reverse cedes to light orange, sky-blue, and purple toning on the obverse. Well preserved, lustrous surfaces exhibit sharp definition.(#7134)

Important 1882-O/S VAM-4 Morgan, MS64

562 **1882-O/S MS64 PCGS.** VAM-4, O/S Recessed. A Top 100 Variety. This brilliant Mint State piece is a Choice example of the popular overmintmark variety. These pieces are usually available in MS64, but almost never any finer. PCGS has only certified two finer examples of the variety (1/10). (#7138)

Superlative 1882-S Morgan, MS68

563 **1882-S MS68 NGC.** Neither NGC or PCGS have certified a finer example of the 1882-S Morgan dollar. This Superb Gem is sharply defined with satiny silver luster and only a trace of gold toning along portions of the obverse and reverse borders. Census: 77 in 68, 0 finer (1/10). (#7140)

564 **1883 MS67 NGC.** Fantastically lustrous with suggestions of pale blue on the reverse of an otherwise silver-white Superb Gem. Well-defined for the issue and notably appealing. NGC has graded only three numerically finer pieces (12/09).(#7142)

Brilliant MS67 1883-CC Dollar

565 **1883-CC MS67 PCGS.** The 1883-CC and 1884-CC are common date dollars from the GSA hoard, but rarely are these dates seen in MS67 condition. As one would expect from a CC dollar, the mint luster is thick and frosted. The striking details are fully brought up on each side, and there are no mentionable abrasions. A wonderful CC type coin. (#7144)

566 **1883-CC MS66 Prooflike NGC.** Both sides of this Premium Gem Prooflike Morgan yield considerable "flash," and each is essentially color-free. Well struck surfaces are nicely preserved. Census: 68 in 66 Prooflike, 2 finer (12/09).(#7145)

567 **1883-O MS64 Deep Mirror Prooflike PCGS.** One of the more available O-mints with reflective fields, this 1883-O is brilliant and fully struck. The fields are deeply mirrored and the frosted devices establish a stark contrast on each side.
From The Classic Collection.(#97147)

568 **1883-S MS62 PCGS.** Essentially untoned surfaces exhibit a nearly unbroken luster flow and well struck design elements. Distributed light marks occur over each side.(#7148)

569 **1883-S MS62 NGC.** The soft frosty luster of this brilliant silver dollar hosts pale champagne toning on each side. Typical weakness is evident over Liberty's ear, but all other design elements are sharp. Here is an attractive example, and a scarce date that is often on collector want lists. (#7148)

570 **1883-S MS63 NGC.** Bright luster endows the untoned surfaces of this Select S-mint coin. A well struck piece that shows a few grade-consistent marks.(#7148)

Impressive Gem 1883-S Dollar

571 **1883-S MS65 PCGS.** The 1883-S Morgan is well known for its similarities and differences from the other S-mint issues preceding it in the series. Similar is that when Mint State specimens of the 1883-S are found, they largely feature sharp strikes and are overall quite well produced. Different is that few were apparently saved, and those that did survive seem to have been handled roughly, resulting in severe bag marks, as a rule.

This is a wonderful example that fortunately escaped the twin fates of melting or severe abrasions. The strike is bold throughout, with only minor weakness on the hair above the ear and the eagle's breast. There are no singular abrasions, and the delightful patina comprises jade in the obverse center, ceding to amber-gold at the rim, with the reverse displaying pinkish-gray and amber accents. PCGS has certified only 15 coins at this level, with three finer (1/10). A prize for the Morgan dollar aficionado, and a coin of rare beauty. (#7148)

572 **1884 MS66 Prooflike NGC.** Virtually brilliant, although hints of gold are noted here and there. Attentively struck and well preserved with flashy fields and impressive eye appeal. Census: 5 in 66 Prooflike, 0 finer (12/09).(#7151)

Attractively Toned MS67 1884-CC Dollar

573 **1884-CC MS67 PCGS.** The 1884-CC was heavily represented in the GSA hoard by 962,638 pieces. When these coins were sold, examples such as this one were sold at a discounted price because the government equated toning with wear! This is a fabulous dollar that has thick mint luster that shines brightly through the golden toning on the obverse. The reverse is mostly brilliant with just a hint of peripheral color. The striking details are complete, and there are no mentionable or noticeable abrasions on either side of this magnificent dollar. Population: 56 in 67, 3 finer (1/10). (#7152)

1884-CC Dollar, MS67 A Magnificent Type Coin

574 **1884-CC MS67 PCGS.** The majority of the mintage of 1.1 million pieces of the 1884-CC remained in government vaults for decades. Bowers (1993) mentions the sale of an 1884-CC in an auction in 1919 that brought an astounding $11.00, underscoring how few of this issue actually were released to the public. The surfaces of this piece have soft, creamy mint luster that is unimpaired by even the tiniest abrasion. Both sides are brilliant throughout. (#7152)

575 **1884-CC MS65 Deep Mirror Prooflike PCGS.** Untoned surfaces yield strong field-motif contrast and are minimally abraded. Sharp definition is apparent on the design features, including the hair over Liberty's ear.(#97153)

576 **1884-CC MS65 Deep Mirror Prooflike NGC.** Sharply struck design features are highlighted by the deeply mirrored fields. Whispers of gold and purple toning concentrate at the margins. A few grade-consistent marks are undisturbing.(#97153)

577 **1884-S PCGS Genuine.** The PCGS number ending in .91 suggests Artificial Color as the reason, or perhaps one of the reasons, that PCGS deemed this coin not gradable. The coin has Unc. Details, but of course this is not indicated on the insert. The surfaces are remarkably lustrous, especially for an 1884-S, but each side is covered with heavy blue and purple toning. The obverse is sharply struck while the center of the reverse show a bit of striking weakness on the eagle's breast.(#7156)

578 **1884-S AU58 PCGS.** The silvery surfaces of this near-Mint State Morgan exhibit ample luster and well defined devices. A few minute marks are noted over each side.(#7156)

Delightful 1884-S Morgan, MS61

579 **1884-S MS61 ANACS.** The 1884-S Morgan dollar is one of the important condition rarities in the series, nearly always available in all circulated grades, but seldom seen in Mint State. Here is an exceptional example for the grade, with fully lustrous silver surfaces and delightful iridescent peripheries. (#7156)

580 **1885 MS67 NGC.** Silver-white brightness on the obverse and right reverse with peach-gold toning over the remainder. NGC has certified only five examples above the MS67 level (1/10). (#7158)

581 **1885 MS66 Deep Mirror Prooflike PCGS.** A lovely Morgan dollar with brilliant silver surfaces that combined deep mirrored fields and frosty, lustrous devices. This example approaches the finest certified, with just one better piece graded by PCGS. Population: 70 in 66 Deep Mirror Prooflike, 1 finer (12/09).(#97159)

582 **1885-CC MS65 NGC.** VAM-4. A Hot 50 Variety. The VAM is undesignated on the PCGS insert. A thick dash beneath the second 8 probably suggests the base of a 7. Strong definition is apparent on the design features of this untoned, highly lustrous Gem. A few light grazes do not distract.(#7160)

583 **1885-CC MS65 NGC. CAC.** Gold, grayish-blue, and purple splashes show on the obverse of this Gem, leaving the reverse essentially untoned. Generally well struck save for minor softness in the centers. A few trivial grazes do not disturb.(#7160)

584 **1885-CC MS65 ★ NGC.** Partially prooflike fields accentuate the well struck design features. Untoned surfaces are very nicely preserved.(#7160)

585 **1885-CC MS65 NGC.** Bright luster endows this sharply struck Gem. Untoned surfaces show just a few light grazes.(#7160)

586 **1885-CC MS65 NGC.** Brightly lustrous with a suggestion of frostiness on the devices. This CC-mint Gem is largely silver-white with splashes of green-gold and brown through the left reverse. (#7160)

587 **1885-CC MS65 PCGS.** Booming luster exudes from both sides of this lovely Gem, each of which shows a wisp or two of light tan color. Well defined and revealing no significant marks. (#7160)

588 **1885-CC MS65 PCGS.** This sharply struck Gem displays good detail in the hair at Liberty's ear and on the breast feathers. Untoned, lustrous, and quite nicely preserved.(#7160)

589 **1885-CC MS66 NGC.** Coruscating luster endows the silvery surfaces of this Premium Gem. A sharply struck, minimally abraded piece with outstanding eye appeal.(#7160)

590 **1885-CC MS66 NGC.** The reddish-gold obverse displays purple and electric-blue accents at the margins, while the reverse is basically untoned. Sharply struck, including the hair at Liberty's ear and the eagle's breast feathers. Nicely preserved, with semiprooflike fields that highlight the devices.(#7160)

591 **1885-CC MS66 PCGS.** Nearly untoned save for a wisp of two of barely discernible gold color on the reverse. Lustrous surfaces are well struck and minimally abraded.(#7160)

592 **1885-CC MS66 PCGS.** Soft sky-blue, purple, and gold patina shows at the margins, especially on the obverse. Lustrous, well struck, and nicely preserved.(#7160)

593 **1885-CC MS66 PCGS. CAC.** Vibrant luster enlivens both sides of this sharply struck Premium Gem; softness is noted in the obverse center, however. Untoned and minimally abraded. (#7160)

594 **1885-CC MS66 NGC.** Strongly struck with ample frosty luster. The upper right obverse shows a suggestion of green patina, while the rest of the coin is pale silver-gray. A luster graze is noted to the left of Liberty's nose.(#7160)

595 **1885-CC MS66 PCGS.** Nearly untoned save for occasional wisps of yellow-gold and tan. Lustrous surfaces exhibit well struck devices and reveal just a few obverse grazes.(#7160)

596 **1885-CC MS66 PCGS.** Yellow-gold splashes run over the radiantly lustrous surfaces of this well struck Premium Gem, accented with electric-blue, lavender, and orange at the margins. Some light grade-consistent marks are undisturbing.(#7160)

597 **1885-CC MS66 NGC.** Dynamic luster adorns the untoned surfaces of this Premium Gem and a decisive strike manifests itself in sharp definition on the design features. Devoid of mentionable marks.(#7160)

598 **1885-O MS67 NGC.** Medium intensity rainbow-like toning gravitates to the upper reverse margin, leaving most of the remaining surfaces color-free. Both sides possess intense luster and are sharply struck and minimally abraded.(#7162)

599 **1885-O MS67 NGC.** Shining luster, silver-white with touches of cream and gray, gives way to a tiny strip of green-gold and blue at the upper reverse border. NGC has graded just nine pieces in grades above MS67 (1/10).(#7162)

600 **1885-S MS65 PCGS. CAC.** Partially prooflike fields highlight the devices on this attractive Gem. Untoned, minimally abraded, and appropriately defined. Difficult to acquire any finer.(#7164)

601 **1886 MS67 NGC. CAC.** This fully brilliant Superb Gem has no evidence of toning on either side. It is sharply struck with essentially pristine surfaces and frosty luster. NGC has only certified 12 finer examples of the date.(#7166)

Deep Mirror Prooflike 1886 Morgan, MS66

602 **1886 MS66 Deep Mirror Prooflike PCGS.** The 1886 is plentiful in Mint State if cartwheel luster is desired. But those who seek dazzling DMPL examples face a much more difficult task. Here is a sharply struck and virtually brilliant Premium Gem with well preserved and prominently reflective fields. Population: 25 in 66 Deep Mirror Prooflike, 0 finer (1/10). (#97167)

Gem 1887/6 Morgan, VAM-2

603 **1887/6 MS65 NGC.** VAM-2. A Top 100 Variety. The lower curved remnants of a 6 are visible below the 7. This overdate was discovered in the mid-1970s. Dazzling luster emanates from each side of this well-struck Gem example, and faint hints of light tan are occasionally seen under magnification. A few minor marks are well within the parameters of the grade designation. Census: 66 in 65, 5 finer (1/10). (#7174)

Elusive 1887/6 VAM-2 Dollar, MS65 Prooflike

604 **1887/6 MS65 Prooflike NGC.** VAM-2. A Top 100 Variety. Only a few years ago, the grading services had never seen an MS65 or finer example of the 1887 over 6 Morgan dollar. Today, such Gem pieces are still seldom encountered, especially with prooflike surfaces like this piece. It is fully brilliant with no evidence of toning, save for faint champagne color on the reverse. Splendid prooflike fields contrast nicely with the lustrous devices. Census: 22 in 65 Prooflike, 1 finer (1/10). (#7175)

605 **1887/6-O MS63 PCGS.** VAM-3. A Top 100 Variety. A faint trace of the 6 shows to the lower right of the 7. Lustrous, essentially untoned surfaces reveal grade-defining obverse marks. Well impressed save for the centers.(#7178)

606 **1887/6-O MS63 ANACS.** VAM-3. A Top 100 variety. This is the highly-collectible New Orleans overdate variety of 1887. The present coin has brilliant silver luster with a lovely frame of gold toning near the borders.(#7178)

Scarce 1887/6-O Dollar, MS64

607 **1887/6-O MS64 PCGS. CAC.** VAM-3. A Top 100 variety. The overdate feature was not discovered until 1972, and then only after the P-mint overdate had been discovered the year before. This is a later die state that shows just the faintest trace of the 6 to the right of the 7. The surfaces are brilliant and exude thick, satiny mint luster. The centers are a bit lightly struck. Population: 97 in 64, 1 finer (1/10). (#7178)

639 **1891-CC MS64 PCGS.** VAM-3. A Top 100 Variety. The "Spitting Eagle" VAM, which apparently comprised much of the GSA holdings for the '91-CC. Vibrant luster sweeps this stone-gray and almond-gold near-Gem.(#7206)

Sharply Defined 1891-CC Gem Dollar

640 **1891-CC MS65 NGC.** The 1891-CC is readily available through near-Gem but can only be located with patience in Gem condition, and is extremely difficult in finer grades. This sharply defined MS65 specimen displays pleasing luster emanating from color-free, minimally abraded surfaces. (#7206)

641 **1891-CC MS64 Prooflike PCGS.** A well executed strike delivers strong definition to the design elements that are highlighted by the prooflike fields. Untoned surfaces reveal some light marks, more so on the obverse, that deny Gem status. PCGS has graded only 13 pieces finer (1/10).(#7207)

642 **1892 MS64 Prooflike PCGS.** This near-Gem offering is almost color-free, save for a few wisps of localized reddish-tan. Well struck and minimally abraded. A planchet defect on Liberty's neck does not detract in the least. Prooflike examples are rarely found any finer. Population: 22 in 64 Prooflike, 3 finer (12/09).(#7213)

643 **1892-CC MS62 NGC.** The lustrous, untoned surfaces of this CC-mint representative exhibit crisply struck design features, including the hair over Liberty's ear. Scattered light to moderate abrasions, more so on the obverse, limit the grade.(#7214)

644 **1892-CC MS62 ANACS.** VAM-2. A minor variety with the second C in the mintmark touching the wreath. Solidly struck with minimal patina save for hints of gold-orange around the rims. (#7214)

645 **1892-CC MS63 NGC.** Splashes of cobalt-blue, lavender, and gold-orange patina gravitate to the borders of this well struck Select specimen. Light surface and rim marks limit the grade. (#7214)

646 **1892-CC MS63 PCGS.** Generally well struck with lustrous, untoned, lightly abraded surfaces. Nice eye appeal for an MS63. (#7214)

647 **1892-CC MS63 PCGS.** Peripheral blushes of tan and medium-gray visit this otherwise essentially silver-white Carson City Morgan dollar. Scattered light abrasions on the cheek affect the technical grade more than the eye appeal.(#7214)

648 **1892-CC MS63 PCGS.** Yellow-gold toning gravitates to the reverse margins of this lustrous, Select CC-mint Morgan. Well struck and exhibiting nice eye appeal despite scattered light grazes. (#7214)

649 **1892-S AU50 PCGS.** Light silver-gray surfaces retain traces of luster in the recessed areas. Both sides are quite clean for a coin having seen some circulation. The '92-S is difficult to locate in Mint State grades.(#7218)

650 **1892-S AU50 ANACS.** VAM-8. A Hit List 40 variety. Doubled and tripled hair strands are evident on the obverse of this elusive variety. Considerable luster remains on each side, with light silver-gray surfaces and traces of iridescent toning.(#7218)

Scarce AU58 1892-S Dollar

651 **1892-S AU58 PCGS.** Most of the 1.2 million 1892-S Morgan dollars entered the channels of commerce within a decade or two of striking. This is evident from the large number of circulated examples certified by PCGS and NGC. Mint State coins are quite rare, however. The two services have graded roughly 110 Uncirculated pieces, most in the lower levels thereof.

The present scarce near-Mint State coin displays considerable luster on its silver-gray surfaces imbued with wisps of light tan. Sharp definition characterizes the design features, despite a bit of wear on the hair at Liberty's ear and on the breast feathers. A few light circulation marks do not detract. (#7218)

652 **1893 MS64 NGC.** Occasional splashes of peripheral orange-gold are joined by wisps of cobalt-blue and lavender at the obverse margins. Nicely struck and showing just a few minor grade-defining marks.(#7220)

653 **1893-CC VF35 NGC.** Whispers of orange-gold patina visit the light gray surfaces of this Choice VF. Relatively clean surfaces and well defined.(#7222)

Reflective 1893-CC Morgan, MS62 VAM-5, Clashed Dies

654 **1893-CC MS62 ANACS.** VAM-5, Clashed Dies. Noticeable die clashing is visible in the fields near the design motifs on both sides of this brilliant Mint State example. This piece has bright silver luster with no toning on either side. The fields are faintly reflective with a hint of cameo contrast visible. (#7222)

Popular 1893-CC Dollar, MS63

655 **1893-CC MS63 PCGS.** The 1893-CC is the final Carson City emission, and is also among the scarcest Morgan issues from that facility. This lustrous and boldly impressed silver dollar has minimal toning and only a moderate number of grazes on the portrait. The fields are well preserved. (#7222)

Appealing 1893-CC Dollar, MS61 Prooflike

656 **1893-CC MS61 Prooflike PCGS.** Housed in a green-label PCGS holder, this fully brilliant and prooflike Mint State piece is an excellent representative of the final Carson City Mint Morgan dollar. It has wonderful eye appeal with essentially untoned silver surfaces. Population: 61 in 61 Prooflike, 92 finer (1/10). (#7223)

657 **1893-O MS60 ANACS.** VAM-2. The mintmark is tilted to the right. This satiny Mint State dollar has mostly light silver surfaces with lovely peripheral iridescence on both sides. The devices are frosty and the fields are satiny.(#7224)

Low Mintage 1893-O Dollar, MS62

658 **1893-O MS62 PCGS.** The small mintage of 300,000 pieces underscores the importance and popularity of this issue with Morgan dollar collectors. This piece is brilliant and displays the usual satiny mint luster. As one would expect from an MS62, there are numerous small to mid-sized abrasions (most of which are on the obverse) that explain the grade. The strike is well brought up but not full, as usual. Each side is brilliant, and the reverse fields display slight reflectivity. (#7224)

Challenging MS63 1893-O Morgan

659 **1893-O MS63 PCGS.** The 1893-O is the lowest mintage New Orleans Morgan dollar, and examples are very scarce in attractive Mint State grades. This lustrous representative has the expected incompleteness of strike at the centers, but the fields are splendidly smooth, and the cheek displays only wispy marks. A few slender russet streaks on the lower left obverse deny full brilliance. (#7224)

660 **1893-S—Rim Damage, Cleaned—NGC. Good Details.** The light gray surfaces of this key date piece display faint hairlines and a few small to moderate rim dings. Appropriately defined.(#7226)

Desirable 1893-S Morgan, Good 6

661 **1893-S Good 6 ANACS.** Although well-worn, this piece is entirely original with deep gray fields and gray-gold devices. The rims are completely intact, and the obverse diagnostics remain visible. A fully desirable piece for the grade, and in fact sharper than the ANACS grade suggests. (#7226)

662 **1893-S—Environmental Damage—NGC. VG Details.** A significantly worn example of the key date which shows extensive environmental effects in the gunmetal-black fields and on the more lightly toned devices. Despite the environmental effects and a number of scattered abrasions, this is a readily collectible example.(#7226)

Always Popular 1893-S Dollar, VG8

663 **1893-S VG8 PCGS.** Scarce in all grades and pursued by collectors in all grades. This VG example has light, nearly brilliant surfaces, quite unlike the dark circulated coins often seen. Each side is peppered with numerous small abrasions, but the only mark worthy of mention is a diagonal abrasion on the eagle's right (facing) wing. There is also a horizontal planchet flaw and grease stain across the bridge of Liberty's nose. (#7226)

Desirable VG10 1893-S Dollar

664 **1893-S VG10 ANACS.** A significantly worn yet fundamentally problem-free representative of this famous key-date Morgan dollar, more accessible than the perhaps more-abundant VF examples for which the issue has become famous. Considerable lavender-blue color drapes the reverse, while the obverse is primarily gold-gray. Scattered abrasions are light and consistent with the amount of wear present. (#7226)

Prized 1893-S Dollar, Fine 12

665 **1893-S Fine 12 PCGS.** A lovely Fine example of this famously low-mintage San Francisco Morgan dollar. Medium-gray surfaces show deeper hues in the protected areas of the devices and along the rims, creating strong and pleasing contrast. A few small digs at Liberty's lower jaw are grade-consistent and expected for a circulated coin. (#7226)

Excellent Choice XF 1893-S Dollar

666 **1893-S XF45 PCGS.** Deep bluish-gray patination displays subtle champagne and gold undertones, and the design elements are well defined. Close inspection reveals no significant contact marks. These attributes add up to making this Choice XF example an excellent candidate for a high grade Morgan dollar collection. (#7226)

Nearly Brilliant 1893-S Dollar, XF45

667 **1893-S XF45 PCGS.** The diagnostic diagonal die scratch at the top of the T in LIBERTY is clearly evident (with a magnifier, of course). Light friction is seen over the high points on each side, and the abrasions present are remarkably light. Each side also shows just the slightest evidence of golden toning, otherwise the surfaces are brilliant. (#7226)

668 **1894 PCGS Genuine.** The PCGS number ending in .98 suggests Damage as the reason, or perhaps one of the reasons, that PCGS deemed this coin not gradable. In our opinion, this coin has the details of an AU specimen that has been cleaned, smoothed, and repaired. Liberty's cheek and the nearby field are smoothed, and both sides are a bit bright from a cleaning. Nonetheless, a minimally circulated example of this low mintage key date.(#7228)

669 **1894 PCGS Genuine.** The PCGS number ending in .92 suggests Cleaned as the reason, or perhaps one of the reasons, that PCGS deemed this coin not gradable. In our opinion, this coin has the details of an XF specimen that has been cleaned. The stone-gray surfaces are mildly subdued, perhaps from exposure to baking soda, and a hair-thin line has darkly toned near the left border of the eagle's breast. Many collectors would nonetheless be pleased with this well detailed and low mintage Morgan dollar.(#7228)

670 **1894 XF45 PCGS.** After the 1893-S and the proof-only 1895, the honor of the third-lowest-mintage Morgan dollar goes to the 1894. The present piece features deep steel-gray and tan-brown toning. Thorough examination with a loupe locates a few moderate marks, near IN GOD and on the right obverse field.(#7228)

671 **1894 XF45 PCGS.** Both sides of this Choice XF Morgan are essentially untoned and display hints of luster in the recessed areas. A nicely defined and minimally abraded piece. One of the lowest-mintage Morgan dollars (110,000 circulation strikes). (#7228)

672 **1894 XF45 ANACS.** Soft gold peripheral patination is joined on the reverse margins by light purple. Well defined and lightly marked. This is a nice example of this key date.(#7228)

673 **1894—Artificially Toned—ANACS. AU50 Details.** This low mintage key date silver dollar has alternating blushes of faded cherry-red and olive-gold toning. Thin marks are noted above ONE and near the D in DOLLAR. Ample luster shimmers across the lightly circulated design.(#7228)

674 **1894 AU53 NGC.** A pleasing example of this key date Morgan. Soft purple and gold patina can be found at the margins. Minimally abraded and well defined.(#7228)

675 **1894 AU55 PCGS.** An important rarity in the Morgan series, the 1894 ranks as the second rarest business strike from the Philadelphia Mint, with an original mintage of just 110,000 coins. This Choice AU piece has light rub, but retains nearly all of its original brilliance.(#7228)

676 **1894 AU58 NGC.** The key date among business strike Philadelphia Mint Morgans, the 1894 had a mintage of only 100,000 coins, and few of those survive today. This is a popular date at the AU58 level, combining quality and price into a good value. Only a trace of wear is evident on the frosty silver surfaces. Hints of peripheral gold toning complete the picture.(#7228)

677 **1894 AU58 PCGS.** A whisper of friction on the eagle's breast confirms a momentary stint in circulation, but the essentially brilliant surfaces still shimmer with cartwheel luster. Minor field grazes and reeding marks are consistent with the near-Mint level. (#7228)

Elusive 1894 Morgan, MS61

678 **1894 MS61 ANACS.** VAM-1. The key Philadelphia Mint issue, and always in demand in all Mint State grades. This specimen has bright silver surfaces with frosty luster and subtle traces of golden toning along the borders. It is nicely defined with surfaces that suggest a higher numerical grade. (#7228)

Challenging MS63 1894 Dollar

679 **1894 MS63 PCGS.** Due to its low mintage, the 1894 is contested in all grades. The scarce issue perhaps provides the most value in the MS63 grade, since an MS64 will set back the buyer an additional $3,000 to $4,000. The present example is untoned and lustrous with an above average strike. Faint obverse marks limit the grade, but not the eye appeal. (#7228)

680 **1894-O MS62 ANACS.** VAM-5. Minute doubling is evident below the upper serif of the 1. This pleasing piece has fully brilliant silver luster with traces of toning. The strike is typical with central design weakness on both sides.(#7230)

681 **1894-O MS60 Prooflike ANACS.** An appreciably reflective piece with gold and violet peripheral toning around silver-white centers. Significantly abraded throughout but with better eye appeal than the MS60 grade might suggest. Housed in a small-format holder.(#7231)

682 **1894-S MS64 NGC.** Essentially untoned surfaces display semiprooflike fields that highlight the sharply struck design elements. Trivial grazes keep from full Gem.(#7232)

Charming Near-Mint 1895-O Dollar

683 **1895-O AU58 PCGS. CAC.** Impressively lustrous with only modest friction visible at the softly struck high points. The luster is virtually intact, the surfaces nearly brilliant save for arcs of orange along parts of the rims. Faint abrasions are consistent with a brief stint in circulation. Overall, a strong example of this popular lower-mintage issue. (#7236)

Lovely 1895-S Dollar, MS61

684 **1895-S MS61 ANACS.** Although the surfaces have myriad abrasions that are consistent with the grade, this is a lovely 1895-S Morgan with brilliant silver luster, sharp design motifs, reflective fields, and splashes of pale gold toning on each side. The 1895-S is the only usually seen Morgan dollar of the date in Mint State grades. (#7238)

685 **1896-O MS60 ANACS.** Although both sides have a number of small abrasions expected at the grade level, this piece has full silver luster with splashes of iridescent toning on both sides. (#7242)

Vibrant Select 1896-S Silver Dollar

686 **1896-S MS63 PCGS.** Lilac, gunmetal-gray, and apricot toning consumes the obverse, while the reverse has only a hint of tan patina. Lustrous with a smooth reverse and only minor incompleteness of strike at the centers. Liberty's cheek and neck are abraded, although no marks are obtrusive. (#7244)

Lovely 1896-S Morgan Dollar, MS63

687 **1896-S MS63 ANACS.** VAM-6. The 1896-O and S Morgan dollars are both condition rarities in Mint State. Of the two issues, the 1896-S is somewhat more available but still in high demand, especially as the numeric grade increases. This lovely example offers full mint brilliance, frosty luster, sharp design definition, and attractive peripheral gold toning. (#7244)

688 **1897-O MS62 ANACS.** A fully brilliant and lustrous example of this conditionally rare Morgan dollar. The 1897-O is normally only encountered in circulated grades, and all Mint State pieces are in high demand. At first glance, this piece appears to be much finer than the numerical grade assigned.(#7248)

689 **1898 MS65 Deep Mirror Prooflike PCGS.** The 1898 is an unusual late-date dollar to locate with prooflike fields and in high grades. The fields on this piece are exceptionally deep, which set up noticeable contrast against the satiny devices. The surfaces are nearly brilliant with just a hint of peripheral toning. The devices are sharply struck throughout. Population: 63 in 65 Deep Mirror Prooflike, 12 finer (1/10).
From The Classic Collection.(#97253)

690 **1898-O MS67 NGC.** A stunning Superb Gem of this hoard issue. The bright, satiny surfaces are sharply struck and the centers are brilliant with golden toning around the rims. An exceptionally pleasing type coin.(#7254)

691 **1898-S MS64 Prooflike PCGS.** Considerable "flash" greets the observer of this color-free S-mint Morgan. Nicely struck and revealing a few grade-consistent marks. Population: 39 in 64 Prooflike, 5 finer (12/09).(#7257)

Prooflike Gem 1898-S Morgan

692 **1898-S MS65 Prooflike PCGS.** Prooflike specimens of the 1898-S Morgan dollar are very rare at the Gem level. The present coin is a well struck specimen, with only slight softness on the hair above the ear and the eagle's breast. The flashy fields provide moderate contrast with the evenly frosty devices. Brilliant throughout. Population: 5 in 65 Prooflike, 0 finer (10/09). (#7257)

Deep Mirror Near-Gem 1898-S Dollar

693 **1898-S MS64 Deep Mirror Prooflike PCGS. CAC.** Orange-red and ocean-blue dominate the obverse margin, but the rest of this flashy near-Gem is virtually untoned. The reverse is beautifully undisturbed by contact, while the portrait and the field near the P in PLURIBUS display moderate marks. Population: 33 in 64 Deep Mirror Prooflike, 7 finer (1/10). (#97257)

Dazzling 1899-S Dollar, MS66

694 **1899-S MS66 PCGS. CAC.** Dazzling luster endows this wonderful Premium Gem, complementing its well struck design motifs, and untoned surfaces are impeccably preserved. Great overall eye appeal. David Bowers (2006) suggests that more than 1 million of the 2.5 million mintage was probably melted. (#7262)

695 **1900-O/CC MS64 PCGS. CAC.** VAM-11. Bold remnants of the former CC mintmark are visible on both sides of the O. This fully brilliant silver dollar has no evidence of toning on either side. The strike is bold and the surfaces are exceptional for the grade. (#7268)

696 **1901 MS61 ANACS.** VAM-19. The Discovery Coin according to the ANACS holder. The variety has Liberty's upper lip minutely doubled. The E in UNITED is also slightly doubled. This piece is brilliant and lustrous with satiny silver surfaces and faint gold toning at the border.(#7272)

Lustrous MS62 1901 Morgan

697 **1901 MS62 PCGS.** Although struck from the same facility and only two years later than the 1899, there is a tremendous discrepancy in high grade survival rates for the two issues. The low mintage 1899 is plentiful in MS64, while the 1901 is very rare in such quality. In fact, any Uncirculated 1901 silver dollar is desirable. This is a lustrous, sharply struck, and lightly toned caramel-gold and steel-blue example that has surprisingly few marks. (#7272)

Elusive MS62 1901 Morgan Dollar

698 **1901 MS62 PCGS.** Light chestnut-brown enriches this lustrous and powerfully struck silver dollar. Marks are surprisingly few for the MS62 level. Despite a mintage of nearly 7 million pieces, the 1901 is increasingly difficult to secure in advancing Mint State grades. AU examples are fairly available, which suggests that bags were released into circulation well into the 20th century. (#7272)

699 **1901 Doubled Die Reverse XF45 ANACS.** VAM-3. A Top 100 Variety. Known as the Shifted Eagle variety, this is a wonderful doubled die reverse with the tail feathers, wings, and beak all clearly doubled. A pleasing Choice XF, this example has desirable light gray surfaces with splashes of gold toning.(#7302)

Appealing 1901-S Dollar, MS65

700 **1901-S MS65 PCGS.** Fairly scarce within the context of S-mint Morgans from the turn of the century. The lustrous surfaces of this Gem are essentially untoned and exhibit relatively well impressed design elements. A few light roller marks are visible on the obverse. Pleasing overall eye appeal. (#7276)

Patinated Gem 1901-S Morgan

701 **1901-S MS65 NGC.** Purple, gold, and electric-blue coloration gravitates to the margins of this well struck Gem, more prominent on the obverse. Some insignificant obverse marks are noted. An elusive Morgan dollar issue, as is the case with the other S-mints from its decade. Census: 86 in 65, 7 finer (1/10). (#7276)

702 **1903 MS65 Prooflike PCGS. CAC.** Apricot toning graces the reverse, but the obverse is virtually brilliant. A well struck and satiny Gem. Scarce in Prooflike, particularly with such clean surfaces. Population: 29 in 65 Prooflike, 5 finer (1/10).(#7285)

703 **1903-S AU53 PCGS.** Silver-gray surfaces show traces of luster in the recesses. Generally well defined and showing just a few small marks.(#7288)

704 **1903-S AU53 NGC.** Whispers of light tan color are noted on the reverse this lightly worn S-mint example. Traces of luster are visible in the recesses of the remarkably clean surfaces.(#7288)

Rim-Toned 1903-S Dollar, MS62

705 **1903-S MS62 ANACS.** VAM-4. A satiny Mint State piece with mostly brilliant silver surfaces that are framed by peripheral gold and iridescent toning on each side. Minor surface marks, especially those on the cheek, prevent a higher grade. An excellent combination of grade and value for the budget-minded collector. (#7288)

Attractive Gem 1904 Morgan Dollar

706 **1904 MS65 PCGS.** A lovely MS65 representative of the last Morgan dollar issue struck at Philadelphia before 1921. It is well struck with strongly lustrous silver-white centers and faint elements of cream and light green at parts of the rims. Minimally marked and undeniably appealing. PCGS has certified 14 finer pieces (1/10). (#7290)

707 **1904-S MS61 ANACS.** VAM-2. The chin is minutely doubled. A pleasing Mint State piece with brilliant, untoned silver surfaces. Faint traces of gold toning are noted on each side, giving this piece additional character.(#7294)

Brilliant Choice 1904-S Dollar

708 **1904-S MS64 PCGS.** San Francisco silver dollars from the first decade of the 20th century are known for their scarcity in Mint State. The 1904-S is no exception. Perhaps Uncirculated bags were last in and first out of the Treasury vault, and participated in the Pittman Act melts. This essentially untoned example has a clean cheek and a well preserved reverse. A few wispy grazes are noted on the field near the profile. (#7294)

Nicely Toned 1904-S Dollar, MS65

709 **1904-S MS65 PCGS.** The 1904-S is a highly respected, late-date issue that has surprisingly few high grade survivors out of the mintage of 2.3 million pieces. Apparently this issue was not available for sale to the public in bag quantity, except for a brief offering through Los Angeles banks in the early 1950s. This piece displays the usual softly frosted mint luster and both sides are toned to varying degrees in rose-golden shades (deeper on the obverse, less so on the reverse). The striking details are above average, but not complete in the centers. Lightly abraded. (#7294)

Brilliant MS65 1904-S Dollar

710 **1904-S MS65 PCGS.** The untoned surfaces of this scarce S-mint dollar allow full appreciation of the uncommonly pronounced soft mint frost seen on this piece. The striking definition is less-than-complete over the ear of Liberty as well as on the eagle's breast, as one would expect. A loupe is required to see the few tiny marks that are on this Gem, otherwise the surfaces appear blemish-free. (#7294)

Conditionally Rare 1921-S Morgan, MS66

711 **1921-S MS66 NGC.** The 1921-S is an issue that was formerly little distinguished, if at all, from its P- and D-mint counterparts. In the last couple of decades, however, it has come to the fore as a condition rarity in the higher Mint State grades. This satiny piece has splendid surfaces with plum and gold accents near the rims. A sharp and pleasing Premium Gem. Census: 53 in 66, 1 finer (1/10). (#7300)

PROOF MORGAN DOLLARS

Gorgeous 1878 Eight Tailfeathers Dollar, PR66

712 **1878 8TF PR66 PCGS.** VAM-14.3. Deeply toned across both sides in gorgeous shades of rose-gray and mottled forest-green. This Premium Gem proof, from the first Morgan dollar type, is crisply and fully struck on all design elements. Excellent preservation has kept the piece from acquiring any unwanted hairlines or bothersome contact marks. From a small mintage of just 500 coins, and highly desirable to type collectors. Population: 9 in 66, 1 finer (1/10). (#7311)

Colorful 1879 Dollar, PR64

713 **1879 PR64 PCGS.** Deep cobalt-blue patination occupies the obverse of this near-Gem proof Morgan, accented with wisps of reddish-gold, while the reverse consists of deep purple and cobalt-blue. Sharply struck except for softness in the obverse center. Both sides appear to be devoid of significant marks. Population: 83 in 64, 34 finer (1/10). (#7314)

Well-Produced 1881 Morgan Dollar, PR64

714 **1881 PR64 NGC.** Fully struck with lovely, smoky purple-violet toning on both sides and a mild degree of cameo contrast on the obverse, where Liberty's portrait is lightly frosted. One of only 975 pieces struck in proof format this year. The 1881 Morgan dollar proofs are known to be well produced and attractive, and this near-Gem is no exception. (#7316)

Premium Gem Proof 1881 Morgan Dollar

715 **1881 PR66 NGC.** This Premium Gem has gleaming mirrors beneath rich crazy-quilt patina. The obverse has subtle shifts between gold, green, and blue shadings, while the reverse has more overt turquoise, cobalt, magenta, and gold-orange elements. Sharply struck and gorgeous. Census: 26 in 66, 18 finer (1/10). (#7316)

Select Proof 1882 Morgan Dollar

716 **1882 PR63 ANACS.** At 1,100 specimens struck, the 1882 is one of several Morgan dollar issues prized by proof type collectors. This Select survivor has watery mirrors draped in dappled green and gold-gray toning with deeper elements in arcs and patches along the rims. Housed in a small-format ANACS holder. (#7317)

Brilliant 1883 Morgan, PR65

717 **1883 PR65 NGC.** This fully brilliant Gem proof is a coin of exquisite beauty with no evidence of toning on either side. The fields are fully and deeply mirrored framing the lustrous and satiny devices with their incredibly sharp design details. This is an important opportunity for type collector and specialist alike. Census: 58 in 65, 36 finer (1/10). (#7318)

718 **1885 PR62 Cameo PCGS. CAC.** Bold green-gold peripheral tints give way to swirling cloud-gray and silver-blue tints through the centers. Well struck with prominent mirrors, though significant hairlines are noted through the left obverse field and elsewhere. Population: 8 in 62 Cameo, 45 finer (12/09).(#87320)

1888 Morgan Dollar, PR64
Rare Double-Punched Date

719 **1888 PR64 NGC.** Breen-5600. This proof variant is allegedly rare (but how many collectors actually examine their proof dollars for die varieties?). According to the BB reference, this double-punched variety was discovered by Walter Breen in 1954. The 1 shows the most obvious signs of repunching, but when closely examined all the other numerals show some evidence. The surfaces are mostly oyster-gray with just a hint of golden patina around the margins. Light hairlining explains the grade. The centers show slight striking weakness from inadequate die spacing, a situation that began in this year and continued until 1893. (#7323)

720 **1891 PR62 PCGS.** Champagne-gold, sky-blue, and bluish-purple toning dominates this proof Morgan. A trifle softly struck at the hair over the ear, as is often the case for this year's proofs, with scattered hairlines and a handful of contact marks.(#7326)

Attractive 1891 Dollar, PR64

721 **1891 PR64 PCGS.** A melange of sky-blue, orange-gold, and forest-green patination assumes slightly deeper hues on the reverse of this near-Gem Morgan proof. A well executed strike sharpens the design elements, except for minor weakness in the obverse center. This nicely preserved specimen resides in a green label holder. (#7326)

Popular PR64 Cameo 1895 Dollar

722 **1895 PR64 Cameo NGC.** Following several years of heavy Morgan dollar production, spurred by first the Bland-Allison Act of 1878 and especially the Sherman Act in 1890, the nation's financial reserves were in crisis. The government had radically overpaid for the silver used for striking the Morgan dollars of the time, and a wrinkle in the Sherman Act—that the government had to pay for the silver with paper money convertible to gold—led to a precipitous drop in the nation's gold reserves. The Panic of 1893 wrecked hundreds of banks and hundreds of thousands of households' finances before Congress repealed the Sherman Act that year, eliminating the reserve-draining subsidy and the monthly influx of silver to be minted into coin.

The years from 1893 to 1895 saw drastically reduced Morgan dollar production; business strikes from those three years combined do not come close to the 16.8 million pieces coined at Philadelphia in 1890 alone. All Morgan dollars in that date range are elusive at best, and two of the greatest Morgan dollar rarities, the 1893-S and the 1895, are among them. This is an example of the latter, a proof as always, since not one of the 12,000 1895 business strike dollars listed in official Mint Reports has ever turned up.

Both sides are appreciably contrasted, as most specimens of this date came originally, with moderately frosted devices offering a contrast to the mirrors. While the centers are minimally toned, the fields offer gold-gray patina that deepens close to the rims. Strong reflectivity with only a few minor hairlines and marks to preclude an even finer designation. Census: 34 in 64 Cameo, 49 finer (12/09). (#87330)

Wonderfully Toned 1896 Morgan, PR67

723 **1896 PR67 NGC.** This Superb Gem proof has impressive cameo contrast under sea-green, champagne, and rose toning on the obverse, and deeper blue-green, violet, and turquoise toning on the reverse. The depth of toning masks the contrast, so this piece has no Cameo designation. Census: 18 in 67, 6 finer (1/10). (#7331)

Contrasted 1899 Morgan, PR66

724 **1899 PR66 NGC. CAC.** Warm golden-tan patination bathes both sides of this Premium Gem proof, accented with whispers of electric-blue, lavender, and russet at the rims. An attentive strike results in virtually complete definition on the design elements, and impeccably preserved surfaces reveal a degree of field-motif contrast, especially when rotated under a light source. Census: 25 in 66, 15 finer (1/10). (#7334)

1900 Morgan Dollar, PR67 Cameo
A Magnificent, Brilliant Coin

725 **1900 PR67 Cameo NGC.** This is a spectacular, turn-of-the-century type coin whose surfaces appear to be unimprovable. Both sides are completely white, which allows the viewer an unimpeded view of the cameo effect between the frosted devices and deeply mirrored fields. The only "flaw" we see is of Mint origin: A tiny bit of porosity is in the field just below the letters U and N in UNUM. Census: 13 in 67 Cameo, 7 finer (12/09). (#87335)

Incredible PR68 1903 Morgan Dollar

726 **1903 PR68 NGC.** While this late-date proof Morgan dollar has limited field-to-device contrast, like the majority of its fellow specimens, it offers exquisite preservation and eye appeal that cannot be ignored. The fields are fantastically mirrored with golden overtones that cover the obverse margins as well as most of the reverse. Light but appreciable frost graces the portrait, and the eagle on the reverse shows a similar, greater effect. The surfaces are virtually perfect to the unaided eye. Tied with five others for numerically finest in the combined certified population (12/09). (#7338)

PEACE DOLLARS

727 **1921 MS65 PCGS. CAC.** A frosty Gem with fully brilliant and lustrous silver surfaces that display faint traces of heather and champagne toning. Central weakness is typical of all 1921 Peace dollars.(#7356)

728 **1921 MS65 NGC.** VAM-1F, R.5. Struck from the same die pair used to coin matte proofs. The variety is undesignated on the NGC insert. Whispers of chestnut-gold visit this lightly toned and lustrous Gem. The centers show moderate inexactness of strike, unavoidable for the issue. Smooth overall with a couple of wispy obverse grazes on the portrait and field.(#7356)

729 **1921 MS65 PCGS.** Softly detailed through the centers but otherwise well struck, this first-year Peace dollar is luminous and frosty. Light silver-white color overall with glimpses of peach and tan near the rims.(#7356)

Splendid 1921 Peace Dollar, MS66

730 **1921 MS66 PCGS.** A high grade example of this famous issue, struck in high relief for circulation only in 1921. Splashes of honey-gold and russet endow lustrous and lightly abraded surfaces. The strike is certainly above average, although incomplete as are all business strikes of the date. The chin and nose exhibit strike doubling. PCGS and NGC combined have certified just 13 pieces finer (1/10). (#7356)

Lustrous 1921 Peace Dollar, MS66

731 **1921 MS66 PCGS.** Sunset-gold and gunmetal-blue toning endow this satiny and virtually immaculate Premium Gem. The hair over the ear and the portion of the wing just above the eagle's leg show some blending of detail, as customary for this lower mintage issue. PCGS has certified a mere seven pieces finer (1/10). (#7356)

732 **1922-S MS65 PCGS.** Bright luster envelops both sides of this Gem, and wisps of light tan on the reverse provide the only color. Well struck and minimally abraded.(#7359)

733 **1922-S MS65 ANACS.** Aside from a touch of the usual striking softness in the centers, this brightly lustrous Gem is well-defined. Brilliant throughout with deeply frosted surfaces.(#7359)

Scarce MS65 1923-S Dollar

734 **1923-S MS65 NGC.** The 1923-S is very common through near-Gem but scarce in MS65 and extremely elusive any finer. Hints of light tan-gold color adhere to the lustrous surfaces of this Gem representative and an above average strike leaves relatively strong definition on the design features. A few minute marks are noted on each side. Census: 75 in 65, 1 finer (12/09). (#7362)

Scintillating Gem 1923-S Silver Dollar

735 **1923-S MS65 NGC.** Attractively toned in peach-gold and sky-blue tints. Lustrous and attentively struck with no conspicuous marks. The 1923-S was struck in prodigious quantity but few were set aside, unlike the much lower mintage 1921 Peace dollar. Encapsulated in a prior generation holder, and essentially unobtainable any finer. Census: 75 in 65, 1 finer (12/09). (#7362)

736 **1924-S MS64 PCGS. CAC.** The lustrous surfaces of this near-Gem yield just an occasional whisper of light gold color and exhibit well struck design features. Minor grazes deny Gem status. Housed in a green label holder.(#7364)

737 **1924-S MS64 NGC.** VAM-1E, R.5. The obverse field is inundated with wispy die polish lines, as made, that provide an unusual textured appearance. The eagle has a prominent "shoulder spike." Lustrous and lightly toned with generally clean surfaces. (#7364)

738 **1924-S MS64 PCGS.** Splashes of light golden-brown toning visit the obverse and are more prominent on the reverse. A lustrous and well struck coin with smooth fields and minor facial marks. (#7364)

Beautiful Gem 1924-S Dollar

739 **1924-S MS65 PCGS.** Light chestnut-gold toning visits the margins of this lustrous and sharply impressed Gem. Marks are elusive to find, and the eye appeal is exemplary. The 1924-S is the first branch mint issue of the series with a mintage of less than 2 million pieces. Population: 70 in 65, 5 finer (1/10). (#7364)

Outstanding MS67 1925 Dollar

740 **1925 MS67 NGC.** A frosty and beautiful P-mint Peace dollar with light green-gold toning gracing much of the fields and fresh silver color prevailing on the well-defined central devices. Virtually unavailable any better; NGC and PCGS have graded just two numerically finer examples between them (1/10). (#7365)

Remarkable 1925 Peace Dollar, MS67

741 **1925 MS67 PCGS.** Subtle champagne toning adds to the character and aesthetic desirability of this Superb Gem 1925 Peace dollar that ranks among the finest existing survivors. Only one coin has ever received a higher PCGS grade. In fact, the MS68 PCGS 1925 Peace dollar and a similar grade 1924 are the only two coins of any date that PCGS has certified at the grade level. This 1925 is one of another 183 coins that they have certified as MS67, out of a total population of more than 372,000 coins of the design. This piece has satiny luster, pristine surfaces, and bold design features. Population: 69 in 67, 1 finer (1/10). (#7365)

742 **1926-S MS65 NGC. CAC.** A condition rarity in finer grades, with just 38 finer NGC certified examples recorded in over 20 years. This brilliant and untoned Gem has extraordinary surfaces and incredible eye appeal.(#7369)

743 **1926-S MS65 PCGS. CAC.** Dazzling luster exudes from the unpatinated, nicely preserved surfaces of this lovely Gem. The design elements are well impressed.(#7369)

Die Doubled Gem 1927 Peace Dollar

744 **1927 MS65 PCGS. CAC.** VAM-3. The obverse is lightly die doubled, most obviously on the TR in TRVST. Minor strike doubling is also present. A well struck and lustrous Gem with a hint of golden toning. The portrait and the left obverse field are remarkably free from contact. A lower mintage issue. (#7370)

Gorgeous 1927 Peace Dollar, MS65

745 **1927 MS65 PCGS.** Light golden accents adorn the pale silver-gray surfaces of this Peace dollar Gem. The strike is substantially above average, and only a few wispy abrasions preclude an even finer designation. This lower mintage Philadelphia issue is a formidable condition rarity any better, with just five such pieces certified by PCGS (12/09). (#7370)

Conditionally Scarce 1927-D Gem Dollar

746 **1927-D MS65 NGC.** The 1927-D is available through the near-Gem level of preservation but becomes quite scarce in MS65. Hints of barely discernible tan color visit the lustrous surfaces of this Gem specimen, and a well executed strike imparts strong definition to the design elements. Light, grade-consistent marks detract minimally from the overall appeal. Census: 75 in 65, 3 finer (12/09). (#7371)

Satiny 1927-D Peace Dollar, MS65

747 **1927-D MS65 PCGS.** The golden-russet toning is slight aside from deeper shadings across the lower obverse periphery. A satiny Gem that is well struck throughout the major devices. The cheek is particularly free from abrasions. PCGS has certified only nine pieces finer (1/10). (#7371)

748 **1928 MS64 NGC. CAC.** Hints of barely discernible gold-tan color reside on the lustrous surfaces of this near-Gem, and a well executed strike sharpens the devices. Light marks preclude Gem status.(#7373)

749 **1928 MS64 PCGS.** A brilliant example of this popular, low-mintage issue. The surfaces are dazzling and the striking details are complete.(#7373)

750 **1928-S MS64 PCGS. CAC.** The mint luster is amazingly bright and thickly frosted, even for a San Francisco issue. Additionally, each side is free from any noticeable abrasions. An impressive, upper-end example of this popular S-mint Peace dollar. (#7374)

751 **1934-D MS65 NGC.** Micro D. Strongly lustrous beneath subtle, pleasing patina. The clean-cheeked obverse exhibits delicate gold-gray shadings, while the reverse shows hints of pink and blue with a touch of orange near the rims. A well struck Gem.(#7376)

Highly Desirable 1934-S Dollar, MS62

752 **1934-S MS62 PCGS.** The lustrous surfaces of this key date 1934-S representative display nearly indiscernible traces of gold-beige and bluish-violet color under magnification. An impressive strike leaves better definition than often seen on the central reverse. A few light marks limit the grade. This issue is highly desirable in all Mint State grades. (#7377)

Pleasing Near-Gem 1934-S Peace Dollar

753 **1934-S MS64 PCGS.** The 1934-S is the key to the Peace dollar series in Mint State. Speckles of light gray patina run over the lustrous surfaces of this near-Gem example. The design elements are generally well impressed, save for the usual softness in the centers. A scattering of grade-consistent marks do not detract from the overall appeal. (#7377)

Toned Gem 1934-S Peace Dollar

754 **1934-S MS65 PCGS. CAC.** This Gem 1934-S Peace dollar is one of the important condition rarities in the series, and a key-date in all grades. The present piece has deep pearlescent luster with hints of darker peripheral toning. PCGS has only certified 24 finer examples of the 1934-S Peace dollar (1/10). (#7377)

COMMEMORATIVE SILVER

755 **1893 Isabella Quarter MS65 PCGS.** Light to medium gray patination is joined on the reverse with lime-green, violet, and orange. Lustrous surfaces exhibit well struck devices and are nicely preserved.(#9220)

756 **1893 Isabella Quarter MS65 NGC.** Considerable liquid reflectivity filters through the veils of toning on each side. Cherry-gold and ruby hues mingle with violet, and a few streaks of the last color stand alone at the right obverse.(#9220)

757 **1900 Lafayette Dollar MS62 NGC.** DuVall 1-B, a plentiful variety. About half of all Lafayette dollars are from the 1-B die pair. This pleasing Mint State example will appeal to a number of collectors who desire the issue without spending the vast sums required for a Gem or finer piece. This specimen has satiny silver luster with a dusting of light iridescent toning.(#9222)

758 **1900 Lafayette Dollar MS63 NGC.** DuVall 3-D. A better die variety identified by obverse repunching on the AT in STATES. Uniform medium to deep gray patina displays gold undertones, and the design elements are sharply struck. A few light marks limit the grade.(#9222)

Radiant 1900 Lafayette Dollar, MS64

759 **1900 Lafayette Dollar MS64 NGC.** DuVall 1-B. This variety is seem as often as the other four varieties combined. A mostly brilliant and frosty near-Gem, this 1900 Lafayette dollar has splashes of peripheral lavender and blue toning on each side. The design elements are bold and the luster is radiant. (#9222)

1900 Lafayette Dollar, MS64 With Attractive Mottled Patina

760 **1900 Lafayette Dollar MS64 PCGS.** DuVall 1-B. This common variety shows the lower right leaf of the branch positioned between the 1 and 9 in the date, and the A in DOLLAR is low and leans left. This piece has obviously been well cared for since the date of issue. The surfaces display mottled gray, brilliant, olive-green, and blue patina in varying degrees on each side. The only mark of note is located on the reverse in the field above the horse's tail. Pleasing satiny mint luster. (#9222)

Satiny 1900 Lafayette Dollar, MS65

761 **1900 Lafayette Dollar MS65 NGC.** Variety 2-C. This is the second most plentiful Lafayette dollar variety behind the 1-B die combination. A survey of 280 Lafayette dollars revealed 12 of variety 1-A, 150 of variety 1-B, 95 of variety 2-C, 23 of variety 3-D, and none of variety 4-E.

This fully brilliant Gem has splendid satin luster with hints of delicate gold toning along the borders. The surfaces are splendid with only a few trivial marks. (#9222)

762 **1921 Alabama MS65 PCGS.** Light grayish-tan patina rides over the lustrous surfaces of this well struck Gem, augmented by speckles of deeper color. Some grade-consistent marks are noted, especially on the eagle's leg. Housed in a green label holder.(#9224)

763 **1921 Alabama MS65 NGC.** High grade Alabama halves consistently display thick mint frost. On this piece it is abundantly evident even through the medium-density gray-rose toning seen on each side. Both obverse and reverse are minimally abraded, as expected.(#9224)

764 **1921 Alabama 2x2 MS65 PCGS.** A melange of gray, greenish-gold, violet, and ice-blue patina endows the lustrous surfaces of this well struck Gem. A few grade-consistent marks do not detract. (#9225)

765 **1937 Antietam MS67 PCGS. CAC.** Yellow-russet patina, deeper on the reverse, washes over this lustrous example of the issue. A small purple spot is noted on General Lee's forehead, but this crisply struck piece shows no individually mentionable marks. Housed in a small-format holder.(#9229)

766 **1937 Antietam MS67 NGC.** The grade pretty much says it all: nearly perfect. What is not included is the satiny mint luster that enhances the light oyster-gray surfaces that deepen slightly around the peripheries.(#9229)

1937 Antietam Half, MS68
A Colorful, Nearly Perfect Example

767 **1937 Antietam MS68 NGC. CAC.** The Battle of Antietam (or Sharpsburg, as it was commonly called in the South), fought on Sept. 17, 1862, was the "bloodiest day of the Civil War," with almost 23,000 dead and wounded. The 1937 Antietam half dollar commemorates the 75th anniversary of that battle. This essentially pristine and beautifully toned example offers deep cherry-red, amber-gold, mint-green, and maroon patina dispersed on both sides. Census: 17 in 68, 2 finer (1/10). (#9229)

Impressive 1937-D Arkansas Half, MS67

768 **1937-D Arkansas MS67 PCGS. CAC.** A satiny and precisely struck pearl-gray Superb Gem with impressively mark-free surfaces. A few light silver-gray flecks appear under a loupe. Only 5,005 pieces were struck, and those were only sold as part of PDS Sets. Population: 14 in 67, 1 finer (12/09). (#9242)

Exquisite 1938-D Arkansas Half, MS67

769 **1938-D Arkansas MS67 NGC.** Hints of honey-gold enliven the borders of this otherwise untoned Superb Gem. A precisely struck and virtually pristine representative of this low mintage issue. The Arkansas state centennial was in 1936, but PDS sets were issued annually between 1935 and 1939. Census: 25 in 67, 2 finer (1/10). (#9246)

770 **1936-S Bay Bridge MS66 PCGS.** The Bay Bridge is a difficult coin to locate with an abrasion-free bear, as seen on this piece. Both sides are covered with finely speckled gray-rose toning and show strong underlying mint luster.(#9254)

771 **1934 Boone MS67 PCGS. CAC.** Violet and beige-gold patina imbued with hints of mint-green adhere to the lustrous surfaces of this charming Superb Gem, and an exacting strike leaves sharp detail on the design elements. Impeccable preservation rounds out the coin's eye appeal. Population: 30 in 67, 1 finer (1/10). (#9257)

772 **1935 Boone MS67 PCGS. CAC.** Bold silver-blue color consumes most of this Superb Gem, though green-gold peripheral arcs also grace each side and the upper reverse adds an element of muted mustard. Strong luster and visual appeal. Population: 32 in 67, 0 finer (12/09).(#9258)

773 **1935-S Boone MS65 PCGS.** This Gem S-mint commemorative is awash with vibrant luster and displays well struck motifs. Wisps of violet, tan, and gold occupy nicely preserved surfaces. (#9260)

774 **1935/34-D Boone MS67 PCGS. CAC.** This piece, from a net mintage of 2,003 pieces, is one of a few dozen so certified at PCGS, with but six coins graded finer (12/09). The silvery, pristine surfaces are virtually untoned and unperturbed, save for a thin ring of amber-gold at the extreme rims.(#9263)

775 **1935/34-D Boone MS67 PCGS.** A Superb Gem example of the infamous Denver edition of the 1935/1934 Boone half dollar, the lowest-mintage classic silver commemorative by one assay coin. Soft silver-blue luster shows elements of olive and mustard-gold at the margins.(#9263)

776 **1936-D Boone MS67 PCGS. CAC.** Gold and lemon-yellow toning are splashed across the brilliant and frosty silver surfaces of this Superb Gem. Both sides are sharply defined and pristine. Population: 22 in 67, 0 finer (12/09).(#9267)

777 **1936-D Boone MS67 NGC. CAC.** Soft violet and champagne patina is joined on the reverse periphery with aqua-green, lilac, and gold. Lustrous surfaces exhibit well struck design motifs and are devoid of significant marks. Census: 10 in 67, 0 finer (1/10). (#9267)

778 **1937 Boone MS65 PCGS.** Dapples of olive-green and purple interact with splashes of orange-gold and bluish-violet to yield a magnificent toning palette. Strong luster exudes from both sides, each of which exhibits sharply struck devices and is nicely preserved.(#9270)

779 **1937 Boone MS67 PCGS. CAC.** Luminous blue-gray toning through the centers with elements of muted green-gold around the rims. This Boone half has solid definition and strong all-around eye appeal. Population: 71 in 67, 3 finer (12/09).(#9270)

780 **1937-S Boone MS67 NGC.** Mottled gray-russet and rose toning is scattered over each side with strong underlying satiny mint luster. An exceptionally pleasing and problem-free Boone type coin. (#9272)

781 **1936 Bridgeport MS66 PCGS.** The soft, frosted mint luster enhances the variegated gray and rose toning over each side of this remarkably clean, problem-free commemorative half. (#9279)

Delicately Toned 1936 Bridgeport Half, MS67

782 **1936 Bridgeport MS67 PCGS. CAC.** Pastel ice-blue and sun-gold toning adorns this lustrous and virtually pristine Superb Gem. Many numismatic wags have commented on the significance of the obverse portrait of promoter P.T. Barnum, best known for his alleged quotation, "there's a sucker born every minute." There is no doubt, however, that in MS67 condition the Bridgeport is both rare and desirable. Encapsulated in a green label holder. Population: 54 in 67, 0 finer (12/09). (#9279)

783 **1925-S California MS66 PCGS. CAC.** Lustrous surfaces are overlain by light gray and faint russet toning along with lime-green and cobalt-blue accents, and are nicely preserved. There are seemingly no significant contact marks over either side. (#9281)

Amazingly Preserved 1925-S California Half, MS68 ★

784 **1925-S California MS68 ★ NGC.** Among early commemoratives, the California half was wedged between the Stone Mountain and the Fort Vancouver. The former was a resounding success, the latter not. As pointed out in Paul Green's 2007 *Numismatic News* article, "the California Diamond Jubilee half dollar had none of the features designed to increase sales." By that he was referring to the stars, Xs, and counterstamps applied to the Alabama, Missouri, Grant, and Stone Mountain coins. This is an amazingly preserved example of this well-designed half. The surfaces are nearly perfect. The mint luster has the bright sheen usually seen on these coins, and each side has lovely peripheral iridescence with nearly untoned centers. This piece is tied with five other MS68 ★ coins, and none are finer at either service (1/10). (#9281)

Superb Gem 1936-D Cincinnati Half

785 **1936-D Cincinnati MS67 NGC.** A Superb Gem example of the infamous Cincinnati design's D-mint issue, among the finest of the 5,005 pieces struck. Light silver-gray luster dominates, though the margins show tan and gold toning and dots of reddish-umber patina come closer to the centers on the obverse. Census: 32 in 67, 2 finer (1/10). (#9284)

786 **1936-S Cincinnati MS66 PCGS.** Dappled gold-orange and deep blue-violet peripheral tints give way to muted olive and silver-gray through the centers. A lustrous Premium Gem example of this challenging design. Population: 49 in 66, 1 finer (12/09). (#9285)

787 **1936 Cincinnati PDS Set MS66 PCGS. CAC.** Each coin has full satin luster with typical design definition, the San Francisco piece having slightly less detail. The Philadelphia coin is mostly brilliant with champagne toning and deeper peripheries. The Denver specimen is brilliant with champagne toning and splashes of gold. The example from the Western mint is darker, with golden-brown and iridescent toning.

788 **1936 Cincinnati PDS Set MS66 PCGS.** All three coins show green, gold, and violet peripheral toning around lustrous silver-gray centers. The **1936** and **1936-D** coins have CAC green labels, while the **1936-S** coin does not.(Total: 3 coins)

789 **1936 Cleveland MS66 PCGS.** An evenly struck and clearly original Premium Gem that possesses milky almond-gold and olive-gray toning. Contact is nearly imperceptible, with the obverse essentially pristine. Certified in a green label holder. (#9288)

790 **1936 Cleveland MS67 NGC.** Lime-green, purple, and russet toning dominates this Superb Gem commemorative, complementing the lustrous, well struck surfaces. Nicely preserved throughout. Census: 51 in 67, 4 finer (1/10).(#9288)

791 **1936 Columbia MS67 PCGS.** Remarkable dappled forest-green, golden-brown, and lilac toning consumes this shimmering and pristine Superb Gem. Housed in an old green label holder. Population: 54 in 67, 0 finer (1/10).(#9291)

792 **1936-D Columbia MS66 PCGS.** This beautifully toned representative displays rich sun-gold, gunmetal-blue, and mauve-gray patina that deepens near the margins. The present Premium Gem is interesting for its two retained laminations (as produced) near the M and C in AMERICA.(#9292)

Fantastic MS67 1892 Columbian Half

793 **1892 Columbian MS67 NGC.** The Columbian half has an enduring popularity with collectors. It also often shows a distinctive patination pattern, "Columbian half toning." This is such a piece. The obverse has teal colored patina for the most part, while the reverse is reddish in the center with a blue margin. The fields are bright and give the coin added zest, yielding a touch of prooflikeness. An exceptional coin and free from the surface distractions normally associated with this issue. (#9296)

794 **1935 Connecticut MS67 NGC.** Coruscating luster enlivens both sides of this Superb Gem commemorative and a well directed strike leaves well defined design features. A couple minuscule surface and rim marks are undisturbing. Census: 65 in 67, 1 finer (1/10). (#9299)

795 **1936 Delaware MS67 NGC.** Lime-green and crimson compete for territory on the lustrous surfaces of this well struck Delaware commemorative. A few obverse marks are mentioned for complete accuracy.(#9301)

796 **1936 Elgin MS65 NGC.** Frosty luster in light silver-gray is the rule on this Elgin Gem. The obverse margins show additional gold-orange and violet elements, particularly at the bottom. (#9303)

797 **1936 Gettysburg MS66 PCGS. CAC.** The lack of abrasions, thick mint luster, and light original color all combine on this one coin to make an exceptional, high grade example of this popular Civil War-themed commemorative. Definitely a high-end coin. (#9305)

798 **1922 Grant No Star MS66 PCGS. CAC.** Light to medium walnut-brown and steel-blue toning enriches this nicely struck and uncommonly unabraded Premium Gem. As is the case with most No Star Grant halves, the obverse is mildly prooflike from its proliferation of fine raised die lines in the field.(#9306)

799 **1922 Grant No Star MS66 NGC.** Pastel lime-green, apricot-gold, rose-red, and stone-gray endow this satiny and unabraded Premium Gem. The tree trunk near the frame house window shows slight incompleteness, but the strike is otherwise bold. Housed in a former generation holder.(#9306)

800 **1922 Grant With Star MS63 NGC.** Soft rose color is barely visible on the lustrous surfaces of this Grant with Star commemorative. Sharply struck and devoid of significant marks.(#9307)

801 **1922 Grant With Star MS63 PCGS. CAC.** Vibrant luster radiates from this Grant commemorative that displays soft pastels of multicolored toning along the margins, and a well executed strike imparts strong definition to the design elements. A couple of marks in the right obverse field barely preclude the next highest grade. Nevertheless, nice overall eye appeal, appropriately recognized by CAC.(#9307)

802 **1928 Hawaiian—Improperly Cleaned—NGC. Unc Details.** Fine hairlines are visible on the bright, essentially untoned surfaces, but mentionable contact marks are absent. Sharply struck throughout. (#9309)

Desirable 1928 Hawaiian Half, MS64

803 **1928 Hawaiian MS64 NGC.** This Choice Mint State 1928 Hawaiian half dollar has splashes of mustard-yellow toning on the reverse, an appearance that is often associated with the Bank of Hawaii hoard that was sold in January 1986. Of course, those coins are all widely dispersed today, more than 20 years later, and pieces appear in the marketplace infrequently. Aside from its peripheral patina, this piece is lustrous and fully brilliant. (#9309)

804 **1935 Hudson MS64 PCGS.** Light olive and chestnut toning visits this lustrous near-Gem. Nicely struck and impressively devoid of abrasions. Among the lowest mintage silver commemorative types. Certified in an old green label holder.(#9312)

805 **1935 Hudson MS65 NGC. CAC.** Light sun-gold and powder-blue shades visit this lustrous and evenly struck Gem. One thin curved mark on the main sail. Among the lowest mintage silver commemorative types. Certified in a prior generation holder. (#9312)

806 **1935 Hudson MS65 NGC.** A softly struck but immensely lustrous Gem with golden splashes against otherwise pale silver-gray surfaces. Minimally abraded and thoroughly charming.(#9312)

807 **1935 Hudson MS65 PCGS.** This Hudson is notably free of the numerous abrasions usually seen on the narwhale and Neptune. The mint luster is soft and frosted with an overlay of light lavender and lilac toning. A solid Gem Hudson half.(#9312)

Colorful MS66 1935 Hudson Half

808 **1935 Hudson MS66 PCGS.** While MS66 examples of the Hudson half dollar cannot properly be termed scarce, they are in high demand, since anything finer is the province of just a handful of Registry collectors. This lustrous Premium Gem offers rich green-gold, rose, and violet toning. Softly struck as usual in the centers, but the overall eye appeal is redeeming. (#9312)

809 **1946 Iowa MS68 ★ NGC.** Reddish-gold and orange-gold patination on the obverse cedes to lime-green, purple, and orange on the reverse. A well executed strike brings out strong detail on the design elements. An immaculately preserved and highly appealing commemorative. Census: 13 in 68 ★, 0 finer (1/10). (#9316)

810 **1936 Long Island MS66 PCGS.** Dappled dove-gray, olive-green, and canary-gold patina confirms the originality of this lustrous and immaculate Premium Gem. An outstanding representative, housed in an old green label holder.(#9322)

811 **1936 Long Island MS66 PCGS.** Beautiful orange-gold, ruby-red, and navy-blue toning dominates the borders of this lustrous Premium Gem. The devices display dappled golden-brown and gunmetal-blue. A slightly incomplete strike at the centers, but otherwise essentially unimprovable.(#9322)

Desirable 1936 Long Island Half, MS67

812 **1936 Long Island MS67 NGC.** A plentiful and popular commemorative issue, except in Superb Gem the Long Island is elusive and highly desirable. This piece has exquisite lavender toning with rainbow iridescence on both sides. The pristine surfaces have satiny underlying luster and are blemish-free. Census: 60 in 67, 3 finer (1/10). (#9322)

Strong MS67 1936 Long Island Half

813 **1936 Long Island MS67 NGC.** Small patches of frosty silver-gray give way to bold bronze, blue-green, cerulean, and umber hues on this Long Island Superb Gem. Each side is carefully preserved, with only a single tiny tick noted on the settler's cheek. NGC has certified just three numerically finer pieces (1/10). (#9322)

Lustrous 1920 Maine Half Dollar, MS67

814 **1920 Maine MS67 NGC.** Potent luster emanates from both sides of this Superb Gem and dapples of olive-green, brown, purple, and sky-blue concentrate at the margins of each. Well preserved surfaces are in receipt of a well executed strike, enhancing the coin's eye appeal. Census: 23 in 67, 1 finer (1/10). (#9326)

815 **1934 Maryland MS65 PCGS.** Moderate mauve toning fills the borders of this lustrous and attentively struck Gem. The reverse is well preserved, and the obverse has only minor contact. In a green label holder.(#9328)

816 **1921 Missouri MS64 NGC.** Gunmetal-blue, lavender, and soft russet toning concentrates at the margins of this radiantly lustrous near-Gem and a solid strike delivers full definition to the design motifs. A few trivial marks are undistracting.(#9330)

1921 'Plain' Missouri Centennial Half, MS65

817 **1921 Missouri MS65 NGC.** A delightful Missouri commemorative half dollar with original iridescent toning and underlying mint frost. This Gem, issued to celebrate the Missouri Centennial, has exceptional surfaces and possesses strong eye appeal. NGC has only certified 31 finer examples of this issue (1/10). (#9330)

818 **1921 Missouri 2x4 MS64 NGC.** The surfaces are attractive and minimally abraded, as indicated by the grade. The centers are untoned but surrounded by golden toning at the margins. Excellent value in this difficult commemorative issue.(#9331)

Pleasing Gem 1921 2x4 Missouri Half

819 **1921 Missouri 2x4 MS65 NGC.** The obverse toning of this 2x4 Gem are vaguely concentric, though the hues—green-gold outside, fading to blue and faded orange with an eventual silver-gray center—form arcs rather than complete circles. The reverse has rich, subdued rose-violet, gold, and orange patina around a near-brilliant core. NGC has graded just 20 numerically finer examples (1/10). (#9331)

820 **1923-S Monroe MS65 NGC.** Brownish-gray patination with gold undertones bathes the lustrous surfaces of this S-mint Monroe commemorative. Sharply struck and revealing just a couple of minor grade-consistent marks. This issue becomes difficult to acquire any finer.(#9333)

821 **1938 New Rochelle MS66 NGC.** Vibrant luster appears to reach out to the observer of this impeccably preserved, sharply struck New Rochelle commemorative. Reddish-gold, russet, and electric-blue patina concentrates at the obverse margin, while golden-orange covers most of the reverse.(#9335)

822 **1925 Norse Thin Planchet MS65 PCGS.** Traces of chestnut toning cling to the rims of this satiny octagonal Gem. The strike is precise, and marks of any size require patience to locate. The thin planchet variety is believed approximately five times scarcer than its thick flan counterpart. Population: 28 in 65, 3 finer (1/10). (#9451)

823 **1926-S Oregon MS67 PCGS. CAC.** The violet and gold hues that dominate the left obverse and the peripheral reverse yield to startling brilliance elsewhere. This glittering Superb Gem is near the top of the PCGS *Population Report*, with just four coins graded finer (12/09).(#9341)

824 **1933-D Oregon MS67 PCGS.** Light silver-gray color overall with dots of deeper pewter and slate-blue close to the rims. A sculptural Superb Gem example of this much-favored Oregon issue. Population: 71 in 67, 0 finer (12/09).(#9343)

825 **1933-D Oregon MS67 PCGS. CAC.** Pink and violet tones cede to deeper plum and orange at parts of the margins. Well struck with lovely luster. This Superb Gem is tied for finest certified by PCGS (12/09).(#9343)

Lovely 1938-D Oregon Half, MS68

826 **1938-D Oregon MS68 NGC.** Both sides of this incredible Superb Gem have peripheral iridescent toning along the borders, serving as a nice frame for the brilliant and frosty silver luster at the centers. This piece is a remarkable example, exceeded for grade by just two NGC submissions and two other PCGS submissions. Census: 59 in 68, 2 finer (1/10). (#9349)

827 **1939 Oregon MS67 PCGS. CAC.** Barely discernible gold and violet coloration rests on the lustrous surfaces of this Superb Gem commemorative, and a well executed strike leaves strong detail on the devices. Pleasing overall eye appeal. Population: 74 in 67, 4 finer (1/10).(#9352)

828 **1936 Rhode Island MS66 PCGS.** Golden-tan and purple freckles run over the lustrous surfaces of this attractive Premium Gem, accented with light green and crimson along the lower obverse margin. This well struck piece reveals no marks worthy of note. (#9363)

829 **1936-D Rhode Island MS66 PCGS.** Grayish-violet, gold, greenish-gold, and crimson toning adorns both sides of this D-mint commemorative, complemented by a well executed strike. Highly lustrous and nicely preserved.(#9364)

830 **1936-D Rhode Island MS67 PCGS. CAC.** Ex: JFS Collection. The surfaces are immaculate and highly lustrous with light, even patina over each side that deepens to golden-russet around the margins. Minimally marked and sharply defined. Population: 46 in 67, 0 finer (12/09).(#9364)

Iridescently Toned 1936-S Rhode Island Half, MS67

831 **1936-S Rhode Island MS67 PCGS. CAC.** A silky-smooth Rhode Island half with pale lilac and pastel-rose obverse toning, intensifying several shades on the reverse into orange, green, and bright carmine iridescence. A one-of-a-kind example that is bound to excite the toned commemorative enthusiast. Population: 14 in 67, 0 finer (12/09). (#9365)

Richly Patinated 1937 Roanoke Commemorative, MS68

832 **1937 Roanoke MS68 NGC.** Crimson, olive-green, forest-green, reddish-orange, and yellow-gold patination dominates the obverse margins ceding to yellow-green in the central area and over most of the reverse. Crisp, uniform definition is apparent on the design elements and both sides are immaculately preserved. Census: 26 in 68, 0 finer (1/10). (#9367)

833 **1936 Robinson MS66 PCGS.** A well executed strike leaves sharp, uniform detail on the lustrous surfaces of this Premium Gem. Whispers of barely discernible ice-blue and gold color are slightly more prevalent on the obverse. A pleasing, impeccably preserved specimen.(#9369)

834 **1936 Robinson MS66 PCGS.** Variegated chestnut-brown and dove-gray drape the obverse of this lustrous and pristine Premium Gem. The reverse provides lighter stone-gray and sun-gold color. Certified in an old green label holder.(#9369)

835 **1935-S San Diego MS67 PCGS. CAC.** A softly lustrous Superb Gem, well struck and richly toned. Dappled gold, blue-green, cerulean, and violet peripheral shadings yield to generally silver-gray centers. PCGS has graded just three coins finer (12/09). (#9371)

836 **1935-S San Diego MS67 NGC.** The remarkably clean and lustrous surfaces are mostly brilliant, but there is an accent of golden toning around the margins on both obverse and reverse. Virtually unobtainable any finer. Census: 81 in 67, 5 finer (1/10). (#9371)

837 **1926 Sesquicentennial MS65 NGC.** A richly toned Gem example of this famously challenging issue, gray-gold in the centers with powder-blue of varying intensity at the rims. NGC has certified just 17 numerically finer pieces (12/09).(#9374)

838 **1935 Spanish Trail MS64 PCGS. CAC.** Light silver-gray color overall with golden tints at the rims. The reverse also has a narrow but stark line of charcoal color through the left field. High eye appeal for the grade, and housed in a prior-generation PCGS holder.(#9376)

839 **1935 Spanish Trail MS65 PCGS. CAC.** Dappled gold and blue-gray toning graces the lustrous surfaces of this Spanish Trail Gem. Well struck for the issue with no individually mentionable flaws. Housed in a green label holder.(#9376)

840 **1935 Spanish Trail MS66 NGC.** A minimally toned Spanish Trail half with uncommonly bright luster for the type. The obverse is minimally marked, though a few small abrasions appear above the map on the reverse.
From The Stan Burger Collection, Part Two.(#9376)

841 **1935 Spanish Trail MS66 NGC.** Typical of the issue, this Premium Gem has satiny silver luster with sharp design motifs. It is mostly brilliant with subtle gold and iridescent toning on each side. (#9376)

1935 Spanish Trail Half, MS67

842 **1935 Spanish Trail MS67 PCGS. CAC.** Edmund J. Senn, the artist who modeled the Spanish Trail half, is best known as having been unemployed at the time L.W. Hoffecker gave him the commission. Classically trained and Austrian-born, the sexagenarian Senn died in 1938, just three years after his brush with the commemorative world. This silver-gray Superb Gem has subtle pink accents and a touch of orange patina at the rims. Well-defined and carefully preserved with a single spot of deeper toning above the L of LIBERTY. Population: 88 in 67, 2 finer (12/09). (#9376)

843 **1925 Stone Mountain MS67 NGC.** We do not see any abrasions on this superior Stone Mountain. Each side is toned in multicolored iridescent colors and is a wonder to behold.(#9378)

Lustrous 1935 Texas Half, MS68

844 **1935 Texas MS68 NGC.** Yellow-green patination imbued with hints of reddish-gold gravitates to the leftmost margins of both obverse and reverse, while dabs of olive-green visit the latter's central area. Radiantly lustrous and exactingly struck. A narrow zone of ejection flatness is seen on the margin of the right (facing) wing. Census: 13 in 68, 0 finer (1/10). (#9382)

845 **1936 Texas MS67 PCGS.** Frosty silver-blue and light gray centers give way to bold green-gold at the obverse margins. A sharply struck and gorgeous Superb Gem. PCGS has graded just six finer examples (12/09).(#9386)

Attractive 1937-D Texas Fifty Cent, MS68 ★ The Finest NGC-Certified

846 **1937-D Texas MS68 ★ NGC.** NGC has seen fit to assign the Star designation to a mere three 1937-D Texas commemorative half dollars, with the present MS68 offering being the finest. Apple-green, golden-orange, and crimson concentrate along the obverse borders, while reddish and golden-tan freckles dominate the reverse periphery. Intense luster radiates from immaculately preserved surfaces that exhibit well delineated devices. (#9391)

Amazing MS67 1938 Texas Half

847 **1938 Texas MS67 NGC.** Deep orange-bronze toning consumes most of the obverse, leaving only small areas of gleaming silver surface, though the toning on the reverse, while similar in color with purple additions, is far more subdued and restricted to the margins. Carefully preserved beneath the patina with a solid strike. Census: 43 in 67, 2 finer (1/10). (#9394)

848 **1938-D Texas MS67 PCGS.** Frosty and gorgeous with a suggestion of powder-blue peripheral toning around silver-white centers on each side. The obverse adds distinct bands of gold and orange. Population: 66 in 67, 0 finer (12/09).(#9395)

849 **1938-S Texas MS67 NGC.** Exceptional luster and remarkably clean surfaces characterize this Superb type coin. Each side has finely speckled gray patina that is interspersed with rose, lilac, and lime-green. Census: 71 in 67, 12 finer (1/10).(#9396)

850 **1925 Vancouver MS66 NGC.** A well-preserved early commemorative half, the toning on this piece sets it apart as well as the exceptionally clean surfaces. Both sides show purplish-russet and cobalt-blue toning, but the reverse more so.(#9399)

851 **1946 Booker T. Washington MS67 PCGS.** PCGS has only certified a single finer example of this common date commemorative half dollar, often chosen to represent the Booker T. Washington design. This lustrous piece has vivid toning over frosty surfaces. Population: 33 in 67, 1 finer (1/10).(#9404)

Spectacular MS67 1946-D BTW Half

852 **1946-D Booker T. Washington MS67 PCGS.** A shining Superb Gem with outstanding, borderline outlandish toning. Crazy-quilt patterns of reddish-orange, gold, forest-green, and magenta-violet appear on each side, as do localized hints of additional colors. Tied for the finest certified by PCGS (1/10), and as such a Registry collector essential. (#9405)

Colorful Superb Gem 1946-D BTW Fifty Cent

853 **1946-D Booker T. Washington MS67 NGC.** Violet-gray and greenish-gold obverse toning cedes to deeper reddish-gold, green, and purple coloration on the reverse. Exquisitely struck and preserved. Conditionally rare at the MS67 level, undoubtedly due to the mediocre strike seen on most examples of the type. Census: 53 in 67, 5 finer (1/10). (#9405)

854 **1947 Booker T. Washington MS66 PCGS.** Vibrant luster radiates from both sides of this delightful commemorative. Russet and aqua-blue toning concentrates around the obverse borders, ceding to olive-green freckles on the reverse margins. A few "chatter marks" do not take from the coin's eye appeal. PCGS has seen a mere four pieces finer (1/10).(#9408)

855 **1947-D Booker T. Washington MS66 PCGS.** Radiantly lustrous surfaces display hints of gold peripheral toning and a well executed strike imparts strong detail to the design elements. Both sides are devoid of mentionable marks. Population: 84 in 66, 1 finer (1/10). (#9409)

856 **1947-S Booker T. Washington MS67 NGC.** Light blue accents visit pale silver-gray surfaces. This second-year Superb Gem is conditionally rare so fine, and neither NGC nor PCGS has graded a numerically finer example (12/09).(#9410)

Prized MS67 1948-D BTW Half

857 **1948-D Booker T. Washington MS67 NGC.** This D-mint Booker T. Washington issue has a low mintage of just 8,000 pieces excluding assay coins, and Superb Gem coins are conditionally rare. This MS67 coin is tied for numerically finest in the combined certified population (1/10), thanks to impressive preservation that brings out the best of the strongly lustrous surfaces, faintly silver-blue with elements of tan. (#9413)

Superb Gem 1948-S BTW Half

858 **1948-S Booker T. Washington MS67 PCGS. CAC.** With just five MS67 examples of this issue certified by PCGS and none finer (12/09), this BTW half is of high importance to the Registry collector. Pale golden toning visits much of each side, though the portrait is minimally patinated. Minor planchet roughness is present, but post-striking flaws are few. (#9414)

859 **1951 Booker T. Washington MS67 NGC.** The combined NGC and PCGS population of 13 Superb Gem MS67 coins, and only one finer piece, help to identify just how important this piece is. Both sides have a high degree of luster beneath deep rainbow toning. Census: 8 in 67, 1 finer (1/10).(#9424)

860 **1951-S Booker T. Washington MS67 PCGS. CAC.** Brilliant throughout, this lovely coin displays bright, frosted mint luster and nearly abrasion-free surfaces. An amazing Superb Gem. Population: 25 in 67, 0 finer (12/09).(#9426)

1951-S Washington-Carver Half, MS67

861 **1951-S Washington-Carver MS67 NGC.** Dappled blue, green, and gold hues grace the outer zones on this Washington-Carver Superb Gem, while the centers remain mostly pale silver-gray. Slight central striking softness is visible on the reverse map, specifically the S superimposed over it, but this is a minor quibble next to the impressive luster. Tied for numerically finest graded by NGC or PCGS (1/10). (#9432)

862 **1952 Washington-Carver MS66 PCGS.** A delicate blend of violet, light green and orange-gold adorns the lustrous surfaces of this Premium Gem. Well preserved surfaces exhibit decisively struck design elements. PCGS has seen a mere six pieces finer (1/10).(#9434)

Lovely MS67 1952 Washington-Carver Half

863 **1952 Washington-Carver MS67 NGC.** The obverse of this Washington-Carver half showcases electric iridescence, with gold, green, blue, violet, rose, and orange hues represented. The reverse, by contrast, has rich infusions of peach and violet with little variation besides. Well struck and carefully preserved. Census: 17 in 67, 1 finer (1/10). (#9434)

864 **1953 Washington-Carver MS66 PCGS. CAC.** Whispers of nearly imperceptible violet and beige-gold patina visit the lustrous surfaces of this Premium Gem commemorative and a solid strike imparts sharp detail to the design features. Both sides have been well cared for. Population: 49 in 66, 1 finer (1/10).(#9438)

865 **1953-S Washington-Carver MS66 PCGS.** This appealing S-mint commemorative shows freckled reddish-gold patina on the violet surfaces of the obverse and a mix of violet, greenish-gold, and orange-gold on the reverse. Both sides exhibit pleasing luster and sharply struck design features. A few grade-consistent marks do not disturb. Population: 81 in 66, 4 finer (1/10).(#9440)

866 **1954-D Washington-Carver MS66 NGC.** The surfaces are untoned and there are remarkably few abrasions for this normally heavily marked type. The mint luster is bright and satiny. A very scarce commemorative to locate in high grades. Census: 18 in 66, 1 finer (1/10).(#9443)

867 **1954-D Washington-Carver MS66 PCGS. CAC.** Light gold and sky-blue dominates, although dabs of deep russet and sea-green are present on the lower obverse. The final year of the Washington-Carver type, which completed the long run of pre-1982 commemorative issues. Population: 24 in 66, 0 finer (1/10). (#9443)

868 **Selection of Original Commemorative Folders.** Includes nine items: a five-coin self-covered folder for Albany half dollars; a three-coin card for Columbia half dollars; a five-coin self-covered folder for Delaware half dollars; a single-coin box for a Lexington half dollar; a single-coin self-covered folder for a New Rochelle half dollar; a five-coin self-covered folder for Norfolk half dollars; a printed envelope for a Panama-Pacific half dollar; a five-coin self-covered folder for Roanoke half dollars; and a single-coin self-covered folder for a Booker T. Washington half dollar titled *Gems of Wisdom*. There are no coins included in this lot.(Total: 9 items)

COMMEMORATIVE GOLD

869 **1903 Louisiana Purchase/Jefferson MS65 NGC.** Strong yellow-gold luster with above-average design definition. The upper reverse rim shows a small copper spot above the space between the AS in PURCHASE.(#7443)

870 **1903 Louisiana Purchase/McKinley MS64 PCGS. CAC.** Variegated peach-gold and mint-green surfaces yield an occasional splash of apricot, especially on the reverse. Pleasing luster radiates from each side, with the central obverse device being nicely frosted. An exacting strike delivers sharp, uniform definition to the design features. A nicely preserved piece.(#7444)

871 **1903 Louisiana Purchase/McKinley MS64 PCGS. CAC.** A lemon-gold Choice Mint State example that has peripheral hints of lime patina. Luster dominates both sides, and the absence of abrasions confirms both the numerical grade and the opinion of CAC. It is true that a 1903 McKinley will always be available for purchase, but perhaps not with the superior quality of the present coin.(#7444)

872 **1903 Louisiana Purchase/McKinley MS66 NGC.** An incredible Premium Gem, this McKinley gold dollar has frosty luster with rich yellow surfaces and substantial design definition. It is a highly appealing piece with few peers, especially among coins available in the market place.(#7444)

873 **1903 Louisiana Purchase/McKinley MS66 NGC.** Sharply defined and fully lustrous, this Premium Gem has satiny yellow surfaces with heavy die polish in the obverse field that imparts a suggestion of reflectivity.(#7444)

874 **1904 Lewis and Clark MS62 PCGS.** The Lewis side displays peach patina, while the Clark side is honey-gold. A satiny and evenly struck representative of this scarce commemorative gold dollar type. In a green label holder.(#7447)

High-End MS64 1904 Lewis and Clark Gold Dollar

875 **1904 Lewis and Clark MS64 PCGS. CAC.** This issue commemorates the 100th anniversary of the Voyage of Discovery. Meriwether Lewis is on the obverse (dated side), and William Clark is on the reverse. The fields are lightly striated and slightly reflective, and each side has an accent of reddish patina. Minimally abraded and high-end. (#7447)

Gem 1904 Lewis and Clark Dollar

876 **1904 Lewis and Clark MS65 NGC.** Bright yellow-gold luster prevails on each side, though glimpses of sun and peach are also present close to the centers. A relatively well struck example with few of the post-striking abrasions so often seen, though a handful of minor faults combine to preclude an even finer designation. (#7447)

Exemplary Near-Gem 1905 Lewis and Clark Gold Dollar

877 **1905 Lewis and Clark MS64 PCGS.** Lustrous and lovely with an unperturbed appearance and a consistently crisp strike. Coin designers must disagree with the maxim that two heads are better than one, since the 1904 and 1905 Lewis and Clark gold dollars remain the only true double-headed U.S. type coin. (#7448)

MS64 1905 Lewis and Clark Dollar

878 **1905 Lewis and Clark MS64 NGC.** A generally well struck and lustrous yellow-gold example from the more challenging second year of the Lewis and Clark gold dollar design. Minor alloy is noted at the peripheries, but aside from a handful of shallow lines in the fields around the portraits, significant abrasions are few. (#7448)

879 **1915-S Panama-Pacific Gold Dollar MS65 NGC. CAC.** Strong butter-yellow luster with orange and peach overtones. Well struck for this classic commemorative gold dollar issue and pleasingly preserved, even by Gem standards.(#7449)

880 **1915-S Panama-Pacific Gold Dollar MS66 PCGS.** A subtle blend of mint-green and apricot resides on the lustrous surfaces of this Premium Gem commemorative gold dollar. Sharply struck and devoid of mentionable marks.(#7449)

MS63 1915-S Panama-Pacific Two and a Half

881 **1915-S Panama-Pacific Quarter Eagle MS63 PCGS.** An attractive Select example of this popular gold commemorative quarter eagle issue, the first of just two classic commemoratives of its denomination. Lustrous butter-yellow surfaces lend the coin considerable eye appeal despite light abrasions. Minor striking softness affects the central figures. (#7450)

Frosty 1915-S Panama-Pacific Quarter Eagle, MS65

882 **1915-S Panama-Pacific Quarter Eagle MS65 NGC.** Part of the famous set of Panama-Pacific commemorative coins that were issued by Farran Zerbe, the quarter eagle is infrequently encountered in Gem or finer grades. This piece has frosty green-gold luster with excellent surfaces with only a few trivial blemishes and no spotting of any type. (#7450)

883 **Pair of 1915-S Panama-Pacific Boxes.** A pair of single-coin boxes for Panama-Pacific fifty dollar gold pieces, one for an octagonal example, the other for a round piece. The boxes are complete and intact, with some scuffing on the outside, but with complete gilt trim. The purple velvet interior of each is excellent, with the gilt lettering bold and vibrant. The holder for the round piece has a printed information card included. There are no coins included in this lot.(Total: 2 items)

884 **1916 McKinley MS65 NGC.** Rich orange-gold coloration is evident with reflective fields and satiny devices. The 1916 and 1917 McKinley gold dollars were fund-raising pieces for the McKinley Birthplace Memorial in Niles, Ohio, midway between Warren and Youngstown in the far eastern part of the state.(#7454)

Marvelous MS66 1917 McKinley Gold Dollar

885 **1917 McKinley MS66 NGC.** The third and last classic gold commemorative to bear an image of the late President McKinley, the 1917 Birthplace dollar was not well-received in its time but has gained considerable popularity since. The bold, slightly satiny orange-gold luster of this well struck Premium Gem lends it excellent eye appeal. (#7455)

Attractive 1917 McKinley Gold Dollar, MS66

886 **1917 McKinley MS66 PCGS.** This Premium Gem commemorative gold dollar gives off ebullient luster from its surfaces that are attractively toned in orange, mint-green, and lilac on the obverse and the first two colors on the reverse. This exquisitely struck piece is devoid of mentionable marks. (#7455)

887 **1922 Grant No Star MS64 PCGS.** Striking yellow-gold luster lends this No Star near-Gem impressive eye appeal. Softly struck devices show a handful of wispy abrasions, as do the fields. (#7458)

Gem No Star 1922 Grant Gold Dollar

888 **1922 Grant No Star MS65 PCGS. CAC.** This yellow-gold Gem appears immaculate aside from two brief hair-thin marks, one above the frame house door and the other on Grant's forehead. Sharply struck save for the inevitable incompleteness on the tree trunk near the window, which is opposite the highpoint of Grant's hair. Encapsulated in a green label holder. (#7458)

Lustrous 1922 Grant No Star Dollar, MS65

889 **1922 Grant No Star MS65 NGC.** Sharp design details and lustrous light yellow-gold surfaces characterize this pristine Gem gold dollar. The famous Civil War general and later U.S. President Ulysses S. Grant is the subject of this commemorative, showing his Ohio birthplace on the reverse. This piece will serve as a nice addition to a commemorative collection or a Civil War historical collection. (#7458)

Bold 1922 Grant Star Dollar, MS65

890 **1922 Grant With Star MS65 NGC.** This boldly detailed Gem has frosty yellow-gold luster with traces of pale green patina on each side and mostly sharp design motifs. Only a few minor marks are evident in the left obverse field, with additional small copper toning spots primarily on the obverse. (#7459)

Bright 1922 Grant With Star Gold Dollar MS66

891 **1922 Grant With Star MS66 PCGS. CAC.** The 1922 Grant With Star memorial gold dollar was the first version of the type, the star later being removed. Bright luster endows this Premium Gem that displays pretty peach-gold color. Additionally, a solid strike imparts strong definition to the design elements. An inoffensive alloy spot occurs on each side. (#7459)

Appealing 1922 Grant With Star Dollar, MS66

892 **1922 Grant With Star MS66 NGC.** A wonderful example of the Grant With Star variety, an unrequested bonus received by the issuing agency, generating additional profits as most collectors required both varieties. This lustrous piece has frosty yellow surfaces with excellent design definition. (#7459)

Popular 1926 Sesquicentennial Quarter Eagle, MS65

893 **1926 Sesquicentennial MS65 NGC.** A fantastically lustrous yellow-gold Gem with mildly frosted design elements. Remarkable overall quality, with only shallow luster grazes where the majority of examples will show light to moderate abrasions. Elusive in better grades; NGC has graded 92 numerically finer examples (1/10). (#7466)

MODERN ISSUE

894 **2000-W Library of Congress PR70 Deep Cameo PCGS.** An utterly unimpeachable specimen of this increasingly popular bimetallic commemorative issue. Both the outer gold ring and inner platinum disc offer excellent reflectivity and contrast.
From The Stan Burger Collection, Part Two.(#99784)

MODERN BULLION COINS

895 **1986 One-Ounce Gold Eagle Gem Uncirculated PCGS.** Per the insert, "Gem Uncirculated" rather than a numeric grade, from "WTC Ground Zero Recovery." Lustrous with deep yellow streaks against lighter straw-gold color.(#9806)

1986-W One-Ounce Gold American Eagle PR69 Deep Cameo, Gerald Ford Autograph

896 **1986-W One-Ounce Gold Eagle PR69 Deep Cameo PCGS.** "President Edition," #500 of 500, insert signed by the late President Ford. Outstandingly contrasted and virtually flawless, with only a few tiny imperfections visible; most appear only under magnification, though the field between the flying eagle's wings does show a handful of modest faults. An unusual and desirable example of this first-year proof one-ounce gold American Eagle issue. (#9807)

Prized PR68 Deep Cameo 1995-W Silver Eagle

897 **1995-W Silver Eagle PR68 Deep Cameo PCGS.** Outstanding contrast and eye appeal for this prized modern key, the greatest obstacle to a complete set of proof silver American eagles. A couple of tiny milk spots can be found in the fields close to the frost-white devices, but a black-and-white appearance dominates otherwise. (#9887)

PR69 Ultra Cameo 1995-W Silver American Eagle

898 **1995-W Silver Eagle PR69 Ultra Cameo NGC.** A virtually perfect representative of the well-known key to the proof silver American Eagle series, one of just over 30,000 specimens coined. The surfaces are profoundly contrasted with an absolute black-and-white appearance. Only under magnification do a handful of minuscule flaws appear. (#9887)

Modern Key 1995-W Silver Eagle, PR69 Ultra Cameo

899 **1995-W Silver Eagle PR69 Ultra Cameo NGC.** This pristine proof, a remarkable near-perfect specimen, survives from a mintage of only 30,125 coins, an ultra-low mintage resulting in a key modern issue rarity. Both sides have impressive field-device contrast with fully brilliant and untoned proof surfaces. (#9887)

900 **2005 Four-Piece Platinum Eagle Set MS69 PCGS.** All four platinum American Eagles are designated by PCGS as "First Strikes." Includes the **tenth-ounce, quarter-ounce, half-ounce,** and **one-ounce** sizes.(Total: 4 coins)

901 **2006-W Four-Piece Gold Eagle Set MS70 NGC.** All four gold American Eagles are described by NGC as "Early Releases." Includes the **tenth-ounce, quarter-ounce, half-ounce,** and **one-ounce** sizes.(Total: 4 coins)

902 **2006-W One-Ounce Gold Eagle MS70 NGC.** Early Releases. Technically flawless with a shining sense of modern perfection. While it does not influence the technical grade, a shallow depression to the left of the main eagle's right wingtip is of some interest.(#89989)

903 **2006 One-Ounce Gold Buffalo MS70 NGC.** An ounce of pure gold, struck to satiny perfection. The butter-yellow surfaces offer exquisite texture and undeniable quality.
From The Stan Burger Collection, Part Two.(#9999)

904 **2006 One-Ounce Gold Buffalo MS70 NGC.** NGC described as "First Strikes." Richly textured and sharply struck with utterly flawless butter-yellow surfaces. A tiny glint appears behind the portrait's neck.(#9999)

905 **2006 One-Ounce Gold Buffalo MS70 NGC.** NGC designation "First Strikes." A delightful and technically perfect example of this popular pure-gold bullion series, boldly impressed with rich yellow color.(#9999)

906 **2006-W One-Ounce American Eagle Gold Reverse Proof PR70 PCGS.** PCGS First Strike designation. A technically flawless specimen of this intriguing one-shot concept from the American Eagle 20th Anniversary celebration. Frosted fields are as carefully preserved as the gleaming devices.
From The Stan Burger Collection, Part Two.(#89995)

907 **2006-W Buffalo One-Ounce Gold PR70 Ultra Cameo NGC.** An utterly flawless proof specimen of this one-ounce gold issue, struck at the West Point Mint. The textured, gleaming fields supply excellent contrast with the frosted devices.
From The Stan Burger Collection, Part Two.(#9990)

908 **2006-W One-Ounce Platinum Eagle PR70 Ultra Cameo NGC.** This white on black beauty has exemplary preservation and an intricate strike. The lower gown has inconspicuous highpoint contact.(#921119)

909 **Four-Piece 2008-W Buffalo Gold Set SP70 ANACS.** The set includes the **tenth-ounce, quarter-ounce, half-ounce,** and **one-ounce** 2008-W Buffalo gold coins. All four examples are fully struck and immaculate. A desirable four-piece set.(Total: 4 coins)

910 **2009 Ultra High Relief MS70 PCGS.** An utterly flawless rendition of the popular Ultra High Relief twenty dollar coin from 2009, exactingly struck and perfectly beautiful. Comes with original packaging and documentation, including a still-shrinkwrapped book about the issue.(#407404)

911 **2009 Ultra High Relief MS70 NGC.** From the gleaming curves of the golden fields to the razor-sharp strike of the devices, every aspect of this modern-day Ultra High Relief coin is unimpeachable. Accompanied by original box and book of issue.(#407404)

912 **2009 Ultra High Relief MS70 NGC.** An utterly faultless example of this popular Ultra High Relief modern issue. Comes with original box and still-shrinkwrapped book.(#407404)

COINS OF HAWAII

Exceptional 1883 Hawaiian Ten Cent, MS65

913 **1883 Hawaii Ten Cents MS65 PCGS.** This Gem is sharply defined with incredible golden-violet toning over frosty silver surfaces and a full quota of original underlying mint luster. The 1883 Hawaiian dime was struck at the San Francisco Mint, and carries the same standard as U.S. dimes. Population: 18 in 65, 11 finer (1/10). (#10979)

914 **1883 Hawaii Quarter MS66 PCGS. CAC.** Dappled green-gold, blue, and violet hues drape the gleaming surfaces of this sharply struck Premium Gem. Uncommonly flashy for this Kalakaua issue. (#10987)

915 **1883 Hawaii Half Dollar MS61 NGC.** Struck at the San Francisco Mint, the 1883 Hawaiian silver coins were produced at the same standard as the U.S. silver coins of the time, utilizing existing planchets. This pleasing Mint State piece is sharply defined with frosty silver luster and splashes of iridescent toning. (#10991)

916 **1883 Hawaii Half Dollar MS63 PCGS.** Whispers of golden-tan patina visit the obverse of this Select half dollar, joined by blushes of sky-blue, lavender, and olive-gray on the reverse. Lustrous and sharply struck with clean surfaces aside from a small curved granular streak near OF.(#10991)

Toned, Near-Gem 1883 Hawaiian Half Seldom Seen in Such High Grade

917 **1883 Hawaii Half Dollar MS64 PCGS.** A deeply toned hapalua with bold design elements and excellent luster, all combining to create incredible aesthetic appeal. This desirable piece, like all 1883 Hawaiian silver coins, was struck at the San Francisco Mint, using planchets of U.S. coinage standards. Population: 55 in 64, 12 finer (12/09). (#10991)

Challenging Choice 1883 Hawaii Half

918 **1883 Hawaii Half Dollar MS64 PCGS.** The 1883 Hawaii quarter is plentiful in Mint State, undoubtedly due to a since-distributed hoard. However, its half dollar counterpart is rare at the MS64 level, yet remains affordable despite its status as a one-year type. Lustrous and boldly struck with lovely golden-brown, lime-green, and cream-gray toning. Distributed unimportant obverse contact fails to affect the considerable eye appeal. Population: 55 in 64, 12 finer (1/10). (#10991)

Lovely 1883 Hawaiian Dollar, MS63

919 **1883 Hawaii Dollar MS63 PCGS. CAC.** This gorgeous Hawaiian dollar has blue, violet, and gray toning over satiny surfaces. The reverse is slightly lighter than the obverse of this important piece. Hawaiian dollars are difficult to locate in higher Mint State grades, as the population data reveals. Population: 14 in 63, 34 finer (1/10). (#10995)

ERRORS

Undated Reverse Die Cap From Copper-Nickel Cent, MS64

920 **Undated Copper-Nickel Indian Cent—Reverse Die Cap—MS64 PCGS.** The combination of a copper-nickel planchet and an oak-wreath-with-shield design suggest an origin between 1860 and 1864. The cap, though shallow in depth, offers impressive distortion on the "inner" face, with the backwards ONE CENT impressively broadened and flattened. An intriguing 19th century error.

921 **1864 Copper-Nickel Indian Cent—Struck 15% Off Center—MS61 NGC.** Struck off center toward 5:30. All legends are intact, although the date is distorted, and there is a broad area of unstruck surface centered at 11:30. A few wispy marks are noted on the reverse exergue and below CENT. Satiny and luminous with light gold and ice-blue toning.

922 **Undated Indian Cent—Struck by Capped Die—XF45 ANACS.** The medium brown reverse has a normal appearance. The obverse, however, shows only a blurry raised indication of the Indian motif. Struck through a relatively late state obverse die cap, which is not included.

923 **Undated Indian Cent—Obverse Struck Through Capped Die—AU58 NGC. Eagle Eye Photo Seal, Card Included.** The reverse has a normal appearance, and is the Bold N subtype of 1870 to 1909. The obverse is featureless aside from a barely identifiable impression of Liberty in a headdress. A late-in-life die cap (not included) blocked the obverse die, but the cap was sufficiently thin that an indication of the design passed through.

25% Off Center Indian Cent, MS63 Brown On a Thin 1.13 Gram Planchet

924 **Undated Indian Cent—Struck 25% Off Center on a 1.13 Gram Planchet—MS63 Brown NGC. Eagle Eye Photo Seal, Card Included.** Struck widely off center toward 1 o'clock, relative to the reverse. The reverse is otherwise normal, and is the Bold N post-1870 subtype. The obverse displays a blurry, reversed, and incused impression of the reverse. Apparently, this wafer-thin planchet was fed off center into a coinage chamber along with a correctly centered second planchet (not included) that obstructed the obverse die.

925 **1907 Indian Cent—Struck Through Reverse Die Cap—AU50 NGC.** The NGC insert asserts the coin is "Uniface Reverse", but the reverse design is in fact vaguely present, although nearly featureless as it was struck through a later stage reverse die cap. A deep brown cent with light wear on the bust tip, forehead, and shoulder curl.

926 **1907 Indian Cent—Reverse Struck Through Capped Die—MS63 Brown NGC.** The chocolate-brown obverse is normal, but the reverse has only a blurry indication of the wreath, shield, and central legend. The reverse die was blocked by a late stage die cap (not included) that blunted detail from that die.

1945 Lincoln on Netherlands East Indies 1/2C Flan VF30 Details

927 **1945 Lincoln Cent—Struck on a Netherlands East Indies Half Cent Planchet—VF30 Details Damaged ANACS.** This pieces is smaller diameter than a Lincoln cent, and has olive-brown surfaces with some minor roughness and a scrape at the lower reverse. Unfortunately, ANACS failed to record the weight of this example on the holder, so the attribution is based solely on their holder.

1962 Lincoln Struck Through Die Cap, MS66 Red

928 **1962 Lincoln Cent—Obverse Struck Through Capped Die—MS66 Red NGC.** Both sides of this Premium Gem show fiery orange mint luster, slightly deeper on the reverse, with a few trivial flyspecks limiting the grade. The obverse is disfigured from the strike thru, while the reverse is fully and sharply defined. (#2878)

929 **1980 Lincoln Cent—Struck over a 1980-P Roosevelt Dime—MS64 NGC.** Sometimes called an 11 cent piece, this error type is extremely popular and highly elusive. Usually only when major error collections come out do these coins become available in the market place, where they remain for an extremely short time. Lustrous with pleasing champagne toning and darker accents.

Astounding 1999 Lincoln Cent Struck on a 1980-D Dime, MS66

930 **1999 Cent—Struck on a 1980-D Dime—MS66 NGC.** A remarkable double-denomination piece with 20 years between strikes! Not only is this a double-denomination, double-date piece, but it is also a dual Mint coin. The first strike occurred in Denver in 1980 and the second in Philadelphia in 1999! One might wonder how that could happen, but happen it did, and the result is an impressive and highly sought-after error. A gorgeous example with fully brilliant and highly lustrous nickel-gray surfaces.

Interesting Superb Gem Double Denomination 2000 Cent Struck on a 2000-P Dime

931 **2000 Lincoln Cent—Double Denomination, Struck on a 2000-P Dime—MS67 NGC.** Double denomination errors are seldom offered for sale and when they are collectors jump at the opportunity. An arc of hazel and deep red patina graces the margins of this "11 cents" error, while the centers are fully brilliant. The first three digits of the dime's date, as well as the mintmark and a significant amount of other undertype, are clearly visible above Lincoln's head. The only marks appear to be mint-made.

Desirable Superb Gem Double Denomination 2001 Cent Struck on a 2001-P Dime

932 **2001 Lincoln Cent—Double Denomination, Struck on a 2001-P Dime—MS67 NGC.** Heritage has offered only about a half-dozen of the popular double denomination errors in the past year. They are rarely seen in today's marketplace. The obverse of this Superb Gem "11 cents" error has a touch of tan patina, while the reverse exhibits soft blue and gold toning. While NGC ascribes a date to the dime undertype, the numerals are difficult to identify, even under magnification. An impeccably preserved example of this interesting error.

Remarkable Double Denomination, MS68 2001 Cent Struck on a 2001-P Dime

933 **2001 Lincoln Cent—Double Denomination, Struck on a 2001-P Dime—MS68 NGC.** With the usually strict quality control at the U.S. mints, it is quite rare to find modern double denominations. Collectors treasure these rare and interesting errors. An impressive amount of the dime's undertype is still visible, including the date. A touch of tan accents the mostly silver-gray surfaces. Both sides appear pristine, and the cent's details are boldly struck. The bust of Roosevelt is upside-down relative to Lincoln. A highly lustrous and appealing specimen.

1943-S Nickel Struck on a Silver Australian Sixpence Flan, AU58

934 **1943-S Jefferson Nickel—Struck on an Australian Sixpence Planchet—AU58 NGC.** 2.8 gm. The San Francisco Mint struck 4,000,000 silver sixpence for a war-isolated Australia (KM-38, 2.82 gm) in 1943. This wrong metal error is struck on a Type Two planchet with raised rims. Slightly uncentered toward 12 o'clock. The mintmark and date are bold. Lustrous and unmarked with no obvious signs of wear.

Choice AU Dime Reverse Die Cap With Brockage, New Orleans Origin

935 **Undated New Orleans Dime—Reverse Die Cap Brockage—AU55 PCGS.** The reverse design, with simple wreath of cereals and only lettering ONE DIME within and an 'O' mintmark below, indicates a New Orleans dime struck in 1860, 1891, or one of a string of Barber dime dates from 1892 to 1909. A shallow but distinctive die cap, richly toned blue and violet with considerable remaining luster, though modest wear is also present.

Curious Undated D-Mint Quarter Struck on a Silver Dime Planchet, MS63

936 **Undated, D-Mint Washington Quarter—Struck on a Silver Dime Planchet—MS63 PCGS.** There was obviously not an obverse die in place when the reverse quarter die struck a well-centered impression on a silver dime planchet. How a dime planchet was mixed in with the production of quarters is another story and one we do not have the answer to. The unstruck, wavy "obverse" is brilliant. The struck reverse side shows light golden toning. A curious striking error.

PR65 Cameo 1972-S Washington Quarter With Rotation Between Obverse Images

937 **1972-S Quarter—Double Struck With Obverse Rotation—PR65 Cameo NGC.** Both sides have watery reflectivity and moderate contrast beneath gold and royal-purple toning. While the reverse appears normal, the obverse die apparently rotated between strikings, resulting in a distinct "spread" is noted on both peripheral and central elements on that side.

1912-D Barber Half on a 1902 Half Dollar Fine 15 A Stunning and Likely Unique Mint Error

938 **1912-D Barber Half—Struck on a 1902 Half Dollar—Fine 15 NGC.** The host coin is a 1902 Barber half dollar, either from the Philadelphia or New Orleans Mint as just a suggestion of a possible previous mintmark is visible, and of course the Denver Mint was barely under construction in 1902 and didn't begin operation until 1906. The host coin then made its way to Denver, where it found its way into the coin press for Barber half dollars a decade later.

All four digits of the 1902 date are clearly visible, overlapping and slightly left of the 1912 date. Considerable additional detail is closely overlapping, appearing as a shift strike if the 1902 date wasn't present.

This is a stunning and almost certainly unique mint error with pleasing surfaces and natural light gray-tan color on both sides. All of LIBERTY is clearly visible, and all other detail is consistent with the assigned grade.

Near-Mint 1963-D Half Struck on a Quarter Dollar Flan

939 **1963-D Franklin Half—Struck on a Silver Quarter Planchet—AU58 PCGS.** Struck on a Type One quarter flan that never made it through the upset mill to raise the rim. LIBERTY is absent, as is most of HALF DOLLAR, but the date and mintmark are complete. This satiny example is unabraded aside from a brief scratch in the left obverse field. Both sides have blushes of peripheral gold and iridescent toning that add to the overall eye appeal of this piece.

940 **90% Silver Type One Dollar Blank AU58 PCGS.** The alloy is 90% silver, which corresponds to 1840 through 1935 U.S. silver dollars. This unstruck planchet is Type One, which indicates it never passed through the upset mill to raise the rims. The "obverse" has a few minute ticks, and the reverse has faint thin marks that appear similar to adjustment marks. Toned cream-gray to russet.

First-Year 1986 Silver American Eagle Struck Through Emery Circle

941 **1986 Silver Eagle—Reverse Struck Through Sanding Disk—MS68 NGC.** What NGC describes as a "sanding disk" is actually a circle of emery paper, used to prepare the Uncirculated versions of the silver American Eagles. Coins would be struck deliberately through the emery paper to impart texture to them. While those coins ordinarily would be condemned and melted, this error and its heavily textured reverse escaped to the outside world. Peripheral tan-orange and violet shadings add color to each side.

HARD TIMES TOKEN

942 **1837 Token MS62 NGC.** HT-73. The famous 1837 half-cent-sized token with legend HALF CENT WORTH OF PURE COPPER within and below the wreath on the reverse. A luminous violet-brown piece that apparently never circulated.(#109)

WASHINGTONIA

943 **1872-Dated George Washington 1/4 California Gold Charm MS65 NGC.** Baker-504A (1885 edition). This octagonal example has vibrant yellow-gold luster. The central fraction shows moderate striking weakness, as it is opposite the portrait of Washington.

944 **1872-Dated George Washington 1/2 California Gold Charm MS67 NGC.** Baker-505 (1885 edition). A flashy yellow-gold octagonal example that displays the expected slight softness of strike on the central reverse.

SO-CALLED DOLLAR

945 **(1897) Bickford Dollar, HK-835, MS67 NGC.** Aluminum with a brass center. Listed as "very rare" in the original Hibler-Kappen reference. New York City resident Dana Bickford traveled to Europe, where he had difficulty exchanging dollars into foreign currency. This experience led him to lobby the U.S. Mint to produce patterns, such as the famous Stellas of 1879 and 1880. He continued his cause in 1897 with a series of informational medals. Lustrous and immaculate with attractive gold and green toning on the brass center.

MISCELLANEOUS

946 **Nevada 50 State Quarters Coin and Die Set.** A die used strike Nevada quarters at the Denver Mint, serial number D6-063070, with die face planed off to prevent unauthorized restriking. Comes with a **2006-D Nevada quarter,** Mint State, near-brilliant, in Mint box of issue with certificate of authenticity.

947 **Nevada 50 State Quarters Coin and Die Set.** A die used strike Nevada quarters at the Denver Mint, serial number D6-063382, with die face planed off to prevent unauthorized restriking. Comes with a **2006-D Nevada quarter,** Mint State, a degree of golden toning, in Mint box of issue with certificate of authenticity.

948 **Nevada 50 State Quarters Coin and Die Set.** A die used strike Nevada quarters at the Philadelphia Mint, serial number P6-121962, with die face planed off to prevent unauthorized restriking. Comes with a **2006-P Nevada quarter,** Mint State, gold-orange toning at rims, in Mint box of issue with certificate of authenticity.

GSA DOLLARS

Capped Die VAM-3 1879-CC Dollar In Black GSA Holder, MS61

949 **1879-CC Capped Die MS61 NGC.** VAM-3. A Top 100 Variety. A strongly lustrous silver-gray example with considerable frostiness to the luster. Numerous tiny abrasions are present on the obverse, including at Liberty's cheek, though the reverse is comparatively clean. Band-certified in the black GSA holder of issue with box and certificate. (#7088)

950 **1882-CC GSA Hoard MS65 Deep Mirror Prooflike NGC.** A staggering 605,029 examples of the 1882-CC were in the GSA holdings and finally distributed in the 1970s. Most were low grade because of heavy abrasions. This is a lovely Gem that has extraordinarily deep fields on each side. The devices are heavily frosted and present strong contrast against the "blackness" of the fields. Fully struck. Band-certified in the original black GSA holder of issue. No box is included.(#97135)

951 **1885-CC MS65 NGC.** Light peach-gray patina visits strongly cartwheeled surfaces that offer a hint of frosty sparkle over the devices. This CC-mint Gem is band-certified in the black holder of issue with accompanying box and certificate.(#7160)

952 **1890-CC MS61 NGC.** An impressively lustrous and minimally toned example of this later Carson City Morgan dollar issue, minimally abraded save for a horizontal line of reed marks along the jaw. Band-certified in the holder of issue with box and certificate. (#7198)

End of Session Two

SESSION THREE

Floor, Telephone, Heritage Live!™, Internet, Fax, and Mail Signature® Auction #1137
Friday, February 5, 2010, 6:00 PM PT, Lots 953-1877
Long Beach, California

A 15% Buyer's Premium ($14 minimum) Will Be Added To All Lots

Visit HA.com to view full-color images and bid.

EARLY HALF DIMES

Popular 1795 Half Dime VF30, V-5, LM-8

953 **1795 VF30 ANACS.** V-5, LM-8, R.3. This variety, familiar to specialists, features a die crack through the 7 in the date and the Y in LIBERTY. Ocean-blue and sun-gold enrich the moderately abraded and slightly wavy surfaces. All legends are bold aside from the top of OF. Certified in an ANA cache holder. (#4251)

XF 1795 Flowing Hair Half Dime V-5, LM-8

954 **1795 XF40 NGC. CAC.** V-5, LM-8, R.3. The slender die crack from Liberty's nose through the Y in LIBERTY is familiar to specialists, but is not diagnostic, since V-6 shares the same obverse die and crack. This mark-free dove-gray half dime has pleasing detail and will satisfy type demand for most collectors. Struck from rotated dies. (#4251)

Attractive 1797 13 Stars Half Dime Rare V-1, LM-4 Variety, XF40

955 **1797 13 Stars XF40 PCGS.** V-1, LM-4, R.6. LM-4, the only die marriage with 13 stars, is the rarest 1797 half dime variety. PCGS and NGC combined have certified just 30 examples of this variety in all levels of preservation.

A medley of violet, reddish-gold, and mint-green patination bathes both sides of this lovely XF specimen, joined by an occasional splash of crimson on the obverse. Relatively strong, uniform definition is seen on the design elements. A minor planchet defect on Liberty's nose and one in the adjacent field do not detract. Population for LM-4: 4 in 40, 9 finer (12/09). (#4260)

Rare 13 Stars 1797 Half Dime Choice XF, V-1, LM-4

956 **1797 13 Stars XF45 PCGS.** V-1, LM-4, R.6. The rarest die marriage of the year, and also the only Valentine variety with 13 stars. Golden-brown, forest-green, and dove-gray blend across this minimally worn example. Two inconspicuous vertical abrasions are concealed within the hair, and the obverse field has a few faint thin marks. Population: 4 in 45, 5 finer (1/10). (#4260)

XF40 15 Stars 1797 Half Dime, V-2, LM-1

957 **1797 15 Stars XF40 PCGS.** V-2, LM-1, R.3. V-2 is the sole die pairing with 15 stars and thus receives a separate *Guide Book* listing. Principally toned in honey-gold and cherry-red, although portions of the reverse border are navy-blue. Well detailed and appealing, with minor inexactness of strike at the centers. Housed in a green label holder. (#4258)

Pleasing 1805 Half Dime, V-1, LM-1, AU58

958 **1805 AU58 PCGS.** V-1, LM-1, R.4. The 1805 half dime is an extremely scarce issue, with a reported mintage of 15,600 pieces produced from a single known die pairing. It is the last Heraldic Eagle Reverse issue, since the next striking of half dimes would not occur until 24 years later, of the Capped Bust design by Chief Engraver William Kneass. The Logan-McCloskey half dime reference (1998) indicates that the 1805 is "rare in grades above VF and almost never available in grades approaching Mint State."

The present near-Mint State offering is the finest grade one can expect to locate, as a single Mint State specimen has thus far been certified. A splash or two of violet visits the predominately soft olive-green obverse, while the two colors show about equal coverage on the reverse. A sharply struck and remarkably clean example. Population: 4 in 58, 0 finer (12/09). (#4272)

BUST HALF DIMES

959 **1830 MS64 PCGS.** V-10, LM-1, R.4. This unabraded and satiny Gem is richly patinated with a palette of forest-green, plum-red, and tan-gold. The centers show moderate incompleteness of strike, but the technical quality is exceptional.(#4277)

960 **1832 MS64 PCGS.** V-8, LM-5, R.1. A lustrous near-Gem example of this popular and available die pair, champagne-orange and silver-gray overall with pockets of deep blue at the reverse margins. Housed in a green label holder.(#4279)

961 **1832 MS64 PCGS. CAC.** V-1, LM-3, R.1. This Choice Mint State half dime is housed in a green-label PCGS holder. It features frosty luster beneath ivory patina with steel-blue, lilac, and green-gold toning.(#4279)

MS65 1832 Half Dime, V-8, LM-5

962 **1832 MS65 NGC.** V-8, LM-5, R.1. An unworn example of this available Bust half dime die pair, strongly struck and impressively lustrous beneath rich blue-green and violet patina. Minimally marked overall, though an old pinscratch (since toned-over) is visible in the field above and to the right of Liberty's cap. (#4279)

963 **1835 Large Date, Large 5C MS64 Prooflike NGC. CAC.** V-2, LM-1, R-2. There is a thick die crack with lumps along the top of the scroll below ITE, the right (facing) wing of the eagle shows a heavy die crack which extends down its length, and additional spidery breaks are found on many of the reverse lettering and devices, all of which are typical of the variety. Hints of barely discernible light tan show at the margins and well struck design features are highlighted by the Prooflike fields. A minute rim ding is noted at 9:00 on the obverse. One of only two Prooflike examples graded by NGC (1/10).(#4282)

Gem 1835 Half Dime, V-3, LM-3
Large Date and 5C

964 **1835 Large Date, Large 5C MS65 NGC.** V-3, LM-3, R.1. This lustrous high grade Capped Bust type coin displays sea-green and plum-mauve shades throughout the peripheries. The devices and fields are predominantly pearl-gray. Crisply struck and minimally abraded. Struck from clashed dies that exhibit several fine cracks. (#4282)

965 **1837 Large 5C PCGS Genuine.** V-5, LM-3, R.6. The PCGS number ending in .GN suggests an unknown reason why PCGS deemed this coin not gradable. In our opinion, this coin has the details of a VG specimen that has a repair and environmental damage. Although evenly micro-granular, this example displays most letters in E PLURIBUS UNUM, and the letters in LIBERTY are faintly evident when inspected beneath a loupe. Repaired left of the 5C, with a flattened appearance opposite on star 7. A hair-thin diagonal line on the bust, probably a lamination, is barely worthy of mention.(#4289)

966 **1837 Large 5C VF20 PCGS.** V-5, LM-3, R.6. The rarest Logan-McCloskey 1836 variety, distinguished by a recut C in AMERICA and a low 3 in the date. The walnut-brown surfaces appear unblemished. All legends are bold, and most star centrils are visible. Softly impressed near the left border of the shield. (#4289)

SEATED HALF DIMES

Splendid MS66 1837 Seated Half Dime
Large Date, No Stars

967 **1837 No Stars, Large Date (Curl Top 1) MS66 NGC.** Honey-gold and ivory-gray cede to deeper forest-green and plum-red near the rims. A satiny and crisply struck Premium Gem with nary an indication of abrasions. The first year of the Seated half dime, and the only year that the No Stars subtype was coined at Philadelphia. (#4311)

968 **1838 Large Stars, No Drapery MS65 PCGS.** Lustrous and unabraded with medium olive and golden-russet toning. Sharply struck save for the leaf near the H in HALF. The lower reverse has a few trivial flecks. Population: 52 in 65, 24 finer (12/09). (#4317)

969 **1841-O MS63 PCGS.** Medium O. This lovely half dime has frosty silver luster with light champagne toning on both sides. Heavy clash marks on each side add to its overall desirability. Here is an excellent opportunity for the advanced collector that knows the difficulty of the issue. Population: 3 in 63, 6 finer (1/10). (#4329)

970 **1844-O XF40 PCGS. CAC.** Small O. Two mintmark sizes are known despite a low New Orleans mintage of 220,000 pieces. Light gold and lilac toning visits this well defined and moderately abraded half dime. Struck with close to medal turn, and certified in a green label holder. Population: 3 in 40, 25 finer (12/09). (#4334)

Appealing 1847 Half Dime, MS66

971 **1847 MS66 PCGS. CAC.** Soft violet, mauve, orange, and sky-blue patina resides on the lustrous surfaces of this Premium Gem. A solid uniform strike adds to the coin's pleasing eye appeal, as do the well preserved surfaces. An inoffensive hair-thin mark on Liberty's cheek is mentioned for complete accuracy. Population: 15 in 66, 2 finer (12/09). (#4337)

Well Struck 1848-O Half Dime, MS66

972 **1848-O MS66 NGC.** Large O. Greenish-gold and orange peripheral toning is joined by splashes of reddish-gold on the reverse margins. The design elements are sharply struck except for minor weakness in the leaf ribbing of the upper left wreath. Both sides have been well cared for. A minute mark on Liberty's jaw might help to identify the coin. Census: 17 in 66, 3 finer (12/09). (#4340)

973 **1851 MS65 PCGS. CAC.** Freckles of light tan-gold run over both sides of this well struck Gem, and partially prooflike fields yield modest variance with the devices. Housed in a green label holder. Population: 11 in 65, 17 finer (12/09).(#4347)

974 **1853 Arrows MS66 NGC.** Lustrous white surfaces display just the slightest hint of gold color on the obverse. Sharply struck and lacking any noticeable marks. The surfaces show significant evidence of metal flow from well-worn dies. Census: 52 in 66, 19 finer (1/10).(#4356)

Delicately Patinated 1858 Half Dime, MS67

975 **1858 MS67 PCGS.** Mint-green, orange, gray, orange-tan, crimson, and sky-blue toning covers the lustrous surfaces of this Superb Gem. The design elements are sharply struck except for Liberty's head. Light clash marks are visible on each side but post-strike impairments are lacking. Population: 11 in 67, 1 finer (1/10). (#4367)

Superb Gem 1860 Half Dime
First Year of the Legend Obverse

976 **1860 MS67 NGC.** First year of the new Legend Obverse design and a highly collectible coin as such. Both sides of this piece show evidence of die striations, which usually imparts reflectivity, and indeed here the fields are brighter than the devices. The centers are generally free from toning, while the margins display deeper gray-russet and sea-green patina. The design elements are fully stuck in all areas. Census: 22 in 67, 7 finer (1/10). (#4377)

977 **1862 MS66 NGC.** Beige-gray peripheral patination frames aqua-blue and lilac centers. Lustrous surfaces are well preserved and exhibit sharply impressed design elements. This is a highly pleasing Civil War-era half dime. Census: 39 in 66, 24 finer (12/09). (#4381)

Key Date 1864 Half Dime, MS67

978 **1864 MS67 PCGS.** The 1864 is one of the key dates of the Seated half dime series. Al Blythe (1992) writes that the reported mintage of 48,000 business strikes is "highly suspect." In any event, fewer than 100 survivors are estimated to exist in all grades. Hints of light peripheral tan color adhere to the highly lustrous, well preserved surfaces of this Superb Gem. Well struck except for weakness in the upper left wreath. Both sides are moderately clash marked. Population: 2 in 67, 0 finer (12/09). (#4384)

979 **1868 MS64 PCGS. CAC.** A coruscating near-Gem that provides light autumn-gold and slate toning. Marks are surprisingly scarce. An excellent opportunity to acquire a high quality example of this low mintage issue. Population: 11 in 64, 24 finer (1/10). (#4392)

980 **1871-S MS64 PCGS.** Light bluish-gray patination adorns this near-Gem S-mint half dime. This well struck piece displays soft luster emanating from minimally marked surfaces. Population: 26 in 64, 8 finer (1/10).(#4399)

981 **1872-S Mintmark Below Bow MS66 PCGS.** This boldly struck Premium Gem displays a melange of low intensity violet, ice-blue, and gold patination that assumes slightly deeper shades on the reverse. Highly lustrous surfaces are nicely preserved. More difficult than the "Above Wreath" variety. Population: 42 in 66, 8 finer (1/10).(#4401)

PROOF SEATED HALF DIMES

982 **1859 PR63 PCGS.** The 800 proof half dimes of 1859 were part of the first silver proof set year to have production exceeding 500 units. This Select proof has strong mirrors beneath light mauve and silver-gray patina. A contact mark is visible in the right obverse field.(#4438)

983 **1863 PR64 Cameo PCGS.** The obverse is lightly toned in violet, purple, and gold, leaving the reverse essentially untoned. Heavy die polish lines are visible in the fields, especially those of the reverse. Frosty devices exhibit strong definition. Population: 8 in 64 Cameo, 7 finer (1/10).(#84446)

Wonderful 1864 PR65 Ultra Cameo Half Dime

984 **1864 PR65 Ultra Cameo NGC.** Surviving 1864 proof half dimes are much scarcer than the 470-piece mintage might suggest. Moreover, Cameos are highly elusive, especially those in the Ultra/Deep category. Indeed, this Gem is tied for one of only two Ultras certified by NGC. Untoned surfaces are sharply struck and impeccably preserved. A small planchet defect in the rock is visible above the 4 in the date. (#94447)

985 **1868 PR65 NGC.** Deep shades of blue and iridescent toning enhance the eye appeal of this elusive Gem proof. Both sides are sharply struck. The obverse has mirrored fields around frosty devices, while the reverse has a satiny look. Census: 24 in 65, 20 finer (1/10).(#4451)

986 **1868 PR66 NGC. CAC.** A gorgeous Premium Gem proof with splashes of gold, turquoise, and iridescent toning on both sides. The fields are fully mirrored around lustrous devices, creating an excellent cameo appearance, though this is unreflected on the holder. Census: 15 in 66, 4 finer (10/09).(#4451)

EARLY DIMES

Pleasing 1796 JR-6 Dime, Good 4

987 **1796 Good 4 PCGS.** JR-6, R.3. The obverse has the diagnostic die break through the date. A pleasing light to medium gray example of the popular first-year dime produced at the young Philadelphia Mint. This piece has light surface roughness, but all of the design motifs are fully defined. (#4461)

Impressive 1796 Dime, JR-6, MS64 ★ Prooflike
Ex: Ed Price Collection

988 **1796 MS64 ★ Prooflike NGC.** Ex: Ed Price Collection. JR-6, R.3. There are two key diagnostics for this variety: all of the letters in LIBERTY are separated, and there is a thick die crack that extends horizontally through the 17 in the date. In this later state of the dies, the crack lengthens from the rim along the left side of 9, upward onto Liberty's neck, through the hair and the upper left obverse field to star 8. On the reverse, another prominent crack appears along the rim near 10 o'clock, angling diagonally downward between ST in STATES, through the left branch to the top of the eagle's left (facing) wing, across the right wing and branch to the left side of M, then to the rim.

According to the John Reich Collectors Society reference work on early U.S. dimes (1984), there were 10,244 examples of this die marriage produced: 3,864 pieces on February 28, 1797, and 6,380 coins on March 21, 1797. These JR-6 examples were struck in addition to the 22,135 pieces that constitute the official mintage figure for 1796-dated dimes, pushing the actual mintage number to 32,359 coins (this information is credited to researcher Robert P. Hilt II, among others). The authors estimate, further, that representatives of the JR-6 variety account for approximately 30% of all 1796 dimes extant.

This near-Gem is in a much better state of preservation than the usual survivors, which tend to appear in grades ranging from Good to Very Fine, and are often impaired by improper cleaning or other problems. Lovely electric-turquoise toning occurs near the peripheries, mingling with gold, rose, and violet iridescence. The design elements are sharply struck, save for typical softness on the eagle, and there are no readily visible marks or blemishes on either side of this impressive specimen. This is the only JR-6 graded with a Star designation and certified as Prooflike (12/09). (#4461)

Challenging 13 Stars 1797 Dime JR-2, VF25

989 **1797 13 Stars VF25 PCGS.** JR-2, R.4. Vividly toned in fire-red, lavender, and aquamarine shades. Liberty's cheek and shoulder exhibit wear, but the hair and wing plumage are well detailed, and consequential marks are absent. Housed in a green label holder. Population: 3 in 25, 38 finer (12/09). (#4463)

990 **1807 VF25 PCGS. CAC.** JR-1, R.2. A pleasing mid-grade example of the Draped Bust, Heraldic Eagle design, this 1807 dime has natural medium gray surfaces with lighter ivory on the high points. A few faint scratches and other microscopic blemishes are consistent with the grade.(#4480)

BUST DIMES

Gem 1825 Dime, JR-3

991 **1825 MS65 NGC.** JR-3, R.3. The obverse is appreciably clashed and cracked through the lower obverse, while the reverse shows bold recutting on the A in STATES, the most prominent diagnostic for the side. This Gem example is brightly lustrous with pale silver surfaces. A degree of striking softness is visible through the stars to the left of Liberty's cap and in the shield area on the reverse, but the rest of the coin is relatively well-defined. For coins not specifically attributed, Census: 7 in 65, 2 finer (12/09). (#4503)

JR-7 1834 Small 4 Dime, MS66

992 **1834 Small 4 MS66 NGC.** JR-7, R.2. The sole Small 4 die pair for the year, distinguished by the long, undamaged serif on the rightmost digit of the date. A colorful and lustrous coin with green and blue-violet outer toning and plum and tan patina at the interiors, with the obverse showing a loosely concentric pattern. Census: 5 in 66, 7 finer (1/10). (#4525)

SEATED DIMES

993 **1838-O No Stars AU50 PCGS.** Soft bluish-gray and champagne patina resides on the surfaces of this well defined O-mint representative. Minor obverse rim bruises occur at 4:00 and 10:00 and a couple of light scrapes are located in the lower right reverse quadrant.(#4564)

Sharply Struck 1839 No Drapery Gem Dime

994 **1839 No Drapery MS65 NGC.** The No Drapery dime, with stars on the obverse, was only produced from 1838 through 1839, and during part of 1840, making this a desirable three-year type for collectors. This lustrous Gem features soft golden-gray patina and sharply struck design motifs. A couple of trivial marks are unimportant. Census: 26 in 65, 34 finer (1/10). (#4571)

Important 1853 Arrows Dime, MS66

995 **1853 Arrows MS66 NGC.** The Arrows edition of the 1853 dime, with its mintage of slightly over 12 million pieces, has long been popular with type enthusiasts. This Premium Gem example should find favor, with its light silver-white central luster and glints of gold and tan near the rims. Census: 42 in 66, 14 finer (1/10). (#4603)

996 **1857 MS65 NGC.** This fully brilliant Gem has satiny silver luster. The design definition is a trifle weak, rather common for the date. However, the surfaces and luster are first-rate. Census: 35 in 65, 13 finer (1/10).(#4614)

997 **1866 MS63 PCGS.** The semiprooflike fields of this Select example display relatively strong contrast with the frosty, well defined design elements. Whispers of light gray visit both sides, each of which reveals fewer marks than what might be expected for the designated grade. Population: 8 in 63, 15 finer (1/10).(#4643)

998 **1876 MS65 NGC. CAC.** Type One Reverse. Sky-blue, rose, and gold-beige patina runs over both sides of this Gem, and semiprooflike fields highlight the mildly frosted, sharply struck design elements. A shallow mark on Liberty's neck is well concealed in the toning. Great overall eye appeal. Census: 42 in 65, 28 finer (1/10).(#4679)

999 **1877 MS65 PCGS.** Type One Reverse. Fortin-107, his "Lazy" I variety. Housed in a green-label PCGS holder, this Gem 1877 dime has a prooflike obverse and a frosty reverse. The obverse is brilliant with subtle gold toning while the reverse is untoned, other than a few tiny brownish spots. Population: 14 in 65, 12 finer (1/10). (#4682)

Brilliant MS67 1879 Dime
Low Mintage of Only 14,000 Business Strikes

1000 **1879 MS67 NGC.** The 1879 dime has the lowest regular mintage in the entire run of Legend Obverse series, with only 14,000 pieces struck. This impressive example displays glowing, semiprooflike fields on each side. The surfaces are brilliant throughout, and the striking details are fully brought up. Exceptionally clean, as one would expect from an MS67. Census: 28 in 67, 3 finer (1/10). (#4687)

1001 **1882 MS66 NGC.** Greenish-gold patina concentrates at the obverse margins of this pleasing Premium Gem and is scattered over the reverse, where it is joined by tints of red-orange. Lustrous surfaces exhibit well struck devices save for minor softness in the hair atop Liberty's head. Devoid of mentionable marks. Census: 42 in 66, 28 finer (12/09).(#4690)

Amazing MS67 1884 Dime

1002 **1884 MS67 NGC.** A subtly lustrous, richly patinated Superb Gem representative of this later Seated dime issue, ideal for the toned type set. Green-gold elements prevail at the margins, while the centers have more blue-green patina as well as boldly defined devices. Census: 24 in 67, 5 finer (1/10). (#4692)

1003 **1888 MS65 PCGS.** Light golden-tan toning adorns this lustrous and nicely struck Gem. Essentially devoid of marks, and a desirable addition to a high grade 19th century type set. Certified in a green label holder. Population: 41 in 65, 24 finer (1/10).(#4700)

1004 **1891 MS66 PCGS.** Solidly struck with gorgeous blue-green, gold, and violet colors that are more extensive and deeper on the reverse. An attractive example of this high-mintage Seated dime issue, one always popular with type collectors.(#4706)

PROOF SEATED DIMES

1005 **1860 PR65 Cameo PCGS.** PCGS and NGC have certified approximately 300 of the 1,000 proof dimes minted in 1860 and have assigned the Cameo label to about 50 specimens. The virtually white surfaces of this Gem Cameo display profound contrast, along with exquisitely struck design elements. Both sides lack mentionable marks. Population: 3 in 65 Cameo, 6 finer (12/09). (#84753)

Elegant PR66 Cameo 1864 Dime

1006 **1864 PR66 Cameo PCGS.** Bold champagne and orange hues take on additional rose elements at the lower and left reverse. Prominently mirrored and carefully preserved with charming contrast, thanks to light to medium frost over the devices. This Civil War-era date is hard to find in such a high grade. Population: 6 in 66 Cameo, 2 finer (1/10). (#84757)

1007 **1869 PR65 PCGS. CAC.** Attractive chestnut-gold, electric-blue, and lime-green toning drape this nicely mirrored Gem. The strike is precise aside from a few cereal grains on the upper left portion of the wreath, and the surfaces are exemplary apart from a faint graze beneath DIME. Population: 19 in 65, 3 finer (12/09).(#4762)

1008 **1873 No Arrows, Closed 3 PR64 NGC.** A sharply struck and detraction-free Choice proof. Mostly brilliant, although glimpses of sun-gold and cobalt-blue visit the upper reverse periphery. Census: 46 in 64, 37 finer (1/10).(#4766)

1009 **1873 Closed 3, No Arrows PR66 Cameo NGC.** Close to an Ultra Cameo designation, since the frost is thick throughout the devices, and the field exhibit pleasing reflectivity. An intricately struck Gem that has peripheral indications of russet-gold patina. Census: 3 in 66 Cameo, 3 finer (1/10).(#84766)

Iridescent 1873 Arrows Dime, PR66

1010 **1873 Arrows PR66 NGC.** The 1873 Arrows dime is the first of a two-year modification to the Legend obverse design, and it is highly desired by type collectors. This Premium Gem has excellent contrast beneath pale gold and iridescent toning. Census: 8 in 66, 3 finer (1/10). (#4769)

1011 **1875 PR66 Cameo NGC.** Bright silver-white centers present a bold cameo effect, while rich champagne and violet peripheral tints offer contrast of their own. Carefully preserved and gorgeous. Census: 13 in 66 Cameo, 4 finer (12/09).(#84772)

1012 **1881 PR65 PCGS.** A stunning Gem with original blue and iridescent toning over fully mirrored fields. Brighter surfaces would probably allow for a cameo designation, although we like this piece just the way it is. Population: 48 in 65, 14 finer (1/10). (#4778)

Attractive 1885 Dime, PR67

1013 **1885 PR67 NGC. CAC.** Attractive cobalt-blue, yellow-gold, and lavender patination runs over both sides of this Superb Gem proof, and a well executed strike imparts strong definition to the design elements, save for the typical minor weakness in the upper left wreath. Exquisitely preserved and exhibiting a degree of field-motif contrast. Census: 12 in 67, 3 finer (12/09). (#4782)

1014 **1885 PR65 Cameo NGC.** Cobalt-blue, lavender, and gold-orange toning resides on the borders of this Gem proof and the sharply struck, frosted design motifs are highlighted by the mirrored fields. Devoid of mentionable handling marks.(#84782)

Pleasing 1885 Dime, PR67 Cameo

1015 **1885 PR67 Cameo NGC.** An essentially untoned Superb Gem proof with notable field-motif contrast, confirming the Cameo designation. Well struck, including most of Liberty's head, an area that is generally weak; minor softness is noted on the upper left wreath. Carefully preserved throughout. Census: 28 in 67 Cameo, 5 finer (12/09). (#84782)

Magnificent PR68 ★ Cameo 1885 Dime

1016 **1885 PR68 ★ Cameo NGC.** The PR68 ★ Cameo grade says much about this coin, which combines splendidly contrasting, pristine silver-white surfaces with tremendous eye appeal. The strike is somewhat blunt on Liberty's head and foot. The only identifying mark for pedigree purposes is a small threadlike strike-through projecting into the field from the left bottom serif of the 1 in the date. Census: 1 in 68 ★ Cameo, none finer (1/10). (#84782)

1017 **1888 PR66 Cameo NGC.** Starkly contrasting devices and fields make this a wonderful example of this popular, late-date Seated dime. The surfaces are mostly brilliant but there is a slight accent of golden patina also present.(#84785)

Stunning 1889 Dime, PR66 Cameo

1018 **1889 PR66 Cameo NGC.** Faint traces of champagne toning grace the surfaces of this boldly defined Premium Gem Cameo proof. Both sides have exceptionally deep mirrors around satiny devices. This is a stunning piece with only a few equals. Census: 6 in 66 Cameo, 5 finer (1/10). (#84786)

1019 **1891 PR65 Cameo NGC.** Purplish toning with orange accents takes on slightly deeper hues on the obverse of this lovely Gem Proof. Strong definition characterizes the design features, all of which are highlighted by the mirrored fields. Exquisitely preserved throughout. Census: 13 in 65 Cameo, 20 finer (1/10). (#84788)

BARBER DIMES

Richly Toned MS67 1892 Barber Dime

1020 **1892 MS67 NGC.** This first-year Superb Gem displays spectacular electric-blue, purple-red, and gold patina that occurs in a mottled fashion on both sides. Intense luster shimmers over the undisturbed surfaces, that reveal crisply made design features throughout. A beautiful and technically impressive Barber dime. Census: 22 in 67, 0 finer (1/10). (#4796)

1021 **1896 MS65 PCGS.** Soft golden-tan patination adheres to the lustrous surfaces of this sharply struck Barber dime. A handful of minuscule obverse marks are concealed within the toning. Population: 15 in 65, 10 finer (12/09).(#4809)

1022 **1897 MS66 NGC.** Attractive luster endows this sharply struck Premium Gem. Well preserved surfaces exhibit distributed freckles of light gray. Census: 25 in 66, 6 finer (12/09).(#4812)

1023 **1902-S MS64 PCGS.** Silver-white surfaces have been in receipt of a decisive strike and display pleasing luster. Minute marks on Liberty's portrait limit the grade. Population: 15 in 64, 17 finer (1/10).(#4829)

Outstanding 1903-O Dime, MS66

1024 **1903-O MS66 PCGS. CAC.** An impressive Premium Gem example of the high-mintage 1903-O Barber dime, a condition rarity seldom found in Gem condition. Nearly all of the more than 8 million coins minted were released to circulation. This splendid Premium Gem is fully lustrous, with brilliant surfaces beneath ivory and iridescent toning. Population: 4 in 66, 0 finer (1/10). (#4831)

Well Struck 1905-O Dime, MS66

1025 **1905-O MS66 PCGS. CAC.** This New Orleans issue is seldom seen in the better levels of Mint State, and when located is often weakly struck. A better-than-average strike characterizes this lustrous, well cared-for Premium Gem. Hints of sea-green and golden-beige patina rest on each side. Population: 16 in 66, 6 finer (12/09). (#4836)

1026 **1907-D MS65 PCGS.** Deep forest-green and golden-brown toning embraces this satiny and razor-sharp Gem. Devoid of contact, and among the nicest survivors of this early Denver Mint issue. Population: 6 in 65 Cameo, 7 finer (12/09).(#4843)

1027 **1908-O MS65 PCGS. CAC.** Bold green-gold and orange colors are present at parts of the rims. The obverse has a violet-gray center, while the reverse shows paler silver. Population: 24 in 65, 11 finer (12/09).(#4848)

1028 **1909-S MS64 PCGS.** A beautiful Choice piece that has strong, pleasing luster on each side. Light gold patination occupies the obverse, leaving the reverse untoned. Localized weakness is noted on the design elements. Faint slide marks are visible on the obverse portrait. Population: 17 in 64, 13 finer (12/09).(#4853)

Surprisingly Scarce 1914-S Dime, MS66

1029 **1914-S MS66 PCGS.** This better date S-mint had a mintage of only 2.1 million pieces. In spite of its late date, few examples were set aside in high grade. This piece shows the bright, thick mint luster that one would expect from a San Francisco product. The surfaces are brilliant except for a few tiny specks of russet and charcoal on each side. Well, but not completely struck up. Population: 11 in 66, 1 finer (1/10). (#4867)

PROOF BARBER DIMES

Sharp 1893 Ten Cent, PR67

1030 **1893 PR67 NGC. CAC.** Medium intensity cobalt-blue toning bathes the obverse of this Superb Gem proof, while champagne-gold patina in the reverse center is flanked by purple and gold-brown at the periphery. Relatively strong field-motif contrast shows on both sides when the coin is rotated slightly under a light source. A solid strike brings out strong definition on all of the design elements. Well preserved throughout. Census: 18 in 67, 7 finer (12/09). (#4877)

1031 **1895 PR64 PCGS.** The 1895 proof Barber dime is popular on a couple counts. First is its association with the 1895 proof Morgan dollars, a premier 19th century railroad. Second is the associated rarity of business strikes that are seldom encountered. Both sides of this beauty have mirrored fields masked by deep blue and iridescent toning.(#4879)

1032 **1897 PR65 PCGS. CAC.** This stunning Gem proof has considerable cameo contrast hidden beneath the iridescent toning on each side. The fields are fully and visibly mirrored with full gold, lilac, and blue-green toning. Population: 44 in 65, 48 finer (12/09). (#4881)

1033 **1897 PR66 Cameo NGC.** Profoundly mirrored with stunning contrast. Light silver-gray color overall with green-gold at the right margins, as well as thin streaks of milky toning through the center of the reverse. Census: 18 in 66 Cameo, 22 finer (12/09). (#84881)

Seemingly Perfect PR68 1898 Barber Dime

1034 **1898 PR68 NGC.** The collector can expect a finer product, grade for grade, in any type coin dated 1898. This dime is a perfect example. The surfaces appear to be flawless. The fields are deeply reflective on each side and backlight the streaky, multicolored toning that is interspersed with occasional areas of original brilliance. Obviously original. There are only six other coins that have been so graded by NGC and none are finer (1/10). (#4882)

Brilliant 1898 Barber Dime, PR66 Cameo

1035 **1898 PR66 Cameo NGC.** An incredible Premium Gem Cameo proof with fully brilliant silver surfaces and no evidence of toning on either side. The deeply mirrored fields set off the frosty devices of this beauty, a borderline Ultra Cameo proof. Census: 16 in 66 Cameo, 27 finer (1/10). (#84882)

1036 **1909 PR66 PCGS.** Splashes of low intensity multicolored toning run over the well cared for surfaces of this Premium Gem. An exquisitely struck proof. Population: 24 in 66, 19 finer (1/10). (#4893)

Flashy Cameo PR66 1910 Barber Dime

1037 **1910 PR66 Cameo NGC.** A visually impressive type coin, the surfaces show deeply reflective mirrors on each side that contrast strongly against the frosted mint luster seen over the devices. There are no reportable contact marks on either side of this brilliant coin, just a tiny planchet flake toward the back of Liberty's neck. Only 551 proofs were minted of this date. Census: 4 in 66 Cameo, 8 finer (1/10). (#84894)

TWENTY CENT PIECES

1038 **1875-CC—Stained—NGC. Unc. Details.** This lightly toned Carson City type coin shimmers with luster, and is refreshingly unabraded. The strike is incomplete only on the lower left portion of the rock, and opposite on the top of the left (facing) wing. Hints of tan-gray toning appear mildly granular when viewed beneath a loupe.(#5297)

Appealing MS64 1875-CC Twenty Cent

1039 **1875-CC MS64 PCGS.** Subtle, swirling luster filters through rich orange, silver-blue, and umber-rose patina. This Carson City near-Gem is solidly struck and uncommonly well-preserved for that Mint's limited output of twenty cent pieces. PCGS has certified a mere 24 finer representatives (1/10). (#5297)

Gorgeous Gem 1875-S Twenty Cent

1040 **1875-S MS65 PCGS.** Pink, gold, and violet elements add to swirling luster with elements of frost and satin. Well struck overall and carefully preserved, an excellent Gem representative of this S-mint twenty cent issue long celebrated by type enthusiasts. PCGS has certified 60 finer examples (1/10). (#5298)

Toned Gem 1876 Twenty Cent Piece

1041 **1876 MS65 NGC.** The 1876 twenty cent comes from a low business strike mintage of 14,640 pieces. Concentric rings of violet, greenish-gold, electric-blue, and lavender patina adorn the lustrous surfaces of this Gem, and an exacting strike delivers strong definition to the design elements. Nicely preserved throughout. Census: 36 in 65, 21 finer (1/10). (#5299)

PROOF TWENTY CENT PIECES

Gem Cameo Proof 1875 Twenty Cent

1042 **1875 PR65 Cameo PCGS.** The twenty cent piece enjoyed a massive official proof mintage in 1875, the first year of the design. The 2,790 specimens struck account for well over half of the total mintage of twenty cent proofs in the Mint's record books. Of the survivors, surprisingly few combine the considerable cameo effect and careful surface preservation offered by this Gem. Moderately mirrored silver-white fields offer considerable contrast to the snowy devices. While a number of die-polish lines are present in the fields, post-striking flaws are minimal. Population: 5 in 65 Cameo, 2 finer (12/09). (#85303)

Appealing 1876 Twenty Cent, PR64

1043 **1876 PR64 NGC.** The proof mintage in this second year was less than half that of the debut 1875's production. A medley of aqua-blue, lavender, and yellow-orange toning bathes this near-Gem proof, and a solid strike imparts strong definition to the design features. Occasional fine hairlines are all that stand in the way of a finer numerical grade. Nevertheless, this coin exudes pleasing eye appeal. Housed in a former generation holder. Census: 70 in 64, 32 finer (12/09).
From The Stan Burger Collection, Part Two. (#5304)

Sharply Struck 1878 Twenty Cent, PR64 Cameo

1044 **1878 PR64 Cameo NGC.** Frosty, sharply struck devices appear to float over the deep watery fields of this near-Gem Cameo twenty cent piece. Whispers of grayish-tan adhere to the edges of some of the obverse design features, while hints of reddish-gold are noted on portions of the reverse. Some wispy handling marks limit the grade. Census: 15 in 64 Cameo, 20 finer (1/10). (#85306)

EARLY QUARTERS

Famous 1796 Quarter, B-1

1045 **1796 PCGS Genuine.** B-1, R.4. Tompkins Die State 3/3. The PCGS number ending in .98 suggests Damage as the reason, or perhaps one of the reasons, that PCGS deemed this coin not gradable. In our opinion, this coin has the details of an Fine specimen with reverse damage. The upper reverse has two small roundish digs, one between the ES in STATES and the other northwest of the O in OF. The second small dig may account for the flattened appearance of the obverse border at 5:30. A dove-gray example with minor granularity on the right obverse field. (#5310)

Scarce B-1 1804 Quarter, AG3

1046 **1804 AG3 PCGS. CAC.** B-1, R.3. Even in this coin's heavily worn state, the usual die scratch is visible between the two stars closest to the Y in LIBERTY. Slate-blue and medium-gray colors prevail, with the latter color in parts of the fields and on the devices. The lower reverse is nearly smooth, but the coin displays well. (#5312)

Original 1804 B-1 Quarter, AG3

1047 **1804 AG3 PCGS.** B-1, R.4. This entirely original quarter has the central motifs outlined but worn smooth, with the borders merged into the peripheral devices. Both sides have medium gray surfaces with darker steel patina. This is an important key date in the early quarter series, in demand regardless of its grade. (#5312)

Collectible 1804 Quarter, B-1, Good 4

1048 **1804 Good 4 PCGS.** B-1, High R.3. The less rare of only two varieties for the year, B-1 has a die scratch between stars 8 and 9. Lavender-gray patina in the fields highlights the light gray devices. The lower reverse legends are partly worn into the rim. However, the shield lines are nearly fully separated and some plumage detail is visible. The portrait has a few wispy slide marks, but there are no unseemly contact marks. The 1804 is a key issue among the early U.S. quarter dollars, from a mintage of only 6,738 coins. Housed in a green label holder. (#5312)

1049 **1806 PCGS Genuine.** B-9, R.1. The PCGS number ending in .94 suggests Altered Surfaces as the reason, or perhaps one of the reasons, that PCGS deemed this coin not gradable. In our opinion, this coin has the details of an Uncirculated specimen that has altered surfaces. This partly lustrous Draped Bust quarter has almond-gold and cream-gray toning. Portions of the devices are softly brought up and display a mildly granular texture, which is also seen on a shallow strike-through near obverse star 3.(#5314)

BUST QUARTERS

Boldly Defined 1820 Large 0 Quarter, B-2, MS64

1050 **1820 Large 0 MS64 NGC.** B-2, R.2. Star 1 points to the second fold of drapery, and a die line connects the leaf point left of the lower berry to the rim. An exacting strike imparts bold delineation to the design elements and medium bluish-gray and golden-brown patina covers both sides. A shallow, scalloped mark is noted in the lower left obverse field. (#5329)

1051 **1825/4/3 VF25 PCGS. CAC.** B-2, R.1. An early die state with no obvious die cracks on the reverse, although the crack from the border to the left serif of the I in UNITED. This is the only common variety of 1825 quarter, the one most often chosen for type collections. This piece exhibits dark steel and medium gray patina in the fields with lighter gray devices.(#5336)

1052 **1825/4/3 AU50 PCGS. CAC.** B-2, R.2. The slightly more accessible 1825/4/3 die pair, distinguished by a reverse with denomination high within the exergue. Peach and violet peripheral tints give way to a luminous silver-gray center.(#5336)

1053 **1831 Small Letters XF45 PCGS.** B-3, R.5. A seldom encountered Browning variety that shares a reverse die with the far more common B-4. The obverse die was also used to produce the plentiful B-2. This is a richly detailed piece with deep peach-gold and steel-gray toning. The fields display subtle marks consistent with the grade.(#5348)

1054 **1831 Small Letters AU53 PCGS.** B-3, R.5. Dark dove-gray toning encompasses this well detailed and only lightly abraded Bust quarter. B-3 is the rarest of the four 1831 Small Letters Browning varieties, and most survivors are in well-worn grades.(#5348)

1055 **1835 VF30 PCGS. CAC.** B-8, High R.4. The rarest die pairing for the date. Star 13 touches the bust, and a die crack rises between the TE in STATES. Dusky cream-gray and olive-green toning embraces this minimally abraded and nicely defined Bust quarter. (#5354)

Elusive MS62 B-4 1836 Quarter

1056 **1836 MS62 PCGS.** B-4, R.4. Prominent bisecting die cracks on both sides make attribution an easy task. Beautifully toned with sea-green centers and rose-gold margins. Sharply struck and only lightly abraded. Luster fills the borders and devices. Population: 7 in 62, 16 finer (12/09). (#5355)

SEATED QUARTERS

1057 **1838 No Drapery XF40 PCGS. CAC.** In a green label holder. The first year of the Seated design on the quarter denomination, although the motif appeared on Gobrecht dollars two years prior. A richly detailed and lightly abraded XF example with blended olive-gray and tan-gold toning.(#5391)

1058 **1840-O No Drapery AU55 NGC.** Large O. The 8 in the date is lightly repunched. Lovely powder-blue and apricot-gold bands adorn the margins of this partly lustrous and sharply struck New Orleans quarter. Scarce this close to Mint State. Census: 9 in 55, 45 finer (1/10).(#5393)

1059 **1842 Large Date MS62 PCGS.** Deep cream-gray and sun-gold toning envelops this intricately struck low mintage quarter. Mildly prooflike, and marks are limited to trivial contact on the upper reverse field. Population: 6 in 62, 5 finer (12/09).(#5401)

Prized Small Date 1842-O Quarter, VF30

1060 **1842-O Small Date VF30 PCGS.** Briggs 1-A. Small Date dies saw only limited use for quarters in 1842; Philadelphia used them to strike proofs only, and New Orleans coined only a tiny fraction of the year's mintage with a Small Date obverse. This midrange example of the latter issue is richly toned with faintly luminous elements beneath the deep violet, slate-blue, and rose patina. Minimally marked and attractive. (#5403)

Sharply Struck 1845 Quarter, MS65

1061 **1845 MS65 NGC.** The 1845 quarter is scarce in near-Gem and rare any finer. Cobalt-blue and orange-gray patination takes on splashes of lavender and golden-orange on the reverse. A decisive strike sharpens the design features, and close inspection reveals no marks of consequence. Census: 5 in 65, 1 finer (1/10). (#5408)

Choice Mint State 1852 Quarter

1062 **1852 MS64 PCGS.** An early 1850s Seated quarter that has survived from before the weight reduction of 1853. These low mintage issues, in this case 177,060 coins, are rarities in higher Mint State grades. This lovely Choice Mint State example has satiny luster beneath gray, gold, and iridescent toning. Population: 10 in 64, 6 finer (12/09). (#5419)

'Huge O' 1854-O Quarter, Fine 15
A Popular, Hand-Engraved Variant

1063 **1854-O Huge O Fine 15 PCGS.** FS-501, formerly FS-004. The "Huge O" is immediately recognizable, and it is an immensely popular variety. The mintmark was obviously hand-cut, and crudely done. The obvious explanation is a non-mintmarked die was shipped to New Orleans and an O was added by hand engraving the mintmark directly into the die. This variety was not appreciated until recent years, the proof of which is in the lack of high grade survivors. This is an attractive coin for the grade with pale gray surfaces and deeper gray patina around the margins. Each side is evenly worn and the coin is well-balanced from side to side. (#5434)

XF Sharpness 1854-O Huge O Quarter

1064 **1854-O Huge O—Improperly Cleaned—NCS. XF Details.** FS-501, formerly FS-004. The famous Huge O *Guide Book* variety, with an oversized and irregular mintmark, misshapen to the point of being grotesque. While this minimally worn example was subjected to a past cleaning, the margins show slight retoning in gold with small zones of deep violet-crimson. (#5434)

Richly Toned MS65 1856 Quarter

1065 **1856 MS65 NGC.** Beautiful reddish-orange toning dominates each side, although the upper reverse also offers cream-gray and electric-blue. Luster shimmers across the minimally marked fields. Nicely struck overall, with blending of detail seen on the fletchings, hair, and upper stars. Encapsulated in a prior generation holder. Census: 12 in 65, 4 finer (12/09). (#5438)

Sharp 1861 Gem Quarter

1066 **1861 MS65 NGC.** Type Two Obverse and Type Two Reverse, with extra shield lines above E in LIBERTY and a convex eye on the eagle. Soft golden-tan peripheral color is slightly deeper on the reverse. Sharply struck and displaying frosty luster. A couple of grade-consistent field marks are noted on each side. Census: 31 in 65, 13 finer (1/10). (#5454)

1067 **1867-S VF20 ANACS.** The 1867-S quarter, from a mintage of 48,000 pieces, is very scarce in all grades. Larry Briggs (1991) assigns it a high R.5 rarity rating in F/VF. Light violet-gray, gold, and sky-blue patina covers both sides of this VF specimen. Appropriately defined, including full clarity in the letters of LIBERTY and IN GOD WE TRUST. An unobtrusive hair-thin mark in the right obverse field is in line with a piece having seen moderate circulation. Highly appealing overall.(#5471)

1068 **1872 MS63 NGC.** The 1872 is a scarce issue in the Seated quarter series from a mintage of only 182,000 coins. Mint State pieces are especially difficult to find, and seem to be quite underrated in the current market place. This lovely example has full design definition with frosty devices and reflective fields, displaying gorgeous iridescent toning. Census: 6 in 63, 8 finer (1/10).(#5481)

Amazingly Preserved MS68 1877 Quarter

1069 **1877 MS68 NGC.** Type Two Reverse. The 1877 is one of the more available dates in the With Motto series. However, at the MS68 level only a handful have survived from the mintage of 10.9 million pieces. This is an exceptionally attractive coin, as one would imagine from the grade. The surfaces are brilliant throughout and the luster glows with radiant mint frost. Perhaps there is an abrasion on this coin somewhere, but we could not find it. Just outstanding quality. Census: 7 in 68, 0 finer (1/10). (#5504)

1070 **1884 MS64 PCGS.** This satiny and boldly struck Choice quarter has medium to deep canary-gold and stone-gray toning. Surprisingly devoid of abrasions. Just 8,000 business strikes were issued. Population: 21 in 64, 39 finer (1/10).(#5516)

Low Mintage 1884 Quarter, MS65

1071 **1884 MS65 NGC.** Only 8,000 circulation strikes were produced in 1884. Because of the low output, when located the 1884 quarter is typically prooflike as the initial polish on the dies never had time to wear off. The prooflike fields on this piece are abundantly evident, even through the more extensive toning on the reverse. The rim on the obverse is deep russet-gray, while the reverse has irregular patches of blue and golden. Fully struck. Census: 10 in 65, 19 finer (1/10). (#5516)

Exemplary MS66 ★ 1888 Quarter

1072 **1888 MS66 ★ NGC.** Blushes of peach and aquamarine congregated near the borders of this lustrous and attractively preserved Premium Gem. The strike is precise save for the star centers. Only 10,000 pieces were struck, presumably due to continued large-scale production of silver dollars. Census: 2 in 66 ★, 3 finer with a Star designation (1/10). (#5520)

Final-Year 1891 Seated Quarter, MS66

1073 **1891 MS66 NGC.** After the decade of low-mintage quarters ended, the final year showed a substantial increase in production, with 3.9 million pieces struck. The mint luster on this example is bright and frosted, shining forcefully through the medium-density golden-rose and cobalt-blue toning. The striking details are sharp throughout. (#5524)

1891 Quarter, MS66
A Second High-Grade Example

1074 **1891 MS66 NGC.** This is a second impressive, high-grade 1891 quarter. Again, the surfaces display thick mint frost that is abundantly evident even through the medium-density iridescent toning. The peripheral stars show some softness, but the centers of each side are strongly struck. Light die clashing is seen in the fields on each side. Census: 32 in 66, 15 finer (1/10). (#5524)

PROOF SEATED QUARTERS

Important 1867 Seated Quarter, PR67 Cameo

1075 **1867 PR67 Cameo NGC.** Navy-blue and plum-red fills the margins, while the fields are light golden-brown and the device are only faintly toned. Exactingly struck with flashy mirrors and obvious frost across the major devices. A stingy 625 proofs were struck. Census: 3 in 67 Cameo, 0 finer (1/10). (#85566)

Sharply Struck 1873 Arrows Quarter, PR64

1076 **1873 Arrows PR64 PCGS.** This brilliant and sharply struck proof has nearly untoned surfaces. The fields are fully mirrored and the devices show a trace of mint frost that imparts light cameo contrast. The With Arrows coins were struck only in 1873 and 1874, and all offerings are popularly received by type collectors. Population: 32 in 64, 15 finer (1/10). (#5574)

1077 **1875 PR64 PCGS. CAC.** Type One Reverse. Splashes of cobalt-blue, lavender, and golden-tan coloration are deeper on the reverse of this near-Gem proof. Well struck minimally abraded surfaces exhibit a degree of field-motif variance, slightly more so on the obverse. Population: 34 in 64, 10 finer (1/10).(#5576)

1078 **1877 PR65 PCGS. CAC.** Type Two Reverse. A low-mintage proof date with only 510 pieces issued. The fields are bright and the mirrorlike effect is evident even through the blue and rose toning seen over each side. A lovely, high-end example.(#5578)

1079 **1878 PR64 NGC.** Orange-red, straw-gold, and ice-blue grace this flashy and precisely struck near-Gem. A mere 800 proofs were struck. Encased in a prior generation holder. Census: 51 in 64, 30 finer (1/10).(#5579)

1080 **1878 PR64 Cameo NGC.** Larry Briggs (1991) says of the 1878 quarter: "Proof issues were very sloppily made." This near-Gem Cameo is a pleasing exception. Its frosty, well struck design motifs are highlighted by reflective fields, and just a touch of nearly imperceptible gold color visits each side. Some wispy handling marks deny Gem classification. Census: 6 in 64 Cameo, 12 finer (12/09).(#85579)

1081 **1880 PR65 PCGS.** Type One Reverse. Medium intensity electric-blue, lavender, and golden-tan patina on the obverse cedes to bluish-purple on the reverse. The well struck design elements show some contrast against the semireflective fields. Housed in a green label holder.(#5581)

1082 **1881 PR63 Cameo NGC.** Field-motif contrast is somewhat stronger on the reverse of this well struck Select Cameo proof. Gunmetal-blue, lavender, and gold-orange patina occupies a large portion of the obverse but is confined to the rim areas on the reverse. Some faint wispy obverse field hairlines do not detract. (#85582)

1083 **1882 PR64 PCGS.** This era of low-mintage business strikes exerts added pressure on the proof issues. In 1882, the 1,100 proof quarters saw a complement of only 15,200 circulation coins that are rare in all levels of preservation. Splashes of bluish-violet and gold-orange visit each side of this near-Gem proof, each of which exhibits well struck devices that are highlighted at most angles by reflective fields.(#5583)

Beautifully Toned PR67 1882 Quarter

1084 **1882 PR67 NGC.** The 1882 quarter is one in a long line of low total-mintage issues that begin in 1879 and continue through 1889. This year had only 15,200 strikes for circulation plus 1,100 proofs. This impressive example has spectacular toning. The obverse has a rose-colored center surrounded by blue at the margin. The reverse, on the other hand, displays uniform blue-green toning. The fields are deeply reflective and the surfaces are problem-free, just as one would expect. Census: 15 in 67, 0 finer (1/10). (#5583)

Appealing 1883 Quarter, PR66

1085 **1883 PR66 NGC.** This Premium Gem proof is from an original mintage of just 1,039 pieces, a number of which have survived to the present day. Sharp definition is apparent on the frosty motifs that display good contrast with the mirrored fields. No significant marks detract from the coin's strong overall eye appeal. Census: 22 in 66, 20 finer (1/10). (#5584)

Amazing PR67 1885 Quarter

1086 **1885 PR67 NGC.** This Superb Gem is one of just 930 proofs struck alongside a limited Philadelphia-only issuance of business strikes. Bold green-gold peripheral hues cede rapidly to azure and violet, which dominate the broad centers. Magnificent visual appeal. Census: 13 in 67, 1 finer (1/10). (#5586)

1087 **1887 PR64 PCGS.** This brilliant proof exhibits undeniable cameo contrast, but is undesignated as such due to its older generation green label holder. The borders show moderate inexactness of strike. A scant 710 proofs were issued, and the associated business strike production was also low.(#5588)

BARBER QUARTERS

1088 **1894 MS66 NGC. CAC.** Whispers of golden-tan patination are joined by occasional accents of sky-blue at the margins. Vibrant luster issues from both sides, and a well executed strike emboldens the design elements, leaving no areas with even a hint of weakness. The surfaces reveal no mentionable contact marks, and a light fingerprint in the lower left obverse quadrant blends in nicely with the toning. Census: 5 in 66, 2 finer (1/10).(#5607)

Gorgeous 1896 Barber Quarter, MS66

1089 **1896 MS66 PCGS. CAC.** An absolutely stunning Premium Gem with rich green and iridescent toning over pearlescent surfaces. The design elements are sharp, and the underlying luster is frosty. This is fully original and highly attractive. Population: 5 in 66, 4 finer (1/10). (#5613)

1090 **1896-S Good 4 PCGS.** The Y and part of the T in LIBERTY remain visible on this Good example. Rich silver-gray color overall with elements of denim-blue. A great example of this popular key. (#5615)

1091 **1898 MS66 PCGS.** Golden-gray patina is joined on the obverse with electric-blue and lavender. A highly lustrous, sharply struck Premium Gem. Population: 18 in 66, 4 finer (1/10).(#5619)

Nearly Brilliant 1900-O Quarter, MS66

1092 **1900-O MS66 NGC.** Type Two Obverse, Type Two Reverse. The surfaces of this impressive piece are brilliant save for the lightest blushes of silver-tinged iridescence. Liberty's portrait is sufficiently sharp for an O-mint delivery of this type, although we note some striking incompleteness on a few of the obverse star centrils and the high points of the reverse eagle. Creamy mint frost overlies both sides, and no abrasions are out of context with the assigned grade. Census: 3 in 66, 3 finer (12/09). (#5626)

1093 **1902-S MS64 NGC.** Rich rose and violet shadings cover much of each side, though the obverse also shows blue accents and the right reverse has a wedge of golden-tan. Well struck and pleasing for a near-Gem. Census: 14 in 64, 15 finer (12/09).(#5633)

1094 **1908-S MS64 PCGS.** Mottled violet and steel-blue toning blankets each side. A sharply struck and smooth near-Gem that exhibits vigorous satin luster. A lower mintage issue of just 784,000 pieces. Population: 18 in 64, 18 finer (1/10).(#5652)

1095 **1913-S Good 6 PCGS. CAC.** Grayish-blue patina with hints of yellow-gold run over the surfaces of this key-date Barber representative. Full rims show some dentilation on the reverse. The LI and Y of LIBERTY show, as does PLURIBUS on the reverse ribbon. Both central devices display a modicum of internal detail, and the date and mintmark are sharp. A couple of linear abrasions are visible in the lower obverse field.(#5666)

Pleasing VG10 1913-S Quarter

1096 **1913-S VG10 PCGS.** This key date issue saw a mintage of only 40,000 pieces, with the majority of surviving examples falling into the AG to Fine grade range. The present Choice VG offering is ideal for a mid- or even better-grade Barber quarter collection. Its design detail stands out for the designated grade. The letters LI and Y of LIBERTY are sharp, as is the upper part of T. The jaw line, eye, and ear are strong, and the obverse rim is full and shows a few worn dentils. The reverse displays considerable dentilation, albeit worn, as expected. Several of the letters in E PLURIBUS UNUM are clear, as is a fair amount of the eagle's plumage, and the right, left, and bottom sides of the shield are completely separate from the eagle. Soft violet-gray and gold patina runs over both sides, each of which is remarkably clean for a coin having seen moderate to heavy circulation. This piece will elicit spirited bidding among Barber coinage specialists, and likely even from those non-specialists simply wanting a nice key date specimen for their collections. (#5666)

1097 **1915-D MS66 PCGS. CAC.** Flickers of peach patina add color to otherwise pale silver-gray surfaces. This charming Premium Gem hails from a now-popular but little-saved Denver issue. Population: 35 in 66, 2 finer (12/09).(#5671)

1098 **1916-D MS66 PCGS.** Traces of ice-blue and gold patina are visible on the lustrous surfaces of this Premium Gem. Sharply struck, save for the often-seen weakness on the upper right shield. (#5674)

1099 **1916-D MS66 PCGS. CAC.** A wonderful acquisition for collectors working on a last-year-of-issue type set, this 1916-D Barber quarter boasts splendid cartwheel luster over radiant silver-white surfaces that appear completely devoid of coloration. Under a loupe a couple of small die cracks appear on each side, signs of die fatigue. PCGS has certified six coins finer (1/10).(#5674)

PROOF BARBER QUARTERS

1100 **1896 PR65 PCGS.** Washes of turquoise and green-gold toning grace the gleaming fields and lightly frosted devices of this attractive Gem. Strong preservation and eye appeal. Population: 34 in 65, 45 finer (12/09).(#5682)

Lovely 1900 Barber Quarter, PR66

1101 **1900 PR66 PCGS. CAC.** Type One Obverse, Type Two Reverse. This piece absolutely qualifies as a cameo proof, despite the lack of any PCGS designation in that regard. Both sides are fully brilliant and untoned with deeply mirrored fields. The obverse motif is satiny and lustrous with obvious cameo contrast, while the reverse motif has heavier mint frost. Population: 22 in 66, 7 finer (1/10). (#5686)

1102 **1901 PR64 Cameo PCGS.** This near-Gem has excellent contrast between the lustrous devices and mirrored fields. Both sides are attractively toned in blue, violet, and gold, the reverse slightly darker. Population: 6 in 64 Cameo, 17 finer (1/10).(#85687)

Glittering PR68 Cameo 1901 Quarter

1103 **1901 PR68 Cameo NGC.** An impressively contrasted and even more impressively preserved specimen from a turn-of-the-century issue, this 1901 proof quarter comes from one of the last issues found routinely with such a strong cameo effect. Both sides are practically black-and-white with only the faintest suggestion of a golden cast. Census: 4 in 68 Cameo, 0 finer (1/10). (#85687)

1104 **1902 PR64 PCGS. CAC.** Splashes of sun-gold toning visit this nicely mirrored and precisely struck Choice specimen. The fields are unperturbed by hairlines, spots, or other visible flaws. One of just 777 proofs struck, and housed in a green label holder. (#5688)

1105 **1905 PR65 PCGS.** Cobalt-blue, lavender, and gold-tan toning graces this marvelous Gem proof, leaving the reverse center nearly untoned. Exquisitely struck, including the upper right corner of the shield, an area often weak. Very nicely preserved for the numerical grade. Population: 48 in 65, 40 finer (1/10).(#5691)

Beautifully Toned 1908 Quarter, PR66

1106 **1908 PR66 PCGS.** A lovely Premium Gem proof, this 1908 quarter has gold toning at the center, surrounded by lemon, blue, green, and violet iridescence. The design features are bold, and both sides show clear cameo contrast despite the lack of such a designation. Population: 14 in 66, 15 finer (1/10). (#5694)

Brilliant, Nearly Perfect PR68 Cameo 1911 Quarter

1107 **1911 PR68 Cameo NGC.** Exquisite and sure to delight high quality proof type collectors, this coin is devoid of even the slightest toning. As such, one can fully appreciate the awe-inspiring cameo contrast between the frosty textured devices and deeply mirrored fields. Pinpoint striking definition is noted throughout, and there ar no grade-limiting blemishes. Census: 12 in 68 Cameo, 2 finer (1/10). (#85697)

1108 **1913 PR65 PCGS.** Honey-gold, emerald-green, violet, and cobalt-blue alternate across this flashy Gem. Minor weakness is noted on the upper right shield corner. Undisturbed and attractively patinated. A meager 613 proofs were issued. Population: 28 in 65, 40 finer (12/09).(#5699)

EARLY HALF DOLLARS

1109 **1795 2 Leaves VG10 NGC.** O-119, R.4. A steel-gray early silver type coin with ample hints of autumn-gold throughout the borders. The right (facing) wing is well detailed, and no marks are consequential for the given grade.(#6052)

1110 **1795 2 Leaves VG10 PCGS.** O-117a, R.4. A radial obverse die crack at 5:30 confirms the Overton variety. Gunmetal-gray and light tan toning encompasses unblemished surfaces. A minor obverse rim ding appears at 1 o'clock, and wear is uneven on the upper right obverse margin and the lower right reverse border. (#6052)

1111 **1795 2 Leaves VG10 PCGS.** O-115, R.5. A slightly scarcer variety, this Flowing Hair half dollar has dark gray surfaces with lighter heather devices. It is an attractive piece for the grade with few unexpected blemishes for the grade.(#6052)

Very Fine Two Leaves 1795 Half
Difficult O-107a Marriage

1112 **1795 2 Leaves VF20 NGC.** O-107a, R.5. A prominent die crack bisects the reverse between 2:30 and 8:30. When viewed beneath a loupe, the cursive initials JB are visible on the upper right obverse field. Otherwise, this cream-gray and caramel-gold Flowing Hair half is surprisingly unmarked for the grade. A solitary adjustment mark, as made, crosses Liberty's chin. (#6052)

Pleasing VF20 1795 Half, O-117

1113 **1795 2 Leaves VF20 ANACS.** O-117, R.4. This Flowing Hair half has light golden-gray toning and an absence of consequential marks, aside from a small nick beneath the R in LIBERTY. Much design detail remains, although the eagle's breast and wingtips are worn. Certified in an ANACS cache holder. (#6052)

1114 **1795 2 Leaves—Repaired, Whizzed—ANACS. XF40 Details.** O-110, R.4. No repair is readily evident, but the surfaces are unnaturally bright and microgranular. Light tan toning adorns the moderately abraded fields. An important and coveted early silver type.(#6052)

Choice XF 1795 Flowing Hair Half Dollar
Two Leaves, O-104

1115 **1795 2 Leaves XF45 PCGS.** O-104, R.4. The 10x7 berry configuration identifies the reverse, while on the obverse, Liberty's looping curl comes close to star 1 but never touches it. As a Choice XF representative of a very scarce Flowing Hair half dollar die pair, this is a coin of interest to both type collectors and variety specialists. The surfaces are remarkably lustrous for an XF-range coin, particularly when one considers the peach, gold, blue-green, and violet patina over each side. Both sides have deeper peripheral colors yielding to light centers, with the contrast on the reverse more stark. Minimally marked and highly appealing, even if worn just past the AU level. (#6052)

1116 **1795 Small Head VG8 PCGS.** O-126, R.4. This elusive Flowing Hair subtype is represented only by Overton varieties 126 through 128. The dusky stone-gray fields and pearl-gray devices exhibit wear consistent with the grade, but there are no detracting marks. Population: 6 in 8, 21 finer (1/10).(#6054)

Scarce 1801 O-101 Half, VF20

1117 **1801 VF20 NGC. CAC.** O-101, R.3. The first year of issue for the Draped Bust, Heraldic Eagle design, and one of the scarce date in the short-lived series that continued only until 1807. This pleasing mid-grade coin has attractive gray-brown surfaces with only a few grade-consistent imperfections. (#6064)

1118 **1801—Improperly Cleaned—NGC. VF Details.** O-101, R.3. A granular rare date half dollar that has pitting on the portrait highpoints. The obverse field is cloudy from hairlines. Generally slate-white, but portions of both sides are gray where metal loss has occurred. Two scratches are noted, one on Liberty's neck and the other through the olive branch.(#6064)

1119 **1802—Improperly Cleaned—NGC. VF Details.** O-101, R.3. Sole die pair for the year and scarce regardless of grade. This midrange example is too bright for the moderate wear shown on the high points, though the silver-gray surfaces have lightly retoned emerald-green and blue.(#6065)

Attractive 1802 O-101 Half Dollar, VF25

1120 **1802 VF25 NGC. CAC.** O-101, R.3. A splendid, fully natural early half dollar with subtle lilac toning over the medium gray surfaces. The obverse has lighter tan on the central device. Here is a delightful middle-grade example of the scarce 1802 half dollar, surviving from a mintage of 29,890 coins. (#6065)

1121 **1803 Large 3 XF40 NGC.** O-103, R.3. Light silver-gray surfaces at the centers are framed by lovely iridescent toning on the obverse. The reverse is entirely untoned with traces of luster.(#6066)

Significant 1803 Small 3 Half Dollar AU50, O-104

1122 **1803 Small 3 AU50 NGC.** O-104, R.3. Deep cobalt-blue and mauve-gray toning is intermixed over each side, with some underlying brightness. Free from any relevant abrasions. The only Small 3 die marriage, and hence Overton-104 receives its own *Guide Book* listing. Census: 4 in 50, 7 finer (1/10). (#6067)

1123 **1805/4 VF30 NGC.** O-102, R.3. Three overdate varieties of the 1805/4 half dollars are known, and B. Max Mehl said that they were the closest anyone could come to owning an 1804 half dollar. Medium to dark gray fields have hints of pale blue toning, with lighter silver on the devices.(#6070)

Condition Census 1805/4 O-102 Half, AU58

1124 **1805/4 AU58 NGC.** O-102, R.3. The second scarcest of three 1805 over 4 overdate half dollars, this piece is a remarkable example with only a touch of rub on the high points of Liberty's cheek and hair on the obverse, and the eagle's wings on the reverse. The surfaces are light silver-gray with little toning, but substantial luster. NGC has certified a single MS65 example of the O-101 overdate variety, and three AU58 coins, including this piece, as the four finest of the overdate that they have encountered (1/10). (#6070)

1125 **1805 VF20 NGC.** O-112, R.2. All letters in E PLURIBUS UNUM are readable, and the lavender-gray surfaces are free from blemish. Considerable design detail is present. A pleasing VF Draped Bust type coin.(#6069)

1126 **1805 VF30 NGC.** O-104, R.5. A scarce and important die marriage. The present piece appears to have seen long-term storage in a cardboard album, as it now has concentric rings of iridescent toning, especially on the obverse.(#6069)

Desirable 1805 O-111 Half, XF45

1127 **1805 XF45 NGC.** O-111, R.2. This Normal Date variety has five berries in the branch on the reverse, while some other 1805 half dollars only have four berries. The *Guide Book* makes no distinction between those varieties, while they do in other series, such as 1805 dimes where there are both four and five berries varieties listed. This attractive piece has silver-gray surfaces with only a few minor imperfections. The surfaces retain ample traces of luster with only the faintest gold toning. (#6069)

O-102 1806/5 Half Dollar
A Scarcer Die Variety

1128 **1806/5 PCGS Genuine.** O-102, High R.3. The PCGS number ending in .91 suggests Questionable Color as the reason, or perhaps one of the reasons, that PCGS deemed this coin not gradable. In our opinion, this coin has the details of an AU specimen that has questionable color. The obverse features rich honey-gold, as does the reverse periphery. The crossbar of the 5 underdigit is apparent, and the radial die crack through the N in UNITED is diagnostic. The obverse field has scattered unimportant marks. The central reverse is softly impressed, although the remainder of the design is bold. Ample luster brightens protected regions. (#6077)

1129 **1806/5 VF30 ANACS.** O-103, R.2. The most available of the various 1806/5 overdate marriages. Moderately worn with contrast between the slate-blue of the fields and the lighter gray of the worn zones.(#6077)

1130 **1806/5 XF45 ANACS.** O-101, R.3. Three different overdate varieties are known from the single obverse die. On the O-101 die combination, the second T of STATES is boldly recut along its left upright. This Choice XF piece has considerable remaining luster beneath light gold and iridescent toning. It is a pleasing and attractive example.(#6077)

1131 **1806 Knobbed 6, Small Stars XF40 NGC.** O-106, R.4. One of just two Knobbed 6, Small Stars die pairs, slightly more available than the O-107 family but still very scarce. This XF example shows scattered light digs, but it remains luminous with sage and slate-blue patina overall.(#6075)

1132 **1806 Pointed 6, No Stem VF30 ANACS.** O-109, R.1. Sole die pair for the type. Pewter-gray and steel-blue surfaces offer considerable eye appeal for the grade.(#6073)

O-109 1806 Pointed 6, No Stem Half, AU

1133 **1806 Pointed 6, No Stem AU50 PCGS.** O-109, R.1. The sole Pointed 6 Obverse, No Stem Reverse die pair for the year. This still-lustrous AU example has a mixture of silver-turquoise, steel-blue, and olive-gold toning across most of each side. Modestly worn with abrasions generally light. For the variety, Population: 24 in 50, 65 finer (1/10).
From The South Texas Collection. (#6073)

1134 **1806 6 Over Inverted 6 VF30 PCGS.** O-111, R.3, with a cud primarily over the E in UNITED. Deep steel-gray patina graces this moderately circulated half. All letters in E PLURIBUS UNUM are clear. A good strike despite characteristic softness opposite the bust type. Population: 10 in 30, 28 finer (12/09).(#6078)

O-118a 1806 Pointed 6, Stem Half

1135 **1806 Pointed 6, Stem PCGS Genuine.** O-118a, R.3. The PCGS number ending in .94 suggests Altered Surfaces as the reason, or perhaps one of the reasons, that PCGS deemed this coin not gradable. In our opinion, this coin has the details of an AU58 specimen that has been cleaned. Luminous orange, silver-steel, and violet-blue colors linger over this minimally worn Bust half. There are few marks on either side, though a diagnostic die crack through the top of most of UNITED on the reverse does supply interest. (#6071)

1136 **1806 Pointed 6, Stem XF45 NGC.** O-115, R.1. The earlier die state without a crack through UNITED, although the dual crack through the first three obverse stars is present, as always. This Choice XF example has a convex reverse and a slightly concave obverse center. Marks are limited to a couple of faint abrasions on Liberty's neck.(#6071)

1137 **1806 Pointed 6, Stem XF45 NGC.** O-118, R.3. A pleasing Choice XF example, this half dollar has dark gray toning at the borders with attractive iridescent toning. Lighter gray appears on the design highpoints.(#6071)

1138 **1807 Draped Bust VF35 PCGS. CAC.** O-105, R.1. The leaf point that is normally below the I in AMERICA is entirely right of that letter on this variety. Both sides have attractive dark gray surfaces. Aside from a few marks in the left obverse field, the surfaces are consistent with the grade.(#6079)

Attractively Toned AU53 1807 Half, O-110a

1139 **1807 Draped Bust AU53 PCGS. CAC.** O-110a, R.3. Attractively toned powder-blue, sun-gold, and rose-red. Impressively void of abrasions, and the strike shows only moderate incompleteness limited to the stars near the beak and opposite on the curls above the shoulder. A partly lustrous representative of the final Draped Bust issue. (#6079)

O-102 1807 Draped Bust Half, AU55

1140 **1807 Draped Bust AU55 NGC.** O-102, R.2. Rich peach, rose, and violet overtones drape otherwise medium-gray surfaces. Remarkably lustrous despite the light wear present over the centers. As a Choice AU example from the last year of the Draped Bust design for half dollars, an excellent choice for the type enthusiast. (#6079)

BUST HALF DOLLARS

1141 **1807 Capped Bust, Small Stars VF30 PCGS.** O-113a, R.3. Distinguished by extensive die cracking on each side. On the obverse, most notably a crack from the end of the bust through all the stars on the left, another from the milling through the 0 in the date up to the drapery. On the reverse, several die cracks encircle most of the periphery on the left side. Golden-gray and violet patina covers both sides of this well defined half, each of which is remarkably clean.(#6087)

Toned 1809 O-102 Half, Certified MS62

1142 **1809 Normal Edge MS62 NGC.** O-102, R.1. Ocean-blue, ruby-red, and gunmetal-gray envelop this satiny early Capped Bust half. The eagle's left (facing) wing is softly defined near the shield, and a trio of light marks are noted on the cheek. Peripheral iridescent luster suggests the grade. Census: 24 in 62, 40 finer (1/10). (#6092)

1143 **1811 Small 8 AU50 PCGS.** O-110a, R.2. Luster brightens the borders, eagle, and cap of the present AU example. Peach-gold and ocean-blue illuminate the borders. Attractive and only lightly abraded.(#6097)

1144 **1813 XF45 PCGS.** O-107a, R.1. This Choice XF half is awash in aqua-blue and lilac-red patina. A few trivial hair-thin marks are noted near the portrait. A late dies example with numerous peripheral die cracks.(#6103)

1145 **1814 E Over A AU55 ANACS.** O-108, R.2. This conditionally scarce *Guide Book* variety exhibits an obvious die engraving blunder: The E in STATES is over an errant A. The eagle's head is softly brought up, but this generally lustrous example lacks obvious marks and is originally toned in aqua and apricot shades.(#6107)

1146 **1818 AU50 PCGS.** O-104a, R.3. Readily attributed by distinctive obverse die cracks. Golden-brown toning drapes the lustrous borders. Occasional minor field marks have little impact on the eye appeal. *Ex: Long Beach Signature (Heritage, 2/2007), lot 8368, which realized* $805.(#6113)

1147 **1819 XF40 PCGS.** O-112, R.3. Medium to deep stone-gray and russet toning consumes this moderately circulated and problem-free XF example.(#6117)

Sharp 1820/19 Square Base 2 Half, O-101, AU58

1148 **1820/19 Square Base 2 AU58 PCGS.** O-101, R.2. The underdigits show clearly. The second S in STATES is lower than E and the I of PLURIBUS is centered under the second T. Luster resides in the recessed areas of this near-Mint State specimen that displays splashes of low to medium intensity multicolored toning. Well defined and minimally marked. A sharp Bust half. (#6125)

1149 **1821 XF45 PCGS.** O-107, R.3. This scarcer date Capped Bust half has medium sea-green and golden-tan toning. Luster glimmers from the borders and plumage. There are no abrasions worthy of individual description.(#6128)

Popular 1824/1 Half Dollar, O-101, MS62

1150 **1824/1 MS62 PCGS.** O-101, R.2. The more common 1824/1 die pair, with the reverse having the serif of the U in UNITED significantly higher than that on the nearby N. Strongly struck with fantastic luster, silver-white in the centers with a mixture of gold, green, and sage at the rims. Population: 9 in 62, 17 finer (1/10). (#6139)

1151 **1824 AU50 PCGS.** O-105, R.2. Deep jade-green and golden-tan toning embraces this well defined AU half dollar. Luster fills protected areas, the fields are minimally abraded, and there are only a couple of moderate marks on the face.(#6137)

1825 O-114 Half, MS64
A High-End Example

1152 **1825 MS64 PCGS. CAC.** O-114, R.1. This plentiful variety has the left side of the 1 recut, and the lower shield border recut between pales 2 and 3. The present near-Gem specimen is fully original with central ivory surfaces that gradually change to sea-green, rose, and iridescent toning toward the borders. The toning is lovely and fully original. (#6142)

1153 **1827 Square Base 2 AU53 PCGS.** O-115, R.2. This satiny representative is well struck save for the left-side stars. The centers are pearl-gray, while the borders offer deeper blue-gray patina. No marks are readily evident.(#6144)

Census Level 1827 O-112a Half, MS64

1154 **1827 Square Base 2 MS64 NGC.** O-112a, R.4. The obverse has two prominent die cracks, the first from the border vertically between the 8 and 2, grazing the left top of the 2. The second extends from the border to the hair curl, continuing into the hair curls well above the drapery. This piece is in the Condition Census for the variety and is possibly the finest of the late-die-state coins. (#6144)

1155 **1828 Square Base 2, Small 8, Large Letters AU53 PCGS.** O-120, R.1. The ball of the 2 is recut, important to identification of the Overton marriage. Lovely autumn-gold and electric-blue toning clings to the margins.
Ex: Central States (Heritage, 5/2007), lot 8329, which realized $470.35.(#6151)

1156 **1829 Small Letters AU50 PCGS.** O-116a, R.4. This scarce die marriage is confirmed by the spindly die crack that forms a semicircle across much of the reverse. Golden-russet and lavender shades dominate the borders. The slightly luminous surfaces lack obtrusive marks.(#6154)

1157 **1829 Small Letters MS62 NGC.** O-108, R.2. Die lines between the edge and end of the bust aid in attribution, as does the recutting at the top of the 5, which is higher than the 0. The last A in AMERICA is incompletely filled to warrant the advanced 108a die state. Mauve-gray and golden patina bathes both sides, and the design elements are sharply impressed.(#6154)

Well Defined 1830 Small 0 Half Dollar O-103, MS64

1158 **1830 Small 0 MS64 PCGS.** O-103, R.1. The obverse stars have round, blunt points, and the 3 in the date is somewhat lower than the remaining digits. On the reverse the first S in STATES is high and distant from TATES. Line 1 of stripe 2 extends to the second crossbar. Light golden-gray patina dominates lustrous surfaces accented with aqua-green, purple, and golden-brown. A nicely defined piece that is devoid of mentionable marks. (#6156)

1159 **1831 MS62 ★ NGC.** O-103, R.1. A plentiful variety, this piece is destined to reside in a date or type collection where it will proudly illustrate the 1831 Capped Bust half dollar coinage. Both sides are brilliant and lustrous with reflective, nearly prooflike fields , the mirrors interrupted by some minor mint frost.(#6159)

1160 **1831 MS62 NGC.** O-106, R.3. A slightly scarcer 1831 half dollar variety and always in demand in Mint State grades. This piece has satiny luster with pale gold and darker steel toning on the obverse, and lighter gold on the reverse.(#6159)

Near-Gem O-102 1831 Half Dollar

1161 **1831 MS64 NGC.** O-102, R.1. The reverse for the O-102 variety is distinctive, with "welded" lines in the first vertical stripe of the shield as well as filling of the right side of the N in UNITED. Warm peach-gold and silver colors dominate the centers, while the margins show elements of blue and violet. (#6159)

1162 **1832 Small Letters AU55 PCGS.** Ex: Benson. O-102, R.1. Exquisite bands of golden-brown and navy-blue enrich the peripheries of this mostly lustrous Choice AU half. Unmarked and highly attractive.
Ex: Ira S. Reed, 6/1944; Benson Collection, Part II (Ira & Larry Goldberg, 2/2002), lot 974; FUN Signature (Heritage, 1/2007), lot 61938, which realized $805.(#6160)

Lightly Patinated 1832 Small Letters Half Dollar O-110, MS64

1163 **1832 Small Letters MS64 PCGS.** O-110, R.1. A "spike" at the top of the cap typically identifies the obverse, but one must exercise caution because this same defect is sometimes seen on O-109, which shares the same obverse. The 5 in the denomination is slightly recut on the outer curve and URI in PLURIBUS is weak, both of which are diagnostic for the reverse. Golden-gray surfaces display peripheral electric-blue and lavender accents. Well delineated save for minor softness on the upper right shield. (#6160)

1164 **1833 AU55 PCGS.** O-112, R.2. Star 8 is recut, diagnostic for this relatively available die pairing. An attractively toned Choice AU Bust half that is bathed in apple-green, ocean-blue, and straw-gold. Thorough inspection locates a few inconsequential faded marks. (#6163)

Gem 1836 Lettered Edge Half, O-117

1165 **1836 Lettered Edge MS65 NGC.** O-117, R.3. The distinctive obverse has the 1 in the date too low relative to the 8 and leaning in toward the latter digit. This Gem example from the last year of Lettered Edge Bust half coinage has impressive luster beneath dappled green-gold, olive, blue, and violet patina. Solidly struck with great eye appeal. (#6169)

1166 **1836 50 Over 00 AU58 PCGS.** O-116, R.2. This *Guide Book* variety has a blundered denomination, an error undoubtedly facilitated by the mirror image aspect of working dies. A lustrous and unmarked chestnut-gray Borderline Uncirculated representative. Population: 4 in 58, 13 finer (12/09).(#6170)

1167 **1836 Reeded Edge—Improperly Cleaned—NGC. VF Details.** The 1836 is the scarcer of the two-year Capped Bust Reeded Edge 50 CENTS design type. Silver-gray surfaces are accented with purple and electric-blue peripheral toning and exhibit appropriate definition on the design elements. Light hairlines are visible under magnification.(#6175)

REEDED EDGE HALF DOLLARS

Popular 1836 Reeded Edge Half, Choice XF

1168 **1836 Reeded Edge XF45 PCGS.** The famous (and famously low-mintage) Reeded Edge half dollar variant of late 1836 marked a new era of Mint technology, combining historic importance with scarcity. This lightly circulated representative, pale silver-gray in the still-lustrous centers, has gold-orange elements near the rims. (#6175)

1169 **1837 AU53 PCGS.** A lightly worn example of this more accessible Reeded Edge, 50 Cents Reverse date. Dappled blue-violet and green-gold toning drapes lightly worn but still-lustrous surfaces. (#6176)

Extremely Rare JR-29 1837 Reeded Edge Half Dollar, AU58, Undiscovered Until 2006

1170 **1837 AU58 NGC.** JR-29. Presumably an Rarity-8 variety. This variety was only discovered during the cataloging of the Jules Reiver Collection, which was sold in January 2006. Since that time we have only sold two examples, and this is a repeat appearance of one of them. In the Reiver catalog the diagnostics were listed as: 83 close, 1 and 7 high. Die crack from star 1 to star 5. Die crack under 837 to star 13. Die lump under A3 on the reverse, close to the wing. Die crack over top of ED STATE. Die crack through the middle of TES, and along the bottoms of OF AMERICA. This appears to be an earlier die state as the die crack is very faint over the top of ED STATE. The silver-gray surfaces have a light overlay of golden toning on each side. There is slight weakness evident at the margins. Nice portions of luster remain around the devices, and there are a few small, scattered field marks on each side, but none are worthy of individual mention. (#6176)

1171 **1837 MS62 PCGS.** This is the more available of the two-year Reeded Edge design type with the 50 CENTS reverse. Lustrous surfaces display traces of light brown color and sharply struck design motifs. Minute obverse marks preclude a higher grade. (#6176)

Brilliant MS63 1837 Reeded Edge Half

1172 **1837 MS63 PCGS.** Reeded Edge halves were struck in such a small quantity in 1836, for many collectors 1837 represents the first truly collectible year. The old bust design was reworked the previous year and given a reeded edge. According to Mint Director Patterson striking in a close collar "gives a mathematical equality to their diameters." This is an attractive example that is brilliant throughout. The steam press was certainly effective in this case as every detail is fully brought up. A few light abrasions can be seen, but none are worthy of individual mention. (#6176)

Appealing 1837 Reeded Edge Half, MS64

1173 **1837 MS64 NGC.** The first Capped Bust, Reeded Edge half dollars, struck late in 1836, are often called pattern coins, making this 1837 the first year of issue for a three-year design. Since the reverse had its denomination changed from 50 CENTS to HALF DOL. in 1838, this 1837 is technically a one-year type coin. This Choice Mint State example is attractively toned with excellent eye appeal. (#6176)

High-Grade 1837 Reeded Edge Half, MS66

1174 **1837 MS66 NGC.** With the 1836 Reeded Edge issue having an extremely limited mintage, the 1837 half dollar is the only accessible date for the variety with denomination expressed as 50 CENTS. Despite a mintage of over 3.6 million pieces, the 1837 Reeded Edge half is understandably rare at the MS66 level and above. This Premium Gem is remarkably bright for a coin over 170 years old, with minimally toned surfaces showing only whispers of golden toning around the lower reverse. The strike is sharp through the centers, though the stars surrounding Liberty are slightly soft. Census: 9 in 66, 3 finer (1/10). (#6176)

1175 **1839 AU58 PCGS.** The cartwheel luster is essentially complete, and the lightly toned cream-gray surfaces are smooth aside from a few faint and slender scuffs. The final year of the long-lived Capped Bust design. Encapsulated in an old green label holder. (#6179)

Lustrous 1839 Capped Bust Half, MS64

1176 **1839 MS64 NGC.** The final year of issue for the Capped Bust, Reeded Edge design. This piece is an exceptional near-Gem with frosty and fully brilliant silver surfaces. All of the design elements are bold, save for slight weakness at the bust tip. Both sides are entirely untoned, and the surfaces show only a few grade-limiting marks. Census: 47 in 64, 6 finer (1/10). (#6179)

1177 **1839-O XF40 NGC.** A lightly worn example with strong contrast between the light silver-gray outlining the devices and the deep slate-blue of the fields and hollows. Two nearly intersecting die cracks travel from the eagle's beak to the bottoms of (STA)TES OF AMERICA and the arrowheads.(#6181)

SEATED HALF DOLLARS

Choice XF 1849 Half Dollar With Dramatically Repunched Date, FS-301

1178 **1849 XF45 PCGS.** FS-301, formerly FS-004.5. WB-102. Curiously, this coin is designated by PCGS as an error. It is in fact a repunched date, and one of the most dramatic in the entire Seated half series. All the digits in the date are repunched with the original punching easily seen to the left. Also present are the remnants of two mispunched 9s; one protrudes from the rock above 49, and the other is faintly seen in the denticles. The surfaces are medium gray on the obverse and light gray on the reverse, with contrasting brilliantish-silver accents over the devices on each side. Several field marks are present. (#6262)

1179 **1850 AU55 PCGS.** It would be a mistake to think of the 1850 as a common date, for its mintage of 227,000 pieces and its low survival rate ensure that this issue is hard to locate in all grades. Although lightly worn as the grade implies, this piece retains considerable luster beneath its deep heather and gold toning. Population: 8 in 55, 40 finer (1/10).(#6264)

Popular 1853 Arrows and Rays Fifty Cent, MS64

1180 **1853 Arrows and Rays MS64 NGC.** The 1853 Arrows and Rays half dollar is a popular one-year type coin. Whispers of electric-blue, lavender, and gold patina visit portions of the margins on this near-Gem example, especially on the obverse. Lustrous surfaces display well struck devices and some die cracks over each side. Minor marks deny Gem status. (#6275)

The Eliasberg 1861-O Half, MS64

1181 **1861-O MS64 PCGS. CAC.** Ex: Eliasberg. The final New Orleans Mint Seated half dollar struck at the beginning of the Civil War, this Choice Mint State piece has pastel gold and iridescent toning with bold design definition.
Ex: J.M. Clapp; John H. Clapp; Clapp Estate; Louis E. Eliasberg, Sr.; Eliasberg Estate (Bowers and Merena, 4/1997), lot 1987. (#6303)

1182 **1872-CC VF25 NGC.** An early Seated half dollar from the Carson City Mint, this 1872-CC is moderately worn with pleasing light to medium gray surfaces. A substantial mintage of 257,000 coins was produced during the year, but most of those have been lost to the perils of time. Survivors are desirable in all grades. (#6334)

Choice AU 1873-CC No Arrows Half

1183 **1873-CC No Arrows AU55 NGC.** Small CC. A lightly circulated but still-lustrous example of the No Arrows 1873-CC half dollar, richly toned peach, olive, and silver-blue over a gray base. Minimally abraded save for a single mark above the F in HALF and crisply defined, an all-around attractive coin. Census: 3 in 55, 9 finer (1/10). (#6338)

1184 **1874-CC Arrows VF20 PCGS.** 1874 is a magical year for silver coins from the Carson City Mint, for they are all rare. It seems that production of gold coins was the more pressing need. The half dollar only had a mintage of 59,000 coins, and examples are elusive in all grades. This pleasing piece has medium to dark gray toning in the fields with lighter tan devices.(#6347)

1185 **1877-CC MS62 NGC.** Type Two Reverse. Luminous silver-gray surfaces show occasional subtle whispers of light tan-gold and well impressed design features. Light cracks are visible in the upper left obverse border and along the reverse margins. A few minute contact marks limit the grade.(#6356)

1186 **1882 MS64 PCGS.** Beneath the rich green-gold and violet patina, this near-Gem has flashy fields and even a measure of frost on the devices, though the striking characteristics are not as uniformly sharp as for a proof. Lightly abraded to the left and right of Liberty, yet attractive. Population: 17 in 64, 18 finer (12/09). (#6364)

PROOF SEATED HALF DOLLARS

Appealing 1857 Half Dollar, PR62

1187 **1857 PR62 PCGS. CAC.** Champagne-gold centers are flanked by deep purple toning at the margins, the latter being somewhat more extensive on the obverse. This sharply struck piece possesses great eye appeal for the numerical grade despite the presence of some inoffensive handling marks. A rare proof issue. Population: 5 in 62, 29 finer (12/09). (#6411)

1857 Half, PR64, Ex: Eliasberg

1188 **1857 PR64 PCGS. CAC.** The population of 1857 proof half dollars is probably about 50 coins, but this is only an estimate. PCGS and NGC have graded about 70 examples, an unknown number of which are likely resubmissions. This exquisitely struck near-Gem displays whispers of delicate golden toning, accented with hints of electric-blue and lavender at the margins.
Ex: Harlan P. Smith (Chapman Brothers, 5/1906); John H. Clapp; Clapp Estate; Louis E. Eliasberg, Sr.; Eliasberg Estate (Bowers and Merena, 4/1997), lot 1970. (#6411)

Toned Near-Gem Proof 1862 Half

1189 **1862 PR64 PCGS. CAC.** The mirrored fields of this near-Gem proof are subdued by the original gray and iridescent toning on both sides, and that is the only reason the grade was limited to PR64. It is a sharply detailed example with excellent, problem-free surfaces. Population: 53 in 64, 20 finer (1/10). (#6416)

Brightly Reflective PR64 1863 Seated Half Mintage of 460 Pieces

1190 **1863 PR64 NGC.** It is a wonder that any proof coinage was struck during the tumultuous days of the Civil War. Specie payments had been suspended and proofs had a two-tiered pricing structure, based on whether greenbacks or coins were used for payment. A tiny mintage of 460 proof halves was struck in 1863, and NGC has only certified 24 in PR64 with 20 pieces finer (1/10). This piece displays deeply mirrored fields with each side showing speckled rose and blue toning. (#6417)

1191 **1866 Motto PR63 PCGS.** A sharp Select proof, minimally contrasted but with rich steel-blue and silver-green patina. Scattered hairlines beneath the toning contribute to the grade. Population: 38 in 63, 45 finer (12/09).(#6424)

Gem Proof 1867 Half Dollar

1192 **1867 PR65 NGC. CAC.** Light peach and silver shadings over parts of each side give way to brilliant blue hues, ranging from pale turquoise to an electric shade. A crisply detailed and delightfully mirrored Gem specimen of this post-Civil War proof half dollar issue, one of just 625 specimens coined. Census: 25 in 65, 7 finer (1/10). (#6425)

Flashy PR64 Cameo 1871 Half

1193 **1871 PR64 Cameo PCGS.** This outstanding Cameo coin has faintly toned yet essentially silver-white mirrors. Strongly impressed devices show only light frost, but the contrast is strong for the amount of frost present. A tiny lint mark in the right obverse field has no influence on the technical grade. Population: 9 in 64 Cameo, 1 finer (12/09). (#86429)

1194 **1874 Arrows PR63 NGC.** Small Arrowheads. Fully struck with pleasing gold, alabaster, and sea-green toning, and noteworthy cameo contrast on the obverse. A handful of wispy slide marks are noted in the right obverse field. The short-lived Arrows design has long been a favorite of collectors, and proofs are elusive. (#6435)

Gorgeous 1878 Seated Half, PR66 Cameo

1195 **1878 PR66 Cameo NGC.** Type Two Reverse. This gorgeous 1878 half dollar has exquisite contrast between the fields and the devices, with mostly brilliant, untoned silver surfaces. Peripheral lilac and electric blue toning is evident on both sides of this Premium Gem. Census: 10 in 66 Cameo, 3 finer (1/10). (#86439)

Fully Struck 1884 Gem Cameo Proof Half Dollar

1196 **1884 PR65 Cameo PCGS.** Proof 1884 half dollars are readily available through near-Gem, and even finer-grade coins can be located with patience. Cameos are another story. They are particularly difficult in Gem and above. Golden-tan patina gravitates to the margins of this Gem Cameo and a full strike is seen over the design elements. Nicely preserved. Population: 5 in 65 Cameo, 2 finer (1/10). (#86445)

1197 **1888 PR62 NGC. CAC.** Fantastically reflective with moderately hairlined fields. If the frost over the devices were slightly stronger, this coin could have had a bold black-and-white effect. (#6449)

Elegant 1890 Half Dollar, PR67 Cameo

1198 **1890 PR67 Cameo NGC.** Orange-gold and purple toning, confined mostly to the margins on the obverse, cover more territory on the reverse of this elegant Superb Gem proof. Sharply struck, satiny devices appear to float over the mirrored fields, confirming the Cameo designation. Proof half dollars of 1890 (590 coins) see added pressure because of the minimal business strike emission of 12,000 pieces. The present coin will stand out in the finest collection. A crack on the holder extends across the bottom of the insert. Census: 8 in 67 Cameo, 0 finer (1/10). (#86451)

BARBER HALF DOLLARS

Lightly Patinated 1894-S Half Dollar, MS64

1199 **1894-S MS64 PCGS.** Whispers of light gray and gold patina visit the lustrous surfaces of this near-Gem S-mint half and an impressive strike leaves strong definition on the design features, though the upper right shield corner is a touch weak. An occasional obverse handling mark precludes Gem classification. Population: 45 in 64, 31 finer (1/10). (#6470)

Semikey 1895-S Barber Half, MS65

1200 **1895-S MS65 PCGS.** The 1895-S is a semikey issue with a mintage of 1.1 million pieces. The typical coin is found with good luster and semiprooflike fields, as seen on this piece. The striking definition is remarkably strong with complete hair details on the forecurls, showing just a bit of softness on the right (facing) talon of the eagle. Pale rose-colored toning is seen over each side. Population: 11 in 65, 3 finer (1/10). (#6473)

MS64 1902-O Barber Half
Conditionally Scarce New Orleans Issue

1201 **1902-O MS64 PCGS.** Delightful purple toning in the periphery yields to pale gray patina in the centers. Impressive satiny luster shines beneath the attractive toning. The northeast corner of the shield and the eagle's right wing are weakly struck, but the rest of the details are sharp. A minimally marked and lustrous example of this conditionally scarce issue. Population: 15 in 64, 6 finer (12/09). (#6493)

Richly Toned MS64 1903 Half

1202 **1903 MS64 PCGS.** Deep violet and blue peripheral shades fade through olive and green-gold before settling into rich silver-gray at the centers. A luminous and satiny near-Gem example of this underrated Barber half dollar issue, little-saved at the time of release. Population: 25 in 64, 8 finer (12/09). (#6495)

1203 **1904-S XF40 PCGS.** The 553,038-piece mintage of the 1904-S is low but unremarkable, given the 505,000-piece production of the 1905-O and the 662,000-piece coinage of the 1905. Certainly, the 1913, 1914, and 1915 all have much lower mintages. Nonetheless, the 1904-S is the rarest Barber half issue in Mint State, excluding the 1892-O Micro O. It is also extremely scarce in nice circulated grades, although uncertified AG3 examples can be obtained with little difficulty. A problem-free pearl-gray representative that has substantial plumage detail.(#6500)

Subtly Toned MS65 1906-D Barber Half

1204 **1906-D MS65 PCGS. CAC.** The 1906-D is surprisingly scarce in high grades for a coin with a mintage in excess of 4 million pieces. PCGS has certified 17 Gems, and eight are finer (1/10). The surfaces of this piece show soft mint frost, and each side has light, speckled rose and gray toning. Sharply struck overall with just a bit of high point softness. (#6505)

Attractively Toned MS65 1907 Barber Half

1205 **1907 MS65 NGC.** This lustrous Gem has distinctive toning on each side, lightly and attractively done. Golden-rose and lilac colors are intermingled in the fields with mostly brilliant devices. The strike is as expected, with softness localized to the eagle's right wing. A small planchet flake is noted just below Liberty's jawline. Census: 17 in 65, 3 finer (12/09). (#6508)

1206 **1907-O MS64 PCGS.** Light violet-gray and beige patination runs over the lustrous surfaces of this near-Gem. The design elements are well struck except for the usual softness in the upper right shield corner. A few minuscule marks deny Gem status. Population: 42 in 64, 21 finer (1/10).(#6510)

1207 **1912 MS63 PCGS.** Peripheral golden color with few spots of deeper charcoal. The luminous centers have satiny silver-gray luster. Housed in a first-generation holder.(#6524)

1208 **1912-D MS64 PCGS.** This richly toned near-Gem is well-defined with subtle luster filtering through layers of gold-orange, umber, and deep violet patina. Minimally marked for the grade. PCGS has certified 65 finer pieces (12/09).(#6525)

1209 **1912-S MS64 PCGS.** Honey-gold and pearl-gray enrich this shimmering and intricately struck Choice Barber half. A few faint obverse luster grazes are all that prevent classification as a full Gem. Population: 50 in 64, 26 finer (12/09).(#6526)

1210 **1913-D MS64 NGC.** Strongly lustrous for this Denver issue with eye appeal that suggests a finer grade than MS64. Minor softness on the obverse stars and a few abrasions on the cap contribute to the coin's near-Gem status. Faint golden toning adds color to otherwise silver-white surfaces. Census: 39 in 64, 17 finer (12/09). (#6528)

Light and Dark Gray-Toned 1915 Half, MS62

1211 **1915 MS62 PCGS.** Final year of issue, this example shows remarkably good luster for the grade. The centers are light gray with significantly deeper gray around the margins. The striking details are strong but not quite complete in all areas, lacking just a bit of high point definition on Liberty's forecurls and the eagle's legs. (#6532)

PROOF BARBER HALF DOLLARS

Interesting 1894 Barber Half, PR67
Repunched 4 in Date

1212 **1894 PR67 NGC.** Breen-5052. The 4 in the date is clearly repunched with extra outlines within the triangle of the digit. This apparently is only seen on proofs, but we do not know what percentage of the 972 proofs struck show this feature. The fields are deeply reflective and shine forcefully through the multiple layers of sea-green, rose, and gray toning that cover most of each side. A lovely early proof Barber half. Census: 20 in 67, 4 finer (1/10). (#6541)

1213 **1894 PR64 Cameo PCGS.** Illimitable depth of mirrored reflectivity is seen in the fields on each side with noticeably contrasting frosted devices, which is evident even through the light covering of golden-rose toning. Pinpoint striking definition. Population: 16 in 64 Cameo, 34 finer (1/10).(#86541)

PR66 Cameo 1895 Barber Half

1214 **1895 PR66 Cameo NGC.** By 1895 whatever lingering enthusiasm might have existed for the Barber designs had evaporated, and from the first-year total of more than 1,200 proof half dollars, by this fourth year of production the net coinage had slumped to 880 pieces. This coin is among the finer survivors, with good field-device contrast and untoned, silver-white surfaces that show the slightest blush of champagne tint on the reverse. Census: 21 in 66 Cameo, 20 finer (1/10). (#86542)

Beautiful 1896 Half, PR66 Cameo

1215 **1896 PR66 Cameo NGC.** A brilliant silver half dollar, this Premium Gem Cameo proof shows bold design motifs with satiny devices and fully mirrored fields. There is no evidence of toning on either side of this beautiful half dollar. Census: 12 in 66 Cameo, 12 finer (1/10). (#86543)

Gem Proof 1898 Half Dollar

1216 **1898 PR65 NGC.** Rich and beautiful patina dominates the eye appeal of this Gem proof, wreathed in plum and deep peach on the obverse with small slots of gleaming silver-white. The reverse has slightly lighter color, blue and turquoise with suggestions of emerald. Census: 28 in 65, 55 finer (1/10). (#6545)

Prized PR66 Cameo 1900 Half Dollar

1217 **1900 PR66 Cameo NGC.** Excellent eye appeal for this turn-of-the-century issue, mildly but distinctly contrasted between the lightly frosted and sharply struck devices and the prominent mirrors, which are generally silver-white but show occasional hints of patina. Carefully preserved with excellent eye appeal. Census: 22 in 66 Cameo, 13 finer (1/10). (#86547)

1218 **1905 PR64 PCGS.** This boldly detailed, deeply toned proof has blue, gold, rose, and violet toning over fully mirrored fields. The devices have a smooth, satiny appearance.(#6552)

Deeply Toned PR67 1905 Barber Half

1219 **1905 PR67 NGC.** The mirrored fields on this Superb Gem proof offer noticeable contrast with the satiny motifs, especially on the reverse. Yellow-gold patina dominates the obverse, with violet splashes. Violet also dominates the reverse, accented with yellow-gold. Exquisitely struck and immaculately preserved. Census: 12 in 67, 4 finer (1/10). (#6552)

Sharp 1907 Half Dollar, PR66

1220 **1907 PR66 NGC.** Freckles of light tan-gold color show under magnification and the design elements are well struck, save for the usual weakness in the upper right shield corner. A few minor handling marks are undisturbing. The 1907 proof can be located with patience through near-Gem but is difficult any finer. Census: 25 in 66, 8 finer (12/09). (#6554)

Nearly Brilliant 1908 Half, PR64 Cameo

1221 **1908 PR64 Cameo PCGS. CAC.** Early 20th century proof Barber half dollars are difficult to find with any degree of contrast, as seen on this piece. It has fully and deeply mirrored fields around sharply defined, satiny devices. There is little evidence of toning on either side, with only subtle gold color. Population: 3 in 64 Cameo, 9 finer (1/10). (#86555)

Solidly Struck 1910 Half Dollar, PR67

1222 **1910 PR67 NGC.** The demand for high-grade 1910 proof half dollars is high owing to the elusiveness of low-mintage circulation strikes (fewer than 500,000 pieces). Dappled cobalt-blue, orange, and lavender toning runs over both sides of this Superb Gem and a solid strike delivers strong definition to the design features. Impeccably preserved. Census: 19 in 67, 7 finer (1/10). (#6557)

EARLY DOLLARS

Plentiful 1795 B-5, BB-27 Dollar, VF20

1223 **1795 Flowing Hair, Three Leaves VF20 ANACS.** B-5, BB-27, R.1. The common 1795 Flowing Hair dollar variety, with the diagonal bar in the upper left obverse field, and seen as often as all other varieties combined. This glossy silver piece has light gray surfaces with iridescent toning on each side. (#6852)

1795 Flowing Hair Dollar, VF25 Three Leaves, B-5, BB-27

1224 **1795 Flowing Hair, Three Leaves VF25 PCGS.** B-5, BB-27, R.1. The slender "bar" behind the uppermost neck curl is diagnostic. Pearl-gray overall with walnut-brown in design recesses. The obverse margin displays minor adjustment marks, as made. The obverse rim is softly defined near 7 o'clock on the obverse and opposite on the reverse, likely due to a flan of slightly uneven thickness. In an old green label holder. (#6852)

Pleasing 1795 B-2, BB-20 Dollar, VG10

1225 **1795 Flowing Hair, Two Leaves VG10 NGC.** B-2, BB-20, R.3. The later, lapped die state with thin stars at the left obverse border. Although well worn, this piece has pleasing surfaces. Both sides have deep steel-gray patina in the fields, with lighter silver-tan devices creating a splendid two-tone appearance. (#6853)

Flowing Hair, Two Leaves 1795 Dollar B-1, BB-21, Choice AU

1226 **1795 Flowing Hair, Two Leaves AU55 PCGS.** B-1, BB-21, R.2. The obverse with "blundered date" showing an underdigit beneath the 7, the reverse with a 9x10 berry configuration and one berry below the right side of the first A in AMERICA. An uncommonly fine example of a Flowing Hair dollar, since most representatives grade VF or below. Each side remains luminous beneath rich blue-green and cobalt-silver toning. Wear is present mostly as "fresh metal" at the highest points of the letters in LIBERTY and through the lower reverse. Minimally abraded save for a handful of small to medium scrapes at the eagle's breast. Population: 16 in 55, 23 finer (12/09). (#6853)

Bold AU Details Centered Draped Bust 1795 Silver Dollar, B-15, BB-52

1227 **1795 Draped Bust, Centered—Improperly Cleaned—NGC. AU Details.** B-15, BB-52, R.2. Bowers-Borckardt Die State III-IV. A splendidly detailed first-year Draped Bust dollar that is bathed in deep sea-green toning, with occasional hints of golden-brown. The right obverse field is slightly glossy and has a couple of small, faint abrasions. The devices on *both* sides have a couple of light adjustment marks (as made), beneath Liberty's ear and on the eagle's right (facing) leg. (#6858)

Well Defined 1795 Draped Bust, Off Center Dollar B-14, BB-51, VF Details

1228 **1795 Draped Bust, Off Center—Improperly Cleaned—NGC. VF Details.** B-14, BB-51, R.2. The bust is off-center left in the die, leaving the highest wave of hair under the B in LIBERTY rather than the E as usually seen on most early dollars. The surfaces are light gray, violet, purple, and gold, and reveal faint hairlines under magnification. Nice design detail and only lightly abraded. Interested bidders should not be dissuaded by the light cleaning. (#96858)

1795 Off Center Bust Dollar, VF35 B-14, BB-51

1229 **1795 Draped Bust, Off Center VF35 NGC.** B-14, BB-51, R.1. If the off-centered bust of Liberty is not an obvious tip-off that this is a B-14, the hair curl that is centered beneath the B in LIBERTY is also a reliable diagnostic. The medium gray surfaces show green and golden accents at the obverse border, and there are no obvious abrasions on either side. (#96858)

1795 Uncentered Bust Dollar B-14, BB-51, AU50

1230 **1795 Draped Bust, Off Center AU50 NGC.** B-14, BB-51, R.2. Perfect dies as always. The Uncentered Bust variety with Liberty crowding the stars along the left obverse border. The position of Liberty on the obverse is diagnostic for each of the two known 1795 Draped Bust varieties. Both varieties are seen on a regular basis, about 60% for this variety and 40% for the other.

The devices of this pleasing Draped Bust dollar are lightly worn, with smooth gray surfaces that host light iridescence. The surfaces are attractive, with only a few minor blemishes on Liberty's profile. (#96858)

Near-Mint 1795 Draped Bust Dollar B-14, BB-51

1231 **1795 Draped Bust, Off Center AU58 PCGS.** B-14, BB-51, R.2. Known as the Off-Center Draped Bust obverse, this variety has been the occasional source of confusion from people who mistakenly think that the actual coin was struck off-center. For that reason we recommend changing the name to the "Uncentered Bust" variety. This piece has nearly full, satiny luster with lovely silver-gray surfaces and equally attractive peripheral iridescence. The strike is good, with only slight weakness at the center of the reverse. A few surface marks are consistent with the grade, but the overall eye appeal is excellent. (#96858)

Desirable 1796 B-4, BB-61 Dollar, VF20

1232 **1796 Small Date, Large Letters VF20 NGC.** B-4, BB-61, R.3. The small die chip centered over the 1 in the date identifies this obverse that was also used for BB-62. The reverse dies are distinguished by the Large Letters of BB-61 and the Small Letters of BB-62. It is believed that this variety was the first die combination struck with the 1796 date. This piece is a pleasing light gray example with lighter silver-gray devices. Only a few grade-consistent blemishes are noted on either side. (#6860)

Lovely 1796 B-4, BB-61 Dollar, AU50

1233 **1796 Small Date, Large Letters AU50 PCGS.** B-4, BB-61, R.3. A die chip high above the 1 in the date identifies this variety. This piece is an attractive silver-gray example with excellent detail on both sides. Faint radial adjustment marks extend in from the border left of the date. Considerable luster is still visible on both sides, with faint rose and iridescent toning. Population: 7 in 50, 11 finer (1/10). (#6860)

Elusive VF Small Date, Small Letters 1796 Dollar, B-1, BB-66

1234 **1796 Small Date, Small Letters VF20 PCGS.** B-1, BB-66, R.4. Incorrectly designated as a Large Date by PCGS. This scarce Small Eagle dollar displays apple-green, navy-blue, and lilac patina. A vertical scratch extends from the left wreath loop and stem, and other abrasions are noted left of the eagle's neck and beneath the hair ribbons. All marks are inconspicuous, and the eye appeal is attractive to the unaided eye. (#6859)

Scarce 1796 B-2, BB-63 Dollar, VF20

1235 **1796 Small Date, Small Letters VF20 PCGS.** B-2, BB-63, R.4. Ex: Hesselgesser. This is a scarcer variety, and the present piece is a duplicate from the marvelous Dr. Hesselgesser Collection, one of the finest collections of Bust dollars ever formed, past or present. An attractive light silver-gray piece, this early dollar will fit nicely in an advanced variety collection, or a design collection. (#6859)

Delightful 1796 B-5, BB-65 Dollar, VF20

1236 **1796 Small Date, Small Letters VF20 NGC.** B-5, BB-65, R.2. This variety is always identified by the variable die chip between the I and C of AMERICA, in this case joining both letters. This pleasing example has an attractive blend of deep steel-blue and gray-brown toning on both sides. Trivial surface marks on each side are consistent with the grade. Overall, a fully natural and delightful early dollar. (#6859)

Scarce 1796 Dollar, Fine Details Large Date, Small Letters, B-5, BB-65

1237 **1796 Large Date, Small Letters—Rim Damage—NGC. Fine Details.** B-5, BB-65, R.2. Bowers-Borckardt Die State IV, the die lump between the IC in AMERICA is well advanced. Each side has a couple of small to medium rim nicks, the most noticeable at 8:30 on the obverse and at 6 o'clock on the reverse. A thin curved mark near the lower reverse rim appears to be post-strike. Attractive golden-brown, blue-green, and stone-gray toning embraces the circulated (but minimally abraded) fields and devices. (#6861)

1238 **1797 10x6 Stars, Large Letters—Repaired—NCS. VF Details.** B-3, BB-71, R.2. Bowers-Borckardt Die State III. The eagle's breast, the right obverse field, and the reverse field near 2 o'clock have been smoothed. This steel-gray Small Eagle dollar retains ample design detail.(#6865)

Bold VF30 1797 Dollar, 10x6 Stars B-3, BB-71, Large Letters

1239 **1797 10x6 Stars, Large Letters VF30 NGC.** B-3, BB-71, R.2. Bowers-Borckardt Die State III. Powder-blue and chestnut shades adorn the margins, but the majority of this Small Eagle dollar is stone-gray. A diagonal mark on the neck was likely on the planchet prior to the strike, and the surfaces are otherwise smooth except for a trivial rim ding on the reverse at 6 o'clock. In a former generation holder. (#6865)

B-1, BB-73 1797 Dollar, VF20 9x7 Stars, Large Letters

1240 **1797 9x7 Stars, Large Letters VF20 PCGS. CAC.** B-1, BB-73, R.3. Bowers-Borckardt Die State I or II; the toning and abrasions in the area of the "pellet" die flaw make it difficult to tell if the "pellet" is better termed bold or faint. Moderately worn with blue and olive overtones gracing medium-gray surfaces. Several old pinscratches are noted in the fields. (#6863)

Die State III B-1, BB-73 1797 Dollar, VF25 9x7 Stars, Large Letters

1241 **1797 9x7 Stars, Large Letters VF25 ANACS.** B-1, BB-73, R.3. Bowers-Borckardt Die State III, with die cracks through hair ribbon but the crack through the second T in STATES not yet visible. A radiant midrange example, silver-gray through most of the centers but with dramatic multicolored toning at the margins and extending into the device areas. An unusual coin that must be seen in person to be truly appreciated. (#6863)

VF Small Letters, 9x7 Stars 1797 Dollar B-2, BB-72

1242 **1797 9x7 Stars, Small Letters VF20 NGC.** B-2, BB-72, R.4. The deep cream-gray toning has olive-green and cobalt-blue undertones. Nicely defined for the VF level, and marks are of little consequence aside from a trio on the field near Liberty's profile. There are only three die marriages of 1797 dollars, and each is sufficiently distinctive to merit a separately listing in the 2010 *Guide Book*. Bolender-2 is scarcest of the three varieties. The prior generation NGC holder has a small chip on the lower right front corner that has no effect on the coin's preservation or the holder integrity. (#6866)

Rarity-3 B-1, BB-82 1798 Dollar Small Eagle, 13 Stars, VF25

1243 **1798 Small Eagle, 13 Stars VF25 PCGS.** B-1, BB-82, R.3. Bowers-Borckardt Die State III, a late state with die crack through the N in UNITED to the nearby branch. The sole 13 Star obverse-Small Eagle reverse die pair is represented here by a VF coin, olive-gray and slate-blue through the fields with lighter silver color at the worn high points. (#6867)

Elusive Small Eagle, 13 Stars 1798 Dollar B-1, BB-82, VF30

1244 **1798 Small Eagle, 13 Stars VF30 ANACS.** B-1, BB-82, R.3. Bowers-Borckardt Die State III. Rich cream-gray and lavender toning cedes to occasional glimpses of almond-gold. No marks are remotely worthy of individual description. B-1 is a separate *Guide Book* variety, as the only other Small Eagle marriage has a 15 Stars reverse. Housed in an ANA cache holder. (#6867)

1245 **1798 Large Eagle, Pointed 9, Four Berries—Polished—NGC. VF Details.** B-8, BB-125, R.2. Obviously polished with bright and glossy silver surfaces that still retain some light toning. A few minor scratches and other imperfections are visible.(#6873)

1246 **1798 Large Eagle, Pointed 9 VF20 PCGS.** B-30, BB-116, R.4. Attractive, smooth medium gray surfaces with lighter gray devices and a uniform underlying brightness. There is a small, ancient scratch extending diagonally through some of the hair on the bust, but one that is hardly noticeable since it has toned naturally and blended in to the rest of the design over the course of time. No other distinct problems for the grade, and overall an appealing specimen of this scarce variety.
Ex: Heritage (9/2002), lot 7797.(#6873)

1247 **1798 Large Eagle, Pointed 9—Improperly Cleaned—NGC. VF Details.** B-8, BB-125, R.2. The Four Berries reverse, an important and distinct *Guide Book* variety represented by this single die marriage. Prominent die cracks and bulges are visible on each side of this later die state example. While described as cleaned, and maybe so, this example has deep steel toning with lighter silver gray on the devices. Minor surface marks on each side are consistent with the grade.(#6873)

Scarce VF30 1798 Heraldic Eagle Dollar
Close Date, Pointed 9, B-28, BB-118

1248 **1798 Large Eagle, Pointed 9, Close Date VF30 PCGS.** B-28, BB-118, R.3. Bowers-Borckardt Die State IV. A memorable Bolender variety due to prominent die cracks on each side. An early dollar with russet-brown fields and pearl-gray highpoints. The wing plumage and hair exhibit a wealth of detail, and no marks merit individual discussion. The reverse is misaligned a few degrees toward 3 o'clock. (#6873)

Attractive VF30 1798 Dollar, B-25, BB-123
Ex: Reiver

1249 **1798 Large Eagle, Pointed 9 VF30 NGC.** Ex: Jules Reiver Collection. B-25, BB-123, R.4. Whisker under chin, die dot in field between neck and star 12; line star pattern, star 12 touches upper beak, points to right edge of B. Reiver die state c. Bowers-Borckardt die state III. Attractive gunmetal-gray in the fields with lighter silver tones on the devices. A well struck coin that boasts strong eye appeal for the grade. There are no surface problems aside from a rim bump on the reverse near the tip of the left wing. On this later die state, the obverse displays encircling die cracks, with an additional radial crack from the rim to star 7.
Ex: Van Horn (February, 1972); Jules Reiver Collection (Heritage, 1/2006), lot 23537. (#6873)

1798 Heraldic Eagle, Pointed 9 Dollar
B-27, BB-113, AU58

1250 **1798 Large Eagle, Pointed 9 AU58 NGC.** B-27, BB-113, R.2. Bowers-Borckardt Die State III, an uncommonly seen late state with delicate curving die crack arcing from the left arrowheads through the field below UNITED, into the left wingtip, and on to the lower part of the STA of STATES. This near-Mint representative has both strong luster and attractive toning, with deep blues and green-golds dominant and violet and olive hues in ancillary roles. Strongly defined with only a touch of rub on the uppermost design elements and few abrasions, though there are a handful of depressions seen in the upper half of the shield.
From The South Texas Collection. (#6873)

Rare Choice VF B-17, BB-101 1798 Dollar
10 Arrows, 5 Stripes, Pointed 9

1251 **1798 5 Stripes, 10 Arrows, Pointed 9 VF35 ANACS.** B-17, BB-101, R.5. Bowers-Borckardt Die State III. B-17 is the sole die marriage with both a Pointed 9 in the date and five vertical lines in each stripe. Forest-green, golden-brown, and stone-gray toning embrace this well defined dollar. Unimportant rim nicks are seen at 1:30 on the obverse and 12:30 on the reverse. (#6874)

1252 **1798 5 Stripes, Pointed 9 VF35 NGC.** Ex: Miller. B-4, BB-92, R.4. Dusky golden-brown and powder-blue encompass this lightly abraded Heraldic Eagle dollar. All letters in E PLURIBUS UNUM are bold. A problem-free collector coin of this better variety early dollar that bears a pedigree to the noted holdings of Warren Miller. (#6874)

Rarity-4 1798 Dollar, B-4, BB-92, AU50

1253 **1798 5 Stripes, Pointed 9 AU50 NGC.** B-4, BB-92, R.4. This very scarce variant enjoys considerable niche popularity, and a high-end example such as the present coin should prove irresistible to the advanced early dollar specialist. Strongly lustrous peach-gold and silver-gray surfaces show only light wear concentrated over the well struck high points. The coin displays excellent eye appeal and a certified grade that compares favorably to other known survivors. (#6874)

1254 **1798 Large Eagle, 10 Arrows—Improperly Cleaned—NGC. VF Details.** B-21, BB-107, R.5. This rare variety Heraldic Eagle dollar has blue-green and tan-gold toning that helps conceal distributed small marks. Slightly glossy, but some luster remains in design recesses.(#6876)

Desirable 1798 B-13, BB-108 Dollar, XF45

1255 **1798 Large Eagle, Pointed 9, 10 Arrows XF45 NGC.** B-13, BB-108, R.3. Rose-gray in color, this is an unusually well-detailed piece which appears to be denied an even higher grade only due to a lack of remaining luster. The surfaces are smooth for the grade, except for numerous adjustment marks in the center of the obverse, which are of Mint origin and common on 18th century coinage. (#6876)

Choice AU 1798 B-6, BB-96 Silver Dollar

1256 **1798 Large Eagle, 10 Arrows AU55 NGC.** B-6, BB-96, R.3. Bowers-Borckardt Die State IV with a die crack near the I in AMERICA. Substantial luster shimmers across this lightly circulated caramel-gold and slate-gray Heraldic Eagle dollar. The obverse has a few deep russet freckles. Criss-cross adjustment marks on the reverse are all of mint origin. (#6876)

1257 **1799 7x6 Stars VG10 PCGS.** B-22, BB-168, R.5. This better Bolender die marriage is promptly identified by the bold horizontal die crack across the central reverse. Gunmetal-gray fields contrast mildly with pearl-gray devices and legends. Void of any obvious marks.(#6878)

1258 **1799 7x6 Stars Fine 12 NGC.** B-16, BB-158, R.2. Bowers-Borckardt Die State III. This cream-gray Draped Bust dollar displays substantial plumage detail for the given grade, and the only detractions are a small obverse rim nick at 7 o'clock and a hair-thin line that descends from the hair ribbon.(#6878)

Pleasing 1799 B-21, BB-169 Dollar, VF25

1259 **1799 7x6 Stars VF25 PCGS.** B-21, BB-169, R.3. An intermediate die state with light obverse and reverse cracks. This piece has intermingled tan and silver-gray toning over ivory surfaces. Perhaps finer than graded, but with a weak strike. Here is a pleasing early dollar that will suit the type, date, or variety collector. (#6878)

XF Sharpness 1799 Dollar
7x6 Stars, B-16, BB-158

1260 **1799 7x6 Stars—Improperly Cleaned—NCS. XF Details.** B-16, BB-158, R.2. Bowers-Borckardt Die State III. This early dollar has only light wear, although the fields are slightly cloudy due to a dip, and the field beneath UNUM is a bit glossy. A slender granular strip is noted above the hair ribbon. Splendidly detailed, and luster lurks within design elements. (#6878)

Impressive Choice XF 7x6 Stars
1799 Dollar, B-12, BB-160

1261 **1799 7x6 Stars XF45 NGC. CAC.** B-12, BB-160, R.3. Bowers-Borckardt Die State III. A walnut-brown Heraldic Eagle dollar with a pleasing problem-free appearance. A couple of faint mint-made adjustment marks are noted on the eagle's shield. Well struck aside from reverse star 10. All letters in E PLURIBUS UNUM are bold. (#6878)

Luminous 1799 7x6 Stars Dollar
B-9, BB-166, AU50

1262 **1799 7x6 Stars AU50 NGC.** B-9, BB-166, R.1. Bowers-Borckardt Die State V, last state with cracks to the left of star 12 on the obverse, along with a host of others. Green-gold and blue toning embraces the lustrous surfaces, with the obverse showing mild color and more electric hues on the reverse. A lightly worn piece that shows the usual scattered marks but no singularly mentionable abrasions. *From The South Texas Collection*. (#6878)

Bold AU53 'Apostrophe' 1799 Dollar
7x6 Stars, B-9, BB-166

1263 **1799 7x6 Stars AU53 NGC.** B-9, BB-166, R.1. Bowers-Borckardt Die State V. The so-called "Apostrophe" variety, named for the die break after the second S in STATES. Lavender and cobalt-blue fields contrast with the lighter stone-gray devices. Luster dominates the margins. Close inspection locates minor thin marks near the lips, fletchings, and horizontal shield stripes, but the overall eye appeal is pleasing. (#6878)

1264 **1799 Irregular Date, 13 Stars Reverse—Improperly Cleaned—NGC. VF Details.** B-15, BB-152, R.3. The more available of two Irregular Date, 13 Stars Reverse die pairs, though still scarce in an absolute sense. Vivid blue-green and iridescent toning covers moderately worn surfaces still glossy from a past cleaning. (#6880)

Second Finest 1799 B-13, BB-151 Dollar, AU58

1265 **1799 Irregular Date, 13 Stars Reverse AU58 NGC.** B-13, BB-151, R.5. The single rarest 1799 silver dollar variety with a total estimated population of 60 to 70 coins. This is a remarkable example of the 1799 Irregular Date obverse, combined with the 13 Stars reverse. The two 9s in the date are improperly placed, both high with the first 9 leaning sharply to the left. The E in STATES has die rust inside and above, consistent with all known examples of the variety.

This lovely near-Mint example is clearly a Condition Census piece. The Bowers-Borckardt reference recorded just four Notable Specimens, grading AU55, AU50 (2), and XF45. The present piece, while weakly struck at the centers as always, is sharper than either of the two Dr. Hesselgesser coins illustrated on the PCGS web site. Both sides have deep steel and violet toning with additional iridescence over considerable original luster. The surfaces have a few trivial marks, along with some light reverse adjustment marks.

This coin is from the famous 1975 ANA Sale, lot 945, where it was described as "iridescent tone with mint frost about the devices. Poorly struck up in the centers, central reverse adjustment marks and has some trivial obverse handling marks before Liberty's face. One of two finest known of this rarity and another exciting coin. Probably ex W.G.C. (F.C.C. Boyd), Austin, Ostheimer." Earlier, the Boyd, Ostheimer coin, although not plated in either catalog, was described almost the same by Lester Merkin, who wrote: "Indefinitely struck up in centers, elsewhere very sharp. Mint frost with iridescent cool tone; light adjustment marks on reverse, trivial handling marks." The similarity of descriptions leads us, as it did Dave Bowers, to feel that the present specimen from the 1975 ANA Sale was earlier from the Boyd and Ostheimer Collections.

The finest pieces we can trace are: The AU58 PCGS coin from the Cardinal Collection, earlier lot 779 in Stack's session of Auction '87; the present AU58 NGC coin from the 1975 ANA Sale; the Dr. Hesselgesser Set 1 coin that PCGS grades XF40, but is really much nicer; and the Bolender Collection coin that later appeared in the Gilhousen sale and two later Superior auctions.

There is little doubt that this coin is the second finest known B-13, BB-151 dollar, and it is virtually as nice as the Cardinal coin. The two coins are each considerably nicer than the remaining coins known for the variety. (#6880)

AU 8x5 Stars 1799 Dollar, B-23, BB-159

1266 **1799 8x5 Stars AU50 NGC.** B-23, BB-159, R.4. Bowers-Borckardt Die State II. The sole 1799 marriage with an 8x5 obverse star arrangement, and thus a significant *Guide Book* variety. Cream-gray, powder-blue, and almond-gold enrich this evenly struck and splendidly defined Heraldic Eagle dollar. Undisturbed aside from a tiny reverse rim nick at 3 o'clock. (#6881)

Elusive B-8, BB-188 1800 Dollar, VF25

1267 **1800 VF25 PCGS.** B-8, BB-188, R.4. Bowers-Borckardt Die State IV. The motifs display wear commensurate with the grade, yet silvery luster lurks near design crevices. Most of the coin is toned deep dove-gray. Both sides are free from noteworthy marks. Certified in an old green label holder. (#6887)

VF25 1800 Silver Dollar, B-8, BB-188

1268 **1800 VF25 PCGS.** B-8, BB-188, R.4. Die State III. Obverse die dot inside lower part of R; only three star points touch clouds. The reverse is cracked through AMER to the border over the right side of the R, with the metal slightly elevated at this spot. This is a later intermediate die state. The B-8 is one of the scarce 1800 varieties with about 100 to 150 pieces known today. Light gray surfaces with considerable champagne toning highlights. A few faint hairlines are evident from an old cleaning. Minor surface marks are visible on each side of this pleasing dollar.
Ex: Lano Balulescu (5/2003); William Luebke (Heritage, 1/2007), lot 5026. (#6887)

1800 Dollar—Struck 3% Off Center—XF40 B-1, BB-181

1269 **1800 XF40 PCGS.** B-1, BB-181, R.5. Die State I. Struck 3% off-center at 1 o'clock. Die flaw at star 1; first T in STATES doubled. The B-1 variety is instantly recognizable by the horizontal bulge between star 1 and the hair curls, present on every example seen to date. Additional intermittent die flaws are present at star 11, apparently also present on every known example. The Bowers *Silver Dollar Encyclopedia* notes that all examples are struck from [otherwise] perfect dies and, earlier, Bolender made no mention of any die defects. This example has faint clash marks on both sides. The obverse has clash marks from dentils below the date, and the reverse has the entire date visible behind TES. In his update of Bolender, Jules Reiver discussed these clash marks.

Several examples of this rare variety are known with less-than-perfect centering, but few or no others have been seen with the degree of off-centeredness found on this piece, enough for PCGS to classify it as a mint error. The variety is a solid R.5 with only about 60 pieces known today, and nearly all in lower grades. Bowers wrote: "Most examples are in lower grades with VG and Fine being quite acceptable for the variety. VF coins are very rare, and any piece over VF, such as the Spies EF, would be a sure-fire Condition Census item. All seen are lightly struck at the centers." A lovely example with violet-gray color on each side, accented by lighter gold toning. Hints of luster are still visible in the protected areas on each side. A few faint hairlines are hidden beneath the toning.
Ex: Craig Eberhart (1/2005). (#6887)

Challenging XF 1800 Dollar, B-4, BB-186

1270 **1800 XF40 PCGS. CAC.** B-4, BB-186, R.4. The base of the T in UNITED is repunched. Deep gunmetal-gray blankets this scarce variety early dollar. Glimmers of luster are visible throughout the reverse periphery, and no marks are noticeable on either side. An impressive acquisition for the variety collector. Housed in a green label holder. (#6887)

Impressive, High Grade 1800 Dollar, AU50
B-13, BB-193

1271 **1800 AU50 PCGS.** B-13, BB-193, R.4. Distributed clash marks identify this scarcer die pairing. Substantial white luster sparkles across the devices and legends of this chestnut and ivory-gray early dollar. Slightly glossy, and surprisingly free from detrimental marks. Light wear on the cheek, forehead, and drapery prevent an even finer grade. (#6887)

1272 **1800 AMERICAI Fine 12 NGC.** B-19, BB-192, R.2. Star 1 closer to hair than star 7 to L; AMERICAI. Reiver die state a. Bowers-Borckardt die state III. **This is the Reiver plate coin for the obverse of this variety.** This coin was struck fairly early in this die pairing's life, although all reported examples of this obverse show clashing, mostly on the lower right portion of the obverse. Identifiable by a short die line or lump below the first star, and on the reverse by the familiar die scratch that appears to be an I after AMERICA. The most logical explanation for this is a major slip by the engraver, as this does not appear to be a misplaced letter. Toned a light silver-gray with slight mottling on the obverse, and a scratch is noted in the left obverse field from the third star nearly to Liberty's hair. Weakly struck on the area above the arrows and on the shield, and similarly weak on the upper portion of Liberty's hair. A relatively plentiful die marriage, but always in demand for the AMERICAI reverse.
Ex: Freeman (September, 1966) lot 1992; Jules Reiver (Heritage, 1/2006), lot 23622.(#6892)

AMERICAI 1800 Dollar
B-19, BB-192, Fine 15

1273 **1800 AMERICAI Fine 15 PCGS.** B-19, BB-192, R.2. The more available of the AMERICAI die pairs; the B-11 (BB-191) is rare. Though significantly worn, this dollar has surprisingly light and radiant silver-gray color, accented in gold and violet that is present mostly at the rims. Several pinscratches are noted behind Liberty's head. (#6892)

Favored XF AMERICAI 1800 Dollar
B-19, BB-192

1274 **1800 AMERICAI XF40 NGC.** B-19, BB-192, R.2. A popular Guide Book reverse distinguished by a mint-made die scratch after the final A in AMERICA. Blended sea-green and dove-gray encompass this attractive early dollar. The reverse has inconsequential rim dings at 4:30 and 7:30, and a slender and faint granular streak crosses the shield. (#6892)

1275 **1800 Dotted Date—Improperly Cleaned—NGC. VF Details.** B-14, BB-194, R.3. The Dotted Date dollar is a distinctive variety with several small die chips around the first 0. This piece has cleaning lines visible beneath lovely blue, gray, and iridescent toning with lighter tan on the devices.(#6889)

Popular 1800 'Dotted Date' Dollar, XF45
B-14, BB-194

1276 **1800 Dotted Date XF45 NGC.** B-14, BB-194, R.3. Dusky plum-gray toning deepens slightly toward the rims. This is a well-defined example of this collectible *Guide Book* marriage, named for the curious series of die dots near the first 0 in the date. Refreshingly unmarked for the grade despite a couple of small hits near the right shield corner, and minor obverse rim dings at 11 and 12 o'clock. (#6889)

1277 **1801 Fine 15 PCGS.** B-2, BB-212, R.3. A lovely middle-grade Draped Bust dollar, this 1801 is housed in an old green-label PCGS holder. The obverse is light gray and the reverse is darker gray. The surfaces are pleasing for the assigned grade.(#6893)

Charming VF 1801 Dollar, B-3, BB-213

1278 **1801 VF20 ANACS.** B-3, BB-213, R.3. Bowers-Borckardt Die State II. A gunmetal-gray representative that retains considerable plumage detail on the eagle's breast. The types display wear consistent with the grade. One thin mark is noted between the left ribbon end and the N in UNITED. Encapsulated in an ANACS cache holder. (#6893)

VF 1801 Dollar, B-1, BB-211

1279 **1801 VF20 PCGS.** B-1, BB-211, R.3. Bowers-Borckardt Die State I, with no die crack visible to the left of the date. A moderately worn example of this scarce variety, surprisingly luminous with gold-rose and violet field color giving way to silver-gray on the devices. Light abrasions overall with a few significant marks on the portrait and a handful of minor pinscratches. Housed in a green label holder. (#6893)

1801 Bust Dollar, VF20, B-1, BB-211
A Surprisingly Clean Coin for the Grade

1280 **1801 VF20 NGC. CAC.** B-1, BB-211, R.3. Die State III with a light die crack descending through STA into the clouds. Golden-brown and gunmetal-blue toning is seen over the surfaces of this circulated but relatively unblemished Bust dollar. Most letters in E PLURIBUS UNUM are clear, and only a couple of minor rim dings are seen on either side. (#6893)

Attractive VF30 1801 Dollar, B-1, BB-211

1281 **1801 VF30 NGC.** B-1, BB-211, R.3. Bowers-Borckardt Die State IV with a descending die crack through the STA in STATES. Delicate caramel-gold toning overlies the minimally abraded stone-gray surfaces. All letters in E PLURIBUS UNUM are at least partly present, and most letters are clear. Pockets of luster brighten design crevices. (#6893)

Bright, Glossy AU50 1801 Dollar
B-3, BB-213

1282 **1801 AU50 ANACS.** B-3, BB-213, R.3. This sharp, slightly glossy Bust dollar possesses a full complement of breast feathers, and marks are surprisingly few and far between Medium golden-brown and lilac toning does not conceal the extensive mint luster, which dominates the borders and devices. An attractive piece likely to command spirited floor bidding. (#6893)

AU 1801 Heraldic Eagle Dollar
B-2, BB-212

1283 **1801 AU50 NGC.** B-2, BB-212, R.3. Bowers-Borckardt Die State II with a double "collar" clashmark near Liberty's throat. Ocean-blue and lavender centers are bounded by peripheral golden-brown. Luster is readily evident, and the only marks of any consequence are limited to the area near OF. (#6893)

1284 **1802/1 Narrow Date VF20 NGC.** B-4, BB-232, R.3. A scarce overdate variety, one of five different 1802 over 1 silver dollars varieties. This piece has deep gray and iridescent toning on both sides. A few scattered marks are consistent with the grade. (#6898)

Impressive AU53 1802/1 Dollar
Wide Date, B-3, BB-234

1285 **1802/1 Wide Date AU53 NGC.** B-3, BB-234, R.3. Bowers-Borckardt Die State III with faint "wave" clashmarks above the date. Subtle plum-red and jade-green shades visit this partly lustrous example. There are no distracting marks, and close inspection reveals only a hint of granularity near the T in LIBERTY. Certified in a former generation holder. (#6899)

Choice VF Narrow Date 1802 Dollar
B-6, BB-241

1286 **1802 Narrow Date VF35 NGC.** B-6, BB-241, R.1. A slate-gray Choice VF silver dollar from the final years of the Heraldic Eagle type. The minutely granular surfaces are uncommonly devoid of abrasions, and all letters in E PLURIBUS UNUM are readable. Light wear on the eagle's breast and other highpoints corresponds with the grade. (#6895)

Popular 1802 Narrow Date Dollar, XF45
B-6, BB-241

1287 **1802 Narrow Date XF45 PCGS.** B-6, BB-241, R.1. The date is spaced 18 02 and the right foot of the T in LIBERTY is missing on this die marriage. The obverse of this bright silver-gray example is attractively framed in rich russet and blue-green iridescent toning. Well detailed overall, with a cluster of glossy old marks beneath Liberty's chin. (#6895)

Noteworthy AU 1802 Dollar
Narrow Date, B-6, BB-241

1288 **1802 Narrow Date AU50 NGC.** B-6, BB-241, R.1. Traces of ice-blue and tan-gold adorn this richly detailed slate-gray Large Eagle dollar. Partial luster illuminates the design, and the eye appeal is significant. Impressively devoid of scratches, and the few nearly imperceptible rim dings will be ignored by most collectors. (#6895)

B-4, BB-254 1803 Small 3 Dollar, VF

1289 **1803 Small 3 VF20 ANACS.** B-4, BB-254, High R.3. Surprisingly radiant for a VF piece with pale silver color overall and blue-green and tawny-gold elements through the peripheral zones. Softly defined at the portrait, though actual wear is in line with the grade assigned. Housed in a small-format ANACS holder. (#6900)

1290 **1803 Small 3—Improperly Cleaned—NGC. VF Details.** B-1, BB-251, R.4. This die pair is slightly scarcer than some other 1803 varieties. The present example has dark steel patina accented by lighter blue toning. The surfaces are smooth and pleasing, despite faint underlying hairlines.(#6900)

1803 Small 3 Dollar, VF30
B-4, BB-254
Ex: Jules Reiver

1291 **1803 Small 3 VF30 NGC.** B-4, BB-254, High R.3. Small 3, star 1 closer than star 7; outer arrow point below leftmost base of N. Reiver die state a. Bowers-Borckardt die state I. **This is the Reiver plate coin, obverse and reverse, for this variety.** All seen are this die state, as the dies were apparently retired prior to any significant deterioration took place. Light silver-gray in color with deeper gray adhering to the devices, making them stand out from the fields. A few trivial surface scratches are present, but no bumps are seen. *Ex: Carl Wattenbarger (December, 1967); Jules Reiver Collection (Heritage, 1/2006), lot 23641.* (#6900)

B-6, BB-255 1803 Large 3 Dollar, VF20

1292 **1803 Large 3 VF20 PCGS. CAC.** B-6, BB-255, R.2. Delicate navy-blue, gold, and forest-green patination enriches this charming large early silver type coin. Unusually sharp for the VF20 grade, particularly on the eagle's wings and motto. A cluster of wispy pinscratches above the hair ribbon are nearly invisible. Certified in an old green label holder. (#6901)

Undisturbed AU 1803 Silver Dollar
Large 3, B-6, BB-255

1293 **1803 Large 3 AU50 NGC.** B-6, BB-255, R.2. Bowers-Borckardt Die State III with a hairline die crack through the right-side obverse stars. A mauve-gray early silver type coin that displays glimpses of lime-green and steel-blue. Abrasions of any relevance are refreshingly absent, and luster beckons from the eagle and reverse legends. Struck from moderately rotated dies.
Ex: Dr. Hesselgesser, Ira & Larry Goldberg, 2/2007, lot 1609.
(#6901)

Exquisite Near-Mint 1803 Dollar
B-6, BB-255, Large 3

1294 **1803 Large 3 AU58 NGC.** B-6, BB-255, R.2. Bowers-Borckardt Die State III. This wonderful Borderline Uncirculated early silver type coin shimmers with luster, and has only slight wear on such highpoints as Liberty's cheek and the eagle's breast feathers. Lightly toned with powder-blue, autumn-gold, and sea-green throughout the margins. Both sides lack memorable marks, and the eye appeal is exemplary. As of (1/10), NGC has certified 3 Large 3 dollars as AU58 with only two finer. The service has graded an additional 13 pieces as AU58 without a Small or Large 3 designation.
Ex: Royal Oak Collection (Heritage, 8/2006), lot 5310.
(#6901)

SEATED DOLLARS

Semiprooflike 1844 Seated Dollar, MS61

1295 **1844 MS61 PCGS.** Always pursued by collectors, the 1844 has a notably low mintage of only 20,000 pieces and it is seldom seen in Uncirculated grades. This is an impressive piece that has the usual bright, semiprooflike fields on each side. The striking details are complete throughout, and the grade is explained by numerous small abrasions scattered over both obverse and reverse. Population: 7 in 61, 24 finer (1/10). (#6930)

Rare MS61 1845 Dollar

1296 **1845 MS61 NGC.** The 1845 is exceedingly rare in Mint State, and none have been certified higher than near-Gem. Soft ice-blue and gold -beige patina dominates both sides of this MS61 example, each of which displays lavender and orange accents. Well struck except for weak centrils in the right-border stars. Light handling marks limit the grade. Census: 8 in 61, 8 finer (12/09). (#6931)

1297 **1846-O AU50 NGC.** This is a well defined New Orleans example. Silver-gray surfaces reveal just a few minor scattered marks.(#6933)

Low Mintage 1846-O Dollar, MS62

1298 **1846-O MS62 NGC.** The 1846-O Seated Liberty, from a small mintage of 59,000 pieces, is the first silver dollar coined at a branch mint. Medium intensity golden-brown, cobalt-blue, and violet patination occupies both sides of this MS62 specimen, and partially prooflike fields exhibit a degree of contrast with the well struck devices. A few minute handling marks limit the grade. Census: 9 in 62, 2 finer (1/10). (#6933)

1299 **1853—Cleaned—AU58 ANACS.** This low mintage No Motto silver dollar has substantial luster and possesses light chestnut toning. Careful rotation reveals wispy hairlines, most prominent on the right obverse field.(#6941)

1300 **1855 PCGS Genuine.** The PCGS number ending in .94 suggests Damage as the reason, or perhaps one of the reasons, that PCGS deemed this coin not gradable. In our opinion, this coin has the details of an AU specimen that has altered surfaces from cleaning. Cream-gray with hints of golden patina. The fields appear smooth but are dull and cloudy. Only 26,000 pieces were struck. (#6943)

1301 **1859-O—Improperly Cleaned—NGC. AU Details. Incorrectly designated as an 1850-O by NGC.** A well struck and moderately glossy New Orleans No Motto dollar that has scattered small marks and dusky autumn-gold and pearl-gray patina.(#6947)

1302 **1860-O MS61 NGC.** The luminous surfaces of this well struck O-mint representative display splashes of orange, violet, and electric-blue, more extensive and deeper on the obverse. Difficult to locate in the better Mint State grades.(#6950)

1303 **1870-CC—Altered Surfaces—ANACS. AU50 Details.** Variety 2-E. A dusky and streaky slate-gray Carson City Seated dollar that has only slight wear, but the reverse rim is somewhat abraded, particularly between 1 and 2 o'clock.(#6964)

Choice AU 1870-CC Dollar

1304 **1870-CC AU55 PCGS.** Variety 2-E. Autumn-brown toning is consistent throughout this well defined and slightly glossy Choice AU dollar. Both sides are surprisingly devoid of marks apart from one hair-thin vertical mark that extends from the forehead to the shield tip. The 1870-CC dollar was the first issue struck at the Carson City Mint. Certified in a green label holder. Population: 36 in 55, 30 finer (1/10). (#6964)

1305 **1871 MS60 PCGS.** A gleaming, partially prooflike Philadelphia Seated dollar with no trace of wear. The well struck devices and mirrored fields show numerous light to moderate abrasions. (#6966)

1306 **1872-S—Improperly Cleaned—NGC. AU Details.** A richly detailed but thickly hairlined dove-gray example of this challenging San Francisco issue. A mere 9,000 pieces were struck, and only a handful of Uncirculated survivors are known.(#6970)

1307 **1872-S—Harshly Cleaned—NGC. AU Details.** This low mintage San Francisco Seated dollar is untoned and unnaturally bright. The fields display distributed similar faint curved brush marks. (#6970)

PROOF SEATED DOLLARS

Attractive 1856 Dollar, PR63

1308 **1856 PR63 PCGS.** Most 1856 proof dollars were probably issued as part of silver proof sets, which in that year were starting to have a wide following among numismatists. The approximately 40 examples thought by Breen to exist are more or less in line with the 60 or so seen by PCGS and NGC, after discounting resubmissions and crossovers.

Both sides of this Select example display soft golden-tan color accented with whispers of electric-blue and lavender at the margins. A well executed strike delivers sharp definition to the design elements, with no areas revealing even hints of weakness. A few faint hairlines limit the grade. Housed in a green label holder. Population: 8 in 63, 11 finer (12/09). (#6999)

Pleasingly Toned PR63 1862 Seated Dollar

1309 **1862 PR63 PCGS.** Only 550 proof dollars were struck in 1862. Because of the uncertainties of the War, the ordering of proof coins from the Mint had a two-tiered structure. A higher price was required for coins purchased with currency or a bank draft, a lower price for those purchased with coins. This is a deeply reflective example that has pinpoint striking definition. Light hairlining can be seen beneath the finely speckled golden-rose toning seen over each side. Population: 49 in 63, 38 finer (1/10). (#7005)

Lovely 1866 With Motto Dollar, PR62 Cameo

1310 **1866 Motto PR62 Cameo NGC.** A splendid representative of the first regular issue with IN GOD WE TRUST on the reverse. This piece has some light hairlines that limit the grade, but it also has exceptional eye appeal with mostly brilliant surfaces and a frame of gold and iridescent toning. It exhibits excellent contrast between the fields and the devices. (#87014)

Spectacular PR64 Cameo 1866 Seated Dollar
First Year of the With Motto Type

1311 **1866 Motto PR64 Cameo NGC.** Only 725 proofs were struck in this first year of the With Motto design, an issue that several advanced collectors have pursued, including Jimmy Hayes. This absolutely stunning Cameo proof offers deeply mirrored silver fields and lustrous white devices. There is slight evidence of toning on each side, occasionally dabbed around the margins. Every design element throughout is fully and sharply delineated. Census: 20 in 64 Cameo, 18 finer (1/10). (#87014)

1312 **1869 PR61 PCGS.** This sharply struck specimen has flashy fields and only a hint of golden toning near the rims. The right obverse field has faint chatter, and minor planchet granularity is noted near Liberty's left (facing) arm. A scant 600 proofs were struck. Encased in a first generation holder.(#7017)

1313 **1870 PR61 PCGS.** This precisely struck specimen is primarily untoned, although the borders offer delicate bands of ocean-blue and pumpkin-gold. The fields lack obvious hairlines, although their reflectivity is slightly subdued.(#7018)

Obviously Original 1870 Seated Dollar
PR66 Cameo

1314 **1870 PR66 Cameo NGC.** The proof Seated Liberty dollar saw a mintage of 1,000 pieces in 1870. A number of these have survived in the better levels of preservation, though pieces with a Cameo finish are scarce. Splashes of medium intensity multicolored toning are seen over each side with an off-center circle of brilliance on both obverse and reverse. The surfaces are remarkably well preserved on this Premium Gem Cameo and show no obvious or mentionable flaws. The design elements exhibit razor-sharp definition. Census: 2 in 66 Cameo, 2 finer (1/10). (#87018)

TRADE DOLLARS

1315 **1873-CC—Environmental Damage, Cleaned—ANACS. MS60 Details.** This rare date Carson City Trade dollar is mostly lustrous but is moderately hairlined and displays a few small patches of charcoal patina along the borders. The obverse field has scattered minute marks. A good strike with minor softness on the right (facing) claw.(#7032)

Well Struck Mint State 1874-CC Trade Dollar

1316 **1874-CC MS61 NGC.** Tall CC. Period after FINE. A hint of golden toning on the rims accents the mostly brilliant centers. Myriad abrasions limit the grade but minimally affect the flow of the stunning satiny luster. Crisply struck save for the typical weakness on Liberty's head and the adjacent stars and on the eagle's right (facing) leg. Delicate die cracks are noted by the date. (#7035)

Attractive 1874-CC Trade Dollar, MS61

1317 **1874-CC MS61 ANACS.** Tall CC. Period after FINE. A veneer of violet and gold patination is more extensive and deeper on the obverse of this CC-mint example. Well struck save for the typical weakness on Liberty's head and the eagle's right (facing) leg. A few small handling marks limit the grade, yet an attractive piece for the MS61 designation. Most were apparently shipped to China. (#7035)

1318 **1874-S MS62 PCGS.** Medium S. Period after FINE. A strongly struck and impressively lustrous example of this Trade dollar issue, available for a price through all circulated grades but elusive in Mint State. Gold-gray outer toning gives way to centers that are silver-white with milky streaks.(#7036)

1319 **1875-S Chop Mark MS62 PCGS.** Type Two Reverse. Large S. This lustrous Trade dollar has five chop marks, two on the obverse and three on the reverse. A curious raised ornament above the right leaf trio is affected by a darkly toned oval abrasion. (#87039)

1320 **1875-S MS63 NGC.** Type One Reverse, Large S. Attractively toned in peach, lemon, and powder-blue shades. A satiny silver type coin that has only minor incompleteness of strike on the eagle's right (facing) leg. Field marks are refreshingly few in number. (#7039)

1321 **1876 MS63 PCGS.** Type One Obverse, Type Two Reverse. Wisps of olive-green adhere to light gray surfaces on the obverse of this Select Trade dollar, while the reverse takes on mauve-gray coloration with cobalt-blue in the recesses. Well struck save for Liberty's hair and the upper stars. Appealing for the grade. (#7041)

Lustrous 1877 Trade Dollar, MS64

1322 **1877 MS64 PCGS.** Soft beige and rose patination runs over both sides of this near-Gem Trade dollar, each of which displays pleasing luster. The design elements are well struck except for the typically-seen weakness on the stars and in Liberty's hair. A few light marks are undisturbing. Population: 64 in 64, 5 finer (1/10). (#7044)

1323 **1877-S MS60 PCGS.** Large S. Light copper-gold toning adorns the peripheries of this lustrous and sharply impressed Uncirculated type coin. The fields are lightly abraded for the grade, despite moderate marks near OF. Encased in a first generation holder. (#7046)

1324 **1877-S MS63 PCGS.** Large S. The 1877-S mintage of more than 9.5 million coins was the heyday of the Trade dollar, struck in the year before the standard silver dollar was returned from an 1873 banishment. This appealing Select piece would make a good choice for a type set, with deep golden-gray surfaces that offer plenty of radiant luster and a bold strike. Light obverse marks account for the grade.(#7046)

1325 **1877-S MS63 NGC.** Large S. Dappled gray-blue patina is joined by a splash of yellow-gold on the reverse. Sharply struck, and revealing just a few minor handling marks.(#7046)

1326 **1877-S MS63 PCGS.** Large S. This flashy Select example displays semiprooflike fields and scattered light toning. A small reddish-brown spot is below the eagle's tail. Scattered wispy marks define the grade.(#7046)

Key 1878-CC Trade Dollar, AU58

1327 **1878-CC AU58 PCGS.** The mintage for the 1878-CC Trade dollar was a mere 97,000 pieces, and many of these were probably part of the 44,148 pieces that were melted on July 19 of this year, thus further reducing the net availability of this key issue. Very rare in mint condition, this near-Mint example represents excellent value for the collector. Some of the original luster still remains and the striking details are sharp overall and are set off by the muted gray toning. Identifiable by a three-reed nick in the field between the left wing of the eagle and the back of his neck. Toned on both obverse and reverse with hazy gray-lilac toning with an occasional dab of golden. Population: 12 in 58, 24 finer (1/10). (#7047)

Richly Toned 1878-S Trade Dollar, MS64

1328 **1878-S MS64 PCGS.** The 1878-S is one of the most plentiful Trade dollar issues, and as a result is a favorite of type coin collectors. This near-Gem has medium-density gray and blue toning over each side with mint luster that shines forcefully through. The strike is full in all areas and there are no noticeable abrasions on either side. (#7048)

PROOF TRADE DOLLARS

Brilliant PR63 1873 Trade Dollar

1329 **1873 PR63 PCGS. CAC.** The 1873 is the rarest date as a proof in the run from 1873 through 1883. While 865 proofs were struck, attrition has taken a heavy toll on this date. Breen believed about 200 pieces were sold to non-collectors and were subsequently spent, accounting for the date's rarity. This is an all-brilliant example that has nicely reflective, flashy mirrors in the fields. It is also fully struck in all areas, which is not a given on 1873 proofs. Both obverse and reverse are lightly hairlined, explaining the grade. Population: 46 in 63, 36 finer (1/10). (#7053)

Cameo Near-Gem Proof 1875 Trade Dollar
A Wondrously Toned Example

1330 **1875 PR64 Cameo NGC.** Type Two Reverse. Highly attractive, variegated gunmetal-blue, lavender, and orange-gold patination gravitates to the margins of this near-Gem, ceding to freckles of light gold in the central areas. Sharply struck, save for minor weakness in Liberty's hair and the adjacent stars. A few faint handling marks preclude Gem status. (#87055)

Starkly Contrasted 1875 Trade Dollar
PR64 Deep Cameo

1331 **1875 PR64 Deep Cameo PCGS.** Type One Obverse, Type One Reverse. Apparently close to two-thirds of proof 1875 Trade dollars are of this variant with the ribbon ends pointing left on the obverse and berry below claw on the reverse. This is a particularly impressive example that is brilliant overall. The devices are thickly frosted allowing strong contrast against the unfathomably deep mirrors in the fields. A visually pleasing coin that has a few stray hairlines that prevent an even higher grade. Population: 6 in 64 Deep Cameo, 2 finer (1/10). (#97055)

Shimmering 1878 Trade Dollar, PR63 Cameo

1332 **1878 PR63 Cameo PCGS.** The proof-only 1878 Trade dollar is infrequently seen with cameo contrast. This light champagne-toned piece has brilliant silver surfaces with fully mirrored fields and satiny, sharply detailed devices, combining to create excellent eye appeal. Population: 25 in 63 Cameo, 26 finer (1/10). (#87058)

Exquisite 1878 Trade Dollar, PR65 Cameo

1333 **1878 PR65 Cameo NGC.** An exquisite Gem representative of the proof-only 1878 Trade dollar, featuring peripheral gold and iridescent toning around brilliant central devices. The thick and frosty white luster on the devices is nearly sufficient for a Ultra Cameo designation. Census: 23 in 65 Cameo, 6 finer (1/10). (#87058)

1334 **1880 PR63 NGC.** Golden overtones grace surfaces that are silver-gray through the centers. A strongly struck Select proof-only Trade dollar with minor hairlines and field scuffing that account for the grade.(#7060)

Well Defined 1880 Trade Dollar, PR62 Cameo

1335 **1880 PR62 Cameo PCGS. CAC.** Whispers of soft gold and violet patina are discernible only under magnification and the field-motif contrast confirms the Cameo designation. An above-average strike leaves strong definition on the design elements, including Liberty's head and the adjacent stars, areas that are often weak. Some wispy handling marks limit the grade but detract little from the pleasing overall eye appeal. (#87060)

Deeply Mirrored PR64 1881 Trade Dollar

1336 **1881 PR64 PCGS.** A highly collectible and sought-after date among the later, proof-only issues. The 1881 had a mintage of only 960 pieces. The remarkably aspect of this piece is how deep the proof mirrors are in spite of the depth of toning seen over each side. The surfaces are murky light gray with underlying multicolored iridescence, a color scheme that may not sound all that appealing, but seen here with the bright mirrors it is definitely attractive. The striking details are complete throughout and there are no obvious or detracting contact marks. (#7061)

Lovely 1883 Trade Dollar, PR64 Cameo

1337 **1883 PR64 Cameo PCGS.** This silver-white near-Gem has some grayish-gold patina but remains largely untoned in the centers. The considerable field-device contrast is duly noted by PCGS, and there are few mentionable abrasions—a lovely example for a type set. The 1883 proof-only Trade dollar is the last regular issue in the series: The 1884 and 1885 are ultrarare fabrications from a later era. Population: 25 in 64 Cameo, 20 finer (12/09). (#87063)

WHITENING ROOM

Rare 1839 Judd-97 Restrike Half Dollar, PR64

1338 **1839 Half Dollar, Judd-97 Restrike, Pollock-107, High R.7, PR64 NGC.** The Backward Head design. The obverse is much like that found on the regular-issue 1839 gold eagles, with a rounded tip on the forward edge of the bust truncation and a pointed tip on the rear edge—but the entire head faces backward from that on the eagle, right rather than left. Thirteen stars ring the rim, with date 1839 below. The reverse is from the regular-issue Seated Liberty die, Large Letters, as used from 1842 through 1853. Struck in silver with a reeded edge.

Commentary. In the 1976 ANA sale the cataloger described this coin as, "Brilliant Proof. Deep blue obverse, pink and russet iridescent toning on the reverse. An extremely rare coin, high Rarity 8, with no recent records." The 1989 cataloger quoted the above while adding, "In our opinion today the Rarity 8 rating stands intact. The only other specimen offered in two decades was the example in Rarcoa's session of Auction '81, lot 327. No specimen was included in the Olsen, Garrett, Malcolm Jackson, Crouch, or even Woodin collections. The only earlier record we have was the Farouk Sale, lot 1733."

It appears from the census below that today we should rate the piece as High R.7 rather than R.8, as perhaps five or even a half-dozen pieces might exist. This still puts the variety in the stratosphere of the super-rare, with—a little numismatic perspective here, please—far fewer known survivors than the 1933 double eagle or the 1804 silver dollar.

USPatterns.com says, "Stewart Witham noted 146 reeds [the edge reeding] on these, which according to a reed count listing from Bill Bugert of the Liberty Seated Collectors Club, means they were likely struck some time between 1854 & 1860 although this reed count was also used in 1869 and 1870."

Physical Description. The splendid original toning present in the 1976 description above is still much in evidence, perhaps a bit more mellowed but just as stunning. This near-Gem boasts a sharp strike, particularly on the reverse, that is equally appealing.

Census. We believe that only four or five separate specimens exist (including one in the Smithsonian), with most of the older appearances representing duplications:
1. Anderson Dupont (Stack's, 11/1954), lot 2416; River Oaks (Bowers and Ruddy, 11/1976), lot 964; Auction '81 (RARCOA), lot 327; Morris Evans Collection-Rarities Sale (Bowers and Merena, 8/1998), lot 2037, which realized $12,650. PR64.
2. ANA (Stack's, 8/1976), lot 3598; Rarities Group; James A. Stack, Sr. Collection (Stack's, 11/1989), lot 716. **The present specimen.**
3. Superior (5/2003), lot 3469, $32,200. PR64 PCGS.
4. Numismatics, Ltd.; Harry W. Bass, Jr. via private treaty sale (8/1974); Bass Collection (Bowers and Merena, 5/1999), lot 1155. PR62 PCGS.
5. Chase Manhattan Bank; Smithsonian Institution. 191.3 grains, 1.204-in. diameter, coin alignment.

Other Appearances.
A. Virgil Brand; Illustrated History (Kosoff, 1962), lot 119.
B. King Farouk; Palace Collections of Egypt (Sotheby's, 5/1954), lot 1733. XF. (#11416)

Judd-168 Original Flying Eagle 1855 Cent, PR63 Brown

1339 **1855 Flying Eagle Cent, Judd-168 Original, Pollock-193, R.4, PR63 Brown PCGS.** Thirteen stars surround an eagle that is flying slightly upward, similar to the Christian Gobrecht/Titian Peale flying eagle design for the Gobrecht dollars (and soon the Flying Eagle cents). The reverse design is similar to the issued large cent. The diameter is intermediate between the large cents struck for commerce in 1855 and the small cents that were first produced in 1856. Struck from clashed dies in bronze with a plain edge. This is a precisely struck cent whose deep brown surfaces exhibit plum-mauve and golden-tan shades once rotated beneath a light. Infrequent minute carbon determines the grade. (#11720)

Choice Transitional 1859 Indian Cent Judd-228, Snow-PT4

1340 **1859 Indian Cent, Judd-228, Pollock-272, R.1, MS64 PCGS.** Snow-PT4. A popular transitional Indian cent pattern. The obverse has the regular issue 1859 Indian cent obverse design, and the reverse displays the issued 1860 Indian cent reverse. Struck in copper-nickel with a plain edge. This is a boldly struck example that shows just a bit of weakness on the upper shield details. Isolated hints of carbon account for the grade. In a green label PCGS holder. (#11932)

Lovely Gem Proof Judd-239 Silver 1859 Half Dollar

1341 **1859 Half Dollar, Judd-239, Pollock-295, R.4, PR65 PCGS.** One of several half dollar patterns from this year that feature the "French Head of Liberty", credited to Longacre. The reverse depicts the denomination as 1/2 DOLLAR, instead of HALF DOLLAR (Judd-237 and Judd-245), 50 CENTS (Judd-241), or HALF DOL. (Judd-243). Struck in silver with a reeded edge. Caramel-gold visits the obverse, while the reverse displays apple-green and walnut-tan shades. Well struck and pleasing with fine vertical die lines (as issued) on the right obverse field. (#11972)

1861 GOD OUR TRUST Half Dollar Judd-279, PR61

1342 **1861 Half Dollar, Judd-279, Pollock-330, Low R.7, PR61 PCGS.** From regular issue dies except that GOD OUR TRUST is present sans scroll in the reverse field above the eagle. Struck in silver with a reeded edge. Probably a dozen or so examples are known of this and the copper variant. This example is mostly brilliant with a faint trace of russet around the margins. The surfaces are obviously hairline, accounting for the grade, and there are a couple of lint marks on the obverse. (#12106)

PR62 Cameo 1863 GOD OUR TRUST Half Dollar Pattern, Judd-338

1343 **1863 Half Dollar, Judd-338, Pollock-410, R.5, PR62 Cameo PCGS.** The obverse is the regular Seated Liberty die for 1863; the reverse is like the regular issue, with the addition of GOD OUR TRUST on a scroll above the eagle's head. Struck in silver with a reeded edge. An early prototype of the religious-motto class, considerably contrasted with deep silver, blue, and violet shadings through the mirrored fields. Scattered hairlines, perhaps more concentrated in the right obverse field, account for the grade. (#60500)

Prized 1865 Judd-453 Twenty Dollar With Motto Pattern in Copper, PR64 Brown

1344 **1865 Twenty Dollar, Judd-453, Pollock-526, High R.6, PR64 Brown PCGS.** Both the obverse and the reverse are similar to the regular issue 1865 double eagle except that the motto IN GOD WE TRUST was added above the eagle as adopted in 1866. Struck in copper with a reeded edge. The Judd-453, both gilt and ungilt (as in the present case), has been a collector favorite from the time of its creation to the present day. The PR64 Brown example offered here is a lovely representative of the very rare pattern, olive-brown with ethereal blue and violet elements that form deep pools in small pockets on the reverse. Excellent definition and visual appeal. Population: 3 in 64 Brown, 1 finer (12/09). (#60640)

Pleasing 1868 Three Cent Nickel Pattern Judd-618, PR64 Cameo

1345 **1868 Three Cent Nickel, Judd-618, Pollock-687, R.4, PR64 Cameo PCGS.** The design is similar to the regular-issue three cent nickel, but with the wreath farther from the rims and no ribs in the reverse columns. Struck in nickel with a plain edge. An attractive Cameo specimen of this very scarce pattern, strongly reflective in the minimally toned fields with delicate but delightful frost over the devices. Population: 3 in 64 Cameo, 1 finer (1/10). (#860834)

Near-Gem Proof Judd-633 1868 Five Cent Pattern

1346 **1868 Five Cents, Judd-633, Pollock-705, R.5, PR64 PCGS.** The obverse design is that of the three cent nickel, as adopted, but on a larger planchet, with minor design modifications appropriate to the larger diameter. The reverse features a Roman numeral V in the center, with a wreath encircling, scroll with IN GOD WE TRUST and Maltese cross above. Struck in nickel with a plain edge. Light blue and green tints on the generally nickel-gray obverse give way to deeper colors on the reverse. An attractive example of this intriguing pattern, housed in a green label holder. (#60851)

Outstanding PR66 Judd-721 1869 Standard Silver Quarter

1347 **1869 Standard Silver Quarter Dollar, Judd-721, Pollock-802, R.5, PR66 PCGS.** The obverse features a bust right of Liberty wearing a cap ornamented with three stars. A scroll bearing IN GOD WE TRUST is below. The reverse depicts 25 CENTS centered in a small wreath of oak and laurel leaves with STANDARD SILVER above and the date 1869 below. Struck in silver with a reeded edge. A magnificent Premium Gem draped in dusky aquamarine and autumn-gold shades. Fully struck and undisturbed. Population: 1 in 66, 0 finer (1/10). (#60948)

Challenging Judd-882 1870 Quarter, PR61

1348 **1870 Quarter Dollar, Judd-882, Pollock-980, High R.7, PR61 PCGS.** A regular issue Motto reverse quarter is paired with a William Barber rendition of the seated Liberty. She faces left and holds an olive branch and a Federal shield. A Liberty pole ascends behind her arm. Struck in silver with a reeded edge. A well struck stone-white specimen that has minor die rust on the reverse. The glassy fields provide noticeable contrast with the radiant devices. (#61126)

Elusive 1870 Standard Silver Quarter
Judd-889, PR63

1349 **1870 Standard Silver Quarter Dollar, Judd-889, Pollock-988, Low R.7, PR63 PCGS.** A bust of Liberty wearing a cap ornamented with three stars facing right, the legend UNITED STATES OF AMERICA surrounds the figure, and a scroll with IN GOD WE TRUST is below. The reverse reads 25 CENTS 1870 in the center and is surrounded by a wreath of cotton and corn. Struck in silver with a plain edge. This boldly struck example has good field reflectivity, and is untoned aside from a deep blush of ruby-red, orange, and cobalt-blue at 1:30 on the obverse. (#61133)

Judd-915 1870 Standard Silver Quarter
Struck in Copper, PR63 Brown

1350 **1870 Standard Silver Quarter Dollar, Judd-915, Pollock-1011, Low R.7, PR63 Brown PCGS.** Standard Silver design with the head of Liberty wearing a diadem and a ribbon inscribed LIBERTY in raised letters. The reverse reads STANDARD SILVER 1870 around the rim with 25 CENTS in the center of an oak and laurel wreath. Struck in copper with a plain edge. This glossy and fully struck representative is vividly toned in magenta-red, sun-gold, and navy-blue. No surface detractions are noted despite examination beneath a lens. (#61159)

Rare Judd-918 1870 Standard Silver Quarter
PR62, Struck in Silver

1351 **1870 Standard Silver Quarter Dollar, Judd-918, Pollock-1022, Low R.7, PR62 PCGS.** The obverse exhibits a bust of Liberty facing right with the legend UNITED STATES OF AMERICA around the upper border. Liberty wears a ribbon inscribed LIBERTY, and the motto IN GOD WE TRUST is on a scroll near the lower border. The reverse displays the denomination 25 CENTS within a wreath of laurel and oak. STANDARD SILVER is at the top, the date 1870 is below. Struck in silver with a reeded edge. A lightly toned and flashy specimen that lacks hairlines, but both sides have several interesting mint-made lintmarks, the most prominent above the hair bun. (#61162)

Difficult 1870 Standard Silver Half
Judd-987, PR63

1352 **1870 Standard Silver Half Dollar, Judd-987, Pollock-1116, High R.6, PR63 PCGS.** Standard Silver design with Liberty facing right wearing a headband with a star, a scroll below, and UNITED STATES OF AMERICA above. The reverse has 50 CENTS in the center and is surrounded by a wreath of oak and laurel with 1870 below and STANDARD SILVER above. Struck in silver with a reeded edge. Honey-gold and powder-blue enrich this moderately toned and well struck representative. The right obverse field displays a few faint contact marks. (#61233)

PR62 1871 Five Cent Pattern, Judd-1053

1353 **1871 Five Cents, Judd-1053, Pollock-1188, High R.6, PR62 NGC.** The bust of Liberty is similar to that seen on the issued three cent nickel. Simple laurel wreath and denomination reverse. Struck in nickel with a plain edge. Though a number of tiny contact marks and a few spots of deep reddish toning are present on this specimen, the surfaces offer a strong nickel-white gleam. High visual appeal for the grade. (#61312)

1885 One Cent Annular Pattern in Silver
Judd-1740, PR45

1354 **1885 One Cent, Judd-1740, Pollock-1950, High R.6, PR45 PCGS.** This annular pattern cent has a central perforation with a smooth, raised edge. The obverse has UNITED STATES OF AMERICA above with the date 1885/3 at the bottom of that side. On the reverse, ONE CENT is in large letters at the top with a small shield below flanked by laurel sprigs. Struck in silver with a plain edge. The Eastman Johnson design, a clever if eventually unadopted concept. This proof shows considerable rub on the sage-silver surfaces, consistent with time spent as a pocket piece, for example. Population: 2 in 45, 8 finer (12/09). (#62181)

Pollock-5465 Private Half Eagle Constitution Commemorative Pattern in Tungsten, MS62

1355 **1987 "Half Eagle" Pollock-5465, R.4 MS62 NGC.** Weight 182.7 grains. Fred Zinkann design for the Bicentennial of the Constitution half eagle commemorative, three fluted columns on one side, heraldic eagle flanked by plants, sun, and stars on the other. Struck in tungsten with a plain edge. One of 88 pieces in tungsten, per Pollock, struck privately by Pressed Metal Products, Vancouver, BC, Canada. "Very softly struck" with "pewter gray surfaces" also per Pollock, with additional gold-green overtones.

GOLD DOLLARS

Pleasing 1849 No L Gem Gold Dollar

1356 **1849 No L MS65 PCGS.** This scarce variety lacks the designer's initial on the bust truncation. Yellow-gold surfaces display pleasing frosty luster, and the design elements are sharply impressed, save for softness in the uppermost stars. This well preserved Gem shows light die cracks on the reverse. Population: 28 in 65, 9 finer (12/09).
From The Longfellow Collection. (#7501)

Exceptional MS66 1849 Gold Dollar Open Wreath, With L

1357 **1849 Open Wreath MS66 PCGS. CAC.** Breen-6001. This Open Wreath variant also has the L initial (for designer James Longacre) prominently punched on the truncation of the neck. The Breen reference calls this and the 6002 listing "Small Head" varieties. Several years ago, John Dannreuther proved conclusively that the head is not actually smaller than on the so-called "Large Head" varieties. Instead, Longacre moved the stars inward on a later hub modification, thus giving the optical illusion of a larger head on that hub and subsequent dies.

This is an exceptionally attractive example of this always-popular first year of issue. The surfaces display lovely, swirling mint frost and yellow-orange gold color. The striking details are full in all areas, and there are no obvious abrasions on this Premium Gem. "Ghosting" of the central obverse device is seen in the center of the reverse. Population: 12 in 66, 2 finer (12/09).
From The Longfellow Collection. (#7502)

Sharp 1849 Closed Wreath Gold Dollar, MS66

1358 **1849 Closed Wreath MS66 PCGS. CAC.** Breen-6006, thin numerals in date. A shining example with heavy mint frost and lovely canary-gold toning across both sides. The design details are produced with astonishing crispness and clarity. Diagonal die striations cover the flashy, semiprooflike reverse. A beautifully preserved Premium Gem example of this first-year gold dollar issue. Population: 4 in 66, 0 finer (12/09).
From The Longfellow Collection. (#7503)

STATES OF A
1
DOLLAR
1849
C

'Near-Mythic' 1849-C Open Wreath Gold Dollar, XF45

1359 **1849-C Open Wreath XF45 NGC.** Nearly every series has its key date(s), important coins that are required to complete a collection. However, throughout the entire panorama of American coinage, there are a few issues that stand out as major rarities. Among the most important is the 1849-C Open Wreath gold dollar, of which there are just four confirmed examples, with a fifth piece rumored. We are delighted to present this XF45 NGC piece, the third finest of the four known coins. The 1849-C is peerless in the field of Southern mint gold coins struck in Charlotte, North Carolina; Dahlonega, Georgia; or New Orleans, Louisiana.

In fact, the 1849-C Open Wreath gold dollar has few peers among all regular issue U.S. gold coins. The unique 1870-S three dollar piece is a special issue; the 1797 Heraldic Eagle half eagles with 16 stars and 15 stars on the obverse are each unique in the Smithsonian Institution; the 1822 half eagle has just three known (including two in the Smithsonian Institution); the 1854-S half eagle has just three known; the 1861 Paquet double eagle has just two known; and the 1933 double eagle has just one in collectors' hands, but 13 are known. Any of those coins would easily bring seven figures if offered at auction today. There are a few additional million-dollar coins, but none are in the same rarity category as the 1849-C Open Wreath gold dollar.

The 1849-C Open Wreath has had difficulty keeping pace with other major rarities. The current auction record for any example of this issue was established in July 2004, when the finest known example realized $690,000. That was a time when eight other coins had already broken the seven-figure barrier. Doug Winter writes in the third edition of *Gold Coins of the Charlotte Mint 1838-1861* that "this variety remains underpublicized among non-specialists. Among Charlotte collectors, it has assumed near-mythic proportions." The time is right for the 1849-C Open Wreath gold dollar to make its own place among auction records for rare coins—and the time is also right for the forward-looking collector to add this coin to his or her collection.

As with most major rarities, the provenance of the known 1849-C Open Wreath gold dollars is subject to continual refinement. The *NGC Census Report* lists this coin and two others, an MS63 Prooflike piece and one that grades Fine 15. A single AU58 coin appears on the *PCGS Population Report*, and all four certified coins are listed in our roster:

1. MS63 Prooflike NGC. Richmond Collection (David Lawrence, 7/2004), lot 1005, $690,000; to a partnership of Heritage Rare Coin Galleries, Martin Paul, and Steve Contursi; sold to a private collector in 2005 for a sum reportedly close to $1 million. Winter writes that this coin "is said to be ex: New Netherlands inventory in the 1950s."

2. AU58 PCGS. The discovery coin for the 1849-C gold dollar. Waldo Newcomer; Belden Roach Collection (B. Max Mehl, 2/1944), lot 1083; Charles Williams Collection; Robert Schermerhorn Collection; 1956 ANA Sale (James Kelly, 8/1956), lot 1571; later, a Midwestern Collection; Auction '79 (Stack's, 7/1979), lot 749, $90,000; New England Rare Coin Galleries; private collection; 1982 FUN Sale (New England Rare Coin Auctions, 1/1982), lot 1350, $55,000; Southern Collection; Kevin Lipton; Winthrop Carner; North Georgia Collection (1999 FUN Sale, Heritage, 1/1999), lot 7722, unsold; Doug Winter and Hancock and Harwell; James Blanchard & Co.; a North Carolina Collection (Heritage, 4/2006, lot 1520, unsold. The 1944 Mehl catalog of the Roach Collection is apparently the earliest record of the variety in print. The March 1951 issue of *The Numismatist* carries a notice from Robert Schermerhorn that he acquired his coin "about eight years ago." Since the Charles Williams Collection was not sold until 1950, Q. David Bowers questions that portion of the provenance.

3. XF45 NGC. New England Rare Coin Galleries, circa 1978-1979; a Delaware Collection; later, Jefferson Coin and Bullion, to a private collector. **This is the present specimen, and its first auction appearance, and to the best of our knowledge its first plated appearance.**

4. Fine 15 NGC. The reverse is scratched and shows traces of an old jewelry mounting. "McReynolds" prior to 1956; Leo Young; Charles Southwick; 1974 GENA Sale (Pine Tree Auctions, 9/1974), lot 1952, $35,000; Elrod Collection (Stack's, 5/1986), lot 1330, $25,850; a California Collection (via Winthrop Carner for a reported $150,000); Heritage Rare Coin Galleries (1997); William Miller Collection; Long Beach Sale (Heritage, 2/1999), lot 6086, unsold; 2000 FUN Sale (Heritage, 1/2000), lot 7549, $86,250; Ashland City Collection (Heritage, 1/2003), lot 4607, $97,750; a North Carolina Collection (via Doug Winter).

In addition to those four coins, Doug Winter records the possible existence of a fifth piece that "was supposedly owned by a Connecticut dealer back in the 1960s or 1970s." Bowers published his own take on the roster of known specimens, giving each of the five coins a distinctive name, although he gives little other information useful for tracing the pedigree of the different coins. He listed the Newcomer specimen (our number 2), the New Netherlands specimen (our number 1), the McReynolds specimen (our number 4), the Lumadue specimen owned by Connecticut dealer Donald Lumadue (the coin Winter mentions), and the Private Collection coin (our number 3, the present piece).

Waldo Newcomer (1867-1934), the famous early 20th century collector, was the first to recognize this important variety, sometime before 1933. Most of the Newcomer Collection was sold to B. Max Mehl in 1931, although remnants of the collection were offered at auction by J.C. Morgenthau in 1939.

All past authors have written that the reason for the change from the Open Wreath to the Close Wreath is unknown. It is virtually certain that the Open Wreath coins were struck before the Closed Wreath coins, and delivery records suggest the date was July 3, 1849. In *A Guide Book of Gold Dollars*, Q. David Bowers writes that "two examples were sent to Mint Director Robert Maskell Patterson in Philadelphia, who replied that the coins were not well made, that the milling was too prominent, and that, in any event, new dies were being sent." The exchange appears to indicate why the change took place from the Open Wreath to the Close Wreath, and why so few of the former pieces were made.

Although two pairs of dies were sent to Charlotte in June 1849, it seems that only one pair was used. All known 1849-C Open Wreath gold dollars have the same characteristics. Doug Winter describes them: "The star opposite the tip of Liberty's nose has a short right point and it is weaker than the other stars. The leaf below the 1 in the date is hollow while the tip of the leaf below the 9 is partly detached. The ribbons are incomplete due to die lapping. A tiny die file mark can be seen above the RI in AMERICA."

Described in print for the first time, this splendid Choice XF piece has a slight greenish appearance with traces of yellow luster visible in the protected areas around the design motifs, letters, and stars. Light wear has flattened the hair strands below the coronet and over the ear, with all other details quite sharp. As Mint Director Patterson mentioned, the obverse and reverse borders are prominent. Trivial surface marks are seen to some degree on each of the known specimens, including this piece, with a prominent mark below Liberty's chin that will serve for future identification.

The current offering is the 13th time that an 1849-C Open Wreath gold dollar has appeared for public competition in any auction sale since 1944, an average of once every five years. Offerings have taken place in 1944, 1956, 1974, 1979, 1982, 1986, 1999 (2), 2000, 2003, 2004, 2006, and now in 2010. It is impossible to predict when the next auction appearance may take place, but the year 2016 seems a reasonable guess. The Charlotte gold specialist who has waited to obtain this "near-mythic" variety may well want to take advantage of the present opportunity.

From The Longfellow Collection. (#7506)

Condition Census 1849-C Closed Wreath Dollar MS64, Tied for Finest Graded

1360 **1849-C Closed Wreath MS64 NGC.** Variety 1. The U.S. Mint was quite late coming to the gold dollar party. The Bechtler family of Rutherford County, North Carolina—capitalizing on the nation's first gold rush nearly two decades before that in California—had produced private gold coinage since 1831, the year of their first gold dollar.

The Mint had fiddled with gold dollar patterns as early as 1836. That was the year in which it produced the derivative Judd-67 dollar patterns, based on the Liberty Cap and Rays design of Mexican silver coinage. The same design would be used on Mint medalets produced that same year that commemorate the first U.S. steam-powered coinage.

But it would be another 13 years, until 1849, before the first federal gold dollars were produced. Meanwhile, the young nation had opened branch mints in New Orleans; Dahlonega, Georgia; and Charlotte, North Carolina, but only New Orleans struck both gold and silver. The two inland mints struck only small-denomination gold, so it came as no surprise when Charlotte struck gold dollars in the first year of the federal coinage, alongside Dahlonega, Philadelphia, and New Orleans. The Charlotte mintage, however, at 11,634 coins was a pittance compared to the much-larger productions in Philadelphia and New Orleans. The fiddling was not yet completely over, as the design went through several iterations in its first year, and later subtypes would appear in 1854 and 1856. The Open Wreath 1849-C is a fabulous rarity, while the Closed (or Close) Wreath is scarce in all grades and a true rarity in Mint State. The 1849-C Closed Wreath dollars are usually found prooflike, with convex obverse fields that give a bulged look to the coins.

The present example offers semiprooflike fields and surfaces that feature full pinpoint strike definition throughout. The bright yellow-gold surfaces show tinges of reddish patina in the protected areas. The grade is accounted for by several minor ticks in the right obverse field. A short but prominent die crack runs on the reverse from the top of the 1 in the date to O(F).

Doug Winter estimates that no more than a dozen pieces of the 1849-C Closed Wreath are known in Mint State. This is the first time we have ever handled this issue in MS64 since we began maintaining our Permanent Auction Archives, and the present piece is tied with one other NGC-certified piece for the finest graded (1/10). The finest certified by PCGS are several pieces in MS63, all of which we have handled, that Doug Winter lists at the top of his Condition Census from 2008.
From The Longfellow Collection. (#7505)

1361 **1849-D—Improperly Cleaned—NGC. XF Details.** Variety 1-A. The Open Wreath design is standard on all known 1849-D gold dollars. This piece is lightly cleaned, yet it retains ample luster over greenish-gold surfaces. Minor marks are evident on both sides. (#7507)

Unworn 1849-D Gold Dollar

1362 **1849-D—Scratches—NCS. Unc Details.** Variety 1-A, with mintmark to the left of the knot on the wreath. This lemon-gold example of this first-year Dahlonega gold dollar shows no evidence of wear, though numerous scratches pass through the fields below and to the right of the portrait, as well as around the 1 in the denomination. (#7507)

Lustrous 1849-D Gold Dollar, MS63

1363 **1849-D MS63 NGC.** Variety 1-A with the mintmark left of center below the bow knot. With a mintage of 21,588 coins, the 1849-D is the most plentiful Dahlonega Mint gold dollar. The production was one-third of the entire gold dollar mintage for all years in Georgia. As it is also the first year of issue for the denomination, the 1849-D is considered the perfect Dahlonega Mint type coin of the Type One gold dollar design. Although shy of the Condition Census for the date, this 1849-D is a lovely piece with brilliant green-gold luster and reflective surfaces. It is sharply struck, although the border is weak in places as always. Census: 17 in 63, 8 finer (12/09).
From The Longfellow Collection. (#7507)

1364 **1849-O Open Wreath MS61 NGC.** This wonderful New Orleans gold dollar has bright yellow surfaces with frosty luster and bold design definition. The 1849-O had a modest mintage of 215,000 coins, with most survivors showing light wear. Several obverse die cracks are present.(#7508)

1365 **1849-O Open Wreath MS62 PCGS.** Yellow-gold surfaces yield well struck motifs, though the 8 and 4 in the date exhibit the usual weakness. Light granularity is noted, especially on the obverse portrait.(#7508)

Sharply Struck 1849-O Open Wreath Gold Dollar, MS64

1366 **1849-O Open Wreath MS64 PCGS.** All known examples of the 1849-O gold dollar are of the Open Wreath variety. This lustrous near-Gem displays apricot-gold and mint-green patination, and a decisive strike delivers sharp definition to the design elements, enhancing the coin's eye appeal. A few trivial marks preclude Gem status. Population: 15 in 64, 4 finer (12/09).
From The Longfellow Collection. (#7508)

Scarce Gem 1850 Gold Dollar

1367 **1850 MS65 PCGS.** Despite a high mintage of nearly 500,000 pieces, 1850 gold dollars are scarce in the better Mint State grades. Rich orange-gold patination is imbued with tints of sky-blue, and lustrous surfaces exhibit well struck design motifs. This nicely preserved piece shows some light reverse cracks. Housed in a green label holder. Population: 13 in 65, 4 finer (12/09).
From The Longfellow Collection. (#7509)

1368 **1850-C XF40 PCGS.** Variety 1. Orange-tinged luster outlines the design elements of this original XF Charlotte Mint dollar. A loupe reveals only inconsequential contact. Just 6,966 pieces were struck. Population: 12 in 40, 58 finer (1/10).(#7510)

1850-C Gold Dollar, MS62
A Notable, Lower Condition Census Coin

1369 **1850-C MS62 PCGS. CAC.** Variety 1. The 1850-C is one of the scarcer gold dollars from the Charlotte Mint. Only 6,966 pieces were produced, and the typical survivor is only VF or XF. Almost Uncirculated pieces are scarce, and Mint State pieces are rare. Probably only five to 10 coins exist in Mint State, from a total of 150 to 250 coins in all grades.

This lower-Condition Census coin is tied with at least three other pieces at the MS62 level. The fields are bright with a glimmer of semireflectivity on each side. Both obverse and reverse lack the granularity often seen, and both sides show pronounced reddish patina. The devices are sharply struck also. Identifiable by a horizontal die flaw just to the left of the middle of the 1 on the reverse. Population: 4 in 62, 1 finer (12/09).
From The Longfellow Collection. (#7510)

Low Mintage 1850-O Gold Dollar, MS63

1370 **1850-O MS63 NGC. CAC.** The 1850-O, with a mintage of 14,000 pieces, is the rarest New Orleans gold dollar, although it trades at lower values than the popular Type Two 1855-O. Most '50-O survivors grade AU, but this example is unworn and sharply struck. The borders display potent luster, and the open fields lack any noticeable marks. Census: 6 in 63, 1 finer (12/09).
From The Longfellow Collection. (#7512)

Lovely MS66 1851 Gold Dollar

1371 **1851 MS66 NGC.** An influx of California-mined gold increased the relative value of silver, which drove Seated coinage out of circulation. Gold dollar mintage peaked between 1851 and 1853, to replace hoarded silver coins in commerce. Few pieces were saved, however, and Premium Gems are rare today. Boldly struck and nearly pristine with a lustrous straw-gold appearance. Census: 18 in 66, 8 finer (12/09).
From The Longfellow Collection. (#7513)

1372 **1851-C AU58 ANACS.** Variety 1, and identified here by the usually seen die crack through the tops of F and AM. This pleasing green-gold representative has sharp definition with only a trace of rub. Virtually full frosty mint luster remains.(#7514)

Spectacular MS66 1851-C Gold Dollar

1373 **1851-C MS66 NGC.** Variety 1. Every now and then, a coin comes along that has no real reason to exist. The nature of production and distribution of the Southern mint gold are such that a survivor of any issue in Premium Gem quality is essentially unheard of. The NGC and PCGS population reports each show two MS66 examples of this date certified, although we tend to think those figures only represent two or three different coins. None have ever received a higher grade.

This Premium Gem has frosty and brilliant yellow-gold luster with a touch of green patina and faint splashes of iridescent toning. It is sharply struck with bold obverse and reverse design details. An impressive, amazing Premium Gem. Census: 2 in 66, 0 finer (12/09).
From The Longfellow Collection. (#7514)

Uncirculated 1851-D Gold Dollar

1374 **1851-D MS61 NGC.** Variety 3-E. The heavy die crack at the right reverse is distinctive for the variety, which Winter speculates may have been struck entirely in June 1851. This sun-gold survivor has noticeable luster and is minimally marked for the grade. The centers are incompletely brought up, as usual for the Dahlonega facility. Census: 19 in 61, 34 finer (12/09).
From The Longfellow Collection. (#7515)

Desirable Gem 1851-O Gold Dollar

1375 **1851-O MS65 PCGS.** A wonderfully original Gem that exhibits orange and olive-gray toning. Only minor marks are evident, and the lustrous fields and devices are well struck except for slight inexactness at the centers. Virtually uncollectible any finer. Population: 28 in 65, 2 finer (12/09).
From The Longfellow Collection. (#7516)

Gorgeous 1852 Gold Dollar, MS67

1376 **1852 MS67 PCGS. CAC.** Although PCGS has certified four finer pieces, including an MS69, this Superb Gem is an amazing type coin with pristine, essentially perfect surfaces, frosty yellow and orange-gold luster, and bold design motifs. The difference between this coin and a higher-grade piece is a judgment call, with a trifle more iridescent toning required for the higher grade. More than 2 million pieces were coined, and survivors are available in any grade desired, providing collectors with an excellent opportunity to choose between market price and grade. Population: 1 in 67, 4 finer (12/09).
From The Longfellow Collection. (#7517)

1377 **1852-C—Improperly Cleaned—NGC. AU Details.** Variety 2. The upright of the 1 in the date extends below the base. This lightly cleaned example retains considerable luster with bright green-gold surfaces.(#7518)

Outstanding 1852-C Gold Dollar, MS65
Tied for Second on the Condition Census

1378 **1852-C MS65 NGC.** Variety 2. Charlotte produced fewer than 10,000 gold dollars in 1852, and though NGC and PCGS combined report over 200 certifications, several authors suggest the survival rate is closer to 100 pieces. This example has the common Mint-made planchet or die problem in the center of the reverse that blurs the definition of LA in DOLLAR. However, from a mint notorious for striking problems, this is a beautiful coin. Liberty's hair, the centers of the obverse stars (save for one below the point of the neck), and the reverse wreath are all strongly defined, though the dentils on the obverse are mushy. This amazing coin also displays vibrant luster and bright honey-gold color. The surfaces are exceptionally clean for the grade; a couple of areas of roughness on the lower neck and before and behind Liberty's neck, and through the reverse denomination, are typical for the issue and neither particularly distracting nor grade-affecting.

The third (2008) edition of Winter's reference on Charlotte Mint gold enumerates one MS66 NGC example as the finest known, and each of the five Gems known are certified by NGC. This coin is listed as tied for second finest on the Condition Census.
From The Longfellow Collection. (#7518)

Low-Mintage 1852-D Gold Dollar, MS61

1379 **1852-D MS61 NGC.** Variety 4-F, the only known variety from a mintage of 6,360 coins. This date is rare in all grades and seldom available in Mint State. This piece is boldly detailed with lustrous light yellow surfaces that display traces or splashes of lilac toning. Census: 16 in 61, 12 finer (12/09).
From The Longfellow Collection. (#7519)

Bright MS64 1852-O Gold Dollar
Third Rarest O-Mint in the Series

1380 **1852-O MS64 NGC.** Mint State specimens of the 1852-O gold dollar are rare, and Garrett and Guth rank it as the third-rarest O-mint behind the 1850-O and 1855-O. This lovely near-Gem is well struck, with honey-gold surfaces and good eye appeal. There is some central striking weakness noted on the reverse, with LA and the 5 in the date soft, but this piece more than compensates in other ways. Census: 12 in 64, 2 finer (12/09).
From The Longfellow Collection. (#7520)

1381 **1853 MS64 NGC.** An intricately struck near-Gem gold type coin that has vibrant luster and exemplary preservation. Apricot fields and devices are encompassed by lime-green borders. Encased in a prior generation holder.(#7521)

Sharp 1853 Dollar, MS66

1382 **1853 MS66 PCGS. CAC.** The 1853 is common through the Gem level of preservation. Premium Gems such as this offering are scarce and finer specimens are rare. Honey-gold patination resides on the lustrous surfaces, and a well executed strike leaves sharp definition on the design elements. Both sides are well cared for. Population: 26 in 66, 11 finer (12/09).
From The Longfellow Collection. (#7521)

Near-Census 1853-C Gold Dollar, MS63

1383 **1853-C MS63 NGC.** Variety 1, the only known die pair from a mintage of 11,515 coins. Doug Winter calls the 1853-C the "worst struck Type One gold dollar from the Charlotte Mint." However, the present piece is a delightful exception to that rule, with bold hair details, sharp star centrils, and strong leaf details. It is a lovely Mint State piece with lustrous green-gold surfaces that exhibit hints of orange toning. Both sides have reflective fields that impart excellent eye appeal. An MS65 and three MS64 coins are the finest certified pieces, followed by this MS63 and 12 others that NGC has certified. PCGS has certified three MS63 coins, with none finer. Here is an amazing opportunity to acquire a solid Mint State example on the outskirts of the Condition Census.
From The Longfellow Collection. (#7522)

1384 **1853-D—Improperly Cleaned—NGC. AU Details.** Variety 5-G, the only dies for this challenging Dahlonega issue, which has a meager mintage of 6,583 pieces. This well defined example has a lightly hairlined obverse. The reverse field above DOLLAR appears tooled.(#7523)

Superlative 1853-D Gold Dollar, MS66
Possibly the Finest Known

1385 **1853-D MS66 NGC. CAC.** Variety 5-G. Before the appearance of this Premium Gem, the finest 1853-D gold dollar that we had ever offered in our auctions graded just MS64. In fact, this is the only piece that is certified as MS66, with none finer. Behind this coin are two PCGS MS65s and two NGC MS64s. In the second edition of his reference, Doug Winter records the existence of two different MS66 NGC coins, both from a Jackson, Tennessee hoard, although only one piece currently appears in the NGC Census Report. No illustrations of the two coins in Winter's Census exist, as far as we know. The piece that Winter lists first is described as prooflike and may be this example.

Winter records the discovery of the Jackson hoard, including gold dollars and other coins mostly dated in the 1850s, during construction of a parking lot. "A frenzy ensued and a number of workers stuffed their pockets with various coins, ranging from gold dollars to eagles."

This example clearly shows the die line from the rim to the star at 9 o'clock, as well as other obverse markers. A vertical die line passes just left of the star at 11 o'clock, and heavy die lines are evident along the profile, especially at the neck and throat. Both sides have incredible mint brilliance with mirrored fields and boldly defined devices. Amazing green-gold luster remains, creating far above-average eye appeal for the issue. Census: 1 in 66, 0 finer (12/09).
From The Longfellow Collection. (#7523)

Popular 1853-O Gold Dollar, MS64

1386 **1853-O MS64 NGC.** A near-Gem representative of this available (and thus popular) Southern gold dollar issue, crisply detailed with remarkable yellow-gold and honey luster. Surface preservation is pleasing, though a few wispy abrasions surrounding the portrait preclude Gem status. NGC has certified 12 numerically finer examples (1/10). (#7524)

Rare Gem 1853-O Gold Dollar

1387 **1853-O MS65 NGC.** If an example that grades between AU58 and MS62 is desired, the 1853-O is fairly plentiful. MS63 pieces are scarce, MS64 coins are very scarce, and full Gems are rarities. This is a precisely struck and lustrous New Orleans gold dollar that has clean surfaces and peripheral orange toning. Census: 10 in 65, 2 finer (12/09).
From The Longfellow Collection. (#7524)

Stunning Type One 1854 Gold Dollar, MS66

1388 **1854 Type One MS66 NGC.** Both the 1854 Type One and Type Two gold dollars were minted in generous quantities in Philadelphia, totaling more than 1.6 million pieces between the two types. This attractive piece shows evidence of die clashing on each side, more prominently on the reverse, and both dies show evidence of fatigue in the form of metal flow lines. Die cracks join a few of the star points with the obverse rim. The poststrike preservation, however, is as exemplary as the eye appeal is superlative. Census: 26 in 66, 7 finer (12/09).
From The Longfellow Collection. (#7525)

AU Sharpness 1854-D Gold Dollar

1389 **1854-D—Improperly Cleaned—NGC. AU Details.** Variety 6-H, the only known die pair. Though recent years have brought greater availability to the 1854-D gold dollar, such availability has made the issue merely "very scarce" in all grades instead of an absolute rarity. This modestly worn example should appeal to a wide range of collectors, though it does show hairlines on its blue-tinged butter-yellow surfaces. (#7526)

AU Details 1854-D Gold Dollar

1390 **1854-D—Improperly Cleaned—NGC. AU Details.** Variety 6-H, the only known dies. Only 2,935 pieces were struck for this difficult Dahlonega issue. An olive-gold example with a hint of wear on the hair near the ear. The obverse field is faintly hairlined, and the reverse rim has been tooled near 6 o'clock. Although slightly granular, the surfaces lack noticeable marks. (#7526)

Mid-Condition Census 1854-D Gold Dollar MS62, Ex: Ashland City

1391 **1854-D MS62 NGC.** Variety 6-H, the only known die pair. Writing in 1965, Walter Breen stated that only 25-30 1854-D gold dollars are extant from a minuscule original mintage of 2,935 pieces. The actual number of survivors is closer to 85-95 pieces (per Winter, 2003), but this does not change the fact that the '54-D is a rare coin that is always in demand among advanced specialists. This date ranks fourth in overall rarity among D-mint gold dollars after the 1855-D, 1856-D, and 1861-D, and third in high grade rarity after only the 1855-D and 1856-D. Since the low end of the Condition Census is two MS60 coins and one MS61 piece, the present MS62 representative also qualifies for this coveted distinction. It is actually ranked #3 on Winter's Condition Census.

The present example displays lovely golden-rose color over satiny surfaces. The diagnostic die scratches (as produced) are evident on both sides, particularly on the reverse around the D mintmark, and the striking bluntness over the lower left reverse is also characteristic of the issue. There are a few moderate distractions in the lower left obverse field, but the eye appeal is above average for the MS62 grade level and extraordinary for a survivor of this often worn and/or impaired date. Identifiable by an obverse abrasion before the star at 12 o'clock and a reverse planchet void (as struck) below the first S in STATES.
Ex: FUN Sale (Heritage, 1/2000), lot 7557, where it realized $11,500; Ashland City Collection, FUN Sale (Heritage, 1/2003), lot 4632, where it brought $10,063.
From The Longfellow Collection. (#7526)

Scarce 1854-S Gold Dollar, MS63

1392 **1854-S MS63 NGC.** The inaugural year of the San Francisco Mint led to two great numismatic rarities, the 1854-S half eagle and quarter eagle. The 1854-S gold dollar is collectible, and has a low mintage of 14,632 pieces. The issue was likely coined to help meet a local need for small denominations, since no silver was struck at the facility that year. The present example has scintillating luster and lovely apricot toning. No marks are consequential, and the strike is sharp throughout. Census: 5 in 63, 9 finer (12/09).
From The Longfellow Collection. (#7527)

Amazing MS64 1854 Type Two Gold Dollar

1393 **1854 Type Two MS64 PCGS.** The short-lived Type Two gold dollar has long provided a focal point for gold type enthusiasts, who often turn their attention to the Philadelphia issues rather than the more challenging mintmarked dates. While the Type Two 1854 gold dollar is available for a price even in MS64, anything finer is decidedly scarce, and few near-Gems approach the eye appeal of this survivor. Frosty, swirling orange-gold luster enlivens minimally marked surfaces. While the central devices show slight softness of detail, the overall eye appeal is redeeming. PCGS has graded 64 finer pieces (1/10). (#7531)

Elusive 1854 Type Two Gold Dollar, MS65

1394 **1854 Type Two MS65 NGC.** The debut issue of the short-lived Type Two design, and a remarkable Gem example. This piece has vibrant yellow-gold luster with frosty surfaces and exceptional eye appeal. The strike is a trifle soft at the centers as usual, but the date is bold, including the 8. Light clash marks are evident, primarily on the reverse. The 1854 (especially) and the 1855 Type Two gold dollars are in high demand for type collections. These pieces are particularly elusive in MS65 or finer grades. In fact, NGC has only certified 38 Gem or finer pieces, from a total population of more than 5,000 coins of the date. Only one out of every 138 submissions has been certified as a Gem at NGC. *From The Longfellow Collection*. (#7531)

Marvelous MS66 ★ 1854 Type Two Gold Dollar

1395 **1854 Type Two MS66 ★ NGC.** The first section of the 1849 Coinage Act reads:

> "Be it enacted by the Senate and House of Representatives of the United States of America in Congress assembled, That there shall be, from time to time, struck and coined at the mint of the United States, and the branches thereof, conformably in all respects to law, (except that on the reverse of the gold dollar the figure of the eagle shall be omitted,) and conformably in all respects to the standard for gold coins now established by law, coins of gold of the following denominations and values, viz.: double eagles, each to be of the value of twenty dollars, or units, and gold dollars, each to be of the value of one dollar, or unit."

Previously, only quarter eagles, half eagles, and ten dollar eagles had been produced by the United States. The significant gold deposits discovered in California the prior year were undoubtedly the motivation behind this coinage act authorizing two additional gold coin denominations. By the end of 1849, nearly 1 million gold dollars had been struck at the four U.S. mints.

In 1854, the size and design of the gold dollar were altered slightly. The coins were made thinner, with the diameter increased from 13 to 15 millimeters. The obverse portrait of Liberty was changed to the likeness of an Indian princess and also made smaller. This new Type Two design had problems, however, like the Type One; Type Twos were only made from 1854 through 1856, creating a scarcer type for coin collectors.

This marvelous Premium Gem example displays intense, shimmering mint frost over honey-gold surfaces. The design elements are sharply struck and the coin is free of poststrike distractions. Moderate clash marks are noted on both obverse and reverse, a typical feature of the Type Twos. Although NGC has graded eight pieces as MS66, this is the only one to also receive the coveted Star designation for exceptional eye appeal. Three coins have been certified numerically finer by NGC, but none of them were awarded the Star (12/09). (#7531)

1396 **1855 MS61 NGC.** Minimally abraded save for a slender mark near the first S in STATES. Luster dominates the wreath and borders. The scarce Type Two gold dollar is known for clashmarks, and they are present on this Uncirculated example, found below the bust truncation and on the field beneath the headdress. Housed in a former generation holder.(#7532)

Miraculously Preserved
1855 Type Two Gold Dollar, MS66

1397 **1855 MS66 PCGS. CAC.** Diminutive yet precious, the gold dollar holds a special place in the hearts of many a collector. The denomination was born out of the flood of gold that came from California beginning in 1849. The nation's mints began producing large quantities of gold dollars, which had their greatest commercial use on the West Coast but gained acceptance nationwide.

Breen comments in his *Complete Encyclopedia* that from 1849 through 1854 "gold dollars formed the bulk of the nation's legal circulating medium between the 3c and the $2.50 denominations," eagerly sought by the public as alternatives to the often worthless and unredeemable private bank notes and store scrip, both of which flooded the country as the value of gold and silver fluctuated. The little gold dollar was hardly worth melting, compared to the eagle, and was highly useful, accounting for its broad acceptance in the 1850s. But the coin proved to be too easily dropped—and lost—in its initial version.

Beginning in August 1854, a new, thinner but wider-diameter version appeared—what we call the Type Two gold dollar. Liberty was replaced by a charming, feathered Indian princess—the first obeisance on national coinage to Native Americans, who were not to become a "national enemy" until the Indian Wars that followed the Civil War and intensified in the 1870s.

Mint Director Snowden requested the new design from his talented engraver, James Longacre, along with a "bigger sister," the three dollar gold piece. Longacre intended the image of Liberty as a Romanesque version of the classic Venus (from a marble statue he saw in a Philadelphia museum) but the public saw the headdress and a classic was named. In fact, it became the inspiration for the Indian cent. The new-style gold dollar, however, lasted only a matter of months. The government's set exchange rate—the ratio of gold to silver—could not be maintained, constantly threatening all gold pieces with private melting for profit. Many gold dollars struck during the period of this type's manufacture (less than two years) failed to survive the decade, accounting in part for their rarity today.

The style was elegant, a deft rendering of Liberty in her feathered bonnet, in noticeable high relief, but as Breen says, "The coins proved unsatisfactory from the beginning. Longacre had miscalculated, overestimating the power of the coining presses then in use." It was a sheer manufacturing problem, especially for the Southern mints, which used older presses discarded by the main facility at Philadelphia. The coins most often were poorly struck, with weak features that wore quickly in use. Many were officially melted. The final type of this denomination, made beginning late in 1856, was the same size but in lower relief yet more deeply engraved, making the coins easier to produce with full details, and therefore they would endure far longer. What did not endure, in any number, were the Type Two issues—most of them unsharp to begin with, easily worn, largely melted and recoined into the new type. High-grade survivors such as this exciting piece somehow escaped, and as such are miraculous reminders of those perilous days so long ago.

The surfaces of this piece are exceptional in every regard, as the grade indicates. The life of the coin, its luster, is thick and frosted, and unbroken by the abrasions that usually afflict Type Two gold dollars. The striking details are uncommonly sharp, with only the slightest hint of softness in the centers. The bright yellow-gold surfaces show a moderate overlay of light reddish patina. One of only 13 pieces so graded by PCGS, with a mere four coins finer (12/09).
From The Longfellow Collection. (#7532)

AU Definition 1855-C Gold Dollar

1398 **1855-C—Scratches—NGC. AU Details.** Variety 2. As a Type Two issue struck by a Southern mint, the 1855-C gold dollar enjoys strong popularity with that specialty. While this well-defined example has a scratch on Liberty's neck, the yellow-gold devices show only the slightest evidence of actual wear. Struck from significantly clashed dies. (#7533)

Rare, High-Grade 1855-C Gold Dollar, AU58
The Only C-Mint Type Two

1399 **1855-C AU58 NGC.** Variety 1. The mintage for the 1855-C is a low 9,803 pieces, but remarkably an estimated 250 to 350 pieces are known in all grades. The majority of those survivors are VF, and only 28 to 45 pieces are believed extant in AU condition. As always, this piece shows a notable lack of high-point definition in the center of each side. This weakness makes the 1855-C a difficult coin to grade, but on this piece slight traces of luster surround the devices. The surfaces are orange-gold with traces of lilac on the reverse. The only mentionable mark is a tiny one just in front of the lower part of Liberty's brow.
From The Longfellow Collection. (#7533)

Scarce 1855-D Gold Dollar, AU58
Variety 7-J

1400 **1855-D AU58 NGC.** Variety 7-J, and slightly scarcer than variety 7-I. The only Type Two gold dollar struck in Dahlonega, the 1855-D had a remarkably low mintage of only 1,811 coins. About 75 of those coins are believed to survive today, about 4% of the original mintage. This piece ranks high among the survivors. NGC has only certified six Mint State pieces, probably including resubmissions. Likewise, the 14 AU58 pieces almost certainly include some resubmissions. This piece is almost identical to another AU58 NGC example, also variety 7-J, that appeared in our 2010 FUN auction. Light green-gold surfaces have a few minor blemishes on each side as expected. Traces of wear on the high points have slightly deeper gold color. Census: 14 in 58, 6 finer (12/09).
From The Longfellow Collection. (#7534)

Near-Gem 1855-O Gold Dollar Tied for Finest Certified

1401 **1855-O MS64 NGC.** The Type Two gold dollar was a short-lived series that was only produced for less than three years. The Type One gold dollar had proven unpopular because its small size rendered it easily lost in pants pockets or purses. The Mint addressed this problem by increasing the planchet's diameter from 13 mm to 15 mm. Of course, the planchet's width was reduced to maintain weight and fineness standards. This measure had the unfortunate effect of making the coins extremely difficult to strike up. Type Two dollars are generally seen with soft strikes, with the 1855-O perhaps better than average in that respect. Such problems caused the design to be abandoned after only three years.

The 1855-O is the last gold dollar from the New Orleans Mint. It is also the only Type Two gold dollar produced at the historic facility. In *Collecting & Investing Strategies for United States Gold Coins*, Jeff Ambio writes of the issue:

> "Of the six issues in the Type II gold dollar series, only two readily present themselves as potential candidates for inclusion in an advanced type set of rarer issues. The first is the 1855-O, which I believe to be among the more underrated coins in the entire U.S. gold dollar series. Survivors from an original mintage of 55,000 pieces are scarce in all grades and decidedly rare in Mint State."

There are currently no specimens graded at the Gem level or above. The present example displays an above-average strike, with some softness on the date and LL of DOLLAR that is seen on almost all Type Two gold dollars. The color is a rich butter-yellow, with traces of golden-brown. Eye appeal is far above average for the issue. NGC and PCGS have certified a combined total of 11 coins at this level, with none finer (12/09).
From The Longfellow Collection. (#7535)

AU53 1856-S Type Two Gold Dollar

1402 **1856-S Type Two AU53 NGC.** Normal mintmark. As the only Type Two gold dollar struck in 1856 (and the only Type Two gold dollar coined at the San Francisco Mint), the 1856-S issue enjoys considerable popularity. This briefly circulated example shows distinct wear across the high points, yet the deep butter-yellow surfaces remain remarkably lustrous. (#7536)

Popular MS62 1856-S Gold Dollar Type Two, Repunched Mintmark

1403 **1856-S Type Two MS62 NGC.** FS-501. The mintmark is widely repunched. A normal mintmark variety also exists. The final issue of the briefly produced Type Two design, and the only issue of the type from the San Francisco Mint. Census: 10 in 62, 6 finer (1/10).
From The Longfellow Collection. (#7536)

Dazzling 1856 Slanted 5 Dollar, MS66

1404 **1856 Slanted 5 MS66 NGC.** Dazzling mint frost radiates over the beautifully toned surfaces of this Premium Gem gold dollar. The 1856 issue features two varieties: the Normal 5 and this, the Slanted 5. This piece offers generally good striking detail, although there is typical weakness on OLL and 85, near the center of the reverse. Shallow planchet flaws appear beside the large denominational 1 and near the lower left reverse border at 8 o'clock, but post-striking defects are minimal. Census: 5 in 66, 1 finer (12/09).
From The Longfellow Collection. (#7540)

Lustrous 1857 Gem Gold Dollar

1405 **1857 MS65 NGC.** Yellow-gold and greenish-gray patination adorns the radiantly lustrous surfaces of this lovely Gem. A well executed strike leaves sharp definition on the design elements, save for the usual softness in the upper leftmost wreath. Clash marks are visible on the reverse. Census: 11 in 65, 8 finer (12/09).
From The Longfellow Collection. (#7544)

Reddish-Gold 1857 Gold Dollar, MS66

1406 **1857 MS66 NGC.** Deep, satiny surfaces on this Type Three example present an even layering of deep reddish-gold patina on both sides. Die clashing is most visible on the reverse. Close examination fails to reveal any singularly mentionable marks or abrasions. Census: 8 in 66, 0 finer (12/09).
From The Longfellow Collection. (#7544)

1857-C Gold Dollar, MS61
A Key Charlotte Mint Issue

1407 **1857-C MS61 NGC.** Variety 1, the only variety known. Although the Mint issued the first Type Three gold dollars in 1856, the first examples were not struck in Charlotte until the following year. Interestingly, the mintage of the 1857-C—13,280 pieces—is on the high side compared to most series issues, it is among the rarest in Mint State. This is partially because the 1857-C is, on average, one of the worst produced gold coins in U.S. history. Only a select few Mint State examples have been certified, none above MS62.

The present coin offers an excellent opportunity to acquire one of the finest representatives of this desirable issue. Pleasing olive-gold patina endows the surfaces of this lightly marked specimen. Although the quality of this issue is notoriously poor, this piece exhibits a significantly sharper strike and fewer defects than typically seen. The fields have a wavy appearance, as usual, and there is minor deterioration on the rims. Nonetheless, the surfaces are fairly smooth overall, and patches of luster appear throughout, remarkable for the issue. A number of die cracks are noted on both sides. This piece has great eye quality compared to the average 1857-C, which is usually seen dull and rather rough. PCGS has certified just one example at the MS61 level, with none finer. NGC reports four MS61 representatives, which may represent multiple submissions of the same coin, along with only two MS62 specimens (12/09).
From The Longfellow Collection. (#7545)

Low Mintage 1857-D Gold Dollar, AU58

1408 **1857-D AU58 PCGS.** Variety 9-L, the only variety for the year. A surprisingly well-preserved example of this popular and low-mintage Dahlonega gold dollar issue. It comes by its grade honestly, with just a touch of light wear at the highest parts over the otherwise undisturbed surfaces. Lemon-gold coloration prevails. Population: 16 in 58, 15 finer (12/09).
From The Longfellow Collection. (#7546)

Sensational 1858 Gold Dollar, MS67

1409 **1858 MS67 PCGS.** The 1858 gold dollar, with a mintage of nearly 118,000 pieces, is fairly available through MS62, but becomes scarcer in MS63 and near-Gem grades. Higher levels of preservation are considerably more difficult to acquire. In MS67, the grade of the present coin, NGC and PCGS combined have certified only five examples, with a mere three specimens graded finer. Moreover, according to our records, only four MS67 examples have appeared for sale in our auctions over the last 17 or so years, as has one MS68 coin.

On this example, fully lustrous surfaces display a softly frosted, nearly satiny texture and are devoid of any mentionable marks. The strike is well executed, emboldening the coin's motifs. Some minor clash marks are noted on each side. A superb specimen for the aficionado of gold dollars. Population: 5 in 67, 2 finer (12/09).
From The Longfellow Collection. (#7548)

1410 **1858-D—Improperly Cleaned—NGC. AU Details.** Variety 10-M. A hairlined representative with a diagonal pinscratch on the upper right reverse. A retained lamination through the mintmark is of Mint origin. Another difficult Dahlonega date, as only 3,477 pieces were coined.(#7549)

Seldom-Seen 1858-D Gold Dollar, MS63

1411 **1858-D MS63 PCGS.** Variety 10-M, the only die pairing. The 1858-D dollar, with a mintage of only 3,477 pieces, is rare in all grades. Douglas Winter, in *Gold Coins of the Dahlonega Mint,* writes that it is fairly easy to locate in Very Fine and Extremely Fine grades. It becomes scarce in About Uncirculated and is rare in Mint State.

The peach-gold surfaces of this Select example display hints of light green and possess nice luster. Most of the design elements are well impressed, though portions of the bonnet and bowknot show the typical softness, as does the 5 in the date. A few minute handling marks occur on the obverse, and clash marks are visible on the reverse. Population: 8 in 63, 4 finer (12/09).
From The Longfellow Collection. (#7549)

Dazzling 1859 Dollar, MS66

1412 **1859 MS66 PCGS.** Premium Gem 1859 gold dollars such as this offering are elusive, and anything finer is nearly unobtainable. Dazzling luster exudes from its yellow-gold surfaces imbued with hints of sky-blue and lavender, and the design elements are uniformly strongly impressed. This nicely preserved coin shows light reverse clash marks. Population: 8 in 66, 6 finer (12/09).
From The Longfellow Collection. (#7551)

Desirable 1859-C Gold Dollar, MS62

1413 **1859-C MS62 NGC.** Variety 1, the only known dies. The 1859-C is the last gold dollar made at the Charlotte Mint and has the lowest mintage (5,235 pieces) of any C-mint issue. In the third edition of *Gold Coins of the Charlotte Mint, 1838-1861*, Douglas Winter estimates that 150 to 250 pieces are known, with a mere eight to 12 in Mint State.

Attractive brass-gold color with faint blushes of light green covers soft luster, and the strike is well above average for the issue. While minor softness is noted on portions of the Indian's hair, the O in DOLLAR, and the 8 in the date, the issue ordinarily displays weak design definition throughout. Winter points out that "the 1859-C is always found with a very weak obverse" and "the reverse is poorly struck as well." Some minute handling marks preclude a higher grade. Census: 15 in 62, 0 finer (12/09).
From The Longfellow Collection. (#7552)

1414 **1859-D—Rim Filing—NGC. Unc. Details.** Variety 11-N. Luster shimmers from the legends and devices of this rare date gold dollar. A minor pinscratch near the first A in AMERICA provides the only relevant mark. The reverse rim at 9:30 has a small filed area. Just 4,952 pieces were struck.(#7553)

Brilliant 1859-D Gold Dollar, MS63

1415 **1859-D MS63 NGC.** Variety 11-N. Survivors of this issue are probably the most frequently encountered Dahlonega Mint Type Three gold dollars, but most of them only grade about AU50 or AU55. Relatively few Mint State examples have been certified. Light clash marks are noted on the both sides. The pretty surfaces are medium golden-yellow, and the central reverse details, the 85 in the date, are somewhat mushy but legible (on some examples, those numbers are completely missing). Some light field chatter accounts for the grade, but there are no singular contact marks. Census: 8 in 63, 6 finer (12/09).
From The Longfellow Collection. (#7553)

1416 **1860 MS64 PCGS. CAC.** Green-gold luster dominates this sharply impressed near-Gem. A loupe locates only unimportant faint field grazes. A low mintage date, particularly when compared with the 1861 and 1862. Population: 14 in 64, 10 finer (12/09).
From The Longfellow Collection.(#7555)

Uncirculated 1860-D Gold Dollar From a Tiny Mintage of Only 1,566 Pieces

1417 **1860-D MS61 NGC.** Variety 12-P, the sole variety for the year. Mint State coins of this issue are quite rare, although a surprising number of survivors, mostly circulated, exist for a date with so tiny a mintage. Only 1,566 business strikes were produced, most of dubious quality including poor strikes and planchets. This example offers a typical strike for the issue, comprising the always-weak U in UNITED and softness on the top of the 6 in the date and the O in DOLLAR, which is nearly obliterated. The reverse rim at 3 o'clock shows little denticulation remaining, also strike weakness, and the bow details are incompletely brought up. But the luster is good and there is strictly no trace of high point rub, as expected. Light field chatter marks and planchet roughness account for the grade, but there are no singular abrasions. Census: 5 in 61, 4 finer (12/09).
From The Longfellow Collection. (#7556)

1418 **1860-S AU58 NGC.** The peach-gold surfaces of this near-Mint State example are imbued with traces of mint-green and retain luster in the recessed areas. Sharply struck, including all letters in LIBERTY and the bow knot. Census: 50 in 58, 35 finer (1/10). (#7557)

Low-Mintage 1860-S Gold Dollar, MS61

1419 **1860-S MS61 NGC.** The 1860-S has a low mintage of 13,000 pieces as well as a low survival rate, making Mint State coins hard to come by. Rich orange-gold coloration runs over this MS61 specimen, and an exacting strike imparts sharp detail to the design motifs. A few light marks are undisturbing. A nice coin for the designated grade. Census: 20 in 61, 14 finer (12/09).
From The Longfellow Collection. (#7557)

Extraordinary 1861 Gold Dollar, MS67

1420 **1861 MS67 PCGS. CAC.** An extraordinary Superb Gem, this gold dollar is one of just two MS67 pieces certified at PCGS, with two others in the same grade certified by NGC. Neither service has graded a nicer piece. The date is readily available in lower Mint State grades and is an excellent choice for type collectors, representing the Type Three design at the beginning of the Civil War. This beauty has satiny yellow-gold luster with incredible iridescent toning. It is boldly detailed despite shallow design motifs. Both sides exhibit clash marks, stronger on the reverse.
From The Longfellow Collection. (#7558)

Famous 1861-D Gold Dollar

1421 **1861-D PCGS Genuine.** Variety 12-Q, the only known dies. The PCGS number ending in .82 suggests Filed Rims as the reason, or perhaps one of the reasons, that PCGS deemed this coin not gradable. In our opinion, this coin has the details of an AU specimen that is scratched and has obverse damage and filed rims. Pinscratched beneath the A in STATES and above the ES in STATES. A brief pinscratch is also present beneath the date. The holder makes the rim filing difficult to observe. This desirable Dahlonega dollar, struck by Georgia or the Confederacy from Federal dies, has apricot-gold color and occasional peripheral softness of strike. (#7559)

Crisply Struck 1862 Dollar, MS66

1422 **1862 MS66 NGC.** With a mintage exceeding 1 million pieces, the 1862 gold dollar is one of the most common dates of the series. That generalization does not fit Premium Gems, however. Ebullient luster endows both sides of this crisply struck specimen, each of which displays attractive greenish-gold coloration. Census: 52 in 66, 8 finer (12/09).
From The Longfellow Collection. (#7560)

Well Struck 1866 Gem Gold Dollar

1423 **1866 MS65 PCGS.** Die striations are visible in the partially prooflike fields of this lovely Gem. Variegated yellow-gold and apricot patina occupies both sides, each of which displays a degree of field-motif variance. A well struck piece with minimal marks. Population: 10 in 65, 13 finer (12/09).
From The Longfellow Collection. (#7565)

Sparkling Prooflike 1867 Gold Dollar, MS66

1424 **1867 MS66 NGC.** It is unsurprising that this piece has bright, shimmering prooflike fields since the mintage is so low. Only 5,250 pieces were produced, and most likely the initial die polish never diminished when the last coin was struck. As Breen notes (1988): "many with clash marks." This piece has dramatic clashing on both sides, but the most interesting by far is the complete word LIBERTY below the date, clashed from the obverse headdress. The surfaces are bright yellow-gold and there are no mentionable abrasions, just a bit of planchet granularity to the right of the denomination on the reverse.
From The Longfellow Collection. (#7566)

Difficult Gem 1868 Gold Dollar

1425 **1868 MS65 NGC.** Gold coins failed to circulate in the years immediately after the Civil War, driven from commerce by unbacked Federal paper money. Thus, only 10,500 gold dollars were struck in 1868, excluding the meager proof mintage of 25 pieces. The present Gem business strike has vibrant luster and an exacting strike. Only a couple of trivial marks on the left obverse field prevent an even finer assessment. Census: 2 in 65, 3 finer (12/09).
From The Longfellow Collection. (#7567)

Remarkable 1874 Gold Dollar, MS67

1426 **1874 MS67 PCGS.** The 1873 and 1874 have much larger mintages than any other post-1862 gold dollars. The Mint apparently anticipated a demand that never emerged, partly because the paper dollar again failed to reach equality with its gold equivalent. That finally occurred in 1878. The relatively high mintage of the 1874 makes the issue prevalent in typical Mint State, but Superb Gems are undeniably rare. The present sharply impressed example has comprehensive luster and rich copper-red toning. Beautifully preserved, and unimprovable from PCGS. Population: 33 in 67, 0 finer (12/09).
From The Longfellow Collection. (#7575)

Significant 1875 Gold Dollar, MS66
Low-Mintage Rarity, Tied for Finest Certified

1427 **1875 MS66 PCGS. CAC.** Three-quarters of the way through the 19th century, the U.S. Mint managed to create a remarkable series of rarities with the memorable date of 1875. The coinage emphasis in that year was large-denomination silver coins and double eagles. Gold and silver coins had not circulated in any significant way since the Civil War year 1862, but the government was gearing up for the "parity" between gold and silver coins and paper currency that was expected to take place in January 1879. Accordingly, the double eagle was produced to the extent of more than 1.6 million pieces at three mints, complementing more than 5 million Liberty Seated quarters and 10 million Seated halves.

Except for the double eagle, all of the 1875 gold coin issues were struck in minuscule quantities; all of them are great rarities today. In the case of the gold dollar, the mintage was a skimpy 400 business strikes, plus 20 proofs, one of the lowest mintages of any "regular-issue" U.S. coin. Akers makes these cogent comments in his still-useful 1975 reference on the gold dollar series:

> "With so low a mintage, essentially all specimens are 'first strikes' and therefore invariably have full proof-like surfaces. This has given rise to the false notion that the 1875 gold dollar is more common in proof than it is in uncirculated condition. Most cataloguers have mistakenly called Uncs. 'proofs' over the years, as one can readily see from the auction records below ... . Actually, the Uncs. are readily distinguishable from the proofs because all uncirculated 1875 gold dollars have a small thorn-like projection from the throat into the field. This projection is seen only on the Uncs., not on the proofs, and no matter how much a particular 1875 may look like a proof, if it has the projection from the throat into the field, it is an Unc."

Akers goes on to say that the proof is a great rarity and deserves recognition. However, the business strikes are quite rare as well, a rarity that increases with condition: NGC has certified 31 pieces in all grades including Prooflike pieces, the highest a single MS66 non-Prooflike piece. PCGS has graded 54 examples in all grades but has certified no Prooflike examples of any gold dollar issue. Nonetheless this MS66 piece is one of the two finest certified at PCGS, and a marvelous coin it is. Rich reddish-gold surfaces offer just a hint of interspersed lilac, especially noticeable over the wreath on the reverse. The fields on each side are fully prooflike and nicely reflective. The piece is problem-free, as expected of the grade, although a couple of faint Mint-made file marks run from the C in AMERICA upward into the field. The small "thorn-like" projection that Akers notes, diagnostic of business strikes, is clear at the throat.

This coin presents a significant opportunity to obtain one of the finest certified examples of this prime rarity, an opportunity that may not soon repeat. Series specialists must act accordingly.
From The Longfellow Collection. (#7576)

1428 **1876 MS64 Prooflike NGC.** The reflective fields are minimally abraded. The strike is bold save for the 8 in the date. As with most other gold denominations from this date and mint, the 1876 mintage was very low. Only 3,200 pieces were struck. Census: 5 in 64 Prooflike, 1 finer (1/10).(#77577)

1429 **1877 MS64 PCGS. CAC.** The 1877 gold dollar is a popular date primarily because of the cachet attached to the date and the many rare coins issued in this year. The gold dollar had a mintage of 3,900 pieces and it is scarce, but not as difficult as the 1876 or 1878. This is a lovely, reddish-tinged example that has the usual semiprooflike fields on each side. The striking details are sharp throughout, and there are no singularly mentionable abrasions on either side.
From The Longfellow Collection.(#7578)

Gorgeous Gem 1878 Gold Dollar

1430 **1878 MS65 PCGS.** Watery reflectivity makes up much of this Gem's luster, with bold sun-yellow and paler lavender-silver colors enlivening each side. Preservation, as expected for a Gem, is excellent. With just four finer examples known to PCGS (1/10), a top-flight example of this low-mintage issue. (#7579)

Impressive 1878 Gold Dollar, MS66

1431 **1878 MS66 NGC.** An issue that is seldom offered as a Premium Gem, the 1878 (3,000 business strikes produced) is the rarest post-1876 gold dollar. The finish is semiprooflike, as expected for a low-mintage gold dollar from the late 1870s, and the devices display pinpoint striking definition in all areas. The reddish-gold surfaces reveal slight counterclockwise die rotation. A few faint lines on each side appear at first glance to be pinscratches, but we believe them to be as struck. Census: 5 in 66, 2 finer (12/09).
From The Longfellow Collection. (#7579)

1432 **1879 MS65 PCGS. CAC.** A gorgeous Gem, this 1879 gold dollar has frosty yellow luster with excellent surfaces and bold design definition. Only 3,000 business strikes were minted. Population: 55 in 65, 39 finer (1/10).(#7580)

Superb Gem 1879 Gold Dollar
A One-Sided Prooflike

1433 **1879 MS67 NGC.** Well struck with rich orange-gold patina over both sides. The obverse fields are notably reflective, while curiously the reverse is not. On the reverse several noticeable clash marks are noted. A few wispy die striations show on each side of this attractive, essentially unmarked Superb Gem. Census: 18 in 67, 0 finer (12/09).
Ex: Palm Beach Signature (Heritage, 3/2005), lot 6830.
From The Longfellow Collection. (#7580)

Stunning 1880 Gold Dollar, MS68

1434 **1880 MS68 NGC.** The 1880 gold dollar has a high survival rate despite a low mintage of just 1,600 circulation strikes. That said, specimens in this lofty grade are infrequently seen. Luminous brassy-gold surfaces appear to reach out to the observer. Additionally, a decisive strike leaves uniformly sharp detail on the design elements. Immaculately preserved throughout. Census: 21 in 68, 0 finer (12/09).
From The Longfellow Collection. (#7581)

Immaculate 1881 Gold Dollar, MS68

1435 **1881 MS68 NGC.** The mintage of three cent nickels spiked in 1881, but there was no such event in the gold dollar series, which continued its trend of minimal production. Just 7,620 pieces were struck. A number of those fell into numismatic hands, but any gold dollar is highly desirable at the pristine MS68 level. This exactingly struck Superb Gem is immaculate and lustrous and is further distinguished by a curly lintmark (as issued) concealed in the hair above the obverse center. Census: 45 in 68, 3 finer (12/09).
From The Longfellow Collection. (#7582)

Fabulous MS68 1882 Gold Dollar

1436 **1882 MS68 NGC.** A pristine representative that possesses a full strike and potent luster. Hints of honey patina are noted throughout. Unimprovable at either major service, and a formidable type coin as well. A mere 5,000 pieces were struck for this later Type Three date. Census: 13 in 68, 0 finer (12/09).
From The Longfellow Collection. (#7583)

Spectacular 1883 Gold Dollar, MS68

1437 **1883 MS68 PCGS.** Housed in a green label PCGS holder, this 1883 is a stunning Superb Gem, one of just eight coins that PCGS has graded MS68 with none finer, and that population includes the possibility of resubmissions. Both sides are prooflike with virtually flawless surfaces. Even a strong glass fails to reveal more than a few trivial blemishes on each side. This piece has brilliant yellow surfaces with lovely iridescent toning that enhances its eye appeal. Among PCGS-certified coins, this piece represents just the fourth auction appearance of an MS68 in our sales since 1993. This is a spectacular coin for the connoisseur who demands the finest possible quality.
From The Longfellow Collection. (#7584)

Outstanding 1884 MS67 Gold Dollar

1438 **1884 MS67 PCGS. CAC.** This breathtaking Superb Gem possesses beautiful yellow-gold and apricot patination. The semiprooflike fields yield pleasing contrast with the devices. Added to this are the sharp strike and impeccable preservation, making for magnificent overall eye appeal aptly recognized by CAC. Population: 14 in 67, 5 finer (12/09).
From The Longfellow Collection. (#7585)

Lovely 1885 Gold Dollar, MS66

1439 **1885 MS66 NGC. CAC.** An incredible Premium Gem from a modest mintage of just 11,156 coins. Unlike some other years, only a few higher grade pieces survive of the 1885. This example is prooflike with mirrored fields around lustrous, sharply defined devices. Census: 63 in 66, 34 finer (1/10). (#7586)

MS68 1885 Gold Dollar
Tied for Finest Certified

1440 **1885 MS68 NGC.** Despite a higher mintage than some of the other late gold dollar issues, the 1885 presents a greater challenge than many in high Mint State grades. Any year, however, would be truly remarkable and extremely rare in MS68. Many collectors have to wait years before there is an opportunity to acquire such a spectacular example, and it is essentially impossible to find a representative any finer. The present specimen is powerfully struck, and the butter-yellow surfaces exhibit vibrant, satiny luster throughout. This simply breathtaking representative appears flawless, even under magnification. PCGS has certified no examples at this level, and NGC reports just three other pieces in MS68, with none finer (12/09).
From The Longfellow Collection. (#7586)

Exemplary Superb Gem 1886 Gold Dollar

1441 **1886 MS67 NGC.** Another low mintage date, as just 5,000 pieces fell from the dies. That omits the 1,016 proofs struck, many or most of which were made into love tokens, a popular fad of the era. The present coin is neither a proof nor a love token. It is a Superb Gem, and as one should demand from such a grade, the surfaces are lustrous, well struck, and virtually pristine. Lightly toned in caramel shades. Census: 14 in 67, 0 finer (12/09).
From The Longfellow Collection. (#7587)

Richly Toned, Prooflike 1887 Gold Dollar, MS66

1442 **1887 MS66 NGC.** An incredible Premium Gem, this gold dollar has rich yellow-gold luster with prooflike fields that are essentially free of marks. Only 7,500 business strikes were coined, and most survivors are in lower Mint State grades. Census: 48 in 66, 25 finer (12/09).
From The Longfellow Collection. (#7588)

1443 **1888 MS65 NGC.** Here is a remarkable gold dollar with brilliant yellow-gold surfaces and exceptional luster. A glass is required to view the few tiny marks.(#7589)

Frosty 1888 Gold Dollar, MS67

1444 **1888 MS67 NGC.** This unusual Superb Gem has frosty greenish-gold luster on both sides, rather than the oft-seen prooflike fields that are so often encountered on these late gold dollars. Both sides of this specimen have sharp design details with hints of pale orange toning. Census: 53 in 67, 3 finer (1/10). (#7589)

Nearly Perfect MS68 1888 Gold Dollar

1445 **1888 MS68 PCGS. CAC.** The 1888 is the next-to-last year of the gold dollar series, a denomination that began in 1849 and was produced annually from then until 1889. Only 15,500 pieces were struck of the 1888. This splendid example offers luxuriant mint luster that illuminates light honey-gold surfaces. The design elements are struck with an overall degree of sharpness that is noticeably better than average on both sides, even though the letters ERTY are imperfectly defined. The surfaces are impressively preserved and nearly pristine. Population: 5 in 68, 0 finer (12/09).
From The Longfellow Collection. (#7589)

Magnificent 1889 Gold Dollar, MS67

1446 **1889 MS67 NGC.** The 1889 gold dollar is one of the more common dates of the type. Rich apricot-gold and mint-green patination endows both sides of this Superb Gem each of which exudes dazzling luster. Exquisitely struck design features and impeccable preservation round out the coin's magnificent eye appeal. (#7590)

Pristine MS68 1889 Gold Dollar

1447 **1889 MS68 NGC.** Born out of the California Gold Rush in 1849, the gold dollar passed from the coinage scene in 1889 rather ignominiously, with a mintage of only 28,950 business strikes. Many examples were apparently saved, as today the 1889 is the most common gold dollar from the 1880s. MS68 coins, however, remain conditionally rare. This gorgeous example displays rich orange-gold coloration over pristine, satiny surfaces. The strike is razor-sharp throughout, and the overall appearance is one of numismatic perfection. Census: 15 in 68, 0 finer (12/09).
From The Longfellow Collection. (#7590)

PROOF GOLD DOLLAR

Glittering PR66 Cameo 1884 Gold Dollar

1448 **1884 PR66 Cameo NGC.** The 1884 issue begins the series-ending string of four-figure proof mintages for gold dollars; production went from 207 pieces the year before to 1,006 specimens. Few survivors from that multitude, however, have the combination of cameo contrast and high preservation offered by this Premium Gem. Glassy golden-black fields host thickly frosted and decisively detailed devices. Several small lint marks are noted on the reverse, particularly at the left side of the portrait area, but they affect neither the technical grade nor the eye appeal. Census: 18 in 66 Cameo, 12 finer (1/10). (#87634)

EARLY QUARTER EAGLES

BD-2 1802/1 Two and a Half, AU58

1449 **1802/1 AU58 NGC.** Breen-6118, BD-2, High R.5. A mere 3,035 pieces were struck of the 1802 quarter eagle. Probably more than 250 pieces exist today in all grades, making the 1802 the second most "common" date in the series—"common" being relative, of course, when speaking of this challenging design type. As with many other dates in the Capped Bust Right series, the 1802 is known for soft central details and adjustment marks. This attractive example has bright surfaces. As expected, the centers are weakly struck, and light diagonal adjustment marks occur on the reverse. The surfaces are lightly abraded, but the only marks worth mentioning are a shallow planchet flake in the exergue above the 8 in the date, and a Z-shaped scratch just below the AM of AMERICA on the reverse. *From The South Texas Collection.* (#7650)

Near-Mint 1833 Quarter Eagle, BD-1

1450 **1833 AU58 NGC. CAC.** Breen-6136, BD-1, R.5. Bass-Dannreuther Die State a/c, the reverse state a holdover from previous years' usage that was nearly steady through the issue's meager mintage of 4,160 pieces, nearly all of which were melted as old-tenor currency after the weight adjustments of 1834. Rich butter-yellow surfaces offer glossy luster on this near-Mint representative, which shows light wear but few overt abrasions on the reverse. The obverse has small cuts at the jawline and neck, as well as the right field. Still, a coin with strong overall eye appeal. Census: 13 in 58, 27 finer (1/10). *From The South Texas Collection.* (#7673)

CLASSIC QUARTER EAGLES

1451 **1837 AU50 NGC.** McCloskey-B, R.2. The usual variety for this lower mintage date. Hints of apricot-tinged luster and traces of recessed dirt confirm the originality. Well struck, save for softness in the stars along the left border.(#7695)

Appealing XF45 1839-C Quarter Eagle

1452 **1839-C XF45 NGC.** Breen-6150, McCloskey-C, Variety 2, R.4. The obverse's mintmark placement, over the space between the two central date digits, is diagnostic. A well struck, lightly abraded Choice XF example of this popular Classic Head Charlotte issue with surprisingly radiant butter-yellow surfaces. (#7699)

Near-Mint 1839-C Quarter Eagle

1453 **1839-C AU58 NGC.** Breen-6150, McCloskey-C, Variety 2, R.4. The mintmark is centered over the space between the 8 and 3 in the date, with a die crack passing just to its right. Coins that combine the allure of Southern gold with the old-style Classic Head design are in high demand from a broad range of collectors, and the 1839-C quarter eagle is no exception. This radiant near-Mint piece has bold gold-orange luster with only slight rub on the softly struck high points. A handful of scattered abrasions are consistent with brief circulation. NGC has graded 17 numerically finer pieces (1/10), though this number is likely inflated by resubmissions. *From The South Texas Collection*. (#7699)

LIBERTY QUARTER EAGLES

Delightful MS61 1840-O Quarter Eagle

1454 **1840-O MS61 PCGS.** Though this earlier New Orleans quarter eagle issue is a frequent resubmission candidate, few coins have ever achieved an MS61 or finer designation. This softly struck but fully lustrous yellow-gold piece is one of the fortunate few. Pleasing overall, though a number of tiny digs and abrasions contribute to the grade. Population: 4 in 61, 7 finer (1/10). (#7720)

Scarce 1841-C Quarter Eagle, AU55

1455 **1841-C AU55 NGC. CAC.** Variety 1, the only variety for the year. The 1841-C is scarce in any grade and rare in Mint State. NGC/PCGS figures show a disproportionate number of AUs, which is likely explained by resubmissions, as the number of coins seen does not support such a high number. The greenish-gold surfaces of this Choice AU exhibit sharply struck devices. There are relatively few marks to report. Census: 28 in 55, 33 finer (1/10). (#7721)

1456 **1843-D Small D—Scratches—NGC. XF Details.** Variety 4-D. This is the usually seen Small D variety. This example has light green-gold surfaces with several minor scratches on each side. (#7730)

Challenging 1844-C Quarter Eagle, XF45

1457 **1844-C XF45 NGC.** Variety 1. The 1844-C quarter eagle is one of the more difficult C-mint issues, with relatively few and often low-quality survivors from a mintage of just 11,622 coins. Also, the striking quality is generally poor and sometimes planchet flaws can be a problem as well. This piece shows the usual softness in the centers, but smooth surfaces without severe marks make it a desirable representative at the XF45 grade level, and worthy of a specialist's attention. (#7735)

Condition Rarity 1845-O Quarter Eagle, AU58

1458 **1845-O AU58 NGC.** The 1845-O, coming from a minuscule mintage of 4,000 pieces, is extremely scarce in circulated grades and a major rarity in Mint State. The yellow-gold surfaces of this near-Mint State specimen retain luster in the recessed areas and are minimally marked. Well struck except for the usual localized weakness on the eagle. The 18 of the date shows the typical recutting. Census: 8 in 58, 2 finer (12/09). (#7739)

1459 **1846 AU58 NGC.** The Liberty quarter eagle specialist will want to take careful consideration of this near-Mint 1846, a scarce date in all grades. Both sides have a few trivial surface marks that are present on virtually all known examples of the 1846. The surfaces are bright greenish-gold with considerable luster.(#7740)

Surprising MS61 1847 Quarter Eagle

1460 **1847 MS61 PCGS.** Pale yellow, with hints of lime in the centers and orange along the peripheries amid traces of reflectivity in the fields. As usual for the date, the left (facing) leg of the eagle is softly struck. The surfaces are quite smooth for the grade. A die crack bisects the reverse, extending from the fraction along the right (facing) wing. Very scarce in Mint State. Population: 4 in 61, 5 finer (1/10). (#7744)

1461 **1847-C—Obverse Damage—NGC. AU Details.** Variety 1, the only known die pair. Despite a few minor scrapes on the obverse, this is an attractive green-gold example with faint orange toning in the fields. Perhaps lightly cleaned, this piece retains considerable luster.(#7745)

1462 **1847-D—Altered Surfaces—ANACS. AU50 Details.** Variety 9-M. This low mintage straw-gold Dahlonega quarter eagle has hints of luster and is free from obvious marks. Slightly bright, perhaps from an encounter with baking soda.(#7746)

Flashy Near-Mint 1847-D Quarter Eagle

1463 **1847-D AU58 NGC. CAC.** Variety 9-M, sole die pair for the year. A remarkably sharp near-Mint representative of this popular Dahlonega issue with virtually intact yellow-gold luster. The coin is temptingly close to Mint State, with only a touch of friction blending with the slight striking softness found on Liberty's central curls. Census: 46 in 58, 17 finer (12/09). (#7746)

Elusive 1848 Quarter Eagle, MS61

1464 **1848 MS61 NGC.** The 1848 quarter eagle, with its small mintage of 6,500 pieces, is a scarce issue. This MS61 example displays apricot-gold surfaces splashed with mint-green. The fields are partially prooflike, especially on the reverse which shows die polish lines. Sharply struck, except for the usual weakness on the eagle's left (facing) leg. Wispy obverse handling marks limit the grade. Census: 9 in 61, 9 finer (12/09). (#7748)

Bright 1848-C Quarter Eagle, AU58

1465 **1848-C AU58 NGC.** Variety 1. The left base of 1 in the date is over a space between dentils and the second 8 is closer to the dentils than to the bust. Bright yellow-gold surfaces reveal just a few small marks. The design features are well defined except for the typical weakness on the eagle's legs. Census: 35 in 58, 16 finer (12/09). (#7750)

Bright 1850-O Quarter Eagle, AU58

1466 **1850-O AU58 PCGS. CAC.** The bright yellow-gold surfaces of this near-Mint State quarter eagle possess ample luster. The peripheral elements are sharply impressed, though the central areas are weak, particularly on the reverse, a major characteristic of surviving examples of this issue. There are no major marks to report. Population: 9 in 58, 19 finer (1/10). (#7758)

Choice AU 1851-D Quarter Eagle

1467 **1851-D AU55 NGC.** Variety 14-M, as always for this issue, from a mintage of 11,264 coins. This piece has pale green-gold color with considerable luster remaining on both sides. The central motifs show some weakness, especially on the eagle's neck and left (facing) leg. Here is an attractive piece for the advanced collector. Census: 14 in 55, 19 finer (1/10). (#7761)

1468 **1853 MS64 NGC.** Here is a remarkable Choice Mint State example of a conditionally rare date, from a large mintage of more than 1.4 million coins. The surfaces are frosty with rich lemon-yellow luster and amazing eye appeal. Census: 66 in 64, 17 finer (1/10).(#7767)

1469 **1854 MS63 PCGS.** Attractive red-gold surfaces are well struck save for the eagle's left (facing) leg and show only a few grade-consistent abrasions. There is a small reverse die crack from ST(ATES) to the rim, and faint evidence of die clashing on the reverse. An appealing example of this historic issue. Population: 40 in 63, 27 finer (12/09).(#7769)

Appealing 1854-O Quarter Eagle, MS62

1470 **1854-O MS62 NGC. CAC.** The 1854-O can be located with minimal difficulty in lower grades, but is a rare coin in Mint State. Certified population figures indicate that examples above MS62, the grade of the current offering, are seldom seen. Lustrous yellow-gold surfaces are well struck, save for the typical weakness on the central reverse. The few minuscule marks present take nothing from the pleasing overall eye appeal. Census: 16 in 62, 2 finer (1/10). (#7772)

Pleasing 1857-S Quarter Eagle, AU58

1471 **1857-S AU58 NGC.** Most 1857-S quarter eagles are in the Extremely Fine to mid-About Uncirculated grade levels, and Mint State pieces are difficult to come by. The yellow-gold surfaces of this near-Mint State example retain a good amount of luster and exhibit well struck design features. A remarkably clean coin for having seen some circulation. (#7785)

Delightful 1858 Quarter Eagle, MS64

1472 **1858 MS64 NGC.** The 1858 quarter eagle is scarce in all grades and rare in near-Gem and finer. This MS64 specimen displays yellow-gold surfaces and sharply struck design motifs, save for the usual softness in the eagle's left (facing) leg. Die polish lines in the fields point to semiprooflike characteristics. An occasional contact mark denies Gem status. Census: 5 in 64, 2 finer (1/10). (#7786)

Old Reverse 1859 Quarter Eagle, MS61

1473 **1859 Old Reverse, Type One MS61 NGC.** In 1859, the Philadelphia Mint modified the reverse of the quarter eagle, shrinking the lettering and the arrowheads on that side, but coins with the old reverse were also struck in 1859 and on into 1860 and 1861. This 1859 Old Reverse piece has strong yellow-gold luster and solid overall detail, though the eagle's legs show a degree of softness. Census: 18 in 61, 14 finer (1/10). (#97788)

1474 **1861 Old Reverse, Type One AU55 NGC.** The Old Reverse, noted for its wider arrowheads and slightly larger letters relative to the New Reverse, was coined for the final time in 1861. Most quarter eagles that bear this date have a Type Two, or "new" reverse, and Old Reverse examples merit a substantial premium. This is an attractive straw-gold Choice AU piece with substantial peripheral luster and no relevant marks. The eagle's legs are incompletely brought up, as usual for the issue.(#97794)

Scarce 1861 Type One Quarter Eagle, MS61

1475 **1861 Old Reverse, Type One MS61 PCGS.** Coinage dies were converted from the fat arrowheads of Type One to the slender arrowheads of Type Two in 1859, although some of the old reverse dies remained unhand. Such was the case when this coin was struck in 1861. Apparently no one noticed at the time that the incorrect reverse die was placed in the press. Here is a splendid example with strong design details, fully brilliant yellow luster, and pleasing surfaces for the grade. (#97794)

Near-Gem 1861 Type Two Quarter Eagle, MS64

1476 **1861 New Reverse, Type Two MS64 PCGS.** The normally seen new reverse has long, slender arrowheads that are separated from each other. This lovely example is fully brilliant with frosty yellow luster and splashes of rose toning. A couple marks on Liberty's cheek prevent a higher grade. PCGS has only certified 30 finer pieces. (#7794)

Low Mintage 1861-S Quarter Eagle, AU53

1477 **1861-S AU53 PCGS.** The 1861-S is a scarce West Coast issue that is even more challenging than its mintage of 24,000 pieces would suggest. Most of the known examples are VF-XF, and only a handful of coins have been certified in Mint State. This AU53 represents excellent value and is one of the finer pieces available. Close examination with a loupe shows light hairlining on each side. Light reddish patina is present, and only slight softness is seen in the centers. (#7795)

1478 **1862 AU58 NGC.** One of the more frequently encountered Civil War gold coins. The mintage was 98,508 pieces, highest in the post-1861 Civil War era. This is a bright yellow-gold example that shows signs of handling in the fields and is peppered with numerous small but individually insignificant abrasions.(#7796)

1479 **1868 AU58 NGC.** Sharply struck with a degree of reflectivity in the watery fields. Lightly abraded throughout but with only a touch of friction on the high points to preclude a strictly Mint State grade. Census: 72 in 58, 20 finer (12/09).(#7807)

Uncirculated 1869 Two and a Half

1480 **1869 MS61 NGC.** A sharply struck pumpkin-gold rare date quarter eagle. A mere 4,320 pieces were struck, most of which were melted long ago. A few minute marks on the field above the eagle are of little account. Cartwheel luster occupies the borders and devices. Encased in a prior generation holder. Census: 12 in 61, 5 finer (12/09). (#7809)

1872-S Quarter Eagle, MS61

1481 **1872-S MS61 PCGS.** A well directed strike leaves strong definition on the design elements except for the usually weak legs of the eagle. Yellow-gold surfaces show a good amount of luster and a few minute contact marks. Mint State coins are seen rather infrequently. Population: 2 in 61, 7 finer (12/09). (#7816)

1482 **1876-S AU55 NGC.** Bold lemon-gold and lighter straw colors converge on this still-lustrous Choice AU coin. Great eye appeal for the grade assigned and the low-mintage issue.(#7825)

1483 **1876-S AU55 PCGS. CAC.** An important date in the quarter eagle series, the 1876-S had an original mintage of just 5,000 coins, and survivors are elusive in all grades. This Choice AU piece has lustrous light yellow surfaces with a few trivial surface marks as expected. Population: 14 in 55, 29 finer (1/10).(#7825)

Infrequently Seen MS62 1877 Quarter Eagle

1484 **1877 MS62 NGC.** Most 1877 quarter eagles appearing at auction are in the XF to AU grade range. Mint State examples, such as this MS62, are infrequently seen. Brass-gold surfaces have partially prooflike fields that offer a degree of variance with the sharply struck design features. Some minor surface and rim marks keep from a finer grade. Census: 8 in 62, 8 finer (1/10). (#7826)

Popular 1877 Select Quarter Eagle

1485 **1877 MS63 NGC.** The 1877 quarter eagle has one of the lowest mintages of the series (1,632 business strikes) and is consequently popular and in high demand. Apricot-gold and mint-green patina runs over both sides of this Select specimen, each of which displays some prooflike tendencies. This sharply struck piece reveals just a few minor handling marks. Census: 5 in 63, 3 finer (12/09). (#7826)

Near-Mint 1881 Quarter Eagle
One of 640 Business Strikes

1486 **1881 AU58 NGC.** With a business strike mintage of just 640 pieces, the 1881 quarter eagle is one of several near-legendary Philadelphia issues in the later half of the long-running Liberty quarter eagle series. This sharply struck, moderately reflective example is scarcely worn, though the blue-accented yellow-gold fields show a number of abrasions. Census: 18 in 58, 15 finer (1/10). (#7833)

Low-Mintage 1886 Quarter Eagle, MS63

1487 **1886 MS63 PCGS. CAC.** Sharply struck with fresh yellow-gold luster. Though this Select coin shows light, scattered abrasions on both obverse and reverse, it offers high eye appeal for its low-mintage issue of only 4,000 business strikes. Housed in a green label holder. Population: 13 in 63, 5 finer (12/09). (#7838)

Shining Gem 1890 Quarter Eagle

1488 **1890 MS65 PCGS.** Distinctly reflective sun-yellow fields yield to paler straw-gold devices, which are well-defined but not sharp in the manner of a true proof. Only a few small, shallow faults are visible in the fields, most noticeably a graze in the field just below Liberty's chin. Housed in a green label holder. Population: 3 in 65, 1 finer (1/10). (#7842)

Challenging 1894 Quarter Eagle, MS64

1489 **1894 MS64 PCGS.** Just 4,000 coins were minted, although few of them actually circulation, so the typical survivor is a lower grade Mint State piece. This one has rich yellow luster and sharp details with reflective fields, especially on the reverse. Population: 20 in 64, 20 finer (1/10). (#7846)

Near-Gem 1894 Quarter Eagle

1490 **1894 MS64 PCGS. CAC.** The 1894 quarter eagle is a popular issue owing to its low mintage of 4,000 circulation strikes. Dazzling luster emanates from the yellow-gold surfaces of this near-Gem and an exacting strike delivers strong definition to the design elements. A few minute marks preclude Gem status. Population: 20 in 64, 20 finer (1/10). (#7846)

Elusive 1896 Quarter Eagle, MS65

1491 **1896 MS65 NGC.** This frosty Gem has brilliant and highly lustrous yellow surfaces with sharp design motifs. Like most late 19th century quarter eagles, the 1896 is a low mintage date with a higher survival rate, although Gem or finer pieces are hard to find. Census: 56 in 65, 32 finer (1/10). (#7848)

Magnificent 1897 Gem Quarter Eagle

1492 **1897 MS65 PCGS.** This Gem is beautifully toned in variegated mint-green, orange-gold, and lilac. Its surfaces radiate stunning luster, and both sides yield modest field-motif variance. This is an exquisitely struck piece that is impeccably preserved. Housed in a green label holder. Population: 70 in 65, 32 finer (1/10). (#7849)

Gorgeous MS66 1899 Quarter Eagle

1493 **1899 MS66 NGC. CAC.** A strongly struck Premium Gem with satiny, swirling luster, light yellow-gold with lemon overtones. The surfaces are exquisitely preserved, smooth delights. Great preservation and eye appeal for this lower-mintage turn-of-the-century issue. NGC has certified just five numerically finer pieces (1/10). (#7851)

PROOF LIBERTY QUARTER EAGLES

Lovely 1883 Quarter Eagle, PR66 Cameo

1494 **1883 PR66 Cameo NGC. CAC.** This is only the 10th auction appearance of a proof 1883 quarter eagle in any of our sales since 1993, and those 10 appearances include nine different coins. It is believed today that about 30 proofs survive from the original 82-coin mintage, most in lower grades. This piece is tied for the finest Cameo proof certified, with three Proof 66 Ultra Cameo coins and two Proof 67 Ultra Cameo pieces. We believe this piece is at the low end of the Condition Census for the proof issue. It is fully and deeply mirrored with exceptional contrast between the mirrors and the fields. Both sides are pristine, with blemish-free surfaces. (#87909)

Cameo PR64 1900 Quarter Eagle

1495 **1900 PR64 Cameo PCGS.** A boldly contrasted specimen of this turn-of-the-century issue, prominently mirrored with pale golden frost enveloping the exquisitely detailed devices. This charming miniature shows a few minor hairlines and points of contact, including a flaw just above star 13 on the obverse, but the eye appeal is strong for the grade. Population: 5 in 64 Cameo, 4 finer (12/09). (#87926)

Sensational 1900 Quarter Eagle PR68 Ultra Cameo

1496 **1900 PR68 Ultra Cameo NGC.** With a mintage of 205 proofs, the 1900 quarter eagle has the second highest proof mintage of all Liberty quarter eagles behind the 223 pieces struck the following year. As such, the 1900 makes a great type coin for the design enthusiast. While the NGC Census Report shows eight coins similarly graded, with three finer PR69 Ultra Cameo examples (1/10), it is difficult to imagine such a quantity of *different* coins in these lofty grades. This Superb Gem exhibits a high degree of mint brilliance with bright yellow surfaces, incredible mirrored fields, and highly lustrous devices. (#97926)

Desirable 1901 Quarter Eagle PR64 Ultra Cameo

1497 **1901 PR64 Ultra Cameo NGC.** A stunning and boldly defined Ultra Cameo proof quarter eagle, this piece has frosty and fully brilliant yellow devices with mirrored fields of unlimited depth. Both sides exhibit a few minuscule contact marks that prevent a higher grade. Otherwise, this pristine piece would rank as one of the best examples available for the date, or for the type.

The mintage of 223 proof quarter eagles in 1901 was the highest for the entire design, and that suggests the importance of this piece as a type coin for the 20th century design collector, as it represents the first year of the new century, according to some. Census: 7 in 64 Ultra Cameo, 28 finer (1/10). (#97927)

INDIAN QUARTER EAGLES

1498 **1908 MS64 NGC.** This first-year Indian quarter eagle has strongly shining yellow-gold surfaces. Well struck for the issue with few abrasions of any significance.
From The Alfred V. Melson Collection, Part Two.(#7939)

1499 **1908 MS64 PCGS.** Apricot-gold surfaces are imbued with traces of mint-green. Well struck, save for the often-seen softness on the eagle's shoulder. Trivial marks prevent Gem status.(#7939)

Beautiful 1908 Indian Quarter Eagle, MS66

1500 **1908 MS66 PCGS.** Only a few Indian quarter eagles can match the quality of this piece, regardless of the date, and the first-year of issue status adds considerable desirability to this specimen. It is sharply struck including the headdress, stars, and hair on the obverse, and the eagle's feathers on the reverse. Only the top of the forewing is indistinct, but that is true of every example of the 1908 that we have seen. The surfaces are fully brilliant with bright yellow luster and full mint frost. A trace of light rose toning adds to its aesthetic appeal. Population: 87 in 66, 2 finer (1/10). (#7939)

Impressive MS66 1908 Quarter Eagle

1501 **1908 MS66 NGC. CAC.** A fantastic Premium Gem representative of this first-year Indian quarter eagle issue, which is available for a price even in MS65 but scarce any better. The strike is remarkably sharp, and gorgeous satin luster enlivens the carefully preserved butter-yellow surfaces. A memorable coin. NGC has certified a mere three numerically finer pieces (12/09). (#7939)

1502 **1909 MS63 NGC.** Impressive mustard and butter shadings dominate the eye appeal of this softly lustrous Indian quarter eagle. Neither side shows any individually significant abrasions.
From The Alfred V. Melson Collection, Part Two.(#7940)

Lustrous Gem 1909 Quarter Eagle

1503 **1909 MS65 PCGS.** The various Indian quarter eagle and half eagle issues are notoriously elusive in better Mint State grades, and for the 1909 quarter eagle, anything finer than this Gem is a condition rarity. Orange-infused wheat-gold surfaces are remarkably smooth with uncommonly strong luster. Well struck with a single mark noted on the jawline. (#7940)

Bold Gem 1909 Two and a Half

1504 **1909 MS65 NGC.** With just 19 numerically finer pieces known to NGC (1/10), any 1909 quarter eagle in higher grade than the present Gem example is conditionally rare. Bold sun-gold surfaces show both orange and emerald glints, the latter mostly in an arc above the eagle's bonnet. Strong overall detail and excellent preservation, as demanded of the grade. (#7940)

1505 **1910 MS63 NGC.** Luminous butter-yellow surfaces host well struck devices. An attractive Select example of this popular Indian quarter eagle issue.
From The Alfred V. Melson Collection, Part Two.(#7941)

Bright MS64 1910 Two and a Half

1506 **1910 MS64 NGC.** This is an excellent coin for type purposes. Satiny mint luster rolls over the granular texture. Overall the coin is bright and mostly yellow-gold, with just a hint of pale rose present. Only a few grade-limiting abrasions appear under a loupe, on the right side of the reverse. Sharply struck.
From The Alfred V. Melson Collection, Part Two. (#7941)

Wonderful MS64 1910 Two and a Half

1507 **1910 MS64 NGC.** Bold lemon-yellow luster defines the centers, while deeper butter and even orange hues occupy parts of the rims. This near-Gem is solidly struck, though the lowest pendant on the necklace shows a degree of softness, and the visual appeal is top-notch. Only a few wispy marks preclude an even finer designation. (#7941)

1508 **1911 MS64 NGC.** Boldly defined, particularly on the Indian's necklace, with uncommonly strong yellow-gold luster that takes on lemony hues at parts of the margins. A near-Gem with noteworthy eye appeal.
From The Alfred V. Melson Collection, Part Two.(#7942)

Entry Level 1911-D Quarter Eagle, AU Details

1509 **1911-D—Obverse Rim Filed—NGC. AU Details.** The obverse rim filing is visible clockwise from 5 o'clock to 10 o'clock. Both sides have stippled surfaces with green-gold color and traces of luster. The D mintmark is boldly evident, even without magnification. A suitable example for the budget-minded collector. (#7943)

Near-Mint 1911-D Quarter Eagle

1510 **1911-D AU58 NGC.** An appealing near-Mint example of this perennially popular Indian quarter eagle issue, strongly lustrous despite mild friction on the high points. Pale yellow-gold surfaces have an orange cast near the rims and occasional pink highlights. Practically Mint State quality at a fraction of the price.
From The Alfred V. Melson Collection, Part Two. (#7943)

Popular MS62 1911-D Quarter Eagle

1511 **1911-D MS62 NGC.** In his 1975 volume *U.S. Quarter Eagles 1796-1929*, David Akers commented:

> "As an *issue*, the 1911-D is the rarest and most famous of the series and its fame actually extends to the whole of the Numismatic Community, an unusual occurrence for a Gold coin. This coin is probably scarce in any grade but all available evidence tends to confirm the thesis that the 1911-D was actively saved within 15 years of issuance."

By the author's logic, then, collectors recognized the rarity of the issue even before the series was through. More than 80 years after the end of the denomination, 1911-D quarter eagles such as the present piece continue to attract collectors of this short-lived, completable series. For the MS62 grade, this coin offers strong visual appeal, thanks to a bold strike and bright lemon-yellow luster. Small, scattered abrasions and a shallow scrape at the far right edge of the headdress contribute to the grade. (#7943)

MS62 1911-D Quarter Eagle

1512 **1911-D MS62 NGC.** The 100 employees of the Denver Mint in 1911 found their work pulled in many different directions, from double eagles that were in high demand to Lincoln cents that were never previously coined at that facility. Throughout the year, the Denver Mint produced 28,841,000 coins of all denominations. According to the *Mint Director's Report*, there were 16 employees in the coiner's department, meaning that each employee was responsible for 1.5 million coins during the year.

Only 55,680 pieces, a tiny fraction of just one employee's allotment, were quarter eagles, which has cemented the 1911-D issue's key status. This strongly yellow-gold example shows wheat and straw accents. Overall definition is strong, and the surfaces are minimally abraded for the grade assigned. Solid eye appeal.
From The Alfred V. Melson Collection, Part Two. (#7943)

Well Struck 1911-D Quarter Eagle, MS62

1513 **1911-D MS62 NGC.** An impressive strike leaves strong definition on the design features of this key date quarter eagle, including the headdress feathers and mintmark. Only the eagle's shoulder feathers are a tad soft. Brass-gold coloration covers both sides. A small hit in the lower obverse field and a couple of more in the reverse field limit the grade. (#7943)

Rarely Seen MS65 1911-D Quarter Eagle

1514 **1911-D MS65 NGC.** The late Paul M. Green turned his attention to the 1911-D quarter eagle in his "Item of the Week" column for the *Numismatic News* dated September 17, 1996. He begins with a simple assertion: "Key-date gold coins are often overlooked and underpriced." He continues by noting that while the various copper and silver series, particularly more modern ones, are accessible to a broad range of collectors, gold coinage demands a substantial budget. Green does highlight the Indian quarter eagle series, however, as a potential exception. It is short, and in his words, "supplies of all dates from the Indian Head quarter eagles ... are ample with the exception of one."

Then this:

> "In all cases the single exception is the 1911-D. The 1911-D had a total mintage of 55,680 pieces, making it far and away the lowest production date of that type. It had not become any more common over the years. It always has, and always will be the key date in the Indian Head quarter eagle set. Its prices routinely run four or five times higher than the prices of common dates. None question that it is the key date to the set and worth the price."

The intervening years have widened the gap between the 1911-D quarter eagle and its peers, validating Green's assertions from 1996. The 1911-D is rarely encountered in Gem condition, in large part because of the way these coins were designed. The sunken relief places the fields as the high points, and extreme care had to be taken so they were not abraded. This is a truly impressive example that shows clear fields, the only exception being a short diagonal mark on the reverse above and to the left of the motto. Light, even reddish color is seen over each side. The diagnostic partial wire rim is easily seen on the right side of the obverse. The striking details are sharp, but not quite fully brought up on the lowest feather in the headdress. Census: 71 in 65, 2 finer (1/10). (#7943)

Solid 1912 Quarter Eagle, MS64

1515 **1912 MS64 NGC.** The 1912 quarter eagle is common in the lower Mint State grades but becomes more difficult in near-Gem. Gems are quite challenging and higher-grade coins are elusive. The lustrous honey-gold surfaces of this MS64 example exhibit well struck devices. Light marks on the raised, exposed fields of the reverse preclude Gem status.
From The Alfred V. Melson Collection, Part Two. (#7944)

1516 **1913 MS64 NGC.** Peach-gold lustrous surfaces exhibit well struck design elements, including the eagle's shoulder feathers. Some inoffensive marks preclude Gem status. Scarce any finer. (#7945)

Important Gem 1913 Quarter Eagle

1517 **1913 MS65 PCGS.** Though the 1913 quarter eagle is readily available in grades through Choice Mint State, MS65 coins are scarce, and anything finer is a condition rarity. This Gem example is delightfully lustrous with bold orange-gold color and hints of rose at the margins. A handful of long, thin abrasions are noted in the fields to the left of the portrait. Housed in a green label holder. (#7945)

Elusive 1914 Quarter Eagle, MS63

1518 **1914 MS63 NGC.** The 1914 quarter eagle is a conditionally scarce issue from a mintage that was limited to just 240,000 coins. Enough examples survive in low and middle Mint State grades that most any collector can obtain one with a little patience. This ideal example provides an excellent combination of grade and value. Both sides are sharply defined, with satiny yellow luster and excellent eye appeal.
From The Alfred V. Melson Collection, Part Two. (#7946)

Luminous MS64 1914 Quarter Eagle

1519 **1914 MS64 NGC.** Rich gold-orange luster is at once satiny and potent, gracing a boldly impressed near-Gem. With just 240,000 pieces struck, the 1914 has gained considerable fame as the Indian quarter eagle issue with the second-lowest mintage, behind only the notorious 1911-D. NGC has graded 42 finer pieces (1/10). (#7946)

1520 **1915 MS64 PCGS.** The 1915 quarter eagle is available through the near-Gem level before becoming moderately challenging in MS65. Rich apricot-gold patina resides on the lustrous surfaces of this attractive MS64, and an exacting strike leaves strong detail on the design motifs. Neither side reveals mentionable marks. (#7948)

1521 **1925-D MS64 NGC.** Brassy-gold luster invigorates this sharply struck D-mint near-Gem. Light handling marks in the raised, exposed fields define the grade.(#7949)

Brilliant 1925-D Quarter Eagle, MS65

1522 **1925-D MS65 NGC. CAC.** Highly lustrous and frosty with brilliant yellow-gold surfaces and bold design definition on both sides. This amazing piece is just shy of top honors for the date, as NGC has only certified 42 finer examples (1/10). This is the most available of the three Denver Mint Indian quarter eagles. (#7949)

Well Struck 1925-D Quarter Eagle, MS65

1523 **1925-D MS65 NGC. CAC.** Inspection of NGC/PCGS population figures indicates that the 1925-D is readily available through the near-Gem level. Gems can be located without too much difficulty, but anything finer is elusive. Lustrous peach-gold surfaces exhibit well struck motifs and reveal just a few minor grade-consistent marks. (#7949)

Condition Census 1925-D Quarter Eagle MS66 ★, One of Two at NGC

1524 **1925-D MS66 ★ NGC.** The 1925-D quarter eagle is the last of only three D-mint Indian Head quarter eagles issues produced at irregular intervals during the series' run. The Denver Mint made quarter eagles, but no half eagles during 1925, making the issue even more interesting as half eagle production figures throughout U.S. numismatic history are generally much higher. The aberrant issue must have been recognized at the time, as clearly many examples were saved. The issue was a generous (for the series) 578,000 coins, amidst the Roaring Twenties and before the great stock market crash of four years later.

Today the issue is available up through the MS66 level, although only a single MS67 NGC piece has been graded finer. The current MS66 ★ example is one of only two so certified at NGC (1/10). PCGS has never certified an example finer than MS66. The surfaces are interesting, with contrasting obverse and reverse. The obverse is frosted, yet the reverse shows die striations in the upper right field and is consequently brighter there. The surfaces are deep reddish-gold overall, with pale hints of lilac on the reverse. The strike is sharp but not full, lacking full definition on the lowest headdress feather. (#7949)

Amazing 1926 Indian Quarter Eagle, MS66

1525 **1926 MS66 PCGS.** All of the Indian quarter eagles from the 1920s are considered common dates, but none are common in Premium Gem preservation. Consider almost 96,000 Indian quarter eagles of all dates that are PCGS certified, with only 230 of those coins graded MS66 or MS67. That is one Premium Gem for every 417 pieces certified. This piece has wonderful brilliant yellow surfaces with frosty luster and exceptional eye appeal. The strike is bold throughout, with only a few tiny marks and spots that prevent an even higher certified grade. Population: 38 in 66, 0 finer (1/10). (#7950)

Attractively Patinated 1927 Gem Quarter Eagle

1526 **1927 MS65 NGC. CAC.** The 1927 quarter eagle is available in any grade from MS65 and below; finer examples are highly elusive. A medley of apricot-gold, apple-green, and rose patination resides on the lustrous surfaces of the present Gem offering. Well cared for surfaces exhibit crisply struck design motifs. (#7951)

1527 **1928 MS64 NGC.** Sharp definition for this later issue with bright yellow-gold luster. This near-Gem Indian quarter eagle is housed in a prior-generation holder.(#7952)

Frosty 1928 Indian Quarter Eagle, MS65

1528 **1928 MS65 NGC.** An extraordinary Gem, and approaching the finest available quality for the date or for any Indian quarter eagle. NGC has only certified 14 finer examples of the date, and only 230 finer examples of the entire series. This Gem has gorgeous rose toning over frosty yellow-gold luster with bold details and excellent surfaces. (#7952)

THREE DOLLAR GOLD PIECES

1529 **1854 AU53 PCGS.** Luster fills the legends and outlines the wreath of the present first-year honey-gold type coin. Unimportant contact is present, but no marks are of singular consequence. Certified in a green label holder.(#7969)

1530 **1854 AU55 PCGS.** Bright orange luster fills the design recesses of this attractive and originally toned three dollar gold piece. No marks are worthy of comment. Encased in a green label holder. (#7969)

Appealing Select 1854 Three Dollar

1531 **1854 MS63 NGC.** As a Select example of the unusual and popular three dollar gold denomination, this first-year representative is automatically in high demand. The present piece blends prominent apricot and peach shadings in a swirl of luster, offering a sharp strike and excellent eye appeal for the grade. (#7969)

Shining MS64 1854 Three Dollar

1532 **1854 MS64 PCGS.** Deep reddish-gold patina graces each side, with wonderful luster emanating from the surfaces. The strike is boldly executed, even on the often-weak bowknot, and neither side reveals much in the way of ticks or abrasions, even under a loupe. The 1854 is usually grouped with the 1874 and 1878 issues for "type" purposes, though with the small ONE DOLLAR denomination it is technically a one-year subtype. PCGS has graded 26 finer pieces (1/10). (#7969)

1533 **1855 AU58 NGC.** Strong yellow-gold luster persists despite friction on the high points. Occasional greenish accents visit minimally abraded surfaces. An appealing near-Mint representative of this second-year odd-denomination issue.(#7972)

Lustrous 1856 Three Dollar, MS64

1534 **1856 MS64 PCGS.** Circulated 1856 three dollar gold pieces are easily enough found, including high-end About Uncirculated specimens. Uncirculated examples become difficult to locate, especially at the Gem level. Indeed, near-Gems are the finest grade collectors are likely to encounter.

The greenish-gold surfaces of this MS64 piece exhibit pleasing luster emanating from a satinlike finish, and a relatively strong impression characterizes the design elements, except for weakness in the bowknot. Occasional minute obverse marks deny Gem classification. Population: 34 in 64, 2 finer (12/09). (#7974)

1535 **1857-S—Removed From Jewelry, Bent—NGC. XF Details.** The reverse border is tooled between 9 and 1 o'clock, and also between 4 and 7 o'clock, to remove evidence of mounts where the piece was once affixed to jewelry. The right obverse field is lightly polished, and a slight bend is evident when the piece is rotated. (#7977)

1536 **1861 PCGS Genuine.** The PCGS number ending in .94 suggests Altered Surfaces as the reason, or perhaps one of the reasons, that PCGS deemed this coin not gradable. In our opinion, this coin has the details of an AU specimen that is scratched and has obverse damage. The obverse has faint scratches on the upper left field and through the top of the bust tip. The open obverse field may have been thumbed in order to reduce the visual impact of abrasions. (#7982)

1537 **1874 AU55 NGC.** A lightly worn yet strongly lustrous example of this popular odd-denomination type issue. Generally yellow-gold surfaces show a distinct patch of violet between STATES and OF on the obverse, a color echoed within the reverse wreath. (#7998)

1538 **1877—Mount Removed, Polished—NCS. XF Details.** Inordinately bright and glossy from polishing. No evidence of a removed mount is readily evident. Still desirable due to a low mintage of 1,468 pieces. Unlike later date scarcities such as the 1882, few if any examples were set aside by Philadelphia-area dealers at the time of issue.(#7999)

1539 **1878—Reverse Scratched—NCS. UNC Details.** The reverse has a single light scratch from the left border across the wreath to the large 3. Otherwise, both sides have excellently preserved surfaces approaching a Choice Mint State grade level.(#8000)

Popular 1878 Three Dollar, MS61

1540 **1878 MS61 NGC.** Strong yellow-gold luster offers elements of peach and honey. The strike is pleasing, if not strictly perfect, and while a handful of light to moderate abrasions appear in the portrait area, the overall eye appeal is far superior to what the grade might suggest. An intriguing choice for the type collector. (#8000)

Gorgeous MS64 1878 Three Dollar

1541 **1878 MS64 PCGS.** The bold and swirling luster that graces the best three dollar gold pieces is in full force on this near-Gem from the last high-mintage issue of the denomination. The strike is strong, and few marks are visible on the yellow-gold surfaces. A single small alloy spot is noted near the tip of Liberty's nose. (#8000)

Appealing MS64 1878 Three Dollar Gold

1542 **1878 MS64 NGC.** The honey-gold obverse offers wonderful, swirling luster, while the reverse has brighter yellow-gold color and displays mildly prooflike tendencies. An excellent strike boosts the eye appeal of this near-Gem, which shows no singularly distracting abrasions. A great coin for the type enthusiast. (#8000)

Dazzling 1888 Three Dollar, MS63

1543 **1888 MS63 PCGS.** Dazzling luster emanates from the yellow-gold and greenish-gray surfaces of this Select three dollar and a well directed strike leaves strong definition on the design elements. Despite the minor handling marks that limit the grade, both sides yield pleasing eye appeal. This will be an excellent selection for a high grade type collection. (#8010)

Sharp 1888 Three Dollar, MS64

1544 **1888 MS64 PCGS.** The 1888 three dollar is one of the most available dates in the series due to hoarding, despite its low mintage of 5,000 circulation strikes. Variegated mint-green and apricot patination enlivens the lustrous, minimally marked surfaces of this near-Gem. Sharply struck except for minor softness in the leaf left of the bowknot. (#8010)

1545 **1889 AU53 PCGS.** Muted green-gold surfaces have accents of light rose toning on each side. This is a splendid example of the final three-dollar gold piece. Most survivors are actually in higher grades, making this a rather unusual situation.(#8011)

Extremely Rare BD-7 1795 Small Eagle Five Dollar, AU53

1546 **1795 Small Eagle AU53 PCGS.** Breen-6415, BD-7, R.7. This extremely rare variety pairs an obverse die with recutting on the 5 on the date and a reverse with four berries on the small wreath, two on each side of the beak, one inside and one outside. Though distinctly rubbed at Liberty's nose and the eagle's breast, this yellow-gold example remains remarkably lustrous, with mildly prooflike elements at the peripheral protected areas. Solid central detail with numerous small but individually inoffensive marks that are consistent with both brief circulation and the grade assigned. (#8066)

Historic Mint State 1795 Half Eagle
Small Eagle Reverse, BD-1

1547 **1795 Small Eagle MS60 NGC.** BD-1, R.5. Two major design types are known for the half eagles with a 1795 date. This Small Eagle design was actually produced in 1795, whereas the Large or Heraldic Eagle design was backdated, and actually coined in 1798. There are 12 individual die varieties of the Small Eagle type, representing the earliest gold coins produced at the Philadelphia Mint. These 12 varieties were produced through various combinations of eight obverse dies and nine reverse dies.

When Walter Breen studied these coins in the 1960s, he assigned numbers 1 through 4 and letters A through D to the four obverse and reverse dies that he believed were first used by the Mint. Adjustments have been made to his sequence, and today, the Bass-Dannreuther reference notes that this was the very first half eagle variety produced in 1795, thus it is possibly **the first U.S. gold coinage variety.** On July 31, 1795, the chief coiner of the Mint delivered 744 half eagles to the Mint treasurer, and this example was probably among those pieces. Minor die cracks and die rust on both sides suggest that this is a later die state of the variety.

The surfaces are pleasing with attractive green-gold coloration. A minor scratch from Liberty's neck crosses the left obverse field to star 5, and this is the only readily apparent imperfection, aside from the usual abrasions that exist on nearly every known example. There is no trace of wear on either side, and the fields exhibit a slightly reflective appearance. This is a lovely example, and an extremely important opportunity for the half eagle specialist or the collector of historic coinage.
From The South Texas Collection. (#8066)

1799 Small Stars Reverse Half Eagle BD-1, AU50

1548 **1799 Small Stars Reverse AU50 NGC. CAC.** Breen-6433, BD-1, High R.5. Bass-Dannreuther Die State b/c, with the faintest beginnings of a die crack through the bottoms of stars 11 and 12. Like all other die pairs of the 1799 half eagle, the BD-1 is rare in an absolute sense. The winning bidder is sure to prize this AU50 example. The yellow-gold surfaces remain amply lustrous, with surprisingly few abrasions for the grade assigned. Only slight striking softness is present through the centers, though this makes the reverse appear perhaps more worn than it really is. Overall, a thoroughly appealing coin.
From The South Texas Collection. (#8081)

Near-Mint BD-4 1800 Half Eagle

1549 **1800 AU58 PCGS.** Breen-6439, BD-4, R.4. Bass-Dannreuther Die State d/b, with clash marks on both obverse and reverse, but not the die cud at the lower left reverse indicating that side's terminal state. Bass and Dannreuther note about the reverse, which was only used once: "The obviously recut M makes this one of the easiest varieties to identify." As an AU58 example, this coin must rank highly among known survivors, though a number of Mint State examples of the issue appear in the combined certified population. Radiant yellow-gold surfaces show only scant evidence of abrasions and friction. All things considered, a strongly appealing early half eagle.
From The South Texas Collection. (#8082)

1802/1 'High Overdate' Half Eagle
Rare BD-7 Die Pair, AU58

1550 **1802/1 AU58 PCGS.** Breen-6440, BD-7, R.5. Bass-Dannreuther Die State b-c/a-b, intriguingly with both obverse and reverse in transition. The obverse has the crack from star 5 to the rim but not the one at star 3; similarly, the reverse shows a faint crack through the last three letters of UNITED but not the one from the arrows through the shield. Luminous orange-gold fields are cut with butter-yellow, creating an intriguing and eye-appealing combination. Well struck and minimally abraded, with only modest wear on the high points to preclude a Mint State designation. (#8083)

BD-3 1803/2 Half Eagle, AU55

1551 **1803/2 AU55 PCGS.** Breen-6441, BD-3, R.4. Recutting on the T in UNITED is a useful diagnostic. The deep yellow-orange surfaces of this Choice AU coin show both age and luster, the latter scarcely dimmed by the modest amount of rub across the high points. Small and scattered marks contribute to the grade.
From The South Texas Collection. (#8084)

Notable MS61 BD-2 1804 Half Eagle

1552 **1804 Small 8 MS61 NGC.** Breen-6443, BD-2, High R.4. Bass-Dannreuther Die State d/f, with die crack through the top of the TY in LIBERTY in addition to the prominent north-to-south bisecting die crack on the obverse. This example has excellent luster characteristics with light canary-yellow color overall that occasionally takes a sun-gold hue. Well-defined for the die state, though constant relapping has robbed the devices of some of their detail. Shallow pinscratches are noted on and to the left of the portrait. For all Small 8 varieties, Census: 26 in 61, 45 finer (1/10).
From The South Texas Collection. (#8085)

Popular Choice XF 1806 Five Dollar
Round Top 6, 7x6 Stars, BD-6

1553 **1806 Round Top 6, 7x6 Stars XF45 NGC.** Breen-6448, BD-6, R.2. The only Round 6 die variety, and also the only Bust Right variety of any date with a 7x6 star arrangement, which crowds the left obverse border. Ample luster shimmers from the design of this early half eagle. Rose-red borders encompass butter-gold centers. The reverse is problem-free aside from a slightly soft central strike, while the reverse is attractive but has a few thin marks, including one above the ear. Certified in a prior generation holder. (#8089)

Popular 1806 Round Top 6 Half Eagle BD-6, AU55

1554 **1806 Round Top 6, 7x6 Stars AU55 NGC.** Breen-6448, BD-6, R.2. The Round Top 6 or "Knobbed 6" variety. Bass Dannreuther Die State a/c, a combination unlisted in the reference but a logical transition point; the obverse does not show the edge-to-lowest-curls die crack needed for Obverse State b, though the curls are thinned, while the reverse shows the die crack through the N in UNITED to the arrowheads that corresponds with Reverse State c. This surprisingly radiant yellow-gold example offers strong eye appeal for the variety. Though numerous tiny ticks are present in the fields, the devices show only slight evidence of wear.
From The South Texas Collection. (#8089)

Difficult Choice XF BD-2 1807 Bust Right Half Eagle

1555 **1807 Bust Right XF45 PCGS.** Small Date, Small Obverse Stars, Large Reverse Stars, Breen-6450, BD-2, R.5. The terminal die state with a prominent cud above the E in LIBERTY. The highpoints display slight wear, but substantial luster remains beneath rich butter-gold toning. No marks merit individual mention. Encapsulated in an old green label holder. (#8092)

Choice AU 1808 Five Dollar Wide Denomination, BD-4

1556 **1808 AU55 NGC.** Wide 5D, Breen-6457, BD-4, High R.3. Bass-Dannreuther Die State c/a. The nonoverdated obverse die, lapped from its previous appearance, paired with a new reverse with a wide space between the 5 and the D in the denomination. Bass and Dannreuther note in *Early U.S. Gold Coin Varieties*, "This variety is the first early gold coin that seems to have a single die state for both dies for the entire production run." Whether struck early or late, this Choice AU example offers rich gold-orange luster and a solid strike. Marks are few, save for a small cluster of abrasions to the left of Liberty's lips.
From The South Texas Collection. (#8102)

Uncirculated Wide 5D 1808 Half Eagle, BD-4

1557 **1808 MS61 NGC. CAC.** Wide 5D, Breen-6457, BD-4, High R.3. This well struck Mint State early five dollar piece has peach-red toning throughout the borders, which along with the devices are illuminated by vivacious luster. The few delicate field marks are of no concern. An impressive example of a scarce gold type. BD-4 is the sole Wide 5D variety among the four 1808-dated die pairings, which are further divided into two normal date and two 1808/7 marriages. The overdate is considered rarer, particularly BD-1, whose production run was apparently limited by a prominent bisecting obverse die crack. (#8102)

Near-Gem 1810 Large Date, Large 5 Half Eagle, BD-4, MS64

1558 **1810 Large Date, Large 5 MS64 NGC.** Breen-6459, BD-4, R.2. Bass-Dannreuther Die State c/b, with clashed obverse showing a faint die crack between the 8 and the second 1 in the date. This is the most frequently seen combination of the two diagnostic aspects for the year, with both large date and large 5 in the denomination. This shining near-Gem is a delightful representative for the type enthusiast, with rich butter-yellow color and solid design definition. Only a few light scuffs and abrasions in the portrait area preclude an even better designation. NGC has certified seven numerically finer examples of the variety (1/10). (#8108)

Partly Lustrous AU53 1812 Five Wide 5D, BD-1

1559 **1812 AU53 PCGS.** Wide 5D, Breen-6466, BD-1, R.3. This butter-gold early five dollar type coin offers its share of billowy luster and has nearly full design detail. A small strike-through is near the chin, the cheek is slightly bright, and the fields have occasional small patches of closely spaced marks. Certified in a green label holder. (#8112)

1812 Wide 5D Five Dollar, BD-1 Uncirculated Sharpness

1560 **1812—Improperly Cleaned—NGC. Unc. Details.** Wide 5D, Breen-6466, BD-1, R.3. Careful rotation beneath a light reveals patches of hairlines in the fields. The cheek has a few parallel thin marks. Mint luster dominates the raised design elements. The 1812 is less available than the 1807 or 1810, although the Capped Bust Left series can be completed by date, unlike the Capped Head Left type that follows. (#8112)

Attractive AU58 1813 BD-1 Half Eagle

1561 **1813 AU58 NGC.** Breen-6467, BD-1, R.2. Bass-Dannreuther Die State b/b, with clash marks from the shield on the reverse visible within the letters of LIBERTY. A pleasing near-Mint representative of this popular Capped Bust half eagle variety, lightly rubbed on the high points with strong yellow-gold luster. A degree of alloy is noted between star 13 and the nearby curl.
From The South Texas Collection. (#8116)

CLASSIC HALF EAGLES

1562 **1834 Plain 4—Improperly Cleaned, Obverse Scratched—NGC. AU Details.** First Head, Breen-6501, McCloskey 3-B, R.1. This richly detailed straw-gold introductory-year type coin has a faint, straight, hair-thin pinscratch between 1 and 8 o'clock. A mild cleaning causes a slightly luminous appearance.(#8171)

1563 **1834 Plain 4 AU55 NGC. CAC.** Second Head, Breen-6502, McCloskey 2-A, R.1. Luster outlines individual stars and fills the legend and eagle. No marks are consequential, and the centers show only slight incompleteness of strike.(#8171)

1564 **1834 Plain 4 AU58 NGC.** Second Head, Breen-6502, McCloskey 2-A, R.1. Canary-gold with traces of lime toning. Luster encompasses all but the open fields and Liberty's cheek and neck. Well struck for the type, and both sides are refreshingly devoid of abrasions.(#8171)

1565 **1834 Plain 4 AU58 NGC.** Second Head, Breen-6502, McCloskey 2-A, R.1. Luster dominates the peripheries and fills the hair and plumage. The fields display only unimportant marks, and the central strike shows expected moderate incompleteness.(#8171)

1566 **1834 Plain 4—Altered Surfaces—ANACS. MS60 Details.** Second Head, Breen-6502, McCloskey 2-A, R.1. The 4 in the date is triple punched, and the D in UNITED is repunched. This unworn example appears unabraded and displays satin luster. The centers show incompleteness of strike typical of the type.(#8171)

1834 Plain 4 Classic Half Eagle, MS61

1567 **1834 Plain 4 MS61 NGC. CAC.** Second Head, Breen-6502, McCloskey 2-A, R.1. An unabraded butter-gold representative that has exemplary luster throughout the devices and borders. As is customary for the Second Head subtype, the left shield border shows moderate incompleteness of die detail, where metal flowed to the recesses of the high relief bust during the strike. (#8171)

Series Key Crosslet 4 1834 Classic Five, AU53

1568 **1834 Crosslet 4 AU53 NGC.** Second Head, Breen-6503, McCloskey 5-D, R.4. The Plain 4 variety is commonplace compared to the Crosslet 4, which is a seldom-seen and eagerly pursued *Guide Book* entry. This apricot-gold example has its share of glistening luster, and the scattered small field marks are of little importance. Census: 4 in 53, 32 finer (12/09). (#8172)

1569 **1836 AU55 PCGS.** Second Head, Large Date, Breen-6509, McCloskey 2-B, R.4. A scarce die marriage distinguished by a prominent vertical die crack that nearly bisects the obverse between 12:30 and 5:30. Splendidly detailed and partly lustrous. One thin obverse mark is noted at 10:30.(#8174)

Enthralling 1836 Classic Five Dollar, MS62

1570 **1836 MS62 PCGS.** Third Head, Breen-6510, McCloskey 3-C, R.2. A lovely butter-gold type representative that has an excellent strike and impressively unabraded surfaces. Bright luster dominates the legends and devices. The only marriage for this obverse die, identified by repunching on the peak of the 1 in the date. Population: 39 in 62, 29 finer (1/10). (#8174)

1571 **1837 AU53 NGC.** McCloskey 2-B. This is the only common variety of the year, although 1837 is scarcer than the earlier dates in the series. This piece has attractive lemon-yellow surfaces with minor grade-consistent marks.(#8175)

LIBERTY HALF EAGLES

1572 **1840 Narrow Mill AU58 NGC.** Immensely lustrous with deep orange-gold surfaces. The strike is crisp, and only modest friction precludes a Mint State designation. Census: 64 in 58, 25 finer (12/09).(#8194)

Rare 1842-C Small Date Five Dollar, XF40

1573 **1842-C Small Date XF40 PCGS. CAC.** Variety 1. One of the rarest coins from the Charlotte Mint and much more difficult to find than its Large Date cousin. Yellow-gold surfaces are accented with greenish-gray and reddish-gold patina and exhibit appropriately defined design elements. Distributed minute marks do not detract. Population: 9 in 40, 18 finer (1/10). (#8208)

Challenging 1842-D Large Date Five, AU50

1574 **1842-D Large Date AU50 PCGS.** Variety 9-G. This radiant apricot-gold Dahlonega half eagle is lustrous for the designated grade and shows only slight wear on the plumage and on Liberty's curls, eyebrow, and shoulder. The fields display minor marks, mostly clustered near star 13. The Large Date variety is substantially scarcer than the Small Date. Population: 5 in 50, 14 finer (1/10). (#8211)

Elusive 1843 Liberty Five, MS62

1575 **1843 MS62 NGC.** In both circulated and lower Mint State grades, the 1843 (611,205 pieces produced) is the most common Liberty Half Eagle from the 1840s after the 1847. Of course, we use the term "common" in a relative sense, as Uncirculated survivors of all early Liberty fives are rare when viewed in the wider context of U.S. numismatics. Satiny in finish, the luster quality is quite pleasing for the grade. Both sides are orange-gold, with scattered light and moderate abrasions seeming to account for the MS62 assessment. Crisply impressed throughout. Census: 15 in 62, 23 finer (1/10). (#8213)

Impressive MS63 1844 Half Eagle

1576 **1844 MS63 NGC.** A remarkable Mint State representative of this pre-California Gold Rush half eagle issue. The devices are sharply struck, and effervescent yellow-gold luster enlivens each side. Though a few small marks and wispy abrasions preclude a numerically finer designation, this coin's eye appeal is impossible to ignore. Census: 12 in 63, 0 finer (12/09). (#8219)

Select 1844-O Five Dollar

1577 **1844-O MS63 NGC.** Garrett and Guth note: "The 1844-O half eagle has one of the highest mintages of any New Orleans gold coin, second only to the 1847-O eagle." That enormous production did not translate into wide availability in Mint State grades, however; the authors term the issue "quite rare" at that level, stating: "Relatively few coins were saved from this high-mintage issue." This Select example has characteristically sharp definition on the portrait and strong yellow-gold luster. Scattered wispy abrasions are present on the mildly mirrored fields, yet the visual appeal is strong for the grade assigned. Census: 11 in 63, 6 finer (12/09). (#8222)

1578 **1845-D—Improperly Cleaned—NGC. AU Details.** Variety 12-I. This is the usually seen variety for the year. The surfaces have muted yellow luster with myriad surface marks and other blemishes, reminiscent of the so-called "salt water" pieces. The design motifs show excellent definition.(#8224)

Choice XF 1846-C Half Eagle

1579 **1846-C XF45 NGC.** Variety 1. An appealing Choice XF representative of this 1840s Charlotte half eagle issue, struck from a single die pair. Pale yellow-gold surfaces remain subtly lustrous despite light overall wear and abrasions. A measure of more significant rub is found on Liberty's brow and through the eagle's central feathers. Census: 10 in 45, 43 finer (12/09). (#8227)

Scarce 1846-C Half Eagle, AU53

1580 **1846-C AU53 NGC.** Variety 1, the only known die pair for the limited mintage of just 12,995 coins. This piece has deep green-gold surfaces with traces of orange toning. The fields are satiny with noticeable luster and the design definition is well above average. Census: 10 in 53, 28 finer (1/10). (#8227)

1581 **1846-D/D AU50 PCGS.** Variety 15-J. The repunched mintmark is blatant, the most prominent such variety with the Dahlonega gold series. This well detailed example has a subtle mint-made strike-through on the cheek and lightly abraded, luminous straw-gold fields.(#8229)

Fantastic AU58 1846-D/D Half Eagle

1582 **1846-D/D AU58 NGC.** The 16-L die combination with broad void at the top of the 6 and boldly repunched mintmark. Strong yellow-gold luster gives the fields a moderately prooflike aura, and the devices exhibit only mild friction on the high points. Truly Mint State examples with the repunched mintmark are rare; NGC has graded only nine such pieces (1/10). (#8229)

1583 **1847-C—Bent—NGC. AU Details.** Variety 1. Only a single die pair is known for this high mintage issue. A total of 84,151 pieces were coined, suggesting the possible existence of at least one additional variety that is just waiting to be found. This example has bright green-gold surfaces with excellent design definition. It is described as bent, but apparently only slightly so.(#8233)

Pleasing AU 1848-D Five Dollar

1584 **1848-D AU50 PCGS.** Variety 18-M, State III. The reverse is prominently cracked through the A in STATES and across the tips of the two uppermost arrowheads. Softly defined at the margins, as usually seen, but mildly prooflike yellow-gold luster persists in the fields. Lightly abraded with small depressions on Liberty's neck, yet strongly appealing. Housed in a green label holder. Population: 19 in 50, 38 finer (1/10). (#8238)

Almost Uncirculated 1849-D Five Dollar

1585 **1849-D AU50 NGC.** Variety 22-N. Of the 39,036 pieces struck for this Dahlonega issue, it is estimated that today only 125-150 coins remain in all grades, the majority of which are VF-XF. This is a well struck example that has bright yellow-gold color. The surfaces are peppered with numerous small abrasions, but the only one worthy of mention is in the obverse field between stars 5 and 6. (#8242)

Important MS61 1851 Five Dollar

1586 **1851 MS61 NGC.** Though half eagle mintages skyrocketed as the California Gold Rush went on, the denomination remained little-saved, and Mint State examples are scarce today. This MS61 example has effusive yellow-gold luster and a sharp strike, though a number of small digs and abrasions preclude a finer designation. Census: 29 in 61, 33 finer (1/10). (#8246)

1587 **1851-C—Harshly Cleaned—NGC. XF Details.** Variety 1. This piece has noticeable hairlines on its light green-gold surfaces. Both sides have the usual surface marks expected at the grade level. Deep iridescent toning is evident around the borders.(#8247)

1588 **1851-C—Improperly Cleaned—NGC. XF Details.** Variety 1, and clearly showing the circular mark on Liberty's earlobe, as struck. This piece is lightly cleaned yet has excellent eye appeal created by the green-gold surfaces and traces of luster.(#8247)

1589 **1852-D—Improperly Cleaned—NGC. XF Details.** Variety 27-U. This is the most common variety of the 1852-D half eagles. Both sides have light hairlines visible in the fields of this green-gold representative.(#8252)

1590 **1852-D XF45 NGC.** Variety 27-U. The obverse has the date left of center and the reverse has a vertical die line through the right side of the final S. This pleasing light yellow-gold example has excellent surfaces for the grade. Here is an important Dahlonega gold piece for the date or type collector.(#8252)

Well Impressed 1854 Select Five Dollar

1591 **1854 MS63 PCGS.** Most 1854 half eagles appear in the XF and AU grade levels. Mint State coins, when available, are usually in the lower levels thereof. This MS63's surfaces possess nearly full luster and are toned in peach-gold and mint-green, and reveal a few minute grade-defining marks. The design elements are well impressed. Population: 8 in 63, 2 finer (1/10). (#8256)

1592 **1856-S AU55 PCGS.** Medium S. A well struck and still-lustrous Choice AU coin with bold color and eye appeal. Stark yellow-gold surfaces show elements of violet alloy at the right reverse. Population: 26 in 55, 14 finer (12/09).(#8270)

1593 **1857-C—Damaged—NGC. XF Details.** Variety-1, the only known die pair for the 1857-C half eagle. This piece has several bulges on the obverse, but nothing on the reverse suggests a source. The surfaces, especially on the reverse, are somewhat rough. However, traces of luster are present on the obverse, and the strike is above average.(#8272)

1594 **1858 AU58 NGC. CAC.** This near-Mint State five dollar retains luster in the recessed areas of its peach-gold surfaces and exhibits strong definition on the devices. Distributed small marks are undisturbing. Census: 15 in 58, 14 finer (1/10).(#8276)

Prized 1864 Half Eagle, AU53

1595 **1864 AU53 NGC.** This Civil War-era issue of just 4,170 business strikes is conditionally rare at and above the AU53 level represented by this still-lustrous survivor. Strong striking definition has withstood the coin's modest wear, and while the orange-influenced yellow-gold surfaces show a number of light marks, the overall eye appeal is remarkable for the designation. Census: 9 in 53, 27 finer (12/09). (#8296)

1596 **1867-S Fine 12 NGC.** Considerable wear is evident on both sides of this piece, quite expected for an issue that was immediately placed in circulation in California, while eastern residents were hoarding the silver and gold coins they encountered. The surfaces are pleasing for the grade, and overall this is a highly desirable example.(#8314)

1597 **1868 XF45 PCGS.** Yellow-gold surfaces imbued with traces of light green exhibit well defined design elements. Distributed small marks are in concert with a coin having seen some circulation. (#8315)

1598 **1871-CC Fine 15 NGC.** Reddish-gold patina covers the reverse and visits the obverse margins. Appropriately detailed. Distributed minute marks are more prevalent on the obverse. One of the scarcest issues in the series.(#8323)

Lustrous 1871-CC Half Eagle, AU55

1599 **1871-CC AU55 PCGS.** An exceptional example with only a few peers and a small number of finer pieces in existence. This Choice AU half eagle has rich yellow-gold luster with traces of peripheral orange toning. The strike is good and the surfaces are free of significant blemishes. Nearly full mint luster remains with only traces of wear on the high points. Although more than 20,000 1871-CC half eagles were minted, most survivors are well-worn, with an average grade of about VF30. NGC and PCGS have graded just 19 pieces in AU55 with only 13 finer, including resubmissions. Population: 9 in 55, 5 finer (1/10). (#8323)

1600 **1873-S AU50 NGC.** A surprising amount of mint luster illuminates the borders and devices of this lightly circulated rare date half eagle. Relatively smooth for the grade and type, since no marks merit individual mention. All 31,000 pieces struck were apparently from the Closed 3 date logotype. Census: 16 in 50, 30 finer (12/09).(#8332)

Choice XF 1874-CC Half Eagle

1601 **1874-CC XF45 NGC.** This Choice XF example offers better-than-expected definition on the reverse, where the degree of wear seems more consistent with an AU designation. Several pronounced "spikes," or heavy die lines, are evident between the eagle's beak and the top of the left (facing) wing. The coin has a nice overall appearance, with mild satiny luster remnants on each side. Census: 26 in 45, 53 finer (12/09). (#8334)

Notable Near-Mint 1874-S Half Eagle

1602 **1874-S AU58 NGC.** This is a Condition Census example of an issue that is, as of this writing, unknown in Mint State grade, although the present AU58 piece is tied with a bit more than a dozen pieces at both services combined (1/10). Even in AU the 1874-S half eagle is rare. This piece displays splendid yellow-gold surfaces with tinges of lilac patina at the obverse rim. A few light abrasions are characteristic, as is the central strike weakness; the latter is most notable on the S mintmark, faint yet discernible. (#8335)

Elusive 1877-CC Five, AU Details

1603 **1877-CC—Plugged, Improperly Cleaned—NCS. AU Details.** Holed and plugged with detail reengraved, including star 7 on the obverse and VE of FIVE on the reverse. The surfaces are bright yellow with additional imperfections from improper cleaning or handling. However, the date is an important rarity in the Carson City half eagle series, and this piece will easily find a happy home. (#8343)

1604 **1877-S AU53 NGC.** Peach-gold surfaces are tinted with light green and are relatively well defined. Light marks are somewhat more plentiful on the obverse.(#8344)

Challenging 1878-CC Half Eagle, AU55

1605 **1878-CC AU55 PCGS.** All Carson City five dollar issues from the 1870s are rare, and the 1878-CC is no exception. Gold bullion depositors preferred payment in double eagles, which were more convenient for accounting purposes. An absence of Old West collectors caused most survivors to remain in circulation for many years. Just one piece has been certified Mint State, which makes an AU example the finest that most collectors can hope to own. The present piece has too much friction on the wingtips and eyebrow to command a higher grade, but luster brightens the borders and major devices. No marks are remotely consequential. Population: 5 in 55, 5 finer (1/10). (#8346)

1606 **1878-S MS62 PCGS.** A splendid example of the conditionally rare 1878-S half eagle, this piece has few peers. It is fully lustrous with lovely orange-gold coloration, and few marks for the grade. Quite undervalued in the market place. Population: 33 in 62, 8 finer (1/10).(#8347)

1607 **1879-S MS62 NGC.** Sharply struck with considerably bright luster. Pale yellow-gold centers give way to deeper butter hues close to the rims. Census: 50 in 62, 25 finer (12/09).(#8350)

Conditionally Rare 1880 Gem Five Dollar

1608 **1880 MS65 NGC.** As might be expected from its high mintage exceeding 3 million circulation strikes, the 1880 is relatively common in all grades below near-Gem. The latter is scarce and Gems are rare. Wheat-gold luster invigorates this sharply struck, minimally abraded MS65. Census: 24 in 65, 1 finer (1/10). (#8351)

1609 **1880-S MS64 NGC. CAC.** Dazzling luster radiates from the yellow-gold surfaces of this highly attractive near-Gem S-mint half eagle. Sharply struck and revealing just a few minor handling marks that preclude Gem status. NGC and PCGS combined have seen only 18 coins finer (1/10).(#8353)

1610 **1880-S MS64 PCGS.** Rich peach-gold and lime toning adorns this thoroughly lustrous, carefully preserved, and precisely struck Choice Liberty five. A better date at the MS64 level, despite a mintage of nearly 1.35 million pieces. Certified in a green label holder. Population: 67 in 64, 1 finer (1/10).(#8353)

1611 **1880-S MS64 PCGS.** This lustrous Choice half eagle has an exacting strike and original olive and apricot toning. The reverse is nearly pristine. Although plentiful in typical Uncirculated grades, this issue is scarce and underappreciated at the MS64 level. Population: 67 in 64, 1 finer (1/10).(#8353)

1612 **1881/0 MS62 PCGS. CAC.** FS-301, formerly FS-005. Only light magnification is required to see the curve of the 0 beneath the 1 in the date. The surfaces are uncommonly lustrous for an MS62. Numerous small abrasions pepper both sides, but none are of individual significance. Population: 15 in 62, 16 finer (1/10). (#8355)

Select 1883-S Half Eagle

1613 **1883-S MS63 NGC.** Luminous gold-orange surfaces have more vibrancy on the reverse, but both sides offer a bold impression on the central devices. An attractive Select example of this challenging San Francisco issue with a five-figure mintage, only modestly abraded for the grade. Census: 11 in 63, 0 finer (1/10). (#8363)

1614 **1884-CC XF45 PCGS.** Rich orange and mint-green patination bathes both sides of this Choice XF half eagle. Nicely defined despite high-point wear and only minimally abraded.(#8365)

1615 **1885 MS64 PCGS.** This sharply defined and fully lustrous 1885 half eagle exhibits brilliant yellow-gold surfaces with only a few trivial marks on each side. It is an excellent example for the grade, and virtually a point finer. Population: 55 in 64, 2 finer (1/10). (#8367)

1616 **1890-CC AU58 PCGS.** Mint-green and apricot-gold patina adorns both sides of this near-Mint State five dollar. Ample luster occurs in the areas around and in the interstices of the well defined design elements. A few trivial marks do not detract.(#8376)

Impressive 1890-CC Half Eagle, MS64

1617 **1890-CC MS64 NGC.** A hoard of between 20 and 30 Uncirculated 1890-CC half eagles entered the market in the fall of 1996, a number of which were in the MS62 to MS64 range (Douglas Winter, 2001). Near-Gems such as the example in the present lot, however, are still scarce. The issue remains very rare in Gem and above.

Lustrous yellow-gold surfaces exhibit well struck design elements, save for the usual minor weakness on the eagle's neck and breast and obverse rim. Minute obverse marks deny Gem classification. Census: 28 in 64, 4 finer (1/10). (#8376)

1618 **1891-CC MS62 PCGS.** Traces of orange patina are present over lustrous green-gold surfaces on this frosty Mint State Carson City half eagle. The date is popular with type collectors due to its high mintage and survival.(#8378)

Lustrous 1891-CC Half Eagle, MS63

1619 **1891-CC MS63 PCGS.** This half eagle has a bold strike with fully defined motifs on both sides. It is a lustrous piece with frosty yellow surfaces and wisps of pale orange toning. Although the date is rather plentiful in MS63, PCGS has graded only a few finer coins. They have only certified 56 better examples, including resubmissions (1/10). (#8378)

1620 **1893-CC AU58 PCGS.** Sharply struck with the luster virtually intact, though modest friction is noted on the yellow-gold devices. Minimally abraded save for a small tick on the cheekbone. (#8384)

1621 **1893-S MS64 PCGS.** The lustrous surfaces are surprisingly clean with the only mentionable abrasion being a milling mark to the right of the eagle. Smooth, even mint luster is covered with a light layer of reddish patina.(#8386)

Surprising 1898-S Five, MS64

1622 **1898-S MS64 PCGS. CAC.** A reasonably available Liberty half eagle that is fully struck with bright mint luster and no large or mentionable abrasions on either side. This issue is conditionally rare, however, with only a handful of Gem quality examples recognized by the grading services. This Choice half eagle is quite affordable in comparison. Population: 30 in 64, 8 finer (1/10). (#8397)

1623 **1899-S MS64 PCGS.** Strong luster enlivens this sharply struck near-Gem. Apricot and mint-green surfaces are minimally abraded for the designated grade. Population: 33 in 64, 8 finer (1/10). (#8399)

Extraordinary 1900-S Liberty Five, MS65

1624 **1900-S MS65 PCGS.** This boldly detailed half eagle is a remarkable and rare coin in Gem preservation. The mintage was adequate at 329,000 coins, but most survivors today are in lower Mint State grades. NGC and PCGS combined have only certified 14 coins in MS65 or finer grades, a total that undoubtedly includes resubmissions. Both sides have full design definition, with brilliant and frosty yellow-gold luster and peripheral accents of olive-green. The surfaces exhibit trivial marks on each side that limit the grade. Population: 5 in 65, 5 finer (1/10). (#8401)

1625 **1901 MS64 PCGS.** This frosty half eagle has brilliant light yellow surfaces, with a few trivial, grade-consistent marks. The strike is excellent, and the overall eye appeal is high. PCGS has only certified 64 finer examples (1/10).(#8402)

Conditionally Scarce 1907 Half Eagle, MS66

1626 **1907 MS66 PCGS. CAC.** The 1907 is one of the most common dates in the Liberty Head series. Premium Gem examples such as the present offering are extremely scarce, however, and higher-grade pieces are almost unobtainable. Ebullient luster exudes from yellow-gold surfaces displaying sharply struck design elements. A few minor ticks do not detract. Population: 16 in 66, 0 finer (1/10). (#8416)

Rare 1903 Five Dollar, PR67 Cameo

1627 **1903 PR67 Cameo NGC.** Proof half eagles saw a production of only 154 coins in 1903. Walter Breen, in his 1988 *Complete Encyclopedia of U.S. and Colonial Coins*, contends that the proof five dollar pieces of 1866-1907—that is, the Coronet Head with Reverse Motto design type—are rarer than their mintages suggest, and that many survivors are impaired. Similarly, David Akers, in his 1979 *United States Gold Coins, An Analysis of Auction Records* reference, states that "Proofs are rare."

NGC and PCGS combined have graded 115 Coronet with Motto half eagle specimens, with the modal grade being in the Select to near-Gem proof range. Fewer than 30 coins have been assigned the Cameo designation, and none the Ultra or Deep Cameo classification.

The current Superb Gem Cameo displays breathtakingly uniform brass-gold coloration. Moderately frosted motifs stand out amidst the deeply mirrored fields, yielding a gold-on-black appearance when the coin is observed from various angles. The design elements are fully struck, as expected, and close examination with a loupe reveals no mentionable marks. Indeed, nothing on the coin's surface yields even a hint of a pedigree marker. In summary, this piece exhibits outstanding technical quality and aesthetically pleasing overall eye appeal, and as such is sure to draw close attention from specialists in proof gold coinage. Census: 5 in 67 Cameo, 1 finer Cameo (12/09). (#88498)

Sparkling 1907 Liberty Five, PR65 Cameo 92 Pieces Minted

1628 **1907 PR65 Cameo NGC.** While the Liberty Head type was minted through 1908, the 1907 was the final year available in proof format. The mintage was predictably low with only 92 proofs produced, but even that number gives a misleading indication of availability. Garrett-Guth 2006) estimate that only 30 to 35 coins exist today, and of those survivors a surprising number are cleaned or otherwise impaired. Also, few examples are known with cameo contrast. This lovely, deeply mirrored example shows noticeable contrast between the fields and devices on each side. A curious area of striking weakness is seen in the centers, but there are no obvious flaws aside from a lint mark in the field in front of Liberty's mouth. Census: 6 in 65 Cameo, 11 finer (1/10). (#88502)

INDIAN HALF EAGLES

Lustrous 1908 Indian Five, MS64

1629 **1908 MS64 PCGS. CAC.** A wonderful example of the first Indian half eagle, struck in the transitional year following production of the 1908 Liberty fives. This piece is sharply detailed with excellent yellow-gold luster and frosty surfaces. The surfaces are remarkably nice for the grade. (#8510)

1630 **1908-D MS62 NGC.** The first year of the Indian Head half eagle series. Sharp definition is found on the design elements of this yellow-gold D-mint representative. A couple of faint linear abrasions in the upper left obverse quadrant limit the grade. (#8511)

Sharply Struck 1908-D Five Dollar, MS64

1631 **1908-D MS64 NGC. CAC.** The 1908-D half eagle is difficult to obtain any finer than near-Gem. The sharply struck design features of the current MS64 example complement the pleasing luster emanating from its brassy-gold surfaces. Inoffensive field marks preclude the Gem grade. (#8511)

Splendid 1908-D Half Eagle, MS64

1632 **1908-D MS64 PCGS. CAC.** This splendid near-Gem Indian half eagle provides an excellent opportunity for the Set Registry collector. While relatively plentiful at this grade level, the 1908-D is a major condition rarity any finer, with just nine better pieces certified by PCGS (1/10). This piece has brilliant and frosty yellow luster with trivial, grade-consistent marks. (#8511)

Near-Gem 1909-D Five Dollar

1633 **1909-D MS64 NGC. CAC.** While the 1909-D five dollar, the most common type issue of the design, remains available for a price in MS64, that price is strong due to sky-high demand. This near-Gem offers attractive yellow coloration on the smooth obverse, while there is more orange-gold luster on the mildly abraded reverse. NGC has certified 66 numerically finer pieces (1/10). (#8514)

1634 **1910-S MS60 NGC.** The surfaces resemble those of a 1909-D five because they have deep green color intermixed with the usual reddish-gold. The strike is full, and as one would expect for an MS60 there are numerous small to medium-sized abrasions on each side.(#8519)

Fully Struck 1910-S Half Eagle, MS64

1635 **1910-S MS64 NGC.** The 1910-S half eagle hails from a plentiful mintage of more than three-quarters of a million coins, and although examples in the higher Mint State levels are scarce, examples up to the near-Gem level of this piece, and occasionally even Gem coins, can be found for a price. Also fortuitous for collectors is that the issue is generally a well-produced one, with a sharp strike, bold mintmark, and lustrous surfaces.

The present example is representative of those sterling qualities, with a full strike that extends even to the headdress feathers at the bottom of the obverse. The lustrous orange-gold surfaces show a hint of reddish patina, and the surfaces are exceptionally clean overall. A couple of small abrasions between stars 9 and 11, and a horizontal nick to the left of the G in GOD on the reverse, are all well within the context of the near-Gem grade. Census: 16 in 64, 2 finer (1/10). (#8519)

Bright Gem 1911 Five Dollar

1636 **1911 MS65 NGC.** Regardless of date, a Gem Indian half eagle is a prize, and this selection, which hails from a popular type issue, is sure to find favor with collectors. Strong yellow-orange luster at the centers trends firmly toward the latter color close to the margins. Well struck with only a handful of scattered flaws that have minimal effect on the eye appeal. Despite a generous mintage of 915,000 pieces, the 1911 five dollar is elusive in MS65 condition and virtually impossible to find any finer; there are only two such pieces in the combined certified population (1/10). (#8520)

1637 **1911-S MS61 NGC.** Yellow-gold surfaces exhibit relatively well struck design elements, though the eagle's shoulder is a tad soft. Some dark areas are visible on the borders of both sides. This issue is fairly scarce in Mint State despite its generous mintage of 1.416 million pieces.(#8522)

Desirable 1911-S Half Eagle, MS62

1638 **1911-S MS62 PCGS. CAC.** A delightful example with fully lustrous yellow-gold surfaces and above average design definition. A few marks are consistent with the grade. The 1911-S is a challenging issue in the higher Mint State grade levels. This piece provides a wonderful opportunity to acquire the issue at a reasonable price. (#8522)

1639 **1912 MS63 NGC.** Honey-gold surfaces display pleasing luster and sharply defined design features. Light marks in the upper reverse field limit the grade.(#8523)

Important MS62 1914-S Half Eagle

1640 **1914-S MS62 PCGS.** This lower-mintage S-mint Indian half eagle issue is challenging regardless of condition, with MS62 coins elusive and anything finer flat-out rare. This dusky yellow-orange example has an uncommonly sharp strike and soft, inviting luster. Scattered wispy marks contribute to the grade. PCGS has certified just 24 higher-graded pieces (12/09). (#8529)

Remarkable 1909 'Roman Finish' Indian Half Eagle, PR67 ★

1641 **1909 PR67 ★ NGC.** Paraphrasing from our description of "The Matte Proofing Process" (page 36) in *The Coinage of Augustus Saint-Gaudens as Illustrated by the Phillip H. Morse Collection*, when the Mint introduced four new gold coinage designs in 1908, it was determined, due to the extreme curvature of the dies, that the old method of producing proof gold could not be used, in which portions of the coins would turn out with brilliant mirrored fields. A "sandblast" method was used, in which the newly produced gold pieces were taken to an industrial cabinet and "carefully sandblasted on each side with a stream of fine, industrial sand to impart a dull, grainy effect. The fineness of the particles and skill of the workman doing the sandblasting governed the shade and appearance of the particular coin, ranging from light yellow-gold, to light brown, to deep khaki-green color."

Some numismatists liked the new finish. Most did not, however, and in the following year 1909 the Mint tried a new so-called Roman gold finish. Breen describes it as "satiny, semi brilliant, pale lemon color." The present coin shows two different perspectives on the Roman finish gold, depending on the distance from which the observer looks at the coin. From a distance, it is remarkable how bright the fields are. The piece appears bright yellow-gold, with a slight hint of reddish patina. Up close, however, the observer notes the fine-grained mattelike surfaces, in which tiny individual grains stand out. As expected of the grade, essential contact is nonexistent, and the NGC Star appellation justly confirms the overwhelming appeal. A fine wire rim appears around the entire reverse and nearly all of the obverse. In PR67 ★ this piece is one of three pieces so graded, and there are two finer, both PR68 without the Star (1/10). (#8540)

Important AU53 1795 Ten Dollar
BD-1, 13 Leaves Reverse

1642 **1795 13 Leaves AU53 PCGS.** Breen-6830, Taraszka-1, BD-1, High R.3. Bass-Dannreuther Die State a/a, without any of the cracks indicating state b for either side. The BD-1 1795 eagle is one of the most available of the Small Eagle ten dollar die pairs, scarce in an absolute but not a relative sense; the authors of *Early U.S. Gold Coin Varieties* state that "there are likely are more known for this variety than all the other 1795 *[eagle]* varieties combined." Still, their estimate of 225 to 325 pieces known leaves far fewer survivors than there are interested collectors, a surefire recipe for high prices, particularly in Extremely Fine and better grades.

Though this AU53 example shows a measure of rub which precludes a Mint State designation, the still-lustrous butter-yellow surfaces show more Mint-made artifacts than post-striking abrasions. Adjustment marks (present across Liberty's face), for example, outnumber other marks; the lower and right obverse show apparent strike-through depressions, possibly from thread; and the upper left reverse field has a shallow planchet depression.

None of this is to suggest that this is in any way an unattractive coin; on the contrary, it has remarkable eye appeal for its age and history. Particularly beguiling is the rose coloration, subtle but easily picked up under magnification, that surrounds the peripheral lettering and stars. Housed in a green label holder. (#8551)

Heraldic Eagle 1797 Ten Dollar BD-4, AU50

1643 **1797 Large Eagle AU50 NGC.** Breen-6834, Taraszka-12, BD-4, High R.4. Bass-Dannreuther Die State d/a-b transitional, with the reverse not showing all die cracks as described in the reference but showing the beginning of the crack through the R in AMERICA. This still-lustrous orange-influenced ten dollar piece comes from the first year of the Heraldic Eagle reverse for that denomination. Shallow adjustment marks are noted at the lower right obverse, but the other marks scattered on each side are luster grazes and abrasions. A slight rim bump is noted near 6 o'clock on the reverse. Despite these minor faults, truly an appealing coin for the grade. *From The South Texas Collection.* (#8559)

1799 Small Stars Ten Dollar, BD-5

1644 **1799 Small Stars Obverse PCGS Genuine.** Breen-6838, Taraszka-17, BD-5, R.6 The PCGS number ending in .92 suggests Cleaning as the reason, or perhaps one of the reasons, that PCGS deemed this coin not gradable. This piece has Unc Details. The reverse die was used only for this single die marriage, and all known examples have a prominent die chip or rust mark between vertical stripes 4 and 5, just inside the lower shield border. This is one of the scarcer varieties of 1799 tens. Only 1,250 to 1,750 pieces are believed to have been struck, and of that low mintage a mere 22 to 30 examples are believed known today. Predictably, the surfaces are bright from cleaning. Close examination reveals that the cleaning has not removed all the mint luster. Small remnants can still be seen around the obverse stars, and there is considerable luster remaining over the reverse. The striking details are strong overall. There are numerous tiny abrasions peppered over each side, but the only marks of any significance are a couple of shallow ones in the upper right obverse field. (#98562)

Well-Defined 1799 Ten Dollar, AU Details BD-7

1645 **1799 Small Stars Obverse—Improperly Cleaned, Rim Damage—NGC. AU Details.** Irregular Date, Small Stars, Breen-6840, Taraszka-19, BD-7, R.3. This appears to be Obverse State a, as there are no clashing or clashing evident. Of the eight Small Star varieties for 1799, the BD-7 is the one most frequently encountered. The surfaces are unnaturally bright from cleaning and there are numerous small to medium sized abrasions on each side. The rim damage mention on the insert apparently refers to smoothing of the rim between 7 and 9 o'clock. The striking details are sharp throughout and the color is bright yellow-gold. (#98562)

Extremely Rare BD-4 1799 Small Stars Obverse Eagle, AU55

1646 **1799 Small Stars Obverse AU55 PCGS.** Breen-6838, Taraszka-16, BD-4, R.7. Since Harry Bass Jr. had a lone example of BD-4 to examine in the course of his research, he could only confirm one die state. But he posited the existence of both earlier and terminal states. The current coin is identical in terms of die state to the BD-4 specimen in Bass' core collection. This variety comprises Bass-Dannreuther obverse die 4 and reverse die A. It is believed that reverse A became terminal during this short die marriage (its final of four uses). Obverse 4 was later paired with two other reverse dies to create BD-5 and BD-6, both of which are rare, but not to the extent of BD-4.

A hint of green accents the light yellow-gold surfaces of this Choice AU piece. The surfaces are lightly abraded, consistent with the grade. A tiny mark above the left top of Y will identify this piece. A minuscule rim nick over the R in LIBERTY is hidden by the PCGS holder. There is no evidence of adjustment marks on either side. (#98562)

XF40 1801 Eagle, BD-2

1647 **1801 XF40 PCGS.** Breen-6843, Taraszka-25, BD-2, R.2. Bass-Dannreuther Die State b/b, with "spikes" (actually lines from the reverse shield) through Liberty's cap. This variety's availability (it does not qualify as "scarce" in an absolute sense) has long been a source of attraction to type collectors, though the corresponding increased demand has elevated the BD-2 1801 eagle close to its less-available counterparts. On this XF coin, faint glimmers of reflective luster are present at the yellow-orange margins. Shallow but significant abrasions are present through the fields and on the devices, though the lower left obverse's parallel lines are die adjustment marks and not flaws picked up in circulation. Housed in a green label holder.
From The South Texas Collection. (#8564)

Near-Mint 1801 Eagle, BD-2

1648 **1801 AU58 PCGS.** Breen-6843, Taraszka-25, BD-2, R.2. Bass-Dannreuther Die State b/b, with clash marks through cap, a frequently seen and important diagnostic. Garrett and Guth write in their *Encyclopedia of U.S. Gold Coins*, "The 1801 eagle has a high mintage and is noted for having the second-highest surviving population (after 1799), thus it is an excellent choice as one of the more affordable dates of the type." This brightly lustrous near-Mint example, yellow-gold with only light marks and a trace of friction, similarly is a strong candidate for the type collector seeking a coin with Mint State-grade eye appeal for less money. (#8564)

BD-2 1801 Eagle, MS61

1649 **1801 MS61 NGC.** Breen-6843, Taraszka-25, BD-2, R.2. Bass-Dannreuther Die State b/b, with clash marks through Liberty's cap. This is an example of the more commonly seen BD-2 die pair, distinguished by the obverse with star 1 distant from Liberty's curl. Bass and Dannreuther note: "This is the most available early eagle variety, as the dies were among the most productive of the type." This availability extends to Mint State, though as may be expected, demand still exceeds supply. This radiant, lightly abraded yellow-gold piece offers strong central definition, though a loss of detail is noted on a handful of the highest design elements. A strongly appealing coin. (#8564)

Choice XF 1803 Ten Dollar Small Stars Reverse, BD-3

1650 **1803 Small Stars Reverse XF45 PCGS.** Breen-6844, Taraszka-28, BD-3, R.4. Bass-Dannreuther Die State b/c, with only light cracking on the reverse. The BD-3, very scarce but still the most available 1803 Small Reverse Stars eagle die pair, brings together two extraordinarily long-lived dies, though the reverse die met its end in this die pair. This Choice XF butter-yellow example has surprisingly radiant butter-yellow surfaces and a pleasing level of remaining detail despite unmistakable signs of wear. In addition to the expected light digs, an old pinscratch is noted at the upper part of Liberty's portrait. (#8565)

Near-Mint 1803 Eagle Small Stars, BD-1

1651 **1803 Small Stars Reverse AU58 NGC. CAC.** Breen-6844, Taraszka-26, BD-1, High R.5. Bass-Dannreuther Die State a/a. While the obverse die used to strike 1803-dated eagles was seemingly charmed, the reverse dies were not; six distinct reverse dies are known paired with the single obverse. Reverse A, as it is known in the Bass-Dannreuther reference, shows die lumps between the first T and the A in STATES. This near-Mint representative offers considerable yellow-gold luster in fields that are almost flashy, though the highest design elements show evidence of rub. Still, a thoroughly delightful example of this rare Small Stars die pair.
From The South Texas Collection. (#8565)

LIBERTY EAGLES

1652 **1843-O AU50 PCGS.** Traces of luster reside in the recesses of this well defined O-mint ten dollar. Yellow-gold surfaces reveal a few minute surface and rim marks.(#8589)

AU53 1845-O Ten Dollar

1653 **1845-O AU53 PCGS.** Bright lemon-yellow surfaces are moderately abraded with appreciable wear, though the protected peripheral fields show glints of prooflike reflectivity. Strong design definition enhances each side, though the feathers on the eagle are particularly sharp. An important example of this O-mint eagle issue. Population: 10 in 53, 12 finer (12/09). (#8593)

1845-O Eagle, AU55 From the S.S. *Republic*

1654 **1845-O AU55 NGC.** Ex: S.S. *Republic*. Variety One. NGC describes this as a "doubled 84" variety (read: repunched date). Radiant yellow-gold surfaces, though moderately abraded, retain considerable prooflike reflectivity. A line of shallow reed marks crosses Liberty's cheek, though the impact on the eye appeal is curiously minimal. (#8593)

1655 **1848-O—Improperly Cleaned—NGC. XF Details.** Unlike the high mintage 1847-O, the 1848-O had a small production of just 35,850 pieces. Only a handful of Mint State coins are known. This moderately circulated representative has hairlined fields but lacks distracting marks. A shield ring is noted atop the second vertical stripe.(#8600)

1656 **1850-O XF45 PCGS.** Here is an amazing green-gold charmer with considerable luster still visible on each side. In fact, this coin is more green than gold in overall color. The surfaces are typically abraded, yet none are significant. Population: 40 in 45, 26 finer (1/10).(#8605)

Scarce 1852-O Eagle, AU53

1657 **1852-O AU53 PCGS.** The 1852-O ten dollar is very scarce in the About Uncirculated grade levels and extremely rare in Mint State. PCGS and NGC have certified a mere three Uncirculated pieces, all MS60 or MS61! The peach-gold surfaces of this AU53 specimen retains luster in the recesses and exhibits well defined devices, save for the usual softness in the star centers. (#8609)

Important 1853 No Motto Eagle, MS61

1658 **1853 MS61 NGC.** Despite the presence of trivial abrasions and a few tiny rim nicks, this 1853 ten is a remarkable example of the No Motto design. The luster is bright with green-gold surfaces and satiny mint brilliance. This is an important issue in Mint State grades. Census: 20 in 61, 9 finer (1/10). (#8610)

Challenging 1854-O Large Date Eagle, AU58

1659 **1854-O Large Date AU58 NGC.** The Large Date variety was made in error when the diesinker mistakenly used a date punch for a silver dollar. There is disagreement as to whether the Large or Small Date is scarcer. In any event, near-Mint State Large Date examples such as the current offering are challenging to acquire. Its yellow-gold surfaces retain a good amount of luster and the centers exhibit the usual softness, though the remaining areas are well impressed. (#98614)

1660 **1855 AU53 PCGS.** Peach-tinged luster beckons from the borders and eagle of this well struck and moderately abraded No Motto eagle. A fairly scarce issue that in the present grade trades for only a modest premium above bullion value.(#8616)

1661 **1855 AU58 NGC.** Considerable luster invigorates the yellow-gold surfaces of this near-Mint State eagle. The design elements are well defined, and distributed small marks are in line with a coin having experienced some circulation. Scarce at this grade level and difficult in Mint State.(#8616)

Choice AU 1857 Ten Dollar

1662 **1857 AU55 NGC.** During the 1850s, heavy production of double eagles limited the mintage of the less convenient eagles. The 1857 ten has a mintage of only 16,606 pieces, and NGC has certified only two examples in Mint State, both as MS60. The present Choice AU representative is nicely struck and provides substantial luster. Marks are generally confined to the cheek and upper reverse field. Census: 18 in 55, 27 finer (12/09). (#8622)

Still-Lustrous XF45 1857-O Eagle

1663 **1857-O XF45 NGC.** A still-lustrous yellow-gold Choice XF example from this O-mint eagle issue of only 5,500 pieces. Strongly defined with pockets of alloy around certain stars and at the nearby rims, which also show a handful of minor flaws. Scattered light abrasions are consistent with the grade. Census: 13 in 45, 48 finer (12/09). (#8623)

1664 **1860-O XF40 PCGS.** An outstanding green-gold example, this 1860-O Liberty eagle is a lovely piece for the grade. Both sides have a few grade-consistent surface marks. A frame of light orange toning enhances the overall eye appeal.(#98631)

1665 **1861 AU55 NGC.** Honey-gold surfaces display hints of light tan and retain traces of luster in the recessed areas. Well defined, and revealing just a few minute circulation marks.(#8633)

1666 **1861 AU55 PCGS.** Five-fold or rounded bun subtype. An original Choice AU No Motto ten from the initial year of the Civil War. Toned orange and olive-green with a good strike and scattered small marks.(#8633)

1667 **1868-S XF45 PCGS.** An attractive Choice XF example of this underrated post-Civil War San Francisco eagle issue, strongly struck with considerable luster remaining in the deep yellow-gold fields, particularly the reverse. Slight weakness on the stars is not uncommon for the time, and the light wear and abrasions visible on each side are grade-consistent. Population: 10 in 45, 25 finer (1/10).(#8654)

1668 **1868-S XF45 PCGS.** Banker and exporter preferences for the more convenient double eagle led to a low mintage for the 1868-S ten. Just 13,500 pieces were coined, and none were set aside by collectors until many years later. Luster fills design crevices, and the moderately marked surfaces display original pumpkin-gold color. Encapsulated in a green label holder. Population: 10 in 45, 25 finer (1/10).(#8654)

1669 **1871 XF40 PCGS.** Well defined, yellow-gold surfaces are tinted with hints of light green and are lightly abraded. From an extremely small mintage of 1,790 circulation strikes. Population: 6 in 40, 22 finer (12/09).(#8660)

Appealing 1873-S Ten Dollar, XF45

1670 **1873-S XF45 PCGS.** An appealing Choice XF example of this elusive San Francisco ten dollar issue, one of only 12,000 pieces struck. Most known examples are in VF and XF condition, and Mint State coins are nearly nonexistent. Apricot-gold surfaces exhibit well defined design motifs and are only lightly abraded. Population: 6 in 45, 14 finer (12/09). (#8668)

1671 **1874 MS61 PCGS.** The 1874 ten is a scarce date overall and difficult to locate in Mint State. This peach-gold MS61 specimen displays luster around and in the interstices of the well struck devices. Distributed small marks determine the grade. Population: 19 in 61, 17 finer (1/10).(#8669)

1672 **1878-S AU55 NGC.** Both sides of this Choice AU ten dollar yield a brass-gold appearance. This well defined piece displays traces of luster in the recessed areas. Distributed small marks—typical of the issue—are noted over both sides. This scarce date is extremely elusive in Mint State grades. Census: 32 in 55, 30 finer (1/10). (#8682)

1673 **1880 MS63 NGC.** A frosty and brilliant yellow example with pleasing surfaces for the grade. The design elements are sharply defined. The 1880 is a high mintage issue that is elusive in Mint State. Census: 31 in 63, 15 finer (1/10).(#8687)

1674 **1880-CC AU50 PCGS.** Yellow-gold surfaces retain traces of luster in the recessed areas. This is a nicely defined piece with no more marks than what would be expected for a coin seeing some circulation. From a low mintage of less than 12,000 pieces. (#8688)

Low Mintage 1880-CC Eagle, AU55

1675 **1880-CC AU55 NGC.** Choice AU is the highest grade most collectors will encounter of this Carson City issue that comes from a mintage of only 11,190 pieces. This example displays traces of luster in the recessed areas of the well struck design elements. Both sides yield yellow-gold hues and are lightly abraded. (#8688)

1676 **1881 MS63 PCGS.** Predominantly pumpkin-gold, although the margins have aqua-green hues. Lustrous and boldly impressed with the scattered minor marks associated with the MS63 level. Encased in a green label holder.(#8691)

1677 **1881-O AU50 NGC.** Splashes of reddish-purple patina make occasional visits to the peach-gold surfaces of this sharply defined ten dollar, and the fields on both sides yield partially prooflike characteristics. A scattering of small surface and rim marks is noted.(#8693)

Conditionally Elusive 1881-S Ten, MS63
Tied for Finest Certified

1678 **1881-S MS63 PCGS. CAC.** With a mintage of 970,000 coins, the 1881-S is a rather available issue for Liberty eagles of the 1880s. But, surprisingly, this MS63 piece is tied for the finest of 50 coins certified by NGC and PCGS combined. This piece is sharply defined with light yellow and pink surfaces and excellent eye appeal. Population: 28 in 63, 0 finer (1/10). (#8694)

Scarce 1883 Ten Dollar, MS63

1679 **1883 MS63 PCGS.** The 1883 ten dollar is common thanks to European bank hoards, where hundreds of examples were found in MS60 to MS62. MS63 specimens such as the present piece are scarce; near-Gems are highly elusive. PCGS and NGC have graded none finer than MS64. Lustrous peach-gold surfaces exhibit traces of mint-green and are sharply struck. Light marks limit the grade. Population: 66 in 63, 4 finer (1/10). (#8699)

1680 **1884-CC XF45 NGC.** This Choice XF ten dollar displays traces of luster in the recesses of its peach-gold surfaces. Well defined and minimally abraded.(#8704)

Prooflike 1885 Liberty Ten, MS63

1681 **1885 MS63 PCGS.** The 1885 Liberty eagle is an extremely important condition rarity, with the typical survivor hovering around the MS60 grade level. This piece has rich yellow-gold luster with prooflike fields, deeper yellow along the borders, and light cameo contrast. Trivial surface marks are inconsequential. Population: 36 in 63, 10 finer (1/10). (#8706)

Seldom Seen Near-Gem 1885 Ten Dollar

1682 **1885 MS64 PCGS.** Unlike the 1880 to 1882 Philadelphia issues, each of which was struck in excess of 1 million pieces, the 1885 has a relatively low mintage of 253,462 pieces. Uncirculated examples are scarcer than expected, but readily collected in grades through MS62. Near-Gems, however, are rare, and none have been certified by PCGS as Gem or finer (1/10). This lustrous and sharply impressed example has lime-green borders and apricot fields and devices. No marks merit mention, and the eye appeal is excellent for this much better date. (#8706)

1683 **1887-S MS63 NGC.** While the 1887-S eagle is readily available through most lower Mint State grades, Select examples are elusive and finer coins are conditionally rare. This MS63 coin has bright luster in pale yellow-gold with a "shadow" ring around the obverse. Sharply struck with small, scattered marks that are grade-consistent. Census: 49 in 63, 5 finer (1/10).(#8711)

1684 **1887-S MS63 PCGS.** Brass-gold surfaces yield pleasing luster and well struck design features. Scattered minute marks account for the grade. Challenging at the Select level and rare any finer. Population: 69 in 63, 2 finer (1/10).(#8711)

1685 **1887-S MS63 PCGS.** Bold design definition and excellent eye appeal are evident on this yellow and pinkish-gold eagle. Traces of peripheral olive patina add to its overall desirability. A lovely example of a condition rarity in the Liberty eagle series. Population: 69 in 63, 2 finer (1/10).(#8711)

Rare Choice 1889-S Ten Dollar

1686 **1889-S MS64 NGC. CAC.** The mintage of the 1889-S eagle—more than 425,000 coins—suggests that it is plentiful, and indeed it is readily secured in MS61 or MS62. MS63 examples are scarce, however, and the issue is a rarity at the MS64 level. Like so many original gold coins, the present piece is predominantly pumpkin-gold with lime-green peripheries. It is lustrous and intricately struck with only one mark of consequence, on the field beneath the left (facing) wing. Census: 7 in 64, 0 finer (1/10). (#8716)

Challenging 1890-CC Eagle, MS61

1687 **1890-CC MS61 NGC.** The 1890-CC eagle is a low-mintage date of 17,500 pieces that offers a significant challenge in Mint State. This MS61 example show a uniformly sharp strike and considerable attractive luster. Distributed small marks limit the grade. Census: 71 in 61, 51 finer (12/09). (#8718)

Charming 1890-CC Ten, MS62

1688 **1890-CC MS62 PCGS.** Subdued green-gold surfaces are exhibited on this pleasing Carson City Mint ten, possessing the charm of the Nevada Mint and the mystique of the Old West. Here is an important opportunity for the type collector to acquire an attractive Nevada gold piece. Population: 31 in 62, 10 finer (1/10). (#8718)

Conditionally Rare 1891 Eagle, MS63

1689 **1891 MS63 PCGS.** The 1891 Liberty eagle is a scarcer issue with a mintage of 91,868 coins. This piece is a remarkable Select Mint State example with fully brilliant and highly lustrous yellow-gold surfaces and frosty luster. An excellent opportunity for the specialist. Population: 33 in 63, 3 finer (1/10). (#8719)

1690 **1891-CC AU58 PCGS.** Bright yellow-gold luster with only modest friction over the high points. Though several light to moderate abrasions appear in the face area, the overall quantity of marks is grade-consistent.(#8720)

1691 **1891-CC MS61 NGC.** FS-501. The mintmark is clearly repunched, a variety first reported by gold specialist Douglas Winter. A frosty and lustrous yellow-gold representative of the Carson City Mint, this pleasing piece has darker patina on the high points, attesting to its originality.(#8720)

1692 **1891-CC MS61 NGC.** Sharply struck with a near-complete luster flow. Brassy-gold surfaces reveal distributed light marks. (#8720)

Pleasing MS62 1891-CC Ten

1693 **1891-CC MS62 PCGS.** Those in search of a quality Mint State ten dollar piece for a Carson City type set inevitably select an 1891-CC, since all other issues of the denomination from the legendary facility are formidable rarities at the MS62 level. This honey-gold representative is sharply struck and has no singularly significant marks. (#8720)

Vibrant Gem 1894 Ten Dollar

1694 **1894 MS65 NGC.** This Gem P-mint eagle offers bold central detail, though a handful of stars show striking softness. Yellow-gold surfaces are delightfully frosty with suggestions of deeper color in tiny dots to the left of Liberty's profile. Tied for numerically finest among NGC-certified examples (1/10). (#8729)

1695 **1895-O MS62 PCGS.** A highly lustrous and brilliant Mint State example, this lovely eagle has generally sharp design definition with excellent eye appeal for the grade. Only a few finer examples have been certified. Population: 73 in 62, 14 finer (1/10).(#8733)

Attractive MS61 1895-S Eagle

1696 **1895-S MS61 NGC.** Like many of its San Francisco fellows, the 1895-S eagle is underrated despite a mintage of just 49,000 pieces. The present MS61 survivor has warm yellow-gold luster and an above-average strike, though small abrasions pepper the obverse and several more overt marks are noted in the right obverse field. Census: 5 in 61, 4 finer (1/10). (#8734)

1697 **1899-S MS63 NGC.** Bright yellow-gold luster and strong design detail. This is a great Select example of its turn-of-the-century issue with few overt abrasions. Unexpectedly scarce at the MS63 level; it seems the issue was little-saved in foreign bank holdings. Census: 35 in 63, 14 finer (12/09).(#8744)

Stunning 1901-S Liberty Ten, MS66

1698 **1901-S MS66 PCGS.** This is a stunning Premium Gem example of a date that is generally considered common; however, it is uncommon in this grade. This specimen has intense yellow-gold luster with delightful olive accents. PCGS has only certified two finer examples of this issue, despite a mintage of almost 3 million coins (1/10). (#8749)

Attractive 1907 Wire Rim Ten, MS63

1699 **1907 Wire Rim MS63 PCGS.** It was Theodore Roosevelt who urged Augustus Saint-Gaudens to place a warbonnet on his figure of Liberty that was used on the 1907 ten dollar. Saint-Gaudens also used a slightly modified version of the standing eagle used on Roosevelt's special inaugural medal from 1905. Then the sculptor submitted the so-called Wire Rim variant to the Mint. However, according to Roger Burdette and Jeff Reichenberger in a *Coin World* article in 2007,

> "Chief Engraver Charles Barber decided that the initial version would never be suitable for commerce. The first variety of $10 coin had no properly defined rim, made a wobbly stack when the experimental pieces were piled, and required use of a medal press to bring up the design. To remedy these defects, Barber made a new set of hubs and dies from the same set of models as before. But this time, he cut a well defined rim into the hubs."

The Wire Rim tens have been relegated to pattern status, although neither the Wire Rim nor the Rolled Rim that followed it are technically patterns. Again, quoting Burdette, "... they might be more accurately described as special issues and withdrawn production pieces (or production trials)."

This example has lovely reddish-golden and lilac patina interspersed over each side. The grade seems unduly harsh, with the only (not-so-obvious) hairlines over the figure of the Native American and eagle. The always-seen die polishing lines are plainly evident in the fields. The surfaces are remarkably free from post-striking defects on both obverse and reverse, and the devices are sharply struck. (#8850)

Gem 1907 No Periods Ten Dollar

1700 **1907 No Periods MS65 PCGS.** A shining Gem example of the first widely distributed Saint-Gaudens eagle issue. Though the centers are softly defined as usual, the sun-gold and lemon-yellow hues of the immensely lustrous surfaces supply immense eye appeal. PCGS has certified just 77 finer examples (12/09). (#8852)

Select No Motto 1908-D Eagle

1701 **1908-D No Motto MS63 NGC.** Slight striking softness through the centers is of little concern in the context of the overall eye appeal. Sun-influenced wheat-gold surfaces are luminously radiant, and aside from a small rim bump at the right reverse, that side is relatively smooth. Wispy abrasions and a few small obverse marks account for the grade. Census: 32 in 63, 37 finer (1/10). (#8854)

MS62 1908-D With Motto Eagle

1702 **1908-D Motto MS62 PCGS.** A strongly detailed example of this first-year With Motto Denver eagle issue, challenging any finer despite a generous mintage. This MS62 example has immense luster that enlivens the pale straw-gold surfaces. A number of light abrasions are present on and around Liberty's face, and the mintmark is curiously flattened. (#8860)

Gorgeous Gem 1908-S Ten Dollar

1703 **1908-S MS65 PCGS.** Garrett and Guth note: "This date is available in gem and even superb gem grades in spite of the very low mintage. Most examples were very sharply struck and quite lustrous, some with a fine granular appearance, and others frostier." This sharp yellow-orange piece has intense luster and the aforementioned crisp detail. Only a handful of tiny ticks are visible, and the small mark above Liberty's eye is entirely grade-consistent. While the writers were literally truthful in that the 1908-S ten dollar exists in Gem and better grades, it is conditionally rare as such, as shown by the PCGS population data: 11 in 65, 21 finer (1/10). (#8861)

1704 **1909 MS62 NGC.** Frosty lemon-yellow surfaces with fully brilliant luster on both sides, this Indian ten is sharply defined with excellent eye appeal. Trivial surface marks are entirely consistent with the grade.(#8862)

Impressive MS64 1910 Eagle

1705 **1910 MS64 PCGS.** Bold sun-gold and butter-yellow hues prevail on this near-Gem, though occasional emerald shadings are also present. Minimally marked on the portrait, which sports bold definition on Liberty's often-weak hair. Housed in a green label holder. PCGS has certified 79 finer examples (1/10). (#8865)

1706 **1910-D MS63 PCGS.** Housed in a green-label PCGS holder, this Select Mint State 1910-D eagle has frosty yellow luster with splendid pink and rose overtones. A few trivial surface marks are expected at the grade level.(#8866)

Well Defined 1910-D Gem Eagle

1707 **1910-D MS65 NGC.** Despite that a vast majority of the 2.3 million mintage was melted during the 1930s, sufficient numbers survived in America and overseas to satisfy collector and type demand. The yellow-gold satiny surfaces of this Gem display above-average definition on the date, stars, and reverse lettering, areas often weak owing to die damage. A nicely preserved piece. (#8866)

1708 **1911-D AU50 PCGS.** Pretty yellow-gold and light green patination endows this D-mint specimen. Generally well defined and minimally marked.(#8869)

1709 **1911-D AU55 PCGS.** Traces of luster reside in the recessed areas of relatively well defined design elements. Yellow-gold surfaces are imbued with hints of mint-green and are lightly marked, including a linear contact on Liberty's cheek.(#8869)

1710 **1911-D AU55 PCGS.** A good amount of luster resides on the yellow-gold surfaces of this Choice AU ten dollar and relatively strong definition occurs on the design elements. A few minute contact marks are unimportant.(#8869)

1711 **1911-D AU55 NGC.** Splashes of greenish-gray visit the peach-gold surfaces of this Choice AU eagle. Both sides show well defined devices and a good amount of luster. Some minute marks are in concert with a coin experiencing brief circulation.(#8869)

Desirable 1911-D Indian Ten, AU58

1712 **1911-D AU58 PCGS.** Only a trace of rub and some dark patina on the high points are evident on this important key issue in the Indian eagle series. This piece has lightly abraded surfaces, as usual for the date and grade. A number of higher-grade pieces have been certified, but they rarely appear for sale in the marketplace. (#8869)

Bright Near-Gem 1913 Eagle

1713 **1913 MS64 NGC.** Bold lemon-gold and sun-yellow luster lights up this near-Gem, well-defined and attractive. Both sides are minimally abraded overall, though a horizontal mark on Liberty's cheek precludes a Gem or better designation. Challenging any better; NGC has graded 92 numerically finer examples (1/10). (#8873)

1714 **1913-S AU55 ANACS.** Rich orange-gold color contributes to the eye appeal of this important Indian ten. Both sides have considerable luster with only a few imperfections.(#8874)

Near-Mint 1913-S Ten Dollar

1715 **1913-S AU58 NGC.** A luminous yellow-orange example with all the characteristics of a briefly circulated coin: minor rub on the high points, nearly intact luster, and an assortment of small to moderate marks. A prominent die erosion line passes through the first two digits in the date and arcs into the nearby field. (#8874)

1716 **1914-D MS62 NGC.** The yellow-gold surfaces of this ten dollar reveal minimal impact on the luster flow from scattered scuffs. Well struck throughout.(#8876)

1717 **1926 MS64 NGC.** Here is a lovely example of the plentiful 1926 Indian ten, one of two dates most often chosen for type collections due to their availability. Light yellow surfaces display traces of green and pink toning. Just a few too many marks are present for a Gem grade determination.(#8882)

1718 **1932 MS64 NGC.** An impressive 1930s gold piece with frosty yellow luster and considerable green patina. Hints of rose add to its overall eye appeal.(#8884)

1719 **1932 MS64 NGC.** Here is a frosty near-Gem 1932 Indian ten, the only collectible gold coin of the 1930s. This piece has brilliant yellow luster with wisps of delightful rose toning.(#8884)

LIBERTY DOUBLE EAGLES

1720 **1850 XF45 PCGS.** This is an attractive Choice XF example of this always-popular first year of issue in the twenty dollar Liberty series. Each side is well-balanced and there are only minute abrasions scattered about.(#8902)

Popular 1850 Double Eagle, AU58

1721 **1850 AU58 NGC.** An attractive example of this popular first-year 1850 double eagle, displaying partial prooflikeness in the fields within the protected areas. Yellow-gold surfaces exhibit well struck design elements and reveal the distributed marks one would expect on a large gold coin that saw brief circulation. (#8902)

1722 **1850-O VF20 NGC.** This popular issue represents the first year of issue for the double eagle series, with examples only coined in Philadelphia and New Orleans. They are especially popular with type collectors. Although noticeably worn, this example has pleasing greenish-gold surfaces with only trivial grade-consistent marks.(#8903)

Attractive XF 1850-O Twenty

1723 **1850-O XF40 NGC.** Both sides have weak peripheral details but stronger central motifs, a common theme for the issue. The surfaces exhibit bright green-gold color, with myriad abrasions, expected for the grade. After even brief circulation, these large and soft gold coins tended to gather numerous handling marks, but this coin has survived well in that regard. (#8903)

Appealing AU 1850-O Double Eagle

1724 **1850-O AU50 PCGS.** While this first O-mint double eagle issue is relatively available in grades through VF, XF coins are elusive, and anything finer than that is genuinely scarce. This AU50 example shows minimal wear and is only lightly abraded on the well-defined central devices, though the peripheral zones exhibit more marks and design weakness, particularly in the stars closest to the coronet. The overall eye appeal is considerable, however, in large part thanks to the generous green-gold mint luster in the protected areas. Population: 19 in 50, 41 finer (1/10). (#8903)

1725 **1852 XF45 NGC.** An attractive light yellow example of this popular double eagle, likely struck from California mined gold that was shipped to Philadelphia. Hints of luster remain, although noticeable wear is evident on each side as expected.(#8906)

Lustrous 1853 Double Eagle

1726 **1853 PCGS Genuine.** The PCGS number ending in .98 suggests Damage as the reason, or perhaps one of the reasons, that PCGS deemed this coin not gradable. In our opinion, this coin has the details of an Uncirculated example with obverse scratches. These are faint, however, and are located near star 1 and on the cheekbone. A patch of delicate hairlines is noted near a small strike-through near star 5. Were it not for these minor problems, the present piece would rank among the finest examples of the issue, since the coin is fully lustrous and has a Gem-quality reverse. (#8908)

1727 **1854 Small Date AU53 NGC.** A lightly circulated yellow-gold example of the Small Date variant that retains considerable luster. The portrait and surrounding fields show a few moderate abrasions, while the reverse shows small pockets of dark encrustation on parts of the devices.(#8911)

Remarkable MS62 1856-S Twenty Likely From the S.S. *Central America*

1728 **1856-S MS62 PCGS.** Remarkable quality for an early S-mint double eagle. A number of 1856-S twenties were recovered from the S.S. *Central America,* and while this coin is not specifically attributed to that source, such an origin is plausible. The effusive, luminous yellow-orange surfaces share the same aura as a number of the shipwreck pieces, and while small abrasions on the cheek contribute to the grade, they have a minimal effect on the eye appeal. Population: 18 in 62, 13 finer (1/10). (#8919)

Brilliant 1857-S Twenty, MS63 From the S.S. *Central America* Treasure

1729 **1857-S Narrow Serif MS63 PCGS.** Ex: S.S. *Central America.* Here is a fully brilliant and highly lustrous double eagle from the S.S. *Central America* treasure, struck just weeks or months before leaving on its fateful voyage. The surfaces are outstanding for the grade, and faint splashes of orange toning add to the overall eye appeal. (#70002)

1730 **1859-S AU55 NGC.** Minted after the loss of the S.S. *Central America* and long enough before the losses of the S.S. *Brother Jonathan* and S.S. *Republic,* so that there is a good chance this coin had been in numismatic circulation before the discovery of those treasures. The 1859-S had a strong mintage of more than 600,000 coins, but survivors are infrequently encountered. This piece is fully lustrous, except for traces of high-point wear.(#8928)

Desirable 1862 Twenty, XF45

1731 **1862 XF45 PCGS.** An important, lower mintage Civil War era double eagle from the Philadelphia Mint, with few high grade survivors. In fact, PCGS has only certified 43 coins in Choice XF or finer grades. Both sides of this greenish-gold piece have splashes of coppery luster. Population: 12 in 45, 31 finer (1/10). (#8937)

Popular 1863-S Twenty, AU58

1732 **1863-S AU58 NGC.** The surfaces are lightly hairlined and exhibit noticeable high-point wear, particularly on the obverse, but the luster is intense and nearly full over both sides. A few minor coin-to-coin marks are evident in the fields. Once a conditionally rare S-mint twenty, almost always seen in VF to XF grades; around 300 pieces were recovered from the S.S. *Republic* and S.S. *Brother Jonathan* shipwrecks, including many in AU condition. (#8940)

Appealing 1864-S Double Eagle, MS62

1733 **1864-S MS62 PCGS.** Prior to the discoveries of the S.S. *Brother Jonathan* and the S.S. *Republic*, the 1864-S was found mostly in Very Fine to Extremely Fine condition. The shipwreck hoards elevated the '64-S population, especially in the About Uncirculated and lower Mint State levels of preservation.

We cannot say one way or the other whether this MS62 specimen came from one of these hoards. Close inspection of its yellow-gold surfaces imbued with hints of light green show no apparent effects of salt water immersion. Both sides yield pleasing luster and well struck design elements. It is only the presence of some scattered surface and rim marks that preclude a finer grade. Nevertheless, it generates nice eye appeal for the designated grade. Population: 10 in 62, 3 finer (1/10). (#8942)

1734 **1865-S XF45 NGC.** The S.S. *Central America*, S.S. *Brother Jonathan*, and S.S. *Republic* treasure discoveries brought a large number of Mint State Type One double eagles to the market, including a fair number of 1865-S twenties. At one time, this piece would have been considered a top tier example, while today, it is a pleasing type coin. Lightly abraded yellow-gold surfaces retain hints of pink toning and traces of luster.(#8944)

1735 **1867 XF45 PCGS.** Luster brightens substantial portions of this Choice XF Type Two twenty. Minor marks are scattered, but only a small reverse rim ding at 1:30 is worthy of passing comment. (#8951)

Distinctive AU53 Prooflike 1868 Twenty

1736 **1868 AU53 Prooflike NGC.** Though both sides of this Type Two double eagle exhibit a degree of wear, the prooflike reflectivity remaining in the fields is unmistakable and adds greatly to the eye appeal. Well struck with scattered light abrasions and several shallow cuts in the field near Liberty's forehead. (#78953)

1870 Double Eagle, Choice AU

1737 **1870 AU55 NGC.** With its Carson City counterpart attracting most of the attention, the 1870 double eagle from Philadelphia is underrated despite a skimpy, little-saved mintage. This well struck example remains delightfully lustrous, with modest wear and light, scattered abrasions affecting the yellow-gold surfaces. (#8957)

High-End MS62 1873 Open 3 Twenty

1738 **1873 Open 3 MS62 NGC. CAC.** With the initial production of Close 3 coins, the public criticized pieces of all denominations, leading the Mint to change over to the Open 3 logotype early in the year. This piece represents the new date style with lustrous yellow-gold surfaces and satiny mint brilliance. (#8967)

Select Mint State 1875 Double Eagle

1739 **1875 MS63 PCGS.** Garrett and Guth note that while the 1875 double eagle is not a rarity in circulated or even lower-level Mint State grades, "the date is unusual and popular as the only collectible *[gold]* issue from the Philadelphia Mint in 1875. All other denominations were made in very limited numbers and are very rare." Moreover, anything finer than this Select example is a condition rarity, with just seven such certification events in the combined NGC and PCGS population (1/10). This MS63 coin is well struck with bold yellow-gold luster that shows glints of honey and orange. Both sides show scattered abrasions, but they are shallow and not individually distracting. Solid eye appeal for the grade assigned. (#8973)

Delightful MS62 1876 Twenty

1740 **1876 MS62 PCGS.** Heavy Motto. Attractive straw-gold color on the obverse with yellow-orange overtones on the reverse. This Mint State coin is well struck for a Type Two double eagle, though the definition on Liberty's hair is not absolute. Scattered wispy abrasions contribute to the grade. PCGS has certified 45 finer pieces (1/10). (#8976)

Colorful MS62 1877 Twenty

1741 **1877 MS62 PCGS.** A shining sun-yellow and wheat-gold representative from the beginning of the Type Three design for Liberty double eagles, well struck with few overt abrasions on the devices. An alloy streak slanting diagonally from the I in UNITED adds character to the reverse. PCGS has graded 14 finer pieces (1/10). (#8982)

Charming XF 1877-CC Twenty

1742 **1877-CC XF40 PCGS.** Liberty's hair and the eagle's wings show moderate wear, but much luster beckons from the design recesses, and the apricot-gold color is original. Marks are relatively few, and only a single brief pinscratch is noted near obverse star 13. Housed in a green label holder. (#8983)

1743 **1878 MS61 NGC.** Here is a pleasing 1878 Type Three double eagle, and a great condition rarity that is seldom seen much nicer. This piece has rich green and rose toning over prooflike surfaces with frosty luster on the devices. Myriad abrasions are expected for the grade.(#8985)

Deeply Toned 1878-CC Twenty, XF45

1744 **1878-CC XF45 PCGS.** Deep green and steel patina is evident over both sides of this scarce Carson City Mint double eagle. Just 13,180 coins were minted, and survivors are scarce in all grades. For the collector who desires an early Carson City Mint double eagle, here is an important opportunity. (#8986)

1745 **1878-S MS61 PCGS.** A nicely struck S-mint representative with honey-gold surfaces. Small surface and rim marks define the grade. (#8987)

1746 **1878-S MS61 ★ NGC.** This delightful double eagle carries the NGC Star designation, an unusual occurrence on coins that grade MS61. However, this coin deserves the designation as it has reflective, nearly prooflike fields and brilliant luster, with trivial marks consistent with the grade.(#8987)

Sharply Struck 1879 Double Eagle, MS61

1747 **1879 MS61 PCGS.** The 1879 is relatively plentiful in circulated condition but scarce in Mint State. A solid strike manifests itself in sharp definition on the design elements that are highlighted by the semiprooflike fields. Numerous distributed ticks limit the grade, yet the coin exudes considerable eye appeal. (#8988)

Scarce 1879-CC Double Eagle

1748 **1879-CC PCGS Genuine.** The PCGS number ending in .92 suggests Cleaning as the reason, or perhaps one of the reasons, that PCGS deemed this coin not gradable. In our opinion, this coin has the details of an XF example that has been cleaned. This green-gold rare date Carson City twenty is hairlined and exhibits highpoint wear, but luster glimmers from design crevices, and there are few bagmarks. (#8989)

Attractive MS61 1879-S Double Eagle

1749 **1879-S MS61 NGC.** Excellent yellow-gold luster with suggestions of wheat and champagne. Solid striking definition and strong eye appeal despite the abrasion on Liberty's cheek and the other assorted marks which account for the grade. For this S-mint issue, NGC has graded 31 numerically finer examples (1/10). (#8991)

Impressive 1880-S Twenty, MS62 Prooflike

1750 **1880-S MS62 Prooflike NGC.** Full Prooflike survivors in the Liberty double eagle series are seldom encountered, and a collection of such coins provides a major challenge. This piece has fully mirrored fields with scattered abrasions consistent with the grade. This piece is the sole finest of just four Prooflike 1880-S double eagles that NGC has certified (1/10). (#78993)

Legendary 1882 Double Eagle, XF45
One of Just 571 Business Strikes

1751 **1882 XF45 PCGS.** No coin can be summed up in a single number, though for the 1882 double eagle, three digits come close: 5-7-1. With just 571 business strike twenty dollar gold pieces made at Philadelphia that year, the 1882 is one of the indisputable rarities of the series, and if not for the continued existence of the two Philadelphia 1861 Paquet coins, it would be *the* key circulation-strike P-mint Liberty twenty. Looking at the wider picture, Garrett and Guth state in their *Encyclopedia of U.S. Gold Coins* that "The 1882 is actually one of the lowest-mintage U.S. gold coins."

Not only was the 1882 double eagle a low-mintage circulation issue, but it passed virtually unnoticed by collectors at the time. Garrett and Guth note that "... very few were saved, as most collectors at the time preferred Proof examples." Further, later: "there are probably fewer than 25 known in all grades," though that projection might be slightly low.

This honey-gold Choice XF survivor has clearly spent time in circulation, though the wear that affects the high points and much of the fields has left considerable reflective luster in the protected areas. The coin's definition, while strong, is clearly not of a proof standard, highlighting its circulation-strike status. Despite a number of abrasions, including marks below Liberty's eye and just south of star 8 on the obverse, the overall eye appeal is considerable. Population: 4 in 45, 10 finer (12/09). (#8996)

Conditionally Scarce 1883-S Twenty, MS63

1752 **1883-S MS63 NGC.** Short Squat S, one of two mintmark sizes known for the issue. Pale apricot centers are bounded by lime-green margins. This lustrous Select double eagle has faint grazes, but is refreshingly free from obtrusive marks. The 1883-S is plentiful in AU58 through MS62, yet is rare any finer, undoubtedly due to indifferent bag shipment and storage. Census: 65 in 63, 5 finer (12/09). (#9000)

Exceptional 1884-CC Double Eagle, MS63

1753 **1884-CC MS63 PCGS.** A significant number of 1884-CC double eagles were shipped overseas for foreign trade and have since returned to the States. Most survivors, however, are in the range of Very Fine to MS61. MS62s are challenging to locate and MS63s, such as the present coin, are highly elusive. PCGS and NGC have seen none finer than MS63.

Lustrous yellow-gold surfaces are imbued with hints of light green and a well executed strike imparts strong definition to the design features. A few light scuffs preclude a finer grade, but this piece shows none of the heavy abrasions, alloy spots, or grease stains frequently encountered on representatives of the issue. Population: 4 in 63, 0 finer (12/09). (#9001)

1754 **1889-CC—Improperly Cleaned—NGC. AU Details.** Light greenish-gold surfaces are slightly brighter than desired on this lightly cleaned Carson City twenty.(#9011)

1890 Double Eagle, MS64
Finest Grade Obtainable

1755 **1890 MS64 PCGS. CAC.** An amazing condition rarity, and a scarce date outright, the 1890 double eagle is seldom encountered in the rare coin marketplace. This near-Gem specimen is tied for the finest that PCGS has certified. It has bold design definition with fully brilliant and frosty orange-gold luster. While critical examination with a magnifier reveals a few trivial blemishes that are consistent with the grade, a first look at this piece suggest a coin of Gem quality. Here is an amazing opportunity for the connoisseur to acquire an example of the 1890 double eagle rarity. Population: 5 in 64, 0 finer (1/10). (#9013)

1756 **1890-CC XF40 PCGS.** Ample sun-yellow luster remains in the moderately abraded fields of this Carson City twenty. A well struck example of this popular Old West issue, housed in a green label holder.(#9014)

Lustrous 1890-CC Twenty, MS61

1757 **1890-CC MS61 NGC.** Unbroken cartwheel luster invigorates this crisply struck Carson City double eagle. Yellow-gold centers are bounded by green-gold margins. The cheek displays moderate contact, usual for the grade, while the fields have fewer than the usual number of bagmarks. As are most '90-CC twenties, the reverse is minutely die doubled, perhaps most evident on the R in PLURIBUS. (#9014)

Prized MS62 1890-CC Double Eagle

1758 **1890-CC MS62 PCGS. CAC.** At 91,209 pieces struck, the 1890-CC double eagle is the highest-mintage Type Three twenty dollar issue from the Carson City Mint. Though this relatively heavy production makes it available through most circulated grades, Mint State examples are elusive, with MS62 coins conditionally scarce and anything finer a rarity. This sharply struck example, lustrous yellow-gold with a touch of wheat, is uncommonly appealing for a coin not awarded the Select designation. Though scattered wispy abrasions are present, only a few substantial marks are visible, with one on Liberty's upper hair most prominent. Population: 49 in 62, 6 finer (12/09). (#9014)

High-End MS62 1890-CC Twenty Dollar

1759 **1890-CC MS62 PCGS. CAC.** The mintage of the 1890-CC would be the most plentiful through the last double eagle issues from the fabled Carson City Mint, in 1893. The 1890-CC production of 91,209 pieces would be followed by the incredibly small production of 5,000 coins for the 1891-CC, and the 1892-CC and 1893-CC emissions both would remain below the 30,000 mark. The 1890-CC is accordingly available in Mint State levels up to the occasional near-Gem. The present coin, graded on the reverse alone, would probably approach that level, but a few ticks on the obverse bring the grade to MS62. The piece is nonetheless high-end for an MS62, with reddish-gold surfaces and excellent eye appeal. The strike is full. Population: 49 in 62, 6 finer (1/10). (#9014)

Scarce 1892 Double Eagle, AU55 Details

1760 **1892—Cleaned—ANACS. AU55 Details.** The 1892 double eagle, from a tiny mintage of only 4,430 business strikes, is scarce in all grades. The luminous surfaces of this AU55 Details specimen display attractive yellow-gold coloration imbued with whispers of apricot, and a well executed strike delivers strong detail to the design elements. Some faint hairlines that show under high magnification should not dissuade the interested bidder as the cleaning is relatively light. Scattered small contact marks do not unduly detract. Overall, a nice looking coin. (#9019)

Elusive Choice 1892-S Twenty

1761 **1892-S MS64 PCGS. CAC.** The 1892-S has returned in some quantity from foreign bank holdings, but a sizeable majority of such pieces display myriad abrasions and grade MS61 or MS62. The present near-Gem is significantly nicer than the typical Uncirculated survivor. Minor grazes are visible, but the lustrous surfaces provide substantial eye appeal. Population: 72 in 64, 1 finer (1/10). (#9021)

Sharply Struck 1892-S Double Eagle, MS64
Important Condition Scarcity

1762 **1892-S MS64 PCGS.** The 1892-S double eagle can be readily located through the MS63 level. Near-Gems are quite scarce and are the finest most collectors will encounter. The yellow-gold lustrous surfaces of this MS64 example exhibit sharply struck design elements. A few minor grazes preclude Gem status. Population: 72 in 64, 1 finer (12/09). (#9021)

Marvelous MS64 1892-S Twenty

1763 **1892-S MS64 NGC.** This is a sharply struck and highly lustrous example with rich honey-gold color. The surfaces are exceptional for the grade, remarkably close in appearance to MS65 quality, and in any event an amazing example of a San Francisco double eagle issue that is uncommon so fine. NGC has certified a mere four numerically finer pieces (1/10). (#9021)

Shining MS64 1893 Twenty

1764 **1893 MS64 PCGS.** This near-Gem is in a tie for finest example of the issue known to PCGS (1/10). Sun-gold and peach-orange luster enlivens each side, and the strike is uncommonly crisp at both margins and centers. Only a single abrasion through the hair below the coronet precludes an even finer designation. (#9022)

Choice AU 1893-CC Double Eagle

1765 **1893-CC AU55 NGC.** The abrupt end of operations at the Carson City Mint in 1893 left its production of double eagles for the year at just 18,402 pieces. This Choice AU example must have circulated only briefly, since its lightly abraded yellow-gold surfaces remain immensely lustrous. Great eye appeal for this popular issue. (#9023)

Attractive MS63 1893-S Twenty

1766 **1893-S MS63 PCGS.** While several light to medium abrasions are noted on Liberty's cheek, the rest of the obverse and the reverse of this Select coin are more consistent with an MS64 or better designation. Strongly yellow-gold surfaces come alive with elements of orange in the fields. PCGS has graded 38 finer examples (1/10). (#9024)

High Grade 1893-S Twenty, MS64

1767 **1893-S MS64 PCGS. CAC.** This splendid Liberty twenty has frosty green-gold luster with trivial grade-limiting abrasions that are expected for the large size gold piece. Hints of rose and traces of green add to its overall aesthetic appeal. Population: 37 in 64, 1 finer (1/10). (#9024)

1768 **1894 MS63 PCGS. CAC.** Here is a splendid 1894 double eagle with frosty yellow luster and pleasing surfaces. The few marks on each side are consistent with the grade. This issue is available at the MS63 grade level, but scarce in higher grades. PCGS has only certified 89 finer pieces (1/10).(#9025)

1769 **1895 MS64 NGC.** A frosty near-Gem, this 1895 double eagle is seldom available any finer. NGC and PCGS have combined to grade a mere 11 better pieces. This one has rich orange-gold patina with faint green tones in the fields. NGC has only certified nine finer examples of the date.(#9027)

Radiant 1897 Double Eagle, MS64

1770 **1897 MS64 NGC.** Radiant luster envelops the peach-gold surfaces of this attractive near-Gem and a well executed strike delivers strong definition to the design elements. Occasional surface and rim marks deny the Gem level of preservation. The 1897 can be located with relative ease through MS63; MS64 pieces are extremely scarce, and locating finer examples is nearly impossible. (#9031)

Near-Gem 1897-S Double Eagle

1771 **1897-S MS64 NGC. CAC.** Boldly impressed with rich sun-yellow luster and distinct orange overtones. While certain other S-mint dates of the same era are readily available for a price even in MS64, the 1897-S is challenging at that level and distinctly rare any finer; NGC has certified just 19 numerically superior pieces (1/10). (#9032)

1772 **1898-S MS64 PCGS. CAC.** One of the more available S-mint twenties, the 1898-S is even available in near-Gem and Gem condition. This piece is just at the threshold of an MS65 grade. Lovely orange-gold color has subtle accents of red and lilac interspersed. The strike is complete. Just a few too many ticks on Liberty's cheek for an even higher grade.(#9034)

1773 **1898-S MS64 PCGS.** The base of the 89 is repunched. Sharply struck and lustrous with lime-green and apricot toning. Minor marks fail to threaten the original eye appeal. Since an MS65 is valued at more than twice as much, many advanced collectors select an MS64 example.(#9034)

Impressive Gem 1898-S Twenty

1774 **1898-S MS65 PCGS. CAC.** Strong wheat-gold and yellow luster with a dot of alloy noted on the hair behind the coronet. Attractively detailed and remarkably well-preserved for a 19th century Liberty double eagle, with only a handful of tiny marks visible on each side. Population: 78 in 65, 2 finer (1/10). (#9034)

Appealing 1898-S Double Eagle, MS65

1775 **1898-S MS65 PCGS.** The 1898-S double eagle is available in large numbers right through the near-Gem level of preservation. Gems are more challenging, but can be located with patience. Finer pieces are virtually unobtainable. Whispers of light green visit the highly lustrous yellow-gold surfaces of the present Gem and a solid strike delivers sharp detail to the design elements. Light grade-consistent marks do not detract from the overall eye appeal. Population: 78 in 65, 2 finer (1/10). (#9034)

Sharp Gem 1898-S Double Eagle

1776 **1898-S MS65 PCGS.** A sharply struck and lovely Gem representative of this late 19th century San Francisco issue. The luster is strongly yellow-gold with both butter and lemon elements. Only a handful of trifling marks preclude an even higher designation. PCGS has graded a mere two coins finer (1/10). (#9034)

1777 **1900-S MS63 PCGS.** An absolutely beautiful double eagle, this piece has frosty yellow luster with satiny surfaces that show slight reflectivity. The trivial surface marks are consistent with the Select Mint State grade.(#9038)

1778 **1901 MS64 NGC.** A fully brilliant near-Gem, this 1901 double eagle is an ideal candidate for the type collector, representing, according to some, the first year of the 20th century. Both sides have brilliant and frosty yellow luster with traces of pale blue patina.(#9039)

Conditionally Rare 1901-S Twenty, MS65

1779 **1901-S MS65 NGC.** The combined population data of NGC and PCGS reveal a total of seven coins that are certified in MS65 or finer grades. Those coins include one MS65 PCGS, one MS66 PCGS, and five MS65 NGC examples. This impressive coin has satiny and reflective fields with rich yellow luster and hints of rose toning. The devices are boldly defined, and all aspects of this piece fully meet or exceed the MS65 grade assigned. A review of our Permanent Auction Archives shows that this Gem specimen is the first MS65 we have handled since 1993 when are archives were first created. (#9040)

Low Mintage 1902 Twenty Dollar, MS64

1780 **1902 MS64 PCGS.** The 1902 double eagle saw an amazingly low mintage of 31,140 circulation strikes. As becomes readily apparent from inspection of PCGS/NGC population data, the issue is scarce in all grades, and near-Gems, such as the specimen in the present offering, are extremely rare. Lustrous peach-gold surfaces display splashes of soft mint-green, and reveal just a few minor obverse marks that preclude Gem classification. A uniform, sharp strike characterizes the design elements. Encapsulated in a green label holder. Population: 8 in 64, 1 finer (12/09). (#9041)

Original 1903 Double Eagle, MS65

1781 **1903 MS65 NGC.** This 20th century Liberty double eagle issue, though not so available as its counterpart from a year later, is nonetheless available for a price even at the MS65 level, though anything finer is a rarity. This Gem displays rich butter-yellow luster and a solid strike. The center-left shield shows an alloy spot that adds character to the reverse. (#9043)

1782 **1904 MS64 NGC.** This frosty and lustrous near-Gem has lovely yellow-gold brilliance with faint traces of rose and green patina. Only a few trivial imperfections prevent a higher grade. (#9045)

1783 **1904 MS60 Prooflike ANACS.** Fully mirrored fields on both sides serve to frame the satiny devices on this lovely piece. At arm's length, it looks like a proof. Only upon closer inspection to the business strike characteristics become obvious. An impressive and attractive double eagle.(#79045)

1784 **1904-S MS64 PCGS.** Strongly struck with vibrant yellow-gold luster. This near-Gem shows only a handful of grade-defining abrasions, though several appear on Liberty's cheek and neck. (#9046)

1785 **1904-S MS64 PCGS.** Strong yellow-orange luster with occasional peach peripheral overtones. Strong definition with light abrasions across Liberty's cheek and a trio of reed marks just above star 13.(#9046)

Popular Gem 1904-S Double Eagle

1786 **1904-S MS65 PCGS.** Outstanding honey-gold coloration with profound cartwheel luster and occasional suggestions of lavender-silver near the rims. Well struck at the margins with even better central definition. A few tiny marks on the portrait are consistent with the grade. PCGS has certified only two finer examples (1/10). (#9046)

Pleasing MS62 1905 Twenty

1787 **1905 MS62 PCGS. CAC.** Vibrant yellow-orange color with strong, slightly satiny luster and an assortment of mild abrasions. In contrast to the mammoth mintage of double eagles at Philadelphia just a year before, 1905 saw only five-figure production of the denomination there. Few coins of Select and better quality survive, and PCGS has graded only 52 such pieces (1/10). (#9047)

Appealing MS62 1905 Double Eagle

1788 **1905 MS62 NGC.** The 1904 output of millions of double eagles must have left a glut at Philadelphia, since the next year saw just a five-figure mintage of the denomination there. This example has effusive yellow-gold luster and strong central definition. A few alloy flecks at the peripheral obverse and into the portrait lend the coin an aura of originality. (#9047)

Sharply Struck 1905 Select Double Eagle

1789 **1905 MS63 PCGS.** The low-mintage 1905 double eagle (58,919 circulation strikes) is most often found in About Uncirculated to MS62 grades. Select examples are very scarce and finer specimens are extremely rare. Intense luster endows both sides of this MS63 coin and a decisive strike imparts strong definition to the design elements, including the borders, areas that are sometimes flat on the denticles, especially those on the obverse (Michael Fuljenz and Douglas Winter, 1999, p. 160). Yellow-gold surfaces are tinted with wisps of light green and apricot, occasionally joined on the reverse margins with sky-blue. A few scattered, inoffensive marks limit the grade. Housed in a green label holder. Population: 42 in 63, 9 finer (12/09). (#9047)

1905-S Twenty, MS63

1790 **1905-S MS63 NGC.** While its S-mint counterpart from a year earlier is readily available in Select Mint State, the 1905-S is considerably more elusive, if not rare. With its solid detail and light yellow-gold surfaces marked by occasional suggestions of alloy, this example offers both beauty and originality. (#9048)

Outstanding 1906 Liberty Twenty, MS65

1791 **1906 MS65 PCGS.** The 1906 Liberty double eagle is an elusive issue in all grades, from a limited mintage of only 69,596 coins. Survivors are infrequently seen in the market place, and the majority of those found in recent years have been imported from overseas, having been exported shortly after they were minted. This Gem is housed in a green label PCGS holder and possesses outstanding aesthetic appeal. The connoisseur will appreciate the exacting strike, the brilliant and frosty luster, and the splendid lemon-yellow surfaces with considerable olive and traces of iridescent toning. Population: 9 in 65, 1 finer (1/10). (#9049)

Lovely MS64 1907-S Twenty

1792 **1907-S MS64 NGC.** A bright Choice coin from the last year of the Longacre Liberty design, pale wheat-gold with impressive luster. The central devices are strongly defined, and only a few shallow luster grazes and small abrasions keep the piece from Gem status. NGC has graded 13 numerically finer pieces (1/10). (#9054)

HIGH RELIEF DOUBLE EAGLES

Unusual 1907 High Relief, XF Details

1793 **1907 High Relief, Wire Rim—Damaged, Rim Filed—NCS. XF Details.** The surfaces appear to have been intentionally damaged by a process that places a number of coins in a bag, vigorously shaking the bag, and then collecting the tiny pieces of gold that were knocked off by the shaking. This explanation would be consistent with the filing also seen on the rim whose intent was to remove small, but salable amounts of gold from the coin. The piece appears to be slightly circulated also. A highly unusual High Relief. (#9135)

Affordable 1907 High Relief Twenty, AU50 Details

1794 **1907 High Relief, Wire Rim—Cleaned—ANACS. AU50 Details.** While the surfaces of this light yellow-gold example show minor signs of cleaning, it is still an attractive and highly desirable representative of the famous and popular MCMVII High Relief double eagle as Augustus Saint-Gaudens intended for the design. Here is an excellent opportunity to acquire a pleasing piece without the expense of a full Mint State example. (#9135)

Coveted MCMVII High Relief Twenty Uncirculated Details

1795 **1907 High Relief, Wire Rim—Improperly Cleaned—NGC. Unc. Details.** Although designated as cleaned by NGC, most collectors will not be able to tell the difference between the present example and one that is unimpaired. The reverse border near 7:30 has a few unimportant marks, but the surfaces are otherwise virtually unabraded. Sharply struck and shimmering with apricot-tinted luster. (#9135)

Ever-Popular 1907 High Relief Twenty Wire Rim, MS62

1796 **1907 High Relief, Wire Rim MS62 PCGS.** He took his French surname from his father, but Augustus Saint-Gaudens was the son of an Irish mother, and it was from Ireland that the couple emigrated. They arrived in New York City when Augustus was an infant, making the artist an "immigrant success story" even though he was raised in the United States. His noble effigy of Liberty standing tall, as seen on the High Relief double eagle, combines the best of American and European mainstream art as it was known at the time. This example of the Saint-Gaudens High Relief design offers strong yellow-gold luster with a measure of patina settled over the concave fields. Both obverse and reverse show strong wire rims. Few marks for the grade, though Liberty's gown and knee are affected. *From The South Texas Collection*. (#9135)

Upper-End MS64 1907 High Relief Twenty

1797 **1907 High Relief, Wire Rim MS64 PCGS. CAC.** The works of Augustus Saint-Gaudens marked a turning point in America's perception of sculpture in the late nineteenth century. Formerly sculpture had been created for public spaces and for a few select, wealthy patrons. Saint-Gaudens' sculptural works were intended for the general public, and his ten and twenty dollar gold pieces are a further extension of this populist sentiment. Saint-Gaudens and the other sculptors and painters in the so-called Gilded Age, were familiar with Classical art, but they simplified their art, which resulted in a moral tone more suited to America. This gave American art a more cosmopolitan style than previously seen from its artists. More than a hundred years after Saint-Gaudens' death, these coins are by far the best known of all his works, and the cosmopolitan composition of his coins are an enduring legacy to this giant 19th century sculptor.

This is an exceptional, high-end example that has thick, satiny mint luster on each side. The surfaces are free from any detracting contact marks, and both sides are bright yellow-gold with just a tinge of reddish patina. (#9135)

1798 **1907 High Relief, Flat Rim—Filed Rims—PCGS Genuine.** This example has AU Details, and will prove to be an affordable piece for the collector who has always wanted a High Relief twenty. The rims are filed with additional surface marks and hairlines that remain from cleaning.(#9136)

Select 1907 High Relief, Flat Rim Twenty

1799 **1907 High Relief, Flat Rim MS63 NGC. CAC.** NGC calls this a Flat Rim, seemingly more based on attempt than success, since even in the rim-obscuring holder evidence of a fin remains at parts of both obverse and reverse. (The fin, regarded as a minting defect in its time, is now seen as part of the High Relief twenties' historic charm.) Closer to the centers, the warmly lustrous yellow-gold surfaces show only a handful of significant marks, most noticeably a line at the tips of the rays to the light of Liberty. Contact at the knee is also of potential interest. As always, boldly struck and immensely evocative, a milestone of U.S. coinage.
From The South Texas Collection. (#9136)

SAINT-GAUDENS DOUBLE EAGLES

1800 **1907 Arabic Numerals MS64 NGC.** This well struck near-Gem exhibits strong design detail and pleasing luster. Yellow-gold surfaces reveal a few minor marks that preclude the attainment of a Gem classification.(#9141)

1801 **1907 Arabic Numerals MS64 PCGS.** A delightful example with brilliant yellow luster. The surfaces are pleasing with only a scattering of trivial surface marks on each side.(#9141)

1802 **1907 Arabic Numerals MS64 NGC. CAC.** This lustrous first-year Saint Gaudens twenty has delightful butter-gold color and fewer than the expected number of minor abrasions. Liberty's chest and raised knee show slight bluntness of detail.(#9141)

Pleasing 1907 Arabic Numerals Twenty, MS65

1803 **1907 Arabic Numerals MS65 NGC.** Here is a splendid Gem 1907 Saint-Gaudens double eagle, the third design modification following the Ultra High Relief and High Relief coins. This piece has frosty lemon-yellow luster with lighter yellow across the standing figure. The surfaces are pleasing with few imperfections. (#9141)

1804 **1908 No Motto MS64 NGC.** Short Rays obverse. This yellow-gold Choice No Motto type coin has booming luster and only moderate inexactness of strike on the eagle's leg.(#9142)

Shining No Motto 1908 Twenty, MS66

1805 **1908 No Motto MS66 NGC. CAC.** Long Rays obverse. The most popular No Motto type issue, with most high-end examples coming from a single hoard but a handful of isolated coins also available from other sources. This impressively lustrous, slightly satiny Premium Gem has rich orange-gold color overall with minor yellow elements close to the centers. Carefully preserved with great visual appeal. (#9142)

Gem No Motto 1908-D Double Eagle

1806 **1908-D No Motto MS65 PCGS.** Short Rays obverse. The 1908 No Motto may be common, but the Denver Mint issue of the same design subtype is considerably less available, at least in the exceptional quality of the present Gem. A lustrous and exquisitely preserved orange-gold example with minor incompleteness of detail on Liberty's raised knee and chest. (#9143)

Extraordinary 1908-D No Motto Twenty, MS66

1807 **1908-D No Motto MS66 NGC.** Short Rays obverse. While the 1908-D No Motto Saint-Gaudens double eagle is a rather plentiful issue, it is extremely difficult to locate in Premium Gem condition like this piece. NGC has only certified five of these in MS66, and PCGS has certified nine pieces, with none finer at either service (1/10). Just 14 collectors can acquire an MS66, assuming no resubmissions are included in those figures. This Premium Gem is frosty and brilliant with beautiful honey-gold luster and pristine surfaces. All design motifs are boldly defined, including a sharp skyline at the lower left obverse. Here is a remarkable coin and an extraordinary opportunity. (#9143)

1808 **1908 Motto MS62 PCGS.** Whispers of mint-green visit apricot-gold surfaces, mostly around the obverse margins of this well struck twenty. Distributed light contact marks occur over each side. (#9147)

1809 **1908 Motto MS63 NGC.** Each side of this Select twenty dollar is awash in yellow-gold luster and is sharply struck, including the panes on the Capitol building, the fingers on Liberty's branch hand, and the eagle's plumage. The surfaces have a frosty finish and are minimally abraded.(#9147)

1810 **1908 Motto MS63 PCGS.** Strong and slightly glossy luster dominates the eye appeal of this With Motto twenty. Rich yellow-gold and straw colors prevail on both sides. Slight die erosion is visible at the margins.(#9147)

1811 **1908-D Motto MS64 PCGS.** This lustrous yellow-gold near-Gem is well impressed. Light surface and rim marks preclude Gem status. (#9148)

Desirable 1909 Twenty, MS65

1812 **1909 MS65 PCGS.** Here is an elusive issue in the Saint-Gaudens series, known from overdate and normal date obverse dies. This 1909 twenty is one of the rare dates in the Saint-Gaudens series. In fact, it is believed that the Normal Date variety is slightly scarcer than the Overdate, although both are extremely rare in Gem MS65 or finer grades. Since 1993 we have offered 15 MS65 or finer examples of the 1909 Normal Date twenty, compared to 18 similarly graded examples of the 1909 over 8 Overdate double eagle. This frosty Gem has gorgeous green-gold luster with traces of pale orange toning. It is sharply defined with excellent eye appeal. Here is an important opportunity for the advanced collection. Population: 21 in 65, 7 finer (1/10). (#9150)

1813 **1909/8 AU58 NGC.** FS-301. This popular overdate near-Mint State representative displays bright yellow-gold surfaces with well defined design motifs. The few light marks scattered about do not detract from the coin's overall appeal.(#9151)

Lustrous MS62 1909-D Twenty

1814 **1909-D MS62 PCGS.** Rich gold-orange color appears at narrow borders, while the centers are pale straw-gold with two prominent alloy streaks on the eagle's head and wings. Lustrous with scattered light abrasions, including a significant mark just below the stem of the olive branch. The 1909-D is a challenging issue, with just 52,500 pieces produced. (#9152)

1815 **1909-S MS64 NGC.** Double eagles dated 1909 are scarce or rare from the Philadelphia and Denver Mints, with only those from San Francisco making candidates for type collections, or one-per-year collections. This piece has pleasing yellow luster with excellent eye appeal.
A hardwood case accompanies this lot, identifying it as a "Florida Hoard Double Eagle." The interior of the case has a place for the coin in its NGC holder, and also has a Medallic Art Company gold plated silver plaque of Augustus Saint-Gaudens (46 mm x 63 mm). Additional documents are also included.(#9153)

1816 **1909-S MS64 NGC.** Attractive luster issues from the peach-gold surfaces of this near-Gem twenty and a decisive strike sharpens the devices, including the Capitol building, Liberty's fingers, and the eagle's plumage. Scattered minuscule marks prevent the attainment of MS65.
A hardwood case accompanies this lot, identifying it as a "Florida Hoard Double Eagle." The interior of the case has a place for the coin in its NGC holder, and also has a Medallic Art Company gold plated silver plaque of Augustus Saint-Gaudens (46 mm x 63 mm).(#9153)

Shining Gem 1910-S Twenty

1817 **1910-S MS65 NGC.** Gold-orange overtones visit the central obverse, while the rest of this lustrous coin is closer to yellow. Minor peripheral striking softness generally corrects itself toward the centers. A great example of this little-saved and potentially underrated San Francisco issue. Census: 63 in 65, 8 finer (1/10). (#9156)

1818 **1911-D MS65 NGC. CAC.** This fully struck Gem has fields that display a pronounced matte-like texture. Bright, satiny mint luster covers both sides. An outstanding example of this popular, early Saint-Gaudens twenty.(#9158)

Popular 1911-D/D Double Eagle, MS65

1819 **1911-D/D MS65 PCGS.** FS-501, formerly FS-1911.5. This *Cherrypickers' Guide* variety is prominent and popular, with a strong undermintmark to the east of the final punch. This is a great Gem example, strongly yellow-gold with undercurrents of green and pleasing luster. For coins specifically certified as FS-501, Population: 47 in 65, 13 finer (1/10). (#145010)

Gem 1911-D/D Saint-Gaudens Twenty

1820 **1911-D/D MS65 PCGS.** FS-501, formerly FS-1911.5. This prominent and important overmintmark is increasingly popular, particularly among those who collect by the *Cherrypickers' Guide*. The present Gem example offers strong yellow-gold luster with gray and wheat accents. The tops of the eagle's wings show a few light but grade-defining abrasions. (#145010)

1911-D/D Double Eagle, MS65

1821 **1911-D/D MS65 PCGS.** FS-501, formerly FS-1911.5. A shining Gem representative of this repunched mintmark variety, which has grown in popularity since its inclusion in the *Cherrypickers' Guide*. Bold sun-yellow luster dominates the eye appeal, supplemented by a strong strike and the careful preservation of the surfaces. Population: 47 in 65, 13 finer (12/09). (#145010)

Outstanding MS66 1911-D/D Twenty

1822 **1911-D/D MS66 PCGS.** FS-501, formerly FS-1911.5. A remarkable high grade example of this readily available Saint-Gaudens issue. Both sides are uncommonly devoid of marks, and the lustrous khaki-gold fields and devices deliver exceptional eye appeal. Not to be missed by the alert specialist. Population: 13 in 66, 0 finer (1/10). (#145010)

1823 **1911-S MS64 PCGS.** Strong frosty-satiny luster dominates the eye appeal of this well struck Premium Gem. The orange-kissed butter-yellow surfaces show few marks in the fields, though a handful of abrasions on the figure of Liberty preclude a finer designation. (#9159)

Scintillating Choice 1912 Double Eagle

1824 **1912 MS64 PCGS.** The rich pumpkin-orange centers are surrounded by green-gold margins. Booming luster sweeps the moderately marked surfaces. A lower mintage issue, despite the absence of branch mint production in 1912. PCGS and NGC combined have certified a scant 53 pieces in higher grades (1/10). (#9160)

Sharply Struck 1914-D Gem Double Eagle

1825 **1914-D MS65 PCGS. CAC.** The 1914-D double eagle is a common date through MS65. Radiant luster emanates from both sides of this Gem, each of which possesses attractive peach-gold coloration. Sharply struck, including strong definition on the Capitol building, Liberty's fingers, and the eagle's plumage. A few trivial marks are unbothersome. (#9165)

Pleasing 1914-D Double Eagle, MS66

1826 **1914-D MS66 PCGS.** Enough 1914-D double eagles survived the meltings to be able to satisfy current collector demand. That said, Premium Gems such as the present offering will take some searching and patience. Lustrous surfaces exhibit sharply struck design motifs and are well preserved. The few minor marks on the reverse sun, while mentioned for complete accuracy, do not detract from the coin's pleasing overall eye appeal. Population: 56 in 66, 1 finer (1/10). (#9165)

Impressive 1915 Twenty, MS65

1827 **1915 MS65 PCGS.** The 1915 is a scarce, low-mintage issue with a production of just 152,050 coins during the year. Examples are frequently available in lower Mint State grades, but they are extremely rare in Gem condition. This remarkable piece has a bold strike including a nearly full skyline at the lower left obverse. The surfaces are brilliant with satiny yellow luster, and have only a few minor marks that prevent a higher grade. Here is an amazing opportunity to acquire a piece that is tied for the finest PCGS has graded. Population: 36 in 65, 0 finer (1/10). (#9167)

1828 **1915-S MS65 NGC.** A sharply struck, Gem example of this scarcer date in the teens that poses a challenge any finer than MS65. Excellent luster characteristics with lovely, bright golden-orange color. A couple of small marks are seen on Liberty's figure. (#9168)

Underrated 1916-S Double Eagle, MS65

1829 **1916-S MS65 PCGS. CAC.** The 1916-S was very scarce until 1983 when a large South American hoard inflated the Mint State population. Radiant luster on this Gem complements well struck design motifs and attractive yellow-gold nicely preserved surfaces. Pleasing overall eye appeal as recognized by CAC. (#9169)

Gem 1922 Double Eagle

1830 **1922 MS65 PCGS.** The 1922 is one of the most plentiful issues in the entire Saint-Gaudens double eagle series. That said, MS65 is the finest one can expect to locate; higher grade pieces are nearly nonexistent. The present Gem offering displays pleasing luster and well struck yellow-gold surfaces. Some grade-consistent marks are unimportant. (#9173)

Appealing 1922 Twenty, MS65

1831 **1922 MS65 NGC.** Delightful light yellow surfaces with brilliant satin luster, this Gem is boldly defined and possesses excellent aesthetic appeal. It is desirable for its overall quality. A Gem MS65 1922 twenty is about all that any collector could hope to acquire. NGC and PCGS have only certified seven and eight better pieces, respectively. (#9173)

Popular Gem 1922 Double Eagle

1832 **1922 MS65 PCGS.** Prominent orange overtones grace otherwise wheat-gold surfaces on this strongly lustrous Gem. Well-defined on the obverse considering the advanced state of that die, as evidenced by a crack through the letters of LIBERTY. Rare any finer; PCGS has certified only seven such pieces (1/10). (#9173)

Bright 1922-S Twenty, MS62

1833 **1922-S MS62 NGC.** The design elements are generally well defined, and lavish luster gives this piece a flashy, radiant appearance. A few moderate marks on the obverse and scattered trivial marks on the reverse limit the grade of this otherwise alluring representative. According to Garrett and Guth: "This is a date that suffered tremendously from the massive meltings of gold coins in the 1930s." (#9174)

Lustrous 1922-S Twenty Dollar, MS64

1834 **1922-S MS64 PCGS.** Relatively few 1922-S double eagles have survived to the present day. Near-Gems, such as the example in the current lot, can only be located with diligent searching, and finer pieces are elusive. Yellow-gold luster endows both sides, each of which exhibits sharply struck design features. Scattered light marks limit the grade. (#9174)

Well Struck 1923 Gem Double Eagle

1835 **1923 MS65 PCGS.** The 1923 is abundantly available through the near-Gem level of preservation. Gems such as the present example can also be located with patience and searching, but higher-grade specimens are very elusive. Honey-gold lustrous surfaces exhibit well struck devices. Faint die cracks are visible on the reverse sun. (#9175)

Bright 1923 Gem Double Eagle

1836 **1923 MS65 PCGS.** Numerous 1923 double eagles managed to survive the mass meltings of the 1930s in overseas hoards to offer collectors a wide choice in various grades. MS65 pieces can be modestly challenging, but finer examples are virtually nonexistent. Bright peach-gold luster enlivens this Gem, and the only area of weakness occurs on the Capitol building. A few grade-consistent marks are visible. (#9175)

1837 **1924 MS65 NGC.** Lustrous yellow-gold surfaces exhibit well struck design features, including Liberty's fingers, the panes of the Capitol building, and the eagle's plumage. A few light marks deny Gem status.(#9177)

1924 Saint-Gaudens Twenty, MS67
A True Upper-End Coin

1838 **1924 MS67 NGC. CAC.** Certainly nothing can be said about the rarity of the 1924 twenty. What sets this coin apart and makes it worth viewing and bidding on is the exceptional quality. It is well-balanced from side to side with pleasing, satiny luster that is uninterrupted by the abrasions that are usually seen even on Gem Saints. One can almost count the marks on this piece, but a strong magnifier would be required. The color is primarily orange-gold with faint traces of red interspersed, and the strike is complete in all areas. Want a finer one? Only three have been graded, two at NGC and one at PCGS (1/10). (#9177)

Important 1924-S Double Eagle, MS64

1839 **1924-S MS64 PCGS. CAC.** Light greenish-gold surfaces with brilliant and frosty yellow luster characterize this amazing 1924-S twenty, an important rarity despite a mintage of almost 3 million coins. Like most of the mintmarked issues of the 1920s, these coins were struck but never released, with large quantities melted in the following decade. This example is a lovely near-Gem with only a few trivial surface marks that prevent a higher grade. Here is an extremely important opportunity for the advanced Saint-Gaudens double eagle collector to obtain this important issue. Population: 95 in 64, 3 finer (1/10). (#9179)

1840 **1925 MS65 PCGS.** The highly lustrous surfaces are beautifully toned in orange, mint-green, lilac, and rose, and the design elements are crisply impressed. A squiggly scratch is visible on the upper reverse.(#9180)

Attractive 1925-S Select Twenty Dollar

1841 **1925-S MS63 PCGS.** The nearly 4 million-piece mintage of the 1925-S twenty dollar cannot be used as an indicator of its survival rate as most coins were melted in 1937 or later. Fewer than 600 examples are believed known today in all grades, making it one of the major rarities in the Saint-Gaudens series.

Both sides of this Select specimen are attractively patinated in peach-gold imbued with traces of mint-green and lavender. Lustrous surfaces yield a frosty finish and well struck design features, including the 5 in the date, a digit that is often weak. Scattered marks, the most noticeable a milling mark above the shoulder of the branch arm, barely preclude the attainment of a higher grade. Population: 79 in 63, 25 finer (1/10). (#9182)

1842 **1926-S—Improperly Cleaned—NCS. Unc Details.** This later S-mint double eagle shows no trace of wear, though scattered hairlines and disturbed luster suggest a past cleaning. Deep peach and green alloy at the upper obverse contrasts with the yellow-gold present elsewhere.(#9185)

1843 **1927 MS64 NGC.** The radiantly lustrous surfaces of this near-Gem double eagle display peach-gold patina imbued with hints of light green. This sharply struck piece reveals a few light marks that preclude Gem classification.(#9186)

Impressive Gem 1929 Double Eagle
Ex: Morse

1844 **1929 MS65 PCGS.** The 1929 opens the final segment of the Saint-Gaudens double eagle series, and every issue from this year through 1933 faced near-annihilation during the gold recall of the Roosevelt Administration. While the 1929 is the least rare of this group—some have gone as far as to suggest that the 1929 should be classified in a separate and lesser tier of rarity from its peers—it is still a coveted key date whose appearance at auction is an occasion of note among specialists. MS65 pieces are rare, with only 26 pieces graded by both services, and a mere six coins finer (12/09).

As we also previously wrote, the typical 1929, with its generally sharp strike and fully lustrous and frosty surfaces, exudes considerable eye appeal. The example we offer in this lot fits that bill perfectly. All of the design elements are sharply delineated, though minor softness is noted on portions of the Capitol dome. The frosty surfaces exhibit vibrant luster and are toned in variegated yellow, peach, orange-gold, and lime-green. The surfaces are well preserved, although a few minor marks on Liberty's head and left leg are mentioned for accuracy. While this issue often contains copper stains, only one tiny spot is located beneath the eagle's neck. All in all, this is an immensely appealing Gem.

Ex: The Philip H. Morse Collection of Saint-Gaudens Coinage (Heritage, 11/2005), lot 6707.

From The Five Point Collection. (#9190)

1845 **1931-D MS64 PCGS. CAC.** Certain issues, especially in the double eagle series, have experienced a sudden and unexpected availability. Type One twenties were formerly almost unobtainable in mint condition, and now several dates are available in grades through MS66. This, of course, is because of the salvage of gold-laden ships from California. It is highly unlikely that any such "guardian angel" exists for the 1931-D twenty. The 100-150 pieces believed known are most likely to be the only ones that will ever be available to collectors.

Among collectors of this series, the conditional availability of such rarities as the 1931-D is seldom discussed. Those who specialize in this series are generally happy with any 1931-D that is available and that they can afford. But here is something to consider regarding this piece: Several dozen pieces have been certified in MS64; in fact, a total of 60 submission events when one combines both of the major services. Above this level, only 15 pieces have been graded. Therefore, the savvy collector would most likely regard a high-end MS64 as the best value. That is just what this piece is. Examination of the clean surfaces shows that, and it is also confirmed by the CAC endorsement.

To the unaided eye, there is only one mark on each side that keeps this magnificent piece from the Gem category. On the obverse there is a horizontal mark across Liberty's upper thigh, and on the reverse one diagonal abrasion is seen on the wing of the eagle. The devices are fully struck throughout, and the mint luster is bright and satiny with a pronounced reddish tinge. Population: 39 in 64, 18 finer (12/09). (#9193)

1846 **(1842-52) A. Bechtler Dollar, 27G. 21C., Plain Edge—Improperly Cleaned—NGC. AU Details.** K-24, R.3. The usually seen Plain Edge Augustus Bechtler gold dollar with pleasing green-gold surfaces and a slight planchet wave. Minor evidence of cleaned is seen on each side of this otherwise attractive piece. (#10040)

Near-Mint August Bechtler Gold Dollar Kagin-24, 27 G., 21 C., Plain Edge

1847 **(1842-52) A. Bechtler Dollar, 27G. 21C., Plain Edge AU58 NGC.** K-24, R.3. The first circulating gold dollar in the United States was privately coined by the Bechtler family, initially in North Carolina and later in Georgia. Kagin-24 is always available at a price, but many examples are impaired. This near-Mint piece has bright sun-gold luster throughout the legends. The open fields are toned orange. A few minor marks are consistent with brief circulation. Housed in a former generation holder, and listed on page 361 of the 2010 *Guide Book*.
From The Longfellow Collection. (#10040)

A. Bechtler K-24 Gold Dollar, AU58 With Two Clips on Planchet

1848 **(1842-52) A. Bechtler Dollar, 27G. 21C., Plain Edge—Double Clipped Planchet—AU58 PCGS.** 27.7 grains. K-24, R.3. Small clips are present at 1:30 and 4 o'clock. This wavy but attractive piece has bright luster throughout the design, and only minor traces of friction are present. The fields are apricot-gold and steel-blue. Listed on page 361 of the 2010 *Guide Book*. (#10040)

Important A. Bechtler Five Dollar 128 G, 22 C, AU50

1849 **(1837-42) A. Bechtler Five Dollar, 128G. 22C. AU50 NGC.** K-28, R.6. This five dollar piece was at one time considered among the rarest of the Bechtler issues, ranked as R.8—"unique or nearly so"— in Kagin's reference. The coin says CAROLINA GOLD rather than GEORGIA GOLD as on the more common K-23 five dollar piece, and A. BECHTLER rather than C. BECHTLER. The 128G. 22C. is in the *center* of the obverse. In the more than 25 years since Kagin published his reference, more coins have surfaced, though the variety remains very rare.

The outer devices are softly struck on both obverse and reverse. We have not seen enough of these to know if this is common to all K-28 pieces. But the coin may be most easily graded by the remaining prooflikeness that surrounds the lettering. A "pinched" appearance is seen on the obverse rim at 3 and 9 o'clock, a striking defect of unknown origin. The yellow-gold surfaces have taken on just the slightest accent of reddish patina, and there are no mentionable post-striking defects. Listed on page 360 of the 2010 *Guide Book*. (#10043)

1850 **1860 Clark, Gruber & Co. Quarter Eagle—Damaged, Cleaned, Scratched—ANACS. AU Details, Net VF30.** K-1, R.4. Softly defined in the centers as usual but with little actual wear. Gold-and-violet surfaces show a scratched "X" to the left of the date, a dig on the cheek, and hairlines from a past cleaning.(#10135)

Desirable 1861 Clark, Gruber Five, AU55

1851 **1861 Clark, Gruber & Co. Five Dollar AU55 PCGS.** K-6, R.4. The Clark, Gruber coins are the predecessors of the Denver Mint coinage that began in 1906. In fact, the Treasury acquired the Clark, Gruber facilities and ran an assay office throughout the late 19th century prior to the opening of the Denver Mint. This piece has lovely green-gold surfaces, light orange toning, satiny luster, and exceptional aesthetic appeal. Here is a great opportunity to acquire a piece of Colorado history. Population: 6 in 55, 9 finer (1/10). (#10140)

VF Sharpness 1851 Humbert Fifty 887 Thous., 50 Reverse

1852 **1851 Humbert Fifty Dollar, 887 Thous. 50 Rev.—Tooled—NGC. VF Details.** A moderately worn, extensively tooled or re-engraved example of the famed Humbert fifty dollar octagonal family. The 887 fineness appears to be reengraved, as does the 50 at the bottom of the obverse. The eagle is almost entirely reengraved, as are many of the letters. The central 50 on the reverse appears to be reengraved, as does the border around the entire coin. All of the tooling work, which was done with a steady hand, makes attribution extremely difficult. It appears that this is an example of Kagin-4, with the reverse reengraved to resemble the Kagin-3 design. (#10208)

Historical 1852/1 K-8 Humbert Ten, VF30

1853 **1852/1 Humbert Ten Dollar VF30 PCGS.** K-8, R.4. It seems that Augustus Humbert planned smaller denomination gold pieces in 1851, as evidence by this overdate. As operations began, only $50 pieces were produced in the earlier year, with 10 and 20 dollar gold coins struck in 1852 and 1853. This rich green-gold example has traces of iridescent toning with pleasing surfaces for the grade. Population: 5 in 30, 34 finer (1/10). (#10190)

Near-Mint K-10 1852 Humbert Ten Dollar

1854 **1852 Humbert Ten Dollar AU58 NGC.** K-10, Low R.4. While the obverse shows a measure of rim crumbling, the reverse rim is essentially intact, and the die break that defines the K-10a variety is not present. Though traces of friction are visible on the high points of this faintly green-gold piece, considerable luster remains, giving the coin a faintly prooflike aura. A handful of tiny abrasions scattered on each side scarcely affect the visual appeal of this historic Augustus Humbert coin. Listed on page 365 of the 2010 *Guide Book*. For all 1852 Humbert ten dollar varieties, Census: 6 in 58, 4 finer (1/10). (#10187)

Choice VF 1850 Moffat & Co. Five Dollar, K-7b

1855 **1850 Moffat & Co. Five Dollar VF35 PCGS.** K-7b, R.4. Distinctly worn over the high points yet with a glimmer of luster in the fields. Light butter-yellow is the main color of this Choice VF coin, though orange accents are also present. A short abrasion is noted on Liberty's cheek, and a shallow pinscratch is present in the left obverse field. Listed on page 363 of the 2010 *Guide Book*. (#10243)

John L. Moffat in later years.

Rarely Seen 1852 Wass Molitor Ten Dollar Small Head, K-3, VF25

1856 **1852 Wass Molitor Ten Dollar, Small Head VF25 PCGS. CAC.** K-3, R.6. All varieties of the 1852 Wass Molitor ten dollar gold piece are rare in an absolute sense; at an R.6, the K-3 is not so elusive as the K-5, or "Small Closed Date," but it is more challenging than the K-4, with its "Large Head, Wide Date." This midrange example, housed in a green label holder, offers considerable radiance despite moderate wear over each side. Soft striking definition is not uncommon for the issue, while the scattered abrasions on the portrait and in the surrounding fields affect the technical grade, they also lend the coin a sense of history. Listed on page 372 of the 2010 *Guide Book*. (#10345)

Important 55-Ounce Harris Marchand Gold Ingot from the S.S. *Central America*

1857 **55.05-Ounce Harris Marchand Gold Ingot.** Recovered from the S.S. *Central America*. CAGB-135, serial number 6526. 55.05 ounces, 875 fineness, stamped value $995.73. From Q. David Bowers, *A California Gold Rush History*: "Large size ingot. All inscriptions on face with bar horizontally oriented. $ leans sharply left. Reverse finessed or dressed by tapping."

The inimitable *California Coiners and Assayers*, by Dan Owens, compiles a wide range of primary documents, such as newspaper commentaries or court records, to present a portrait of its subjects and the firms they created. From his simple introduction, "H. Harris, D.C. Marchand & C.L. Farrington formed an assaying partnership in Sacramento," a wealth of detail emerges.

They described themselves in an advertisement in the October 4, 1855 edition of the *Sacramento Union* as follows:

"Harris, Marchand & Co., Assay Office, 107 J Street, between Fourth and Fifth, Sacramento.

"H. Harris, Melter and Refiner, formerly employed in the U.S. Mints at New Orleans and San Francisco, and in the assay offices of Kellogg & Co., and Justh & Hunter, San Francisco.

"D. Marchand, Assayer, passed his examination at the Mint of Paris, and holds a private stamp, there registered, which makes his bars recognized and merchantable in France.

"C.L. Farrington, Treasurer, late in the employ of Wells, Fargo & Co.

"Gold and ores of every description assayed promptly and faithfully, and returns made within from 6 to 24 hours in bars or coin.

"We guarantee our assays and will pay all differences that may arise in the same with the assays of the United States Mints.

"Spanish, French, English, German, Swedish, and Danish languages spoken in the office."

[The advertisement continues with a list of references.]

From this advertisement emerges an image of a remarkable firm. Harvey Harris, a Danish national then in his early 40s, had previously worked for Justh & Hunter and Kellogg & Co., both of which were associated (the latter as Kellogg & Humbert) with assayers of gold ingots also found in the S.S. *Central America* treasure.

Desiré Charles Marchand, a French-speaking Belgian (and later naturalized American) whose credentials from the Mint of Paris are mentioned in the advertisement, was extremely young at the formation of the firm; varying accounts are given of his date of birth, but in no case could he have been so old as 20 at the time of the advertisement, and might have been as young as 16. This exceedingly young age could explain why Marchand cited his credentials as opposed to his (possibly nonexistent) work experience.

Charles L. Farrington, the "& Co." of the firm, was an American from the state of Maine, but little else is written about him in *California Coiners & Assayers*, except to note that he "retired from the firm" per a *Sacramento Union* item dated May 30, 1857. The reason is not listed, though age is a distinct possibility. The firm continued without him as Harris & Marchand Assayers.

Though the firm Harris, Marchand & Co. did not last into June 1857, the gold bars stamped that way did, and three dozen bars from the Sacramento office received an unexpected gift of numismatic immortality: they were loaded onto the S.S. *Central America*, and instead of going to New York to be melted down, they landed at the bottom of the ocean, and over the course of more than a century, they transformed into historic treasures.

Like the majority of known Harris, Marchand & Co. ingots, this example shows irregular punching on the serial number, weight, fineness, and value. The arcing HARRIS MARCHAND & CO imprint and circular MARCHAND / ESSAYEUR stamp, however, are precise and elegant as ever. The ingot's surfaces are bright yellow-gold with the usual casting irregularities on most faces, though the bottom is smoother than usually seen (as referenced by Bowers). Corner cuts are at the upper left of the top face and its absolute diagonal opposite. The ingot measures 42 x 112 x 20 mm.

Ex: FUN 2002 Auction (Heritage, 1/2002), lot 7905.

Small to Medium Size 23-Ounce Justh & Hunter Gold Ingot from the S.S. *Central America*

1858 **Small to Medium Size Justh & Hunter Gold Ingot.** CAGB-352. Q. David Bowers, in his *A California Gold Rush History*, offers general notes about the Justh & Hunter ingots recovered from the S.S. *Central America*, including two key observations. First, "Surfaces often irregular, particularly on the reverse." Second, "Some ingots from San Francisco *[assay office]* have part of the serial number, the last two digits, repeated on the reverse." Both are true in the case of this ingot, a small to medium-sized example in the Bowers scale.

All faces show considerable irregularities, with the top face surprising by showing the most irregularities of all. Through the valleys, the punched information from top to bottom: NO. 4341 / [arcing Justh & Hunter imprint] / 23.00 OZ / 890 FINE. / $423.15 *[in 1857 terms]*.

Corner cuts at the upper right of the top face and its diagonal opposite; both corner cuts show rust stains, as does the bottom face, in and near the hollow from the ingot-casting process. This rust is prone to flaking, and appears to have done so within the plastic holder. As noted above, the digits 41 appear at the upper right part of the bottom face, a San Francisco office characteristic for Justh & Hunter ingots. The ingot measures 43 x 61 x 16 mm.

At just 23 ounces, this ingot is accessible to a variety of collectors and researchers, and the Justh & Hunter imprint also falls in a "sweet spot" of sorts, not so elusive as to be inaccessible, but at the same time it is not so broadly available as the Kellogg & Humbert ingots. In sum, it is a prize for the tasteful California gold collector.

Medium-Size Kellogg & Humbert Gold Ingot Salvaged from the *S.S. Central America*

1859 **38.76 Ounce Kellogg & Humbert Gold Ingot.** CAGB-635. Mold K&H-02, per *A California Gold Rush History* by Q. David Bowers. Recovered from the *S.S. Central America*, information on the top face: No. 838 / 38.76 oz. / 892 fine / $714.70 (in 1857 value). Bowers notes the ingot's unusual dimensions, calling it "Thick, almost cubic." On this small and compact ingot, the assayer's imprint is visible on the north face relative to the main information, while the bottom face repeats the serial number just above a prominent hollow from the ingot-making process. Corner-cuts are at the bottom right of the information face and its exact opposite. Medium size, falling just below the 40-ounce cutoff for medium-to-large set by Bowers.

Recent Heritage auctions have brought a number of sizable *S.S. Central America* gold ingots to the market, including several massive ingots weighing in at over 100 ounces in the recent January 2010 FUN Auction. On the other hand, smaller ingots such as this Kellogg & Humbert example or the 23-ounce Justh & Hunter ingot also in this catalog also have an esteemed place in the collecting community, providing opportunities for Old West enthusiasts with a passion for assayer ingots but not necessarily the desire to own a massive "brick" of California gold. This Kellogg & Humbert representative, though small enough to rest on the palm of one's hand, is weighty atop it—and the weight of its history is even greater. The ingot measures 41 x 51 x 30 mm.

Medium to Large Size Kellogg & Humbert Gold Ingot, Ex: S.S. *Central America*

1860 **48.65 Ounce Kellogg & Humbert Gold Ingot.** Kellogg & Humbert Assayers, serial number 947, 48.65 oz, 780 fineness, $784.43 face value. Medium to large size, per the classification system by Q. David Bowers in his *A California Gold Rush History*. Bowers devotes a solid paragraph to the unusual characteristics of this ingot (italics his):

> "Inscriptions on face. 48 in weight double punched. *Fineness first punched as 87, then corrected to 78 ($784.42), with erroneous under digits still visible. $ sign high, leans right, and touches upper left of 7.* Vertically oriented. Reverse stamped with repetition of serial number, but in different font. One of the most amateurishly punched of the many Kellogg & Humbert ingots."

The top face also shows numerous air bubbles and weakness on the "Kellogg & Humbert Assayers" stamp. Bowers does allow, however, that the S.S. *Central America* ingots' individuality is core to their appeal, noting that "[s]uch idiosyncrasies make them fascinating to study."

Beyond the air bubbles, this ingot has a distinctive overall appearance. While most ingots show a measure of rust staining on one or more faces, this pieces' surfaces are bright yellow, with evidence of rust and other dark stains virtually nil. There is a milky area is present over the "78" of 780 FINE. Corner cuts are visible at the bottom right corner of the top face (relative to the punches) and its diagonal opposite on the bottom face. In sum, an attractive and distinctive example of the medium-to-large class of Kellogg & Humbert gold ingots found on the S.S. *Central America*. The ingot measures 42 x 98 x 22 mm.

S.S.C.A. RELIC GOLD MEDALS

1861 **1855 SSCA Relic Gold Medal "1855 Kellogg & Co. Fifty" Gem Proof PCGS.** Struck August 20, 2001. An earlier example of this "commemorative restrike," minted in metal from S.S. *Central America* ingots. Restrike only; box, papers, etc. not included. (#10358)

1862 **2008 SSCA "Humbert Commemorative" Gem Proof NGC.** #61 of 375. Struck with gold recovered from S.S. *Central America*, Kellogg & Humbert gold ingots 830 and 555. Struck on September 12, 2008, missing the sesquicentennial of the sinking by a single year. The design is similar to Kagin-11, but the reverse has a rectangular area with an inscription that states its recent production.

CALIFORNIA FRACTIONAL GOLD

1863 **1853 Liberty Octagonal 25 Cents, BG-101, Low R.5, MS64 PCGS.** Yellow-gold lustrous surfaces display occasional splashes of bluish-purple at the margins of this near-Gem. Well struck for the issue, except for the usual softness in the 8 of the date. Devoid of mentionable marks. This is the single finest certified of the BG-101 variety. Population: 1 in 64, 0 finer (12/09).(#10370)

1864 **1854 Liberty Octagonal 25 Cents, BG-105, R.3, MS65 Prooflike NGC.** This absolutely gorgeous Period One gold 25 cent piece has fully prooflike surfaces and lovely cameo contrast. A remarkable survivor, and nearly as nice as any we have seen. Census: 10 in 65 Prooflike, 4 finer (1/10).(#10374)

1865 **1855 Liberty Round 25 Cents, BG-225, Low R.7, MS62 PCGS.** The formidable rarity of BG-225 is undoubtedly due to its many die cracks, especially the heavy crack between Liberty's ear and the rim at 7 o'clock. This peach-gold Period One round quarter has a few thin marks on the left obverse, and these are all that limit the grade. Population: 3 in 62, 5 finer (12/09).(#10410)

1866 **1853 Peacock Reverse 50 Cents, BG-302, Low R.4, AU58 PCGS.** Those are glory rays above the eagle's back, and the tail is obvious beneath the arrow. Yet the "Peacock" nickname has stuck, and it remains among the most coveted types within the Period One series. Considerable die rust marks this as a Die State II example. There is a retained rim cud joining the star behind Liberty's head. Considerable luster remains on the golden-smoky surfaces.(#10422)

1867 **1853 Liberty Octagonal 1 Dollar, BG-530, R.2, MS63 PCGS.** A shining Select example of this popular, relatively accessible Liberty octagonal one dollar issue. Pale canary-gold surfaces offer satiny luster.(#10507)

1868 **1872 Liberty Octagonal 25 Cents, BG-726, High R.5, MS64 PCGS.** A luminous example of this rarer small octagonal variant. Surfaces are generally butter-yellow with significant lime accents. As always for BG-726, the central reverse displays bluntness, although the strike is sharper than on the Breen-Gillio Second Edition plate coin. Population: 5 in 64, 0 finer (1/10).(#10553)

1869 **1866 Liberty Octagonal 25 Cents, BG-740, Low R.6, MS63 PCGS.** Ex: Bass. Lemon-gold with peripheral suggests of ruby-red. The central reverse exhibits the incompleteness of strike characteristic of the series, but no marks are evident. Population: 6 in 63, 1 finer (1/10).
Ex: Isadore Herman, 11/1973; Harry W. Bass, Jr. Collection, Part I (Bowers and Merena, 5/1999), lot 2532.(#10567)

1870 **1881 Indian Octagonal 25 Cents, BG-799O, Low R.4, MS66 Prooflike NGC.** The Indian design California fractional gold pieces are highly popular with collectors. This piece displays amazing contrast with brilliant and highly lustrous devices and deeply mirrored fields. The surfaces are nearly perfect.(#710641)

1871 **1868 Liberty Round 25 Cents, BG-806, R.3, MS66 PCGS.** A gorgeous example with fully brilliant and frosty yellow-gold luster and excellent details, considering the crude die work of these pieces. Subtle orange toning adds to its overall eye appeal. (#10667)

1872 **1876 Indian Round 25 Cents, BG-879, R.4, MS65 PCGS.** Yellow-gold surfaces display occasional splashes of light orange and are very well preserved. Semiprooflike fields accentuate the frosty design motifs, all of which are relatively sharp except for the top of A in DOLLAR. This round Gem quarter dollar yields considerable eye appeal. Population: 11 in 65, 2 finer (12/09).(#10740)

1873 **1878/6 Indian Round 25 Cents, BG-883, High R.4, MS65 NGC.** Strong yellow-gold with rose overtones and a measure of contrast on the obverse. Carefully preserved, as required of a Gem. (#10744)

1874 **1881 Indian Round 25 Cents, BG-887, R.3, MS66 NGC.** Bright yellow-gold with amply reflective fields (though not strictly of Prooflike quality, in NGC's judgment). Strong eye appeal for this scarce round issue. Census: 2 in 66, 0 finer (1/10).(#10748)

1875 **1870 Liberty Round 50 Cents, BG-1010, R.3, MS66 PCGS.** A remarkable butter-gold Premium Gem of this popular Period Two variety. The strike is above average, and there is no indication of post-strike contact. Population: 1 in 66, 1 finer (1/10). (#10839)

1876 **1868 Liberty Round 50 Cents, BG-1019, R.5, MS62 NGC.** Attractive yellow-gold luster with suggestions of orange. This rare variety can be found with reflective surfaces, as is the case here. As of (1/10), NGC has certified only three examples.(#10848)

1877 **1874 Indian Octagonal 1 Dollar, BG-1124, High R.4, MS62 PCGS.** This moderately mirrored octagonal dollar has lovely orange-gold toning. Both sides are nicely struck and appear smooth aside from a pair of slender, straight mint-made laminations, one through the chin and another through the A in DOLLAR. Population: 12 in 62, 21 finer (1/10).(#10935)

End of Session Three

SESSION FOUR

(NO FLOOR OR PHONE BIDDING)

Heritage Live!™, Internet, Fax, and Mail Signature® Auction #1137
Sunday, February 7, 2010, 2:00 PM CT, Lots 7001-8721

A 15% Buyer's Premium ($14 minimum) Will Be Added To All Lots

Visit HA.com to view full-color images and bid.

SPECIAL INTERNET BIDDING FEATURE:

Online proxy bidding ends at HA.com two hours prior to the opening of the live auction. Check the Time Remaining on individual lots for details. After Internet proxy bidding closes, live bidding will take place through Heritage Live, our NEW bidding software that lets you bid live during the actual auction. Your secret maximum will compete against those bids, and win all ties. To maximize your chances of winning, enter realistic secret maximum bids before live bidding begins. (Important note: Due to software and Internet latency, bids placed through Live Internet Bidding may not register in time and those bidders could lose lots they would otherwise have won, so be sure to place your proxy bids in advance.)

COLONIALS

7001 **1723 Hibernia Farthing, DEI GRATIA MS62 Brown PCGS.** PCGS Population (11/52). NGC Census: (3/9). (#176)

7002 **1723 Hibernia Halfpenny VF30 NGC.** NGC Census: (8/86). PCGS Population (18/332). (#180)

7003 **1723 Hibernia Halfpenny XF40 PCGS.** PCGS Population (29/273). NGC Census: (5/79). (#180)

7004 **1723 Hibernia Halfpenny AU55 PCGS.** PCGS Population (57/145). NGC Census: (14/42). (#180)

7005 **1723 Hibernia Halfpenny MS62 Brown PCGS.** PCGS Population (23/65). NGC Census: (11/17). (#180)

7006 **1723 Hibernia Halfpenny MS63 Brown PCGS.** PCGS Population (38/27). NGC Census: (7/10). (#180)

7007 **1724 Hibernia Halfpenny XF40 PCGS.** PCGS Population (6/26). NGC Census: (1/6). (#190)

7008 **1773 Virginia Halfpenny, Period—Reverse Scratched—NCS. AU Details.** NGC Census: (1/73). PCGS Population (5/208). (#240)

7009 **1773 Virginia Halfpenny, Period MS63 Red and Brown PCGS.** PCGS Population (84/90). NGC Census: (13/27). (#241)

7010 **1773 Virginia Halfpenny, Period MS63 Red and Brown PCGS.** PCGS Population (84/90). NGC Census: (13/27). (#241)

7011 **1760 Hibernia-Voce Populi Halfpenny XF40 PCGS.** PCGS Population (27/107). NGC Census: (3/43). (#262)

7012 **1760 Hibernia-Voce Populi Halfpenny, P Below Bust VF30 PCGS.** PCGS Population (5/16). NGC Census: (2/3). (#268)

7013 **1787 Connecticut Copper, Mailed Bust Left VF30 NGC.** NGC Census: (6/19). PCGS Population (6/28). (#349)

7014 **1787 Connecticut Copper, Draped Bust Left VF30 PCGS.** PCGS Population (53/166). NGC Census: (6/24). (#370)

7015 **1775 Machin's Mills Halfpenny Fine 12 PCGS.** PCGS Population (1/7). NGC Census: (0/0). (#457)

7016 **1778 'Georgivs' Machin's Mills Halfpenny—Corroded, Scratched—NCS. VF Details.** NGC Census: (0/2). PCGS Population (2/6). (#466)

7017 **1787 New Jersey Copper, Camel Head VF30 PCGS.** PCGS Population (8/31). NGC Census: (0/4). (#515)

7018 **1785 Nova Constellatio Copper, Pointed Rays, Large Date VF30 PCGS.** PCGS Population (19/167). NGC Census: (4/39). (#813)

7019 **1785 Nova Constellatio Copper, Pointed Rays, Large Date VF35 NGC.** NGC Census: (4/35). PCGS Population (29/138). (#813)

7020 **1785 Nova Constellatio Copper, Pointed Rays, Large Date XF40 NGC.** NGC Census: (5/30). PCGS Population (37/101). (#813)

7021 **1781 North American Token VF30 NGC.** NGC Census: (9/8). PCGS Population (24/67). (#589)

7022 **(1792-94) Kentucky Token, Plain Edge VF35 PCGS.** PCGS Population (20/289). NGC Census: (3/66). (#614)

7023 **(1792-94) Kentucky Token, Plain Edge MS63 Brown PCGS.** PCGS Population (17/20). NGC Census: (8/5). (#614)

7024 **1794 Franklin Press Token MS63 Brown NGC.** NGC Census: (12/4). PCGS Population (17/7). (#630)

7025 **1794 Talbot, Allum & Lee Cent, NEW YORK VF35 PCGS.** PCGS Population (15/71). NGC Census: (0/19). (#634)

7026 **1795 Talbot Allum & Lee Cent MS62 Brown PCGS.** PCGS Population (25/78). NGC Census: (11/21). (#640)

7027 **1783 Washington & Independence Cent, Draped Bust, No Button VF30 NGC.** NGC Census: (2/20). PCGS Population (7/93). (#676)

7028 **1783 Washington & Independence Cent, Draped Bust, No Button, Copper Restrike, Engrailed Edge PR64 Brown PCGS.** PCGS Population (35/45). NGC Census: (6/7). (#685)

7029 **1795 Washington Grate Halfpenny, Large Buttons, Reeded Edge XF45 PCGS.** PCGS Population (7/173). NGC Census: (1/41). (#746)

7030 **1795 Washington Liberty & Security Halfpenny, LONDON Edge XF40 NGC.** NGC Census: (2/3). PCGS Population (6/30). (#755)

HALF CENTS

7031 **1795 Lettered Edge, Punctuated Date—Damage—PCGS Genuine.** (#1015)

7032 **1797 1 Above 1, Plain Edge—Damage—PCGS Genuine.** (#1042)

7033 **1804 Plain 4, No Stems VF25 ANACS.** C-13. NGC Census: (4/188). PCGS Population (29/519). Mintage: 1,055,312. Numismedia Wsl. Price for problem free NGC/PCGS coin in VF25: $184. (#1063)

7034 **1804 Spiked Chin VG8 ANACS.** C-7. NGC Census: (0/160). PCGS Population (1/203). Numismedia Wsl. Price for problem free NGC/PCGS coin in VG8 : $83. (#1075)

7035 **1805 Large 5, Stems VF25 PCGS.** PCGS Population (3/46). NGC Census: (0/0). Numismedia Wsl. Price for problem free NGC/PCGS coin in VF25: $215. (#1090)

7036 **1806 Small 6, No Stems XF40 PCGS.** PCGS Population (55/243). NGC Census: (12/351). Mintage: 356,000. Numismedia Wsl. Price for problem free NGC/PCGS coin in XF40: $300. (#1093)

7037 **1806 Small 6, No Stems—Recolored, Surface Residue—ANACS. AU58 Details.** C-4. NGC Census: (94/162). PCGS Population (35/69). Mintage: 356,000. Numismedia Wsl. Price for problem free NGC/PCGS coin in AU58: $875. (#1093)

7038 **1826—Improperly Cleaned—NGC. Unc Details.** NGC Census: (3/84). PCGS Population (0/69). Mintage: 234,000. Numismedia Wsl. Price for problem free NGC/PCGS coin in MS60: $350. (#1144)

7039 **1828 13 Stars AU58 NGC.** NGC Census: (139/345). PCGS Population (94/211). Mintage: 606,000. Numismedia Wsl. Price for problem free NGC/PCGS coin in AU58: $200. (#1147)

7040 **1832 AU58 PCGS.** PCGS Population (35/96). NGC Census: (47/115). Mintage: 154,000. Numismedia Wsl. Price for problem free NGC/PCGS coin in AU58: $190. (#1159)

7041 **1835 MS63 Brown PCGS.** PCGS Population (109/128). NGC Census: (108/162). Mintage: 398,000. Numismedia Wsl. Price for problem free NGC/PCGS coin in MS63: $340. (#1168)

7042 **1849 Large Date MS63 Brown PCGS.** PCGS Population (36/22). NGC Census: (33/45). Mintage: 39,864. Numismedia Wsl. Price for problem free NGC/PCGS coin in MS63: $500. (#1218)

7043 **1850 MS62 Brown PCGS. CAC.** PCGS Population (15/56). NGC Census: (39/40). Mintage: 39,800. Numismedia Wsl. Price for problem free NGC/PCGS coin in MS62: $430. (#1221)

7044 **1851 MS63 Brown NGC.** NGC Census: (86/83). PCGS Population (65/31). Mintage: 147,672. Numismedia Wsl. Price for problem free NGC/PCGS coin in MS63: $320. (#1224)

7045 **1853 MS63 Brown PCGS.** PCGS Population (131/157). NGC Census: (140/310). Mintage: 129,694. Numismedia Wsl. Price for problem free NGC/PCGS coin in MS63: $310. (#1227)

7046 **1856—Improperly Cleaned—NCS. Unc Details.** C-1. NGC Census: (3/181). PCGS Population (7/110). Mintage: 40,430. Numismedia Wsl. Price for problem free NGC/PCGS coin in MS60: $185. (#1236)

7047 **1857 MS62 Brown PCGS. CAC.** PCGS Population (49/110). NGC Census: (55/183). Mintage: 35,180. Numismedia Wsl. Price for problem free NGC/PCGS coin in MS62: $330. (#1239)

7048 **1857 MS63 Brown PCGS.** PCGS Population (80/30). NGC Census: (94/89). Mintage: 35,180. Numismedia Wsl. Price for problem free NGC/PCGS coin in MS63: $420. (#1239)

LARGE CENTS

7049 **1793 Wreath Cent, Vine and Bars Poor 1 PCGS.** PCGS Population (6/441). NGC Census: (2/171). Mintage: 63,353. (#1347)

7050 **1794 Head of 1794 Good 6 PCGS.** PCGS Population (18/433). NGC Census: (0/0). Numismedia Wsl. Price for problem free NGC/PCGS coin in Good 6 : $411. (#901374)

7051 **1794 Head of 1795—Scratched—ANACS. VG8 Details.** S-72. NGC Census: (2/124). PCGS Population (16/404). Mintage: 918,521. Numismedia Wsl. Price for problem free NGC/PCGS coin in VG8 : $475. (#1365)

7052 **1794 Head of 1795—Burnished—NCS. VF Details.** S-24. NGC Census: (9/103). PCGS Population (47/284). Mintage: 918,521. Numismedia Wsl. Price for problem free NGC/PCGS coin in VF20: $1,775. (#1365)

7053 **1795 Plain Edge—Corroded—ANACS. VG8 Details.** S-76B. NGC Census: (0/30). PCGS Population (15/265). Mintage: 501,500. Numismedia Wsl. Price for problem free NGC/PCGS coin in VG8 : $500. (#1380)

7054 **1796 Liberty Cap AG3 ANACS.** S-89. NGC Census: (3/76). PCGS Population (4/125). Mintage: 109,825. (#1392)

7055 **1800 Fine 15 ANACS.** S-204. NGC Census: (3/41). PCGS Population (10/54). Mintage: 2,822,175. Numismedia Wsl. Price for problem free NGC/PCGS coin in Fine 15: $419. (#1449)

7056 **1803 Small Date, Large Fraction VF20 PCGS.** PCGS Population (11/76). NGC Census: (1/7). Numismedia Wsl. Price for problem free NGC/PCGS coin in VF20: $340. (#1485)

7057 **1805—Environmental Damage—PCGS Genuine.** Mintage: 941,116. (#1510)

7058 **1805—Cleaned—ANACS. VF30 Details.** S-267. NGC Census: (2/19). PCGS Population (19/74). Mintage: 941,116. Numismedia Wsl. Price for problem free NGC/PCGS coin in VF30: $665. (#1510)

7059 **1812 Small Date—Corroded—ANACS. VF20 Details.** S-288. NGC Census: (6/121). PCGS Population (13/156). Mintage: 1,075,500. Numismedia Wsl. Price for problem free NGC/PCGS coin in VF20: $550. (#1561)

7060 **1813 VG10 ANACS.** S-292. NGC Census: (0/16). PCGS Population (6/145). Mintage: 418,000. Numismedia Wsl. Price for problem free NGC/PCGS coin in VG10: $186. (#1570)

7061 **1816 AU58 PCGS.** PCGS Population (28/110). NGC Census: (13/45). Mintage: 2,820,982. Numismedia Wsl. Price for problem free NGC/PCGS coin in AU58: $375. (#1591)

7062 **1816 MS62 Brown ANACS.** N-2. NGC Census: (8/34). PCGS Population (32/73). Mintage: 2,820,982. Numismedia Wsl. Price for problem free NGC/PCGS coin in MS62: $525. (#1591)

7063 **1817 13 Stars AU58 PCGS.** PCGS Population (36/91). NGC Census: (37/159). Mintage: 3,948,400. Numismedia Wsl. Price for problem free NGC/PCGS coin in AU58: $310. (#1594)

7064 **1817 13 Stars MS63 Red and Brown PCGS.** PCGS Population (31/19). NGC Census: (3/6). Mintage: 3,948,400. Numismedia Wsl. Price for problem free NGC/PCGS coin in MS63: $725. (#1595)

7065 **1818 MS62 Brown NGC.** N-10. NGC Census: (16/33). PCGS Population (87/163). Mintage: 3,167,000. Numismedia Wsl. Price for problem free NGC/PCGS coin in MS62: $300. (#1600)

7066 **1819 Large Date AU58 PCGS.** PCGS Population (20/54). NGC Census: (27/139). Mintage: 2,671,000. Numismedia Wsl. Price for problem free NGC/PCGS coin in AU58: $375. (#1603)

7067 **1819/8 Large Date MS62 Brown NGC.** N-1. NGC Census: (3/2). PCGS Population (4/14). Mintage: 2,671,000. Numismedia Wsl. Price for problem free NGC/PCGS coin in MS62: $825. (#1612)

7068 **1820 Large Date MS63 Brown PCGS.** PCGS Population (76/296). NGC Census: (60/344). Mintage: 4,407,550. Numismedia Wsl. Price for problem free NGC/PCGS coin in MS63: $440. (#1615)

7069 **1822 AU50 NGC.** N-5. NGC Census: (1/56). PCGS Population (11/49). Mintage: 2,072,339. Numismedia Wsl. Price for problem free NGC/PCGS coin in AU50: $475. (#1624)

7070 **1823/2—Damage—PCGS Genuine.** Mintage: 1,262,000. (#1630)

7071 **1823/2 VG8 PCGS.** PCGS Population (7/53). NGC Census: (4/44). Mintage: 1,262,000. Numismedia Wsl. Price for problem free NGC/PCGS coin in VG8 : $160. (#1630)

7072 **1829 Large Letters VF35 ANACS.** N-2. NGC Census: (1/29). PCGS Population (4/34). Mintage: 1,414,500. Numismedia Wsl. Price for problem free NGC/PCGS coin in VF35: $215. (#1663)

7073 **1831 Large Letters AU53 ANACS.** N-3. NGC Census: (4/70). PCGS Population (6/80). Mintage: 3,359,260. Numismedia Wsl. Price for problem free NGC/PCGS coin in AU53: $250. (#1678)

7074 **1834 Large 8, Small Stars, Medium Letters MS63 Brown PCGS.** PCGS Population (16/8). NGC Census: (6/19). Mintage: 1,855,100. Numismedia Wsl. Price for problem free NGC/PCGS coin in MS63: $555. (#1699)

7075 **1834 Large 8, Small Stars, Medium Letters MS63 Brown PCGS.** PCGS Population (16/8). NGC Census: (6/19). Mintage: 1,855,100. Numismedia Wsl. Price for problem free NGC/PCGS coin in MS63: $555. (#1699)

7076 **1836 AU58 PCGS.** PCGS Population (16/45). NGC Census: (14/43). Mintage: 2,111,000. Numismedia Wsl. Price for problem free NGC/PCGS coin in AU58: $200. (#1726)

7077 **1838 MS63 Brown NGC.** N-9. NGC Census: (19/60). PCGS Population (74/127). Mintage: 6,370,200. Numismedia Wsl. Price for problem free NGC/PCGS coin in MS63: $440. (#1741)

7078 **1838 MS63 Brown PCGS.** PCGS Population (74/127). NGC Census: (19/60). Mintage: 6,370,200. Numismedia Wsl. Price for problem free NGC/PCGS coin in MS63: $440. (#1741)

7079 **1839 Booby Head—Cleaned—ANACS. AU55 Details.** N-13. NGC Census: (12/105). PCGS Population (11/77). Mintage: 3,128,661. Numismedia Wsl. Price for problem free NGC/PCGS coin in AU55: $500. (#1751)

7080 **1839 Booby Head AU58 PCGS.** PCGS Population (18/58). NGC Census: (10/95). Mintage: 3,128,661. Numismedia Wsl. Price for problem free NGC/PCGS coin in AU58: $575. (#1751)

7081 **1840 Small Date MS63 Brown PCGS.** PCGS Population (4/8). NGC Census: (0/0). (#1823)

7082 **1841 AU58 PCGS.** PCGS Population (6/27). NGC Census: (7/28). Mintage: 1,597,367. Numismedia Wsl. Price for problem free NGC/PCGS coin in AU58: $275. (#1832)

7083 **1843 Petite Head, Small Letters AU58 PCGS.** PCGS Population (11/52). NGC Census: (10/81). Mintage: 2,425,342. (#1844)

7084 **1843 Petite Head, Small Letters MS63 Brown PCGS.** PCGS Population (11/27). NGC Census: (16/39). Mintage: 2,425,342. (#1844)

7085 **1846 Small Date MS63 Brown PCGS.** PCGS Population (33/21). NGC Census: (20/57). Mintage: 4,120,800. Numismedia Wsl. Price for problem free NGC/PCGS coin in MS63: $380. (#1865)

7086 **1848 AU58 PCGS.** PCGS Population (24/94). NGC Census: (34/182). Mintage: 6,415,799. Numismedia Wsl. Price for problem free NGC/PCGS coin in AU58: $140. (#1883)

7087 **1849 MS63 Red and Brown PCGS.** PCGS Population (8/11). NGC Census: (1/4). Mintage: 4,178,500. Numismedia Wsl. Price for problem free NGC/PCGS coin in MS63: $625. (#1887)

7088 **1850 MS63 Red and Brown PCGS.** PCGS Population (46/227). NGC Census: (2/28). Mintage: 4,426,844. Numismedia Wsl. Price for problem free NGC/PCGS coin in MS63: $300. (#1890)

7089 **1851 MS64 Brown PCGS.** PCGS Population (120/63). NGC Census: (54/96). Mintage: 9,889,707. Numismedia Wsl. Price for problem free NGC/PCGS coin in MS64: $300. (#1892)

7090 **1851 MS64 Red and Brown PCGS.** PCGS Population (81/54). NGC Census: (3/14). Mintage: 9,889,707. Numismedia Wsl. Price for problem free NGC/PCGS coin in MS64: $565. (#1893)

7091 **1853 MS63 Red and Brown NGC.** NGC Census: (51/304). PCGS Population (74/287). Mintage: 6,641,131. Numismedia Wsl. Price for problem free NGC/PCGS coin in MS63: $300. (#1902)

7092 **1853 MS64 Red and Brown PCGS.** PCGS Population (198/89). NGC Census: (154/150). Mintage: 6,641,131. Numismedia Wsl. Price for problem free NGC/PCGS coin in MS64: $560. (#1902)

7093 **1854 MS63 Brown PCGS.** PCGS Population (74/122). NGC Census: (26/118). Mintage: 4,236,156. Numismedia Wsl. Price for problem free NGC/PCGS coin in MS63: $230. (#1904)

7094 **1854 MS63 Brown PCGS.** PCGS Population (74/122). NGC Census: (26/118). Mintage: 4,236,156. Numismedia Wsl. Price for problem free NGC/PCGS coin in MS63: $230. (#1904)

7095 **1855 Upright 5s MS64 Red and Brown NGC.** N-3. NGC Census: (84/123). PCGS Population (157/65). Mintage: 1,574,829. Numismedia Wsl. Price for problem free NGC/PCGS coin in MS64: $440. (#1908)

7096 **1856 Slanted 5 MS63 Brown NGC.** N-14. NGC Census: (21/85). PCGS Population (109/112). Mintage: 2,690,463. Numismedia Wsl. Price for problem free NGC/PCGS coin in MS63: $220. (#1919)

FLYING EAGLE CENTS

7097 **1857 XF45 NGC.** NGC Census: (7/92). PCGS Population (89/2630). Mintage: 17,450,000. Numismedia Wsl. Price for problem free NGC/PCGS coin in XF45: $136. (#2016)

7098 **1858 Large Letters MS63 PCGS.** PCGS Population (378/642). NGC Census: (47/102). Mintage: 24,600,000. Numismedia Wsl. Price for problem free NGC/PCGS coin in MS63: $685. (#2019)

7099 **1858 Large Letters MS63 PCGS.** PCGS Population (378/647). NGC Census: (47/102). Mintage: 24,600,000. Numismedia Wsl. Price for problem free NGC/PCGS coin in MS63: $685. (#2019)

INDIAN CENTS

7100 **1859 MS63 PCGS.** PCGS Population (463/670). NGC Census: (1/7). Mintage: 36,400,000. Numismedia Wsl. Price for problem free NGC/PCGS coin in MS63: $540. (#2052)

7101 **1859 MS64 NGC.** NGC Census: (5/2). PCGS Population (536/133). Mintage: 36,400,000. Numismedia Wsl. Price for problem free NGC/PCGS coin in MS64: $850. (#2052)

7102 **1859 MS64 PCGS.** PCGS Population (537/133). NGC Census: (5/2). Mintage: 36,400,000. Numismedia Wsl. Price for problem free NGC/PCGS coin in MS64: $850. (#2052)

7103 **1860 MS64 NGC. CAC.** NGC Census: (35/10). PCGS Population (393/203). Mintage: 20,566,000. Numismedia Wsl. Price for problem free NGC/PCGS coin in MS64: $380. (#2058)

7104 **1861 MS62 ANACS.** NGC Census: (68/555). PCGS Population (80/775). Mintage: 10,100,000. Numismedia Wsl. Price for problem free NGC/PCGS coin in MS62: $200. (#2061)

7105 **(2)1862—Improperly Cleaned—NCS. Unc Details.** NGC Census: (8/1175). PCGS Population (14/1503). Mintage: 28,075,000. Numismedia Wsl. Price for problem free NGC/PCGS coin in MS60: $77. (#2064) (Total: 2 coins)

7106 **1862 MS65 NGC.** NGC Census: (166/35). PCGS Population (195/65). Mintage: 28,075,000. Numismedia Wsl. Price for problem free NGC/PCGS coin in MS65: $750. (#2064)

7107 **1863 MS64 PCGS.** PCGS Population (627/173). NGC Census: (547/198). Mintage: 49,840,000. Numismedia Wsl. Price for problem free NGC/PCGS coin in MS64: $325. (#2067)

7108 **1863 MS64 NGC.** NGC Census: (547/198). PCGS Population (629/174). Mintage: 49,840,000. Numismedia Wsl. Price for problem free NGC/PCGS coin in MS64: $325. (#2067)

7109 **1864 Bronze No L MS65 Red PCGS.** PCGS Population (107/33). NGC Census: (0/0). Mintage: 39,233,712. Numismedia Wsl. Price for problem free NGC/PCGS coin in MS65: $800. (#2078)

7110 **1864 L On Ribbon—Cleaned—ANACS. AU50 Details.** NGC Census: (1/14). PCGS Population (60/313). Mintage: 39,233,712. Numismedia Wsl. Price for problem free NGC/PCGS coin in AU50: $260. (#2079)

7111 **1864 L On Ribbon MS62 Brown ANACS.** NGC Census: (1/5). PCGS Population (22/120). Mintage: 39,233,712. Numismedia Wsl. Price for problem free NGC/PCGS coin in MS62: $380. (#2079)

7112 **1864 L On Ribbon MS64 Brown NGC.** NGC Census: (2/1). PCGS Population (51/5). Mintage: 39,233,712. Numismedia Wsl. Price for problem free NGC/PCGS coin in MS64: $625. (#2079)

7113 **1864 L On Ribbon MS62 Red and Brown NGC.** NGC Census: (1/5). PCGS Population (25/415). Mintage: 39,233,712. Numismedia Wsl. Price for problem free NGC/PCGS coin in MS62: $425. (#2080)

7114 **1865 Fancy 5 MS64 Red and Brown NGC.** NGC Census: (175/168). PCGS Population (231/77). Mintage: 35,429,288. Numismedia Wsl. Price for problem free NGC/PCGS coin in MS64: $250. (#2083)

7115 **1865 Fancy 5 MS65 Red and Brown NGC.** NGC Census: (149/19). PCGS Population (73/4). Mintage: 35,429,288. Numismedia Wsl. Price for problem free NGC/PCGS coin in MS65: $390. (#2083)

7116 **1865 Fancy 5 MS64 Red PCGS.** PCGS Population (105/49). NGC Census: (2/4). Mintage: 35,429,288. Numismedia Wsl. Price for problem free NGC/PCGS coin in MS64: $400. (#2084)

7117 **1867 Brown—Improperly Cleaned—NCS. Unc Details.** NGC Census: (0/18). PCGS Population (0/86). Mintage: 9,821,000. Numismedia Wsl. Price for problem free NGC/PCGS coin in MS60: $210. (#2088)

7118 **1869—Obverse Damage—NCS. Unc Details.** VP-001, FS-301. NGC Census: (0/65). PCGS Population (0/408). Mintage: 6,420,000. Numismedia Wsl. Price for problem free NGC/PCGS coin in MS60: $475. (#2095)

7119 **1869—Improperly Cleaned—NCS. Unc Details.** VP-001, FS-301. NGC Census: (0/65). PCGS Population (0/408). Mintage: 6,420,000. Numismedia Wsl. Price for problem free NGC/PCGS coin in MS60: $475. (#2095)

7120 **1870—Corroded—ANACS. AU53 Details.** NGC Census: (6/183). PCGS Population (17/131). Mintage: 5,275,000. Numismedia Wsl. Price for problem free NGC/PCGS coin in AU53: $365. (#2097)

7121 **1871 VF35 NGC.** NGC Census: (0/0). PCGS Population (17/300). Mintage: 3,929,500. Numismedia Wsl. Price for NGC/PCGS coin in VF35: $286. (#2100)

7122 **1872 XF40 PCGS.** PCGS Population (54/329). NGC Census: (0/0). Mintage: 4,042,000. Numismedia Wsl. Price for problem free NGC/PCGS coin in XF40: $440. (#2103)

7123 **1872—Improperly Cleaned—NCS. Unc Details.** NGC Census: (0/0). PCGS Population (1/91). Mintage: 4,042,000. Numismedia Wsl. Price for problem free NGC/PCGS coin in MS60: $620. (#2103)

7124 **1872 MS62 Red and Brown PCGS.** PCGS Population (17/344). NGC Census: (0/0). Mintage: 4,042,000. Numismedia Wsl. Price for problem free NGC/PCGS coin in MS62: $775. (#2104)

7125 **1875 AU55 NGC.** NGC Census: (11/166). PCGS Population (33/81). Mintage: 13,528,000. Numismedia Wsl. Price for problem free NGC/PCGS coin in AU55: $120. (#2121)

7126 **1877—Improperly Cleaned, Corrosion—NCS. Good Details.** NGC Census: (133/1177). PCGS Population (305/2187). Mintage: 852,500. Numismedia Wsl. Price for problem free NGC/PCGS coin in Good 4 : $750. (#2127)

7127 **1877—Damaged—ANACS. VG Details Net Good 4.** NGC Census: (133/1176). PCGS Population (305/2180). Mintage: 852,500. Numismedia Wsl. Price for problem free NGC/PCGS coin in Good 4 : $750. (#2127)

7128 **1881 MS64 Red and Brown PCGS.** PCGS Population (249/67). NGC Census: (0/0). Mintage: 39,211,576. Numismedia Wsl. Price for problem free NGC/PCGS coin in MS64: $210. (#2140)

7129 **1882—Broad Struck and Triple Struck—VG10 NGC.** Eagle Eye Photo Seal. Mintage: 38,581,100.

7130 **1885 MS64 Red PCGS.** PCGS Population (66/64). NGC Census: (12/20). Mintage: 11,765,384. Numismedia Wsl. Price for problem free NGC/PCGS coin in MS64: $535. (#2153)

7131 **1887 MS65 Red and Brown NGC.** NGC Census: (52/6). PCGS Population (19/0). Mintage: 45,226,484. Numismedia Wsl. Price for problem free NGC/PCGS coin in MS65: $350. (#2158)

7132 **1895—Triple Struck in Collar—AU58 NGC.** Eagle Eye Photo Seal. Mintage: 38,343,636.

7133 **1895 MS65 Red PCGS.** PCGS Population (107/35). NGC Census: (89/40). Mintage: 38,343,636. Numismedia Wsl. Price for problem free NGC/PCGS coin in MS65: $680. (#2192)

7134 **1896 MS64 Red PCGS.** PCGS Population (144/61). NGC Census: (76/60). Mintage: 39,057,292. Numismedia Wsl. Price for problem free NGC/PCGS coin in MS64: $230. (#2195)

7135 **1898—Triple Struck Rotated in Collar—XF40 NGC.** Mintage: 49,823,080.

7136 **1899 MS65 Red PCGS.** PCGS Population (247/88). NGC Census: (154/63). Mintage: 53,600,032. Numismedia Wsl. Price for problem free NGC/PCGS coin in MS65: $460. (#2204)

7137 **1901—Double Struck in Collar—Fine 15 PCGS.** Eagle Eye Photo Seal. Mintage: 79,611,144.

7138 **1902—Double Struck in Collar—VG8 ANACS.** Mintage: 87,376,720.

7139 **1902 MS65 Red PCGS.** PCGS Population (130/54). NGC Census: (112/111). Mintage: 87,376,720. Numismedia Wsl. Price for problem free NGC/PCGS coin in MS65: $480. (#2213)

7140 **1902 MS65 Red PCGS.** PCGS Population (130/55). NGC Census: (112/111). Mintage: 87,376,720. Numismedia Wsl. Price for problem free NGC/PCGS coin in MS65: $480. (#2213)

7141 **1906 MS65 Red PCGS.** PCGS Population (168/15). NGC Census: (128/34). Mintage: 96,022,256. Numismedia Wsl. Price for problem free NGC/PCGS coin in MS65: $450. (#2225)

7142 **1908-S MS62 Red and Brown NGC.** NGC Census: (21/394). PCGS Population (28/637). Mintage: 1,115,000. Numismedia Wsl. Price for problem free NGC/PCGS coin in MS62: $290. (#2233)

7143 **1909 MS64 Red PCGS.** PCGS Population (879/740). NGC Census: (300/284). Mintage: 14,370,645. Numismedia Wsl. Price for problem free NGC/PCGS coin in MS64: $170. (#2237)

7144 **1909 MS64 Red PCGS.** PCGS Population (879/739). NGC Census: (300/284). Mintage: 14,370,645. Numismedia Wsl. Price for problem free NGC/PCGS coin in MS64: $170. (#2237)

7145 **1909 MS65 Red PCGS.** PCGS Population (586/154). NGC Census: (252/32). Mintage: 14,370,645. Numismedia Wsl. Price for problem free NGC/PCGS coin in MS65: $430. (#2237)

7146 **1909-S VF30 NGC.** NGC Census: (103/619). PCGS Population (225/1006). Mintage: 309,000. Numismedia Wsl. Price for problem free NGC/PCGS coin in VF30: $636. (#2238)

PROOF INDIAN CENTS

7147 **1862 PR62 NGC.** NGC Census: (6/231). PCGS Population (13/273). Mintage: 550. Numismedia Wsl. Price for problem free NGC/PCGS coin in PR62: $475. (#2259)

7148 **1870 PR63 Red PCGS.** PCGS Population (2/56). NGC Census: (1/33). Mintage: 1,000. Numismedia Wsl. Price for problem free NGC/PCGS coin in PR63: $650. (#2299)

7149 **1872 PR64 Red and Brown PCGS.** PCGS Population (111/72). NGC Census: (49/50). Mintage: 950. Numismedia Wsl. Price for problem free NGC/PCGS coin in PR64: $600. (#2304)

7150 **1878 PR62 Red and Brown NGC.** NGC Census: (5/164). PCGS Population (5/259). Mintage: 2,350. Numismedia Wsl. Price for problem free NGC/PCGS coin in PR62: $175. (#2322)

7151 **1878 PR64 Red and Brown PCGS.** PCGS Population (146/47). NGC Census: (81/62). Mintage: 2,350. Numismedia Wsl. Price for problem free NGC/PCGS coin in PR64: $440. (#2322)

7152 **1880 PR64 Red and Brown PCGS.** PCGS Population (206/78). NGC Census: (86/98). Mintage: 3,955. Numismedia Wsl. Price for problem free NGC/PCGS coin in PR64: $285. (#2328)

7153 **1884 PR62 Red and Brown NGC.** NGC Census: (0/0). PCGS Population (8/355). Mintage: 3,942. Numismedia Wsl. Price for problem free NGC/PCGS coin in PR62: $150. (#2340)

7154 **1884 PR64 Red PCGS.** PCGS Population (46/89). NGC Census: (10/42). Mintage: 3,942. Numismedia Wsl. Price for problem free NGC/PCGS coin in PR64: $380. (#2341)

7155 **1890 PR65 Red and Brown PCGS.** PCGS Population (22/2). NGC Census: (37/2). Mintage: 2,740. Numismedia Wsl. Price for problem free NGC/PCGS coin in PR65: $420. (#2358)

7156 **1896 PR64 Red PCGS.** PCGS Population (22/11). NGC Census: (13/9). Mintage: 1,862. Numismedia Wsl. Price for problem free NGC/PCGS coin in PR64: $440. (#2377)

7157 **1906 PR63 Red PCGS.** PCGS Population (5/64). NGC Census: (0/31). Mintage: 1,725. Numismedia Wsl. Price for problem free NGC/PCGS coin in PR63: $170. (#2407)

7158 **1908 PR64 Brown PCGS.** PCGS Population (18/7). NGC Census: (16/16). Mintage: 1,620. Numismedia Wsl. Price for problem free NGC/PCGS coin in PR64: $180. (#2411)

LINCOLN CENTS

7159 **1909 VDB MS66 Red and Brown PCGS.** PCGS Population (78/0). NGC Census: (0/0). Mintage: 27,995,000. Numismedia Wsl. Price for problem free NGC/PCGS coin in MS66: $115. (#2424)

7160 **1909 VDB MS66 Red and Brown NGC. CAC.** NGC Census: (0/0). PCGS Population (77/0). Mintage: 27,995,000. Numismedia Wsl. Price for problem free NGC/PCGS coin in MS66: $115. (#2424)

7161 **1909 VDB MS66 Red PCGS.** PCGS Population (1783/190). NGC Census: (1274/95). Mintage: 27,995,000. Numismedia Wsl. Price for problem free NGC/PCGS coin in MS66: $310. (#2425)

7162 **1909 VDB MS66 Red PCGS.** PCGS Population (1785/190). NGC Census: (1274/95). Mintage: 27,995,000. Numismedia Wsl. Price for problem free NGC/PCGS coin in MS66: $310. (#2425)

7163 **1909-S VDB VF30 ANACS.** NGC Census: (169/2123). PCGS Population (450/3903). Mintage: 484,000. Numismedia Wsl. Price for problem free NGC/PCGS coin in VF30: $1,060. (#2426)

7164 **1909-S VDB—Improperly Cleaned—NCS. AU Details.** NGC Census: (108/1396). PCGS Population (306/1889). Mintage: 484,000. Numismedia Wsl. Price for problem free NGC/PCGS coin in AU50: $1,160. (#2426)

7165 **1909-S MS64 Brown NGC.** NGC Census: (0/0). PCGS Population (57/6). Mintage: 1,825,000. Numismedia Wsl. Price for problem free NGC/PCGS coin in MS64: $330. (#2432)

7166 **1910-S MS64 Red and Brown NGC.** NGC Census: (155/118). PCGS Population (363/158). Mintage: 6,045,000. Numismedia Wsl. Price for problem free NGC/PCGS coin in MS64: $220. (#2439)

7167 **1910-S MS65 Red and Brown PCGS.** PCGS Population (158/2). NGC Census: (105/13). Mintage: 6,045,000. Numismedia Wsl. Price for problem free NGC/PCGS coin in MS65: $340. (#2439)

7168 **1910-S MS66 Red and Brown NGC.** NGC Census: (13/0). PCGS Population (2/0). Mintage: 6,045,000. Numismedia Wsl. Price for problem free NGC/PCGS coin in MS66: $575. (#2439)

7169 **1911-S—Altered Color—NCS. Unc Details.** NGC Census: (0/142). PCGS Population (1/164). Mintage: 4,026,000. Numismedia Wsl. Price for problem free NGC/PCGS coin in MS60: $145. (#2447)

7170 **1912-S MS64 Red and Brown PCGS.** PCGS Population (166/28). NGC Census: (91/37). Mintage: 4,431,000. Numismedia Wsl. Price for problem free NGC/PCGS coin in MS64: $360. (#2457)

7171 **1913-S MS64 Red and Brown PCGS.** PCGS Population (152/24). NGC Census: (74/42). Mintage: 6,101,000. Numismedia Wsl. Price for problem free NGC/PCGS coin in MS64: $575. (#2466)

7172 **1914-D VF20 PCGS.** PCGS Population (348/1766). NGC Census: (144/1060). Mintage: 1,193,000. Numismedia Wsl. Price for problem free NGC/PCGS coin in VF20: $365. (#2471)

7173 **1914-D—Scratches—NCS. VF Details.** NGC Census: (146/1061). PCGS Population (348/1772). Mintage: 1,193,000. Numismedia Wsl. Price for problem free NGC/PCGS coin in VF20: $365. (#2471)

7174 **1914-D VF25 PCGS.** PCGS Population (264/1502). NGC Census: (161/899). Mintage: 1,193,000. Numismedia Wsl. Price for problem free NGC/PCGS coin in VF25: $424. (#2471)

7175 **1914-D XF40 NGC.** NGC Census: (110/526). PCGS Population (269/661). Mintage: 1,193,000. Numismedia Wsl. Price for problem free NGC/PCGS coin in XF40: $785. (#2471)

7176 **1917-D MS65 Red and Brown NGC.** NGC Census: (47/5). PCGS Population (26/1). Mintage: 55,120,000. Numismedia Wsl. Price for problem free NGC/PCGS coin in MS65: $525. (#2499)

7177 **1918-D MS65 Red and Brown NGC.** NGC Census: (22/0). PCGS Population (21/0). Mintage: 47,830,000. Numismedia Wsl. Price for problem free NGC/PCGS coin in MS65: $950. (#2508)

7178 **1918-S MS64 Brown NGC.** NGC Census: (0/0). PCGS Population (43/7). Mintage: 34,680,000. Numismedia Wsl. Price for problem free NGC/PCGS coin in MS64: $290. (#2510)

7179 **1920 MS65 Red PCGS.** PCGS Population (395/119). NGC Census: (85/58). Mintage: 310,164,992. Numismedia Wsl. Price for problem free NGC/PCGS coin in MS65: $190. (#2524)

7180 **1920-D MS64 Red NGC.** NGC Census: (49/20). PCGS Population (194/89). Mintage: 49,280,000. Numismedia Wsl. Price for problem free NGC/PCGS coin in MS64: $325. (#2527)

7181 **1922-D MS64 Red PCGS.** PCGS Population (231/92). NGC Census: (96/25). Mintage: 15,274,000. Numismedia Wsl. Price for problem free NGC/PCGS coin in MS64: $360. (#2539)

7182 **1922 No D Strong Reverse Good 6 NGC.** NGC Census: (0/0). PCGS Population (58/3305). Numismedia Wsl. Price for problem free NGC/PCGS coin in Good 6 : $572. (#3285)

7183 **1925 MS65 Red PCGS.** PCGS Population (464/379). NGC Census: (0/0). Mintage: 139,948,992. Numismedia Wsl. Price for problem free NGC/PCGS coin in MS65: $130. (#2560)

7184 **1925 MS66 Red PCGS.** PCGS Population (324/55). NGC Census: (0/0). Mintage: 139,948,992. Numismedia Wsl. Price for problem free NGC/PCGS coin in MS66: $400. (#2560)

7185 **1925 MS66 Red PCGS.** PCGS Population (324/55). NGC Census: (0/0). Mintage: 139,948,992. Numismedia Wsl. Price for problem free NGC/PCGS coin in MS66: $400. (#2560)

7186 **1925 MS66 Red PCGS.** PCGS Population (324/55). NGC Census: (0/0). Mintage: 139,948,992. Numismedia Wsl. Price for problem free NGC/PCGS coin in MS66: $400. (#2560)

7187 **1925 MS66 Red PCGS.** PCGS Population (324/55). NGC Census: (0/0). Mintage: 139,948,992. Numismedia Wsl. Price for problem free NGC/PCGS coin in MS66: $400. (#2560)

7188 **1926 MS66 Red PCGS.** PCGS Population (439/77). NGC Census: (206/25). Mintage: 157,088,000. Numismedia Wsl. Price for problem free NGC/PCGS coin in MS66: $280. (#2569)

7189 **1926 MS66 Red PCGS.** PCGS Population (439/77). NGC Census: (206/25). Mintage: 157,088,000. Numismedia Wsl. Price for problem free NGC/PCGS coin in MS66: $280. (#2569)

7190 **1928-D MS64 Red PCGS. CAC.** PCGS Population (304/85). NGC Census: (0/0). Mintage: 31,170,000. Numismedia Wsl. Price for problem free NGC/PCGS coin in MS64: $225. (#2590)

7191 **1929-D MS64 Red PCGS. CAC.** PCGS Population (238/162). NGC Census: (66/32). Mintage: 41,730,000. Numismedia Wsl. Price for problem free NGC/PCGS coin in MS64: $165. (#2599)

7192 **1929-S MS65 Red PCGS.** PCGS Population (229/21). NGC Census: (144/24). Mintage: 50,148,000. Numismedia Wsl. Price for problem free NGC/PCGS coin in MS65: $430. (#2602)

7193 **1931-S MS63 Brown PCGS.** PCGS Population (59/56). NGC Census: (48/125). Mintage: 866,000. Numismedia Wsl. Price for problem free NGC/PCGS coin in MS63: $145. (#2618)

7194 **1931-S MS65 Brown PCGS.** PCGS Population (12/0). NGC Census: (25/4). Mintage: 866,000. Numismedia Wsl. Price for problem free NGC/PCGS coin in MS65: $190. (#2618)

7195 **1931-S MS64 Red and Brown PCGS.** PCGS Population (601/94). NGC Census: (556/259). Mintage: 866,000. Numismedia Wsl. Price for problem free NGC/PCGS coin in MS64: $210. (#2619)

7196 **1931-S MS64 Red and Brown NGC.** NGC Census: (556/259). PCGS Population (601/94). Mintage: 866,000. Numismedia Wsl. Price for problem free NGC/PCGS coin in MS64: $210. (#2619)

7197 **1931-S MS64 Red ANACS.** NGC Census: (0/0). PCGS Population (1117/822). Mintage: 866,000. Numismedia Wsl. Price for problem free NGC/PCGS coin in MS64: $265. (#2620)

7198 **1945—Double Struck, Cleaned—ANACS. AU53 Details.** Mintage: 1,040,515,008.

7199 **1960-D Small Over Large Date MS65 Red PCGS.** PCGS Population (72/11). NGC Census: (0/0). (#82869)

7200 **1972 Doubled Die Obverse MS65 Red PCGS.** PCGS Population (1168/501). NGC Census: (518/150). Mintage: 75,000. Numismedia Wsl. Price for problem free NGC/PCGS coin in MS65: $550. (#2950)

7201 **1982 Large Date, Zinc MS67 Red ANACS.** NGC Census: (0/0). PCGS Population (309/19). Numismedia Wsl. Price for problem free NGC/PCGS coin in MS67: $44. (#3047)

7202 **1983 Doubled Die Reverse MS64 Red and Brown NGC.** (#3055)

7203 **1995 Doubled Die Obverse MS68 Red NGC.** NGC Census: (0/0). PCGS Population (2661/1). Numismedia Wsl. Price for problem free NGC/PCGS coin in MS68: $102. (#3127)

PROOF LINCOLN CENTS

7204 **1910—Altered Surface—Proof. PCGS Genuine.** Mintage: 4,118. (#3306)

7205 **1911 PR64 Red and Brown PCGS.** PCGS Population (88/79). NGC Census: (0/0). Mintage: 1,725. Numismedia Wsl. Price for problem free NGC/PCGS coin in PR64: $675. (#3310)

7206 **1913 Matte Proof, PR62 Red ANACS.** NGC Census: (0/68). PCGS Population (0/133). Mintage: 2,983. (#3317)

7207 **1915 Matte Proof, PR63 Red and Brown ANACS.** NGC Census: (5/60). PCGS Population (19/105). Mintage: 1,150. Numismedia Wsl. Price for problem free NGC/PCGS coin in PR63: $330. (#3322)

7208 **1939 PR66 Red PCGS.** PCGS Population (279/27). NGC Census: (146/27). Mintage: 13,520. Numismedia Wsl. Price for problem free NGC/PCGS coin in PR66: $280. (#3344)

7209 **1960 DDO, Large Over Small Date PR66 Red PCGS.** FS-101 (FS-025). PCGS Population (21/61). NGC Census: (9/25). (#3410)

7210 **1960 DDO, Small Over Large Date PR66 Red PCGS.** FS-102 (FS-024). PCGS Population (42/54). NGC Census: (12/32). (#3413)

7211 **1970-S Small Date PR68 Cameo NGC.** NGC Census: (12/1). PCGS Population (36/1). Numismedia Wsl. Price for problem free NGC/PCGS coin in PR68: $500. (#83426)

7212 **1970-S DDO, Large Date/Small Date PR65 Red NGC.** VP-001. NGC Census: (22/286). PCGS Population (61/336). Mintage: 2,632,810. Numismedia Wsl. Price for problem free NGC/PCGS coin in PR65: $5. (#3430)

7213 **1998-S Close AM PR68 Red Deep Cameo PCGS.** PCGS Population (10/39). NGC Census: (1/8). (#93529)

7214 **1999-S Close AM PR69 Red Deep Cameo PCGS.** PCGS Population (65/0). NGC Census: (3989/360). (#38222)

TWO CENT PIECES

7215 **1864 Large Motto MS65 Brown NGC.** NGC Census: (1/0). PCGS Population (41/2). Mintage: 19,847,500. Numismedia Wsl. Price for problem free NGC/PCGS coin in MS65: $330. (#3576)

7216 **1864 Large Motto MS64 Red and Brown PCGS.** PCGS Population (851/285). NGC Census: (2/4). Mintage: 19,847,500. Numismedia Wsl. Price for problem free NGC/PCGS coin in MS64: $260. (#3577)

7217 **1864 Large Motto MS64 Red and Brown PCGS.** PCGS Population (851/285). NGC Census: (2/4). Mintage: 19,847,500. Numismedia Wsl. Price for problem free NGC/PCGS coin in MS64: $260. (#3577)

7218 **1864 Large Motto MS65 Red and Brown NGC.** NGC Census: (4/0). PCGS Population (275/10). Mintage: 19,847,500. Numismedia Wsl. Price for problem free NGC/PCGS coin in MS65: $450. (#3577)

7219 **1866 MS64 Brown NGC.** NGC Census: (56/38). PCGS Population (30/9). Mintage: 3,177,000. Numismedia Wsl. Price for problem free NGC/PCGS coin in MS64: $210. (#3588)

7220 **1867 MS63 Brown NGC.** NGC Census: (47/75). PCGS Population (49/30). Mintage: 2,938,750. Numismedia Wsl. Price for problem free NGC/PCGS coin in MS63: $160. (#3591)

7221 **1869-18/18 VF25 NCS.** FS-004. NGC Census: (1/167). PCGS Population (2/157). Mintage: 1,546,500. Numismedia Wsl. Price for problem free NGC/PCGS coin in VF25: $34. (#3603)

7222 **1871 MS64 Brown NGC.** NGC Census: (68/27). PCGS Population (42/4). Mintage: 721,100. Numismedia Wsl. Price for problem free NGC/PCGS coin in MS64: $480. (#3609)

7223 **1872 VG10 PCGS.** PCGS Population (7/200). NGC Census: (5/98). Mintage: 64,000. Numismedia Wsl. Price for problem free NGC/PCGS coin in VG10: $358. (#3612)

PROOF TWO CENT PIECES

7224 **1866 PR63 Red and Brown PCGS.** PCGS Population (23/112). NGC Census: (4/77). Mintage: 725. Numismedia Wsl. Price for problem free NGC/PCGS coin in PR63: $510. (#3631)

7225 **1871 Doubled Die Obverse PR64 Brown PCGS.** PCGS Population (16/9). NGC Census: (13/24). Mintage: 960. Numismedia Wsl. Price for problem free NGC/PCGS coin in PR64: $440. (#3645)

THREE CENT SILVER

7226 **1852 MS63 PCGS.** PCGS Population (328/605). NGC Census: (245/715). Mintage: 18,663,500. Numismedia Wsl. Price for problem free NGC/PCGS coin in MS63: $235. (#3666)

7227 **1859 MS63 NGC.** NGC Census: (54/136). PCGS Population (74/116). Mintage: 364,200. Numismedia Wsl. Price for problem free NGC/PCGS coin in MS63: $340. (#3677)

7228 **1860 MS64 NGC.** NGC Census: (67/24). PCGS Population (67/34). Mintage: 286,000. Numismedia Wsl. Price for problem free NGC/PCGS coin in MS64: $420. (#3678)

7229 **1861 MS63 NGC.** NGC Census: (108/397). PCGS Population (148/340). Mintage: 497,000. Numismedia Wsl. Price for problem free NGC/PCGS coin in MS63: $250. (#3679)

7230 **1861 MS63 NGC.** NGC Census: (108/399). PCGS Population (148/340). Mintage: 497,000. Numismedia Wsl. Price for problem free NGC/PCGS coin in MS63: $250. (#3679)

7231 **1861 MS63 PCGS.** PCGS Population (148/340). NGC Census: (108/397). Mintage: 497,000. Numismedia Wsl. Price for problem free NGC/PCGS coin in MS63: $250. (#3679)

7232 **1862 MS64 PCGS.** PCGS Population (252/306). NGC Census: (285/360). Mintage: 343,000. Numismedia Wsl. Price for problem free NGC/PCGS coin in MS64: $440. (#3680)

7233 **1862/1 MS63 ANACS.** NGC Census: (30/203). PCGS Population (57/236). Mintage: 343,000. Numismedia Wsl. Price for problem free NGC/PCGS coin in MS63: $350. (#3681)

PROOF THREE CENT SILVER

7234 **1864 PR63 NGC.** NGC Census: (11/120). PCGS Population (31/103). Mintage: 470. Numismedia Wsl. Price for problem free NGC/PCGS coin in PR63: $460. (#3714)

7235 **1869 PR64 PCGS.** PCGS Population (68/56). NGC Census: (49/66). Mintage: 600. Numismedia Wsl. Price for problem free NGC/PCGS coin in PR64: $750. (#3719)

THREE CENT NICKELS

7236 **1865 MS64 PCGS.** PCGS Population (443/149). NGC Census: (502/147). Mintage: 11,382,000. Numismedia Wsl. Price for problem free NGC/PCGS coin in MS64: $185. (#3731)

7237 **1871 MS65 PCGS. CAC.** PCGS Population (38/22). NGC Census: (33/10). Mintage: 603,000. Numismedia Wsl. Price for problem free NGC/PCGS coin in MS65: $680. (#3737)

PROOF THREE CENT NICKELS

7238 **1880 PR64 NGC.** NGC Census: (181/587). PCGS Population (311/600). Mintage: 3,955. Numismedia Wsl. Price for problem free NGC/PCGS coin in PR64: $345. (#3776)

7239 **1882 PR66 Cameo NGC.** NGC Census: (41/25). PCGS Population (62/59). (#83778)

7240 **1887/6 PR66 NGC.** NGC Census: (80/4). PCGS Population (54/3). Mintage: 2,900. Numismedia Wsl. Price for problem free NGC/PCGS coin in PR66: $885. (#3784)

7241 **1888 PR65 NGC.** NGC Census: (360/179). PCGS Population (404/189). Mintage: 4,582. Numismedia Wsl. Price for problem free NGC/PCGS coin in PR65: $490. (#3785)

7242 **1889 PR65 PCGS. CAC.** PCGS Population (389/302). NGC Census: (368/256). Mintage: 3,436. Numismedia Wsl. Price for problem free NGC/PCGS coin in PR65: $490. (#3786)

SHIELD NICKELS

7243 **1866 Rays MS64 PCGS. CAC.** PCGS Population (404/152). NGC Census: (505/181). Mintage: 14,742,500. Numismedia Wsl. Price for problem free NGC/PCGS coin in MS64: $620. (#3790)

7244 **1867 Rays AU50 PCGS.** PCGS Population (10/421). NGC Census: (5/428). Mintage: 2,019,000. Numismedia Wsl. Price for problem free NGC/PCGS coin in AU50: $210. (#3791)

7245 **1867 Rays MS63 NGC.** NGC Census: (71/231). PCGS Population (114/161). Mintage: 2,019,000. Numismedia Wsl. Price for problem free NGC/PCGS coin in MS63: $520. (#3791)

7246 **1879 Fine 12 NGC.** NGC Census: (2/60). PCGS Population (0/107). Mintage: 25,900. Numismedia Wsl. Price for problem free NGC/PCGS coin in Fine 12: $492. (#3808)

7247 **1881—Cleaned—ANACS. VG8 Details.** NGC Census: (1/115). PCGS Population (6/166). Mintage: 68,800. Numismedia Wsl. Price for problem free NGC/PCGS coin in VG8 : $285. (#3811)

7248 **1882 MS65 PCGS.** PCGS Population (173/74). NGC Census: (162/59). Mintage: 11,476,000. Numismedia Wsl. Price for problem free NGC/PCGS coin in MS65: $525. (#3812)

7249 **1883 MS64 PCGS.** PCGS Population (463/332). NGC Census: (393/370). Mintage: 1,456,919. Numismedia Wsl. Price for problem free NGC/PCGS coin in MS64: $240. (#3813)

PROOF SHIELD NICKELS

7250 **1880 PR62 NGC.** NGC Census: (21/618). PCGS Population (28/844). Mintage: 3,955. Numismedia Wsl. Price for problem free NGC/PCGS coin in PR62: $265. (#3835)

7251 **1880 PR63 PCGS.** PCGS Population (87/759). NGC Census: (54/567). Mintage: 3,955. Numismedia Wsl. Price for problem free NGC/PCGS coin in PR63: $300. (#3835)

7252 **1881 PR65 PCGS.** PCGS Population (273/164). NGC Census: (227/194). Mintage: 3,575. Numismedia Wsl. Price for problem free NGC/PCGS coin in PR65: $565. (#3836)

7253 **1882 PR66 NGC.** NGC Census: (214/37). PCGS Population (217/38). Mintage: 3,100. Numismedia Wsl. Price for problem free NGC/PCGS coin in PR66: $735. (#3837)

LIBERTY NICKELS

7254 **1883 No Cents MS66 NGC. CAC.** NGC Census: (428/52). PCGS Population (341/15). Mintage: 5,479,519. Numismedia Wsl. Price for problem free NGC/PCGS coin in MS66: $380. (#3841)

7255 **1886 XF40 PCGS.** PCGS Population (23/357). NGC Census: (8/237). Mintage: 3,330,290. Numismedia Wsl. Price for problem free NGC/PCGS coin in XF40: $590. (#3847)

7256 **1887 MS65 PCGS.** PCGS Population (88/15). NGC Census: (71/17). Mintage: 15,263,652. Numismedia Wsl. Price for problem free NGC/PCGS coin in MS65: $825. (#3848)

7257 **1888 MS64 ANACS.** NGC Census: (101/58). PCGS Population (120/52). Mintage: 10,720,483. Numismedia Wsl. Price for problem free NGC/PCGS coin in MS64: $450. (#3849)

7258 **1890 MS64 PCGS.** PCGS Population (146/53). NGC Census: (106/49). Mintage: 16,259,272. Numismedia Wsl. Price for problem free NGC/PCGS coin in MS64: $320. (#3851)

7259 **1891 MS64 PCGS.** PCGS Population (160/80). NGC Census: (131/80). Mintage: 16,834,350. Numismedia Wsl. Price for problem free NGC/PCGS coin in MS64: $285. (#3852)

7260 **1900 MS64 PCGS.** PCGS Population (301/185). NGC Census: (280/190). Mintage: 27,255,996. Numismedia Wsl. Price for problem free NGC/PCGS coin in MS64: $175. (#3861)

7261 **1901 MS64 PCGS.** PCGS Population (276/198). NGC Census: (242/194). Mintage: 26,480,212. Numismedia Wsl. Price for problem free NGC/PCGS coin in MS64: $170. (#3862)

7262 **1904 MS65 PCGS.** PCGS Population (164/69). NGC Census: (120/35). Mintage: 21,404,984. Numismedia Wsl. Price for problem free NGC/PCGS coin in MS65: $420. (#3865)

7263 **1905 MS64 PCGS.** PCGS Population (386/271). NGC Census: (261/192). Mintage: 29,827,276. Numismedia Wsl. Price for problem free NGC/PCGS coin in MS64: $170. (#3866)

7264 **1907 MS65 PCGS. CAC.** PCGS Population (75/26). NGC Census: (71/12). Mintage: 39,214,800. Numismedia Wsl. Price for problem free NGC/PCGS coin in MS65: $610. (#3868)

7265 **1911 MS65 PCGS.** PCGS Population (199/35). NGC Census: (163/24). Mintage: 39,559,372. Numismedia Wsl. Price for problem free NGC/PCGS coin in MS65: $410. (#3872)

7266 **1912-D MS63 PCGS.** PCGS Population (175/431). NGC Census: (133/395). Mintage: 8,474,000. Numismedia Wsl. Price for problem free NGC/PCGS coin in MS63: $340. (#3874)

PROOF LIBERTY NICKELS

7267 **1883 No Cents PR64 ANACS.** NGC Census: (252/363). PCGS Population (331/396). Mintage: 5,219. Numismedia Wsl. Price for problem free NGC/PCGS coin in PR64: $330. (#3878)

7268 **1883 With Cents PR64 PCGS.** PCGS Population (285/212). NGC Census: (200/248). Mintage: 6,783. Numismedia Wsl. Price for problem free NGC/PCGS coin in PR64: $280. (#3881)

7269 **1884 PR63 PCGS.** PCGS Population (119/551). NGC Census: (62/485). Mintage: 3,942. Numismedia Wsl. Price for problem free NGC/PCGS coin in PR63: $200. (#3882)

7270 **1884 PR65 Cameo NGC.** NGC Census: (36/45). PCGS Population (37/31). (#83882)

7271 **1886 PR66 NGC.** NGC Census: (119/19). PCGS Population (70/17). Mintage: 4,290. Numismedia Wsl. Price for problem free NGC/PCGS coin in PR66: $965. (#3884)

7272 **1891 PR66 Cameo NGC.** NGC Census: (26/4). PCGS Population (7/1). (#83889)

7273 **1896 PR64 PCGS.** PCGS Population (200/92). NGC Census: (134/139). Mintage: 1,862. Numismedia Wsl. Price for problem free NGC/PCGS coin in PR64: $280. (#3894)

7274 **1897 PR64 PCGS.** PCGS Population (176/173). NGC Census: (144/178). Mintage: 1,938. Numismedia Wsl. Price for problem free NGC/PCGS coin in PR64: $300. (#3895)

7275 **1909 PR66 NGC.** NGC Census: (266/95). PCGS Population (197/35). Mintage: 4,763. Numismedia Wsl. Price for problem free NGC/PCGS coin in PR66: $665. (#3907)

BUFFALO NICKELS

7276 **1913 Type One MS65 NGC.** NGC Census: (2134/1431). PCGS Population (2944/2059). Mintage: 30,993,520. Numismedia Wsl. Price for problem free NGC/PCGS coin in MS65: $120. (#3915)

7277 **1913 Type One MS66 NGC.** NGC Census: (1143/288). PCGS Population (1652/407). Mintage: 30,993,520. Numismedia Wsl. Price for problem free NGC/PCGS coin in MS66: $190. (#3915)

7278 **1913-S Type One MS65 PCGS.** PCGS Population (292/126). NGC Census: (210/64). Mintage: 2,105,000. Numismedia Wsl. Price for problem free NGC/PCGS coin in MS65: $510. (#3917)

7279 **1913-S Type Two AU50 PCGS.** PCGS Population (64/1285). NGC Census: (6/877). Mintage: 1,209,000. Numismedia Wsl. Price for problem free NGC/PCGS coin in AU50: $475. (#3923)

7280 **1914-D MS62 NGC.** NGC Census: (103/427). PCGS Population (60/733). Mintage: 3,912,000. Numismedia Wsl. Price for problem free NGC/PCGS coin in MS62: $400. (#3925)

7281 **1914-D MS64 PCGS.** PCGS Population (315/191). NGC Census: (213/79). Mintage: 3,912,000. Numismedia Wsl. Price for problem free NGC/PCGS coin in MS64: $635. (#3925)

7282 **1917 MS64 PCGS.** PCGS Population (477/407). NGC Census: (329/170). Mintage: 51,424,020. Numismedia Wsl. Price for problem free NGC/PCGS coin in MS64: $185. (#3934)

7283 **1923 MS64 PCGS.** PCGS Population (484/405). NGC Census: (309/212). Mintage: 35,715,000. Numismedia Wsl. Price for problem free NGC/PCGS coin in MS64: $175. (#3949)

7284 **1925 MS65 PCGS. CAC.** PCGS Population (456/185). NGC Census: (182/89). Mintage: 35,565,100. Numismedia Wsl. Price for problem free NGC/PCGS coin in MS65: $350. (#3954)

7285 **1925 MS65 PCGS.** PCGS Population (456/185). NGC Census: (182/89). Mintage: 35,565,100. Numismedia Wsl. Price for problem free NGC/PCGS coin in MS65: $350. (#3954)

7286 **1925 MS65 PCGS.** PCGS Population (456/185). NGC Census: (182/89). Mintage: 35,565,100. Numismedia Wsl. Price for problem free NGC/PCGS coin in MS65: $350. (#3954)

7287 **1925 MS65 PCGS.** PCGS Population (456/185). NGC Census: (182/89). Mintage: 35,565,100. Numismedia Wsl. Price for problem free NGC/PCGS coin in MS65: $350. (#3954)

7288 **1925 MS65 PCGS.** PCGS Population (460/187). NGC Census: (182/88). Mintage: 35,565,100. Numismedia Wsl. Price for problem free NGC/PCGS coin in MS65: $350. (#3954)

7289 **1925 MS66 PCGS.** PCGS Population (178/7). NGC Census: (85/4). Mintage: 35,565,100. Numismedia Wsl. Price for problem free NGC/PCGS coin in MS66: $700. (#3954)

7290 **1925 MS66 PCGS.** PCGS Population (178/7). NGC Census: (85/4). Mintage: 35,565,100. Numismedia Wsl. Price for problem free NGC/PCGS coin in MS66: $700. (#3954)

7291 **1926-S VF20 PCGS.** PCGS Population (185/809). NGC Census: (148/739). Mintage: 970,000. Numismedia Wsl. Price for problem free NGC/PCGS coin in VF20: $240. (#3959)

7292 **1927 MS65 PCGS.** PCGS Population (636/263). NGC Census: (283/84). Mintage: 37,981,000. Numismedia Wsl. Price for problem free NGC/PCGS coin in MS65: $225. (#3960)

7293 **1927-S AU58 PCGS.** PCGS Population (95/518). NGC Census: (69/325). Mintage: 3,430,000. Numismedia Wsl. Price for problem free NGC/PCGS coin in AU58: $340. (#3962)

7294 **1929-S MS66 NGC.** NGC Census: (55/5). PCGS Population (169/5). Mintage: 7,754,000. Numismedia Wsl. Price for problem free NGC/PCGS coin in MS66: $575. (#3968)

7295 **1930-S MS65 NGC.** NGC Census: (170/26). PCGS Population (404/131). Mintage: 5,435,000. Numismedia Wsl. Price for problem free NGC/PCGS coin in MS65: $325. (#3970)

7296 **1934-D MS64 PCGS.** PCGS Population (852/361). NGC Census: (585/106). Mintage: 7,480,000. Numismedia Wsl. Price for problem free NGC/PCGS coin in MS64: $185. (#3973)

7297 **1935 MS66 PCGS.** PCGS Population (590/108). NGC Census: (286/33). Mintage: 58,264,000. Numismedia Wsl. Price for problem free NGC/PCGS coin in MS66: $165. (#3974)

7298 **1935 Doubled Die Reverse VF35 NGC.** FS-018. NGC Census: (0/0). PCGS Population (9/40). (#93974)

7299 **1937 MS67 PCGS. CAC.** PCGS Population (298/4). NGC Census: (342/6). Mintage: 79,485,768. Numismedia Wsl. Price for problem free NGC/PCGS coin in MS67: $240. (#3980)

7300 **1937-D Three-Legged VG10 PCGS.** PCGS Population (40/5327). NGC Census: (18/4608). Mintage: 17,826,000. Numismedia Wsl. Price for problem free NGC/PCGS coin in VG10: $564. (#3982)

7301 **1937-D Three-Legged XF40 PCGS.** PCGS Population (425/3699). NGC Census: (186/3799). Mintage: 17,826,000. Numismedia Wsl. Price for problem free NGC/PCGS coin in XF40: $910. (#3982)

7302 **1937-D Three-Legged XF40 NGC.** NGC Census: (186/3799). PCGS Population (425/3699). Mintage: 17,826,000. Numismedia Wsl. Price for problem free NGC/PCGS coin in XF40: $910. (#3982)

7303 **1937-D Three-Legged XF40 PCGS.** PCGS Population (425/3703). NGC Census: (186/3802). Mintage: 17,826,000. Numismedia Wsl. Price for problem free NGC/PCGS coin in XF40: $910. (#3982)

7304 **1937-D Three-Legged—Cleaned—ANACS. XF45 Details.** NGC Census: (341/3453). PCGS Population (621/3061). Mintage: 17,826,000. Numismedia Wsl. Price for problem free NGC/PCGS coin in XF45: $964. (#3982)

7305 **1938-D/D Buffalo MS67 PCGS.** PCGS Population (58/0). NGC Census: (0/0). Mintage: 7,020,000. (#93984)

7306 **1938-D/S MS66 PCGS.** PCGS Population (1439/172). NGC Census: (758/89). Mintage: 7,020,000. Numismedia Wsl. Price for problem free NGC/PCGS coin in MS66: $160. (#3985)

JEFFERSON NICKELS

7307 **1938 MS66 Full Steps PCGS.** PCGS Population (138/8). NGC Census: (12/3). (#84000)

7308 **1938-S MS66 Full Steps PCGS.** PCGS Population (52/4). NGC Census: (2/0). (#84002)

7309 **1939 Doubled MONTICELLO MS64 PCGS.** PCGS Population (38/85). NGC Census: (15/23). (#4004)

7310 **1939-D Reverse of 1938 MS66 NGC.** NGC Census: (203/275). PCGS Population (488/67). Mintage: 3,514,000. Numismedia Wsl. Price for problem free NGC/PCGS coin in MS66: $87. (#4005)

7311 **1940 MS67 Full Steps PCGS.** PCGS Population (32/0). NGC Census: (22/0). (#84007)

7312 **1941-S MS66 Full Steps PCGS.** Ex:Omaha Bank Hoard. PCGS Population (46/4). NGC Census: (6/1). (#84012)

7313 **1942 Type One, DDO MS65 PCGS.** FS-026. PCGS Population (128/231). NGC Census: (128/239). Mintage: 49,818,600. Numismedia Wsl. Price for problem free NGC/PCGS coin in MS65: $24. (#4013)

7314 **1942 Type One MS66 Full Steps PCGS.** PCGS Population (36/2). NGC Census: (36/3). (#84013)

7315 **1942-D MS67 Full Steps PCGS.** PCGS Population (45/0). NGC Census: (14/0). (#84014)

7316 **1942-P Type 2 MS66 PCGS.** Set includes 1942-S and 1943 to 1945 PDS Set. all graded MS66 PCGS. (Total: 11 coins)

7317 **1942-P Type Two MS67 Full Steps PCGS.** PCGS Population (30/0). NGC Census: (27/0). (#84016)

7318 **1943-P MS67 Full Steps PCGS.** PCGS Population (38/1). NGC Census: (21/0). (#84018)

7319 **1943-P Doubled Die Obverse MS66 NGC.** VP-002, FS-106. NGC Census: (0/0). PCGS Population (44/0). (#4174)

7320 **1943-S MS67 Full Steps PCGS.** PCGS Population (55/0). NGC Census: (16/0). (#84021)

7321 **1945-P MS67 PCGS.** Ex:Benson. PCGS Population (35/0). NGC Census: (326/2). Mintage: 119,408,096. Numismedia Wsl. Price for problem free NGC/PCGS coin in MS67: $170. (#4025)

7322 **1945-P MS66 Full Steps PCGS.** PCGS Population (93/5). NGC Census: (27/3). (#84025)

7323 **1945-P Doubled Die Reverse MS65 PCGS.** PCGS Population (56/10). NGC Census: (5/6). (#4173)

7324 **1945-D MS67 Full Steps PCGS.** PCGS Population (68/0). NGC Census: (38/0). (#84026)

7325 **1946-S MS66 Full Steps PCGS.** PCGS Population (36/1). NGC Census: (5/0). (#84030)

7326 **1947 MS66 Full Steps PCGS.** PCGS Population (44/0). NGC Census: (7/0). (#84031)

7327 **1947-S MS66 Full Steps PCGS.** PCGS Population (44/1). NGC Census: (7/0). (#84033)

7328 **1949-D/S MS65 PCGS.** PCGS Population (178/47). NGC Census: (16/12). Mintage: 36,498,000. Numismedia Wsl. Price for problem free NGC/PCGS coin in MS65: $360. (#4039)

7329 **1949-D/S MS66 PCGS.** PCGS Population (46/1). NGC Census: (12/0). Mintage: 36,498,000. Numismedia Wsl. Price for problem free NGC/PCGS coin in MS66: $800. (#4039)

7330 **1950 MS66 Full Steps PCGS.** PCGS Population (29/2). NGC Census: (5/2). (#84041)

7331 **1951-D MS66 Full Steps PCGS.** PCGS Population (39/0). NGC Census: (4/1). (#84044)

7332 **1952 MS65 Full Steps PCGS.** PCGS Population (9/3). NGC Census: (0/2). (#84046)

7333 **1952-D MS66 Full Steps PCGS.** PCGS Population (27/0). NGC Census: (4/1). (#84047)

7334 **1952-S MS65 Full Steps PCGS.** PCGS Population (50/6). NGC Census: (4/2). (#84048)

7335 **1953-D MS66 Full Steps PCGS.** PCGS Population (12/0). NGC Census: (4/0). (#84050)

7336 **1954 MS65 Full Steps PCGS.** PCGS Population (38/3). NGC Census: (7/5). (#84052)

7337 **1954-D MS65 Full Steps PCGS.** PCGS Population (22/1). NGC Census: (0/0). (#84053)

7338 **1954-S/D MS65 PCGS.** PCGS Population (84/3). NGC Census: (44/32). Mintage: 29,384,000. Numismedia Wsl. Price for problem free NGC/PCGS coin in MS65: $220. (#4055)

7339 **1955 MS65 Full Steps PCGS.** PCGS Population (30/2). NGC Census: (1/2). (#84056)

7340 **1955-D MS64 Full Steps PCGS.** PCGS Population (18/5). NGC Census: (0/0). (#84057)

7341 **1955-D/S MS65 PCGS.** PCGS Population (50/2). NGC Census: (41/6). Mintage: 74,464,096. Numismedia Wsl. Price for problem free NGC/PCGS coin in MS65: $320. (#4058)

7342 **1956 MS66 Full Steps PCGS.** PCGS Population (42/1). NGC Census: (27/2). (#84059)

7343 **1956-D MS65 Full Steps PCGS.** PCGS Population (21/6). NGC Census: (0/2). (#84060)

7344 **1958 MS65 Full Steps PCGS.** PCGS Population (15/0). NGC Census: (5/3). (#84063)

7345 **1960-D MS66 PCGS.** PCGS Population (26/0). NGC Census: (105/10). Mintage: 192,582,176. Numismedia Wsl. Price for problem free NGC/PCGS coin in MS66: $24. (#4068)

7346 **1962 MS66 Full Steps PCGS.** PCGS Population (26/0). NGC Census: (11/2). (#84071)

7347 **1962-D MS64 Full Steps PCGS.** PCGS Population (38/1). NGC Census: (1/2). (#84072)

7348 **1964 MS65 Full Steps PCGS.** PCGS Population (36/5). NGC Census: (1/3). (#84075)

7349 **1964-D MS65 Full Steps PCGS.** PCGS Population (25/3). NGC Census: (4/5). (#84076)

7350 **1969-S MS66 PCGS.** PCGS Population (36/1). NGC Census: (28/2). Mintage: 123,009,632. Numismedia Wsl. Price for problem free NGC/PCGS coin in MS66: $300. (#4083)

7351 **1969-S MS66 PCGS.** PCGS Population (36/1). NGC Census: (28/2). Mintage: 123,009,632. Numismedia Wsl. Price for problem free NGC/PCGS coin in MS66: $300. (#4083)

7352 **1970-D MS66 PCGS.** PCGS Population (40/0). NGC Census: (65/8). Mintage: 515,485,376. Numismedia Wsl. Price for problem free NGC/PCGS coin in MS66: $280. (#4084)

7353 **1970-S MS65 Full Steps PCGS.** PCGS Population (17/2). NGC Census: (0/1). (#84085)

7354 **1971-D MS67 Full Steps PCGS.** PCGS Population (12/0). NGC Census: (74/1). (#84087)

7355 **1972 MS66 Full Steps PCGS.** PCGS Population (24/1). NGC Census: (2/0). (#84088)

7356 **1972-D MS66 Full Steps PCGS.** PCGS Population (21/1). NGC Census: (5/0). (#84089)

7357 **1974 MS65 Full Steps PCGS.** PCGS Population (36/12). NGC Census: (1/3). (#84092)

7358 **1974-D MS67 Full Steps PCGS.** PCGS Population (4/0). NGC Census: (0/0). (#84093)

7359 **1975 MS66 Full Steps PCGS.** PCGS Population (23/1). NGC Census: (18/0). (#84094)

7360 **1975-D MS66 Full Steps PCGS.** PCGS Population (20/0). NGC Census: (7/0). (#84095)

7361 **1976 MS65 Full Steps PCGS.** PCGS Population (22/8). NGC Census: (0/2). (#84096)

7362 **1976-D MS66 Full Steps PCGS.** PCGS Population (22/0). NGC Census: (4/0). (#84097)

7363 **1977 MS66 Full Steps PCGS.** PCGS Population (13/0). NGC Census: (0/0). (#84098)

7364 **1977-D MS66 Full Steps PCGS.** PCGS Population (22/0). NGC Census: (5/0). (#84099)

7365 **1978 MS66 Full Steps PCGS.** PCGS Population (10/1). NGC Census: (2/1). (#84100)

7366 **1979 MS66 Full Steps PCGS.** PCGS Population (13/0). NGC Census: (0/0). (#84102)

7367 **1980-P MS66 Full Steps PCGS.** PCGS Population (25/0). NGC Census: (5/0). (#84104)

7368 **1980-D MS66 Full Steps PCGS.** PCGS Population (21/0). NGC Census: (9/0). (#84105)

7369 **1981-D MS66 Full Steps PCGS.** PCGS Population (26/0). NGC Census: (2/0). (#84107)

7370 **1982-P MS66 Full Steps PCGS.** PCGS Population (32/0). NGC Census: (3/0). (#84108)

7371 **1982-D MS66 Full Steps PCGS.** PCGS Population (24/1). NGC Census: (1/0). (#84109)

7372 **1983-P MS65 Full Steps PCGS.** PCGS Population (22/9). NGC Census: (0/0). (#84110)

7373 **1983-D MS66 Full Steps PCGS.** PCGS Population (11/0). NGC Census: (0/0). (#84111)

7374 **1986-P MS66 Full Steps PCGS.** PCGS Population (38/0). NGC Census: (37/5). (#84116)

7375 **1986-D MS66 Full Steps PCGS.** PCGS Population (19/1). NGC Census: (15/0). (#84117)

7376 **1987-P MS67 Full Steps PCGS.** PCGS Population (24/0). NGC Census: (22/0). (#84118)

7377 **1989-P MS67 Full Steps PCGS.** PCGS Population (7/1). NGC Census: (14/0). (#84122)

7378 **1989-P MS67 Full Steps PCGS.** PCGS Population (7/1). NGC Census: (14/0). (#84122)

7379 **1989-D MS66 Full Steps PCGS.** PCGS Population (27/0). NGC Census: (13/3). (#84123)

7380 **1990-D MS66 Full Steps PCGS.** PCGS Population (25/0). NGC Census: (11/2). (#84125)

7381 **1990-D MS66 Full Steps PCGS.** PCGS Population (25/0). NGC Census: (11/2). (#84125)

7382 **1991-D MS66 Full Steps PCGS.** PCGS Population (41/1). NGC Census: (10/3). (#84127)

7383 **1991-D MS66 Full Steps PCGS.** PCGS Population (41/1). NGC Census: (10/3). (#84127)

7384 **1993-D MS67 Full Steps PCGS.** PCGS Population (12/0). NGC Census: (1/0). (#84131)

7385 **1995-P MS67 Full Steps PCGS.** PCGS Population (13/0). NGC Census: (2/0). (#84136)

7386 **1996-P MS67 Full Steps PCGS.** PCGS Population (26/2). NGC Census: (0/0). (#84137)

7387 **1996-P MS67 Full Steps PCGS.** PCGS Population (26/2). NGC Census: (0/0). (#84137)

7388 **1996-D MS67 Full Steps PCGS.** PCGS Population (23/0). NGC Census: (0/0). (#84138)

7389 **1997-P MS67 Full Steps PCGS.** PCGS Population (9/3). NGC Census: (0/0). (#84139)

7390 **1998-D MS66 Full Steps PCGS.** PCGS Population (11/0). NGC Census: (0/0). (#84143)

7391 **1999-P MS67 Full Steps PCGS.** PCGS Population (19/1). NGC Census: (1/0). (#84144)

7392 **2000-P MS67 Full Steps PCGS.** PCGS Population (9/0). NGC Census: (1/0). (#84146)

7393 **2004-P Peace Medal MS67 PCGS.** PCGS Population (66/7). NGC Census: (278/62). Numismedia Wsl. Price for problem free NGC/PCGS coin in MS67: $35. (#4154)

7394 **2004-D Peace Medal MS68 PCGS.** PCGS Population (17/0). NGC Census: (0/0). (#4155)

7395 **2004-P Keel Boat MS68 PCGS.** PCGS Population (22/0). NGC Census: (0/0). Numismedia Wsl. Price for problem free NGC/PCGS coin in MS68: $200. (#4156)

7396 **2005-D Speared Bison MS66 PCGS.** PCGS Population (19/1). NGC Census: (0/0). (#84159)

7397 **2005-D Bison Satin MS69 PCGS.** PCGS Population (12/0). NGC Census: (0/0). Numismedia Wsl. Price for problem free NGC/PCGS coin in MS69: $625. (#94159)

SMS JEFFERSON NICKELS

7398 **1966 SMS MS68 PCGS.** PCGS Population (6/0). NGC Census: (92/0). Mintage: 2,260,000. Numismedia Wsl. Price for problem free NGC/PCGS coin in MS68: $125. (#4198)

7399 **1966 SMS MS65 Deep Cameo PCGS.** PCGS Population (5/31). NGC Census: (2/20). (#94198)

7400 **1967 SMS MS68 PCGS.** PCGS Population (6/0). NGC Census: (97/1). Mintage: 1,860,000. Numismedia Wsl. Price for problem free NGC/PCGS coin in MS68: $200. (#4199)

7401 **1967 SMS MS66 Deep Cameo PCGS.** PCGS Population (42/27). NGC Census: (0/0). (#94199)

7402 **1967 SMS MS67 Deep Cameo PCGS.** PCGS Population (26/1). NGC Census: (0/0). (#94199)

7403 **1997-P SMS MS70 Full Steps PCGS.** PCGS Population (78). NGC Census: (88). (#84140)

PROOF JEFFERSON NICKELS

7404 **1938 PR67 PCGS.** PCGS Population (211/11). NGC Census: (171/10). Mintage: 19,365. Numismedia Wsl. Price for problem free NGC/PCGS coin in PR67: $200. (#4175)

7405 **1939 Reverse of 1938 PR67 PCGS.** PCGS Population (117/7). NGC Census: (66/3). Mintage: 12,535. Numismedia Wsl. Price for problem free NGC/PCGS coin in PR67: $370. (#4176)

7406 **1940 Reverse of 1940 PR67 PCGS.** PCGS Population (107/2). NGC Census: (49/0). Mintage: 14,158. Numismedia Wsl. Price for problem free NGC/PCGS coin in PR67: $260. (#4177)

7407 **1940 Reverse of 1940 PR67 PCGS.** PCGS Population (107/2). NGC Census: (49/0). Mintage: 14,158. Numismedia Wsl. Price for problem free NGC/PCGS coin in PR67: $260. (#4177)

7408 **1940 Reverse of 1940 PR65 Cameo PCGS.** PCGS Population (6/0). NGC Census: (0/0). (#84177)

7409 **1940 Reverse of 1938 PR65 PCGS.** PCGS Population (22/43). NGC Census: (20/28). Numismedia Wsl. Price for problem free NGC/PCGS coin in PR65: $320. (#94177)

7410 **1940 Reverse of 1938 PR66 PCGS.** PCGS Population (28/16). NGC Census: (19/9). Numismedia Wsl. Price for problem free NGC/PCGS coin in PR66: $740. (#94177)

7411 **1941 PR67 PCGS.** Ex:Ed Wielawski. PCGS Population (79/3). NGC Census: (62/0). Mintage: 18,720. Numismedia Wsl. Price for problem free NGC/PCGS coin in PR67: $350. (#4178)

7412 **1942-P Type Two PR67 PCGS.** PCGS Population (306/12). NGC Census: (336/20). Mintage: 27,600. Numismedia Wsl. Price for problem free NGC/PCGS coin in PR67: $185. (#4180)

7413 **1950 PR67 Cameo PCGS.** PCGS Population (35/0). NGC Census: (49/6). Numismedia Wsl. Price for problem free NGC/PCGS coin in PR67: $535. (#84182)

7414 **1951 DDO PR67 PCGS.** FS-101 (FS-032.5). PCGS Population (258/13). NGC Census: (305/135). Mintage: 57,500. Numismedia Wsl. Price for problem free NGC/PCGS coin in PR67: $78. (#4183)

7415 **1951 DDO PR66 Cameo PCGS.** FS-101 (FS-032.5). PCGS Population (103/87). NGC Census: (60/204). Numismedia Wsl. Price for problem free NGC/PCGS coin in PR66: $93. (#84183)

7416 **1953 DDO PR67 PCGS.** FS-101 (FS-032.7). PCGS Population (607/147). NGC Census: (333/375). Mintage: 128,800. Numismedia Wsl. Price for problem free NGC/PCGS coin in PR67: $41. (#4185)

7417 **1953 DDO PR67 Cameo PCGS.** FS-101 (FS-032.7). PCGS Population (145/32). NGC Census: (2/10). Numismedia Wsl. Price for problem free NGC/PCGS coin in PR67: $140. (#84185)

7418 **1953 PR68 Cameo PCGS.** PCGS Population (31/1). NGC Census: (9/1). Numismedia Wsl. Price for problem free NGC/PCGS coin in PR68: $600. (#84185)

7419 **1954 PR68 Cameo PCGS.** PCGS Population (69/4). NGC Census: (94/48). Numismedia Wsl. Price for problem free NGC/PCGS coin in PR68: $180. (#84186)

7420 **1954 PR68 Cameo PCGS.** PCGS Population (69/4). NGC Census: (94/48). Numismedia Wsl. Price for problem free NGC/PCGS coin in PR68: $180. (#84186)

7421 **1955 TDR PR68 PCGS.** FS-801 (FS-035). PCGS Population (184/5). NGC Census: (790/79). Mintage: 378,200. Numismedia Wsl. Price for problem free NGC/PCGS coin in PR68: $41. (#4187)

7422 **1955 PR67 Deep Cameo PCGS.** PCGS Population (41/22). NGC Census: (11/23). Numismedia Wsl. Price for problem free NGC/PCGS coin in PR67: $260. (#94187)

7423 **1956 PR69 PCGS.** PCGS Population (6/0). NGC Census: (90/0). Mintage: 669,384. Numismedia Wsl. Price for problem free NGC/PCGS coin in PR69: $60. (#4188)

7424 **1956 PR68 Cameo PCGS.** PCGS Population (33/2). NGC Census: (70/28). Numismedia Wsl. Price for problem free NGC/PCGS coin in PR68: $185. (#84188)

7425 **1957 PR68 Cameo PCGS.** PCGS Population (16/0). NGC Census: (47/19). Numismedia Wsl. Price for problem free NGC/PCGS coin in PR68: $400. (#84189)

7426 **1959 PR67 Deep Cameo PCGS.** PCGS Population (10/11). NGC Census: (3/3). Numismedia Wsl. Price for problem free NGC/PCGS coin in PR67: $525. (#94191)

7427 **1960 PR68 Deep Cameo PCGS.** PCGS Population (48/4). NGC Census: (16/6). Numismedia Wsl. Price for problem free NGC/PCGS coin in PR68: $340. (#94192)

7428 **1960 PR68 Deep Cameo PCGS.** PCGS Population (48/4). NGC Census: (16/6). Numismedia Wsl. Price for problem free NGC/PCGS coin in PR68: $340. (#94192)

7429 **1961 PR69 Ultra Cameo NGC.** NGC Census: (6/0). PCGS Population (11/0). Numismedia Wsl. Price for problem free NGC/PCGS coin in PR69: $625. (#94193)

7430 **1962 PR69 Deep Cameo PCGS.** PCGS Population (53/0). NGC Census: (22/0). Numismedia Wsl. Price for problem free NGC/PCGS coin in PR69: $400. (#94194)

7431 **1962 PR69 Deep Cameo PCGS.** PCGS Population (54/0). NGC Census: (22/0). Numismedia Wsl. Price for problem free NGC/PCGS coin in PR69: $400. (#94194)

7432 **1963 PR69 Deep Cameo PCGS.** PCGS Population (69/1). NGC Census: (42/0). Numismedia Wsl. Price for problem free NGC/PCGS coin in PR69: $210. (#94195)

7433 **1963 PR69 Deep Cameo PCGS.** PCGS Population (70/1). NGC Census: (43/0). Numismedia Wsl. Price for problem free NGC/PCGS coin in PR69: $210. (#94195)

7434 **1964 PR69 Deep Cameo PCGS.** PCGS Population (187/0). NGC Census: (0/0). Numismedia Wsl. Price for problem free NGC/PCGS coin in PR69: $110. (#94196)

7435 **1964 PR69 Deep Cameo PCGS.** PCGS Population (188/0). NGC Census: (0/0). Numismedia Wsl. Price for problem free NGC/PCGS coin in PR69: $110. (#94196)

7436 **1964 PR69 Deep Cameo PCGS.** PCGS Population (188/0). NGC Census: (0/0). Numismedia Wsl. Price for problem free NGC/PCGS coin in PR69: $110. (#94196)

7437 **1969-S PR69 Deep Cameo PCGS.** PCGS Population (69/0). NGC Census: (51/0). Numismedia Wsl. Price for problem free NGC/PCGS coin in PR69: $260. (#94201)

7438 **1970-S PR69 Deep Cameo PCGS.** PCGS Population (61/0). NGC Census: (40/0). Numismedia Wsl. Price for problem free NGC/PCGS coin in PR69: $255. (#94202)

7439 **1971-S PR69 Deep Cameo PCGS.** PCGS Population (53/0). NGC Census: (23/0). Numismedia Wsl. Price for problem free NGC/PCGS coin in PR69: $480. (#94203)

7440 **1971-S PR69 Deep Cameo PCGS.** PCGS Population (53/0). NGC Census: (23/0). Numismedia Wsl. Price for problem free NGC/PCGS coin in PR69: $480. (#94203)

7441 **1971-S PR69 Deep Cameo PCGS.** PCGS Population (53/0). NGC Census: (23/0). Numismedia Wsl. Price for problem free NGC/PCGS coin in PR69: $480. (#94203)

7442 **1978-S PR70 Deep Cameo PCGS.** PCGS Population (41). NGC Census: (3). Numismedia Wsl. Price for problem free NGC/PCGS coin in PR70: $320. (#94211)

7443 **1979-S Type One PR70 Deep Cameo PCGS.** PCGS Population (29). NGC Census: (0). Numismedia Wsl. Price for problem free NGC/PCGS coin in PR70: $500. (#94212)

7444 **1980-S PR70 Deep Cameo PCGS.** PCGS Population (28). NGC Census: (1). Numismedia Wsl. Price for problem free NGC/PCGS coin in PR70: $580. (#94214)

7445 **1981-S Type Two PR70 Deep Cameo PCGS.** PCGS Population (12). NGC Census: (0). Numismedia Wsl. Price for problem free NGC/PCGS coin in PR70: $500. (#94216)

7446 **1985-S PR70 Deep Cameo PCGS.** PCGS Population (25). NGC Census: (5). Numismedia Wsl. Price for problem free NGC/PCGS coin in PR70: $420. (#94220)

7447 **1988-S PR70 Deep Cameo PCGS.** PCGS Population (31). NGC Census: (8). Numismedia Wsl. Price for problem free NGC/PCGS coin in PR70: $250. (#94223)

BUST HALF DIMES

7448 **1829 AU58 NGC. CAC.** NGC Census: (84/403). PCGS Population (83/297). Mintage: 1,230,000. Numismedia Wsl. Price for problem free NGC/PCGS coin in AU58: $270. (#4276)

7449 **1830 MS63 PCGS.** PCGS Population (91/125). NGC Census: (79/169). Mintage: 1,200,000. Numismedia Wsl. Price for problem free NGC/PCGS coin in MS63: $690. (#4277)

7450 **1832 MS63 PCGS.** PCGS Population (91/192). NGC Census: (127/289). Mintage: 965,000. Numismedia Wsl. Price for problem free NGC/PCGS coin in MS63: $750. (#4279)

7451 **1833 MS62 PCGS.** PCGS Population (57/205). NGC Census: (56/281). Mintage: 1,370,000. Numismedia Wsl. Price for problem free NGC/PCGS coin in MS62: $440. (#4280)

7452 **1835 Large Date, Large 5C MS62 ANACS.** LM-10. NGC Census: (95/389). PCGS Population (68/226). Mintage: 2,760,000. Numismedia Wsl. Price for problem free NGC/PCGS coin in MS62: $425. (#4282)

7453 **1836 Large 5C AU55 ANACS.** LM-6. NGC Census: (13/277). PCGS Population (23/181). Mintage: 1,900,000. Numismedia Wsl. Price for problem free NGC/PCGS coin in AU55: $215. (#4287)

7454 **1837 Large 5C MS61 NGC.** NGC Census: (9/93). PCGS Population (3/64). Mintage: 871,000. Numismedia Wsl. Price for problem free NGC/PCGS coin in MS61: $425. (#4289)

SEATED HALF DIMES

7455 **1838 Large Stars, No Drapery MS64 PCGS. CAC.** PCGS Population (104/76). NGC Census: (123/151). Mintage: 2,225,000. Numismedia Wsl. Price for problem free NGC/PCGS coin in MS64: $600. (#4317)

7456 **1846 Fine 12 NGC.** NGC Census: (1/28). PCGS Population (2/44). Mintage: 27,000. Numismedia Wsl. Price for problem free NGC/PCGS coin in Fine 12: $665. (#4336)

7457 **1854-O Arrows—Improperly Cleaned—NCS. Unc Details.** NGC Census: (0/55). PCGS Population (3/34). Mintage: 1,560,000. Numismedia Wsl. Price for problem free NGC/PCGS coin in MS60: $270. (#4359)

7458 **1856 MS62 NGC.** NGC Census: (31/269). PCGS Population (31/174). Mintage: 4,880,000. Numismedia Wsl. Price for problem free NGC/PCGS coin in MS62: $150. (#4363)

7459 **1857-O MS63 PCGS.** PCGS Population (24/63). NGC Census: (20/78). Mintage: 1,380,000. Numismedia Wsl. Price for problem free NGC/PCGS coin in MS63: $375. (#4366)

7460 **1864—Harshly Cleaned—NCS. XF Details.** NGC Census: (0/41). PCGS Population (0/49). Mintage: 48,000. Numismedia Wsl. Price for problem free NGC/PCGS coin in XF40: $615. (#4384)

7461 **1866—Scratches—NCS. Fine Details.** NGC Census: (0/44). PCGS Population (1/62). Mintage: 10,000. Numismedia Wsl. Price for problem free NGC/PCGS coin in Fine 12: $330. (#4388)

7462 **1867—Improperly Cleaned—NCS. VG Details.** NGC Census: (0/77). PCGS Population (0/80). Mintage: 8,000. Numismedia Wsl. Price for problem free NGC/PCGS coin in VG8 : $422. (#4390)

7463 **1868—Improperly Cleaned—NCS. AU Details.** NGC Census: (0/61). PCGS Population (2/56). Mintage: 88,600. Numismedia Wsl. Price for problem free NGC/PCGS coin in AU50: $310. (#4392)

7464 **1868—Improperly Cleaned—NCS. Unc Details.** NGC Census: (0/57). PCGS Population (0/50). Mintage: 88,600. Numismedia Wsl. Price for problem free NGC/PCGS coin in MS60: $475. (#4392)

PROOF SEATED HALF DIMES

7465 **1860 PR62 ANACS.** NGC Census: (5/90). PCGS Population (18/81). Mintage: 1,000. Numismedia Wsl. Price for problem free NGC/PCGS coin in PR62: $300. (#4443)

7466 **1861 PR63 PCGS.** PCGS Population (26/27). NGC Census: (15/62). Mintage: 1,000. Numismedia Wsl. Price for problem free NGC/PCGS coin in PR63: $500. (#4444)

EARLY DIME

7467 **1798/97 16 Stars on Reverse Good 4 ANACS.** JR-1. NGC Census: (1/43). PCGS Population (0/61). Mintage: 27,550. Numismedia Wsl. Price for problem free NGC/PCGS coin in Good 4 : $550. (#4468)

BUST DIMES

7468 **1809—Damaged—ANACS. VG8 Details.** JR-1. NGC Census: (0/33). PCGS Population (2/50). Mintage: 51,065. Numismedia Wsl. Price for problem free NGC/PCGS coin in VG8 : $220. (#4486)

7469 **1830 Medium 10C—Improperly Cleaned—NCS. Unc Details.** JR-6. NGC Census: (0/103). PCGS Population (3/93). Mintage: 510,000. Numismedia Wsl. Price for problem free NGC/PCGS coin in MS60: $625. (#4516)

7470 **1833 AU58 NGC.** NGC Census: (41/155). PCGS Population (27/102). Mintage: 485,000. Numismedia Wsl. Price for problem free NGC/PCGS coin in AU58: $485. (#4522)

7471 **1833 AU58 NGC.** NGC Census: (42/149). PCGS Population (27/103). Mintage: 485,000. Numismedia Wsl. Price for problem free NGC/PCGS coin in AU58: $485. (#4522)

7472 **1836 AU58 NGC.** NGC Census: (39/102). PCGS Population (22/80). Mintage: 1,190,000. Numismedia Wsl. Price for problem free NGC/PCGS coin in AU58: $450. (#4528)

SEATED DIMES

7473 **1839-O No Drapery AU58 NGC.** NGC Census: (13/37). PCGS Population (9/20). Mintage: 1,323,000. Numismedia Wsl. Price for problem free NGC/PCGS coin in AU58: $475. (#4572)

7474 **1844—Cleaned—ANACS. VF Details Net F15.** NGC Census: (4/35). PCGS Population (15/105). Mintage: 72,500. Numismedia Wsl. Price for problem free NGC/PCGS coin in Fine 15: $454. (#4585)

7475 **1853 Arrows MS61 NGC.** NGC Census: (33/481). PCGS Population (12/440). Mintage: 12,078,010. Numismedia Wsl. Price for problem free NGC/PCGS coin in MS61: $325. (#4603)

7476 **1855 Arrows MS63 PCGS.** PCGS Population (22/20). NGC Census: (19/35). Mintage: 2,075,000. Numismedia Wsl. Price for problem free NGC/PCGS coin in MS63: $800. (#4607)

7477 **1856 Small Date MS64 NGC.** NGC Census: (30/26). PCGS Population (22/23). Mintage: 5,780,000. Numismedia Wsl. Price for problem free NGC/PCGS coin in MS64: $810. (#4609)

7478 **1856-S—Corroded—ANACS. VG Details.** NGC Census: (1/19). PCGS Population (1/40). Mintage: 70,000. Numismedia Wsl. Price for problem free NGC/PCGS coin in VG8 : $140. (#4613)

7479 **1860-O Fair 2 ANACS.** NGC Census: (0/33). PCGS Population (0/60). Mintage: 40,000. Numismedia Wsl. Price for problem free NGC/PCGS coin in Fair 2 : $113. (#4632)

7480 **1864 AG3 ANACS.** NGC Census: (0/36). PCGS Population (0/50). Mintage: 11,000. Numismedia Wsl. Price for problem free NGC/PCGS coin in AG3 : $108. (#4639)

7481 **1865 VG8 ANACS.** NGC Census: (0/49). PCGS Population (1/33). Mintage: 10,000. Numismedia Wsl. Price for problem free NGC/PCGS coin in VG8 : $421. (#4641)

7482 **1872-CC—Bent—NCS. VG Details.** NGC Census: (2/30). PCGS Population (6/40). Mintage: 35,480. Numismedia Wsl. Price for problem free NGC/PCGS coin in VG8 : $1,675. (#4657)

7483 **1880 VG8 ANACS.** NGC Census: (0/129). PCGS Population (1/133). Mintage: 36,000. Numismedia Wsl. Price for problem free NGC/PCGS coin in VG8 : $161. (#4688)

7484 **1881 VF30 NGC.** NGC Census: (1/61). PCGS Population (2/71). Mintage: 24,000. Numismedia Wsl. Price for problem free NGC/PCGS coin in VF30: $289. (#4689)

7485 **1885 MS65 PCGS.** PCGS Population (45/28). NGC Census: (55/44). Mintage: 2,532,497. Numismedia Wsl. Price for problem free NGC/PCGS coin in MS65: $715. (#4694)

7486 **1885-S AG3 NGC.** NGC Census: (1/52). PCGS Population (1/58). Mintage: 43,690. Numismedia Wsl. Price for problem free NGC/PCGS coin in AG3 : $275. (#4695)

7487 **1887 MS64 PCGS.** PCGS Population (153/106). NGC Census: (130/107). Mintage: 11,283,229. Numismedia Wsl. Price for problem free NGC/PCGS coin in MS64: $300. (#4698)

7488 **1890 MS64 PCGS.** PCGS Population (132/89). NGC Census: (130/132). Mintage: 9,910,951. Numismedia Wsl. Price for problem free NGC/PCGS coin in MS64: $325. (#4704)

7489 **1891-S MS62 PCGS.** PCGS Population (24/85). NGC Census: (23/109). Mintage: 3,196,116. Numismedia Wsl. Price for problem free NGC/PCGS coin in MS62: $210. (#4708)

PROOF SEATED DIMES

7490 **1862 PR64 NGC.** NGC Census: (42/16). PCGS Population (31/5). Mintage: 550. Numismedia Wsl. Price for problem free NGC/PCGS coin in PR64: $800. (#4755)

7491 **1873 No Arrows PR63 Cameo NGC.** NGC Census: (1/9). PCGS Population (3/21). (#84766)

7492 **1886 PR62 PCGS.** PCGS Population (27/171). NGC Census: (15/206). Mintage: 886. Numismedia Wsl. Price for problem free NGC/PCGS coin in PR62: $325. (#4783)

BARBER DIMES

7493 **1892-O MS64 NGC.** NGC Census: (54/22). PCGS Population (50/23). Mintage: 3,841,700. Numismedia Wsl. Price for problem free NGC/PCGS coin in MS64: $400. (#4797)

7494 **1898 MS64 PCGS.** PCGS Population (89/91). NGC Census: (109/95). Mintage: 16,320,735. Numismedia Wsl. Price for problem free NGC/PCGS coin in MS64: $240. (#4815)

7495 **1898-S AU55 PCGS.** PCGS Population (4/50). NGC Census: (3/38). Mintage: 1,702,507. Numismedia Wsl. Price for problem free NGC/PCGS coin in AU55: $160. (#4817)

7496 **1899-O AU53 NGC.** NGC Census: (3/52). PCGS Population (5/50). Mintage: 2,650,000. Numismedia Wsl. Price for problem free NGC/PCGS coin in AU53: $220. (#4819)

7497 **1900-S MS62 PCGS.** PCGS Population (21/73). NGC Census: (16/57). Mintage: 5,168,270. Numismedia Wsl. Price for problem free NGC/PCGS coin in MS62: $230. (#4823)

7498 **1905-O Micro O VF25 PCGS.** PCGS Population (5/21). NGC Census: (0/0). (#94836)

7499 **1906 MS63 PCGS.** PCGS Population (93/144). NGC Census: (51/140). Mintage: 19,958,406. Numismedia Wsl. Price for problem free NGC/PCGS coin in MS63: $140. (#4838)

7500 **1911-D MS65 PCGS. CAC.** PCGS Population (53/46). NGC Census: (35/21). Mintage: 11,209,000. Numismedia Wsl. Price for problem free NGC/PCGS coin in MS65: $480. (#4858)

7501 **1914 MS66 PCGS.** PCGS Population (51/5). NGC Census: (32/1). Mintage: 17,360,656. Numismedia Wsl. Price for problem free NGC/PCGS coin in MS66: $850. (#4865)

7502 **1915 MS65 PCGS. CAC.** PCGS Population (48/9). NGC Census: (41/9). Mintage: 5,620,450. Numismedia Wsl. Price for problem free NGC/PCGS coin in MS65: $480. (#4868)

7503 **1915 MS65 NGC.** NGC Census: (41/9). PCGS Population (48/9). Mintage: 5,620,450. Numismedia Wsl. Price for problem free NGC/PCGS coin in MS65: $480. (#4868)

7504 **1916 MS64 NGC.** NGC Census: (281/146). PCGS Population (299/148). Mintage: 18,490,000. Numismedia Wsl. Price for problem free NGC/PCGS coin in MS64: $215. (#4870)

PROOF BARBER DIMES

7505 **1892 PR63 PCGS.** PCGS Population (70/147). NGC Census: (30/170). Mintage: 1,245. Numismedia Wsl. Price for problem free NGC/PCGS coin in PR63: $455. (#4875)

7506 **1902 PR64 PCGS.** PCGS Population (68/36). NGC Census: (65/64). Mintage: 777. Numismedia Wsl. Price for problem free NGC/PCGS coin in PR64: $675. (#4886)

7507 **1903 PR63 NGC.** NGC Census: (27/149). PCGS Population (48/117). Mintage: 755. Numismedia Wsl. Price for problem free NGC/PCGS coin in PR63: $450. (#4887)

7508 **1905 PR64 NGC.** NGC Census: (47/88). PCGS Population (52/91). Mintage: 727. Numismedia Wsl. Price for problem free NGC/PCGS coin in PR64: $675. (#4889)

MERCURY DIMES

7509 **1916 MS67 Full Bands PCGS. CAC.** PCGS Population (87/8). NGC Census: (85/14). Mintage: 22,180,080. Numismedia Wsl. Price for problem free NGC/PCGS coin in MS67: $675. (#4905)

7510 **1916-D Fair 2 PCGS.** PCGS Population (206/4017). NGC Census: (252/1631). Mintage: 264,000. Numismedia Wsl. Price for problem free NGC/PCGS coin in Fair 2 : $308. (#4906)

7511 **1916-D AG3 PCGS.** PCGS Population (1304/2713). NGC Census: (754/877). Mintage: 264,000. Numismedia Wsl. Price for problem free NGC/PCGS coin in AG3 : $535. (#4906)

7512 **1916-D AG3 PCGS.** PCGS Population (1304/2713). NGC Census: (754/877). Mintage: 264,000. Numismedia Wsl. Price for problem free NGC/PCGS coin in AG3 : $535. (#4906)

7513 **1916-D Good 4 PCGS.** PCGS Population (879/1843). NGC Census: (219/659). Mintage: 264,000. Numismedia Wsl. Price for problem free NGC/PCGS coin in Good 4 : $875. (#4906)

7514 **1916-D Full Bands—Damage—PCGS Genuine.** Mintage: 264,000. (#4907)

7515 **1921 VF30 PCGS.** PCGS Population (31/207). NGC Census: (22/143). Mintage: 1,230,000. Numismedia Wsl. Price for problem free NGC/PCGS coin in VF30: $326. (#4934)

7516 **1921 XF40 PCGS.** PCGS Population (45/127). NGC Census: (29/93). Mintage: 1,230,000. Numismedia Wsl. Price for problem free NGC/PCGS coin in XF40: $455. (#4934)

7517 **1921-D VF25 PCGS.** PCGS Population (46/359). NGC Census: (10/241). Mintage: 1,080,000. Numismedia Wsl. Price for problem free NGC/PCGS coin in VF25: $357. (#4936)

7518 **1921-D VF30 PCGS.** PCGS Population (54/305). NGC Census: (23/218). Mintage: 1,080,000. Numismedia Wsl. Price for problem free NGC/PCGS coin in VF30: $426. (#4936)

7519 **1921-D VF30 PCGS.** PCGS Population (54/305). NGC Census: (23/218). Mintage: 1,080,000. Numismedia Wsl. Price for problem free NGC/PCGS coin in VF30: $426. (#4936)

7520 **1923 MS65 Full Bands PCGS.** PCGS Population (284/216). NGC Census: (179/119). Mintage: 50,130,000. Numismedia Wsl. Price for problem free NGC/PCGS coin in MS65: $250. (#4939)

7521 **1924 MS65 Full Bands NGC.** NGC Census: (83/61). PCGS Population (134/82). Mintage: 24,010,000. Numismedia Wsl. Price for problem free NGC/PCGS coin in MS65: $430. (#4943)

7522 **1924-D MS62 Full Bands PCGS.** PCGS Population (30/339). NGC Census: (16/242). Mintage: 6,810,000. Numismedia Wsl. Price for problem free NGC/PCGS coin in MS62: $280. (#4945)

7523 **1924-S MS64 PCGS.** PCGS Population (47/18). NGC Census: (55/22). Mintage: 7,120,000. Numismedia Wsl. Price for problem free NGC/PCGS coin in MS64: $590. (#4946)

7524 **1925 MS64 NGC.** NGC Census: (43/37). PCGS Population (40/27). Mintage: 25,610,000. Numismedia Wsl. Price for problem free NGC/PCGS coin in MS64: $105. (#4948)

7525 **1925 MS66 PCGS.** PCGS Population (9/2). NGC Census: (9/1). Mintage: 25,610,000. Numismedia Wsl. Price for problem free NGC/PCGS coin in MS66: $425. (#4948)

7526 **1925 MS67 PCGS.** PCGS Population (2/0). NGC Census: (1/0). Mintage: 25,610,000. Numismedia Wsl. Price for problem free NGC/PCGS coin in MS67: $965. (#4948)

7527 **1925-D AU55 PCGS.** PCGS Population (14/77). NGC Census: (4/77). Mintage: 5,117,000. Numismedia Wsl. Price for problem free NGC/PCGS coin in AU55: $217. (#4950)

7528 **1926 MS65 Full Bands NGC.** NGC Census: (84/31). PCGS Population (144/86). Mintage: 32,160,000. Numismedia Wsl. Price for problem free NGC/PCGS coin in MS65: $360. (#4955)

7529 **1926-D MS62 Full Bands PCGS.** PCGS Population (24/364). NGC Census: (16/153). Mintage: 6,828,000. Numismedia Wsl. Price for problem free NGC/PCGS coin in MS62: $250. (#4957)

7530 **1927-S AU58 PCGS.** PCGS Population (36/132). NGC Census: (17/119). Mintage: 4,770,000. Numismedia Wsl. Price for problem free NGC/PCGS coin in AU58: $170. (#4964)

7531 **1927-S MS64 PCGS.** PCGS Population (51/24). NGC Census: (40/37). Mintage: 4,770,000. Numismedia Wsl. Price for problem free NGC/PCGS coin in MS64: $650. (#4964)

7532 **1931-D MS64 Full Bands PCGS.** PCGS Population (290/489). NGC Census: (82/186). Mintage: 1,260,000. Numismedia Wsl. Price for problem free NGC/PCGS coin in MS64: $185. (#4985)

7533 **1935 MS67 Full Bands NGC.** NGC Census: (111/1). PCGS Population (217/6). Mintage: 58,830,000. Numismedia Wsl. Price for problem free NGC/PCGS coin in MS67: $240. (#4993)

7534 **1936-D MS65 Full Bands PCGS.** PCGS Population (309/301). NGC Census: (93/87). Mintage: 16,132,000. Numismedia Wsl. Price for problem free NGC/PCGS coin in MS65: $190. (#5001)

7535 **1937-S MS67 PCGS.** PCGS Population (44/0). NGC Census: (124/3). Mintage: 9,740,000. Numismedia Wsl. Price for problem free NGC/PCGS coin in MS67: $135. (#5008)

7536 **1942/1 XF40 PCGS.** PCGS Population (237/630). NGC Census: (129/552). Mintage: 205,432,336. Numismedia Wsl. Price for problem free NGC/PCGS coin in XF40: $640. (#5036)

7537 **1942/1 XF40 ANACS.** NGC Census: (129/552). PCGS Population (237/630). Mintage: 205,432,336. Numismedia Wsl. Price for problem free NGC/PCGS coin in XF40: $640. (#5036)

7538 **1942/1 XF45 ANACS.** NGC Census: (114/438). PCGS Population (188/442). Mintage: 205,432,336. Numismedia Wsl. Price for problem free NGC/PCGS coin in XF45: $761. (#5036)

7539 **1942/1-D VF30 PCGS.** PCGS Population (63/361). NGC Census: (61/317). Mintage: 60,740,000. Numismedia Wsl. Price for problem free NGC/PCGS coin in VF30: $622. (#5040)

7540 **1945-S Micro S MS66 PCGS.** PCGS Population (1499/170). NGC Census: (385/138). Mintage: 41,920,000. Numismedia Wsl. Price for problem free NGC/PCGS coin in MS66: $115. (#5062)

PROOF MERCURY DIMES

7541 **1938 PR67 PCGS. CAC.** PCGS Population (155/6). NGC Census: (213/35). Mintage: 8,728. Numismedia Wsl. Price for problem free NGC/PCGS coin in PR67: $710. (#5073)

7542 **1940 PR66 PCGS. CAC.** PCGS Population (840/298). NGC Census: (819/366). Mintage: 11,827. Numismedia Wsl. Price for problem free NGC/PCGS coin in PR66: $200. (#5075)

7543 **1942 PR66 PCGS. CAC.** PCGS Population (1467/582). NGC Census: (1395/807). Mintage: 22,329. Numismedia Wsl. Price for problem free NGC/PCGS coin in PR66: $170. (#5077)

7544 **1942 PR67 PCGS.** PCGS Population (546/37). NGC Census: (693/113). Mintage: 22,329. Numismedia Wsl. Price for problem free NGC/PCGS coin in PR67: $285. (#5077)

7545 **1942 PR67 NGC.** NGC Census: (692/112). PCGS Population (545/37). Mintage: 22,329. Numismedia Wsl. Price for problem free NGC/PCGS coin in PR67: $285. (#5077)

7546 **1942 PR67 NGC.** NGC Census: (692/112). PCGS Population (545/37). Mintage: 22,329. Numismedia Wsl. Price for problem free NGC/PCGS coin in PR67: $285. (#5077)

ROOSEVELT DIMES

7547 **1949-S MS68 ★ NGC.** NGC Census: (14/0). PCGS Population (3/0). Mintage: 13,510,000. Numismedia Wsl. Price for problem free NGC/PCGS coin in MS68: $1,075. (#5093)

7548 **1982 No P MS65 PCGS.** PCGS Population (697/537). NGC Census: (75/106). Numismedia Wsl. Price for problem free NGC/PCGS coin in MS65: $250. (#5162)

PROOF ROOSEVELT DIME

7549 **1983 No S PR68 Deep Cameo PCGS.** PCGS Population (53/72). NGC Census: (0/0). Numismedia Wsl. Price for problem free NGC/PCGS coin in PR68: $885. (#95265)

TWENTY CENT PIECES

7550 **1875 AU55 NGC.** NGC Census: (27/228). PCGS Population (64/247). Mintage: 36,900. Numismedia Wsl. Price for problem free NGC/PCGS coin in AU55: $570. (#5296)

7551 **1875-CC—Improperly Cleaned—NCS. AU Details.** NGC Census: (13/353). PCGS Population (35/443). Mintage: 133,290. Numismedia Wsl. Price for problem free NGC/PCGS coin in AU50: $725. (#5297)

7552 **1875-S—Improperly Cleaned—NCS. AU Details.** NGC Census: (40/1645). PCGS Population (128/1805). Mintage: 1,155,000. Numismedia Wsl. Price for problem free NGC/PCGS coin in AU50: $290. (#5298)

7553 **1875-S—Improperly Cleaned—NCS. AU Details.** NGC Census: (40/1645). PCGS Population (128/1805). Mintage: 1,155,000. Numismedia Wsl. Price for problem free NGC/PCGS coin in AU50: $290. (#5298)

7554 **1875-S MS62 NGC.** NGC Census: (230/898). PCGS Population (236/988). Mintage: 1,155,000. Numismedia Wsl. Price for problem free NGC/PCGS coin in MS62: $825. (#5298)

7555 **1876—Scratches—NCS. AU Details.** NGC Census: (11/308). PCGS Population (36/348). Mintage: 14,600. Numismedia Wsl. Price for problem free NGC/PCGS coin in AU50: $460. (#5299)

7556 **1876—Improperly Cleaned—NCS. Unc Details.** NGC Census: (4/240). PCGS Population (13/239). Mintage: 14,600. Numismedia Wsl. Price for problem free NGC/PCGS coin in MS60: $730. (#5299)

EARLY QUARTERS

7557 **1805 Good 4 PCGS.** PCGS Population (24/357). NGC Census: (8/191). Mintage: 121,394. Numismedia Wsl. Price for problem free NGC/PCGS coin in Good 4 : $440. (#5313)

7558 **1806 AG3 PCGS.** PCGS Population (16/546). NGC Census: (14/316). Mintage: 206,124. Numismedia Wsl. Price for problem free NGC/PCGS coin in AG3 : $261. (#5314)

7559 **1806 Good 4 PCGS.** PCGS Population (39/506). NGC Census: (16/300). Mintage: 206,124. Numismedia Wsl. Price for problem free NGC/PCGS coin in Good 4 : $425. (#5314)

BUST QUARTERS

7560 **1831 Small Letters VF35 ANACS.** B-5. NGC Census: (5/403). PCGS Population (21/363). Mintage: 398,000. Numismedia Wsl. Price for problem free NGC/PCGS coin in VF35: $247. (#5348)

7561 **1832—Cleaned—ANACS. XF40 Details.** B-2. NGC Census: (3/91). PCGS Population (12/105). Mintage: 320,000. Numismedia Wsl. Price for problem free NGC/PCGS coin in XF40: $300. (#5351)

SEATED QUARTERS

7562 **1840-O No Drapery XF40 NGC.** NGC Census: (11/77). PCGS Population (13/47). Mintage: 382,200. Numismedia Wsl. Price for problem free NGC/PCGS coin in XF40: $400. (#5393)

7563 **1848 XF40 ANACS.** NGC Census: (0/23). PCGS Population (5/27). Mintage: 146,000. Numismedia Wsl. Price for problem free NGC/PCGS coin in XF40: $200. (#5412)

7564 **1853 Arrows and Rays AU58 NGC.** NGC Census: (111/357). PCGS Population (81/323). Mintage: 15,210,020. Numismedia Wsl. Price for problem free NGC/PCGS coin in AU58: $480. (#5426)

7565 **1854-O Huge O AG3 NGC.** NGC Census: (3/23). PCGS Population (4/34). Mintage: 1,484,000. Numismedia Wsl. Price for problem free NGC/PCGS coin in AG3 : $474. (#5434)

7566 **1863 AU50 NGC.** NGC Census: (2/42). PCGS Population (0/54). Mintage: 191,600. Numismedia Wsl. Price for problem free NGC/PCGS coin in AU50: $300. (#5458)

7567 **1865—Improperly Cleaned—NGC. Unc Details.** NGC Census: (0/13). PCGS Population (0/19). Mintage: 58,800. Numismedia Wsl. Price for problem free NGC/PCGS coin in MS60: $775. (#5461)

7568 **1866 Motto Good 6 ANACS.** NGC Census: (0/38). PCGS Population (0/38). Mintage: 16,800. Numismedia Wsl. Price for problem free NGC/PCGS coin in Good 6 : $413. (#5468)

7569 **1874-S Arrows VF35 ANACS.** NGC Census: (0/125). PCGS Population (1/199). Mintage: 392,000. Numismedia Wsl. Price for problem free NGC/PCGS coin in VF35: $215. (#5495)

7570 **1877 AU58 ANACS.** NGC Census: (20/273). PCGS Population (26/283). Mintage: 10,911,710. Numismedia Wsl. Price for problem free NGC/PCGS coin in AU58: $190. (#5504)

7571 **1877 MS64 NGC.** NGC Census: (76/122). PCGS Population (62/144). Mintage: 10,911,710. Numismedia Wsl. Price for problem free NGC/PCGS coin in MS64: $725. (#5504)

7572 **1877 MS64 PCGS.** PCGS Population (62/144). NGC Census: (76/123). Mintage: 10,911,710. Numismedia Wsl. Price for problem free NGC/PCGS coin in MS64: $725. (#5504)

7573 **1879 VG8 ANACS.** NGC Census: (0/191). PCGS Population (0/209). Mintage: 13,600. Numismedia Wsl. Price for problem free NGC/PCGS coin in VG8 : $190. (#5511)

7574 **1879—Harshly Cleaned—NCS. Unc Details.** NGC Census: (0/0). PCGS Population (0/0). Mintage: 13,600. (#5511)

7575 **1881—Cleaned—ANACS. VG8 Details.** NGC Census: (0/93). PCGS Population (1/114). Mintage: 12,000. Numismedia Wsl. Price for problem free NGC/PCGS coin in VG8 : $200. (#5513)

7576 **1883—Rev Improperly Cleaned—NCS. AU Details.** NGC Census: (1/69). PCGS Population (2/74). Mintage: 14,400. Numismedia Wsl. Price for problem free NGC/PCGS coin in AU50: $340. (#5515)

7577 **1885—Damaged—ANACS. Fine 12 Details.** NGC Census: (0/78). PCGS Population (0/113). Mintage: 13,600. Numismedia Wsl. Price for problem free NGC/PCGS coin in Fine 12: $240. (#5517)

7578 **1887—Improperly Cleaned—NCS. XF Details.** NGC Census: (0/0). PCGS Population (0/0). Mintage: 10,000. (#5519)

7579 **1889—Cleaned—ANACS. Fine 15 Details.** NGC Census: (0/168). PCGS Population (0/187). Mintage: 12,000. Numismedia Wsl. Price for problem free NGC/PCGS coin in Fine 15: $259. (#5522)

PROOF SEATED QUARTERS

7580 **1870 PR60 PCGS.** PCGS Population (7/134). NGC Census: (2/100). Mintage: 1,000. Numismedia Wsl. Price for problem free NGC/PCGS coin in PR60: $475. (#5569)

7581 **1882 PR63 PCGS.** PCGS Population (60/151). NGC Census: (42/172). Mintage: 1,100. Numismedia Wsl. Price for problem free NGC/PCGS coin in PR63: $750. (#5583)

BARBER QUARTERS

7582 **1893-O MS63 PCGS.** PCGS Population (38/64). NGC Census: (18/56). Mintage: 3,396,000. Numismedia Wsl. Price for problem free NGC/PCGS coin in MS63: $420. (#5605)

7583 **1896-O XF40 ANACS.** NGC Census: (1/59). PCGS Population (2/90). Mintage: 1,484,000. Numismedia Wsl. Price for problem free NGC/PCGS coin in XF40: $350. (#5614)

7584 **1896-S AG3 PCGS. CAC.** PCGS Population (69/485). NGC Census: (44/181). Mintage: 188,039. Numismedia Wsl. Price for problem free NGC/PCGS coin in AG3 : $487. (#5615)

7585 **1898 MS63 NGC.** NGC Census: (48/101). PCGS Population (58/106). Mintage: 11,100,735. Numismedia Wsl. Price for problem free NGC/PCGS coin in MS63: $260. (#5619)

7586 **1902-S AU53 PCGS.** PCGS Population (4/92). NGC Census: (1/72). Mintage: 1,524,612. Numismedia Wsl. Price for problem free NGC/PCGS coin in AU53: $210. (#5633)

7587 **1909 MS63 PCGS.** PCGS Population (119/200). NGC Census: (74/160). Mintage: 9,268,650. Numismedia Wsl. Price for problem free NGC/PCGS coin in MS63: $300. (#5653)

7588 **1916-D MS62 ANACS.** NGC Census: (137/831). PCGS Population (218/1234). Mintage: 6,540,800. Numismedia Wsl. Price for problem free NGC/PCGS coin in MS62: $190. (#5674)

7589 **1916-D MS64 NGC.** NGC Census: (397/221). PCGS Population (485/401). Mintage: 6,540,800. Numismedia Wsl. Price for problem free NGC/PCGS coin in MS64: $385. (#5674)

PROOF BARBER QUARTER

7590 **1905—Obv Spot Removed—NCS. Proof.** NGC Census: (0/220). PCGS Population (6/238). Mintage: 727. Numismedia Wsl. Price for problem free NGC/PCGS coin in PR60: $315. (#5691)

STANDING LIBERTY QUARTERS

7591 **1917 Type One MS63 PCGS.** PCGS Population (480/852). NGC Census: (240/717). Mintage: 8,740,000. Numismedia Wsl. Price for problem free NGC/PCGS coin in MS63: $230. (#5706)

7592 **1917 Type One MS63 Full Head PCGS. CAC.** PCGS Population (964/2881). NGC Census: (530/2145). Mintage: 8,740,000. Numismedia Wsl. Price for problem free NGC/PCGS coin in MS63: $340. (#5707)

7593 **1917 Type One MS63 Full Head NGC.** NGC Census: (529/2142). PCGS Population (964/2875). Mintage: 8,740,000. Numismedia Wsl. Price for problem free NGC/PCGS coin in MS63: $340. (#5707)

7594 **1917 Type One MS63 Full Head ANACS.** NGC Census: (531/2144). PCGS Population (963/2872). Mintage: 8,740,000. Numismedia Wsl. Price for problem free NGC/PCGS coin in MS63: $340. (#5707)

7595 **1917-D Type One MS62 Full Head ANACS.** NGC Census: (104/714). PCGS Population (105/1041). Mintage: 1,509,200. Numismedia Wsl. Price for problem free NGC/PCGS coin in MS62: $325. (#5709)

7596 **1917 Type Two MS64 Full Head PCGS.** PCGS Population (303/237). NGC Census: (221/172). Mintage: 13,880,000. Numismedia Wsl. Price for problem free NGC/PCGS coin in MS64: $480. (#5715)

7597 **1918 MS64 Full Head PCGS.** PCGS Population (138/116). NGC Census: (98/72). Mintage: 14,240,000. Numismedia Wsl. Price for problem free NGC/PCGS coin in MS64: $565. (#5721)

7598 **1919 MS63 Full Head PCGS.** PCGS Population (75/316). NGC Census: (42/220). Mintage: 11,324,000. Numismedia Wsl. Price for problem free NGC/PCGS coin in MS63: $360. (#5729)

7599 **1924-D MS65 PCGS. CAC.** PCGS Population (462/100). NGC Census: (398/291). Mintage: 3,112,000. Numismedia Wsl. Price for problem free NGC/PCGS coin in MS65: $480. (#5748)

7600 **1924-D MS66 PCGS. CAC.** PCGS Population (91/9). NGC Census: (247/44). Mintage: 3,112,000. Numismedia Wsl. Price for problem free NGC/PCGS coin in MS66: $600. (#5748)

7601 **1925 MS64 Full Head PCGS.** PCGS Population (229/205). NGC Census: (168/131). Mintage: 12,280,000. Numismedia Wsl. Price for problem free NGC/PCGS coin in MS64: $420. (#5753)

7602 **1926-D MS64 NGC.** NGC Census: (871/248). PCGS Population (1286/187). Mintage: 1,716,000. Numismedia Wsl. Price for problem free NGC/PCGS coin in MS64: $220. (#5756)

7603 **1926-D MS64 NGC.** NGC Census: (870/248). PCGS Population (1284/187). Mintage: 1,716,000. Numismedia Wsl. Price for problem free NGC/PCGS coin in MS64: $220. (#5756)

7604 **1927 MS64 PCGS.** PCGS Population (242/119). NGC Census: (176/99). Mintage: 11,912,000. Numismedia Wsl. Price for problem free NGC/PCGS coin in MS64: $250. (#5760)

7605 **1927 MS64 PCGS.** PCGS Population (242/119). NGC Census: (176/99). Mintage: 11,912,000. Numismedia Wsl. Price for problem free NGC/PCGS coin in MS64: $250. (#5760)

7606 **1927 MS64 Full Head NGC. CAC.** NGC Census: (159/99). PCGS Population (212/159). Mintage: 11,912,000. Numismedia Wsl. Price for problem free NGC/PCGS coin in MS64: $450. (#5761)

7607 **1927-S VF35 NGC.** NGC Census: (52/309). PCGS Population (70/516). Mintage: 396,000. Numismedia Wsl. Price for problem free NGC/PCGS coin in VF35: $662. (#5764)

7608 **1928-D MS63 PCGS.** PCGS Population (297/1392). NGC Census: (125/958). Mintage: 1,627,600. Numismedia Wsl. Price for problem free NGC/PCGS coin in MS63: $160. (#5768)

7609 **1930 MS64 Full Head NGC.** NGC Census: (728/595). PCGS Population (866/951). Mintage: 5,632,000. Numismedia Wsl. Price for problem free NGC/PCGS coin in MS64: $375. (#5779)

7610 **1930 MS65 Full Head PCGS.** PCGS Population (664/284). NGC Census: (406/187). Mintage: 5,632,000. Numismedia Wsl. Price for problem free NGC/PCGS coin in MS65: $565. (#5779)

7611 **1930-S MS64 PCGS.** PCGS Population (244/318). NGC Census: (115/172). Mintage: 1,556,000. Numismedia Wsl. Price for problem free NGC/PCGS coin in MS64: $270. (#5780)

WASHINGTON QUARTERS

7612 **1932 MS65 NGC.** NGC Census: (301/89). PCGS Population (442/145). Mintage: 5,404,000. Numismedia Wsl. Price for problem free NGC/PCGS coin in MS65: $260. (#5790)

7613 **1932-D AU50 ANACS.** NGC Census: (75/1432). PCGS Population (126/2481). Mintage: 436,800. Numismedia Wsl. Price for problem free NGC/PCGS coin in AU50: $325. (#5791)

7614 **1932-D AU50 NGC.** NGC Census: (76/1435). PCGS Population (127/2486). Mintage: 436,800. Numismedia Wsl. Price for problem free NGC/PCGS coin in AU50: $325. (#5791)

7615 **1932-S—Cleaned—ANACS. AU55 Details.** NGC Census: (209/1989). PCGS Population (305/2978). Mintage: 408,000. Numismedia Wsl. Price for problem free NGC/PCGS coin in AU55: $225. (#5792)

7616 **1932-S—Cleaned—ANACS. MS60 Details.** NGC Census: (10/1590). PCGS Population (28/2426). Mintage: 408,000. Numismedia Wsl. Price for problem free NGC/PCGS coin in MS60: $410. (#5792)

7617 **1932-S MS62 PCGS.** PCGS Population (466/1909). NGC Census: (416/1035). Mintage: 408,000. Numismedia Wsl. Price for problem free NGC/PCGS coin in MS62: $510. (#5792)

7618 **1932-S MS64 NGC.** NGC Census: (511/63). PCGS Population (934/97). Mintage: 408,000. Numismedia Wsl. Price for problem free NGC/PCGS coin in MS64: $810. (#5792)

7619 **1934-D Heavy Motto MS65 PCGS.** PCGS Population (38/12). NGC Census: (0/0). (#85796)

7620 **1935-D MS63 ANACS.** NGC Census: (99/639). PCGS Population (185/1166). Mintage: 5,780,000. Numismedia Wsl. Price for problem free NGC/PCGS coin in MS63: $240. (#5798)

7621 **1936-D AU53 ANACS.** NGC Census: (13/827). PCGS Population (20/1528). Mintage: 5,374,000. Numismedia Wsl. Price for problem free NGC/PCGS coin in AU53: $220. (#5801)

7622 **1938 MS66 ANACS.** NGC Census: (210/55). PCGS Population (203/26). Mintage: 9,480,045. Numismedia Wsl. Price for problem free NGC/PCGS coin in MS66: $270. (#5806)

7623 **1944-S MS67 PCGS.** PCGS Population (97/2). NGC Census: (256/3). Mintage: 12,560,000. Numismedia Wsl. Price for problem free NGC/PCGS coin in MS67: $340. (#5826)

7624 **1949-D MS67 ★ NGC** and **1950-S MS64 NGC.** (Total: 2 coins)

7625 **1952-D Large D, MS65 PCGS.** FS-501. PCGS Population (615/248). NGC Census: (232/353). Mintage: 49,795,200. Numismedia Wsl. Price for problem free NGC/PCGS coin in MS65: $29. (#5850)

SMS WASHINGTON QUARTER

7626 **1967 SMS MS67 Ultra Cameo NGC.** NGC Census: (6/3). PCGS Population (12/2). (#95999)

PROOF WASHINGTON QUARTERS

7627 **1936 PR61 NGC.** NGC Census: (7/824). PCGS Population (19/1069). Mintage: 3,837. Numismedia Wsl. Price for problem free NGC/PCGS coin in PR61: $450. (#5975)

7628 **1950 PR64 Cameo NGC.** NGC Census: (21/146). PCGS Population (15/71). Numismedia Wsl. Price for problem free NGC/PCGS coin in PR64: $160. (#85982)

7629 **1952 Superbird PR67 PCGS.** FS-901. PCGS Population (64/0). NGC Census: (0/0). (#144443)

STATEHOOD QUARTERS

7630 **2004-D Wisconsin Extra Leaf Low MS65 PCGS.** PCGS Population (1049/201). NGC Census: (0/0). Numismedia Wsl. Price for problem free NGC/PCGS coin in MS65: $170. (#814033)

7631 **2004-D Wisconsin Extra Leaf High MS65 PCGS.** PCGS Population (758/144). NGC Census: (0/0). Numismedia Wsl. Price for problem free NGC/PCGS coin in MS65: $250. (#914033)

EARLY HALF DOLLARS

7632 **1795 2 Leaves—Improperly Cleaned—NCS. VG Details.** O-113A. NGC Census: (62/677). PCGS Population (133/1008). Mintage: 299,680. Numismedia Wsl. Price for problem free NGC/PCGS coin in VG8 : $1,250. (#6052)

7633 **1803 Large 3 VF20 ANACS.** O-103. NGC Census: (13/582). PCGS Population (34/258). Mintage: 188,234. Numismedia Wsl. Price for problem free NGC/PCGS coin in VF20: $650. (#6066)

7634 **1803 Small 3—Scratches—NCS. VF Details.** O-104. NGC Census: (0/0). PCGS Population (8/46). Numismedia Wsl. Price for problem free NGC/PCGS coin in VF20: $725. (#6067)

7635 **1806/5—Improperly Cleaned—NCS. VF Details.** O-103. NGC Census: (9/116). PCGS Population (24/106). Numismedia Wsl. Price for problem free NGC/PCGS coin in VF20: $665. (#6077)

7636 **1806 Pointed 6, No Stem VF25 NGC.** O-109. NGC Census: (0/0). PCGS Population (19/191). (#6073)

7637 **1806 Pointed 6, Stem VG10 NGC.** NGC Census: (28/1193). PCGS Population (32/823). Mintage: 839,576. Numismedia Wsl. Price for problem free NGC/PCGS coin in VG10: $255. (#6071)

7638 **1807 Draped Bust—Cleaned—ANACS. Fine 12 Details.** O-105. NGC Census: (53/679). PCGS Population (36/867). Mintage: 301,076. Numismedia Wsl. Price for problem free NGC/PCGS coin in Fine 12: $300. (#6079)

7639 **1807 Draped Bust VF20 NGC.** O-103. NGC Census: (33/607). PCGS Population (90/690). Mintage: 301,076. Numismedia Wsl. Price for problem free NGC/PCGS coin in VF20: $575. (#6079)

7640 **1807 Draped Bust—Harshly Cleaned, Graffiti—NCS. XF Details.** O-105. NGC Census: (86/365). PCGS Population (101/342). Mintage: 301,076. Numismedia Wsl. Price for problem free NGC/PCGS coin in XF40: $1,350. (#6079)

BUST HALF DOLLARS

7641 **1808 VF20 ANACS.** NGC Census: (8/369). PCGS Population (17/398). Mintage: 1,368,600. Numismedia Wsl. Price for problem free NGC/PCGS coin in VF20: $180. (#6090)

7642 **1808 AU53 NGC.** NGC Census: (33/170). PCGS Population (33/151). Mintage: 1,368,600. Numismedia Wsl. Price for problem free NGC/PCGS coin in AU53: $725. (#6090)

7643 **1809 Normal Edge Fine 15 ANACS.** NGC Census: (2/418). PCGS Population (19/441). Mintage: 1,405,810. Numismedia Wsl. Price for problem free NGC/PCGS coin in Fine 15: $115. (#6092)

7644 **1809 Normal Edge—Cleaned—ANACS. XF40 Details.** O-106. NGC Census: (34/328). PCGS Population (41/296). Mintage: 1,405,810. Numismedia Wsl. Price for problem free NGC/PCGS coin in XF40: $300. (#6092)

7645 **1809 Normal Edge—Improperly Cleaned—NCS. AU Details.** O-105. NGC Census: (29/233). PCGS Population (47/179). Mintage: 1,405,810. Numismedia Wsl. Price for problem free NGC/PCGS coin in AU50: $510. (#6092)

7646 **1810 VF30 PCGS.** PCGS Population (31/425). NGC Census: (18/391). Mintage: 1,276,276. Numismedia Wsl. Price for problem free NGC/PCGS coin in VF30: $231. (#6095)

7647 **1810 AU50 PCGS.** PCGS Population (53/216). NGC Census: (37/243). Mintage: 1,276,276. Numismedia Wsl. Price for problem free NGC/PCGS coin in AU50: $525. (#6095)

7648 **1811 Large 8—Cleaned—ANACS. AU50 Details.** O-106. NGC Census: (30/385). PCGS Population (33/206). Mintage: 1,203,644. Numismedia Wsl. Price for problem free NGC/PCGS coin in AU50: $425. (#6096)

7649 **1811 Large 8—Improperly Cleaned—NCS. AU Details.** NGC Census: (30/385). PCGS Population (33/206). Mintage: 1,203,644. Numismedia Wsl. Price for problem free NGC/PCGS coin in AU50: $425. (#6096)

7650 **1811 Large 8—Cleaned—ANACS. AU55 Details.** O-108A. NGC Census: (60/292). PCGS Population (47/141). Mintage: 1,203,644. Numismedia Wsl. Price for problem free NGC/PCGS coin in AU55: $625. (#6096)

7651 **1812 AU58 ANACS.** O-105. NGC Census: (126/241). PCGS Population (81/169). Mintage: 1,628,059. Numismedia Wsl. Price for problem free NGC/PCGS coin in AU58: $950. (#6100)

7652 **1814—Cleaned—ANACS. AU53 Details.** O-104a. NGC Census: (18/245). PCGS Population (18/213). Mintage: 1,039,075. Numismedia Wsl. Price for problem free NGC/PCGS coin in AU53: $610. (#6105)

7653 **1814 AU55 NGC.** NGC Census: (40/205). PCGS Population (51/162). Mintage: 1,039,075. Numismedia Wsl. Price for problem free NGC/PCGS coin in AU55: $725. (#6105)

7654 **1814 AU58 ANACS.** NGC Census: (82/123). PCGS Population (53/110). Mintage: 1,039,075. Numismedia Wsl. Price for problem free NGC/PCGS coin in AU58: $1,100. (#6105)

7655 **1820/19 Square Base 2—Cleaned—ANACS. XF45 Details.** O-102. NGC Census: (15/103). PCGS Population (12/56). Numismedia Wsl. Price for problem free NGC/PCGS coin in XF45: $676. (#6125)

7656 **1821—Cleaned—ANACS. AU50 Details.** O-104. NGC Census: (36/301). PCGS Population (50/286). Mintage: 1,305,797. Numismedia Wsl. Price for problem free NGC/PCGS coin in AU50: $390. (#6128)

7657 **1822/1—Scratched—ANACS. AU50 Details.** O-101. NGC Census: (6/60). PCGS Population (5/49). Numismedia Wsl. Price for problem free NGC/PCGS coin in AU50: $585. (#6130)

7658 **1824 AU55 NGC.** O-117. NGC Census: (91/396). PCGS Population (107/269). Mintage: 3,504,954. Numismedia Wsl. Price for problem free NGC/PCGS coin in AU55: $475. (#6137)

7659 **1825 AU53 PCGS.** PCGS Population (76/537). NGC Census: (54/600). Mintage: 2,900,000. Numismedia Wsl. Price for problem free NGC/PCGS coin in AU53: $330. (#6142)

7660 **1826 AU53 ANACS.** O-107. NGC Census: (94/1211). PCGS Population (102/790). Mintage: 4,000,000. Numismedia Wsl. Price for problem free NGC/PCGS coin in AU53: $350. (#6143)

7661 **1828 Square Base 2, Small 8, Large Letters AU50 PCGS.** PCGS Population (30/202). NGC Census: (0/0). (#6151)

7662 **1829 Small Letters AU53 NGC.** NGC Census: (73/587). PCGS Population (72/537). Mintage: 3,712,156. Numismedia Wsl. Price for problem free NGC/PCGS coin in AU53: $325. (#6154)

7663 **1829 Small Letters—Corroded—ANACS. AU55 Details.** O-112. NGC Census: (126/461). PCGS Population (160/377). Mintage: 3,712,156. Numismedia Wsl. Price for problem free NGC/PCGS coin in AU55: $360. (#6154)

7664 **1830 Small 0 AU53 ANACS.** O-107. NGC Census: (111/985). PCGS Population (93/682). Mintage: 4,764,800. Numismedia Wsl. Price for problem free NGC/PCGS coin in AU53: $280. (#6156)

7665 **1832 Small Letters AU58 PCGS.** PCGS Population (250/352). NGC Census: (402/436). Mintage: 4,797,000. Numismedia Wsl. Price for problem free NGC/PCGS coin in AU58: $500. (#6160)

7666 **1833 AU50 ANACS.** NGC Census: (56/839). PCGS Population (115/740). Mintage: 5,206,000. Numismedia Wsl. Price for problem free NGC/PCGS coin in AU50: $250. (#6163)

7667 **1834 Large Date, Large Letters AU53 ANACS.** O-117. NGC Census: (121/1259). PCGS Population (64/541). Mintage: 6,412,004. Numismedia Wsl. Price for problem free NGC/PCGS coin in AU53: $280. (#6164)

7668 **1835 XF40 PCGS.** PCGS Population (69/563). NGC Census: (27/613). Mintage: 5,352,006. Numismedia Wsl. Price for problem free NGC/PCGS coin in XF40: $130. (#6168)

REEDED EDGE HALF DOLLARS

7669 **1837 AU53 PCGS.** PCGS Population (60/661). NGC Census: (34/802). Mintage: 3,629,820. Numismedia Wsl. Price for problem free NGC/PCGS coin in AU53: $300. (#6176)

7670 **1837 AU58 NGC.** NGC Census: (244/444). PCGS Population (155/325). Mintage: 3,629,820. Numismedia Wsl. Price for problem free NGC/PCGS coin in AU58: $625. (#6176)

7671 **1839 AU55 PCGS.** PCGS Population (50/142). NGC Census: (47/187). Mintage: 1,392,976. Numismedia Wsl. Price for problem free NGC/PCGS coin in AU55: $440. (#6179)

7672 **1839 AU58 NGC.** NGC Census: (72/114). PCGS Population (39/103). Mintage: 1,392,976. Numismedia Wsl. Price for problem free NGC/PCGS coin in AU58: $825. (#6179)

SEATED HALF DOLLARS

7673 **1840 Reverse of 1839, Small Letters—Whizzed—NCS. AU Details.** (#6234)

7674 **1842 Medium Date, Large Letters VF30 NGC.** VP-002, FS-301. NGC Census: (0/60). PCGS Population (1/130). Mintage: 2,012,764. Numismedia Wsl. Price for problem free NGC/PCGS coin in VF30: $98. (#6239)

7675 **1848 MS61 ANACS.** WB-101. NGC Census: (0/29). PCGS Population (2/21). Mintage: 580,000. Numismedia Wsl. Price for problem free NGC/PCGS coin in MS61: $950. (#6260)

7676 **1853-O Arrows and Rays XF40 PCGS.** PCGS Population (26/103). NGC Census: (9/104). Mintage: 1,328,000. Numismedia Wsl. Price for problem free NGC/PCGS coin in XF40: $260. (#6276)

7677 **1854-O Arrows AU55 PCGS.** PCGS Population (59/247). NGC Census: (52/294). Mintage: 5,240,000. Numismedia Wsl. Price for problem free NGC/PCGS coin in AU55: $350. (#6280)

7678 **1855 Arrows MS62 NGC.** NGC Census: (11/36). PCGS Population (8/31). Mintage: 759,500. Numismedia Wsl. Price for problem free NGC/PCGS coin in MS62: $875. (#6281)

7679 **1856-O AU55 PCGS.** PCGS Population (30/107). NGC Census: (20/127). Mintage: 2,658,000. Numismedia Wsl. Price for problem free NGC/PCGS coin in AU55: $275. (#6288)

7680 **1858-S XF40 PCGS.** PCGS Population (12/57). NGC Census: (4/42). Mintage: 476,000. Numismedia Wsl. Price for problem free NGC/PCGS coin in XF40: $180. (#6295)

7681 **1860 AU55 NGC.** NGC Census: (5/42). PCGS Population (6/66). Mintage: 302,700. Numismedia Wsl. Price for problem free NGC/PCGS coin in AU55: $275. (#6299)

7682 **1860-O AU58 NGC.** NGC Census: (25/101). PCGS Population (17/85). Mintage: 1,290,000. Numismedia Wsl. Price for problem free NGC/PCGS coin in AU58: $375. (#6300)

7683 **1860-S—Cleaned—ANACS. AU58 Details.** NGC Census: (12/23). PCGS Population (11/24). Mintage: 472,000. Numismedia Wsl. Price for problem free NGC/PCGS coin in AU58: $635. (#6301)

7684 **1861 MS63 PCGS.** PCGS Population (58/96). NGC Census: (53/92). Mintage: 2,888,400. Numismedia Wsl. Price for problem free NGC/PCGS coin in MS63: $925. (#6302)

7685 **1863-S AU55 NGC.** NGC Census: (5/64). PCGS Population (15/66). Mintage: 916,000. Numismedia Wsl. Price for problem free NGC/PCGS coin in AU55: $300. (#6310)

7686 **1869—Improperly Cleaned—NCS. AU Details.** NGC Census: (5/73). PCGS Population (5/96). Mintage: 795,300. Numismedia Wsl. Price for problem free NGC/PCGS coin in AU50: $175. (#6325)

7687 **1873 Arrows—Polished—ANACS. MS60 Details.** NGC Census: (1/104). PCGS Population (7/116). Mintage: 1,815,700. Numismedia Wsl. Price for problem free NGC/PCGS coin in MS60: $775. (#6343)

7688 **1876 MS61 NGC.** NGC Census: (21/145). PCGS Population (16/194). Mintage: 8,419,150. Numismedia Wsl. Price for problem free NGC/PCGS coin in MS61: $425. (#6352)

7689 **1876-CC—Cleaned—ANACS. AU50 Details.** NGC Census: (3/98). PCGS Population (16/129). Mintage: 1,956,000. Numismedia Wsl. Price for problem free NGC/PCGS coin in AU50: $275. (#6353)

7690 **1876-S AU58 PCGS.** PCGS Population (20/132). NGC Census: (20/99). Mintage: 4,528,000. Numismedia Wsl. Price for problem free NGC/PCGS coin in AU58: $275. (#6354)

7691 **1890—Harshly Cleaned—NCS. AU Details.** NGC Census: (0/66). PCGS Population (1/96). Mintage: 12,000. Numismedia Wsl. Price for problem free NGC/PCGS coin in AU50: $500. (#6372)

PROOF SEATED HALF DOLLARS

7692 **1869 PR61 NGC.** NGC Census: (7/122). PCGS Population (11/154). Mintage: 600. Numismedia Wsl. Price for problem free NGC/PCGS coin in PR61: $480. (#6427)

7693 **1873 Arrows—Altered Surface—NCS. Proof.** NGC Census: (0/108). PCGS Population (5/131). Mintage: 550. Numismedia Wsl. Price for problem free NGC/PCGS coin in PR60: $800. (#6434)

BARBER HALF DOLLARS

7694 **1892—Environmental Damage—ANACS. MS60 Details.** NGC Census: (3/619). PCGS Population (12/726). Mintage: 934,000. Numismedia Wsl. Price for problem free NGC/PCGS coin in MS60: $390. (#6461)

7695 **1892-S VG8 ANACS.** NGC Census: (5/119). PCGS Population (11/226). Mintage: 1,029,028. Numismedia Wsl. Price for problem free NGC/PCGS coin in VG8 : $300. (#6464)

7696 **1894 AU58 NGC.** NGC Census: (17/110). PCGS Population (14/109). Mintage: 1,148,972. Numismedia Wsl. Price for problem free NGC/PCGS coin in AU58: $400. (#6468)

7697 **1896-O XF40 PCGS.** PCGS Population (13/46). NGC Census: (0/29). Mintage: 924,000. Numismedia Wsl. Price for problem free NGC/PCGS coin in XF40: $475. (#6475)

7698 **1898 AU58 NGC.** NGC Census: (23/101). PCGS Population (16/148). Mintage: 2,956,735. Numismedia Wsl. Price for problem free NGC/PCGS coin in AU58: $385. (#6480)

7699 **1898 MS62 PCGS.** PCGS Population (30/110). NGC Census: (16/76). Mintage: 2,956,735. Numismedia Wsl. Price for problem free NGC/PCGS coin in MS62: $575. (#6480)

7700 **1900—Scratches—NCS. Unc Details.** NGC Census: (4/161). PCGS Population (8/175). Mintage: 4,762,912. Numismedia Wsl. Price for problem free NGC/PCGS coin in MS60: $375. (#6486)

7701 **1900-S—Cleaned, Scratched—ANACS. AU55 Details.** NGC Census: (10/42). PCGS Population (20/61). Mintage: 2,560,322. Numismedia Wsl. Price for problem free NGC/PCGS coin in AU55: $375. (#6488)

7702 **1904 MS62 NGC.** NGC Census: (14/42). PCGS Population (14/86). Mintage: 2,992,670. Numismedia Wsl. Price for problem free NGC/PCGS coin in MS62: $520. (#6498)

7703 **1905-O AU58 ANACS.** NGC Census: (7/79). PCGS Population (14/95). Mintage: 505,000. Numismedia Wsl. Price for problem free NGC/PCGS coin in AU58: $535. (#6502)

7704 **1906-D XF45 PCGS.** PCGS Population (17/250). NGC Census: (5/145). Mintage: 4,028,000. Numismedia Wsl. Price for problem free NGC/PCGS coin in XF45: $187. (#6505)

7705 **1909 VF25 PCGS.** PCGS Population (5/422). NGC Census: (2/281). Mintage: 2,368,650. Numismedia Wsl. Price for problem free NGC/PCGS coin in VF25: $82. (#6516)

7706 **1909 AU53 NGC.** NGC Census: (7/252). PCGS Population (10/364). Mintage: 2,368,650. Numismedia Wsl. Price for problem free NGC/PCGS coin in AU53: $280. (#6516)

7707 **1909-S XF45 PCGS.** PCGS Population (4/97). NGC Census: (2/64). Mintage: 1,764,000. Numismedia Wsl. Price for problem free NGC/PCGS coin in XF45: $205. (#6518)

7708 **1912-D AU58 NGC.** NGC Census: (41/274). PCGS Population (41/347). Mintage: 2,300,800. Numismedia Wsl. Price for problem free NGC/PCGS coin in AU58: $350. (#6525)

7709 **1915-S—Improperly Cleaned—NCS. AU Details.** NGC Census: (4/277). PCGS Population (12/308). Mintage: 1,604,000. Numismedia Wsl. Price for problem free NGC/PCGS coin in AU50: $270. (#6534)

PROOF BARBER HALF DOLLARS

7710 **1901 PR58 PCGS.** PCGS Population (3/228). NGC Census: (2/229). Mintage: 813. (#6548)

7711 **1909 PR63 PCGS.** PCGS Population (49/108). NGC Census: (31/174). Mintage: 650. Numismedia Wsl. Price for problem free NGC/PCGS coin in PR63: $925. (#6556)

WALKING LIBERTY HALF DOLLARS

7712 **1916 MS64 PCGS.** PCGS Population (372/270). NGC Census: (304/195). Mintage: 608,000. Numismedia Wsl. Price for problem free NGC/PCGS coin in MS64: $765. (#6566)

7713 **1916-D MS64 NGC.** NGC Census: (315/187). PCGS Population (443/243). Mintage: 1,014,400. Numismedia Wsl. Price for problem free NGC/PCGS coin in MS64: $720. (#6567)

7714 **1921-D Good 4 ANACS.** NGC Census: (54/511). PCGS Population (118/988). Mintage: 208,000. Numismedia Wsl. Price for problem free NGC/PCGS coin in Good 4 : $275. (#6584)

7715 **1921-D Good 6 PCGS.** PCGS Population (159/833). NGC Census: (82/430). Mintage: 208,000. Numismedia Wsl. Price for problem free NGC/PCGS coin in Good 6 : $296. (#6584)

7716 **1929-D AU55 PCGS.** PCGS Population (47/942). NGC Census: (31/561). Mintage: 1,001,200. Numismedia Wsl. Price for problem free NGC/PCGS coin in AU55: $200. (#6589)

7717 **1929-S—Stained—NCS. Unc Details.** NGC Census: (2/473). PCGS Population (4/665). Mintage: 1,902,000. Numismedia Wsl. Price for problem free NGC/PCGS coin in MS60: $400. (#6590)

7718 **1935 MS65 PCGS.** PCGS Population (974/398). NGC Census: (635/232). Mintage: 9,162,000. Numismedia Wsl. Price for problem free NGC/PCGS coin in MS65: $265. (#6595)

7719 **1935 MS66 NGC.** NGC Census: (214/18). PCGS Population (381/17). Mintage: 9,162,000. Numismedia Wsl. Price for problem free NGC/PCGS coin in MS66: $500. (#6595)

7720 **1935-D MS64 PCGS.** PCGS Population (609/524). NGC Census: (419/152). Mintage: 3,003,800. Numismedia Wsl. Price for problem free NGC/PCGS coin in MS64: $365. (#6596)

7721 **1936 MS66 NGC.** NGC Census: (512/91). PCGS Population (745/105). Mintage: 12,617,901. Numismedia Wsl. Price for problem free NGC/PCGS coin in MS66: $270. (#6598)

7722 **1937-D MS65 PCGS. CAC.** PCGS Population (689/338). NGC Census: (315/172). Mintage: 1,676,000. Numismedia Wsl. Price for problem free NGC/PCGS coin in MS65: $560. (#6602)

7723 **1937-D MS65 NGC.** NGC Census: (315/173). PCGS Population (689/335). Mintage: 1,676,000. Numismedia Wsl. Price for problem free NGC/PCGS coin in MS65: $560. (#6602)

7724 **1939 MS66 PCGS. CAC.** PCGS Population (1052/238). NGC Census: (716/286). Mintage: 6,820,808. Numismedia Wsl. Price for problem free NGC/PCGS coin in MS66: $250. (#6606)

7725 **1939-D MS65 PCGS.** PCGS Population (1827/718). NGC Census: (1067/620). Mintage: 4,267,800. Numismedia Wsl. Price for problem free NGC/PCGS coin in MS65: $160. (#6607)

7726 **1941 MS66 NGC.** NGC Census: (2072/487). PCGS Population (2498/441). Mintage: 24,207,412. Numismedia Wsl. Price for problem free NGC/PCGS coin in MS66: $195. (#6611)

7727 **1941 MS66 NGC.** NGC Census: (2072/487). PCGS Population (2498/441). Mintage: 24,207,412. Numismedia Wsl. Price for problem free NGC/PCGS coin in MS66: $195. (#6611)

7728 **1941 MS67 PCGS. CAC.** PCGS Population (428/12). NGC Census: (471/16). Mintage: 24,207,412. Numismedia Wsl. Price for problem free NGC/PCGS coin in MS67: $625. (#6611)

7729 **1941-S MS65 NGC.** NGC Census: (821/217). PCGS Population (1993/378). Mintage: 8,098,000. Numismedia Wsl. Price for problem free NGC/PCGS coin in MS65: $835. (#6613)

7730 **1942 MS66 PCGS. CAC.** PCGS Population (2359/196). NGC Census: (2164/304). Mintage: 47,839,120. Numismedia Wsl. Price for problem free NGC/PCGS coin in MS66: $185. (#6614)

7731 **1942 MS66 PCGS.** PCGS Population (2355/197). NGC Census: (2165/304). Mintage: 47,839,120. Numismedia Wsl. Price for problem free NGC/PCGS coin in MS66: $185. (#6614)

7732 **1943 MS66 PCGS.** PCGS Population (2642/312). NGC Census: (2519/458). Mintage: 53,190,000. Numismedia Wsl. Price for problem free NGC/PCGS coin in MS66: $185. (#6618)

7733 **1943 MS66 PCGS. CAC.** PCGS Population (2642/312). NGC Census: (2519/458). Mintage: 53,190,000. Numismedia Wsl. Price for problem free NGC/PCGS coin in MS66: $185. (#6618)

7734 **1943-D MS67 PCGS.** PCGS Population (208/2). NGC Census: (252/4). Mintage: 11,346,000. Numismedia Wsl. Price for problem free NGC/PCGS coin in MS67: $725. (#6619)

7735 **1944 MS66 PCGS.** PCGS Population (998/68). NGC Census: (757/83). Mintage: 28,206,000. Numismedia Wsl. Price for problem free NGC/PCGS coin in MS66: $195. (#6621)

7736 **1944-D MS65 PCGS.** FS-901. Hand Engraved Initials. PCGS Population (3602/1690). NGC Census: (2073/1390). Mintage: 9,769,000. Numismedia Wsl. Price for problem free NGC/PCGS coin in MS65: $130. (#6622)

7737 **1944-S MS65 NGC.** NGC Census: (1073/174). PCGS Population (2366/345). Mintage: 8,904,000. Numismedia Wsl. Price for problem free NGC/PCGS coin in MS65: $385. (#6623)

7738 **1944-S MS65 PCGS.** PCGS Population (2366/345). NGC Census: (1073/174). Mintage: 8,904,000. Numismedia Wsl. Price for problem free NGC/PCGS coin in MS65: $385. (#6623)

7739 **1944-S MS65 PCGS.** PCGS Population (2355/344). NGC Census: (1071/173). Mintage: 8,904,000. Numismedia Wsl. Price for problem free NGC/PCGS coin in MS65: $385. (#6623)

7740 **1945-S MS66 PCGS. CAC.** PCGS Population (725/4). NGC Census: (543/23). Mintage: 10,156,000. Numismedia Wsl. Price for problem free NGC/PCGS coin in MS66: $375. (#6626)

7741 **1946 MS66 PCGS.** PCGS Population (857/32). NGC Census: (547/32). Mintage: 12,118,000. Numismedia Wsl. Price for problem free NGC/PCGS coin in MS66: $240. (#6627)

7742 **1946-D MS66 NGC.** NGC Census: (1708/100). PCGS Population (1596/35). Mintage: 2,151,000. Numismedia Wsl. Price for problem free NGC/PCGS coin in MS66: $185. (#6628)

7743 **1946-D MS66 PCGS.** PCGS Population (1596/35). NGC Census: (1708/100). Mintage: 2,151,000. Numismedia Wsl. Price for problem free NGC/PCGS coin in MS66: $185. (#6628)

7744 **1946-S MS66 NGC.** NGC Census: (1097/52). PCGS Population (1388/22). Mintage: 3,724,000. Numismedia Wsl. Price for problem free NGC/PCGS coin in MS66: $300. (#6629)

PROOF WALKING LIBERTY HALF DOLLARS

7745 **1940 PR66 NGC.** NGC Census: (736/385). PCGS Population (748/314). Mintage: 11,279. Numismedia Wsl. Price for problem free NGC/PCGS coin in PR66: $590. (#6640)

7746 **1941 No 'AW' PR65 NGC.** NGC Census: (805/1409). PCGS Population (1374/1199). Mintage: 15,412. Numismedia Wsl. Price for problem free NGC/PCGS coin in PR65: $500. (#6641)

7747 **1941 PR65 NGC.** NGC Census: (805/1409). PCGS Population (1374/1199). Mintage: 15,412. Numismedia Wsl. Price for problem free NGC/PCGS coin in PR65: $500. (#6641)

7748 **1942 PR64 PCGS.** PCGS Population (1236/3835). NGC Census: (604/3143). Mintage: 21,120. Numismedia Wsl. Price for problem free NGC/PCGS coin in PR64: $450. (#6642)

7749 **1942 PR65 NGC.** NGC Census: (888/2255). PCGS Population (1608/2227). Mintage: 21,120. Numismedia Wsl. Price for problem free NGC/PCGS coin in PR65: $480. (#6642)

7750 **1942 PR65 NGC.** NGC Census: (889/2259). PCGS Population (1609/2228). Mintage: 21,120. Numismedia Wsl. Price for problem free NGC/PCGS coin in PR65: $480. (#6642)

7751 **1942 PR66 NGC.** NGC Census: (1298/957). PCGS Population (1504/723). Mintage: 21,120. Numismedia Wsl. Price for problem free NGC/PCGS coin in PR66: $550. (#6642)

7752 **1942 PR67 NGC.** NGC Census: (795/162). PCGS Population (688/35). Mintage: 21,120. Numismedia Wsl. Price for problem free NGC/PCGS coin in PR67: $845. (#6642)

FRANKLIN HALF DOLLARS

7753 **1949 MS65 Full Bell Lines PCGS.** PCGS Population (756/145). NGC Census: (258/31). Numismedia Wsl. Price for problem free NGC/PCGS coin in MS65: $110. (#86653)

7754 **1951-D MS66 Full Bell Lines PCGS.** PCGS Population (66/0). NGC Census: (11/0). Numismedia Wsl. Price for problem free NGC/PCGS coin in MS66: $950. (#86659)

7755 **1952 MS66 PCGS.** PCGS Population (39/0). NGC Census: (87/8). Mintage: 21,100,000. Numismedia Wsl. Price for problem free NGC/PCGS coin in MS66: $180. (#6661)

PROOF FRANKLIN HALF DOLLARS

7756 **1950 PR64 ANACS.** NGC Census: (517/1036). PCGS Population (1073/1473). Mintage: 51,386. Numismedia Wsl. Price for problem free NGC/PCGS coin in PR64: $350. (#6691)

7757 **1951 PR66 PCGS.** PCGS Population (446/91). NGC Census: (429/165). Mintage: 57,500. Numismedia Wsl. Price for problem free NGC/PCGS coin in PR66: $330. (#6692)

7758 **1951 PR67 PCGS.** PCGS Population (89/1). NGC Census: (160/5). Mintage: 57,500. Numismedia Wsl. Price for problem free NGC/PCGS coin in PR67: $640. (#6692)

7759 **1956 Type Two PR68 Deep Cameo PCGS. CAC.** PCGS Population (362/39). NGC Census: (0/0). Numismedia Wsl. Price for problem free NGC/PCGS coin in PR68: $350. (#96697)

SMS KENNEDY HALF DOLLAR

7760 **1966 No "FG" SMS MS66 PCGS.** FS-901 (FS-013.9). PCGS Population (691/824). NGC Census: (83/82). Mintage: 2,200,000. Numismedia Wsl. Price for problem free NGC/PCGS coin in MS66: $18. (#6846)

PROOF KENNEDY HALF DOLLARS

7761 **1970-S PR69 Deep Cameo PCGS.** PCGS Population (223/0). NGC Census: (209/0). Numismedia Wsl. Price for problem free NGC/PCGS coin in PR69: $190. (#96806)

7762 **1988-S PR70 Deep Cameo PCGS.** PCGS Population (78). NGC Census: (48). Numismedia Wsl. Price for problem free NGC/PCGS coin in PR70: $205. (#96829)

EARLY DOLLARS

7763 **1795 Flowing Hair, Three Leaves—Plugged, Polished, Repaired—ANACS. Fine 12 Details.** BB-27, B-5. NGC Census: (62/832). PCGS Population (107/1072). Mintage: 160,295. Numismedia Wsl. Price for problem free NGC/PCGS coin in Fine 12: $3,950. (#6852)

7764 **1800—Scratch / Rim Dent—PCGS Genuine.** Mintage: 220,920. (#6887)

7765 **1800—Improperly Cleaned—NCS. VG Details.** BB-195, B-15. NGC Census: (10/759). PCGS Population (14/889). Mintage: 220,920. Numismedia Wsl. Price for problem free NGC/PCGS coin in VG8 : $900. (#6887)

SEATED DOLLARS

7766 **1842 AU50 PCGS.** PCGS Population (63/195). NGC Census: (35/253). Mintage: 184,618. Numismedia Wsl. Price for problem free NGC/PCGS coin in AU50: $675. (#6928)

7767 **1843 XF45 PCGS.** PCGS Population (81/209). NGC Census: (42/219). Mintage: 165,100. Numismedia Wsl. Price for problem free NGC/PCGS coin in XF45: $545. (#6929)

7768 **1846 XF40 ICG.** NGC Census: (19/307). PCGS Population (49/342). Mintage: 110,600. Numismedia Wsl. Price for problem free NGC/PCGS coin in XF40: $450. (#6932)

7769 **1849 AU50 PCGS.** PCGS Population (32/169). NGC Census: (14/167). Mintage: 62,600. Numismedia Wsl. Price for problem free NGC/PCGS coin in AU50: $635. (#6936)

7770 **1850—Cleaned, Repaired—NCS. VF Details.** NGC Census: (1/96). PCGS Population (1/144). Mintage: 7,500. Numismedia Wsl. Price for problem free NGC/PCGS coin in VF20: $1,025. (#6937)

7771 **1850-O—Improperly Cleaned—NGC. VF Details.** NGC Census: (0/100). PCGS Population (4/126). Mintage: 40,000. Numismedia Wsl. Price for problem free NGC/PCGS coin in VF20: $710. (#6938)

7772 **1859-O—Cleaned—ANACS. XF45 Details.** NGC Census: (13/378). PCGS Population (53/534). Mintage: 360,000. Numismedia Wsl. Price for problem free NGC/PCGS coin in XF45: $513. (#6947)

7773 **1860-O—Improperly Cleaned—NCS. AU Details.** NGC Census: (18/530). PCGS Population (49/817). Mintage: 515,000. Numismedia Wsl. Price for problem free NGC/PCGS coin in AU50: $630. (#6950)

7774 **1867 VF30 NGC.** NGC Census: (1/52). PCGS Population (3/125). Mintage: 46,900. Numismedia Wsl. Price for problem free NGC/PCGS coin in VF30: $455. (#6960)

7775 **1867 XF40 PCGS.** PCGS Population (9/114). NGC Census: (3/48). Mintage: 46,900. Numismedia Wsl. Price for problem free NGC/PCGS coin in XF40: $500. (#6960)

7776 **1871—Cleaned, Scratched—ANACS. VF20 Details.** NGC Census: (5/425). PCGS Population (12/578). Mintage: 1,074,760. Numismedia Wsl. Price for problem free NGC/PCGS coin in VF20: $330. (#6966)

7777 **1871 XF45 NGC. CAC.** NGC Census: (59/305). PCGS Population (98/356). Mintage: 1,074,760. Numismedia Wsl. Price for problem free NGC/PCGS coin in XF45: $525. (#6966)

7778 **1872 AU50 PCGS.** PCGS Population (46/185). NGC Census: (19/179). Mintage: 1,106,450. Numismedia Wsl. Price for problem free NGC/PCGS coin in AU50: $630. (#6968)

TRADE DOLLARS

7779 **1874-CC AU53 PCGS.** PCGS Population (13/197). NGC Census: (3/175). Mintage: 1,373,200. Numismedia Wsl. Price for problem free NGC/PCGS coin in AU53: $620. (#7035)

7780 **1874-S—Improperly Cleaned—NCS. Unc Details.** NGC Census: (12/178). PCGS Population (17/207). Mintage: 2,549,000. Numismedia Wsl. Price for problem free NGC/PCGS coin in MS60: $850. (#7036)

7781 **1875-CC—Cleaned—ANACS. MS60 Details.** NGC Census: (12/125). PCGS Population (12/154). Mintage: 1,573,700. Numismedia Wsl. Price for problem free NGC/PCGS coin in MS60: $1,950. (#7038)

7782 **1878-S AU55 PCGS.** PCGS Population (97/490). NGC Census: (47/466). Mintage: 4,162,000. Numismedia Wsl. Price for problem free NGC/PCGS coin in AU55: $325. (#7048)

MORGAN DOLLARS

7783 **1878 8TF MS65 ANACS.** NGC Census: (331/20). PCGS Population (454/31). Mintage: 699,300. Numismedia Wsl. Price for problem free NGC/PCGS coin in MS65: $1,150. (#7072)

7784 **1878 7/8TF Strong MS64 PCGS.** PCGS Population (1357/212). NGC Census: (935/91). Mintage: 544,000. Numismedia Wsl. Price for problem free NGC/PCGS coin in MS64: $400. (#7078)

7785 **1878 7/8TF Strong MS64 NGC.** NGC Census: (936/91). PCGS Population (1360/213). Mintage: 544,000. Numismedia Wsl. Price for problem free NGC/PCGS coin in MS64: $400. (#7078)

7786 **1878 7/8TF Strong MS64 PCGS.** PCGS Population (1350/211). NGC Census: (933/91). Mintage: 544,000. Numismedia Wsl. Price for problem free NGC/PCGS coin in MS64: $400. (#7078)

7787 **1878 7/8TF Strong MS64 PCGS.** PCGS Population (1357/212). NGC Census: (935/91). Mintage: 544,000. Numismedia Wsl. Price for problem free NGC/PCGS coin in MS64: $400. (#7078)

7788 **1878 7TF Reverse of 1878 MS64 NGC.** NGC Census: (3134/471). PCGS Population (2275/488). Mintage: 4,900,000. Numismedia Wsl. Price for problem free NGC/PCGS coin in MS64: $210. (#7074)

7789 **1878 7TF Reverse of 1878 MS64 PCGS.** PCGS Population (2275/488). NGC Census: (3134/471). Mintage: 4,900,000. Numismedia Wsl. Price for problem free NGC/PCGS coin in MS64: $210. (#7074)

7790 **1878 7TF Reverse of 1878 MS64 Prooflike NGC.** NGC Census: (238/30). PCGS Population (156/37). Numismedia Wsl. Price for problem free NGC/PCGS coin in MS64: $335. (#7075)

7791 **1878 7TF Reverse of 1878 MS63 Deep Mirror Prooflike ANACS.** NGC Census: (0/0). PCGS Population (136/80). Numismedia Wsl. Price for problem free NGC/PCGS coin in MS63: $320. (#97075)

7792 **1878-CC MS61 NGC.** GSA Soft Pack. NGC Census: (530/11089). PCGS Population (631/16890). Mintage: 2,212,000. Numismedia Wsl. Price for problem free NGC/PCGS coin in MS61: $190. (#7080)

7793 **1878-CC MS62 NGC.** NGC Census: (1938/9151). PCGS Population (2863/14027). Mintage: 2,212,000. Numismedia Wsl. Price for problem free NGC/PCGS coin in MS62: $220. (#7080)

7794 **1878-CC MS63 NGC.** NGC Census: (4016/5158). PCGS Population (6667/7361). Mintage: 2,212,000. Numismedia Wsl. Price for problem free NGC/PCGS coin in MS63: $265. (#7080)

7795 **1878-CC MS64 PCGS.** PCGS Population (5630/1731). NGC Census: (3957/1201). Mintage: 2,212,000. Numismedia Wsl. Price for problem free NGC/PCGS coin in MS64: $425. (#7080)

7796 **1878-CC MS64 ANACS.** NGC Census: (3957/1201). PCGS Population (5630/1731). Mintage: 2,212,000. Numismedia Wsl. Price for problem free NGC/PCGS coin in MS64: $425. (#7080)

7797 **1878-CC MS62 Prooflike PCGS.** PCGS Population (309/1004). NGC Census: (168/824). Numismedia Wsl. Price for problem free NGC/PCGS coin in MS62: $250. (#7081)

7798 **1878-S MS66 NGC. CAC.** NGC Census: (457/31). PCGS Population (502/21). Mintage: 9,774,000. Numismedia Wsl. Price for problem free NGC/PCGS coin in MS66: $710. (#7082)

7799 **1878-S MS66 PCGS.** PCGS Population (502/21). NGC Census: (458/31). Mintage: 9,774,000. Numismedia Wsl. Price for problem free NGC/PCGS coin in MS66: $710. (#7082)

7800 **1878-S MS66 NGC. CAC.** NGC Census: (457/31). PCGS Population (502/21). Mintage: 9,774,000. Numismedia Wsl. Price for problem free NGC/PCGS coin in MS66: $710. (#7082)

7801 **1879 MS65 PCGS.** PCGS Population (845/86). NGC Census: (585/51). Mintage: 14,807,100. Numismedia Wsl. Price for problem free NGC/PCGS coin in MS65: $685. (#7084)

7802 **1879 MS65 NGC.** NGC Census: (583/51). PCGS Population (836/86). Mintage: 14,807,100. Numismedia Wsl. Price for problem free NGC/PCGS coin in MS65: $685. (#7084)

7803 **1879-CC Capped Die—Cleaned—ANACS. VF30 Details.** VAM-3 Top 100. NGC Census: (25/1017). PCGS Population (50/1602). Numismedia Wsl. Price for problem free NGC/PCGS coin in VF30: $375. (#7088)

7804 **1879-O MS64 PCGS. CAC.** PCGS Population (1815/281). NGC Census: (1178/139). Mintage: 2,887,000. Numismedia Wsl. Price for problem free NGC/PCGS coin in MS64: $440. (#7090)

7805 **1879-O MS64 PCGS.** PCGS Population (1821/282). NGC Census: (1178/139). Mintage: 2,887,000. Numismedia Wsl. Price for problem free NGC/PCGS coin in MS64: $440. (#7090)

7806 **1879-O MS64 NGC.** NGC Census: (1178/139). PCGS Population (1811/280). Mintage: 2,887,000. Numismedia Wsl. Price for problem free NGC/PCGS coin in MS64: $440. (#7090)

7807 **1879-S MS66 PCGS.** PCGS Population (6495/1231). NGC Census: (6035/1931). Mintage: 9,110,000. Numismedia Wsl. Price for problem free NGC/PCGS coin in MS66: $235. (#7092)

7808 **1879-S MS66 PCGS.** PCGS Population (6495/1231). NGC Census: (6035/1931). Mintage: 9,110,000. Numismedia Wsl. Price for problem free NGC/PCGS coin in MS66: $235. (#7092)

7809 **1879-S MS66 PCGS.** PCGS Population (6485/1229). NGC Census: (5990/1908). Mintage: 9,110,000. Numismedia Wsl. Price for problem free NGC/PCGS coin in MS66: $235. (#7092)

7810 **1879-S Reverse of 1878 MS62 ANACS.** VAM-43 Top 100. NGC Census: (269/660). PCGS Population (618/1241). Numismedia Wsl. Price for problem free NGC/PCGS coin in MS62: $165. (#7094)

7811 **1879-S Reverse of 1878 MS63 NGC.** Top 100. NGC Census: (376/280). PCGS Population (654/569). Numismedia Wsl. Price for problem free NGC/PCGS coin in MS63: $325. (#7094)

7812 **1879-S Reverse of 1878 MS63 Prooflike NGC.** NGC Census: (42/10). PCGS Population (23/8). Numismedia Wsl. Price for problem free NGC/PCGS coin in MS63: $1,150. (#7095)

7813 **1880-CC VG8 ANACS.** NGC Census: (2/5537). PCGS Population (10/10732). Mintage: 591,000. Numismedia Wsl. Price for problem free NGC/PCGS coin in VG8 : $125. (#7100)

7814 **1880-CC MS62 NGC.** NGC Census: (457/4912). PCGS Population (939/9395). Mintage: 591,000. Numismedia Wsl. Price for problem free NGC/PCGS coin in MS62: $455. (#7100)

7815 **1880-CC MS62 ANACS.** VAM-8. NGC Census: (459/4952). PCGS Population (940/9419). Mintage: 591,000. Numismedia Wsl. Price for problem free NGC/PCGS coin in MS62: $455. (#7100)

7816 **1880-CC MS63 NGC.** NGC Census: (1257/3655). PCGS Population (2653/6742). Mintage: 591,000. Numismedia Wsl. Price for problem free NGC/PCGS coin in MS63: $480. (#7100)

7817 **1880-CC MS63 PCGS.** PCGS Population (2654/6757). NGC Census: (1258/3673). Mintage: 591,000. Numismedia Wsl. Price for problem free NGC/PCGS coin in MS63: $480. (#7100)

7818 **1880-CC MS64 PCGS.** PCGS Population (3980/2762). NGC Census: (2238/1417). Mintage: 591,000. Numismedia Wsl. Price for problem free NGC/PCGS coin in MS64: $560. (#7100)

7819 **1880-CC MS64 NGC.** NGC Census: (2238/1417). PCGS Population (3980/2762). Mintage: 591,000. Numismedia Wsl. Price for problem free NGC/PCGS coin in MS64: $560. (#7100)

7820 **1880-CC MS64 PCGS.** PCGS Population (3988/2775). NGC Census: (2257/1430). Mintage: 591,000. Numismedia Wsl. Price for problem free NGC/PCGS coin in MS64: $560. (#7100)

7821 **1880-CC MS63 Prooflike NGC.** NGC Census: (186/384). PCGS Population (240/381). Numismedia Wsl. Price for problem free NGC/PCGS coin in MS63: $555. (#7101)

7822 **1880-CC 8 Over High 7 MS63 PCGS.** PCGS Population (123/570). NGC Census: (0/0). (#7102)

7823 **1880/79-CC Reverse of 1878 MS62 ANACS.** VAM-4 Top 100. NGC Census: (135/1073). PCGS Population (267/2405). Mintage: 591,000. Numismedia Wsl. Price for problem free NGC/PCGS coin in MS62: $490. (#7108)

7824 **1880/79-CC Reverse of 1878 MS62 PCGS.** PCGS Population (267/2416). NGC Census: (135/1075). Mintage: 591,000. Numismedia Wsl. Price for problem free NGC/PCGS coin in MS62: $490. (#7108)

7825 **1880/79-CC Reverse of 1878 MS63 ANACS.** VAM-4 Top 100. NGC Census: (388/685). PCGS Population (747/1658). Mintage: 591,000. Numismedia Wsl. Price for problem free NGC/PCGS coin in MS63: $535. (#7108)

7826 **1880/79-CC Reverse of 1878 MS64 ANACS.** VAM-4 Top 100. NGC Census: (538/148). PCGS Population (1165/503). Mintage: 591,000. Numismedia Wsl. Price for problem free NGC/PCGS coin in MS64: $925. (#7108)

7827 **1880/79-CC Reverse of 1878 MS64 ANACS.** VAM-4. NGC Census: (538/148). PCGS Population (1165/503). Mintage: 591,000. Numismedia Wsl. Price for problem free NGC/PCGS coin in MS64: $925. (#7108)

7828 **1880-CC 8/7 Reverse of 1878 MS64 ANACS.** VAM-5. NGC Census: (0/0). PCGS Population (189/132). (#7110)

7829 **1880-O MS63 PCGS.** PCGS Population (2025/1125). NGC Census: (1619/904). Mintage: 5,305,000. Numismedia Wsl. Price for problem free NGC/PCGS coin in MS63: $300. (#7114)

7830 **1880/79-O MS62 ANACS.** VAM-4. A Top 100 Variety. (#7116)

7831 **(3)1880-S MS65 NGC.** Also includes an **1885-O and 1887 Morgan Dollars. All graded MS65 NGC.** NGC Census: (28035/12974). PCGS Population (30215/10815). Mintage: 8,900,000. Numismedia Wsl. Price for problem free NGC/PCGS coin in MS65: $126. (#7118) (Total: 5 coins)

7832 **1880-S MS66 NGC.** NGC Census: (9804/3147). PCGS Population (9075/1734). Mintage: 8,900,000. Numismedia Wsl. Price for problem free NGC/PCGS coin in MS66: $235. (#7118)

7833 **1880-S MS66 PCGS. CAC.** PCGS Population (9075/1734). NGC Census: (9804/3147). Mintage: 8,900,000. Numismedia Wsl. Price for problem free NGC/PCGS coin in MS66: $235. (#7118)

7834 **1880-S MS65 Prooflike PCGS.** PCGS Population (2408/785). NGC Census: (1886/877). Numismedia Wsl. Price for problem free NGC/PCGS coin in MS65: $210. (#7119)

7835 **1880/9-S MS66 Prooflike NGC.** Medium S, VAM-11 Hot-50. NGC Census: (0/0). PCGS Population (5/0). (#7123)

7836 **1881 MS64 Prooflike NGC.** NGC Census: (94/6). PCGS Population (58/11). Numismedia Wsl. Price for problem free NGC/PCGS coin in MS64: $290. (#7125)

7837 **1881-CC MS63 NGC.** NGC Census: (1537/5473). PCGS Population (3525/12015). Mintage: 296,000. Numismedia Wsl. Price for problem free NGC/PCGS coin in MS63: $450. (#7126)

7838 **1881-CC MS63 ANACS.** NGC Census: (1548/5509). PCGS Population (3528/12047). Mintage: 296,000. Numismedia Wsl. Price for problem free NGC/PCGS coin in MS63: $450. (#7126)

7839 **1881-CC MS64 PCGS.** PCGS Population (6394/5648). NGC Census: (2850/2657). Mintage: 296,000. Numismedia Wsl. Price for problem free NGC/PCGS coin in MS64: $515. (#7126)

7840 **1881-CC MS64 NGC.** NGC Census: (2850/2659). PCGS Population (6390/5657). Mintage: 296,000. Numismedia Wsl. Price for problem free NGC/PCGS coin in MS64: $515. (#7126)

7841 **1881-CC MS64 NGC.** NGC Census: (2850/2657). PCGS Population (6394/5648). Mintage: 296,000. Numismedia Wsl. Price for problem free NGC/PCGS coin in MS64: $515. (#7126)

7842 **1881-CC MS65 NGC.** NGC Census: (1799/842). PCGS Population (4079/1553). Mintage: 296,000. Numismedia Wsl. Price for problem free NGC/PCGS coin in MS65: $930. (#7126)

7843 **1881-O MS64 PCGS.** PCGS Population (2881/483). NGC Census: (3460/475). Mintage: 5,708,000. Numismedia Wsl. Price for problem free NGC/PCGS coin in MS64: $160. (#7128)

7844 **1881-S MS65 PCGS.** PCGS Population (44140/12968). NGC Census: (43325/16573). Mintage: 12,760,000. Numismedia Wsl. Price for problem free NGC/PCGS coin in MS65: $126. (#7130)

7845 **1881-S MS65 PCGS.** PCGS Population (44055/12942). NGC Census: (43115/16394). Mintage: 12,760,000. Numismedia Wsl. Price for problem free NGC/PCGS coin in MS65: $126. (#7130)

7846 **1881-S MS66 NGC.** NGC Census: (13249/3324). PCGS Population (11475/1493). Mintage: 12,760,000. Numismedia Wsl. Price for problem free NGC/PCGS coin in MS66: $230. (#7130)

7847 **1881-S MS66 NGC.** NGC Census: (13249/3324). PCGS Population (11475/1493). Mintage: 12,760,000. Numismedia Wsl. Price for problem free NGC/PCGS coin in MS66: $230. (#7130)

7848 **1881-S MS66 PCGS.** PCGS Population (11475/1493). NGC Census: (13249/3324). Mintage: 12,760,000. Numismedia Wsl. Price for problem free NGC/PCGS coin in MS66: $230. (#7130)

7849 **1881-S MS66 PCGS.** PCGS Population (11475/1493). NGC Census: (13249/3324). Mintage: 12,760,000. Numismedia Wsl. Price for problem free NGC/PCGS coin in MS66: $230. (#7130)

7850 **1881-S MS66 PCGS.** PCGS Population (11475/1493). NGC Census: (13249/3324). Mintage: 12,760,000. Numismedia Wsl. Price for problem free NGC/PCGS coin in MS66: $230. (#7130)

7851 **1881-S MS66 PCGS.** PCGS Population (11475/1493). NGC Census: (13249/3324). Mintage: 12,760,000. Numismedia Wsl. Price for problem free NGC/PCGS coin in MS66: $230. (#7130)

7852 **1881-S MS66 PCGS.** PCGS Population (11475/1493). NGC Census: (13249/3324). Mintage: 12,760,000. Numismedia Wsl. Price for problem free NGC/PCGS coin in MS66: $230. (#7130)

7853 **1881-S MS66 PCGS. CAC.** PCGS Population (11463/1493). NGC Census: (13242/3324). Mintage: 12,760,000. Numismedia Wsl. Price for problem free NGC/PCGS coin in MS66: $230. (#7130)

7854 **1881-S MS67 NGC.** NGC Census: (3148/176). PCGS Population (1398/92). Mintage: 12,760,000. Numismedia Wsl. Price for problem free NGC/PCGS coin in MS67: $700. (#7130)

7855 **1881-S MS65 Prooflike PCGS. CAC.** PCGS Population (1820/552). NGC Census: (1565/621). Numismedia Wsl. Price for problem free NGC/PCGS coin in MS65: $210. (#7131)

7856 **1881-S MS65 Deep Mirror Prooflike NGC.** NGC Census: (317/109). PCGS Population (217/80). Numismedia Wsl. Price for problem free NGC/PCGS coin in MS65: $625. (#97131)

7857 **1882 MS65 NGC.** NGC Census: (1027/194). PCGS Population (1122/182). Mintage: 11,101,100. Numismedia Wsl. Price for problem free NGC/PCGS coin in MS65: $430. (#7132)

7858 **1882 MS64 Deep Mirror Prooflike NGC.** NGC Census: (56/8). PCGS Population (93/19). Numismedia Wsl. Price for problem free NGC/PCGS coin in MS64: $865. (#97133)

7859 **1882-CC MS65 PCGS. CAC.** PCGS Population (4499/1080). NGC Census: (2362/540). Mintage: 1,133,000. Numismedia Wsl. Price for problem free NGC/PCGS coin in MS65: $440. (#7134)

7860 **1882-CC MS65 PCGS. CAC.** PCGS Population (4496/1079). NGC Census: (2362/537). Mintage: 1,133,000. Numismedia Wsl. Price for problem free NGC/PCGS coin in MS65: $440. (#7134)

7861 **1882-CC MS65 ANACS.** NGC Census: (2363/540). PCGS Population (4496/1084). Mintage: 1,133,000. Numismedia Wsl. Price for problem free NGC/PCGS coin in MS65: $440. (#7134)

7862 **1882-CC MS64 Deep Mirror Prooflike ANACS.** NGC Census: (295/93). PCGS Population (759/391). Numismedia Wsl. Price for problem free NGC/PCGS coin in MS64: $650. (#97135)

7863 **1882-O MS64 Cameo Deep Mirror Prooflike ANACS.** NGC Census: (105/6). PCGS Population (136/21). Numismedia Wsl. Price for problem free NGC/PCGS coin in MS64: $875. (#97137)

7864 **1882-O/S MS62 ANACS.** VAM-4 Top 100. NGC Census: (427/714). PCGS Population (607/547). Mintage: 1,039. Numismedia Wsl. Price for problem free NGC/PCGS coin in MS62: $360. (#7138)

7865 **1882-S MS66 NGC.** NGC Census: (5567/1581). PCGS Population (4245/628). Mintage: 9,250,000. Numismedia Wsl. Price for problem free NGC/PCGS coin in MS66: $280. (#7140)

7866 **1882-S MS66 NGC.** NGC Census: (5539/1549). PCGS Population (4237/624). Mintage: 9,250,000. Numismedia Wsl. Price for problem free NGC/PCGS coin in MS66: $280. (#7140)

7867 **1882-S MS66 PCGS. CAC.** PCGS Population (4241/628). NGC Census: (5560/1575). Mintage: 9,250,000. Numismedia Wsl. Price for problem free NGC/PCGS coin in MS66: $280. (#7140)

7868 **1882-S MS67 ★ NGC.** NGC Census: (1504/77). PCGS Population (595/33). Mintage: 9,250,000. Numismedia Wsl. Price for problem free NGC/PCGS coin in MS67: $835. (#7140)

7869 **1882-S MS64 Deep Mirror Prooflike NGC.** NGC Census: (167/81). PCGS Population (75/40). Numismedia Wsl. Price for problem free NGC/PCGS coin in MS64: $400. (#97141)

7870 **1883 MS66 PCGS. CAC.** PCGS Population (757/56). NGC Census: (748/107). Mintage: 12,291,039. Numismedia Wsl. Price for problem free NGC/PCGS coin in MS66: $520. (#7142)

7871 **1883 MS66 NGC. CAC.** NGC Census: (748/107). PCGS Population (747/56). Mintage: 12,291,039. Numismedia Wsl. Price for problem free NGC/PCGS coin in MS66: $520. (#7142)

7872 **1883-CC MS66 PCGS.** GSA. PCGS Population (1685/133). NGC Census: (865/95). Mintage: 1,204,000. Numismedia Wsl. Price for problem free NGC/PCGS coin in MS66: $760. (#7144)

7873 **1883-CC MS66 ICG.** NGC Census: (865/95). PCGS Population (1685/133). Mintage: 1,204,000. Numismedia Wsl. Price for problem free NGC/PCGS coin in MS66: $760. (#7144)

7874 **1883-CC MS64 Prooflike NGC.** NGC Census: (582/366). PCGS Population (1119/685). Numismedia Wsl. Price for problem free NGC/PCGS coin in MS64: $250. (#7145)

7875 **1883-CC MS64 Prooflike PCGS.** PCGS Population (1120/687). NGC Census: (583/365). Numismedia Wsl. Price for problem free NGC/PCGS coin in MS64: $250. (#7145)

7876 **1883-CC MS65 Prooflike PCGS. CAC.** PCGS Population (557/128). NGC Census: (296/70). Numismedia Wsl. Price for problem free NGC/PCGS coin in MS65: $420. (#7145)

7877 **1883-CC MS65 Prooflike ANACS.** NGC Census: (295/70). PCGS Population (558/130). Numismedia Wsl. Price for problem free NGC/PCGS coin in MS65: $420. (#7145)

7878 **1883-CC MS62 Deep Mirror Prooflike NGC.** NGC Census: (80/1107). PCGS Population (258/2920). Numismedia Wsl. Price for problem free NGC/PCGS coin in MS62: $225. (#97145)

7879 **1883-CC MS63 Deep Mirror Prooflike ANACS.** NGC Census: (338/769). PCGS Population (908/2012). Numismedia Wsl. Price for problem free NGC/PCGS coin in MS63: $350. (#97145)

7880 **1883-CC MS64 Deep Mirror Prooflike PCGS.** PCGS Population (1239/780). NGC Census: (527/242). Numismedia Wsl. Price for problem free NGC/PCGS coin in MS64: $540. (#97145)

7881 **1883-O MS65 Deep Mirror Prooflike NGC.** NGC Census: (58/2). PCGS Population (93/13). Numismedia Wsl. Price for problem free NGC/PCGS coin in MS65: $1,000. (#97147)

7882 **1883-S AU58 PCGS.** PCGS Population (361/2372). NGC Census: (510/1501). Mintage: 6,250,000. Numismedia Wsl. Price for problem free NGC/PCGS coin in AU58: $240. (#7148)

7883 **1883-S MS61 ANACS.** VAM-6. NGC Census: (279/1150). PCGS Population (375/1854). Mintage: 6,250,000. Numismedia Wsl. Price for problem free NGC/PCGS coin in MS61: $605. (#7148)

7884 1884-CC MS65 PCGS. PCGS Population (6469/1400). NGC Census: (3614/818). Mintage: 1,136,000. Numismedia Wsl. Price for problem free NGC/PCGS coin in MS65: $370. (#7152)

7885 1884-CC MS65 PCGS. PCGS Population (6445/1390). NGC Census: (3600/808). Mintage: 1,136,000. Numismedia Wsl. Price for problem free NGC/PCGS coin in MS65: $370. (#7152)

7886 1884-CC MS65 NGC. NGC Census: (3600/808). PCGS Population (6445/1390). Mintage: 1,136,000. Numismedia Wsl. Price for problem free NGC/PCGS coin in MS65: $370. (#7152)

7887 1884-CC MS65 PCGS. CAC. PCGS Population (6463/1394). NGC Census: (3610/818). Mintage: 1,136,000. Numismedia Wsl. Price for problem free NGC/PCGS coin in MS65: $370. (#7152)

7888 1884-CC MS66 NGC. NGC Census: (725/93). PCGS Population (1341/59). Mintage: 1,136,000. Numismedia Wsl. Price for problem free NGC/PCGS coin in MS66: $775. (#7152)

7889 1884-CC MS66 Cameo Prooflike ANACS. NGC Census: (53/6). PCGS Population (88/1). Numismedia Wsl. Price for problem free NGC/PCGS coin in MS66: $1,025. (#7153)

7890 1884-CC MS64 Deep Mirror Prooflike PCGS. PCGS Population (1301/672). NGC Census: (590/250). Numismedia Wsl. Price for problem free NGC/PCGS coin in MS64: $460. (#97153)

7891 1884-S AU50 PCGS. PCGS Population (829/2736). NGC Census: (716/3564). Mintage: 3,200,000. Numismedia Wsl. Price for problem free NGC/PCGS coin in AU50: $200. (#7156)

7892 1884-S AU50 ANACS. NGC Census: (714/3554). PCGS Population (825/2722). Mintage: 3,200,000. Numismedia Wsl. Price for problem free NGC/PCGS coin in AU50: $200. (#7156)

7893 1884-S AU50 NGC. NGC Census: (714/3554). PCGS Population (825/2722). Mintage: 3,200,000. Numismedia Wsl. Price for problem free NGC/PCGS coin in AU50: $200. (#7156)

7894 1884-S AU53 PCGS. PCGS Population (770/1952). NGC Census: (798/2756). Mintage: 3,200,000. Numismedia Wsl. Price for problem free NGC/PCGS coin in AU53: $280. (#7156)

7895 1884-S AU53 ANACS. NGC Census: (798/2760). PCGS Population (770/1962). Mintage: 3,200,000. Numismedia Wsl. Price for problem free NGC/PCGS coin in AU53: $280. (#7156)

7896 1884-S AU55 PCGS. PCGS Population (1117/835). NGC Census: (1148/1608). Mintage: 3,200,000. Numismedia Wsl. Price for problem free NGC/PCGS coin in AU55: $400. (#7156)

7897 1884-S AU55 PCGS. PCGS Population (1122/840). NGC Census: (1149/1611). Mintage: 3,200,000. Numismedia Wsl. Price for problem free NGC/PCGS coin in AU55: $400. (#7156)

7898 1885-CC—Altered Surfaces—PCGS Genuine. Mintage: 228,000. (#7160)

7899 1885-CC AG3 PCGS. NGC Census: (1/7380). PCGS Population (4/16706). Mintage: 228,000. Numismedia Wsl. Price for problem free NGC/PCGS coin in AG3 : $168. (#7160)

7900 1885-CC MS62 ANACS. NGC Census: (532/6722). PCGS Population (1220/15156). Mintage: 228,000. Numismedia Wsl. Price for problem free NGC/PCGS coin in MS62: $540. (#7160)

7901 1885-CC MS63 PCGS. PCGS Population (3957/11172). NGC Census: (1761/4948). Mintage: 228,000. Numismedia Wsl. Price for problem free NGC/PCGS coin in MS63: $555. (#7160)

7902 1885-CC MS64 PCGS. PCGS Population (6529/4643). NGC Census: (2821/2127). Mintage: 228,000. Numismedia Wsl. Price for problem free NGC/PCGS coin in MS64: $600. (#7160)

7903 1885-CC MS65 ANACS. NGC Census: (1572/558). PCGS Population (3707/952). Mintage: 228,000. Numismedia Wsl. Price for problem free NGC/PCGS coin in MS65: $960. (#7160)

7904 1885-CC MS62 Prooflike PCGS. PCGS Population (147/916). NGC Census: (77/462). Numismedia Wsl. Price for problem free NGC/PCGS coin in MS62: $560. (#7161)

7905 1885-S MS62 NGC. NGC Census: (711/2843). PCGS Population (1345/5000). Mintage: 1,497,000. Numismedia Wsl. Price for problem free NGC/PCGS coin in MS62: $210. (#7164)

7906 1885-S MS63 NGC. NGC Census: (1355/1488). PCGS Population (2507/2493). Mintage: 1,497,000. Numismedia Wsl. Price for problem free NGC/PCGS coin in MS63: $260. (#7164)

7907 1885-S MS64 NGC. CAC. NGC Census: (1280/212). PCGS Population (2066/448). Mintage: 1,497,000. Numismedia Wsl. Price for problem free NGC/PCGS coin in MS64: $580. (#7164)

7908 1885-S MS64 PCGS. PCGS Population (2062/450). NGC Census: (1280/212). Mintage: 1,497,000. Numismedia Wsl. Price for problem free NGC/PCGS coin in MS64: $580. (#7164)

7909 1885-S MS64 PCGS. CAC. PCGS Population (2062/450). NGC Census: (1280/212). Mintage: 1,497,000. Numismedia Wsl. Price for problem free NGC/PCGS coin in MS64: $580. (#7164)

7910 1886 MS66 NGC. NGC Census: (4007/683). PCGS Population (2315/214). Mintage: 19,963,886. Numismedia Wsl. Price for problem free NGC/PCGS coin in MS66: $310. (#7166)

7911 1886 MS66 NGC. NGC Census: (3999/682). PCGS Population (2310/213). Mintage: 19,963,886. Numismedia Wsl. Price for problem free NGC/PCGS coin in MS66: $310. (#7166)

7912 1886 MS64 Deep Mirror Prooflike PCGS. PCGS Population (232/144). NGC Census: (213/77). Numismedia Wsl. Price for problem free NGC/PCGS coin in MS64: $310. (#97167)

7913 1886-O AU58 ANACS. NGC Census: (1083/1339). PCGS Population (716/1912). Mintage: 10,710,000. Numismedia Wsl. Price for problem free NGC/PCGS coin in AU58: $195. (#7168)

7914 1886-O AU58 NGC. NGC Census: (1084/1342). PCGS Population (718/1918). Mintage: 10,710,000. Numismedia Wsl. Price for problem free NGC/PCGS coin in AU58: $195. (#7168)

7915 1886-O MS60 ANACS. NGC Census: (153/1194). PCGS Population (184/1733). Mintage: 10,710,000. Numismedia Wsl. Price for problem free NGC/PCGS coin in MS60: $500. (#7168)

7916 **1886-O MS61 ANACS.** NGC Census: (405/786). PCGS Population (323/1414). Mintage: 10,710,000. Numismedia Wsl. Price for problem free NGC/PCGS coin in MS61: $750. (#7168)

7917 **1886-O MS61 NGC.** NGC Census: (404/785). PCGS Population (323/1411). Mintage: 10,710,000. Numismedia Wsl. Price for problem free NGC/PCGS coin in MS61: $750. (#7168)

7918 **1886-S MS60 ANACS.** VAM-1A. NGC Census: (29/2316). PCGS Population (77/4169). Mintage: 750,000. Numismedia Wsl. Price for problem free NGC/PCGS coin in MS60: $225. (#7170)

7919 **1887 MS65 PCGS.** PCGS Population (13544/1297). NGC Census: (22056/3391). Mintage: 20,290,710. Numismedia Wsl. Price for problem free NGC/PCGS coin in MS65: $126. (#7172)

7920 **1887 MS66 NGC.** NGC Census: (3121/262). PCGS Population (1232/65). Mintage: 20,290,710. Numismedia Wsl. Price for problem free NGC/PCGS coin in MS66: $300. (#7172)

7921 **1887 MS66 NGC.** NGC Census: (3121/262). PCGS Population (1227/65). Mintage: 20,290,710. Numismedia Wsl. Price for problem free NGC/PCGS coin in MS66: $300. (#7172)

7922 **1887 MS66 PCGS.** PCGS Population (1227/64). NGC Census: (3121/261). Mintage: 20,290,710. Numismedia Wsl. Price for problem free NGC/PCGS coin in MS66: $300. (#7172)

7923 **1887 MS64 Deep Mirror Prooflike PCGS. CAC.** PCGS Population (335/200). NGC Census: (413/135). Numismedia Wsl. Price for problem free NGC/PCGS coin in MS64: $300. (#97173)

7924 **1887 MS64 Deep Mirror Prooflike PCGS.** PCGS Population (335/200). NGC Census: (413/134). Numismedia Wsl. Price for problem free NGC/PCGS coin in MS64: $300. (#97173)

7925 **1887 MS65 Deep Mirror Prooflike NGC.** NGC Census: (123/12). PCGS Population (170/30). Numismedia Wsl. Price for problem free NGC/PCGS coin in MS65: $900. (#97173)

7926 **1887 MS65 Deep Mirror Prooflike NGC.** NGC Census: (122/12). PCGS Population (170/30). Numismedia Wsl. Price for problem free NGC/PCGS coin in MS65: $900. (#97173)

7927 **1887/6 MS62 ANACS.** VAM-2 Top 100. NGC Census: (133/557). PCGS Population (285/888). Numismedia Wsl. Price for problem free NGC/PCGS coin in MS62: $400. (#7174)

7928 **1887/6 MS62 ANACS.** VAM-2 Top 100. NGC Census: (133/557). PCGS Population (285/893). Numismedia Wsl. Price for problem free NGC/PCGS coin in MS62: $400. (#7174)

7929 **1887/6 MS64 Prooflike NGC.** VAM-2 Top 100. NGC Census: (60/23). PCGS Population (63/39). Numismedia Wsl. Price for problem free NGC/PCGS coin in MS64: $1,425. (#7175)

7930 **1887-O MS64 NGC.** NGC Census: (1681/101). PCGS Population (2217/302). Mintage: 11,550,000. Numismedia Wsl. Price for problem free NGC/PCGS coin in MS64: $360. (#7176)

7931 **1887-O MS64 PCGS.** PCGS Population (2214/302). NGC Census: (1681/101). Mintage: 11,550,000. Numismedia Wsl. Price for problem free NGC/PCGS coin in MS64: $360. (#7176)

7932 **1887-S MS63 PCGS.** PCGS Population (2315/1994). NGC Census: (1371/1012). Mintage: 1,771,000. Numismedia Wsl. Price for problem free NGC/PCGS coin in MS63: $210. (#7180)

7933 **1887-S MS63 PCGS.** PCGS Population (2318/2001). NGC Census: (1371/1012). Mintage: 1,771,000. Numismedia Wsl. Price for problem free NGC/PCGS coin in MS63: $210. (#7180)

7934 **1888-S AU53 ANACS.** NGC Census: (42/2865). PCGS Population (83/5122). Mintage: 657,000. Numismedia Wsl. Price for problem free NGC/PCGS coin in AU53: $175. (#7186)

7935 **1888-S—Struck Thru at Date—MS62 ANACS.** VAM-4. NGC Census: (595/1775). PCGS Population (961/3457). Mintage: 657,000. Numismedia Wsl. Price for problem free NGC/PCGS coin in MS62: $290. (#7186)

7936 **1888-S MS63 PCGS.** PCGS Population (1825/1632). NGC Census: (828/947). Mintage: 657,000. Numismedia Wsl. Price for problem free NGC/PCGS coin in MS63: $350. (#7186)

7937 **1888-S MS63 PCGS.** PCGS Population (1824/1631). NGC Census: (826/944). Mintage: 657,000. Numismedia Wsl. Price for problem free NGC/PCGS coin in MS63: $350. (#7186)

7938 **1888-S MS64 PCGS.** PCGS Population (1376/263). NGC Census: (831/116). Mintage: 657,000. Numismedia Wsl. Price for problem free NGC/PCGS coin in MS64: $700. (#7186)

7939 **1889 MS65 PCGS.** PCGS Population (1506/172). NGC Census: (1709/130). Mintage: 21,726,812. Numismedia Wsl. Price for problem free NGC/PCGS coin in MS65: $290. (#7188)

7940 **1889 MS65 PCGS.** PCGS Population (1523/172). NGC Census: (1716/133). Mintage: 21,726,812. Numismedia Wsl. Price for problem free NGC/PCGS coin in MS65: $290. (#7188)

7941 **1889 MS65 NGC.** NGC Census: (1716/133). PCGS Population (1523/172). Mintage: 21,726,812. Numismedia Wsl. Price for problem free NGC/PCGS coin in MS65: $290. (#7188)

7942 **1889-CC PCGS Genuine.** Mintage: 350,000. (#7190)

7943 **1889-CC AG3 NGC.** NGC Census: (17/2576). PCGS Population (46/4074). Mintage: 350,000. Numismedia Wsl. Price for problem free NGC/PCGS coin in AG3 : $280. (#7190)

7944 **1889-CC VG8 PCGS.** PCGS Population (147/3681). NGC Census: (74/2390). Mintage: 350,000. Numismedia Wsl. Price for problem free NGC/PCGS coin in VG8 : $550. (#7190)

7945 **1889-CC—Improperly Cleaned—NCS. Fine Details.** NGC Census: (126/2174). PCGS Population (225/3284). Mintage: 350,000. Numismedia Wsl. Price for problem free NGC/PCGS coin in Fine 12: $750. (#7190)

7946 **1889-CC—Rim Bumps—Fine 12 ANACS. Fine 12 Details.** NGC Census: (126/2174). PCGS Population (225/3284). Mintage: 350,000. Numismedia Wsl. Price for problem free NGC/PCGS coin in Fine 12: $750. (#7190)

7947 **1889-CC—Improperly Cleaned—NCS. VF Details.** NGC Census: (150/1896). PCGS Population (242/2728). Mintage: 350,000. Numismedia Wsl. Price for problem free NGC/PCGS coin in VF20: $1,150. (#7190)

7948 **1889-CC—Cleaned—ANACS. VF20 Details.** NGC Census: (150/1895). PCGS Population (241/2720). Mintage: 350,000. Numismedia Wsl. Price for problem free NGC/PCGS coin in VF20: $1,150. (#7190)

7949 **1889-O MS63 ANACS.** NGC Census: (1194/897). PCGS Population (1773/1487). Mintage: 11,875,000. Numismedia Wsl. Price for problem free NGC/PCGS coin in MS63: $325. (#7192)

7950 **1889-S MS60 PCGS.** PCGS Population (75/6281). NGC Census: (36/3567). Mintage: 700,000. Numismedia Wsl. Price for problem free NGC/PCGS coin in MS60: $160. (#7194)

7951 **1889-S MS62 ANACS.** NGC Census: (674/2670). PCGS Population (1075/4903). Mintage: 700,000. Numismedia Wsl. Price for problem free NGC/PCGS coin in MS62: $220. (#7194)

7952 **1889-S MS63 NGC.** NGC Census: (1233/1437). PCGS Population (2281/2622). Mintage: 700,000. Numismedia Wsl. Price for problem free NGC/PCGS coin in MS63: $275. (#7194)

7953 **1889-S MS63 PCGS.** PCGS Population (2279/2635). NGC Census: (1227/1433). Mintage: 700,000. Numismedia Wsl. Price for problem free NGC/PCGS coin in MS63: $275. (#7194)

7954 **1889-S MS63 ANACS.** Redfield, VAM-2. NGC Census: (1233/1437). PCGS Population (2281/2622). Mintage: 700,000. Numismedia Wsl. Price for problem free NGC/PCGS coin in MS63: $275. (#7194)

7955 **1889-S MS64 NGC. CAC.** NGC Census: (1188/248). PCGS Population (2003/642). Mintage: 700,000. Numismedia Wsl. Price for problem free NGC/PCGS coin in MS64: $490. (#7194)

7956 **1889-S MS64 NGC.** NGC Census: (1191/246). PCGS Population (1999/623). Mintage: 700,000. Numismedia Wsl. Price for problem free NGC/PCGS coin in MS64: $490. (#7194)

7957 **1890-CC MS62 ANACS.** NGC Census: (1023/2255). PCGS Population (1963/5325). Mintage: 2,309,041. Numismedia Wsl. Price for problem free NGC/PCGS coin in MS62: $500. (#7198)

7958 **1890-CC MS63 PCGS.** PCGS Population (3058/2232). NGC Census: (1301/938). Mintage: 2,309,041. Numismedia Wsl. Price for problem free NGC/PCGS coin in MS63: $665. (#7198)

7959 **1890-O MS64 PCGS. CAC.** PCGS Population (3003/441). NGC Census: (2347/165). Mintage: 10,701,000. Numismedia Wsl. Price for problem free NGC/PCGS coin in MS64: $240. (#7200)

7960 **1890-O MS64 PCGS.** PCGS Population (3001/435). NGC Census: (2349/167). Mintage: 10,701,000. Numismedia Wsl. Price for problem free NGC/PCGS coin in MS64: $240. (#7200)

7961 **1890-O MS64 ANACS.** NGC Census: (2335/166). PCGS Population (2992/437). Mintage: 10,701,000. Numismedia Wsl. Price for problem free NGC/PCGS coin in MS64: $240. (#7200)

7962 **1891 MS63 PCGS.** PCGS Population (2436/1622). NGC Census: (1748/1105). Mintage: 8,694,206. Numismedia Wsl. Price for problem free NGC/PCGS coin in MS63: $135. (#7204)

7963 **1891 MS64 PCGS.** PCGS Population (1516/106). NGC Census: (1028/77). Mintage: 8,694,206. Numismedia Wsl. Price for problem free NGC/PCGS coin in MS64: $520. (#7204)

7964 **1891 MS64 PCGS.** PCGS Population (1494/106). NGC Census: (1028/77). Mintage: 8,694,206. Numismedia Wsl. Price for problem free NGC/PCGS coin in MS64: $520. (#7204)

7965 **1891-CC MS61 ANACS.** VAM-3 Top 100. NGC Census: (551/5102). PCGS Population (846/9902). Mintage: 1,618,000. Numismedia Wsl. Price for problem free NGC/PCGS coin in MS61: $345. (#7206)

7966 **1891-CC MS61 NGC.** NGC Census: (551/5102). PCGS Population (846/9902). Mintage: 1,618,000. Numismedia Wsl. Price for problem free NGC/PCGS coin in MS61: $345. (#7206)

7967 **1891-CC MS62 ANACS.** VAM-3 Top 100. NGC Census: (1494/3626). PCGS Population (2375/7583). Mintage: 1,618,000. Numismedia Wsl. Price for problem free NGC/PCGS coin in MS62: $415. (#7206)

7968 **1891-CC MS63 PCGS.** PCGS Population (4104/3464). NGC Census: (2050/1577). Mintage: 1,618,000. Numismedia Wsl. Price for problem free NGC/PCGS coin in MS63: $560. (#7206)

7969 **1891-CC MS64 NGC.** Spitting Eagle, VAM-3 Top 100. NGC Census: (1424/153). PCGS Population (2948/516). Mintage: 1,618,000. Numismedia Wsl. Price for problem free NGC/PCGS coin in MS64: $1,050. (#7206)

7970 **1891-CC MS64 NGC.** NGC Census: (1424/153). PCGS Population (2957/519). Mintage: 1,618,000. Numismedia Wsl. Price for problem free NGC/PCGS coin in MS64: $1,050. (#7206)

7971 **1891-CC MS63 Prooflike PCGS.** PCGS Population (152/122). NGC Census: (108/73). Numismedia Wsl. Price for problem free NGC/PCGS coin in MS63: $725. (#7207)

7972 **1892 MS63 NGC.** NGC Census: (944/783). PCGS Population (1574/1502). Mintage: 1,037,245. Numismedia Wsl. Price for problem free NGC/PCGS coin in MS63: $350. (#7212)

7973 **1892 MS63 ANACS.** NGC Census: (944/783). PCGS Population (1574/1509). Mintage: 1,037,245. Numismedia Wsl. Price for problem free NGC/PCGS coin in MS63: $350. (#7212)

7974 **1892 MS63 ANACS.** VAM-5. NGC Census: (945/783). PCGS Population (1574/1511). Mintage: 1,037,245. Numismedia Wsl. Price for problem free NGC/PCGS coin in MS63: $350. (#7212)

7975 **1892-CC Fine 12 ANACS.** NGC Census: (11/3631). PCGS Population (35/6511). Mintage: 1,352,000. Numismedia Wsl. Price for problem free NGC/PCGS coin in Fine 12: $175. (#7214)

7976 **1892-CC XF40 ANACS.** NGC Census: (25/3533). PCGS Population (80/6219). Mintage: 1,352,000. Numismedia Wsl. Price for problem free NGC/PCGS coin in XF40: $410. (#7214)

7977 **1892-CC—Obverse Improperly Cleaned—MS60 NCS. Unc Details.** NGC Census: (82/3098). PCGS Population (133/5601). Mintage: 1,352,000. Numismedia Wsl. Price for problem free NGC/PCGS coin in MS60: $1,150. (#7214)

7978 **1892-O MS63 ANACS.** Double Ear VAM-7 Top 100. NGC Census: (1358/1228). PCGS Population (2197/1811). Mintage: 2,744,000. Numismedia Wsl. Price for problem free NGC/PCGS coin in MS63: $250. (#7216)

7979 **1892-O MS64 PCGS.** PCGS Population (1663/171). NGC Census: (1149/78). Mintage: 2,744,000. Numismedia Wsl. Price for problem free NGC/PCGS coin in MS64: $675. (#7216)

7980 **1892-S XF40 ANACS.** NGC Census: (268/1698). PCGS Population (343/1485). Mintage: 1,200,000. Numismedia Wsl. Price for problem free NGC/PCGS coin in XF40: $280. (#7218)

7981 **1892-S XF40 ANACS.** NGC Census: (268/1698). PCGS Population (346/1501). Mintage: 1,200,000. Numismedia Wsl. Price for problem free NGC/PCGS coin in XF40: $280. (#7218)

7982 **1892-S XF45 NGC.** NGC Census: (803/895). PCGS Population (720/780). Mintage: 1,200,000. Numismedia Wsl. Price for problem free NGC/PCGS coin in XF45: $593. (#7218)

7983 **1893—Scratched—ANACS. AU Details Net XF45.** NGC Census: (188/2546). PCGS Population (276/4092). Mintage: 389,792. Numismedia Wsl. Price for problem free NGC/PCGS coin in XF45: $235. (#7220)

7984 **1893 XF45 ANACS.** NGC Census: (188/2548). PCGS Population (277/4095). Mintage: 389,792. Numismedia Wsl. Price for problem free NGC/PCGS coin in XF45: $235. (#7220)

7985 **1893—Cleaned—ANACS. MS60 Details.** NGC Census: (31/1843). PCGS Population (47/3388). Mintage: 389,792. Numismedia Wsl. Price for problem free NGC/PCGS coin in MS60: $580. (#7220)

7986 **1893 MS63 ANACS.** NGC Census: (575/739). PCGS Population (1157/1372). Mintage: 389,792. Numismedia Wsl. Price for problem free NGC/PCGS coin in MS63: $975. (#7220)

7987 **1893-CC—Cleaned—ANACS. VF20 Details.** NGC Census: (75/2093). PCGS Population (118/4060). Mintage: 677,000. Numismedia Wsl. Price for problem free NGC/PCGS coin in VF20: $525. (#7222)

7988 **1893-CC—Improperly Cleaned—NCS. VF Details.** NGC Census: (75/2093). PCGS Population (118/4060). Mintage: 677,000. Numismedia Wsl. Price for problem free NGC/PCGS coin in VF20: $525. (#7222)

7989 **1893-CC VF30 ANACS.** NGC Census: (102/1910). PCGS Population (139/3829). Mintage: 677,000. Numismedia Wsl. Price for problem free NGC/PCGS coin in VF30: $745. (#7222)

7990 **1893-CC VF35 PCGS.** PCGS Population (154/3658). NGC Census: (76/1829). Mintage: 677,000. Numismedia Wsl. Price for problem free NGC/PCGS coin in VF35: $861. (#7222)

7991 **1893-O VF20 NGC.** NGC Census: (34/1663). PCGS Population (60/2275). Mintage: 300,000. Numismedia Wsl. Price for problem free NGC/PCGS coin in VF20: $265. (#7224)

7992 **1893-O XF40 ANACS.** NGC Census: (80/1452). PCGS Population (135/1928). Mintage: 300,000. Numismedia Wsl. Price for problem free NGC/PCGS coin in XF40: $460. (#7224)

7993 **1893-O—Scratched—ANACS. AU50 Details.** NGC Census: (94/1210). PCGS Population (155/1549). Mintage: 300,000. Numismedia Wsl. Price for problem free NGC/PCGS coin in AU50: $700. (#7224)

7994 **1894-O AU53 NGC.** NGC Census: (290/1869). PCGS Population (258/1995). Mintage: 1,723,000. Numismedia Wsl. Price for problem free NGC/PCGS coin in AU53: $210. (#7230)

7995 **1894-O AU53 NGC.** NGC Census: (290/1869). PCGS Population (258/1995). Mintage: 1,723,000. Numismedia Wsl. Price for problem free NGC/PCGS coin in AU53: $210. (#7230)

7996 **1894-O AU55 NGC.** NGC Census: (384/1485). PCGS Population (440/1555). Mintage: 1,723,000. Numismedia Wsl. Price for problem free NGC/PCGS coin in AU55: $260. (#7230)

7997 **1894-O AU55 NGC.** NGC Census: (385/1490). PCGS Population (442/1560). Mintage: 1,723,000. Numismedia Wsl. Price for problem free NGC/PCGS coin in AU55: $260. (#7230)

7998 **1894-S AU55 ANACS.** NGC Census: (95/1727). PCGS Population (152/3061). Mintage: 1,260,000. Numismedia Wsl. Price for problem free NGC/PCGS coin in AU55: $400. (#7232)

7999 **1894-S MS63 ANACS.** VAM-4. NGC Census: (495/432). PCGS Population (1012/933). Mintage: 1,260,000. Numismedia Wsl. Price for problem free NGC/PCGS coin in MS63: $900. (#7232)

8000 **1895-O VG8 ANACS.** NGC Census: (40/3014). PCGS Population (85/3403). Mintage: 450,000. Numismedia Wsl. Price for problem free NGC/PCGS coin in VG8 : $255. (#7236)

8001 **1895-O VG8 ANACS.** NGC Census: (40/3033). PCGS Population (86/3429). Mintage: 450,000. Numismedia Wsl. Price for problem free NGC/PCGS coin in VG8 : $255. (#7236)

8002 **1895-O Fine 12 NGC.** NGC Census: (58/2934). PCGS Population (88/3268). Mintage: 450,000. Numismedia Wsl. Price for problem free NGC/PCGS coin in Fine 12: $300. (#7236)

8003 **1895-O VF30 NGC.** NGC Census: (93/2650). PCGS Population (162/2752). Mintage: 450,000. Numismedia Wsl. Price for problem free NGC/PCGS coin in VF30: $422. (#7236)

8004 **1895-O—Cleaned, Corroded—ANACS. XF45 Details.** NGC Census: (594/1731). PCGS Population (641/1586). Mintage: 450,000. Numismedia Wsl. Price for problem free NGC/PCGS coin in XF45: $658. (#7236)

8005 **1895-O XF45 ANACS.** NGC Census: (595/1742). PCGS Population (646/1591). Mintage: 450,000. Numismedia Wsl. Price for problem free NGC/PCGS coin in XF45: $658. (#7236)

8006 **1895-O AU50 NGC.** NGC Census: (323/1420). PCGS Population (402/1191). Mintage: 450,000. Numismedia Wsl. Price for problem free NGC/PCGS coin in AU50: $950. (#7236)

8007 **1895-O AU50 ANACS.** NGC Census: (323/1419). PCGS Population (402/1189). Mintage: 450,000. Numismedia Wsl. Price for problem free NGC/PCGS coin in AU50: $950. (#7236)

8008 **1895-O AU50 ANACS.** NGC Census: (323/1420). PCGS Population (402/1191). Mintage: 450,000. Numismedia Wsl. Price for problem free NGC/PCGS coin in AU50: $950. (#7236)

8009 **1895-S VG8 ANACS.** NGC Census: (35/1269). PCGS Population (63/2300). Mintage: 400,000. Numismedia Wsl. Price for problem free NGC/PCGS coin in VG8 : $350. (#7238)

8010 **1895-S—Cleaned—ANACS. VF20 Details.** NGC Census: (22/1141). PCGS Population (70/1990). Mintage: 400,000. Numismedia Wsl. Price for problem free NGC/PCGS coin in VF20: $475. (#7238)

8011 **1895-S VF20 PCGS.** PCGS Population (70/1990). NGC Census: (22/1141). Mintage: 400,000. Numismedia Wsl. Price for problem free NGC/PCGS coin in VF20: $475. (#7238)

8012 **1896 MS66 PCGS. CAC.** PCGS Population (633/24). NGC Census: (562/52). Mintage: 9,976,762. Numismedia Wsl. Price for problem free NGC/PCGS coin in MS66: $460. (#7240)

8013 **1896-O AU55 ANACS.** NGC Census: (699/2240). PCGS Population (702/2009). Mintage: 4,900,000. Numismedia Wsl. Price for problem free NGC/PCGS coin in AU55: $180. (#7242)

8014 **1896-O AU55 NGC.** NGC Census: (699/2243). PCGS Population (702/2017). Mintage: 4,900,000. Numismedia Wsl. Price for problem free NGC/PCGS coin in AU55: $180. (#7242)

8015 **1896-O AU58 NGC.** NGC Census: (1145/1090). PCGS Population (769/1228). Mintage: 4,900,000. Numismedia Wsl. Price for problem free NGC/PCGS coin in AU58: $350. (#7242)

8016 **1896-O AU58 NGC.** NGC Census: (1148/1095). PCGS Population (775/1238). Mintage: 4,900,000. Numismedia Wsl. Price for problem free NGC/PCGS coin in AU58: $350. (#7242)

8017 **1896-S—Cleaned—ANACS. AU50 Details.** NGC Census: (50/775). PCGS Population (43/1535). Mintage: 5,000,000. Numismedia Wsl. Price for problem free NGC/PCGS coin in AU50: $635. (#7244)

8018 **1897 MS65 PCGS.** PCGS Population (1353/277). NGC Census: (1325/170). Mintage: 2,822,731. Numismedia Wsl. Price for problem free NGC/PCGS coin in MS65: $260. (#7246)

8019 **1897 MS65 PCGS.** PCGS Population (1353/277). NGC Census: (1325/170). Mintage: 2,822,731. Numismedia Wsl. Price for problem free NGC/PCGS coin in MS65: $260. (#7246)

8020 **1897-S MS65 PCGS.** PCGS Population (1021/229). NGC Census: (653/121). Mintage: 5,825,000. Numismedia Wsl. Price for problem free NGC/PCGS coin in MS65: $525. (#7250)

8021 **1897-S MS65 NGC. CAC.** NGC Census: (644/122). PCGS Population (1003/227). Mintage: 5,825,000. Numismedia Wsl. Price for problem free NGC/PCGS coin in MS65: $525. (#7250)

8022 **1897-S MS65 Prooflike PCGS.** PCGS Population (131/24). NGC Census: (102/23). Numismedia Wsl. Price for problem free NGC/PCGS coin in MS65: $635. (#7251)

8023 **1898 MS66 PCGS.** PCGS Population (530/26). NGC Census: (388/17). Mintage: 5,884,735. Numismedia Wsl. Price for problem free NGC/PCGS coin in MS66: $615. (#7252)

8024 **1898 MS66 NGC.** NGC Census: (388/17). PCGS Population (533/26). Mintage: 5,884,735. Numismedia Wsl. Price for problem free NGC/PCGS coin in MS66: $615. (#7252)

8025 **1898 MS66 PCGS.** PCGS Population (529/26). NGC Census: (383/17). Mintage: 5,884,735. Numismedia Wsl. Price for problem free NGC/PCGS coin in MS66: $615. (#7252)

8026 **1898 MS66 PCGS. CAC.** PCGS Population (530/26). NGC Census: (387/17). Mintage: 5,884,735. Numismedia Wsl. Price for problem free NGC/PCGS coin in MS66: $615. (#7252)

8027 **1898-S MS62 ANACS.** NGC Census: (272/1145). PCGS Population (470/2559). Mintage: 4,102,000. Numismedia Wsl. Price for problem free NGC/PCGS coin in MS62: $280. (#7256)

8028 **1899 MS61 ANACS.** NGC Census: (241/5866). PCGS Population (191/8659). Mintage: 330,846. Numismedia Wsl. Price for problem free NGC/PCGS coin in MS61: $240. (#7258)

8029 **1899 MS61 ANACS.** NGC Census: (242/5911). PCGS Population (191/8671). Mintage: 330,846. Numismedia Wsl. Price for problem free NGC/PCGS coin in MS61: $240. (#7258)

8030 **1899 MS62 ANACS.** NGC Census: (756/5155). PCGS Population (1064/7607). Mintage: 330,846. Numismedia Wsl. Price for problem free NGC/PCGS coin in MS62: $250. (#7258)

8031 **1899 MS62 ANACS.** NGC Census: (756/5155). PCGS Population (1064/7607). Mintage: 330,846. Numismedia Wsl. Price for problem free NGC/PCGS coin in MS62: $250. (#7258)

8032 **1899 MS63 NGC.** NGC Census: (2051/3104). PCGS Population (3123/4484). Mintage: 330,846. Numismedia Wsl. Price for problem free NGC/PCGS coin in MS63: $270. (#7258)

8033 **1899 MS63 NGC.** NGC Census: (2048/3096). PCGS Population (3122/4482). Mintage: 330,846. Numismedia Wsl. Price for problem free NGC/PCGS coin in MS63: $270. (#7258)

8034 **1899 MS63 PCGS.** PCGS Population (3122/4482). NGC Census: (2048/3096). Mintage: 330,846. Numismedia Wsl. Price for problem free NGC/PCGS coin in MS63: $270. (#7258)

8035 **1899 MS64 PCGS.** PCGS Population (3308/1176). NGC Census: (2479/625). Mintage: 330,846. Numismedia Wsl. Price for problem free NGC/PCGS coin in MS64: $325. (#7258)

8036 **1899 MS64 PCGS.** PCGS Population (3303/1177). NGC Census: (2459/619). Mintage: 330,846. Numismedia Wsl. Price for problem free NGC/PCGS coin in MS64: $325. (#7258)

8037 **1899-O MS66 NGC.** NGC Census: (900/88). PCGS Population (1110/88). Mintage: 12,290,000. Numismedia Wsl. Price for problem free NGC/PCGS coin in MS66: $330. (#7260)

8038 **1899-S MS61 ANACS.** NGC Census: (100/1532). PCGS Population (90/3035). Mintage: 2,562,000. Numismedia Wsl. Price for problem free NGC/PCGS coin in MS61: $270. (#7262)

8039 **1900-O MS66 NGC. CAC.** NGC Census: (858/64). PCGS Population (830/29). Mintage: 12,590,000. Numismedia Wsl. Price for problem free NGC/PCGS coin in MS66: $440. (#7266)

8040 **1900-O/CC—Cleaned—ANACS. MS60 Details.** Top 100. NGC Census: (10/1861). PCGS Population (27/4584). Numismedia Wsl. Price for problem free NGC/PCGS coin in MS60: $250. (#7268)

8041 **1900-O/CC MS62 ANACS.** VAM-8A Top 100. NGC Census: (282/1506). PCGS Population (529/3995). Numismedia Wsl. Price for problem free NGC/PCGS coin in MS62: $425. (#7268)

8042 **1900-O/CC MS63 NGC.** Top 100. NGC Census: (618/884). PCGS Population (1442/2525). Numismedia Wsl. Price for problem free NGC/PCGS coin in MS63: $620. (#7268)

8043 **1900-O/CC MS63 PCGS.** PCGS Population (1446/2538). NGC Census: (618/888). Numismedia Wsl. Price for problem free NGC/PCGS coin in MS63: $620. (#7268)

8044 **1900-O/CC MS64 NGC.** Top 100. NGC Census: (717/171). PCGS Population (1779/768). Numismedia Wsl. Price for problem free NGC/PCGS coin in MS64: $865. (#7268)

8045 **1900-S MS62 ANACS.** NGC Census: (321/1703). PCGS Population (478/3326). Mintage: 3,540,000. Numismedia Wsl. Price for problem free NGC/PCGS coin in MS62: $285. (#7270)

8046 **1900-S MS63 NGC.** NGC Census: (722/977). PCGS Population (1318/2004). Mintage: 3,540,000. Numismedia Wsl. Price for problem free NGC/PCGS coin in MS63: $325. (#7270)

8047 **1900-S MS63 NGC.** NGC Census: (724/979). PCGS Population (1321/2006). Mintage: 3,540,000. Numismedia Wsl. Price for problem free NGC/PCGS coin in MS63: $325. (#7270)

8048 **1900-S MS64 PCGS.** PCGS Population (1433/573). NGC Census: (805/174). Mintage: 3,540,000. Numismedia Wsl. Price for problem free NGC/PCGS coin in MS64: $510. (#7270)

8049 **1900-S MS65 ANACS.** NGC Census: (152/22). PCGS Population (480/93). Mintage: 3,540,000. Numismedia Wsl. Price for problem free NGC/PCGS coin in MS65: $1,225. (#7270)

8050 **1901 AU50 ANACS.** NGC Census: (281/2679). PCGS Population (369/2453). Mintage: 6,962,813. Numismedia Wsl. Price for problem free NGC/PCGS coin in AU50: $225. (#7272)

8051 **1901 AU58 ANACS.** NGC Census: (1072/600). PCGS Population (711/596). Mintage: 6,962,813. Numismedia Wsl. Price for problem free NGC/PCGS coin in AU58: $785. (#7272)

8052 **1901-S AU58 ANACS.** NGC Census: (116/1421). PCGS Population (90/2485). Mintage: 2,284,000. Numismedia Wsl. Price for problem free NGC/PCGS coin in AU58: $225. (#7276)

8053 **1901-S MS62 ANACS.** VAM-9. NGC Census: (237/1063). PCGS Population (396/1985). Mintage: 2,284,000. Numismedia Wsl. Price for problem free NGC/PCGS coin in MS62: $450. (#7276)

8054 **1902-S AU50 PCGS.** PCGS Population (52/3795). NGC Census: (27/2131). Mintage: 1,530,000. Numismedia Wsl. Price for problem free NGC/PCGS coin in AU50: $200. (#7282)

8055 **1902-S MS62 NGC.** NGC Census: (280/1502). PCGS Population (536/2885). Mintage: 1,530,000. Numismedia Wsl. Price for problem free NGC/PCGS coin in MS62: $380. (#7282)

8056 **1902-S MS63 ANACS.** VAM-6. NGC Census: (653/851). PCGS Population (1282/1597). Mintage: 1,530,000. Numismedia Wsl. Price for problem free NGC/PCGS coin in MS63: $480. (#7282)

8057 **1902-S MS64 PCGS.** PCGS Population (1307/293). NGC Census: (741/109). Mintage: 1,530,000. Numismedia Wsl. Price for problem free NGC/PCGS coin in MS64: $780. (#7282)

8058 **1903 MS65 PCGS.** PCGS Population (2600/858). NGC Census: (2050/559). Mintage: 4,652,755. Numismedia Wsl. Price for problem free NGC/PCGS coin in MS65: $250. (#7284)

8059 **1903 MS66 PCGS.** PCGS Population (793/64). NGC Census: (469/87). Mintage: 4,652,755. Numismedia Wsl. Price for problem free NGC/PCGS coin in MS66: $460. (#7284)

8060 **1903-O—Scratched—ANACS. MS60 Details.** NGC Census: (13/5393). PCGS Population (33/9409). Mintage: 4,450,000. Numismedia Wsl. Price for problem free NGC/PCGS coin in MS60: $333. (#7286)

8061 **1903-O MS63 PCGS.** PCGS Population (2488/6042). NGC Census: (1179/3701). Mintage: 4,450,000. Numismedia Wsl. Price for problem free NGC/PCGS coin in MS63: $375. (#7286)

8062 **1903-O MS64 NGC.** NGC Census: (2142/1554). PCGS Population (3552/2484). Mintage: 4,450,000. Numismedia Wsl. Price for problem free NGC/PCGS coin in MS64: $400. (#7286)

8063 **1903-O MS64 ANACS.** NGC Census: (2143/1558). PCGS Population (3555/2487). Mintage: 4,450,000. Numismedia Wsl. Price for problem free NGC/PCGS coin in MS64: $400. (#7286)

8064 **1903-O MS64 PCGS.** PCGS Population (3555/2487). NGC Census: (2143/1558). Mintage: 4,450,000. Numismedia Wsl. Price for problem free NGC/PCGS coin in MS64: $400. (#7286)

8065 **1903-O MS65 ANACS.** NGC Census: (1193/365). PCGS Population (1877/603). Mintage: 4,450,000. Numismedia Wsl. Price for problem free NGC/PCGS coin in MS65: $610. (#7286)

8066 **1903-S Small S—Whizzed—ANACS. AU Details Net XF40.** VAM-2 Top 100. NGC Census: (0/0). PCGS Population (20/38). (#7306)

8067 **1904-S XF45 ANACS.** NGC Census: (202/845). PCGS Population (179/1461). Mintage: 2,304,000. Numismedia Wsl. Price for problem free NGC/PCGS coin in XF45: $274. (#7294)

8068 **1904-S—Cleaned—ANACS. AU50 Details.** NGC Census: (85/758). PCGS Population (90/1367). Mintage: 2,304,000. Numismedia Wsl. Price for problem free NGC/PCGS coin in AU50: $440. (#7294)

PROOF MORGAN DOLLARS

8069 **1879 PR58 ANACS.** NGC Census: (2/247). PCGS Population (3/281). Mintage: 1,100. (#7314)

8070 **1885—Polished—ANACS. Net PR55.** NGC Census: (0/183). PCGS Population (0/204). Mintage: 930. (#7320)

8071 **1892—Cleaned—ANACS. Proof 60 Details.** NGC Census: (5/257). PCGS Population (11/306). Mintage: 1,245. Numismedia Wsl. Price for problem free NGC/PCGS coin in PR60: $1,125. (#7327)

PEACE DOLLARS

8072 **1921—Reverse Wheel Mark—NCS. Unc Details.** NGC Census: (28/8277). PCGS Population (90/9756). Mintage: 1,006,473. Numismedia Wsl. Price for problem free NGC/PCGS coin in MS60: $215. (#7356)

8073 **1921 MS63 PCGS.** PCGS Population (3144/4700). NGC Census: (2362/4143). Mintage: 1,006,473. Numismedia Wsl. Price for problem free NGC/PCGS coin in MS63: $370. (#7356)

8074 **1921 MS64 NGC.** NGC Census: (3066/1070). PCGS Population (3437/1251). Mintage: 1,006,473. Numismedia Wsl. Price for problem free NGC/PCGS coin in MS64: $630. (#7356)

8075 **1921 MS64 PCGS.** PCGS Population (3448/1252). NGC Census: (3069/1074). Mintage: 1,006,473. Numismedia Wsl. Price for problem free NGC/PCGS coin in MS64: $630. (#7356)

8076 **1922 MS66 NGC.** NGC Census: (708/14). PCGS Population (531/21). Mintage: 51,737,000. Numismedia Wsl. Price for problem free NGC/PCGS coin in MS66: $525. (#7357)

8077 **1922-D MS65 PCGS. CAC.** PCGS Population (1025/145). NGC Census: (767/200). Mintage: 15,063,000. Numismedia Wsl. Price for problem free NGC/PCGS coin in MS65: $400. (#7358)

8078 **1922-D MS65 PCGS.** PCGS Population (1025/145). NGC Census: (767/200). Mintage: 15,063,000. Numismedia Wsl. Price for problem free NGC/PCGS coin in MS65: $400. (#7358)

8079 **1922-S MS64 NGC.** NGC Census: (1544/224). PCGS Population (1548/271). Mintage: 17,475,000. Numismedia Wsl. Price for problem free NGC/PCGS coin in MS64: $200. (#7359)

8080 **1923 MS65 NGC. CAC.** NGC Census: (25369/1781). PCGS Population (14259/1572). Mintage: 30,800,000. Numismedia Wsl. Price for problem free NGC/PCGS coin in MS65: $112. (#7360)

8081 **1923 MS66 PCGS.** PCGS Population (1521/51). NGC Census: (1724/57). Mintage: 30,800,000. Numismedia Wsl. Price for problem free NGC/PCGS coin in MS66: $500. (#7360)

8082 **1923 MS66 NGC.** NGC Census: (1724/57). PCGS Population (1521/51). Mintage: 30,800,000. Numismedia Wsl. Price for problem free NGC/PCGS coin in MS66: $500. (#7360)

8083 **1923-D MS64 PCGS.** PCGS Population (1237/455). NGC Census: (910/235). Mintage: 6,811,000. Numismedia Wsl. Price for problem free NGC/PCGS coin in MS64: $230. (#7361)

8084 **1923-D MS65 PCGS.** PCGS Population (387/72). NGC Census: (212/22). Mintage: 6,811,000. Numismedia Wsl. Price for problem free NGC/PCGS coin in MS65: $1,100. (#7361)

8085 **1923-S MS64 PCGS. CAC.** PCGS Population (1628/114). NGC Census: (1625/76). Mintage: 19,020,000. Numismedia Wsl. Price for problem free NGC/PCGS coin in MS64: $245. (#7362)

8086 **1924 MS66 NGC.** NGC Census: (930/75). PCGS Population (475/22). Mintage: 11,811,000. Numismedia Wsl. Price for problem free NGC/PCGS coin in MS66: $550. (#7363)

8087 **1924 MS66 NGC.** NGC Census: (935/75). PCGS Population (476/22). Mintage: 11,811,000. Numismedia Wsl. Price for problem free NGC/PCGS coin in MS66: $550. (#7363)

8088 **1925 MS66 PCGS. CAC.** PCGS Population (1354/70). NGC Census: (1179/55). Mintage: 10,198,000. Numismedia Wsl. Price for problem free NGC/PCGS coin in MS66: $515. (#7365)

8089 **1925 MS66 PCGS.** PCGS Population (1354/70). NGC Census: (1179/55). Mintage: 10,198,000. Numismedia Wsl. Price for problem free NGC/PCGS coin in MS66: $515. (#7365)

8090 **1925 MS66 NGC.** NGC Census: (1179/55). PCGS Population (1365/70). Mintage: 10,198,000. Numismedia Wsl. Price for problem free NGC/PCGS coin in MS66: $515. (#7365)

8091 **1925-S MS64 NGC.** NGC Census: (1470/58). PCGS Population (1589/36). Mintage: 1,610,000. Numismedia Wsl. Price for problem free NGC/PCGS coin in MS64: $650. (#7366)

8092 **1925-S MS64 NGC.** NGC Census: (1469/58). PCGS Population (1594/36). Mintage: 1,610,000. Numismedia Wsl. Price for problem free NGC/PCGS coin in MS64: $650. (#7366)

8093 **1926 MS65 NGC.** NGC Census: (592/45). PCGS Population (1132/155). Mintage: 1,939,000. Numismedia Wsl. Price for problem free NGC/PCGS coin in MS65: $385. (#7367)

8094 **1926-D MS65 NGC.** NGC Census: (457/117). PCGS Population (644/177). Mintage: 2,348,700. Numismedia Wsl. Price for problem free NGC/PCGS coin in MS65: $655. (#7368)

8095 **1926-S MS63 PCGS.** PCGS Population (1911/2429). NGC Census: (1224/1957). Mintage: 6,980,000. Numismedia Wsl. Price for problem free NGC/PCGS coin in MS63: $86. (#7369)

8096 **1926-S MS64 PCGS.** PCGS Population (1789/640). NGC Census: (1573/384). Mintage: 6,980,000. Numismedia Wsl. Price for problem free NGC/PCGS coin in MS64: $195. (#7369)

8097 **1926-S MS65 NGC.** NGC Census: (346/38). PCGS Population (573/67). Mintage: 6,980,000. Numismedia Wsl. Price for problem free NGC/PCGS coin in MS65: $810. (#7369)

8098 **1926-S MS65 PCGS. CAC.** PCGS Population (560/67). NGC Census: (346/38). Mintage: 6,980,000. Numismedia Wsl. Price for problem free NGC/PCGS coin in MS65: $810. (#7369)

8099 **1927 MS64 NGC.** NGC Census: (805/88). PCGS Population (1448/267). Mintage: 848,000. Numismedia Wsl. Price for problem free NGC/PCGS coin in MS64: $410. (#7370)

8100 **1927-D MS64 PCGS.** PCGS Population (1058/143). NGC Census: (671/78). Mintage: 1,268,900. Numismedia Wsl. Price for problem free NGC/PCGS coin in MS64: $785. (#7371)

8101 **1927-S MS64 NGC.** NGC Census: (970/71). PCGS Population (1236/62). Mintage: 866,000. Numismedia Wsl. Price for problem free NGC/PCGS coin in MS64: $955. (#7372)

8102 **1927-S MS64 NGC.** NGC Census: (971/71). PCGS Population (1233/62). Mintage: 866,000. Numismedia Wsl. Price for problem free NGC/PCGS coin in MS64: $955. (#7372)

8103 **1928—Improperly Cleaned—NCS. VF Details.** NGC Census: (4/4391). PCGS Population (6/6734). Mintage: 360,649. Numismedia Wsl. Price for problem free NGC/PCGS coin in VF20: $285. (#7373)

8104 **1928—Rim Damage—NCS. VF Details.** NGC Census: (4/4391). PCGS Population (6/6734). Mintage: 360,649. Numismedia Wsl. Price for problem free NGC/PCGS coin in VF20: $285. (#7373)

8105 **1928—Cleaned—ANACS. AU55 Details.** NGC Census: (177/4068). PCGS Population (371/6011). Mintage: 360,649. Numismedia Wsl. Price for problem free NGC/PCGS coin in AU55: $365. (#7373)

8106 **1928 MS60 ANACS.** NGC Census: (64/3452). PCGS Population (77/5226). Mintage: 360,649. Numismedia Wsl. Price for problem free NGC/PCGS coin in MS60: $450. (#7373)

8107 **1928 MS61 PCGS.** PCGS Population (251/4973). NGC Census: (363/3084). Mintage: 360,649. Numismedia Wsl. Price for problem free NGC/PCGS coin in MS61: $485. (#7373)

8108 **1928 MS64 NGC.** NGC Census: (858/84). PCGS Population (1589/241). Mintage: 360,649. Numismedia Wsl. Price for problem free NGC/PCGS coin in MS64: $960. (#7373)

8109 **1928-S MS64 PCGS.** PCGS Population (1656/47). NGC Census: (1160/40). Mintage: 1,632,000. Numismedia Wsl. Price for problem free NGC/PCGS coin in MS64: $875. (#7374)

8110 **1928-S MS64 PCGS.** PCGS Population (1656/47). NGC Census: (1160/40). Mintage: 1,632,000. Numismedia Wsl. Price for problem free NGC/PCGS coin in MS64: $875. (#7374)

8111 **1928-S MS64 PCGS. CAC.** PCGS Population (1641/47). NGC Census: (1159/40). Mintage: 1,632,000. Numismedia Wsl. Price for problem free NGC/PCGS coin in MS64: $875. (#7374)

8112 **1928-S MS64 PCGS.** PCGS Population (1630/47). NGC Census: (1159/40). Mintage: 1,632,000. Numismedia Wsl. Price for problem free NGC/PCGS coin in MS64: $875. (#7374)

8113 **1934 MS64 NGC.** NGC Census: (1416/365). PCGS Population (1505/677). Mintage: 954,057. Numismedia Wsl. Price for problem free NGC/PCGS coin in MS64: $325. (#7375)

8114 **1934 MS64 PCGS.** PCGS Population (1506/681). NGC Census: (1416/365). Mintage: 954,057. Numismedia Wsl. Price for problem free NGC/PCGS coin in MS64: $325. (#7375)

8115 **1934-D MS63 NGC.** DDO Motto, Large D, VAM-3 Top 50. NGC Census: (1005/916). PCGS Population (1284/1590). Mintage: 1,569,500. Numismedia Wsl. Price for problem free NGC/PCGS coin in MS63: $325. (#7376)

8116 **1934-D MS64 PCGS.** PCGS Population (1130/464). NGC Census: (688/229). Mintage: 1,569,500. Numismedia Wsl. Price for problem free NGC/PCGS coin in MS64: $510. (#7376)

8117 **1934-S—Cleaned—ANACS. AU53 Details.** NGC Census: (106/1548). PCGS Population (117/2391). Mintage: 1,011,000. Numismedia Wsl. Price for problem free NGC/PCGS coin in AU53: $430. (#7377)

8118 **1934-S AU58 NGC.** NGC Census: (304/1039). PCGS Population (316/1829). Mintage: 1,011,000. Numismedia Wsl. Price for problem free NGC/PCGS coin in AU58: $865. (#7377)

8119 **1935 MS64 PCGS.** PCGS Population (1926/860). NGC Census: (1663/691). Mintage: 1,576,000. Numismedia Wsl. Price for problem free NGC/PCGS coin in MS64: $175. (#7378)

8120 **1935 MS65 NGC.** NGC Census: (634/58). PCGS Population (697/162). Mintage: 1,576,000. Numismedia Wsl. Price for problem free NGC/PCGS coin in MS65: $545. (#7378)

8121 **1935-S MS63 ICG.** NGC Census: (514/1236). PCGS Population (921/1987). Mintage: 1,964,000. Numismedia Wsl. Price for problem free NGC/PCGS coin in MS63: $320. (#7379)

8122 **1935-S MS65 NGC.** NGC Census: (362/51). PCGS Population (569/111). Mintage: 1,964,000. Numismedia Wsl. Price for problem free NGC/PCGS coin in MS65: $975. (#7379)

PROOF SUSAN B. ANTHONY DOLLAR

8123 **1981-S Type Two PR69 Deep Cameo PCGS.** PCGS Population (1774/49). NGC Census: (792/8). Numismedia Wsl. Price for problem free NGC/PCGS coin in PR69: $180. (#99595)

SACAGAWEA DOLLAR

8124 **2000-P Goodacre MS67 PCGS.** PCGS Population (245/457). NGC Census: (0/0). Numismedia Wsl. Price for problem free NGC/PCGS coin in MS67: $28. (#99584)

PRESIDENTIAL DOLLAR

8125 **(2007) John Adams, Missing Edge MS65 ANACS.** NGC Census: (0/0). PCGS Population (461/67). Numismedia Wsl. Price for problem free NGC/PCGS coin in MS65: $325. (#151053)

MODERN BULLION COINS

8126 **2007-S Jefferson Presidential Dollar PR70 Ultra Cameo NGC** and **2007-W Jefferson's Liberty Gold Ten Dollar PR70 Ultra Cameo NGC.** Housed in a custom two-coin holder. (Total: 2 coins)

GOLD DOLLARS

8127 **1849 Open Wreath AU53 ANACS.** NGC Census: (7/1608). PCGS Population (23/999). Mintage: 687,500. Numismedia Wsl. Price for problem free NGC/PCGS coin in AU53: $208. (#7502)

8128 **1849 Open Wreath MS61 NGC.** NGC Census: (293/1072). PCGS Population (99/705). Mintage: 687,500. Numismedia Wsl. Price for problem free NGC/PCGS coin in MS61: $415. (#7502)

8129 **1850-O—Bent—NCS. AU Details.** NGC Census: (6/165). PCGS Population (20/42). Mintage: 14,000. Numismedia Wsl. Price for problem free NGC/PCGS coin in AU50: $775. (#7512)

8130 **1851 MS62 NGC.** NGC Census: (1137/1011). PCGS Population (467/845). Mintage: 3,317,671. Numismedia Wsl. Price for problem free NGC/PCGS coin in MS62: $340. (#7513)

8131 **1851-O AU58 NGC.** Ex:Bass. NGC Census: (229/360). PCGS Population (56/166). Mintage: 290,000. Numismedia Wsl. Price for problem free NGC/PCGS coin in AU58: $300. (#7516)

8132 **1852 MS62 NGC.** NGC Census: (1028/840). PCGS Population (444/598). Mintage: 2,045,351. Numismedia Wsl. Price for problem free NGC/PCGS coin in MS62: $340. (#7517)

8133 **1852-C—Improperly Cleaned—NCS. AU Details.** NGC Census: (7/122). PCGS Population (13/47). Mintage: 9,434. Numismedia Wsl. Price for problem free NGC/PCGS coin in AU50: $1,535. (#7518)

8134 **1852-O—Improperly Cleaned—NCS. AU Details.** NGC Census: (12/377). PCGS Population (19/126). Mintage: 140,000. Numismedia Wsl. Price for problem free NGC/PCGS coin in AU50: $335. (#7520)

8135 **1852-O AU53 ANACS.** NGC Census: (24/354). PCGS Population (12/114). Mintage: 140,000. Numismedia Wsl. Price for problem free NGC/PCGS coin in AU53: $380. (#7520)

8136 **1853 MS61 NGC.** NGC Census: (1912/4879). PCGS Population (453/2730). Mintage: 4,076,051. Numismedia Wsl. Price for problem free NGC/PCGS coin in MS61: $265. (#7521)

8137 **1853 MS63 NGC.** NGC Census: (1148/986). PCGS Population (866/712). Mintage: 4,076,051. Numismedia Wsl. Price for problem free NGC/PCGS coin in MS63: $930. (#7521)

8138 **1853-C—Improperly Cleaned—NCS. AU Details.** NGC Census: (4/102). PCGS Population (8/52). Mintage: 11,515. Numismedia Wsl. Price for problem free NGC/PCGS coin in AU50: $1,700. (#7522)

8139 **1854 Type One AU53 ANACS.** NGC Census: (7/2969). PCGS Population (19/1813). Mintage: 855,502. Numismedia Wsl. Price for problem free NGC/PCGS coin in AU53: $208. (#7525)

8140 **1854 Type One AU58 ANACS.** NGC Census: (305/2632). PCGS Population (450/1183). Mintage: 855,502. Numismedia Wsl. Price for problem free NGC/PCGS coin in AU58: $230. (#7525)

8141 **1854 Type Two AU50 NGC.** NGC Census: (178/4618). PCGS Population (347/2450). Mintage: 783,943. Numismedia Wsl. Price for problem free NGC/PCGS coin in AU50: $420. (#7531)

8142 **1854 Type Two—Improperly Cleaned—NCS. AU Details.** NGC Census: (178/4622). PCGS Population (347/2452). Mintage: 783,943. Numismedia Wsl. Price for problem free NGC/PCGS coin in AU50: $420. (#7531)

8143 **1854 Type Two AU58 PCGS.** PCGS Population (500/1158). NGC Census: (2076/1486). Mintage: 783,943. Numismedia Wsl. Price for problem free NGC/PCGS coin in AU58: $775. (#7531)

8144 **1854 Type Two—Scratches—NCS. Unc Details.** NGC Census: (74/1415). PCGS Population (46/1119). Mintage: 783,943. Numismedia Wsl. Price for problem free NGC/PCGS coin in MS60: $1,325. (#7531)

8145 **1855 AU50 NGC.** NGC Census: (188/4205). PCGS Population (338/2386). Mintage: 758,269. Numismedia Wsl. Price for problem free NGC/PCGS coin in AU50: $440. (#7532)

8146 **1855—Improperly Cleaned—NCS. AU Details.** NGC Census: (188/4205). PCGS Population (338/2386). Mintage: 758,269. Numismedia Wsl. Price for problem free NGC/PCGS coin in AU50: $440. (#7532)

8147 **1858 AU55 ANACS.** NGC Census: (6/173). PCGS Population (26/145). Mintage: 117,995. Numismedia Wsl. Price for problem free NGC/PCGS coin in AU55: $213. (#7548)

8148 **1858-S—Scratches—NCS. AU Details.** NGC Census: (8/67). PCGS Population (9/42). Mintage: 10,000. Numismedia Wsl. Price for problem free NGC/PCGS coin in AU50: $1,000. (#7550)

8149 **1859 AU58 ANACS.** NGC Census: (55/243). PCGS Population (49/187). Mintage: 168,244. Numismedia Wsl. Price for problem free NGC/PCGS coin in AU58: $225. (#7551)

8150 **1860 AU53 ANACS.** NGC Census: (3/78). PCGS Population (8/98). Mintage: 217,600. Numismedia Wsl. Price for problem free NGC/PCGS coin in AU53: $675. (#6949)

8151 **1860-S—Improperly Cleaned—NGC. AU Details.** NGC Census: (8/117). PCGS Population (10/65). Mintage: 13,000. Numismedia Wsl. Price for problem free NGC/PCGS coin in AU50: $565. (#7557)

8152 **1861 MS61 NGC.** NGC Census: (248/663). PCGS Population (109/572). Mintage: 527,499. Numismedia Wsl. Price for problem free NGC/PCGS coin in MS61: $350. (#7558)

8153 **1867—Altered Surfaces—ANACS. AU55 Details.** NGC Census: (0/58). PCGS Population (3/48). Mintage: 5,250. Numismedia Wsl. Price for problem free NGC/PCGS coin in AU55: $635. (#7566)

8154 **1873 Open 3 MS61 NGC.** NGC Census: (339/1191). PCGS Population (202/1077). Mintage: 123,300. Numismedia Wsl. Price for problem free NGC/PCGS coin in MS61: $340. (#7573)

8155 **1873 Open 3 MS62 NGC.** NGC Census: (622/568). PCGS Population (454/621). Mintage: 123,300. Numismedia Wsl. Price for problem free NGC/PCGS coin in MS62: $410. (#7573)

8156 **1873 Closed 3—Whizzed—NCS. XF Details.** NGC Census: (0/81). PCGS Population (0/67). Mintage: 1,825. Numismedia Wsl. Price for problem free NGC/PCGS coin in XF40: $650. (#7574)

8157 **1878 MS62 PCGS.** PCGS Population (26/66). NGC Census: (35/44). Mintage: 3,020. Numismedia Wsl. Price for problem free NGC/PCGS coin in MS62: $700. (#7579)

8158 **1882 MS62 NGC.** NGC Census: (19/156). PCGS Population (31/185). Mintage: 5,000. Numismedia Wsl. Price for problem free NGC/PCGS coin in MS62: $535. (#7583)

8159 **1887 MS61 PCGS.** PCGS Population (36/487). NGC Census: (28/396). Mintage: 7,500. Numismedia Wsl. Price for problem free NGC/PCGS coin in MS61: $400. (#7588)

LIBERTY QUARTER EAGLES

8160 **1842-O VF20 PCGS.** PCGS Population (4/86). NGC Census: (4/127). Mintage: 19,800. Numismedia Wsl. Price for problem free NGC/PCGS coin in VF20: $500. (#7726)

8161 **1843-O Small Date, Crosslet 4 AU53 NGC.** NGC Census: (66/352). PCGS Population (14/86). Mintage: 288,002. Numismedia Wsl. Price for problem free NGC/PCGS coin in AU53: $360. (#7731)

8162 **1846-O XF40 NGC.** NGC Census: (21/214). PCGS Population (9/75). Mintage: 62,000. Numismedia Wsl. Price for problem free NGC/PCGS coin in XF40: $420. (#7743)

8163 **1847-O AU53 NGC.** NGC Census: (34/116). PCGS Population (7/25). Mintage: 124,000. Numismedia Wsl. Price for problem free NGC/PCGS coin in AU53: $785. (#7747)

8164 **1851-O AU53 NGC.** NGC Census: (50/250). PCGS Population (9/39). Mintage: 148,000. Numismedia Wsl. Price for problem free NGC/PCGS coin in AU53: $810. (#7762)

8165 **1852 MS62 NGC.** NGC Census: (207/131). PCGS Population (98/109). Mintage: 1,159,681. Numismedia Wsl. Price for problem free NGC/PCGS coin in MS62: $545. (#7763)

8166 **1852 MS63 NGC.** NGC Census: (73/58). PCGS Population (67/42). Mintage: 1,159,681. Numismedia Wsl. Price for problem free NGC/PCGS coin in MS63: $1,125. (#7763)

8167 **1852-O XF45 NGC.** NGC Census: (55/321). PCGS Population (46/95). Mintage: 140,000. Numismedia Wsl. Price for problem free NGC/PCGS coin in XF45: $462. (#7766)

8168 **1852-O AU55 NGC.** NGC Census: (82/148). PCGS Population (22/25). Mintage: 140,000. Numismedia Wsl. Price for problem free NGC/PCGS coin in AU55: $800. (#7766)

8169 **1854-O AU58 PCGS. CAC.** PCGS Population (25/19). NGC Census: (152/38). Mintage: 153,000. Numismedia Wsl. Price for problem free NGC/PCGS coin in AU58: $625. (#7772)

8170 **1860 New Reverse, Type Two AU55 NGC.** NGC Census: (9/63). PCGS Population (16/49). Mintage: 22,675. Numismedia Wsl. Price for problem free NGC/PCGS coin in AU55: $420. (#7791)

8171 **1861 New Reverse, Type Two XF45 NGC.** NGC Census: (7/1339). PCGS Population (26/899). Mintage: 1,283,878. Numismedia Wsl. Price for problem free NGC/PCGS coin in XF45: $285. (#7794)

8172 **1871-S AU58 PCGS. CAC.** PCGS Population (14/15). NGC Census: (59/29). Mintage: 22,000. Numismedia Wsl. Price for problem free NGC/PCGS coin in AU58: $750. (#7814)

8173 **1876 XF40 ANACS.** NGC Census: (3/106). PCGS Population (5/49). Mintage: 4,100. Numismedia Wsl. Price for problem free NGC/PCGS coin in XF40: $525. (#7824)

8174 **1887—Improperly Cleaned—NCS. Unc Details.** NGC Census: (5/90). PCGS Population (4/71). Mintage: 6,160. Numismedia Wsl. Price for problem free NGC/PCGS coin in MS60: $700. (#7839)

8175 **1891 Doubled Die Reverse AU55 ANACS.** Mintage: 10,900. (#7843)

8176 **1904 AU58 PCGS.** PCGS Population (245/3462). NGC Census: (128/3428). Mintage: 160,700. Numismedia Wsl. Price for problem free NGC/PCGS coin in AU58: $320. (#7856)

8177 **1906 MS63 NGC.** NGC Census: (952/1690). PCGS Population (1319/1771). Mintage: 176,300. Numismedia Wsl. Price for problem free NGC/PCGS coin in MS63: $1,080. (#7858)

INDIAN QUARTER EAGLES

8178 **1908 MS61 PCGS.** PCGS Population (345/4121). NGC Census: (1260/5058). Mintage: 564,800. Numismedia Wsl. Price for problem free NGC/PCGS coin in MS61: $410. (#7939)

8179 **1908 MS63 NGC.** NGC Census: (1252/1563). PCGS Population (1261/1728). Mintage: 564,800. Numismedia Wsl. Price for problem free NGC/PCGS coin in MS63: $900. (#7939)

8180 **1909 MS61 PCGS.** PCGS Population (256/2258). NGC Census: (1038/3528). Mintage: 441,700. Numismedia Wsl. Price for problem free NGC/PCGS coin in MS61: $415. (#7940)

8181 **1911 MS62 PCGS.** PCGS Population (1516/1665). NGC Census: (3282/2562). Mintage: 704,000. Numismedia Wsl. Price for problem free NGC/PCGS coin in MS62: $510. (#7942)

8182 **1912 MS62 NGC.** NGC Census: (2000/1407). PCGS Population (994/1139). Mintage: 616,000. Numismedia Wsl. Price for problem free NGC/PCGS coin in MS62: $540. (#7944)

8183 **1913 MS61 NGC.** NGC Census: (2080/5432). PCGS Population (577/3210). Mintage: 722,000. Numismedia Wsl. Price for problem free NGC/PCGS coin in MS61: $410. (#7945)

8184 **1913 MS62 PCGS.** PCGS Population (1451/1746). NGC Census: (3158/2280). Mintage: 722,000. Numismedia Wsl. Price for problem free NGC/PCGS coin in MS62: $480. (#7945)

8185 **1913 MS63 NGC.** NGC Census: (1440/840). PCGS Population (997/749). Mintage: 722,000. Numismedia Wsl. Price for problem free NGC/PCGS coin in MS63: $885. (#7945)

8186 **1914—Improperly Cleaned—NCS. Unc Details.** NGC Census: (155/4394). PCGS Population (44/1982). Mintage: 240,000. Numismedia Wsl. Price for problem free NGC/PCGS coin in MS60: $375. (#7946)

8187 **1914-D MS61 PCGS.** PCGS Population (535/3072). NGC Census: (1756/4984). Mintage: 448,000. Numismedia Wsl. Price for problem free NGC/PCGS coin in MS61: $420. (#7947)

8188 **1914-D MS61 PCGS.** PCGS Population (522/3053). NGC Census: (1746/4953). Mintage: 448,000. Numismedia Wsl. Price for problem free NGC/PCGS coin in MS61: $420. (#7947)

8189 **1914-D MS62 NGC.** NGC Census: (2925/2057). PCGS Population (1542/1540). Mintage: 448,000. Numismedia Wsl. Price for problem free NGC/PCGS coin in MS62: $500. (#7947)

8190 **1914-D MS62 PCGS.** PCGS Population (1542/1540). NGC Census: (2925/2057). Mintage: 448,000. Numismedia Wsl. Price for problem free NGC/PCGS coin in MS62: $500. (#7947)

8191 **1914-D MS62 NGC.** NGC Census: (2927/2057). PCGS Population (1530/1542). Mintage: 448,000. Numismedia Wsl. Price for problem free NGC/PCGS coin in MS62: $500. (#7947)

8192 **1915—Rev Improperly Cleaned—NCS. Unc Details.** NGC Census: (128/7494). PCGS Population (92/3666). Mintage: 606,000. Numismedia Wsl. Price for problem free NGC/PCGS coin in MS60: $280. (#7948)

8193 **1915 MS62 NGC.** NGC Census: (2905/2683). PCGS Population (1382/1775). Mintage: 606,000. Numismedia Wsl. Price for problem free NGC/PCGS coin in MS62: $470. (#7948)

8194 **1925-D AU58 PCGS.** PCGS Population (1137/9965). NGC Census: (950/15274). Mintage: 578,000. Numismedia Wsl. Price for problem free NGC/PCGS coin in AU58: $255. (#7949)

8195 **1925-D MS62 PCGS.** PCGS Population (3166/5352). NGC Census: (5214/7467). Mintage: 578,000. Numismedia Wsl. Price for problem free NGC/PCGS coin in MS62: $450. (#7949)

8196 **1925-D MS63 NGC.** NGC Census: (3685/3782). PCGS Population (2806/2546). Mintage: 578,000. Numismedia Wsl. Price for problem free NGC/PCGS coin in MS63: $805. (#7949)

8197 **1925-D MS64 NGC.** NGC Census: (3008/774). PCGS Population (2061/485). Mintage: 578,000. Numismedia Wsl. Price for problem free NGC/PCGS coin in MS64: $1,250. (#7949)

8198 **1926 MS61 PCGS.** PCGS Population (1019/8384). NGC Census: (2045/11684). Mintage: 446,000. Numismedia Wsl. Price for problem free NGC/PCGS coin in MS61: $400. (#7950)

8199 **1926 MS62 PCGS.** PCGS Population (2775/5662). NGC Census: (4763/6993). Mintage: 446,000. Numismedia Wsl. Price for problem free NGC/PCGS coin in MS62: $450. (#7950)

8200 **1926 MS63 PCGS.** PCGS Population (2751/2911). NGC Census: (3573/3420). Mintage: 446,000. Numismedia Wsl. Price for problem free NGC/PCGS coin in MS63: $805. (#7950)

8201 **1926 MS64 NGC.** NGC Census: (2956/464). PCGS Population (2284/627). Mintage: 446,000. Numismedia Wsl. Price for problem free NGC/PCGS coin in MS64: $1,250. (#7950)

8202 **1927—Obverse Damage—MS60 NCS. Unc Details.** NGC Census: (148/11329). PCGS Population (176/7755). Mintage: 388,000. Numismedia Wsl. Price for problem free NGC/PCGS coin in MS60: $280. (#7951)

8203 **1927—Improperly Cleaned—NCS. Unc Details.** NGC Census: (148/11253). PCGS Population (175/7703). Mintage: 388,000. Numismedia Wsl. Price for problem free NGC/PCGS coin in MS60: $280. (#7951)

8204 **1927 MS64 NGC.** NGC Census: (2213/343). PCGS Population (1731/381). Mintage: 388,000. Numismedia Wsl. Price for problem free NGC/PCGS coin in MS64: $1,250. (#7951)

8205 **1927 MS64 NGC.** NGC Census: (2213/343). PCGS Population (1731/381). Mintage: 388,000. Numismedia Wsl. Price for problem free NGC/PCGS coin in MS64: $1,250. (#7951)

8206 **1928 MS61 NGC.** NGC Census: (1631/10710). PCGS Population (1114/6837). Mintage: 416,000. Numismedia Wsl. Price for problem free NGC/PCGS coin in MS61: $400. (#7952)

8207 **1928 MS63 NGC.** NGC Census: (3621/2529). PCGS Population (2514/1551). Mintage: 416,000. Numismedia Wsl. Price for problem free NGC/PCGS coin in MS63: $805. (#7952)

8208 **1928 MS64 PCGS.** PCGS Population (1283/268). NGC Census: (2164/365). Mintage: 416,000. Numismedia Wsl. Price for problem free NGC/PCGS coin in MS64: $1,250. (#7952)

8209 **1929 MS61 ANACS.** NGC Census: (2012/12838). PCGS Population (1586/8387). Mintage: 532,000. Numismedia Wsl. Price for problem free NGC/PCGS coin in MS61: $400. (#7953)

8210 **1929 MS64 NGC.** NGC Census: (1995/152). PCGS Population (1308/106). Mintage: 532,000. Numismedia Wsl. Price for problem free NGC/PCGS coin in MS64: $1,300. (#7953)

8211 **1929 MS64 PCGS.** PCGS Population (1308/106). NGC Census: (1995/152). Mintage: 532,000. Numismedia Wsl. Price for problem free NGC/PCGS coin in MS64: $1,300. (#7953)

THREE DOLLAR GOLD PIECES

8212 **1856—Countermarked—XF40 NCS. XF Details.** NGC Census: (15/611). PCGS Population (12/424). Mintage: 26,010. Numismedia Wsl. Price for problem free NGC/PCGS coin in XF40: $1,199. (#7974)

8213 **1862—Improperly Cleaned, Improperly Cleaned—NCS. XF Details.** NGC Census: (1/180). PCGS Population (10/136). Mintage: 5,750. Numismedia Wsl. Price for problem free NGC/PCGS coin in XF40: $1,550. (#7983)

CLASSIC HALF EAGLE

8214 **1834 Plain 4—Improperly Cleaned—NCS. VF Details.** NGC Census: (5/1726). PCGS Population (4/1047). Mintage: 657,460. Numismedia Wsl. Price for problem free NGC/PCGS coin in VF20: $480. (#8171)

LIBERTY HALF EAGLES

8215 **1843-D Medium D AG3 NGC.** NGC Census: (1/214). PCGS Population (0/185). Mintage: 98,452. (#8215)

8216 **1853 AU58 PCGS.** PCGS Population (34/68). NGC Census: (136/80). Mintage: 305,770. Numismedia Wsl. Price for problem free NGC/PCGS coin in AU58: $500. (#8253)

8217 **1856—Rotated Dies—AU53 NGC.** NGC Census: (40/203). PCGS Population (26/84). Mintage: 197,990. Numismedia Wsl. Price for problem free NGC/PCGS coin in AU53: $425. (#8266)

8218 **1863-S Good 4 PCGS.** PCGS Population (2/38). NGC Census: (0/57). Mintage: 17,000. (#8295)

8219 **1872-CC VG8 NGC.** NGC Census: (4/51). PCGS Population (3/66). Mintage: 16,980. Numismedia Wsl. Price for problem free NGC/PCGS coin in VG8 : $550. (#8326)

8220 **1879-CC—Harshly Cleaned—NCS. AU Details.** NGC Census: (16/60). PCGS Population (13/34). Mintage: 17,281. Numismedia Wsl. Price for problem free NGC/PCGS coin in AU50: $2,975. (#8349)

8221 **1880 MS61 ANACS.** NGC Census: (701/811). PCGS Population (132/415). Mintage: 3,166,436. Numismedia Wsl. Price for problem free NGC/PCGS coin in MS61: $520. (#8351)

8222 **1880-S MS63 NGC.** NGC Census: (227/129). PCGS Population (214/68). Mintage: 1,348,900. Numismedia Wsl. Price for problem free NGC/PCGS coin in MS63: $1,065. (#8353)

8223 **1881 MS63 NGC.** NGC Census: (2168/685). PCGS Population (1063/253). Mintage: 5,708,802. Numismedia Wsl. Price for problem free NGC/PCGS coin in MS63: $1,075. (#8354)

8224 **1883 MS62 NGC.** NGC Census: (86/59). PCGS Population (42/74). Mintage: 233,461. Numismedia Wsl. Price for problem free NGC/PCGS coin in MS62: $525. (#8361)

8225 **1884 MS62 PCGS.** PCGS Population (27/19). NGC Census: (53/21). Mintage: 191,078. Numismedia Wsl. Price for problem free NGC/PCGS coin in MS62: $845. (#8364)

8226 **1884-S MS61 NGC.** NGC Census: (104/159). PCGS Population (32/122). Mintage: 177,000. Numismedia Wsl. Price for problem free NGC/PCGS coin in MS61: $520. (#8366)

8227 **1884-S MS62 PCGS.** PCGS Population (71/51). NGC Census: (94/65). Mintage: 177,000. Numismedia Wsl. Price for problem free NGC/PCGS coin in MS62: $545. (#8366)

8228 **1885 MS61 PCGS.** PCGS Population (84/460). NGC Census: (220/663). Mintage: 601,400. Numismedia Wsl. Price for problem free NGC/PCGS coin in MS61: $520. (#8367)

8229 **1887-S MS61 ICG.** NGC Census: (847/1333). PCGS Population (333/790). Mintage: 1,912,000. Numismedia Wsl. Price for problem free NGC/PCGS coin in MS61: $520. (#8371)

8230 **1888-S MS61 NGC.** NGC Census: (33/21). PCGS Population (13/25). Mintage: 293,900. Numismedia Wsl. Price for problem free NGC/PCGS coin in MS61: $910. (#8373)

8231 **1893-S MS62 NGC.** NGC Census: (292/158). PCGS Population (154/120). Mintage: 224,000. Numismedia Wsl. Price for problem free NGC/PCGS coin in MS62: $510. (#8386)

8232 **1893-S MS62 NGC.** NGC Census: (292/158). PCGS Population (154/120). Mintage: 224,000. Numismedia Wsl. Price for problem free NGC/PCGS coin in MS62: $510. (#8386)

8233 **1894-S AU58 NGC.** NGC Census: (45/25). PCGS Population (10/12). Mintage: 55,900. Numismedia Wsl. Price for problem free NGC/PCGS coin in AU58: $685. (#8389)

8234 **1895 MS60 PCGS.** PCGS Population (262/2082). NGC Census: (336/5303). Mintage: 1,345,936. Numismedia Wsl. Price for problem free NGC/PCGS coin in MS60: $410. (#8390)

8235 **1898 MS61 PCGS.** PCGS Population (158/400). NGC Census: (516/1134). Mintage: 633,495. Numismedia Wsl. Price for problem free NGC/PCGS coin in MS61: $500. (#8396)

8236 **1904-S AU53 NGC.** NGC Census: (14/186). PCGS Population (13/115). Mintage: 97,000. Numismedia Wsl. Price for problem free NGC/PCGS coin in AU53: $375. (#8410)

8237 **1907 MS63 NGC.** NGC Census: (1542/923). PCGS Population (1398/672). Mintage: 626,192. Numismedia Wsl. Price for problem free NGC/PCGS coin in MS63: $1,075. (#8416)

INDIAN HALF EAGLES

8238 **1908 MS60 NGC.** NGC Census: (101/4254). PCGS Population (98/3511). Mintage: 577,800. Numismedia Wsl. Price for problem free NGC/PCGS coin in MS60: $460. (#8510)

8239 **1908 MS62 NGC.** NGC Census: (1814/1470). PCGS Population (1271/1869). Mintage: 577,800. Numismedia Wsl. Price for problem free NGC/PCGS coin in MS62: $900. (#8510)

8240 **1908-D MS62 PCGS.** PCGS Population (936/1558). NGC Census: (776/1247). Mintage: 148,000. Numismedia Wsl. Price for problem free NGC/PCGS coin in MS62: $940. (#8511)

8241 **1908-D MS62 NGC.** NGC Census: (777/1250). PCGS Population (923/1526). Mintage: 148,000. Numismedia Wsl. Price for problem free NGC/PCGS coin in MS62: $940. (#8511)

8242 **1909 MS62 NGC.** NGC Census: (1408/824). PCGS Population (1015/1028). Mintage: 627,138. Numismedia Wsl. Price for problem free NGC/PCGS coin in MS62: $890. (#8513)

8243 **1909-D AU58 PCGS.** PCGS Population (2148/22799). NGC Census: (2551/22356). Mintage: 3,423,560. Numismedia Wsl. Price for problem free NGC/PCGS coin in AU58: $410. (#8514)

8244 **1909-D MS62 NGC.** NGC Census: (8427/8772). PCGS Population (8418/10883). Mintage: 3,423,560. Numismedia Wsl. Price for problem free NGC/PCGS coin in MS62: $800. (#8514)

8245 **1909-D MS62 PCGS.** PCGS Population (8361/10838). NGC Census: (8366/8681). Mintage: 3,423,560. Numismedia Wsl. Price for problem free NGC/PCGS coin in MS62: $800. (#8514)

8246 **1910-S AU58 NGC.** NGC Census: (365/214). PCGS Population (105/159). Mintage: 770,200. Numismedia Wsl. Price for problem free NGC/PCGS coin in AU58: $550. (#8519)

8247 **1911 MS62 NGC.** NGC Census: (2261/1021). PCGS Population (1573/1166). Mintage: 915,000. Numismedia Wsl. Price for problem free NGC/PCGS coin in MS62: $925. (#8520)

8248 **1912 AU58 NGC.** NGC Census: (1222/5594). PCGS Population (887/4557). Mintage: 790,000. Numismedia Wsl. Price for problem free NGC/PCGS coin in AU58: $430. (#8523)

8249 **1912 MS62 NGC.** NGC Census: (2520/1052). PCGS Population (2082/1438). Mintage: 790,000. Numismedia Wsl. Price for problem free NGC/PCGS coin in MS62: $890. (#8523)

8250 **1912-S AU53 ANACS.** NGC Census: (83/801). PCGS Population (35/322). Mintage: 392,000. Numismedia Wsl. Price for problem free NGC/PCGS coin in AU53: $410. (#8524)

8251 **1913 MS61 PCGS.** PCGS Population (924/3962). NGC Census: (2146/4249). Mintage: 915,900. Numismedia Wsl. Price for problem free NGC/PCGS coin in MS61: $540. (#8525)

LIBERTY EAGLES

8252 **1842 Large Date AU50 NGC.** NGC Census: (11/20). PCGS Population (15/24). Mintage: 81,507. Numismedia Wsl. Price for problem free NGC/PCGS coin in AU50: $950. (#8584)

8253 **1846-O XF40 ANACS.** NGC Census: (17/81). PCGS Population (16/19). Mintage: 81,780. Numismedia Wsl. Price for problem free NGC/PCGS coin in XF40: $1,275. (#8595)

8254 **1847-O XF45 NGC.** NGC Census: (158/448). PCGS Population (106/148). Mintage: 571,500. Numismedia Wsl. Price for problem free NGC/PCGS coin in XF45: $752. (#8598)

8255 **1847-O AU53 NGC.** NGC Census: (114/238). PCGS Population (30/39). Mintage: 571,500. Numismedia Wsl. Price for problem free NGC/PCGS coin in AU53: $785. (#8598)

8256 **1848—Cleaned, Scratched—ANACS. AU53 Details.** NGC Census: (43/131). PCGS Population (9/26). Mintage: 145,484. Numismedia Wsl. Price for problem free NGC/PCGS coin in AU53: $810. (#8599)

8257 **1849 XF40 PCGS.** PCGS Population (54/235). NGC Census: (62/629). Mintage: 653,618. Numismedia Wsl. Price for problem free NGC/PCGS coin in XF40: $715. (#8601)

8258 **1851-O—Environmental Damage—NCS. AU Details.** NGC Census: (106/426). PCGS Population (67/92). Mintage: 263,000. Numismedia Wsl. Price for problem free NGC/PCGS coin in AU50: $900. (#8607)

8259 **1852 AU50 NGC.** NGC Census: (78/342). PCGS Population (51/88). Mintage: 263,106. Numismedia Wsl. Price for problem free NGC/PCGS coin in AU50: $755. (#8608)

8260 **1853 AU53 NGC.** NGC Census: (81/315). PCGS Population (47/77). Mintage: 201,253. Numismedia Wsl. Price for problem free NGC/PCGS coin in AU53: $735. (#8610)

8261 **1853-O VF30 NGC.** NGC Census: (2/227). PCGS Population (2/160). Mintage: 51,000. Numismedia Wsl. Price for problem free NGC/PCGS coin in VF30: $732. (#8612)

8262 **1854 AU55 NGC.** NGC Census: (52/64). PCGS Population (14/16). Mintage: 54,250. Numismedia Wsl. Price for problem free NGC/PCGS coin in AU55: $975. (#8613)

8263 **1861—Cleaning—PCGS Genuine.** Mintage: 113,100. (#8633)

8264 **1874 AU58 NGC.** NGC Census: (118/71). PCGS Population (41/44). Mintage: 53,160. Numismedia Wsl. Price for problem free NGC/PCGS coin in AU58: $800. (#8669)

8265 **1879-S AU58 NGC.** NGC Census: (193/112). PCGS Population (53/50). Mintage: 224,000. Numismedia Wsl. Price for problem free NGC/PCGS coin in AU58: $765. (#8686)

8266 **1881 MS60 ANACS.** NGC Census: (1067/8094). PCGS Population (898/2981). Mintage: 3,877,260. Numismedia Wsl. Price for problem free NGC/PCGS coin in MS60: $750. (#8691)

8267 **1881-S MS62 ★ NGC.** NGC Census: (417/20). PCGS Population (284/28). Mintage: 970,000. Numismedia Wsl. Price for problem free NGC/PCGS coin in MS62: $900. (#8694)

8268 **1882-S MS62 NGC.** NGC Census: (70/21). PCGS Population (58/11). Mintage: 132,000. Numismedia Wsl. Price for problem free NGC/PCGS coin in MS62: $1,050. (#8698)

8269 **1883-S AU58 NGC.** NGC Census: (37/49). PCGS Population (16/46). Mintage: 38,000. Numismedia Wsl. Price for problem free NGC/PCGS coin in AU58: $765. (#8702)

8270 **1885-S MS62 NGC.** NGC Census: (188/48). PCGS Population (236/61). Mintage: 228,000. Numismedia Wsl. Price for problem free NGC/PCGS coin in MS62: $860. (#8707)

8271 **1888 MS61 PCGS.** PCGS Population (31/21). NGC Census: (108/34). Mintage: 132,996. Numismedia Wsl. Price for problem free NGC/PCGS coin in MS61: $925. (#8712)

8272 **1891 MS62 PCGS.** PCGS Population (103/36). NGC Census: (171/38). Mintage: 91,868. Numismedia Wsl. Price for problem free NGC/PCGS coin in MS62: $875. (#8719)

8273 **1893 MS62 ★ NGC.** NGC Census: (10526/6192). PCGS Population (5817/2067). Mintage: 1,840,895. Numismedia Wsl. Price for problem free NGC/PCGS coin in MS62: $850. (#8725)

8274 **1893 MS62 NGC.** NGC Census: (10400/6114). PCGS Population (5786/2048). Mintage: 1,840,895. Numismedia Wsl. Price for problem free NGC/PCGS coin in MS62: $850. (#8725)

8275 **1893 MS62 NGC.** NGC Census: (10504/6184). PCGS Population (5819/2062). Mintage: 1,840,895. Numismedia Wsl. Price for problem free NGC/PCGS coin in MS62: $850. (#8725)

8276 **1894 MS62 NGC.** NGC Census: (11818/4839). PCGS Population (5819/1463). Mintage: 2,470,778. Numismedia Wsl. Price for problem free NGC/PCGS coin in MS62: $850. (#8729)

8277 **1896-S AU58 PCGS.** PCGS Population (34/68). NGC Census: (122/65). Mintage: 123,750. Numismedia Wsl. Price for problem free NGC/PCGS coin in AU58: $800. (#8736)

8278 **1898-S MS62 NGC.** NGC Census: (103/21). PCGS Population (123/37). Mintage: 473,600. Numismedia Wsl. Price for problem free NGC/PCGS coin in MS62: $855. (#8741)

8279 **1899-S MS62 NGC.** NGC Census: (121/49). PCGS Population (103/69). Mintage: 841,000. Numismedia Wsl. Price for problem free NGC/PCGS coin in MS62: $890. (#8744)

8280 **1900 MS62 NGC.** NGC Census: (2108/1745). PCGS Population (1461/846). Mintage: 293,960. Numismedia Wsl. Price for problem free NGC/PCGS coin in MS62: $900. (#8745)

8281 **1901—Damage—PCGS Genuine.** Mintage: 1,718,825. (#8747)

8282 **1901-S—Obverse Improperly Cleaned—NCS. Unc Details.** NGC Census: (207/13909). PCGS Population (418/13770). Mintage: 2,812,750. Numismedia Wsl. Price for problem free NGC/PCGS coin in MS60: $750. (#8749)

8283 **1906-S MS62 NGC.** NGC Census: (0/0). PCGS Population (56/31). Mintage: 457,000. Numismedia Wsl. Price for problem free NGC/PCGS coin in MS62: $900. (#8762)

8284 **1906-S MS62 PCGS.** PCGS Population (56/31). NGC Census: (0/0). Mintage: 457,000. Numismedia Wsl. Price for problem free NGC/PCGS coin in MS62: $900. (#8762)

8285 **1907 MS61 NGC.** NGC Census: (4618/14259). PCGS Population (2563/9639). Mintage: 1,203,973. Numismedia Wsl. Price for problem free NGC/PCGS coin in MS61: $800. (#8763)

8286 **1907 MS61 NGC.** NGC Census: (4618/14259). PCGS Population (2563/9639). Mintage: 1,203,973. Numismedia Wsl. Price for problem free NGC/PCGS coin in MS61: $800. (#8763)

8287 **1907-S MS62 NGC.** NGC Census: (69/46). PCGS Population (42/24). Mintage: 210,500. Numismedia Wsl. Price for problem free NGC/PCGS coin in MS62: $975. (#8765)

INDIAN EAGLES

8288 **1907 No Periods MS60 PCGS.** PCGS Population (159/3906). NGC Census: (138/4373). Mintage: 239,400. Numismedia Wsl. Price for problem free NGC/PCGS coin in MS60: $805. (#8852)

8289 **1907 No Periods MS61 NGC.** NGC Census: (1018/3371). PCGS Population (515/3402). Mintage: 239,400. Numismedia Wsl. Price for problem free NGC/PCGS coin in MS61: $950. (#8852)

8290 **1908 No Motto AU58 PCGS.** PCGS Population (102/501). NGC Census: (107/447). Mintage: 33,500. Numismedia Wsl. Price for problem free NGC/PCGS coin in AU58: $765. (#8853)

8291 **1908-D No Motto AU58 PCGS.** PCGS Population (189/372). NGC Census: (252/389). Mintage: 210,000. Numismedia Wsl. Price for problem free NGC/PCGS coin in AU58: $820. (#8854)

8292 **1908 Motto—Improperly Cleaned—NCS. Unc Details.** NGC Census: (79/2379). PCGS Population (54/1948). Mintage: 341,300. Numismedia Wsl. Price for problem free NGC/PCGS coin in MS60: $800. (#8859)

8293 **1908-D Motto AU58 PCGS.** PCGS Population (115/266). NGC Census: (155/312). Mintage: 836,500. Numismedia Wsl. Price for problem free NGC/PCGS coin in AU58: $820. (#8860)

8294 **1908-S AU55 ANACS.** NGC Census: (101/305). PCGS Population (79/253). Mintage: 59,850. Numismedia Wsl. Price for problem free NGC/PCGS coin in AU55: $915. (#8861)

8295 **1909 MS61 NGC.** NGC Census: (420/577). PCGS Population (133/543). Mintage: 184,700. Numismedia Wsl. Price for problem free NGC/PCGS coin in MS61: $865. (#8862)

8296 **1909-D XF40 PCGS.** PCGS Population (4/866). NGC Census: (3/718). Mintage: 121,540. Numismedia Wsl. Price for problem free NGC/PCGS coin in XF40: $765. (#8863)

8297 **1909-D AU58 PCGS.** PCGS Population (180/530). NGC Census: (212/422). Mintage: 121,540. Numismedia Wsl. Price for problem free NGC/PCGS coin in AU58: $840. (#8863)

8298 **1909-D MS61 NGC.** NGC Census: (166/217). PCGS Population (154/329). Mintage: 121,540. Numismedia Wsl. Price for problem free NGC/PCGS coin in MS61: $1,025. (#8863)

8299 **1910 MS62 PCGS.** PCGS Population (1148/980). NGC Census: (1412/1188). Mintage: 318,500. Numismedia Wsl. Price for problem free NGC/PCGS coin in MS62: $985. (#8865)

8300 **1910-D MS62 NGC.** NGC Census: (3246/2486). PCGS Population (2676/2429). Mintage: 2,356,640. Numismedia Wsl. Price for problem free NGC/PCGS coin in MS62: $985. (#8866)

8301 **1910-S AU58 ANACS.** NGC Census: (440/373). PCGS Population (257/458). Mintage: 811,000. Numismedia Wsl. Price for problem free NGC/PCGS coin in AU58: $815. (#8867)

8302 **1910-S AU58 NGC.** NGC Census: (441/372). PCGS Population (251/453). Mintage: 811,000. Numismedia Wsl. Price for problem free NGC/PCGS coin in AU58: $815. (#8867)

8303 **1911—Improperly Cleaned—NCS. Unc Details.** NGC Census: (126/5753). PCGS Population (128/4182). Mintage: 505,595. Numismedia Wsl. Price for problem free NGC/PCGS coin in MS60: $800. (#8868)

8304 **1911—Improperly Cleaned—NCS. Unc Details.** NGC Census: (126/5753). PCGS Population (128/4182). Mintage: 505,595. Numismedia Wsl. Price for problem free NGC/PCGS coin in MS60: $800. (#8868)

8305 **1912 MS60 NGC.** NGC Census: (114/3859). PCGS Population (109/2794). Mintage: 405,083. Numismedia Wsl. Price for problem free NGC/PCGS coin in MS60: $800. (#8871)

8306 **1913 MS63 NGC.** NGC Census: (516/381). PCGS Population (590/324). Mintage: 442,071. Numismedia Wsl. Price for problem free NGC/PCGS coin in MS63: $1,700. (#8873)

8307 **1915—Improperly Cleaned—NCS. Unc Details.** NGC Census: (77/2431). PCGS Population (56/1713). Mintage: 351,075. Numismedia Wsl. Price for problem free NGC/PCGS coin in MS60: $800. (#8878)

8308 **1926 MS62 PCGS.** PCGS Population (9390/11142). NGC Census: (9579/13437). Mintage: 1,014,000. Numismedia Wsl. Price for problem free NGC/PCGS coin in MS62: $960. (#8882)

8309 **1926 MS62 PCGS.** PCGS Population (9390/11142). NGC Census: (9579/13437). Mintage: 1,014,000. Numismedia Wsl. Price for problem free NGC/PCGS coin in MS62: $960. (#8882)

8310 **1926 MS63 NGC.** NGC Census: (9025/4218). PCGS Population (8006/2961). Mintage: 1,014,000. Numismedia Wsl. Price for problem free NGC/PCGS coin in MS63: $1,600. (#8882)

LIBERTY DOUBLE EAGLES

8311 **1855-S—Scratched—ICG. XF45 Details.** NGC Census: (123/546). PCGS Population (142/226). Mintage: 879,675. Numismedia Wsl. Price for problem free NGC/PCGS coin in XF45: $1,546. (#8916)

8312 **1873 Open 3 MS61 PCGS.** PCGS Population (971/894). NGC Census: (1862/733). Numismedia Wsl. Price for problem free NGC/PCGS coin in MS61: $1,900. (#8967)

8313 **1877—Obverse Scratched—NCS. Unc Details.** NGC Census: (170/354). PCGS Population (115/277). Mintage: 397,670. Numismedia Wsl. Price for problem free NGC/PCGS coin in MS60: $1,600. (#8982)

8314 **1878-S MS61 NGC.** NGC Census: (376/77). PCGS Population (243/126). Mintage: 1,739,000. Numismedia Wsl. Price for problem free NGC/PCGS coin in MS61: $1,650. (#8987)

8315 **1878-S MS61 NGC.** NGC Census: (374/77). PCGS Population (249/131). Mintage: 1,739,000. Numismedia Wsl. Price for problem free NGC/PCGS coin in MS61: $1,650. (#8987)

8316 **1885-S MS61 PCGS.** PCGS Population (424/1047). NGC Census: (772/721). Mintage: 683,500. Numismedia Wsl. Price for problem free NGC/PCGS coin in MS61: $1,625. (#9005)

8317 **1891-S MS62 PCGS.** PCGS Population (1599/727). NGC Census: (1679/466). Mintage: 1,288,125. Numismedia Wsl. Price for problem free NGC/PCGS coin in MS62: $1,710. (#9018)

8318 **1894 MS63 NGC.** NGC Census: (1199/128). PCGS Population (918/89). Mintage: 1,368,990. Numismedia Wsl. Price for problem free NGC/PCGS coin in MS63: $2,625. (#9025)

8319 **1894 MS63 PCGS.** PCGS Population (918/89). NGC Census: (1199/128). Mintage: 1,368,990. Numismedia Wsl. Price for problem free NGC/PCGS coin in MS63: $2,625. (#9025)

8320 **1897 MS62 NGC.** NGC Census: (6266/2595). PCGS Population (4206/1371). Mintage: 1,383,261. Numismedia Wsl. Price for problem free NGC/PCGS coin in MS62: $1,685. (#9031)

8321 **1897-S MS63 NGC.** NGC Census: (1684/292). PCGS Population (1498/337). Mintage: 1,470,250. Numismedia Wsl. Price for problem free NGC/PCGS coin in MS63: $2,575. (#9032)

8322 **1899 MS63 NGC.** NGC Census: (4210/1092). PCGS Population (1769/351). Mintage: 1,669,384. Numismedia Wsl. Price for problem free NGC/PCGS coin in MS63: $2,575. (#9035)

8323 **1899-S MS63 PCGS.** PCGS Population (1096/232). NGC Census: (1104/278). Mintage: 2,010,300. Numismedia Wsl. Price for problem free NGC/PCGS coin in MS63: $2,575. (#9036)

8324 **1900 MS62 NGC.** NGC Census: (13929/15849). PCGS Population (10818/11554). Mintage: 1,874,584. Numismedia Wsl. Price for problem free NGC/PCGS coin in MS62: $1,685. (#9037)

8325 **1900 MS63 NGC.** NGC Census: (12118/3731). PCGS Population (8455/3099). Mintage: 1,874,584. Numismedia Wsl. Price for problem free NGC/PCGS coin in MS63: $2,625. (#9037)

8326 **1900 MS63 NGC.** NGC Census: (12103/3730). PCGS Population (8435/3089). Mintage: 1,874,584. Numismedia Wsl. Price for problem free NGC/PCGS coin in MS63: $2,625. (#9037)

8327 **1900 MS63 PCGS.** PCGS Population (8435/3089). NGC Census: (12103/3730). Mintage: 1,874,584. Numismedia Wsl. Price for problem free NGC/PCGS coin in MS63: $2,625. (#9037)

8328 **1900 MS63 PCGS.** PCGS Population (8455/3099). NGC Census: (12118/3731). Mintage: 1,874,584. Numismedia Wsl. Price for problem free NGC/PCGS coin in MS63: $2,625. (#9037)

8329 **1900 MS63 PCGS.** PCGS Population (8455/3099). NGC Census: (12118/3731). Mintage: 1,874,584. Numismedia Wsl. Price for problem free NGC/PCGS coin in MS63: $2,625. (#9037)

8330 **1900-S MS63 PCGS.** PCGS Population (751/108). NGC Census: (621/91). Mintage: 2,459,500. Numismedia Wsl. Price for problem free NGC/PCGS coin in MS63: $2,650. (#9038)

8331 **1901 MS63 PCGS.** PCGS Population (1506/1615). NGC Census: (1235/1574). Mintage: 111,400. Numismedia Wsl. Price for problem free NGC/PCGS coin in MS63: $2,575. (#9039)

8332 **1904 MS62 PCGS.** PCGS Population (51161/80923). NGC Census: (61521/100126). Mintage: 6,256,797. Numismedia Wsl. Price for problem free NGC/PCGS coin in MS62: $1,685. (#9045)

8333 **1904 MS63 NGC.** NGC Census: (63987/36139). PCGS Population (49154/31769). Mintage: 6,256,797. Numismedia Wsl. Price for problem free NGC/PCGS coin in MS63: $2,575. (#9045)

8334 **1906-S MS63 NGC.** NGC Census: (611/101). PCGS Population (1025/239). Mintage: 2,065,750. Numismedia Wsl. Price for problem free NGC/PCGS coin in MS63: $2,625. (#9051)

SAINT-GAUDENS DOUBLE EAGLES

8335 **1907 Arabic Numerals MS62 PCGS.** PCGS Population (2223/9756). NGC Census: (2810/5328). Mintage: 361,667. Numismedia Wsl. Price for problem free NGC/PCGS coin in MS62: $1,700. (#9141)

8336 **1907 Arabic Numerals MS62 PCGS.** PCGS Population (2223/9756). NGC Census: (2810/5328). Mintage: 361,667. Numismedia Wsl. Price for problem free NGC/PCGS coin in MS62: $1,700. (#9141)

8337 **1908 No Motto MS62 PCGS.** PCGS Population (16812/77872). NGC Census: (24331/84569). Mintage: 4,271,551. Numismedia Wsl. Price for problem free NGC/PCGS coin in MS62: $1,685. (#9142)

8338 **1908 No Motto MS63 NGC.** NGC Census: (41310/42799). PCGS Population (29862/47438). Mintage: 4,271,551. Numismedia Wsl. Price for problem free NGC/PCGS coin in MS63: $1,825. (#9142)

8339 **1909 MS61 NGC.** NGC Census: (264/616). PCGS Population (193/1355). Mintage: 161,282. Numismedia Wsl. Price for problem free NGC/PCGS coin in MS61: $1,700. (#9150)

8340 **1909-S MS64 NGC.** NGC Census: (1320/223). PCGS Population (1606/258). Mintage: 2,774,925. Numismedia Wsl. Price for problem free NGC/PCGS coin in MS64: $2,125. (#9153)

8341 **1909-S MS64 PCGS.** PCGS Population (1606/258). NGC Census: (1320/223). Mintage: 2,774,925. Numismedia Wsl. Price for problem free NGC/PCGS coin in MS64: $2,125. (#9153)

8342 **1910 MS61 PCGS.** PCGS Population (466/5026). NGC Census: (752/5684). Mintage: 482,000. Numismedia Wsl. Price for problem free NGC/PCGS coin in MS61: $1,700. (#9154)

8343 **1910-D MS62 NGC.** NGC Census: (1482/3948). PCGS Population (952/4148). Mintage: 429,000. Numismedia Wsl. Price for problem free NGC/PCGS coin in MS62: $1,735. (#9155)

8344 **1911-D MS63 PCGS.** PCGS Population (2401/5319). NGC Census: (2594/5625). Mintage: 846,500. Numismedia Wsl. Price for problem free NGC/PCGS coin in MS63: $1,835. (#9158)

8345 **1911-S MS61 PCGS.** PCGS Population (167/3740). NGC Census: (265/4467). Mintage: 775,750. Numismedia Wsl. Price for problem free NGC/PCGS coin in MS61: $1,700. (#9159)

8346 **1914-S MS64 NGC.** NGC Census: (5494/1469). PCGS Population (4608/1895). Mintage: 1,498,000. Numismedia Wsl. Price for problem free NGC/PCGS coin in MS64: $2,025. (#9166)

8347 **1924—Obverse Struck Thru—MS62 NGC.**

8348 **1924 MS62 PCGS.** PCGS Population (39827/184981). NGC Census: (43743/216505). Mintage: 4,323,500. Numismedia Wsl. Price for problem free NGC/PCGS coin in MS62: $1,685. (#9177)

8349 **1924 MS63 PCGS.** PCGS Population (71588/113487). NGC Census: (91115/125536). Mintage: 4,323,500. Numismedia Wsl. Price for problem free NGC/PCGS coin in MS63: $1,825. (#9177)

8350 **1924 MS64 NGC.** NGC Census: (92297/33239). PCGS Population (70664/42823). Mintage: 4,323,500. Numismedia Wsl. Price for problem free NGC/PCGS coin in MS64: $2,000. (#9177)

8351 **1925 MS63 NGC.** NGC Census: (15349/17889). PCGS Population (12220/17375). Mintage: 2,831,750. Numismedia Wsl. Price for problem free NGC/PCGS coin in MS63: $1,825. (#9180)

8352 **1925 MS64 NGC.** NGC Census: (13716/4173). PCGS Population (11067/6308). Mintage: 2,831,750. Numismedia Wsl. Price for problem free NGC/PCGS coin in MS64: $2,000. (#9180)

8353 **1926 MS63 NGC.** NGC Census: (5820/11791). PCGS Population (5815/10661). Mintage: 816,750. Numismedia Wsl. Price for problem free NGC/PCGS coin in MS63: $1,825. (#9183)

8354 **1927—Reverse Struck Thru—MS63 NGC.** NGC Census: (0/0). PCGS Population (0/0). (#661000)

8355 **1927 MS63 NGC.** NGC Census: (35832/66252). PCGS Population (34503/66714). Mintage: 2,946,750. Numismedia Wsl. Price for problem free NGC/PCGS coin in MS63: $1,825. (#9186)

8356 **1927 MS64 NGC.** NGC Census: (46651/19631). PCGS Population (39339/27238). Mintage: 2,946,750. Numismedia Wsl. Price for problem free NGC/PCGS coin in MS64: $2,000. (#9186)

8357 **1927 MS64 NGC.** NGC Census: (46651/19631). PCGS Population (39339/27238). Mintage: 2,946,750. Numismedia Wsl. Price for problem free NGC/PCGS coin in MS64: $2,000. (#9186)

COMMEMORATIVE SILVER

8358 **1893 Isabella Quarter—Improperly Cleaned—NCS. AU Details.** NGC Census: (6/3144). PCGS Population (35/4325). Mintage: 24,214. Numismedia Wsl. Price for problem free NGC/PCGS coin in AU50: $435. (#9220)

8359 **1893 Isabella Quarter MS62 PCGS.** PCGS Population (757/2801). NGC Census: (437/2279). Mintage: 24,214. Numismedia Wsl. Price for problem free NGC/PCGS coin in MS62: $535. (#9220)

8360 **1893 Isabella Quarter MS64 PCGS.** PCGS Population (1135/562). NGC Census: (988/605). Mintage: 24,214. Numismedia Wsl. Price for problem free NGC/PCGS coin in MS64: $800. (#9220)

8361 **1900 Lafayette Dollar—Improperly Cleaned—NCS. Unc Details.** NGC Census: (21/1972). PCGS Population (63/2459). Mintage: 36,026. Numismedia Wsl. Price for problem free NGC/PCGS coin in MS60: $800. (#9222)

8362 **1921 Alabama AU58 ANACS.** NGC Census: (54/1622). PCGS Population (81/1960). Mintage: 59,038. Numismedia Wsl. Price for problem free NGC/PCGS coin in AU58: $175. (#9224)

8363 **1921 Alabama 2x2—Improperly Cleaned—NCS. Unc Details.** NGC Census: (0/1479). PCGS Population (9/1853). Mintage: 6,006. Numismedia Wsl. Price for problem free NGC/PCGS coin in MS60: $275. (#9225)

8364 **1936 Albany AU58 ANACS.** NGC Census: (3/2654). PCGS Population (7/4353). Mintage: 17,671. Numismedia Wsl. Price for problem free NGC/PCGS coin in AU58: $240. (#9227)

8365 **1937 Antietam MS61 ANACS.** NGC Census: (3/2327). PCGS Population (1/4278). Mintage: 18,028. Numismedia Wsl. Price for problem free NGC/PCGS coin in MS61: $575. (#9229)

8366 **1937 Antietam MS63 NGC.** NGC Census: (89/2214). PCGS Population (349/3879). Mintage: 18,028. Numismedia Wsl. Price for problem free NGC/PCGS coin in MS63: $620. (#9229)

8367 **1936-S Arkansas MS66 PCGS.** PCGS Population (125/9). NGC Census: (62/6). Mintage: 9,662. Numismedia Wsl. Price for problem free NGC/PCGS coin in MS66: $420. (#9239)

8368 **1935-S Boone MS66 ANACS.** NGC Census: (162/36). PCGS Population (175/20). Mintage: 5,005. Numismedia Wsl. Price for problem free NGC/PCGS coin in MS66: $325. (#9260)

8369 **1935/34-S Boone MS64 ANACS.** NGC Census: (144/291). PCGS Population (216/295). Mintage: 2,004. Numismedia Wsl. Price for problem free NGC/PCGS coin in MS64: $376. (#9264)

8370 **1938-S Boone MS66 PCGS. CAC.** PCGS Population (121/31). NGC Census: (90/31). Mintage: 2,100. Numismedia Wsl. Price for problem free NGC/PCGS coin in MS66: $725. (#9276)

8371 **1936 Bridgeport MS64 ANACS.** NGC Census: (999/1446). PCGS Population (1739/2167). Mintage: 25,015. Numismedia Wsl. Price for problem free NGC/PCGS coin in MS64: $150. (#9279)

8372 **1936 Bridgeport MS66 PCGS. CAC.** PCGS Population (625/54). NGC Census: (321/19). Mintage: 25,015. Numismedia Wsl. Price for problem free NGC/PCGS coin in MS66: $355. (#9279)

8373 **1925-S California MS64 ANACS.** NGC Census: (1371/1399). PCGS Population (1365/1091). Mintage: 86,394. Numismedia Wsl. Price for problem free NGC/PCGS coin in MS64: $350. (#9281)

8374 **1925-S California MS65 PCGS.** PCGS Population (713/378). NGC Census: (862/537). Mintage: 86,394. Numismedia Wsl. Price for problem free NGC/PCGS coin in MS65: $740. (#9281)

8375 **1936 Cincinnati—Cleaned—ANACS. MS60 Details.** NGC Census: (1/755). PCGS Population (1/1356). Mintage: 5,005. Numismedia Wsl. Price for problem free NGC/PCGS coin in MS60: $252. (#9283)

8376 **1936-D Columbia MS67 PCGS. CAC.** PCGS Population (155/17). NGC Census: (213/44). Mintage: 8,009. Numismedia Wsl. Price for problem free NGC/PCGS coin in MS67: $800. (#9292)

8377 **1935 Connecticut MS62 ANACS.** NGC Census: (67/3019). PCGS Population (175/3910). Mintage: 25,018. Numismedia Wsl. Price for problem free NGC/PCGS coin in MS62: $230. (#9299)

8378 **1936 Delaware MS66 ★ NGC.** NGC Census: (438/102). PCGS Population (594/68). Mintage: 20,993. Numismedia Wsl. Price for problem free NGC/PCGS coin in MS66: $525. (#9301)

8379 **1936 Gettysburg—Improperly Cleaned—NCS. Unc Details.** NGC Census: (0/2829). PCGS Population (3/4801). Mintage: 26,928. Numismedia Wsl. Price for problem free NGC/PCGS coin in MS60: $352. (#9305)

8380 **1924 Huguenot MS65 NGC.** NGC Census: (974/322). PCGS Population (897/348). Mintage: 142,080. Numismedia Wsl. Price for problem free NGC/PCGS coin in MS65: $320. (#9314)

8381 **1946 Iowa MS67 PCGS.** PCGS Population (680/57). NGC Census: (621/41). Mintage: 100,057. Numismedia Wsl. Price for problem free NGC/PCGS coin in MS67: $310. (#9316)

8382 **1925 Lexington MS65 PCGS. CAC.** PCGS Population (880/276). NGC Census: (807/152). Mintage: 162,013. Numismedia Wsl. Price for problem free NGC/PCGS coin in MS65: $410. (#9318)

8383 **1936 Lynchburg MS61 ANACS.** NGC Census: (5/2272). PCGS Population (8/3632). Mintage: 20,013. Numismedia Wsl. Price for problem free NGC/PCGS coin in MS61: $215. (#9324)

8384 **1936 Lynchburg MS64 PCGS.** PCGS Population (1256/1814). NGC Census: (665/1447). Mintage: 20,013. Numismedia Wsl. Price for problem free NGC/PCGS coin in MS64: $240. (#9324)

8385 **1921 Missouri—Improperly Cleaned—NCS. AU Details.** NGC Census: (1/1800). PCGS Population (8/1955). Mintage: 10,428. Numismedia Wsl. Price for problem free NGC/PCGS coin in AU50: $322. (#9330)

8386 **1923-S Monroe MS64 PCGS. CAC.** PCGS Population (1449/405). NGC Census: (1486/362). Mintage: 274,077. Numismedia Wsl. Price for problem free NGC/PCGS coin in MS64: $310. (#9333)

8387 **1938 New Rochelle—Cleaned—ANACS. AU58 Details.** NGC Census: (1/2086). PCGS Population (1/3911). Mintage: 15,266. Numismedia Wsl. Price for problem free NGC/PCGS coin in AU58: $335. (#9335)

8388 **1938 New Rochelle MS64 NGC.** NGC Census: (488/1532). PCGS Population (1221/2390). Mintage: 15,266. Numismedia Wsl. Price for problem free NGC/PCGS coin in MS64: $380. (#9335)

8389 **1936 Norfolk MS62 ANACS.** NGC Census: (2/2434). PCGS Population (30/4406). Mintage: 16,936. Numismedia Wsl. Price for problem free NGC/PCGS coin in MS62: $420. (#9337)

8390 **1936 Norfolk MS65 ANACS.** NGC Census: (540/1694). PCGS Population (1074/2563). Mintage: 16,936. Numismedia Wsl. Price for problem free NGC/PCGS coin in MS65: $470. (#9337)

8391 **1925 Norse Thick Planchet MS65 PCGS. CAC.** PCGS Population (164/29). NGC Census: (0/0). (#9450)

8392 **1925 Norse Thin Planchet MS64 PCGS.** PCGS Population (93/30). NGC Census: (0/0). (#9451)

8393 **1926 Oregon MS66 PCGS.** PCGS Population (349/58). NGC Census: (306/51). Mintage: 47,955. Numismedia Wsl. Price for problem free NGC/PCGS coin in MS66: $360. (#9340)

8394 **1934-D Oregon MS65 PCGS.** PCGS Population (782/348). NGC Census: (542/206). Mintage: 7,006. Numismedia Wsl. Price for problem free NGC/PCGS coin in MS65: $260. (#9344)

8395 **1936-S Oregon MS67 PCGS.** PCGS Population (117/4). NGC Census: (141/13). Mintage: 5,006. Numismedia Wsl. Price for problem free NGC/PCGS coin in MS67: $900. (#9346)

8396 **1937-D Oregon MS65 ANACS.** NGC Census: (492/1413). PCGS Population (924/1668). Mintage: 12,008. Numismedia Wsl. Price for problem free NGC/PCGS coin in MS65: $275. (#9347)

8397 **1915-S Panama-Pacific—Cleaned—ANACS. AU50 Details.** NGC Census: (4/2392). PCGS Population (11/2859). Mintage: 27,134. Numismedia Wsl. Price for problem free NGC/PCGS coin in AU50: $340. (#9357)

8398 **1915-S Panama-Pacific—Cleaned—ANACS. AU50 Details.** NGC Census: (4/2393). PCGS Population (11/2863). Mintage: 27,134. Numismedia Wsl. Price for problem free NGC/PCGS coin in AU50: $340. (#9357)

8399 **1915-S Panama-Pacific—Cleaned—ANACS. MS60 Details.** NGC Census: (1/2291). PCGS Population (28/2600). Mintage: 27,134. Numismedia Wsl. Price for problem free NGC/PCGS coin in MS60: $420. (#9357)

8400 **1921 Pilgrim MS65 NGC.** NGC Census: (669/171). PCGS Population (656/264). Mintage: 20,053. Numismedia Wsl. Price for problem free NGC/PCGS coin in MS65: $400. (#9360)

8401 **1937 Roanoke MS62 ANACS.** NGC Census: (14/3317). PCGS Population (62/5350). Mintage: 29,030. Numismedia Wsl. Price for problem free NGC/PCGS coin in MS62: $205. (#9367)

8402 **1937 Roanoke MS67 PCGS. CAC.** PCGS Population (243/12). NGC Census: (213/25). Mintage: 29,030. Numismedia Wsl. Price for problem free NGC/PCGS coin in MS67: $775. (#9367)

8403 **1936 Robinson MS66 PCGS. CAC.** PCGS Population (389/61). NGC Census: (187/27). Mintage: 25,265. Numismedia Wsl. Price for problem free NGC/PCGS coin in MS66: $650. (#9369)

8404 **1926 Sesquicentennial MS64 PCGS. CAC.** PCGS Population (1944/251). NGC Census: (1704/272). Mintage: 141,120. Numismedia Wsl. Price for problem free NGC/PCGS coin in MS64: $280. (#9374)

8405 **1935-D Texas MS66 PCGS.** PCGS Population (680/197). NGC Census: (635/160). Mintage: 10,007. Numismedia Wsl. Price for problem free NGC/PCGS coin in MS66: $310. (#9383)

8406 **1937-D Texas MS66 PCGS. CAC.** PCGS Population (454/111). NGC Census: (424/82). Mintage: 6,605. Numismedia Wsl. Price for problem free NGC/PCGS coin in MS66: $360. (#9391)

8407 **1925 Vancouver—Cleaned—ANACS. AU58 Details.** NGC Census: (31/2005). PCGS Population (69/2829). Mintage: 14,994. Numismedia Wsl. Price for problem free NGC/PCGS coin in AU58: $280. (#9399)

8408 **1925 Vancouver MS64 PCGS.** PCGS Population (956/970). NGC Census: (801/849). Mintage: 14,994. Numismedia Wsl. Price for problem free NGC/PCGS coin in MS64: $460. (#9399)

8409 **1927 Vermont MS65 PCGS. CAC.** PCGS Population (844/286). NGC Census: (730/181). Mintage: 28,142. Numismedia Wsl. Price for problem free NGC/PCGS coin in MS65: $715. (#9401)

8410 **1951-S Booker T. Washington MS66 PCGS.** PCGS Population (317/25). NGC Census: (245/54). Mintage: 7,004. Numismedia Wsl. Price for problem free NGC/PCGS coin in MS66: $160. (#9426)

8411 **1952 Washington-Carver MS66 PCGS. CAC.** PCGS Population (192/6). NGC Census: (226/18). Mintage: 2,006,292. Numismedia Wsl. Price for problem free NGC/PCGS coin in MS66: $300. (#9434)

8412 **1952 Washington-Carver MS66 PCGS.** PCGS Population (192/6). NGC Census: (225/18). Mintage: 2,006,292. Numismedia Wsl. Price for problem free NGC/PCGS coin in MS66: $300. (#9434)

8413 **1952 Washington-Carver MS66 PCGS. CAC.** PCGS Population (189/6). NGC Census: (227/18). Mintage: 2,006,292. Numismedia Wsl. Price for problem free NGC/PCGS coin in MS66: $300. (#9434)

8414 **1953-S Washington-Carver MS66 PCGS.** PCGS Population (80/4). NGC Census: (95/14). Mintage: 108,020. Numismedia Wsl. Price for problem free NGC/PCGS coin in MS66: $300. (#9440)

8415 **1953-S Washington-Carver MS66 NGC.** NGC Census: (95/14). PCGS Population (80/4). Mintage: 108,020. Numismedia Wsl. Price for problem free NGC/PCGS coin in MS66: $300. (#9440)

8416 **1954 Washington-Carver MS66 PCGS. CAC.** PCGS Population (57/0). NGC Census: (51/2). Mintage: 12,006. Numismedia Wsl. Price for problem free NGC/PCGS coin in MS66: $525. (#9442)

8417 **1954-D Washington-Carver MS65 NGC.** NGC Census: (206/19). PCGS Population (299/24). Mintage: 12,000. Numismedia Wsl. Price for problem free NGC/PCGS coin in MS65: $160. (#9443)

8418 **1936 Wisconsin MS65 ANACS.** NGC Census: (1258/1494). PCGS Population (2125/1810). Mintage: 25,015. Numismedia Wsl. Price for problem free NGC/PCGS coin in MS65: $275. (#9447)

8419 **1936 Wisconsin MS67 PCGS. CAC.** PCGS Population (371/21). NGC Census: (309/21). Mintage: 25,015. Numismedia Wsl. Price for problem free NGC/PCGS coin in MS67: $800. (#9447)

8420 **1936 York MS66 NGC.** NGC Census: (1199/387). PCGS Population (1372/512). Mintage: 25,015. Numismedia Wsl. Price for problem free NGC/PCGS coin in MS66: $320. (#9449)

8421 **1936 York MS67 NGC.** NGC Census: (357/30). PCGS Population (491/21). Mintage: 25,015. Numismedia Wsl. Price for problem free NGC/PCGS coin in MS67: $545. (#9449)

8422 **1936 York MS67 PCGS. CAC.** PCGS Population (491/21). NGC Census: (357/30). Mintage: 25,015. Numismedia Wsl. Price for problem free NGC/PCGS coin in MS67: $545. (#9449)

COMMEMORATIVE GOLD

8423 **1904 Lewis and Clark—Whizzed—NCS. AU Details.** NGC Census: (1/1120). PCGS Population (6/1896). Mintage: 10,025. Numismedia Wsl. Price for problem free NGC/PCGS coin in AU50: $700. (#7447)

8424 **1915-S Panama-Pacific Gold Dollar—Reverse Scratched—NCS. Unc Details.** NGC Census: (6/3171). PCGS Population (42/5021). Mintage: 15,000. Numismedia Wsl. Price for problem free NGC/PCGS coin in MS60: $550. (#7449)

8425 **1916 McKinley—Improperly Cleaned—NCS. Unc Details.** NGC Census: (16/2223). PCGS Population (34/4142). Mintage: 9,977. Numismedia Wsl. Price for problem free NGC/PCGS coin in MS60: $470. (#7454)

8426 **1916 McKinley MS64 PCGS.** PCGS Population (1347/1558). NGC Census: (729/819). Mintage: 9,977. Numismedia Wsl. Price for problem free NGC/PCGS coin in MS64: $775. (#7454)

8427 **1926 Sesquicentennial Fine 12 NGC.** NGC Census: (1/6644). PCGS Population (0/10798). Mintage: 46,019. Numismedia Wsl. Price for problem free NGC/PCGS coin in Fine 12: $144. (#7466)

8428 **1926 Sesquicentennial—Improperly Cleaned—NCS. AU Details.** NGC Census: (7/6633). PCGS Population (19/10722). Mintage: 46,019. Numismedia Wsl. Price for problem free NGC/PCGS coin in AU50: $350. (#7466)

8429 **1926 Sesquicentennial MS62 ANACS.** NGC Census: (1038/4880). PCGS Population (1301/8281). Mintage: 46,019. Numismedia Wsl. Price for problem free NGC/PCGS coin in MS62: $450. (#7466)

MODERN ISSUES

8430 **1982-D Washington Silver Half Dollar MS69 PCGS.** PCGS Population (235/0). NGC Census: (71/0). Mintage: 2,210,458. Numismedia Wsl. Price for problem free NGC/PCGS coin in MS69: $300. (#9600)

8431 **1986-W Statue of Liberty Gold Five Dollar PR69 Ultra Cameo NGC.** NGC Census: (151/1). PCGS Population (6431/306). Mintage: 404,013. Numismedia Wsl. Price for problem free NGC/PCGS coin in PR69: $320. (#9623)

8432 **1987-W Constitution Gold Five Dollar PR70 Deep Cameo PCGS.** PCGS Population (847). NGC Census: (7). Mintage: 651,659. Numismedia Wsl. Price for problem free NGC/PCGS coin in PR70: $330. (#9627)

8433 **1988-W Olympic Gold Five Dollar PR69 Deep Cameo ANACS.** NGC Census: (77/1). PCGS Population (5138/283). Mintage: 281,000. Numismedia Wsl. Price for problem free NGC/PCGS coin in PR69: $315. (#9631)

8434 **1991-P Korean War Silver Dollar PR70 Deep Cameo PCGS.** PCGS Population (13). NGC Census: (1). Mintage: 618,488. Numismedia Wsl. Price for problem free NGC/PCGS coin in PR70: $460. (#9653)

8435 **1992-D Columbus Silver Dollar MS70 PCGS.** PCGS Population (59). NGC Census: (207). Mintage: 106,949. Numismedia Wsl. Price for problem free NGC/PCGS coin in MS70: $180. (#9664)

8436 **1991-1995W World War II Gold Five Dollar MS70 NGC.** NGC Census: (720). PCGS Population (110). Mintage: 23,089. Numismedia Wsl. Price for problem free NGC/PCGS coin in MS70: $360. (#9678)

8437 **1995-D Olympic/Paralympics Silver Dollar MS70 PCGS.** PCGS Population (107). NGC Census: (226). Numismedia Wsl. Price for problem free NGC/PCGS coin in MS70: $150. (#9718)

8438 **1996-D Olympic/Paralympics Silver Dollar MS69 PCGS.** PCGS Population (664/53). NGC Census: (429/82). Numismedia Wsl. Price for problem free NGC/PCGS coin in MS69: $200. (#9726)

8439 **1996-D Olympic/Paralympics Silver Dollar MS69 PCGS.** PCGS Population (664/53). NGC Census: (429/82). Numismedia Wsl. Price for problem free NGC/PCGS coin in MS69: $200. (#9726)

8440 **1996-W Olympic/Cauldron Gold Five Dollar PR70 Deep Cameo PCGS.** PCGS Population (80). NGC Census: (0). Numismedia Wsl. Price for problem free NGC/PCGS coin in PR70: $525. (#9739)

8441 **1996-D Smithsonian Silver Dollar MS70 PCGS.** PCGS Population (129). NGC Census: (268). Mintage: 31,320. Numismedia Wsl. Price for problem free NGC/PCGS coin in MS70: $260. (#9742)

8442 **1997-P Law Enforcement Silver Dollar PR70 Deep Cameo PCGS.** PCGS Population (37). NGC Census: (54). Numismedia Wsl. Price for problem free NGC/PCGS coin in PR70: $300. (#9762)

8443 **1998-S Robert F. Kennedy Silver Dollar MS70 PCGS.** PCGS Population (90). NGC Census: (378). Numismedia Wsl. Price for problem free NGC/PCGS coin in MS70: $135. (#9763)

8444 **1998-S Black Patriots Silver Dollar MS70 NGC.** NGC Census: (196). PCGS Population (38). Numismedia Wsl. Price for problem free NGC/PCGS coin in MS70: $320. (#9769)

8445 **2000-P Leif Ericson Silver Dollar MS70 PCGS.** PCGS Population (72). NGC Census: (340). Numismedia Wsl. Price for problem free NGC/PCGS coin in MS70: $200. (#9785)

8446 **2001-D Buffalo Silver Dollar MS69 PCGS.** 36th U.S. Mint Director Jay W. Johnson. PCGS Population (9331/330). NGC Census: (8031/1241). Numismedia Wsl. Price for problem free NGC/PCGS coin in MS69: $155. (#9793)

8447 **2001-D Buffalo Silver Dollar MS70 PCGS.** 36th U.S. Mint Director Jay W. Johnson. PCGS Population (330). NGC Census: (1241). Numismedia Wsl. Price for problem free NGC/PCGS coin in MS70: $425. (#9793)

8448 **2001-D Buffalo Silver Dollar MS70 PCGS.** PCGS Population (331). NGC Census: (1256). Numismedia Wsl. Price for problem free NGC/PCGS coin in MS70: $425. (#9793)

8449 **2001-P Buffalo Silver Dollar PR69 Deep Cameo PCGS.** 36th U.S. Mint Director Jay W. Johnson. PCGS Population (10716/299). NGC Census: (8412/1351). Numismedia Wsl. Price for problem free NGC/PCGS coin in PR69: $165. (#99793)

8450 **2001-P Buffalo Silver Dollar PR69 Ultra Cameo NGC.** NGC Census: (8549/1355). PCGS Population (10747/305). Numismedia Wsl. Price for problem free NGC/PCGS coin in PR69: $165. (#99793)

8451 **2001-P Buffalo Silver Dollar PR70 Deep Cameo PCGS.** 36th U.S. Mint Director Jay W. Johnson. PCGS Population (299). NGC Census: (1351). Numismedia Wsl. Price for problem free NGC/PCGS coin in PR70: $540. (#99793)

8452 **2001-P Buffalo Silver Dollar PR70 Deep Cameo PCGS.** PCGS Population (305). NGC Census: (1355). Numismedia Wsl. Price for problem free NGC/PCGS coin in PR70: $540. (#99793)

8453 **2001-P Buffalo Silver Dollar PR70 Deep Cameo ICG.** NGC Census: (1355). PCGS Population (305). Numismedia Wsl. Price for problem free NGC/PCGS coin in PR70: $540. (#99793)

8454 **2005-P Marine Corps Silver Dollar PR70 Deep Cameo PCGS.** PCGS Population (662). NGC Census: (2852). Numismedia Wsl. Price for problem free NGC/PCGS coin in PR70: $150. (#921007)

8455 **2006-S Old San Francisco Mint Gold Five Dollar MS70 PCGS.** PCGS Population (268). NGC Census: (1746). Numismedia Wsl. Price for problem free NGC/PCGS coin in MS70: $335. (#21012)

8456 **2007-W Jamestown Gold Five Dollar MS70 PCGS.** PCGS Population (555). NGC Census: (2333). Numismedia Wsl. Price for problem free NGC/PCGS coin in MS70: $335. (#147441)

8457 **2007-W Abigail Adams MS70 NGC.** NGC Census: (0). PCGS Population (428). (#150889)

8458 **2007-W Abigail Adams PR70 Deep Cameo PCGS.** PCGS Population (260). NGC Census: (0). Numismedia Wsl. Price for problem free NGC/PCGS coin in PR70: $650. (#150892)

8459 **2007-W Jefferson MS70 NGC.** NGC Census: (0). PCGS Population (760). (#152120)

8460 **2007-W Jefferson PR70 Deep Cameo PCGS.** NGC Census: (0). PCGS Population (157). Numismedia Wsl. Price for problem free NGC/PCGS coin in PR70: $700. (#152123)

8461 **2007-W Madison MS70 PCGS.** PCGS First Strike Designation. PCGS Population (393). NGC Census: (0). (#152122)

8462 **2008-W Monroe First Strike MS70 PCGS.** PCGS Population (150). NGC Census: (0). (#395697)

8463 **2008-W Van Buren MS70 PCGS.** PCGS First Strike Designation. PCGS Population (59). NGC Census: (0). (#395702)

8464 **2008-P Bald Eagle Silver Dollar PR70 Deep Cameo PCGS.** PCGS Population (194). NGC Census: (3663). Numismedia Wsl. Price for problem free NGC/PCGS coin in PR70: $110. (#394418)

8465 **2008-W Bald Eagle Gold Five Dollar MS70 PCGS.** PCGS Population (359). NGC Census: (755). Numismedia Wsl. Price for problem free NGC/PCGS coin in MS70: $335. (#394419)

MODERN BULLION COINS

8466 **1986-W One-Ounce Gold Eagle PR69 Ultra Cameo NGC.** NGC Census: (6953/930). PCGS Population (10141/154). Mintage: 446,290. Numismedia Wsl. Price for problem free NGC/PCGS coin in PR69: $1,750. (#9807)

8467 **1995-P Silver Eagle PR70 Ultra Cameo NGC.** NGC Census: (626). PCGS Population (68). Numismedia Wsl. Price for problem free NGC/PCGS coin in PR70: $625. (#9896)

8468 **1996-P Silver Eagle PR70 Ultra Cameo NGC.** NGC Census: (2332). PCGS Population (99). Numismedia Wsl. Price for problem free NGC/PCGS coin in PR70: $700. (#9910)

8469 **1997 Half-Ounce Platinum Eagle MS68 PCGS.** PCGS Population (150/546). NGC Census: (39/458). Mintage: 20,500. Numismedia Wsl. Price for problem free NGC/PCGS coin in MS68: $700. (#99752)

8470 **1997 Half-Ounce Platinum Eagle MS68 PCGS.** PCGS Population (150/546). NGC Census: (39/458). Mintage: 20,500. Numismedia Wsl. Price for problem free NGC/PCGS coin in MS68: $700. (#99752)

8471 **1999-W Quarter-Ounce Gold Eagle MS69 PCGS.** Unfinished PR Dies. PCGS Population (745/0). NGC Census: (785/10). Numismedia Wsl. Price for problem free NGC/PCGS coin in MS69: $800. (#99942)

8472 **2000-P Silver Eagle PR70 Ultra Cameo NGC.** NGC Census: (1762). PCGS Population (51). Numismedia Wsl. Price for problem free NGC/PCGS coin in PR70: $420. (#99949)

8473 **2000 Half-Ounce Platinum Eagle MS69 PCGS.** PCGS Population (947/0). NGC Census: (1030/12). Mintage: 18,892. Numismedia Wsl. Price for problem free NGC/PCGS coin in MS69: $720. (#9781)

8474 **2001 Quarter-Ounce Platinum Eagle MS68 PCGS.** PCGS Population (94/1140). NGC Census: (95/1406). Mintage: 21,815. Numismedia Wsl. Price for problem free NGC/PCGS coin in MS68: $340. (#9787)

8475 **2001 Quarter-Ounce Platinum Eagle MS68 PCGS.** PCGS Population (94/1140). NGC Census: (95/1406). Mintage: 21,815. Numismedia Wsl. Price for problem free NGC/PCGS coin in MS68: $340. (#9787)

8476 **2002 Quarter-Ounce Platinum Eagle MS69 PCGS.** PCGS Population (6533/103). NGC Census: (4029/641). Mintage: 27,405. Numismedia Wsl. Price for problem free NGC/PCGS coin in MS69: $360. (#9795)

8477 **2002 Quarter-Ounce Platinum Eagle MS69 PCGS.** PCGS Population (6533/103). NGC Census: (4029/641). Mintage: 27,405. Numismedia Wsl. Price for problem free NGC/PCGS coin in MS69: $360. (#9795)

8478 **2003 Quarter-Ounce Platinum Eagle MS69 PCGS.** PCGS Population (12359/249). NGC Census: (4200/851). Numismedia Wsl. Price for problem free NGC/PCGS coin in MS69: $360. (#21101)

8479 **2004 Quarter-Ounce Platinum Eagle MS69 PCGS.** PCGS Population (8415/195). NGC Census: (4552/2488). Numismedia Wsl. Price for problem free NGC/PCGS coin in MS69: $360. (#21105)

8480 **2004 Half-Ounce Platinum Eagle MS69 PCGS.** PCGS Population (4027/75). NGC Census: (1335/1034). Numismedia Wsl. Price for problem free NGC/PCGS coin in MS69: $720. (#21106)

8481 **2004 Half-Ounce Platinum Eagle MS69 PCGS.** PCGS Population (4027/75). NGC Census: (1335/1034). Numismedia Wsl. Price for problem free NGC/PCGS coin in MS69: $720. (#21106)

8482 **2004 Half-Ounce Platinum Eagle MS69 PCGS.** PCGS Population (4027/75). NGC Census: (1335/1034). Numismedia Wsl. Price for problem free NGC/PCGS coin in MS69: $720. (#21106)

8483 **2004 Half-Ounce Platinum Eagle MS69 PCGS.** PCGS Population (4027/75). NGC Census: (1335/1034). Numismedia Wsl. Price for problem free NGC/PCGS coin in MS69: $720. (#21106)

8484 **2004 Half-Ounce Platinum Eagle MS69 PCGS.** PCGS Population (4027/75). NGC Census: (1335/1034). Numismedia Wsl. Price for problem free NGC/PCGS coin in MS69: $720. (#21106)

8485 **2004 Half-Ounce Platinum Eagle MS69 PCGS.** PCGS Population (4027/75). NGC Census: (1335/1034). Numismedia Wsl. Price for problem free NGC/PCGS coin in MS69: $720. (#21106)

8486 **2005 Quarter-Ounce Platinum, First Strike MS69 PCGS.** PCGS Population (1715/38). NGC Census: (0/0). (#21109)

8487 **2005 Quarter-Ounce Platinum, First Strike MS69 PCGS.** PCGS Population (1715/38). NGC Census: (0/0). (#21109)

8488 **2005 Quarter-Ounce Platinum, First Strike MS69 PCGS.** PCGS Population (1715/38). NGC Census: (0/0). (#21109)

8489 **2005 Quarter-Ounce Platinum, First Strike MS69 PCGS.** PCGS Population (1715/38). NGC Census: (0/0). (#21109)

8490 **2005 Half-Ounce Platinum MS70 NGC.** NGC Census: (0). PCGS Population (46). (#21110)

8491 **2006-W 20th Anniversary Silver Eagle MS70 PCGS.** PCGS Population (235). NGC Census: (6515). Numismedia Wsl. Price for problem free NGC/PCGS coin in MS70: $525. (#89990)

8492 **Three-Coin 2006 Silver American Eagle Set.** Includes: **2006-W Silver Eagle MS69 PCGS; 2006-W Silver Eagle PR69 Deep Cameo PCGS;** and a **2006-P 20th Anniversary Reverse Proof Silver Eagle PR69 PCGS.** (Total: 3 coins)

8493 **2006-W Silver Eagle MS70 PCGS.** PCGS Population (323). NGC Census: (7598). Numismedia Wsl. Price for problem free NGC/PCGS coin in MS70: $150. (#9996)

8494 **2006-W Silver Eagle MS70 PCGS.** PCGS Population (323). NGC Census: (7610). Numismedia Wsl. Price for problem free NGC/PCGS coin in MS70: $150. (#9996)

8495 **2006-W Silver Eagle 20th Ann. PR70 Deep Cameo PCGS.** PCGS Population (1222). NGC Census: (0). Numismedia Wsl. Price for problem free NGC/PCGS coin in PR70: $120. (#89998)

8496 **2006-P Reverse Proof Silver Eagle, 20th Anniversary PR69 PCGS.** PCGS Population (11290/1497). NGC Census: (0/0). Numismedia Wsl. Price for problem free NGC/PCGS coin in PR69: $170. (#799977)

8497 **2006-P Reverse Proof Silver Eagle, 20th Anniversary PR69 NGC.** NGC Census: (0/0). PCGS Population (11302/1501). Numismedia Wsl. Price for problem free NGC/PCGS coin in PR69: $170. (#799977)

8498 **2006-P Reverse Proof Silver Eagle, 20th Anniversary PR69 PCGS.** PCGS Population (11302/1501). NGC Census: (0/0). Numismedia Wsl. Price for problem free NGC/PCGS coin in PR69: $170. (#799977)

8499 **2006-P Reverse Proof Silver Eagle, 20th Anniversary PR70 PCGS.** PCGS Population (1497). NGC Census: (0). Numismedia Wsl. Price for problem free NGC/PCGS coin in PR70: $460. (#799977)

8500 **2006-P Reverse Proof Silver Eagle, 20th Anniversary PR70 NGC.** NGC Census: (0). PCGS Population (1501). Numismedia Wsl. Price for problem free NGC/PCGS coin in PR70: $460. (#799977)

8501 **2006-P Reverse Proof Silver Eagle, 20th Anniversary PR70 PCGS.** PCGS Population (1501). NGC Census: (0). Numismedia Wsl. Price for problem free NGC/PCGS coin in PR70: $460. (#799977)

8502 **2006-P Reverse Proof Silver Eagle, 20th Anniversary PR70 NGC.** NGC Census: (0). PCGS Population (1507). Numismedia Wsl. Price for problem free NGC/PCGS coin in PR70: $460. (#799977)

8503 **2006-W Quarter-Ounce Gold Eagle, Early Releases MS70 NGC.** NGC Census: (4164). PCGS Population (963). Numismedia Wsl. Price for problem free NGC/PCGS coin in MS70: $400. (#79982)

8504 **2006-W Half Ounce Gold Eagle, Early Releases MS70 NGC.** NGC Census: (4072). PCGS Population (1188). Numismedia Wsl. Price for problem free NGC/PCGS coin in MS70: $750. (#79983)

8505 **2006-W Buffalo One-Ounce Gold PR69 Deep Cameo PCGS.** PCGS Population (7176/3044). NGC Census: (11986/13260). Numismedia Wsl. Price for problem free NGC/PCGS coin in PR69: $1,330. (#9990)

8506 **2006 Buffalo One-Ounce Gold, First Strike MS69 PCGS.** PCGS Population (49816/3338). NGC Census: (37012/42993). (#89999)

8507 **2006 Quarter-Ounce Platinum First Strikes MS69 NGC.** NGC Census: (0/0). PCGS Population (315/29). (#821117)

8508 **2006 Quarter-Ounce Platinum First Strikes MS69 NGC.** NGC Census: (0/0). PCGS Population (315/29). (#821117)

8509 **2006 Quarter-Ounce Platinum First Strikes MS69 NGC.** NGC Census: (0/0). PCGS Population (315/29). (#821117)

8510 **2006 Quarter-Ounce Platinum First Strikes MS69 NGC.** NGC Census: (0/0). PCGS Population (315/29). (#821117)

8511 **2006 Quarter-Ounce Platinum First Strikes MS69 NGC.** NGC Census: (0/0). PCGS Population (315/29). (#821117)

8512 **2007 One Ounce Buffalo MS70 PCGS.** PCGS First Strike Designation. PCGS Population (843). NGC Census: (0). (#149122)

CALIFORNIA FRACTIONAL GOLD

8513 **1855 Liberty Octagonal 25 Cents, BG-110, High R.4, MS62 NGC.** NGC Census: (4/3). PCGS Population (28/39). (#10379)

8514 **(1853) Liberty Round 25 Cents, BG-207, High R.5,—Scratched—NCS. AU Details.** NGC Census: (0/4). PCGS Population (1/24). (#10392)

8515 **(1853) Liberty Round 25 Cents, BG-221, R.3, MS63 NGC.** NGC Census: (9/5). PCGS Population (54/43). (#10406)

8516 **Undated Liberty Round 25 Cents, BG-222, R.2, MS62 PCGS.** PCGS Population (133/227). NGC Census: (15/41). (#10407)

8517 **Undated Liberty Round 25 Cents, BG-222, R.2, MS62 PCGS.** PCGS Population (133/227). NGC Census: (15/41). (#10407)

8518 **(1854) Liberty Round 25 Cents, BG-224, R.3, MS62 NGC.** NGC Census: (8/13). PCGS Population (65/88). (#10409)

8519 **1855 Liberty Round 25 Cents, BG-226A, R.5,—Damage—PCGS Genuine.**
(#10417)

8520 **1855 Liberty Octagonal 50 Cents, BG-309, R.5, MS63 PCGS.** PCGS Population (7/2). NGC Census: (1/0). (#10429)

8521 **1856 Liberty Octagonal 50 Cents, BG-311, Low R.4, AU53 PCGS.** PCGS Population (3/110). NGC Census: (0/24). (#10436)

8522 **1852 Liberty Round 50 Cents, BG-401, R.3, AU58 PCGS.** PCGS Population (37/85). NGC Census: (3/7). (#10437)

8523 **1853 Liberty Round 50 Cents, BG-428, R.3, AU58 PCGS.** PCGS Population (61/151). NGC Census: (6/27). (#10464)

8524 **1853 Liberty Round 50 Cents, BG-428, R.3, MS63 NGC.** NGC Census: (4/3). PCGS Population (27/6). (#10464)

8525 **1853 Liberty Round 50 Cents, BG-428, R.3, MS64 NGC.** NGC Census: (2/0). PCGS Population (5/1). (#10464)

8526 **1853 Liberty Round 50 Cents, BG-430, R.3, MS62 NGC.** NGC Census: (9/8). PCGS Population (58/63). (#10466)

8527 **1853 Liberty Octagonal 1 Dollar, BG-518, R.5,—Cleaning—PCGS Genuine.** (#10495)

8528 **1859 Liberty Octagonal 25 Cents, BG-702, R.3, MS64 PCGS.** PCGS Population (74/16). NGC Census: (10/29). (#10529)

8529 **1867 Liberty Octagonal 25 Cents, BG-709, R.4, MS64 PCGS.** PCGS Population (23/35). NGC Census: (2/9). (#10536)

8530 **1871 Liberty Octagonal 25 Cents, BG-717, R.3, MS64 PCGS.** PCGS Population (62/70). NGC Census: (8/13). (#10544)

8531 **1873 Liberty Octagonal 25 Cents, BG-728, R.3, MS63 NGC.** NGC Census: (5/15). PCGS Population (31/112). (#10555)

8532 **1871 Liberty Octagonal 25 Cents, BG-765, R.3, MS60 PCGS.** PCGS Population (16/209). NGC Census: (0/20). (#10592)

8533 **1880 Indian Octagonal 25 Cents, BG-799W, High R.6, MS64 NGC.** NGC Census: (0/1). PCGS Population (8/2). (#10649)

8534 **1880 Indian Octagonal 25 Cents, BG-799X, R.3, MS64 PCGS.** PCGS Population (61/17). NGC Census: (15/9). (#10650)

8535 **1859 Liberty Round 25 Cents, BG-801, R.3, MS64 NGC.** NGC Census: (12/22). PCGS Population (37/12). (#10662)

8536 **1866 Liberty Round 25 Cents, BG-804, R.4, MS63 NGC.** NGC Census: (5/6). PCGS Population (15/52). (#10665)

8537 **1868 Liberty Round 25 Cents, BG-806, R.3, MS66 NGC.** NGC Census: (12/1). PCGS Population (16/1). (#10667)

8538 **1871 Liberty Round 25 Cents, BG-813, R.3, MS64 Prooflike NGC.** NGC Census: (3/1). PCGS Population (0/0). (#710674)

8539 **1863 Liberty Round 25 Cents, BG-820, R.5, AU58 PCGS.** PCGS Population (6/17). NGC Census: (1/3). (#10681)

8540 **1864 Liberty Round 25 Cents, BG-821, Low R.5, MS63 PCGS.** Ex:Jay Roe. PCGS Population (2/1). NGC Census: (0/0). (#10682)

8541 **1869 Liberty Round 25 Cents, BG-826, R.4,—Improperly Cleaned—NCS. AU Details.** NGC Census: (1/6). PCGS Population (1/70). (#10687)

8542 **1870 Liberty Round 25 Cents, BG-835, R.3, AU53 NGC.** NGC Census: (2/38). PCGS Population (9/195). (#10696)

8543 **1870 Liberty Round 25 Cents, BG-835, R.3, AU58 PCGS.** PCGS Population (44/126). NGC Census: (11/26). (#10696)

8544 **1870 Liberty Round 25 Cents, BG-835, R.3, MS62 NGC.** NGC Census: (16/7). PCGS Population (58/28). (#10696)

8545 **1871 Liberty Round 25 Cents, BG-840, Low R.4, AU58 NGC.** NGC Census: (2/27). PCGS Population (12/92). (#10701)

8546 **1871 Liberty Round 25 Cents, BG-840, Low R.4, MS62 NGC.** NGC Census: (11/13). PCGS Population (33/36). (#10701)

8547 **1875 Indian Round 25 Cents, BG-847, R.4, MS64 PCGS.** PCGS Population (27/2). NGC Census: (1/0). (#10708)

8548 **1852 Indian Round 25 Cents, BG-891, Low R.5, MS63 PCGS.** PCGS Population (9/23). NGC Census: (2/3). (#10752)

8549 **1867 Liberty Octagonal 50 Cents, BG-905, Low R.5, MS64 PCGS.** PCGS Population (14/14). NGC Census: (1/3). (#10763)

8550 **1870 Liberty Octagonal 50 Cents, BG-921, Low R.5, AU58 PCGS.** PCGS Population (7/24). NGC Census: (2/0). (#10779)

8551 **1871 Liberty Octagonal 50 Cents, BG-923, R.5, MS62 PCGS.** PCGS Population (11/14). NGC Census: (1/2). (#10781)

8552 **1859 Liberty Round 50 Cents, BG-1002, High R.4, MS61 NGC.** NGC Census: (2/10). PCGS Population (2/44). (#10831)

8553 **1870 Liberty Round 50 Cents, BG-1010, R.3, MS64 PCGS.** PCGS Population (41/19). NGC Census: (6/2). (#10839)

8554 **1869 Liberty Round 50 Cents, BG-1020, Low R.4, MS63 Prooflike NGC.** NGC Census: (2/0). PCGS Population (0/0). (#710849)

8555 **1881 Indian Round 50 Cents, BG-1070, R.5, MS64 PCGS.** PCGS Population (9/1). NGC Census: (2/2). (#10899)

COINS OF HAWAII

8556 **1847 Hawaii Cent Fine 15 PCGS.** PCGS Population (1/326). NGC Census: (0/190). Mintage: 100,000. (#10965)

8557 **1847 Hawaii Cent—Scratches—NCS. AU Details.** NGC Census: (6/168). PCGS Population (22/273). Mintage: 100,000. (#10965)

8558 **1883 Hawaii Half Dollar XF45 ANACS.** NGC Census: (32/250). PCGS Population (50/374). Mintage: 700,000. (#10991)

8559 **1883 Hawaii Half Dollar AU55 NGC.** NGC Census: (31/187). PCGS Population (52/243). Mintage: 700,000. (#10991)

8560 **1883 Hawaii Dollar—Improperly Cleaned—NCS. VF Details.** NGC Census: (2/275). PCGS Population (1/535). Mintage: 500,000. (#10995)

ERRORS

8561 **ND Flying Eagle Cent—Split After Strike, Corroded—ANACS. VG Details Net Good 4.**

8562 **1857 Flying Eagle Cent—Obverse Struck Thru Forgn Object—XF45 PCGS.**

8563 **1857 Flying Eagle Cent—Obverse and Reverse Struck Thru—MS63 NGC.**

8564 **1858 Flying Eagle Cent—Struck 10% Off-Center—VG8 NGC.** Eagle Eye Photo Seal.

8565 **1861 Indian Cent—Broadstruck—AU58 NGC.** Eagle Eye Photo Seal.

8566 **1862 Indian Cent—Split After Strike—Fine 12 ANACS.**

8567 **1862 Indian Cent—Struck Thru Fragment Part Collar, Cleaned—ANACS. AU Details Net XF45.**

8568 **1862 Indian Cent—Broadstruck—XF45 NGC.** Eagle Eye Photo Seal.

8569 **1864 Indian Cent—Double Struck 2nd Strike 95% Off-Center—Bronze No L VG10 PCGS.**

8570 **1864 Indian Cent—Struck 5% Off-Center—Bronze No L AU50 PCGS.**

8571 **1865 Indian Cent—Struck 30% Off-Center—VG8 PCGS.** Eagle Eye Photo Seal.

8572 **1866 Indian Cent—Double Strike-2nd Strike 95% Off-Center—Fine 12 PCGS.** Eagle Eye Photo Seal.

8573 **1879 Indian Cent—Struck 15% Off Center—AU58 NGC.**

8574 **1880 Indian Cent—Reverse Brockage—Good 6 NGC.** Eagle Eye Photo Seal.

8575 **1889 Indian Cent—Broadstruck, RPD—Good 4 ANACS.** S-3.

8576 **1890 Indian Cent—Obverse Lamination—MS62 Brown NGC.** Eagle Eye Photo Seal.

8577 **1891 Indian Cent—Broadstruck on T-1 Planchet—MS62 Brown PCGS.**

8578 **1892 Indian Cent—10% Off-Center With Reverse Indent—VF35 NGC.** Eagle Eye Photo Seal.

8579 **1893 Indian Cent—Double Struck 2nd Strike 90% Off-Center—AU58 NGC.**

8580 **1895 Indian Cent—Double Struck Off-Center 10% and 95%—XF40 PCGS.**

8581 **1895 Indian Cent—Off-Center—AU58 ANACS.**

8582 **1896 Indian Cent—Double Struck 2nd Strike 90% Off-Center—XF40 PCGS.** Eagle Eye Photo Seal.

8583 **1897 Indian Cent—Double Struck 2nd 90% Off-Center—XF45 Brown NGC.**

8584 **1897 Indian Cent—Off-Center—MS63 Red and Brown ANACS.**

8585 **1898 Indian Cent—Struck 5% Off-Center—MS63 Brown PCGS.** Eagle Eye Photo Seal.

8586 **1899 Indian Cent—Broadstruck—MS62 Brown ANACS.**

8587 **1899 Indian Cent—Broadstruck—MS65 Brown NGC.**

8588 **1902 Indian Cent—Struck 10% Off Center, Obverse Die Gouge Thru Eye—MS63 Brown NGC.**

8589 **1903 Indian Cent—Flipover Double Struck—VG8 ANACS.**

8590 **1905 Indian Cent—Off-Center—MS62 Brown ANACS.**

8591 **1905 Indian Cent—Struck 25% Off Center—MS63 Brown NGC.**

8592 **1908-S Indian Cent—Struck in Metal on Obverse—AU58 NGC.** Eagle Eye Photo Seal.

8593 **No Date Lincoln Cent—70% Off Center on Foreign Planchet—MS63 Red and Brown NGC.** 3.9 Grams.

8594 **ND Lincoln Cent—100% Struck Through Wheat Reverse—AU55 PCGS.**

8595 **1919-S Lincoln Cent—Struck 75% Off Center, Environmental Damage—MS60 Brown NCS. Unc Details.**

8596 **1925-D Lincoln Cent—Struck 15% Off Center, Environmental Damage—AU50 NCS. AU Details.**

8597 **1939 Lincoln Cent—Obverse Brockage—MS64 Brown NGC.**

8598 **1956 Lincoln Cent—Struck on 10C Planchet—AU55 PCGS.**

8599 **1956 Lincoln Cent—Struck on Silver 10C Planchet—XF40 PCGS.**

8600 **1957 Lincoln Cent—On 10C Planchet—AU58 ANACS.**

8601 **1960 Large Date, Lincoln Cent—On 10C Planchet—AU50 ANACS.**

8602 **1960-D Small Date, Lincoln Cent—Struck on 10C Planchet—AU55 PCGS.** Ex:Alfred V. Melson Collection.

8603 **1963 Lincoln Cent—Struck on Silver 10C Planchet—MS62 PCGS.** Ex:Alfred V. Melson Collection.

8604 **1964 Lincoln Cent—Struck on 10C Planchet—AU55 PCGS.**

8605 **1965 Lincoln Cent—On 10C Planchet—MS60 ANACS.**

8606 **1966 Lincoln Cent—On 10C Planchet—MS64 Prooflike ANACS.**

8607 **1967 Lincoln Cent—On 10C Planchet—MS62 ANACS.**

8608 **1968-D Lincoln Cent—1C Struck on a 10C Planchet—MS64 NGC.**

8609 **1968-S Lincoln Cent—Struck on Clad 10C Planchet—MS63 PCGS.**

8610 **1969 Lincoln Cent—On 10C Planchet—MS63 ANACS.**

8611 **1969-D Lincoln Cent—On 10C Planchet—MS63 NGC.**

8612 1970 Lincoln Cent—1C Struck on a 10C Planchet—MS65 NGC.

8613 1970-D Lincoln Cent—Struck on Clad 10C Planchet—AU55 PCGS.

8614 1971-D Lincoln Cent—Struck on Clad 10C Planchet—MS61 PCGS. Ex:Alfred V. Melson Collection.

8615 1971-D Lincoln Cent—Struck on Clad 10C Planchet—MS62 PCGS.

8616 1973-D Lincoln Cent—On 10C Planchet—MS61 ANACS.

8617 1975 Lincoln Cent—Fold Over Strike—MS65 Red and Brown PCGS.

8618 1975 Lincoln Cent—Struck on Clad 10C Planchet—MS63 PCGS. Ex:Alfred V. Melson Collection.

8619 1975-D Lincoln Cent—On 10C Planchet—MS62 ANACS..

8620 1976 Lincoln Cent—Struck on Type 1 10C Planchet 2.3 Grams—MS64 NGC.

8621 1976-D Lincoln Cent—On 10C Planchet—MS63 ANACS.

8622 1977 Lincoln Cent—On 10C Planchet—MS66 ANACS.

8623 1978 Lincoln Cent—Struck on Clad 10C Planchet—MS64 PCGS. Ex:Alfred V. Melson Collection.

8624 1980 Lincoln Cent—On 10C Planchet—MS63 ANACS.

8625 1980-D Lincoln Cent—Struck on Clad 10C Planchet—MS63 PCGS. Ex:Alfred V. Melson Collection.

8626 1981 Lincoln Cent—On 10C Planchet—MS64 ANACS.

8627 1981-D Lincoln Cent—On 10C Planchet—MS65 ANACS.

8628 1982 Large Date, Lincoln Cent—On 10C Planchet— MS63 ANACS.

8629 1982 Small Date Cent—On 10C Planchet—MS66 ANACS.

8630 1984 Lincoln Cent—On 10C Planchet—MS63 ANACS.

8631 1985 Lincoln Cent—Struck on Clad 10C Planchet—MS62 PCGS. Ex:Alfred V. Melson Collection.

8632 1985-D Lincoln Cent—Struck on an Unplated Planchet—MS64 NGC.

8633 1989 Lincoln Cent—On 10C Planchet—MS64 ANACS.

8634 1989 Lincoln Cent—Struck on Clad 10C Planchet—MS62 PCGS. Ex:Alfred V. Melson Collection.

8635 1989 Lincoln Cent—Struck on Clad 10C Planchet—MS64 PCGS.

8636 1990 Lincoln Cent—Foldover Strike—MS62 Brown NGC.

8637 1990 Lincoln Cent—Struck on Clad 10C Planchet—MS64 PCGS. Ex:Alfred V. Melson Collection.

8638 1990 Lincoln Cent—Struck on Clad 10C Planchet—MS65 PCGS. Ex:Alfred V. Melson Collection.

8639 1990 Lincoln Cent—Struck on Clad 10C Planchet—MS65 PCGS. Ex:Alfred V. Melson Collection.

8640 1991 Lincoln Cent—Struck on a 10C Planchet—MS66 NGC.

8641 1995 Lincoln Cent—On 10C Planchet—MS64 ANACS.

8642 1996 Lincoln Cent—On 10C Planchet—MS63 ANACS.

8643 1996 Lincoln Cent—Struck on Clad 10C Planchet—MS65 PCGS. Ex:Alfred V. Melson Collection.

8644 1997 Lincoln Cent—Struck on Clad 10C Planchet—MS64 PCGS. Ex:Alfred V. Melson Collection.

8645 1998 Lincoln Cent—Struck on Clad 10C Planchet—MS62 PCGS. Ex:Alfred V. Melson Collection.

8646 1998 Lincoln Cent—Struck on Clad 10C Planchet—MS64 PCGS. Ex:Alfred V. Melson Collection.

8647 1998 Lincoln Cent—Struck on Clad 10C Planchet—MS66 PCGS. Ex:Alfred V. Melson Collection.

8648 1998 Lincoln Cent—Obverse Die Cap—MS66 Red NGC.

8649 1998 Lincoln Cent—Obverse Die Cap—MS67 Red NGC.

8650 1998-D Lincoln Cent—On 10C Planchet—MS65 ANACS.

8651 1999 Lincoln Cent—Struck on Type 1 10C Planchet 2.2 Grams—MS65 NGC.

8652 1999 Lincoln Cent—Mated pair-Coin #1—MS65 Red PCGS and a ND—Mated Pair-Coin #2—MS65 Red PCGS. (Total: 2 coins)

8653 1999 Lincoln Cent—Struck on Clad 10C Planchet—MS66 PCGS. Ex:Alfred V. Melson Collection.

8654 1999-D Lincoln Cent—Struck on Clad 10C Planchet—MS64 PCGS. Ex:Alfred V. Melson Collection.

8655 2000 Lincoln Cent—Struck on Clad 10C Planchet—MS65 PCGS. Ex:Alfred V. Melson Collection.

8656 2001 Lincoln Cent—Struck on Clad 10C Planchet—MS64 PCGS. Ex:Alfred V. Melson Collection.

8657 1865 Three Cent Nickel—2% Clipped Planchet—AU53 PCGS.

8658 1907 Liberty Nickel—4% Clipped Planchet—MS62 PCGS.

8659 1935 Buffalo Nickel—Struck 10% Off Center—MS62 NGC.

8660 1937 Buffalo Nickel—Obverse Struck Thru—MS62 NGC.

8661 1939 Jefferson Nickel—Quad Die Reverse—MS66 PCGS. FS-022.5.

8662 1941 Jefferson Nickel—Uncentered Broadstruck—MS64 PCGS.

8663 1964-D Jefferson Nickel—Struck on 1C Planchet—MS63 Red and Brown PCGS.

8664 1968-S Jefferson Nickel—Struck on 1C Planchet—MS64 PCGS.

8665 **1974-D Jefferson Nickel—On Damaged 1C Planchet 3.1 Grams—MS63 Red NGC.**

8666 **1998-P Jefferson Nickel—Struck on Clad 10C Planchet—MS65 PCGS.**

8667 **1999-P Jefferson Nickel—Obverse Struck Thru Capped Die—MS64 Full Steps PCGS.**

8668 **1999-P Jefferson Nickel—30% Brockage Obverse and Broadstrike—MS65 Full Steps PCGS.**

8669 **1904 Barber Dime—Struck 10% Off Center—MS63 NGC.**

8670 **1999-P Roosevelt Dime—Deep Die Cap—MS64 PCGS.**

8671 **1970-D Washington Quarter—On 5C Planchet, Cleaned—ANACS. AU55 Details.**

8672 **2000-D Maryland—Clad Layer Missing on Obverse—MS63 NGC.**

8673 **1974 Kennedy Half Dollar—Double Struck 2nd 85% Off Center—MS64 NGC.**

8674 **1923 Peace Dollar—Reverse Lamination—MS64 NGC.**

8675 **1999-P S.B. Anthony Dollar—Uncentered Broadstrike Type 1 Planchet—MS65 PCGS.**

8676 **1925-D Indian Quarter Eagle—Reverse Struck Thru—AU58 NGC.**

8677 **1924 Saint-Gaudens Double Eagle—Reverse Struck Thru—MS62 NGC.**

8678 **1935 Spanish Trail Half Dollar—Reverse Struck Thru—MS63 NGC.**

GSA DOLLARS

8679 **1880-CC MS63 NGC.** NGC Census: (1257/3655). PCGS Population (2653/6742). Mintage: 591,000. Numismedia Wsl. Price for problem free NGC/PCGS coin in MS63: $480. (#7100)

8680 **1880-CC MS64 NGC.** NGC Census: (2257/1429). PCGS Population (3985/2775). Mintage: 591,000. Numismedia Wsl. Price for problem free NGC/PCGS coin in MS64: $560. (#7100)

8681 **1880/79-CC Reverse of 1878 MS62 NGC.** NGC Census: (135/1073). PCGS Population (267/2405). Mintage: 591,000. Numismedia Wsl. Price for problem free NGC/PCGS coin in MS62: $490. (#7108)

8682 **1880-S MS66 NGC.** NGC Census: (9823/3151). PCGS Population (9080/1735). Mintage: 8,900,000. Numismedia Wsl. Price for problem free NGC/PCGS coin in MS66: $235. (#7118)

8683 **1881-CC MS63 NGC.** NGC Census: (1537/5473). PCGS Population (3525/12015). Mintage: 296,000. Numismedia Wsl. Price for problem free NGC/PCGS coin in MS63: $450. (#7126)

8684 **1881-CC MS65 NGC.** NGC Census: (1806/851). PCGS Population (4085/1563). Mintage: 296,000. Numismedia Wsl. Price for problem free NGC/PCGS coin in MS65: $930. (#7126)

8685 **1883-CC MS65 NGC.** NGC Census: (3571/959). PCGS Population (6882/1824). Mintage: 1,204,000. Numismedia Wsl. Price for problem free NGC/PCGS coin in MS65: $370. (#7144)

8686 **1883-CC MS66 NGC.** NGC Census: (865/95). PCGS Population (1685/133). Mintage: 1,204,000. Numismedia Wsl. Price for problem free NGC/PCGS coin in MS66: $760. (#7144)

8687 **1884-CC MS66 NGC.** NGC Census: (725/93). PCGS Population (1340/57). Mintage: 1,136,000. Numismedia Wsl. Price for problem free NGC/PCGS coin in MS66: $775. (#7152)

8688 **1884-CC MS66 NGC. CAC.** NGC Census: (725/93). PCGS Population (1341/59). Mintage: 1,136,000. Numismedia Wsl. Price for problem free NGC/PCGS coin in MS66: $775. (#7152)

8689 **1884-CC MS66 NGC.** NGC Census: (725/93). PCGS Population (1341/59). Mintage: 1,136,000. Numismedia Wsl. Price for problem free NGC/PCGS coin in MS66: $775. (#7152)

8690 **1884-CC MS63 Prooflike NGC.** NGC Census: (380/946). PCGS Population (833/1686). Numismedia Wsl. Price for problem free NGC/PCGS coin in MS63: $215. (#7153)

8691 **1884-CC MS63 Deep Mirror Prooflike NGC.** NGC Census: (319/840). PCGS Population (747/1979). Numismedia Wsl. Price for problem free NGC/PCGS coin in MS63: $330. (#97153)

8692 **1884-CC MS63 Deep Mirror Prooflike NGC.** NGC Census: (318/839). PCGS Population (747/1971). Numismedia Wsl. Price for problem free NGC/PCGS coin in MS63: $330. (#97153)

8693 **1885-CC MS62 NGC.** NGC Census: (529/6675). PCGS Population (1218/15110). Mintage: 228,000. Numismedia Wsl. Price for problem free NGC/PCGS coin in MS62: $540. (#7160)

8694 **1885-CC MS63 NGC.** NGC Census: (1752/4923). PCGS Population (3950/11160). Mintage: 228,000. Numismedia Wsl. Price for problem free NGC/PCGS coin in MS63: $555. (#7160)

8695 **1885-CC MS65 NGC.** NGC Census: (1566/539). PCGS Population (3700/938). Mintage: 228,000. Numismedia Wsl. Price for problem free NGC/PCGS coin in MS65: $960. (#7160)

PATTERNS

8696 **C.1967 General Motors "Cent" Pollock-4060, MS62 Red and Brown NGC.** Control Code 2-R.

8697 **C.1967 General Motors "Cent", Pollock-4060, AU58 Brown NGC.** Control Code 5-R.

8698 **C.1967 General Motors "Cent", Pollock-4060, AU58 NGC.** Control Code 10-R.

8699 **C.1967 General Motors "Cent", Pollock-4060, MS61 Brown NGC.** Control Code 21-L.

8700 **C.1967 General Motors "Cent", Pollock-4060, MS62 Brown NGC.** Control Code 24-M.

WASHINGTONIA

8701 **(1917) Elder Restrike Civil War Dog Tag MS62 NGC.** Gilt Bronze. Baker-621A. DeLorey-10.

EXPOSITIONS AND FAIRS

8702 **1904 Louisiana Purchase Expo 10 Stars, 1/4 Louisiana Gold MS64 NGC.** St. Louis, MO. Hendershott-61-310.

8703 **1904 Louisiana Purchase Expo 10 Stars, 1/4 Louisiana Gold MS64 NGC.** St. Louis, MO. Hendershott-61-310.

8704 **1904 Louisiana Purchase Expo 1/2 Louisiana Gold MS64 NGC.** St. Louis, MO. Hendershott-61-330.

8705 **1915 Panama-Pacific Exposition Award Medal MS64 Brown NGC.** Bronze, 70.5mm. San Francisco, CA.

HARD TIMES TOKEN

8706 **1837 Half Cent of Pure Copper AU58 NGC.** HT-73.

CIVIL WAR TOKENS

8707 **(1961) Bashlow Restrike Confederate Cent MS66 Red NGC.** Copper. Breen-8013.

8708 **Cancelled J.A. Garman, PA Sutler Token AU50 NGC.** 54th PA Vols. S-I10Bb.

8709 **Cancelled J.A. Garman, PA Sutler Token AU50 NGC.** 54th PA Vols. S-I10Bb.

8710 **J.A. Garman, PA Sutler Token AU50 NGC.** 54th PA Vols. S-I25B.

8711 **J.A. Garman, PA Sutler Token XF45 NGC.** 54th PA Vols. S-I25B.

8712 **J.A. Garman, PA Sutler Token AU53 NGC.** 54th PA Vols. S-I25B.

8713 **J.A. Garman, PA Sutler Token MS63 NGC.** 54th PA Vols. S-I25B.

8714 **J.A. Garman, PA Sutler Token MS64 NGC.** 54th PA Vols. S-I25B.

8715 **J.A. Garman, PA Sutler Token MS63 NGC.** 54th PA Vols. S-I100B.

U.S. TRADE TOKEN (1866-1889)

8716 **1874 Seated Half, Parisian Varieties Counterstamp—Improperly Cleaned—NCS. XF Details.** Rulau-NY-NY-230.

SO-CALLED DOLLARS

8717 **(1897) Bickford Dollar, HK-834, MS63 NGC.**

8718 **(1897) Bickford Dollar, HK-834, MS64 NGC.**

8719 **(1897) Bickford Dollar, HK-834, MS65 NGC.**

8720 **(1897) Bickford Dollar, HK-834, MS66 NGC.**

ADDITIONAL CERTIFIED COIN

8721 **1900-S Morgan Dollar Paramount MS65 (MS64).** Ex: Redfield Collection. Mintage: 3,540,000. (#7270)

End of Auction

Heritage Auction Galleries Staff

Steve Ivy - Co-Chairman and CEO

Steve Ivy began collecting and studying rare coins as a youth, and as a teenager began advertising coins for sale in national publications in 1963. Seven years later, at the age of 20, he opened for business in downtown Dallas, and in 1976, incorporated as an auction company. Steve managed the business as well as serving as chief buyer, buying and selling hundreds of millions of dollars of coins during the 1970s and early 1980s. In early 1983, James Halperin became a full partner, and the name of the corporation was changed to Heritage Auctions. Steve's primary responsibilities now include management of the marketing and selling efforts of the company, the formation of corporate policy for long-term growth, and corporate relations with financial institutions. He remains intimately involved in all the various categories Heritage Auctions deals in today. Steve engages in daily discourse with industry leaders on all aspects of the fine art and collectibles business, and his views on market trends and developments are respected throughout the industry. He previously served on both the Board of Directors of the Professional Numismatists Guild (past president), and The Industry Council for Tangible Assets (past Chairman). Steve's keen appreciation of history is reflected in his active participation in other organizations, including past board positions on the Texas Historical Foundation and the Dallas Historical Society (where he also served as Exhibits Chairman). Steve is an avid collector of Texas books, manuscripts, and national currency, and he owns one of the largest and finest collections in private hands. He is also a past Board Chair of Dallas Challenge, and is currently the Finance Chair of the Phoenix House of Texas.

James Halperin - Co-Chairman

Born in Boston in 1952, Jim formed a part-time rare coin business at age 15 after discovering he had a knack (along with a nearly photographic memory) for coins. Jim scored a perfect 800 on his math SATs and received early acceptance to Harvard College, but after attending three semesters took a permanent leave of absence to pursue his full-time numismatic career. In 1975, Jim supervised the protocols for the first mainframe computer system in the numismatic business, which would catapult New England Rare Coin Galleries to the top of the industry in less than four years. In 1982, Jim's business merged with that of his friend and former archrival Steve Ivy. Their partnership has become Heritage Auctions, the third-largest auction house in the world. Jim is also a well-known futurist, an active collector of EC comics and early 20th-century American art (visit www.jhalpe.com), venture capital investor, philanthropist (he endows a multimillion-dollar health education foundation), and part-time novelist. His first fiction book, *The Truth Machine*, was published in 1996, became an international science fiction bestseller, and was optioned for movie development by Warner Brothers and Lions Gate. Jim's second novel, *The First Immortal*, was published in early 1998 and immediately optioned as a Hallmark Hall of Fame television miniseries.

Greg Rohan - President

At the age of eight, Greg Rohan started collecting coins as well as buying them for resale to his schoolmates. By 1971, at the age of 10, he was already buying and selling coins from a dealer's table at trade shows in his hometown of Seattle. His business grew rapidly, and by 1985 he had offices in both Seattle and Minneapolis. He joined Heritage in 1987 as Executive Vice-President. Today, as a partner and as President of Heritage, his responsibilities include overseeing the firm's private client group and working with top collectors in every field in which Heritage is active. Greg has been involved with many of the rarest items and most important collections handled by the firm, including the purchase and/or sale of the Ed Trompeter Collection (the world's largest numismatic purchase according to the Guinness Book of World Records). During his career, Greg has handled more than $1 billion of rare coins, collectibles and art. He has provided expert testimony for the United States Attorneys in San Francisco, Dallas, and Philadelphia, and for the Federal Trade Commission (FTC). He has worked with collectors, consignors, and their advisors regarding significant collections of books, manuscripts, comics, currency, jewelry, vintage movie posters, sports and entertainment memorabilia, decorative arts, and fine art. Greg is a past Chapter Chairman for North Texas of the Young Presidents' Organization (YPO), and is an active supporter of the arts. Greg co-authored "The Collectors Estate Handbook," winner of the NLG's Robert Friedberg Award for numismatic book of the year. He previously served on the seven-person Advisory Board to the Federal Reserve Bank of Dallas, in his second appointed term.

Paul Minshull - Chief Operating Officer

As Chief Operating Officer, Paul Minshull's managerial responsibilities include integrating sales, personnel, inventory, security and MIS for Heritage. His major accomplishments include overseeing the hardware migration from mainframe to PC, the software migration of all inventory and sales systems, and implementation of a major Internet presence. Heritage's successful employee-suggestion program has generated 200 or more ideas each month since 1995, and has helped increase employee productivity, expand business, and improve employee retention. Paul oversees the company's highly-regarded IT department, and has been the driving force behind Heritage's Web development, now a significant portion of Heritage's future plans. As the first auction house that combined traditional floor bidding with active Internet bidding, the totally interactive system has catapulted Heritage to the top collectible and Fine Art website (Forbes Magazine's "Best of the Web"). Paul came to Heritage in 1984. Since 1987, he has been Chief Operating Officer for all Heritage companies and affiliates.

Todd Imhof - Executive Vice President

Unlike most of his contemporaries, Todd Imhof did not start collecting in his teens. Shortly after graduating college, Todd declined offers from prestigious Wall Street banks to join a former classmate at a small rare coin firm in the Seattle area. In the mid-1980s, the rare coin industry was rapidly changing, with the advent of third-party grading and growing computer technologies. As a newcomer, Todd more easily embraced these new dynamics and quickly emerged as a highly respected dealer. In 1991, he co-founded Pinnacle Rarities, a firm specialized in servicing the savviest and most preeminent collectors in numismatics. At only 25, he was accepted into the PNG, and currently serves on its Consumer Protection Committee and its Legislation/Taxation Issues Committee. In 1992, he was invited to join the Board of Directors for the Industry Council for Tangible Assets, later serving as its Chairman (2002-2005). Since joining Heritage in 2006, Todd continues to advise most of Heritage's largest and most prominent clients.

Leo Frese - Vice President
Leo has been involved in numismatics for nearly 40 years, a professional numismatist since 1971, and has been with Heritage for more than 20 years. He literally worked his way up the Heritage "ladder," working with Bob Merrill for nearly 15 years, then becoming Director of Consignments. Leo has been actively involved in assisting clients sell nearly $500,000,000 in numismatic material. Leo was recently accepted as a member of PNG, is a life member of the ANA, and holds membership in FUN, CSNS, and other numismatic organizations.

Jim Stoutjesdyk - Vice President
Jim Stoutjesdyk was named Vice President of Heritage Rare Coin Galleries in 2004. He was named ANA's Outstanding Young Numismatist of the Year in 1987. A University of Michigan graduate, he was first employed by Superior Galleries, eventually becoming their Director of Collector Sales. Since joining Heritage in 1993, Jim has served in many capacities. Jim's duties now include buying and selling, pricing all new purchases, assisting with auction estimates and reserves, and overseeing the daily operations of the rare coin department.

Norma L. Gonzalez - VP of Auction Operations
Norma Gonzalez joined the U.S. Navy in August of 1993 and received her Bachelor's Degree in Resource Management. She joined Heritage in 1998 and was promoted to Vice President in 2003. She currently manages the operations departments, including Coins, Currency, World & Ancient Coins, Sportscards & Memorabilia, Comics, Movie Posters, Pop Culture and Political Memorabilia.

Debbie Rexing - VP - Marketing
Debbie Rexing joined the Heritage team in 2001 and her marketing credentials include degrees in Business Administration and Human Resources from The Ohio State University. Debbie has worked across many categories within the company leading to her comprehensive and integrative approach to the job. She guides all aspects of Heritage's print marketing strategies – advertisements, brochures, direct mail campaigns, coordination of print buying, catalog design and production, The Heritage Magazine, and media and press relations.

Ron Brackemyre - Vice President
Ron Brackemyre began his career at Heritage Auction Galleries in 1998 as the Manager of the Shipping Department, was promoted to Consignment Operations Manager for Numismatics in 2004 and in 2009 added oversight of the entire photography operation at Heritage, wherein his department coordinates all photography, scanning and photoshopping. He is also responsible for the security of all of Heritage's coin and currency consignments, both at the Dallas world headquarters and at shows, as well as cataloging of coins for upcoming auctions, coordination of auction planning, security and transportation logistics, lot-view, auction prep and oversight for the entire shipping department.

Marti Korver - Manager - Credit/Collections
Marti Korver was recruited out of the banking profession by Jim Ruddy, and she worked with Paul Rynearson, Karl Stephens, and Judy Cahn on ancients and world coins at Bowers & Ruddy Galleries, in Hollywood, CA. She migrated into the coin auction business, and represented bidders as agent at B&R auctions for 10 years. She also worked as a research assistant for Q. David Bowers for several years.

Mark Prendergast - Director, Trusts & Estates
Mark Prendergast earned his degree in Art History from Vanderbilt University and began his career in the arts working with a national dealer in private sales of 20th Century American Art. Joining Christie's in 1998 and advancing during a 10 year tenure to the position of Vice President, he was instrumental in bringing to market many important and prominent works of art, collections and estates. Having established a Houston office for Heritage, he serves as Director of Business Development, Trusts & Estates, providing assistance to fiduciary professionals and private clients with appraisals, collection assessments and auction consignments in all areas of art and collectibles.

Jared Green - Vice President of Corporate & Institutional Client Development
Jared Green primarily works on developing institutional clients, including corporations and non-profits, and championing new ventures for Heritage's collectibles and art businesses. He maintains relationships with a number of Fortune 500 companies that have collections of rarities and fine art. Prior to joining Heritage, Mr. Jared worked for several years as a business analyst with Cap Gemini-Ernst & Young in its Strategic Advisory Services group. He is a native of North Carolina and graduated with honors from Duke University with a degree in Public Policy. He completed his MBA at Emory University, where he focused on Strategy and Entrepreneurship.

Coin Department

David Mayfield - Vice President, Numismatics
David Mayfield has been collecting and trading rare coins and currency for over 35 years. A chance encounter with his father's coin collection at the age of nine led to his lifetime interest. David has been buying and selling at coin shows since the age of 10. He became a full time coin and currency dealer in the mid-1980s. David's main collecting interest is in all things Texas, specializing in currency and documents from the Republic of Texas.

Jim Jelinski - Consignment Director & Senior Numismatist
Jim Jelinski has been involved in numismatics for more than five decades as a collector, dealer and educator. He started as Buyer for Paramount International Coin Corporation in 1972, opened Essex Numismatic Properties in 1975 in New Hampshire and has held numerous executive positions at M.B. Simmons & Associates of Narberth, Pennsylvania. He works at Heritage as a Senior Numismatist and Consignment Coordinator.

Bob Marino - Consignment Director & Senior Numismatist
Bob Marino joined Heritage in 1999, managing and developing Internet coin sales, and building Heritage's client base through eBay and other Internet auction Web sites. He has successfully concluded more than 40,000 transactions on eBay. He is now a Consignment Director, assisting consignors in placing their coins and collectibles in the best of the many Heritage venues.

Sam Foose - Consignment Director and Auctioneer
Sam Foose joined Heritage Numismatic Auctions, Inc., in 1993 as an Auction Coordinator. He rose to Assistant Auction Director in 1998, and began calling auctions. After a stint serving as a Senior Manager and Consignment Director in other collectible fields, he returned to Heritage in 2002 as a Consignment Director to help Heritage's expansion into other collectibles fields. Besides calling auctions as one of Heritage's primary auctioneers, he travels the nation assisting clients who wish to liquidate their collections of coins, paper money, decorative arts, and sports collectibles.

Katherine Kurachek - Consignment Director
Katherine Kurachek graduated from the University of Mississippi in 1993 as an art major. She came to Heritage in January 2003, working alongside Leo Frese for several years, learning the numismatic wholesale trade. Katherine frequently travels to coin shows to represent Heritage and service her dealer accounts along with her wide ranging duties as Consignment Director.

Shaunda Fry - Consignment Director
Shaunda Fry ran her own textile company for 22 years before meeting Leo Frese while co-coordinating a local school auction. She followed his suggestion to add auctioneering to her list of talents and, after training, worked part-time at Heritage auctions and began to call. She became a Consignment Director and now travels to shows as part of the "Wholesale Dealers Team."

Mike Sadler - Consignment Director
Mike Sadler joined the Heritage team in September 2003. He attended the United States Air Force Academy, flew jets for the military and is a longtime pilot with American Airlines. Before coming to Heritage, his unlimited access to air travel enabled Mike to attend coin shows around the nation, and to build a world class collection that was auctioned by Heritage in 2004. He is known for his tremendous knowledge of rare coins, making him a trusted colleague to many of today's most active collectors.

Chris Dykstra - Consignment Director
Chris Dykstra joined Heritage October 2006. He has held a number of jobs at Heritage including a stint in Wholesale Sales assisting Heritage's dealer clients in locating specific coins and travelling to shows to work the Heritage booth. In August 2008 Chris was promoted into the US Coin Consignments department as a Consignment Director where he now assists consignors in bringing their collections to auction.

Jason Friedman - Consignment Director
Jason's interest in rare coins, which began at 12 and expanded into his own numismatic business, allowed him to pay for most of his college tuition at the University of North Texas, from which he graduated in 2005. He joined Heritage soon after. He is a member of the American Numismatic Association (ANA) and Florida United Numismatists (FUN).

Bert DeLaGarza - Consignment Director
Bert DeLaGarza joined Heritage in 2008, capitalizing on a longtime passion for, and expertise in rare coins from a very young age. Prior to Heritage, Bert spent over 25 years in Landscape Construction and Estate Management having achieved the Texas Master Nurseryman certification. A member of the ANA, Bert is known for his strong knowledge of U.S. coins and an eye for rare U.S. stamps.

Win Callender - Consignment Director & Senior Numismatist
Win Callender has joined Heritage Auction Galleries as a professional numismatist and consignment director. A lifelong numismatist - he found a 1770 Russian 5 Kopek when he was just 5 years old - Callender parlayed his hobby into a fulltime business when he was in his mid-30s, starting his own business in Broken Arrow, Okla., in 1993. He subsequently worked for Carter Numismatics and David Lawrence Rare Coins, working his way up to Vice President in both firms.

Jessica Aylmer - Consignment Director
Jessica joined the Heritage staff as a Consignment Coordinator in 2007, shortly after graduating with a Bachelor's in Art History from the University of North Texas. She was moved up to Consignment Director in 2009, where her main focus is now on working as part of the Heritage dealer consignment team. Jessica has become a familiar face to the numismatic community, attending coin shows and expositions across the country on a weekly basis. Jessica is a member of the American Numismatic Association, Florida United Numismatists and Women In Numismatics.

Diedre Buchmoyer - Consignment Director
Diedre has worked full-time in the numismatic arena for the past eight years buying and selling rare coins, and assisted in several prestigious auctions including the John J. Ford, Jr. Collection. An honors graduate from Hood College in Frederick, Maryland, Diedre received her BA in Art History with a concentration in Archaeology and a double minor in Business Management and Studio Art. She is a member of the American Numismatic Association, Florida United Numismatics, Women in Numismatics and the Industry Council for Tangible Assets.

Mark Van Winkle - Chief Cataloger
Mark has worked for Heritage, and Steve Ivy, since 1979. He has been Chief Cataloger since 1990, and has handled some of the premier numismatic rarities sold at public auction. Mark was editor of Legacy magazine, won the 1989 NLG award for Best U.S. Commercial Magazine, and has won numerous awards for his writing, including the 1990 NLG award for Best Article for his *Interview With John Ford*, the 1996 NLG Best Numismatic Article for *Changing Concepts of Liberty*. He has published extensively and written articles for *Coin World*, *Numismatic News* and has contributed to editions of the *Red Book*, *United States Patterns and Related Issues*, and *The Guide Book of Double Eagle Gold Coins*.

Mark Borckardt - Senior Cataloger
Mark started attending coin shows and conventions as a dealer in 1970, and has been a full-time professional numismatist since 1980. He received the Early American Coppers Literary Award, and the Numismatic Literary Guild's Book of the Year Award, for the *Encyclopedia of Early United States Cents, 1793-1814*, published in 2000. He serves as a contributor to *A Guide Book of United States Coins*, and has contributed to many references, including the Harry W. Bass, Jr. Sylloge, and the *Encyclopedia of Silver Dollars and Trade Dollars of the United States*. Most recently, he was Senior Numismatist with Bowers and Merena Galleries. Mark is a life member of the A. N. A., and an active member of numerous organizations.

Brian Koller - Cataloger & Catalog Production Manager
Brian Koller has been a Heritage cataloger since 2001, before that working as a telecom software engineer for 16 years. He is a graduate of Iowa State University with a Bachelor's degree in Computer Engineering, and is an avid collector of U.S. gold coins. His attention to detail ensures that every catalog, printed and on-line, is as error free as technology and human activity allows. In addition to his coin cataloging duties, he also helps with consignor promises and client service issues.

Dr. Jon Amato - Cataloger
Jon Amato has been with Heritage since 2004. He earned his Ph. D. from the University of Toronto, and was previously a Program Manager in the NY State Dept. of Economic Development, and an Adjunct Professor at the State University of New York at Albany. He is currently writing a monograph on the draped bust, small eagle half dollars of 1796-1797. He has published numerous articles in prestigious numismatic publications and belongs to many numismatic organizations, including the ANA, ANS, John Reich Collectors Society, and the Liberty Seated Collectors Club, and has made several presentations at ANA Numismatic Theaters.

John Dale Beety - Cataloger
John Dale Beety served an internship at Heritage during the summer of 2004 and started full-time as a cataloger in 2006, immediately after graduating from Rose-Hulman Institute of Technology. In addition to catalog writing and editing, he creates the Coin Monday posts that appear weekly on the official Heritage Auction Galleries blog, heritageauctions.blogspot.com.

Cataloged by: Mark Van Winkle, Chief Cataloger
Mark Borckardt, Senior Numismatist; Jon Amato, John Beety, George Huber, Brian Koller, Dave Stone
Edited by: Mark Van Winkle, John Beety, George Huber, Stewart Huckaby
Operations Support by: Christina Gonzales, San Juana Gonzalez, Manuela Bueno, Christina Ibarra, Ira Reynolds, Cinthya Pina, Daisy Manhard, Maria Flores, Jose Martinez
Catalog and Internet Imaging by: Travis Awalt, Maribel Cazares, Joel Gonzalez, Colleen McInerney, Sharon Johnson, Nancy Ramos, Jason Young, Tony Webb, Donna Rusnak
Production and Design by: Lisa Fox, Mark Masat, Mary Hermann, Debbie Rexing

Terms and Conditions of Auction

Auctioneer and Auction:

1. This Auction is presented by Heritage Auction Galleries, a d/b/a/ of Heritage Auctions, Inc., or its affiliates Heritage Numismatic Auctions, Inc., or Heritage Vintage Sports Auctions, Inc., or Currency Auctions of America, Inc., as identified with the applicable licensing information on the title page of the catalog or on the HA.com Internet site (the "Auctioneer"). The Auction is conducted under these Terms and Conditions of Auction and applicable state and local law. Announcements and corrections from the podium and those made through the Terms and Conditions of Auctions appearing on the Internet at HA.com supersede those in the printed catalog.

Buyer's Premium:

2. On bids placed through Auctioneer, a Buyer's Premium of fifteen percent (15%) will be added to the successful hammer price bid on lots in Coin, Currency, and Philatelic auctions or nineteen and one-half percent (19.5%) on lots in all other auctions. There is a minimum Buyer's Premium of $14.00 per lot. In Gallery Auctions (sealed bid auctions of mostly bulk numismatic material), the Buyer's Premium is 19.5%.

Auction Venues:

3. The following Auctions are conducted solely on the Internet: Heritage Weekly Internet Auctions (Coin, Currency, Comics, and Vintage Movie Poster); Heritage Monthly Internet Auctions (Sports, and Stamps). Signature® Auctions and Grand Format Auctions accept bids from the Internet, telephone, fax, or mail first, followed by a floor bidding session; Heritage Live and real-time telephone bidding are available to registered clients during these auctions.

Bidders:

4. Any person participating or registering for the Auction agrees to be bound by and accepts these Terms and Conditions of Auction ("Bidder(s)").
5. All Bidders must meet Auctioneer's qualifications to bid. Any Bidder who is not a client in good standing of the Auctioneer may be disqualified at Auctioneer's sole option and will not be awarded lots. Such determination may be made by Auctioneer in its sole and unlimited discretion, at any time prior to, during, or even after the close of the Auction. Auctioneer reserves the right to exclude any person from the auction.
6. If an entity places a bid, then the person executing the bid on behalf of the entity agrees to personally guarantee payment for any successful bid.

Credit:

7. Bidders who have not established credit with the Auctioneer must either furnish satisfactory credit information (including two collectibles-related business references) well in advance of the Auction or supply valid credit card information. Bids placed through our Interactive Internet program will only be accepted from pre-registered Bidders; Bidders who are not members of HA.com or affiliates should pre-register at least 48 hours before the start of the first session (exclusive of holidays or weekends) to allow adequate time to contact references. Credit may be granted at the discretion of Auctioneer. Additionally Bidders who have not previously established credit or who wish to bid in excess of their established credit history may be required to provide their social security number or the last four digits thereof to us so a credit check may be performed prior to Auctioneer's acceptance of a bid.

Bidding Options:

8. Bids in Signature® Auctions or Grand Format Auctions may be placed as set forth in the printed catalog section entitled "Choose your bidding method." For auctions held solely on the Internet, see the alternatives on HA.com. Review at HA.com/common/howtobid.php.
9. Presentment of Bids: Non-Internet bids (including but not limited to podium, fax, phone and mail bids) are treated similar to floor bids in that they must be on-increment or at a half increment (called a cut bid). Any podium, fax, phone, or mail bids that do not conform to a full or half increment will be rounded up or down to the nearest full or half increment and this revised amount will be considered your high bid.
10. Auctioneer's Execution of Certain Bids. Auctioneer cannot be responsible for your errors in bidding, so carefully check that every bid is entered correctly. When identical mail or FAX bids are submitted, preference is given to the first received. To ensure the greatest accuracy, your written bids should be entered on the standard printed bid sheet and be received at Auctioneer's place of business at least two business days before the Auction start. Auctioneer is not responsible for executing mail bids or FAX bids received on or after the day the first lot is sold, nor Internet bids submitted after the published closing time; nor is Auctioneer responsible for proper execution of bids submitted by telephone, mail, FAX, e-mail, Internet, or in person once the Auction begins. Internet bids may not be withdrawn until your written request is received and acknowledged by Auctioneer (FAX: 214-4438425); such requests must state the reason, and may constitute grounds for withdrawal of bidding privileges. Lots won by mail Bidders will not be delivered at the Auction unless prearranged.
11. Caveat as to Bid Increments. Bid increments (over the current bid level) determine the lowest amount you may bid on a particular lot. Bids greater than one increment over the current bid can be any whole dollar amount. It is possible under several circumstances for winning bids to be between increments, sometimes only $1 above the previous increment. Please see: "How can I lose by less than an increment?" on our website. Bids will be accepted in whole dollar amounts only. No "buy" or "unlimited" bids will be accepted.

   The following chart governs current bidding increments.

Current Bid	Bid Increment	Current Bid	Bid Increment
<$10	$1	$20,000 - $29,999	$2,000
$10 - $29	$2	$30,000 - $49,999	$2,500
$30 - $49	$3	$50,000 - $99,999	$5,000
$50 - $99	$5	$100,000 - $199,999	$10,000
$100 - $199	$10	$200,000 - $299,999	$20,000
$200 - $299	$20	$300,000 - $499,999	$25,000
$300 - $499	$25	$500,000 - $999,999	$50,000
$500 - $999	$50	$1,000,000 - $1,999,999	$100,000
$1,000 - $1,999	$100	$2,000,000 - $2,999,999	$200,000
$2,000 - $2,999	$200	$3,000,000 - $4,999,999	$250,000
$3,000 - $4,999	$250	$5,000,000 - $9,999,999	$500,000
$5,000 - $9,999	$500	>$10,000,000	$1,000,000
$10,000 - $19,999	$1,000		

12. If Auctioneer calls for a full increment, a bidder may request Auctioneer to accept a bid at half of the increment ("Cut Bid") only once per lot. After offering a Cut Bid, bidders may continue to participate only at full increments. Off-increment bids may be accepted by the Auctioneer at Signature® Auctions and Grand Format Auctions. If the Auctioneer solicits bids other than the expected increment, these bids will not be considered Cut Bids.

Conducting the Auction:

13. Notice of the consignor's liberty to place bids on his lots in the Auction is hereby made in accordance with Article 2 of the Texas Business and Commercial Code. A "Minimum Bid" is an amount below which the lot will not sell. THE CONSIGNOR OF PROPERTY MAY PLACE WRITTEN "Minimum Bids" ON HIS LOTS IN ADVANCE OF THE AUCTION; ON SUCH LOTS, IF THE HAMMER PRICE DOES NOT MEET THE "Minimum Bid", THE CONSIGNOR MAY PAY A REDUCED COMMISSION ON THOSE LOTS. "Minimum Bids" are generally posted online several days prior to the Auction closing. For any successful bid placed by a consignor on his Property on the Auction floor, or by any means during the live session, or after the "Minimum Bid" for an Auction have been posted, we will require the consignor to pay full Buyer's Premium and Seller's Commissions on such lot.
14. The highest qualified Bidder recognized by the Auctioneer shall be the buyer. In the event of any dispute between any Bidders at an Auction, Auctioneer may at his sole discretion reoffer the lot. Auctioneer's decision and declaration of the winning Bidder shall be final and binding upon all Bidders. Bids properly offered, whether by floor Bidder or other means of bidding, may on occasion be missed or go unrecognized; in such cases, the Auctioneer may declare the recognized bid accepted as the winning bid, regardless of whether a competing bid may have been higher.
15. Auctioneer reserves the right to refuse to honor any bid or to limit the amount of any bid, in its sole discretion. A bid is considered not made in "Good Faith" when made by an insolvent or irresponsible person, a person under the age of eighteen, or is not supported by satisfactory credit, collectibles references, or otherwise. Regardless of the disclosure of his identity, any bid by a consignor or his agent on a lot consigned by him is deemed to be made in "Good Faith." Any person apparently appearing on the OFAC list is not eligible to bid.
16. Nominal Bids. The Auctioneer in its sole discretion may reject nominal bids, small opening bids, or very nominal advances. If a lot bearing estimates fails to open for 40–60% of the low estimate, the Auctioneer may pass the item or may place a protective bid on behalf of the consignor.
17. Lots bearing bidding estimates shall open at Auctioneer's discretion (approximately 50%-60% of the low estimate). In the event that no bid meets or exceeds that opening amount, the lot shall pass as unsold.
18. All items are to be purchased per lot as numerically indicated and no lots will be broken. Auctioneer reserves the right to withdraw, prior to the close, any lots from the Auction.
19. Auctioneer reserves the right to rescind the sale in the event of nonpayment, breach of a warranty, disputed ownership, auctioneer's clerical error or omission in exercising bids and reserves, or for any other reason and in Auctioneer's sole discretion. In cases of nonpayment, Auctioneer's election to void a sale does not relieve the Bidder from their obligation to pay Auctioneer its fees (seller's and buyer's premium) and any other damages or expenses pertaining to the lot.
20. Auctioneer occasionally experiences Internet and/or Server service outages, and Auctioneer periodically schedules system downtime for maintenance and other purposes, during which Bidders cannot participate or place bids. If such outages occur, we may at our discretion extend bidding for the Auction. Bidders unable to place their Bids through the Internet are directed to contact Client Services at 1-800-872-6467.
21. The Auctioneer or its affiliates may consign items to be sold in the Auction, and may bid on those lots or any other lots. Auctioneer or affiliates expressly reserve the right to modify any such bids at any time prior to the hammer based upon data made known to the Auctioneer or its affiliates. The Auctioneer may extend advances, guarantees, or loans to certain consignors, and may extend financing or other credits at varying rates to certain Bidders in the auction.
22. The Auctioneer has the right to sell certain unsold items after the close of the Auction. Such lots shall be considered sold during the Auction and all these Terms and Conditions shall apply to such sales including but not limited to the Buyer's Premium, return rights, and disclaimers.

Payment:

23. All sales are strictly for cash in United States dollars (including U.S. currency, bank wire, cashier checks, travelers checks, eChecks, and bank money orders, all subject to reporting requirements). All are subject to clearing and funds being received In Auctioneer's account before delivery of the purchases. Auctioneer reserves the right to determine if a check constitutes "good funds" when drawn on a U.S. bank for ten days, and thirty days when drawn on an international bank. Credit Card (Visa or Master Card only) and PayPal payments may be accepted up to $10,000 from non-dealers at the sole discretion of the Auctioneer, subject to the following limitations: a) sales are only to the cardholder, b) purchases are shipped to the cardholder's registered and verified address, c) Auctioneer may pre-approve the cardholder's credit line, d) a credit card transaction may not be used in conjunction with any other financing or extended terms offered by the Auctioneer, and must transact immediately upon invoice presentation, e) rights of return are governed by these Terms and Conditions, which supersede those conditions promulgated by the card issuer, f) floor Bidders must present their card.
24. Payment is due upon closing of the Auction session, or upon presentment of an invoice. Auctioneer reserves the right to void an invoice if payment in full is not received within 7 days after the close of the Auction. In cases of nonpayment, Auctioneer's election to void a sale does not relieve the Bidder from their obligation to pay Auctioneer its fees (seller's and buyer's premium) on the lot and any other damages pertaining to the lot.
25. Lots delivered to you, or your representative in the States of Texas, California, **New York**, or other states where the Auction may be held, are subject to all applicable state and local taxes, unless appropriate permits are on file with Auctioneer. Bidder agrees to pay Auctioneer the actual amount of tax due in the event that sales tax is not properly collected due to: 1) an expired, inaccurate, inappropriate tax certificate or declaration, 2) an incorrect interpretation of the applicable statute, 3) or any other reason. The appropriate form or certificate must be on file at and verified by Auctioneer five days prior to Auction or tax must be paid; only if such form or certificate is received by Auctioneer within 4 days after the Auction can a refund of tax paid be made. Lots from different Auctions may not be aggregated for sales tax purposes.
26. In the event that a Bidder's payment is dishonored upon presentment(s), Bidder shall pay the maximum statutory processing fee set by applicable state law. If you attempt to pay via eCheck and your financial institution denies this transfer from your bank account, or the payment cannot be completed using the selected funding source, you agree to complete payment using your credit card on file.
27. If any Auction invoice submitted by Auctioneer is not paid in full when due, the unpaid balance will bear interest at the highest rate permitted by law from the date of invoice until paid. Any invoice not paid when due will bear a three percent (3%) late fee on the invoice amount or three percent (3%) of any installment that is past due. If the Auctioneer refers any invoice to an attorney for collection, the buyer agrees to pay attorney's fees, court costs, and other collection costs incurred by Auctioneer. If Auctioneer assigns collection to its in-house legal staff, such attorney's time expended on the matter shall be compensated at a rate comparable to the hourly rate of independent attorneys.
28. In the event a successful Bidder fails to pay any amounts due, Auctioneer reserves the right to sell the lot(s) securing the invoice to any underbidders in the Auction that the lot(s) appeared, or at subsequent private or public sale, or relist the lot(s) in a future auction conducted by Auctioneer. A defaulting Bidder agrees to pay for the reasonable costs of resale (including a 10% seller's commission, if consigned to an auction conducted by Auctioneer). The defaulting Bidder is liable to pay any difference between his total original invoice for the lot(s), plus any applicable interest, and the net proceeds for the lot(s) if sold at private sale or the subsequent hammer price of the lot(s) less the 10% seller's commissions, if sold at an Auctioneer's auction.

29. Auctioneer reserves the right to require payment in full in good funds before delivery of the merchandise.
30. Auctioneer shall have a lien against the merchandise purchased by the buyer to secure payment of the Auction invoice. Auctioneer is further granted a lien and the right to retain possession of any other property of the buyer then held by the Auctioneer or its affiliates to secure payment of any Auction invoice or any other amounts due the Auctioneer or affiliates from the buyer. With respect to these lien rights, Auctioneer shall have all the rights of a secured creditor under Article 9 of the Texas Uniform Commercial Code, including but not limited to the right of sale. In addition, with respect to payment of the Auction invoice(s), the buyer waives any and all rights of offset he might otherwise have against the Auctioneer and the consignor of the merchandise included on the invoice. If a Bidder owes Auctioneer or its affiliates on any account, Auctioneer and its affiliates shall have the right to offset such unpaid account by any credit balance due Bidder, and it may secure by possessory lien any unpaid amount by any of the Bidder's property in their possession.
31. Title shall not pass to the successful Bidder until all invoices are paid in full. It is the responsibility of the buyer to provide adequate insurance coverage for the items once they have been delivered to a common carrier or third-party shipper.

Delivery; Shipping; and Handling Charges:

32. Buyer is liable for shipping and handling. Please refer to Auctioneer's website www.HA.com/common/shipping.php for the latest charges or call Auctioneer. Auctioneer is unable to combine purchases from other auctions or affiliates into one package for shipping purposes. Lots won will be shipped in a commercially reasonable time after payment in good funds for the merchandise and the shipping fees is received or credit extended, except when third-party shipment occurs.
33. Successful international Bidders shall provide written shipping instructions, including specified customs declarations, to the Auctioneer for any lots to be delivered outside of the United States. NOTE: Declaration value shall be the item'(s) hammer price together with its buyer's premium and Auctioneer shall use the correct harmonized code for the lot. Domestic Buyers on lots designated for third-party shipment must designate the common carrier, accept risk of loss, and prepay shipping costs.
34. All shipping charges will be borne by the successful Bidder. Any risk of loss during shipment will be borne by the buyer following Auctioneer's delivery to the designated common carrier or third-party shipper, regardless of domestic or foreign shipment.
35. Due to the nature of some items sold, it shall be the responsibility for the successful bidder to arrange pick-up and shipping through third-parties; as to such items Auctioneer shall have no liability. Failure to pick-up or arrange shipping in a timely fashion (within ten days) shall subject Lots to storage and moving charges, including a $100 administration fee plus $10 daily storage for larger items and $5.00 daily for smaller items (storage fee per item) after 35 days. In the event the Lot is not removed within ninety days, the Lot may be offered for sale to recover any past due storage or moving fees, including a 10% Seller's Commission.
36. The laws of various countries regulate the import or export of certain plant and animal properties, including (but not limited to) items made of (or including) ivory, whalebone, turtleshell, coral, crocodile, or other wildlife. Transport of such lots may require special licenses for export, import, or both. Bidder is responsible for: 1) obtaining all information on such restricted items for both export and import; 2) obtaining all such licenses and/or permits. Delay or failure to obtain any such license or permit does not relieve the buyer of timely compliance with standard payment terms. For further information, please contact Ron Brackemyre at 800-872-6467 ext. 1312.
37. Any request for shipping verification for undelivered packages must be made within 30 days of shipment by Auctioneer.

Cataloging, Warranties and Disclaimers:

38. NO WARRANTY, WHETHER EXPRESSED OR IMPLIED, IS MADE WITH RESPECT TO ANY DESCRIPTION CONTAINED IN THIS AUCTION OR ANY SECOND OPINE. Any description of the items or second opine contained in this Auction is for the sole purpose of identifying the items for those Bidders who do not have the opportunity to view the lots prior to bidding, and no description of items has been made part of the basis of the bargain or has created any express warranty that the goods would conform to any description made by Auctioneer. Color variations can be expected in any electronic or printed imaging, and are not grounds for the return of any lot. NOTE: Auctioneer, in specified auction venues, for example, Fine Art, may have express written warranties and you are referred to those specific terms and conditions. .
39. Auctioneer is selling only such right or title to the items being sold as Auctioneer may have by virtue of consignment agreements on the date of auction and disclaims any warranty of title to the Property. Auctioneer disclaims any warranty of merchantability or fitness for any particular purposes. All images, descriptions, sales data, and archival records are the exclusive property of Auctioneer, and may be used by Auctioneer for advertising, promotion, archival records, and any other uses deemed appropriate.
40. Translations of foreign language documents may be provided as a convenience to interested parties. Auctioneer makes no representation as to the accuracy of those translations and will not be held responsible for errors in bidding arising from inaccuracies in translation.
41. Auctioneer disclaims all liability for damages, consequential or otherwise, arising out of or in connection with the sale of any Property by Auctioneer to Bidder. No third party may rely on any benefit of these Terms and Conditions and any rights, if any, established hereunder are personal to the Bidder and may not be assigned. Any statement made by the Auctioneer is an opinion and does not constitute a warranty or representation. No employee of Auctioneer may alter these Terms and Conditions, and, unless signed by a principal of Auctioneer, any such alteration is null and void.
42. Auctioneer shall not be liable for breakage of glass or damage to frames (patent or latent); such defects, in any event, shall not be a basis for any claim for return or reduction in purchase price.

Release:

43. In consideration of participation in the Auction and the placing of a bid, Bidder expressly releases Auctioneer, its officers, directors and employees, its affiliates, and its outside experts that provide second opines, from any and all claims, cause of action, chose of action, whether at law or equity or any arbitration or mediation rights existing under the rules of any professional society or affiliation based upon the assigned description, or a derivative theory, breach of warranty express or implied, representation or other matter set forth within these Terms and Conditions of Auction or otherwise. In the event of a claim, Bidder agrees that such rights and privileges conferred therein are strictly construed as specifically declared herein; e.g., authenticity, typographical error, etc. and are the exclusive remedy. Bidder, by non-compliance to these express terms of a granted remedy, shall waive any claim against Auctioneer.
44. Notice: Some Property sold by Auctioneer are inherently dangerous e.g. firearms, cannons, and small items that may be swallowed or ingested or may have latent defects all of which may cause harm to a person. Purchaser accepts all risk of loss or damage from its purchase of these items and Auctioneer disclaims any liability whether under contract or tort for damages and losses, direct or inconsequential, and expressly disclaims any warranty as to safety or usage of any lot sold.

Dispute Resolution and Arbitration Provision:

45. By placing a bid or otherwise participating in the auction, Bidder accepts these Terms and Conditions of Auction, and specifically agrees to the dispute resolution provided herein. Consumer disputes shall be resolved through court litigation which has an exclusive Dallas, Texas venue clause and jury waiver. Non-consumer dispute shall be determined in binding arbitration which arbitration replaces the right to go to court, including the right to a jury trial.
46. Auctioneer in no event shall be responsible for consequential damages, incidental damages, compensatory damages, or any other damages arising or claimed to be arising from the auction of any lot. In the event that Auctioneer cannot deliver the lot or subsequently it is established that the lot lacks title, or other transfer or condition issue is claimed, In such cases the sole remedy shall be limited to rescission of sale and refund of the amount paid by Bidder; in no case shall Auctioneer's maximum liability exceed the high bid on that lot, which bid shall be deemed for all purposes the value of the lot. After one year has elapsed, Auctioneer's maximum liability shall be limited to any commissions and fees Auctioneer earned on that lot.
47. In the event of an attribution error, Auctioneer may at its sole discretion, correct the error on the Internet, or, if discovered at a later date, to refund the buyer's purchase price without further obligation.
48. Dispute Resolution for Consumers and Non-Consumers: Any claim, dispute, or controversy in connection with, relating to and /or arising out of the Auction, participation in the Auction. Award of lots, damages of claims to lots, descriptions, condition reports, provenance, estimates, return and warranty rights, any interpretation of these Terms and Conditions, any alleged verbal modification of these Terms and Conditions and/or any purported settlement whether asserted in contract, tort, under Federal or State statute or regulation shall or any other matter: a) if presented by a consumer, be exclusively heard by, and the parties consent to, exclusive in personam jurisdiction in the State District Courts of Dallas County, Texas. THE PARTIES EXPRESSLY WAIVE ANY RIGHT TO TRIAL BY JURY. Any appeals shall be solely pursued in the appellate courts of the State of Texas; or b) for any claimant other than a consumer, the claim shall be presented in confidential binding arbitration before a single arbitrator, that the parties may agree upon, selected from the JAMS list of Texas arbitrators. The case is not to be administrated by JAMS; however, if the parties cannot agree on an arbitrator, then JAMS shall appoint the arbitrator and it shall be conducted under JAMS rules. The locale shall be Dallas Texas. The arbitrator's award may be enforced in any court of competent jurisdiction. Any party on any claim involving the purchase or sale of numismatic or related items may elect arbitration through binding PNG arbitration. Any claim must be brought within one (1) year of the alleged breach, default or misrepresentation or the claim is waived. This agreement and any claims shall be determined and construed under Texas law. The prevailing party (party that is awarded substantial and material relief on its claim or defense) may be awarded its reasonable attorneys' fees and costs.
49. No claims of any kind can be considered after the settlements have been made with the consignors. Any dispute after the settlement date is strictly between the Bidder and consignor without involvement or responsibility of the Auctioneer.
50. In consideration of their participation in or application for the Auction, a person or entity (whether the successful Bidder, a Bidder, a purchaser and/or other Auction participant or registrant) agrees that all disputes in any way relating to, arising under, connected with, or incidental to these Terms and Conditions and purchases, or default in payment thereof, shall be arbitrated pursuant to the arbitration provision. In the event that any matter including actions to compel arbitration, construe the agreement, actions in aid or arbitration or otherwise needs to be litigated, such litigation shall be exclusively in the Courts of the State of Texas, in Dallas County, Texas, and if necessary the corresponding appellate courts. For such actions, the successful Bidder, purchaser, or Auction participant also expressly submits himself to the personal jurisdiction of the State of Texas.
51. These Terms & Conditions provide specific remedies for occurrences in the auction and delivery process. Where such remedies are afforded, they shall be interpreted strictly. Bidder agrees that any claim shall utilize such remedies; Bidder making a claim in excess of those remedies provided in these Terms and Conditions agrees that in no case whatsoever shall Auctioneer's maximum liability exceed the high bid on that lot, which bid shall be deemed for all purposes the value of the lot.

Miscellaneous:

52. Agreements between Bidders and consignors to effectuate a non-sale of an item at Auction, inhibit bidding on a consigned item to enter into a private sale agreement for said item, or to utilize the Auctioneer's Auction to obtain sales for non-selling consigned items subsequent to the Auction, are strictly prohibited. If a subsequent sale of a previously consigned item occurs in violation of this provision, Auctioneer reserves the right to charge Bidder the applicable Buyer's Premium and consignor a Seller's Commission as determined for each auction venue and by the terms of the seller's agreement.
53. Acceptance of these Terms and Conditions qualifies Bidder as a client who has consented to be contacted by Heritage in the future. In conformity with "do-not-call" regulations promulgated by the Federal or State regulatory agencies, participation by the Bidder is affirmative consent to being contacted at the phone number shown in his application and this consent shall remain in effect until it is revoked in writing. Heritage may from time to time contact Bidder concerning sale, purchase, and auction opportunities available through Heritage and its affiliates and subsidiaries.
54. Rules of Construction: Auctioneer presents properties in a number of collectible fields, and as such, specific venues have promulgated supplemental Terms and Conditions. Nothing herein shall be construed to waive the general Terms and Conditions of Auction by these additional rules and shall be construed to give force and effect to the rules in their entirety.

State Notices:

Notice as to an Auction in California. Auctioneer has in compliance with Title 2.95 of the California Civil Code as amended October 11, 1993 Sec. 1812.600, posted with the California Secretary of State its bonds for it and its employees, and the auction is being conducted in compliance with Sec. 2338 of the Commercial Code and Sec. 535 of the Penal Code.

Notice as to an Auction in New York City. These Terms and Conditions are designed to conform to the applicable sections of the New York City Department of Consumer Affairs Rules and Regulations as Amended. This is a Public Auction Sale conducted by Auctioneer. The New York City licensed Auctioneers are Harvey Bennett, No. 0924050, and Samuel W. Foose, No.0952360, who will conduct the Auction on behalf of Heritage Auctions, Inc. ("Auctioneer"). All lots are subject to: the consignor's right to bid thereon in accord with these Terms and Conditions of Auction, consignor's option to receive advances on their consignments, and Auctioneer, in its sole discretion, may offer limited extended financing to registered bidders, in accord with Auctioneer's internal credit standards. A registered bidder may inquire whether a lot is subject to an advance or reserve. Auctioneer has made advances to various consignors in this sale.

Notice as to an Auction in Texas. In compliance with TDLR rule 67.100(c)(1), notice is hereby provided that this auction is covered by a Recovery Fund administered by the Texas Department of Licensing and Regulation, P.O. Box 12157, Austin, Texas 78711 (512) 463-6599. Any complaints may be directed to the same address.

Notice as to an Auction in Ohio: Auction firm and Auctioneer are licensed by the Dept. of Agriculture, and either the licensee is bonded in favor of the state or an aggrieved person may initiate a claim against the auction recovery fund created in Section 4707.25 of the Revised Code as a result of the licensee's actions, whichever is applicable.

Rev. 10-20-09

Additional Terms & Conditions: COINS & CURRENCY

COINS and CURRENCY TERM A: Signature. Auctions are not on approval. No certified material may be returned because of possible differences of opinion with respect to the grade offered by any third-party organization, dealer, or service. No guarantee of grade is offered for uncertified Property sold and subsequently submitted to a third-party grading service. There are absolutely no exceptions to this policy. Under extremely limited circumstances, (e.g. gross cataloging error) a purchaser, who did not bid from the floor, may request Auctioneer to evaluate voiding a sale: such request must be made in writing detailing the alleged gross error; submission of the lot to the Auctioneer must be pre-approved by the Auctioneer; and bidder must notify Ron Brackemyre (1-800-8726467 Ext. 1312) in writing of such request within three (3) days of the non-floor bidder's receipt of the lot. Any lot that is to be evaluated must be in our offices within 30 days after Auction. Grading or method of manufacture do not qualify for this evaluation process nor do such complaints constitute a basis to challenge the authenticity of a lot. AFTER THAT 30-DAY PERIOD, NO LOTS MAY BE RETURNED FOR REASONS OTHER THAN AUTHENTICITY. Lots returned must be housed intact in their original holder. No lots purchased by floor Bidders may be returned (including those Bidders acting as agents for others) except for authenticity. Late remittance for purchases may be considered just cause to revoke all return privileges.

COINS and CURRENCY TERM B: Auctions conducted solely on the Internet THREE (3) DAY RETURN POLICY: Certified Coin and Uncertified and Certified Currency lots paid for within seven days of the Auction closing are sold with a three (3) day return privilege. You may return lots under the following conditions: Within three days of receipt of the lot, you must first notify Auctioneer by contacting Client Service by phone (1-800-872-6467) or e-mail (Bid@HA.com), and immediately ship the lot(s) fully insured to the attention of Returns, Heritage, 3500 Maple Avenue, 17th Floor, Dallas TX 75219-3941. Lots must be housed intact in their original holder and condition. You are responsible for the insured, safe delivery of any lots. A non-negotiable return fee of 5% of the purchase price ($10 per lot minimum) will be deducted from the refund for each returned lot or billed directly. Postage and handling fees are not refunded. After the three-day period (from receipt), no items may be returned for any reason. Late remittance for purchases revokes these Return privileges.

COINS and CURRENCY TERM C: Bidders who have inspected the lots prior to any Auction, or attended the Auction, or bid through an Agent, will not be granted any return privileges, except for reasons of authenticity.

COINS and CURRENCY TERM D: Coins sold referencing a third-party grading service are sold "as is" without any express or implied warranty, except for a guarantee by Auctioneer that they are genuine. Certain warranties may be available from the grading services and the Bidder is referred to them for further details: Numismatic Guaranty Corporation (NGC), P.O. Box 4776, Sarasota, FL 34230; Professional Coin Grading Service (PCGS), PO Box 9458, Newport Beach, CA 92658; ANACS, 6555 S. Kenton St. Ste. 303, Englewood, CO 80111; and Independent Coin Grading Co. (ICG), 7901 East Belleview Ave., Suite 50, Englewood, CO 80111.

COINS and CURRENCY TERM E: Notes sold referencing a third-party grading service are sold "as is" without any express or implied warranty, except for guarantee by Auctioneer that they are genuine. Grading, condition or other attributes of any lot may have a material effect on its value, and the opinion of others, including third-party grading services such as PCGS Currency, PMG, and CGA may differ with that of Auctioneer. Auctioneer shall not be bound by any prior or subsequent opinion, determination, or certification by any grading service. Bidder specifically waives any claim to right of return of any item because of the opinion, determination, or certification, or lack thereof, by any grading service. Certain warranties may be available from the grading services and the Bidder is referred to them for further details: Paper Money Guaranty (PMG), PO Box 4711, Sarasota FL 34230; PCGS Currency, PO Box 9458, Newport Beach, CA 92658; Currency Grading & Authentication (CGA), PO Box 418, Three Bridges, NJ 08887. Third party graded notes are not returnable for any reason whatsoever.

COINS and CURRENCY TERM F: Since we cannot examine encapsulated coins or notes, they are sold "as is" without our grading opinion, and may not be returned for any reason. Auctioneer shall not be liable for any patent or latent defect or controversy pertaining to or arising from any encapsulated collectible. In any such instance, purchaser's remedy, if any, shall be solely against the service certifying the collectible.

COINS and CURRENCY TERM G: Due to changing grading standards over time, differing interpretations, and to possible mishandling of items by subsequent owners, Auctioneer reserves the right to grade items differently than shown on certificates from any grading service that accompany the items. Auctioneer also reserves the right to grade items differently than the grades shown in the prior catalog should such items be reconsigned to any future auction.

COINS and CURRENCY TERM H: Although consensus grading is employed by most grading services, it should be noted as aforesaid that grading is not an exact science. In fact, it is entirely possible that if a lot is broken out of a plastic holder and resubmitted to another grading service or even to the same service, the lot could come back with a different grade assigned.

COINS and CURRENCY TERM I: Certification does not guarantee protection against the normal risks associated with potentially volatile markets. The degree of liquidity for certified coins and collectibles will vary according to general market conditions and the particular lot involved. For some lots there may be no active market at all at certain points in time.

COINS and CURRENCY TERM J: All non-certified coins and currency are guaranteed genuine, but are not guaranteed as to grade, since grading is a matter of opinion, an art and not a science, and therefore the opinion rendered by the Auctioneer or any third party grading service may not agree with the opinion of others (including trained experts), and the same expert may not grade the same item with the same grade at two different times. Auctioneer has graded the non-certified numismatic items, in the Auctioneer's opinion, to their current interpretation of the American Numismatic Association's standards as of the date the catalog was prepared. There is no guarantee or warranty implied or expressed that the grading standards utilized by the Auctioneer will meet the standards of any grading service at any time in the future.

COINS and CURRENCY TERM K: Storage of purchased coins and currency: Purchasers are advised that certain types of plastic may react with a coin's metal or transfer plasticizer to notes and may cause damage. Caution should be used to avoid storage in materials that are not inert.

COINS and CURRENCY TERM L: Storage of purchased coins and currency: Purchasers are advised that certain types of plastic may react with a coin's metal or transfer plasticizer to notes and may cause damage. Caution should be used to avoid storage in materials that are not inert.

COINS and CURRENCY TERM M: NOTE: Purchasers of rare coins or currency through Heritage have available the option of arbitration by the Professional Numismatists Guild (PNG); if an election is not made within ten (10) days of an unresolved dispute, Auctioneer may elect either PNG or A.A.A. Arbitration.

COINS and CURRENCY TERM N: For more information regarding Canadian lots attributed to the Charlton reference guides, please contact: Charlton International, PO Box 820, Station Willowdale B, North York, Ontario M2K 2R1 Canada.

WIRING INSTRUCTIONS:

BANK INFORMATION:
Wells Fargo Bank
420 Montgomery Street
San Francisco, CA 94104-1207

ACCOUNT NAME: Heritage Auction Galleries

ABA NUMBER: 121000248

ACCOUNT NUMBER: 4121930028

SWIFT CODE: WFBIUS6S

Your five most effective bidding techniques:

1 Interactive Internet™ Proxy Bidding

(leave your maximum Bid at HA.com before the auction starts)

Heritage's exclusive Interactive Internet™ system is fun and easy! Before you start, you must register online at HA.com and obtain your Username and Password.

1. Login to the HA.com website, using your Username and Password.
2. Chose the specialty you're interested in at the top of the homepage (i.e. coins, currency, comics, movie posters, fine art, etc.).
3. Search or browse for the lots that interest you. Every auction has search features and a 'drop-down' menu list.
4. Select a lot by clicking on the link or the photo icon. Read the description, and view the full-color photography. Note that clicking on the image will enlarge the photo with amazing detail.
5. View the current opening bid. Below the lot description, note the historic pricing information to help you establish price levels. Clicking on a link will take you directly to our Permanent Auction Archives for more information and images.
6. If the current price is within your range, Bid! At the top of the lot page is a box containing the Current Bid and an entry box for your "Secret Maximum Bid" – the maximum amount you are willing to pay for the item before the Buyer's Premium is added. Click the button marked "Place Bid" (if you are not logged in, a login box will open first so you can enter your username (or e-mail address) and password.
7. After you are satisfied that all the information is correct, confirm your "Secret Maximum Bid" by clicking on the "Confirm Absentee Bid" button. You will receive immediate notification letting you know if you are now the top bidder, or if another bidder had previously bid higher than your amount. If you bid your maximum amount and someone has already bid higher, you will immediately know so you can concentrate on other lots.
8. Before the auction, if another bidder surpasses your "Secret Maximum Bid", you will be notified automatically by e-mail containing a link to review the lot and possibly bid higher.
9. Interactive Internet™ bidding closes at 10 P.M. Central Time the night before the session is offered in a floor event. Interactive Internet™ bidding closes two hours before live sessions where there is no floor bidding.
10. The Interactive Internet™ system generally opens the lot at the next increment above the second highest bid. As the high bidder, your "Secret Maximum Bid" will compete for you during the floor auction. Of course, it is possible in a Signature® or Grand Format live auction that you may be outbid on the floor or by a Heritage Live bidder after Internet bidding closes. Bid early, as the earliest bird wins in the event of a tie bid. For more information about bidding and bid increments, please see the section labeled "Bidding Options" found in the Terms & Conditions of this catalog.
11. After the auction, you will be notified of your success. It's that easy!

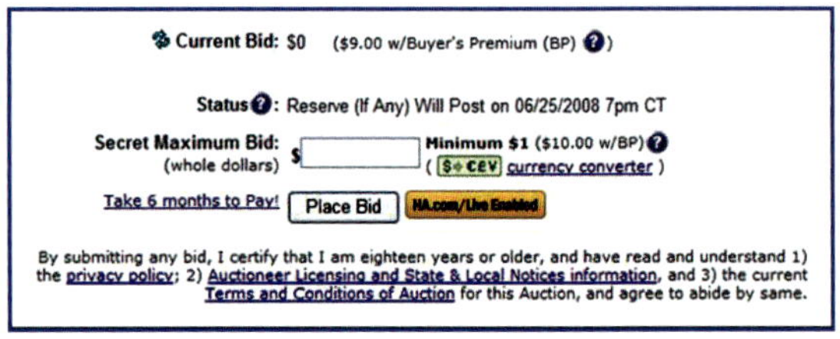

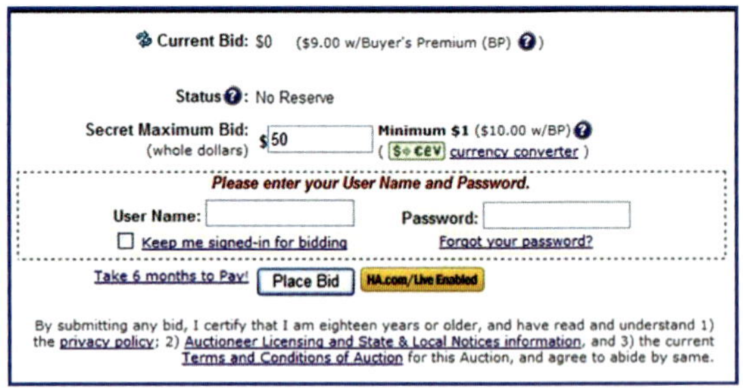

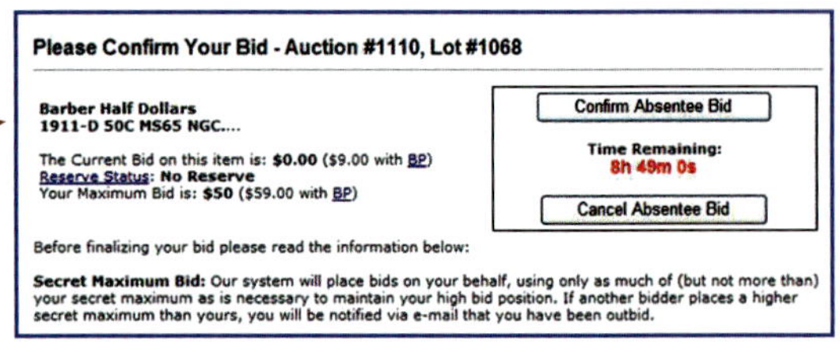

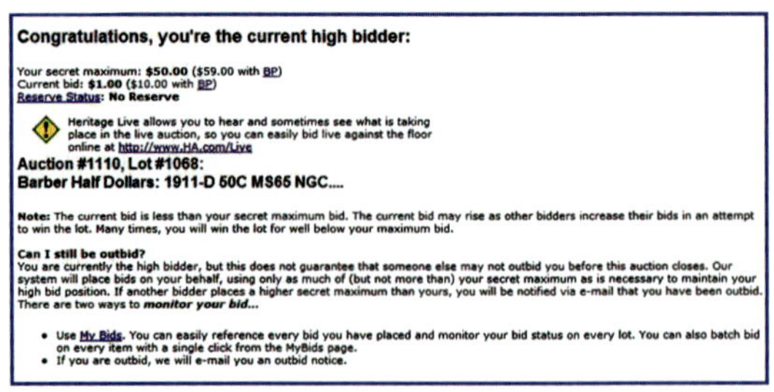

2 HERITAGE Live!™ Bidding
(participate in the Live auction via the Internet)

1. Look on each auction's homepage to verify whether that auction is "HA.com/Live Enabled." All Signature® and Grand Format auctions use the HERITAGE Live!™ system, and many feature live audio and/or video. Determine your lots of interest and maximum bids.
2. Note on the auction's homepage the session dates and times (and especially time zones!) so you can plan your participation. You actually have two methods of using HERITAGE Live!™: a) you can leave a proxy bid through this system, much like the Interactive Internet™ (we recommend you do this before the session starts), or b) you can sit in front of your computer much as the audience is sitting in the auction room during the actual auction.
3. Login at HA.com/Live.
4. Until you become experienced (and this happens quickly!) you will want to login well before your lot comes up so you can watch the activity on other lots. It is as intuitive as participating in a live auction.
5. When your lot hits the auction block, you can continue to bid live against the floor and other live bidders by simply clicking the "Bid" button; the amount you are bidding is clearly displayed on the console.

3 Mail Bidding
(deposit your maximum Bid with the U.S.P.S. well before the auction starts)

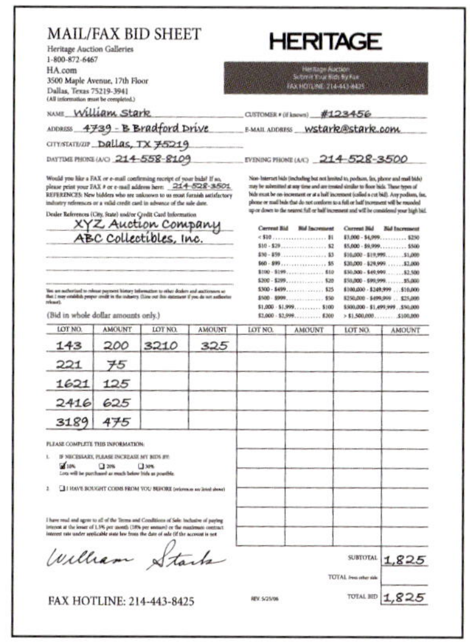

MAIL/FAX BID SHEET
Heritage Auction Galleries
1-800-872-6467
HA.com
3500 Maple Avenue, 17th Floor
Dallas, Texas 75219-3941
(All information must be completed.)

HERITAGE

NAME William Stark — CUSTOMER # (if known) #123456
ADDRESS 4739 - B Bradford Drive — E-MAIL ADDRESS wstark@stark.com
CITY/STATE/ZIP Dallas, TX 75219
DAYTIME PHONE (A/C) 214-558-8109 — EVENING PHONE (A/C) 214-528-3500

Dealer References (City, State) and/or Credit Card Information
XYZ Auction Company
ABC Collectibles, Inc.

(Bid in whole dollar amounts only.)

LOT NO.	AMOUNT	LOT NO.	AMOUNT	LOT NO.	AMOUNT	LOT NO.	AMOUNT
143	200	3210	325				
221	75						
1621	125						
2416	625						
3189	475						

SUBTOTAL 1,825
TOTAL BID 1,825

FAX HOTLINE: 214-443-8425

Mail bidding at auction is fun and easy, but by eliminating the interactivity of our online systems, some of your bids may be outbid before you lick the stamp, and you will have no idea of your overall chances until the auction is over!

1. Look through the printed catalog, and determine your lots of interest.
2. Research their market value by checking price lists and other price guidelines.
3. Fill out your bid sheet, entering your maximum bid on each lot. Bid using whole dollar amounts only. Verify your bids, because you are responsible for any errors you make! Please consult the Bidding Increments chart in the Terms & Conditions.
4. Please fill out your bid sheet completely! We also need: a) Your name and complete address for mailing invoices and lots; b) Your telephone number if any problems or changes arise; c) Your references; if you have not established credit with Heritage, you must send a 25% deposit, or list dealers with whom you have credit established; d) Total your bid sheet; add up all bids and list that total in the box; e) Sign your bid sheet, thereby agreeing to abide by the Terms & Conditions of Auction printed in the catalog.
5. Mail early, because preference is given to the first bid received in case of a tie.
6. When bidding by mail, you frequently purchase items at less than your maximum bid. Bidding generally opens at the next published increment above the second highest mail or Internet bid previously received; if additional floor, phone, or HERITAGE Live!™ bids are made, we act as your agent, bidding in increments over any additional bid until you win the lot or are outbid. For example, if you submitted a bid of $750, and the second highest bid was $375, bidding would start at $400; if no other bids were placed, you would purchase the lot for $400.
7. You can also Fax your Bid Sheet if time is short. Use our exclusive Fax Hotline: 214-443-8425.

4 Telephone Bidding (when you are traveling, or do not have access to HERITAGE Live!™)

1. To participate in an auction by telephone, you must make preliminary arrangements with Client Services (Toll Free 866-835-3243) at least three days before the auction.
2. We strongly recommend that you place preliminary bids by mail or Internet if you intend to participate by telephone. On many occasions, this dual approach has reduced disappointments due to telephone (cell) problems, unexpected travel, late night sessions, and time zone differences. Keep a list of your preliminary bids, and we will help you avoid bidding against yourself.

5 Attend in Person (whenever possible)

Auctions are fun, and we encourage you to attend as many as possible – although our HERITAGE Live!™ system brings all of the action right to your computer screen. Auction dates and session times are printed on the title page of each catalog, and appear on the homepage of each auction at HA.com. Join us if you can!

Take 4 Months to Pay...

Heritage will Finance Your Purchase

We're collectors too, and we understand that on occasion there is more to buy than there is cash. Consider Heritage's Extended Payment Plan [EPP] for your purchases totaling $2,500 or more.

Extended Payment Plan [EPP] Conditions

- Minimum invoice total is $2,500.
- Minimum Down Payment is 25% of the total invoice.
- A signed and returned EPP Agreement is required.
- The EPP is subject to a 3% *fully refundable* Set-up Fee (based on the total invoice amount) payable as part of the first monthly payment.
- The 3% Set-up Fee is refundable provided all monthly payments are made by eCheck, bank draft, personal check drawn on good funds, or cash; and if all such payments are made according to the EPP schedule.
- Monthly payments can be automatically processed with an eCheck, Visa, or MasterCard.
- You may take up to four equal monthly payments to pay the balance.
- Interest is calculated at only 1% per month on the unpaid balance.
- Your EPP must be kept current or additional interest may apply.
- There is no penalty for paying off early.
- Shipment will be made when final payment is received.
- All traditional auction and sales policies still apply.

There is no return privilege once you have confirmed your sale, and penalties can be incurred on cancelled invoices. To avoid additional fees, you must make your down payment within 14 days of the auction. All material purchased under the EPP will be physically secured by Heritage until paid in full.

To exercise the EPP option, please notify **Eric Thomas** at **214.409.1241** or email at **EricT@HA.com** upon receipt of your invoice.

We appreciate your business and wish you good luck with your bidding.

HERITAGE

OUR MISSION

To be the world's most trusted and efficient marketplace and information resource for owners of fine art, collectibles, and other objects of enduring value

OUR VALUES

INTEGRITY
Honesty and fairness must define every facet of our business

TRANSPARENCY
We embrace clarity and freedom of information, enabling clients, partners and coworkers to make informed, confident decisions

TEAMWORK
We collaborate unselfishly, sharing credit for our accomplishments

EFFICIENCY
We seek to help clients, partners and coworkers save valuable time and resources

EXPERTISE
We never stop studying and learning, because our success depends upon providing our clients with the best possible advice

INNOVATION
We continually make our services more accessible and useful to clients, often rendering our own products obsolete by creating better ones

LONG-TERM OUTLOOK
We strive to carefully construct win-win agreements with clients and partners

HERITAGE HA.com
Auction Galleries
The World's Largest Collectibles Auctioneer

3500 Maple Avenue
Dallas, Texas 75219